THE AUTHENTIC
NEW TESTAMENT

EDITED AND TRANSLATED FROM THE
GREEK FOR THE GENERAL READER

by Hugh J. Schonfield

Maps and Illustrations by
J. F. HORRABIN

A MENTOR RELIGIOUS CLASSIC

Published by THE NEW AMERICAN LIBRARY

DEDICATION

To the English-speaking Peoples
of the World, who share the heritage
of the Bible—that great Book of the
People—with the 'People of the Book'

Published as a MENTOR BOOK
By Arrangement with Dobson Books Ltd.

FIRST PRINTING, FEBRUARY, 1958

MENTOR BOOKS are published by
The New American Library of World Literature, Inc.
501 Madison Avenue, New York 22, New York

PRINTED IN THE UNITED STATES OF AMERICA

The Authentic New Testament

Rich insight into the spiritual and historical meaning of the New Testament distinguishes this brilliant new translation, edited by an eminent Jewish scholar.

Hugh J. Schonfield, who worked for thirty years on his modern version of the original Greek text, has created a vivid and readable translation that captures the character, mood and style of each individual author.

Dr. Schonfield has provided a comprehensive introduction covering the historical and geographical background as well as helpful notes on social and religious customs. Included too, for reference use, are maps, illustrations and an index of persons and places.

This incisive translation offers the modern reader a clear understanding of the original meaning of the New Testament and a dramatic picture of Biblical times.

"An excellent translation which is fully entitled to a place alongside those of Goodspeed, Moffatt and Knox. It is scholarly, sensitive and idiomatic." —*London Times Educational Supplement*

Other Books of Special Interest

The Holy Bible in Brief
edited and arranged by James Reeves

The basic story of the Old and New Testaments, a continuous narrative in the words of the King James text. (#Ms116—50¢)

The Meaning of the Dead Sea Scrolls
by A. Powell Davies

A fascinating interpretation of the ancient documents which revolutionize religious teachings and beliefs. (#MD219—50¢)

The Ten Commandments *by A. Powell Davies*

The exciting story of the Ten Commandments and their color and majesty, in the light of modern developments. (Signet Key #Ks343—35¢)

The Living Talmud: The Wisdom of the Fathers and Its Classical Commentaries selected and translated by Judah Goldin. (#MD199—50¢)

OLDEST KNOWN FRAGMENT OF ANY PART OF THE NEW
TESTAMENT. SCRAP FROM A SECOND CENTURY PAPYRUS
CODEX OF THE FOURTH GOSPEL (Jn. xviii. 31-33, 37-38).

By Courtesy of the John Rylands Library.

The letter kills, but the spirit vitalizes

II. Cor. iii. 6.

As an unknown, yet well known

II. Cor. vi. 9.

PREFACE

IN THE FIRST CENTURY OF OUR ERA there erupted from Palestine into the Roman Empire a Movement denounced by the authorities as seditious, subversive and atheistic, a 'pest' which threatened the entire civilized world. That Movement received the name of Christianity, and as one of the great religions it continues to be represented in our time by the various sections of the Christian Church.

In its origins the Movement was Jewish, centred on the person of a wonder-working rabbi from Galilee, accepted by his followers as the King-Messiah and subsequently proclaimed among the nations as the World Deliverer and future Ruler. He had died by crucifixion, was buried, had risen from the dead and ascended into heaven, and his invisible presence— liable at any moment to become vengefully and catastrophically visible—challenged and doomed the imperial regime and the existing order. The Movement was all the more dangerous because of its hidden and inaccessible potentialities.

From whatever point of view the circumstances may now be regarded, Christianity was an extraordinary historical phenomenon. The native climate of its thought and teaching was that of pietistic and prophetic Judaism substantially based on the sacred literature of the Hebrews; but it drew also upon the mysticism and mythology of the non-Jewish world, fusing the longings and expectations of a sick and superstitious age in its own apocalyptic crucible, and generating in the process a white heat of fanatical zeal and anticipation. The electrifying Message, the Good News, spread madly, eagerly, like a raging flame, for the God who had sent it forth was 'an all-consuming fire.'

A number of valuable documents have fortunately been preserved to us from the first hundred years of the Movement's existence, histories, letters, treatises and tracts, which in a selected and collected form are known as the New Testament or New Covenant. These records throw a flood of light on the nature of Christianity, the life and personality of its Founder, its development, fortunes and vicissitudes. The documents are of major importance, not only for what they tell us of the Movement itself, but also for their reflection of many aspects of the social, political and religious life of the period, both among the Jews and in the Graeco-Roman world. As contemporary, or very near contemporary, accounts they are singularly revealing, and in certain respects the information they furnish is obtainable from no other source. But their chief claim on our attention is that they offer us the 'inside story' of Christianity, and what makes the letters especially so excitingly fresh and stimulating is that they were written almost on the spur of the moment, with no thought of general publication, in emotional reaction to internal needs and situations.

The language in which these documents have come down to us is Greek, not for the most part the polished Greek of polite and educated society, but more the commercial and domestic Greek of the multi-national Near East, sometimes even Yiddish-Greek, as colourful in imagery and metaphor as it is often careless in grammatical construction. To read these records is a thrilling experience. They are a real 'discovery'. But how can one convey their atmosphere, their rich and varied flavours, to the reader who is forced to depend on a translation? And what is of greater consequence, how can one break through the condescension of his willingness to hear again a tale he has heard so many times before, and convince him that he never has heard the whole story and the true story?

So many people already know all about the New Testament, or believe they do. Has it not been translated so many times, read and studied for centuries? Is there not widespread familiarity with its language and contents? Yes, of course. Only let us consider this New Testament that is so well known. It is the volume held by Christians to be divinely inspired, the second part of the Holy Bible. It is a work of religious authority, read for devotional and doctrinal purposes. The translation of it, even in the very latest versions, has been almost exclusively the work of Christian theologians and conforms to a pattern ecclesiastical. A great deal of its terminology is the verbal currency of the Christian Faith as this has become stereotyped in the course of a long tradition. This New Testament has somehow been isolated and set apart from its own time for the solace and instruction of believers of all times: it is Holy Writ, the Word of God.

It is perfectly right and proper that the Church should have its authoritative versions of its sacred books. There must be some norm to sustain the common life of the Church in faith and worship. There can be improvement in accuracy of rendering on the basis of fresh evidence, and within limits the diction and presentation can be modernized. But the purpose of such versions obviously excludes any fundamental reassessment of ideas and values, any high-spirited kicking over of the ecclesiastical traces.

Yet to reveal the authentic New Testament a certain abandon and lack of refinement is imperative. The records in the original simply do not read as they are reproduced to serve the spiritual needs of the Christian Faith. There is a diversity of style, often an absence of literary grace, infelicity of phrasing, much use of colloquialisms. There is passionate fervour as well as gentleness and moderation, bluntness and crudity, sarcasm as well as courtesy, both beauty and ugliness. There is also close reasoning alongside simplicity, the employment of dialectical skill and what seems to us to-day to be quite extraordinary methods of exegesis. The New Testament is not the result of planning or set purpose. It is like the dragnet of the Gospel parable which enclosed fish of many kinds. The books deemed good have been retained and the rest discarded; but even those which have been kept still differ greatly in type and quality. The translator, to do justice to his material, has to endeavour to be as many persons as his strongly individualistic authors with their diverse characteristics, abilities and aims. What we have been accustomed to reading is a largely idealized interpretation created by the various schools of Christian faith and piety. Set beside these hallowed versions the real New Testament is an Epstein among the Old Masters, which may first shock and even antagonize traditionalists before it comes to be understood and appreciated.

There must be no intention, of course, wilfully to run counter to cherished belief. But equally, consideration of the possible effects and consequences must not induce the translator to sacrifice literary and historical integrity. The New Testament belongs to its own time, and for purposes of non-ecclesiastical publication must be dealt with in its own way for its own sake. This inevitably affects questions of style, treatment, arrangement and presentation: it also vitally affects the sense and meaning. These venerable documents cannot rightly be comprehended unless they are related to the life and thought of their period. Especially is this the case with Jewish matters with which the New Testament is continually concerned. It is not without justification that Victor Gollancz has said: 'There are things in Christianity, I feel certain, that can be better understood for a previous understanding of orthodox Judaism. I often wonder, indeed, whether a Gentile, however imaginative, can really live as a Jew can in the New Testament atmosphere'.[1] The present version is, so far as I am aware, the first to give the Jewish sources their proper place in elucidating the text of the New Testament.

In the General Introduction to this book the reader will find the distinctive features of the work fully explained. There has been a bold breaking away from convention and tradition because it was essential to my purpose that as far as possible Christianity as now taught and expressed should not be in the forefront either of my own or the reader's consciousness. I will not go into details here; but I must state in more general terms what my aim has been as historian, editor and translator.

What I have attempted is to recapture in the idiom of to-day and with the use of our ampler vocabulary the nuances and flavour of an age that has long gone from us and is alien to most of us. I have not sought to adapt the New Testament to

[1] *My Dear Timothy*, p. 111. Owing to centuries of Christian persecution the New Testament, even to-day, is little read by Jews. The present writer would appear to be the first Jew to translate the New Testament into English.

any 'let's have a man to man drop-the-dog-collar' kind of religion. I have not had an eye to modern theological requirements. I have approached these records as if they had recently
been recovered from a cave in Palestine or from beneath the
sands of Egypt, and had never previously been given to the
public. Such an approach could be much more experimental
and exploratory. One could look at everything freshly, and ask
oneself and try to answer, not always with finality or complete
assurance, all kinds of exciting questions. This has been my
attitude of mind, though naturally I have availed myself of the
labours of a host of scholarly authorities without whose in-
defatigable investigations it would have been impossible for
me to embark on an enterprise of such magnitude and difficulty. But one cannot become intimate with people solely
through study and learning: there must be sympathy, feeling
and association. Otherwise one may misunderstand and mis-
interpret. For this reason, so far as the New Testament writers
are concerned, I have spent to the best of my historical competence and imagination a great many years in their company
and climate of ideas, so that I might represent them more faithfully and enable the first century to speak directly to the
twentieth. As translator I have used only such liberty of trans-
ference from language to language as would convey 'them' to
'us', instead of superimposing 'us' on 'them'. The consequence
is that many passages will sound strangely to ears attuned to the
ecclesiastical versions and their phraseology. I trust, however,
that I have sufficiently clarified in the footnotes and references
things that are unfamiliar or somewhat obscure.

It is, then, a New Testament authentic in accent and atmosphere that I have striven to reproduce, and I shall be abundant-
ly satisfied if I shall have persuaded some, no matter what their
creeds or convictions may be, that it is well worth reading. To
those to whom the New Testament is God's Revelation I am
sure it will be evident that I have handled it in no materialistic
spirit and without any polemical purpose. I do not offer what I
have set down as binding on anyone's mind or conscience, and
if I have offended or distressed anyone I am deeply sorry. But
I hope that even those who may feel that I have failed to perceive the full implications of the Christian Faith will yet discover some things of worth that are new to them and useful to
them. For myself I will only say that I shall consider the
arduous, but to me infinitely rewarding, labours now completed
as sufficiently justified if I shall have managed graphically to
bring before my readers one of mankind's most pregnant
yesterdays. Here, then, are the circumstances of a Movement
and the terms of a Message which nineteen centuries ago
brought Faith, Hope and Love to a world which is still so sadly
in need of all three.

I have received so many kindnesses during the progress of
this work towards publication that in mentioning some of those

who have assisted me I may seem to appear ungrateful to others. I am indeed warmly indebted to them all, named and unnamed alike, and not least to the many scholars of whose studies and researches I have availed myself. But there are certain friends I must expressly thank for their encouragement and for sustaining me in my endeavours, Margaret Watson, Sydney Walton, Dr. W. A. L. Elmslie, Sir Kenneth Grubb and John Stirling. To the latter and to Sir Robert Evans I am further indebted for reading the original draft and making many valuable suggestions. Anthony Hayter and Stuart Holroyd aided nobly in the successive stages of preparing the typescript; Stuart Holroyd also helped in compiling the indexes and correcting the proofs. J. F. (Frank) Horrabin not only contributed his skilled artistry in executing the maps and illustrations, but was very patient in meeting all my requirements. Professor Edward Robertson, Librarian of the John Rylands Library, most courteously supplied the photograph for the illustration on page v. The Printers and Publishers have had the work so much at heart, that they have proved devoted friends as well as skilled collaborators.

It must not go without saying, though she does not need that it should be said, that my dear wife has throughout given solace and cheer to a husband weary and downcast at times with the cares and vicissitudes of his undertaking, and additionally proposed a number of distinct improvements of the text. To my dear mother's memory I would also pay loving tribute; for this work, which she did not survive to see in print, meant much to her because it meant so much to me.

Hugh J. Schonfield

Highgate, 1955

NOTE ON THE TITLE OF THIS WORK

In order to remove the possibility of misunderstanding I wish to make it quite clear that the title *The Authentic New Testament* is in no way intended to imply that my translation is the only genuine one. Manifestly any such suggestion would be both boastful and absurd. The term 'authentic' relates to the quality of the New Testament itself, as it may be read in the Greek, its accurate reflection of the atmosphere of the period in which the documents were written. The only claim I make is that I have endeavoured as faithfully as possible to convey that authenticity to the English reader. The translation may be far from perfect, and other renderings may be better in places; but if I have succeeded in reproducing something of the true flavour and realism of these writings I shall be satisfied. For this reason I have thought it better to employ an appropriate descriptive title, desiring to sink my own identity in that of the authors I was translating, so that the work might never be known as Schonfield's New Testament.

H. J. S.

CONTENTS

ILLUSTRATIONS

MAPS AND PLANS

INTRODUCTION

1. *The First Century of Christianity*

CHRISTIANITY DID NOT REALLY BEGIN with Jesus Christ, though it was the recognition of him by many Jews as the Christ, or Messiah, that centred the already existing Messianic Movement on the teaching and experiences of a living, unique and inspired person. He who was the Founder was also the Completer and Fulfiller, and the one who was seen prophetically to be the 'foundation stone laid in Zion' was equally seen at the same time to be the 'coping-stone'.

Before the advent of Jesus there was a part of Israel that was 'awaiting the consolation', groups and communities of the Saints, believing themselves to be the Elect, dreaming dreams of the coming Redemption, seeing apocalyptic visions of the Day of Judgment and the inauguration of the Reign of God on earth. The ideas and doctrines emanating from these circles, and the books produced by them, contributed in no small measure to the form and content of the Christian Message as reflected in the New Testament. Without these 'Preparations for the Gospel' Jesus could not have taught as he did, or been the Messiah that he was. Nor after his passing from the earthly scene would so many thousands of Jews have attached themselves to his cause, and found in faith in his Resurrection and Ascension the key to the mystery of God's dealings with his people. They were Christians because Jesus had made concrete the prophetic intimations of which they were so profoundly and sublimely conscious. Perhaps at no other time than the first century A.D., and in no other place than Palestine, could such an action and reaction of the spiritual on the physical, such a response of external events to internal convictions, have taken place. Either then, or never, Messiah had to appear, the Word to be made flesh.

So far as can be known, Jesus of Nazareth was born not long before the death of Herod king of Judea in 4 B.C., and grew to manhood among the pleasant hills of Galilee in northern Palestine. He was the eldest of a large family, having four brothers and at least two sisters, and followed his father's trade as a carpenter. The family could pride itself on descent from the famous David, king of Israel, and was therefore one from which the Messiah might spring according to the expectation of many. Jesus appears while still in his teens to have lost his father Joseph, and thus at an early age to have had to assume manly responsibilities of providing for his widowed mother Mary and the younger children.

Whatever may have gone before, the great turning point in his life came about A.D. 26 when Jews were flocking from all parts of the country to listen to the burning words of a strange prophet from the wilderness known as John the Baptist, or Immerser, because he proclaimed the near advent of the Kingdom of God and called upon the people to be dipped in the River Jordan as a sign of their repentance. Jesus was himself immersed by John, and from that moment received the assurance of his divine appointment as Messiah. After retirement into the wilderness, he took up the Baptist's call to national repentance and embarked upon his own public ministry.

As the brief career of Jesus is depicted in the first three Gospels, he was by any reckoning a man of remarkable insight, powers of observation, and knowledge of human nature, and gifted with special powers of teaching and healing. He spoke with authority, and his interpretation of his office differed considerably from popular expectations of a warrior-king; so that he created much uncertainty about himself, whether he was simply a religious teacher, a prophet, or indeed the Messiah, since he seemed to be something of all these. In particular he was opposed, contrary to the inclinations of the more extreme, to any acts of violence against the Roman authorities and their representatives, then ruling the country. Instead he advocated a policy of no reprisals and returning good for evil, and called for penitence and amendment of life as the means of expediting the coming of the Kingdom of God over which he would reign. In spite of this policy, which had the endorsement of a substantial section of the Pharisean party, he fell foul of the Pharisees by relegating their ceremonial observances to a place a good way down in his scale of values, while he opposed the Sadducees, the ruling aristocratic party, as time-servers and exploiters. By both he was regarded as a dangerous demagogue. On the one hand his large following and Messianic pretensions might be used as a pretext by the Romans to take away even the remnants of national self-government, and on the other hand any weakening of loyalty to the religious institutions of Judaism would open the door wide to the subversive influence of paganism, no less destructive of the nation and its hopes of the future.

Because the activities of Jesus were relatively harmless for the present there was no guarantee that they would long remain so in view of the critical state of the nation's affairs. It was best to nip the Movement in the bud. This, however, presented a difficulty. If Jesus was arrested openly, there was a serious risk of a popular rising, especially at the always inflammable season of the Passover, festival of national liberation, which was the very season Jesus chose at which to make a triumphal entry into Jerusalem. A crisis might easily be precipitated instead of avoided. As it happened, one of his inner circle of disciples betrayed Jesus and he was arrested secretly at night and brought before a hastily convened meeting of the Jewish Council, the Sanhedrin. When a capital charge in Jewish law of practising wizardry failed, the capital charge in Roman law of lese-majesty was pressed and succeeded. Jesus agreed that he was the Messiah, king of the Jews, and was thus technically guilty of treason against the Roman Emperor Tiberius. The next day he was brought before the Roman procurator of Judea and sentenced to immediate execution by crucifixion for high treason, even though he had not been found in arms or inciting to rebellion. His quiet demeanour and refusal to defend himself created a favourable impression, but he would not deny that he was the Messiah, the one thing that might have saved him. The whole proceedings were conspiratorial rather than judicial, the formalities of a trial being the merest pretence for purposes of the records.

The death of Jesus, however, was only the end of the beginning. Our documents tell of the disappearance of his body from the tomb, and how his disciples became convinced that he was alive again, having risen from the dead. There were a number of testimonies to having seen and spoken with him, not as a ghost but as a living physical being. As required by prophetic interpretation he had then ascended to heaven, and would ere long return with the angels at his back to inaugurate his reign on earth and the establishment of the Kingdom of God. To this belief many Jews responded, and the Messianic Movement, or Community of the Saints of God, received a new and startling impetus. To other Jews the followers of Jesus became known as Nazoreans (*Notsrim*), while among Gentiles they were dubbed Christians (*Christianoi*), the Greek *Christos* (Christ) being the translation of the Hebrew *Meshiach* (Messiah), meaning the Anointed One.

The *Acts of the Envoys* (Apostles) describes how the Movement developed with its headquarters in Jerusalem, and how it was organized on a communal basis, and of the vain efforts of the authorities to suppress it. Jesus had appointed twelve primary envoys, and these twelve, Matthias having been elected to take the place of the defunct traitor Judas, formed the nucleus of the Community's government, headed by the Galilean ex-fisherman Simeon Kepha (Peter). Soon, however, the Movement was sufficiently powerful, claiming as it did to represent loyal Israel, to create its own senate under the presidency of Jacob (James) the eldest surviving brother of Jesus, a man noted for his piety and asceticism. Non-violence was still the policy of the Movement, but now its rapidly increasing numerical strength and its emphasis on the speedy return of Jesus as God's Messiah made it far more a problem to the Government than it had been while Jesus was proclaiming his message. The political situation in Palestine was steadily deteriorating, due to resentment at pagan domination, and also partly due to the avarice and tyranny both of the Roman procurators and the leading high-priestly families. Very little was needed to cause a general uprising. Advocates of revolt, known as the Zealots, were becoming increasingly active, and bands of patriot, or professed patriot, guerillas were abroad. Other messianic claimants and leaders appeared and easily procured a following. Intense religious fervour was manifested, and on all sides signs and portents were seen or looked for that the Day of Deliverance was at hand.

Nazarenism could not help but be the gainer by the general tension and popular expectations, and not only in Palestine. The leaders believed that they had been called by Jesus to proclaim his message to all their Jewish co-religionists throughout the world. Some escaping from persecution at home, some of set purpose, set out on missionary journeys to the cities of the Roman Empire where Jews were settled. They were not the only Jewish envoys. The Sanhedrin had its own emissaries attending to the religious supervision of the Dispersion and the collection of funds for the Temple; and besides these were other from the Zealot camp bent on instigating revolt against Rome among the Jews of Asia, Greece, Egypt, and even in Rome itself. It became extremely difficult to distinguish between Nazarene and Zealot envoys. This was proved in the case of the most notable recruit to Nazarenism, the Pharisee scholar and Roman citizen Saul, otherwise Paul, of Tarsus. He had been a fanatical opponent of the Nazarenes, but while on the road to Damascus to arrest followers of Jesus there, he had had a vision in which Jesus had appeared to him and appointed him envoy to the Gentiles. Already a number of non-Jews had been won over to the Messianic Faith. These were mainly those who attended Jewish worship and had abandoned paganism. Since much of the service in the foreign synagogues was conducted in Greek they could follow it without difficulty. Paul invariably went first with his message to the synagogues and prayer-centres; but he did not restrict himself to them, and openly proclaimed Jesus as Messiah to pagan Gentiles. By adopting this course he fell foul both of the orthodox Jewish and Nazarene authorities, who regarded it as essential that if Gentile converts were to be incorporated in the Community of Israel they must accept and observe the Mosaic ordinances. Paul argued that if they had faith in the Messiah such Gentiles were automatically Children of Abraham, and did not require to be circumcised and fulfil the obligations of the Mosaic Law.

There might easily have been a fatal split in the Movement as a result of Paul's uncompromising stand on behalf of converts from the Gentiles; but this was avoided when the case came before the Nazarene Council by agreement that believers from the Gentiles would be received into full fellowship provided that they complied with the fundamental requirements of abstention from idolatry and immorality, and observed the minimum dietary regulations. There were those who regarded this decision as too lenient, and some of them visited the communities founded by Paul and had considerable success in persuading the converts to become full proselytes to Judaism. The attacks on Paul and his retaliation enter into several of his letters preserved in our Collection. Paul's correspondence with the communities in Greece and Asia Minor, and his treatise addressed to the believers at Rome display to the full his dialectical skill, his personal views and theological concepts, his passionate faith, his tireless energy and organizing capacity, and provide a most revealing self-portrait. We can well understand how it was this little bald-headed bow-legged Jew,[1] as early Christian tradition depicts him, who really put Christianity on the map.

Part of Paul's work was inevitably the adaptation of the Messianic message to meet Gentile needs. To this he had devoted a great deal of thought and meditation, building on his knowledge of mystical Judaism. There was no playing down at this stage that Jesus was the promised Messiah of Israel; but he was now seen, though non-politically, to be the real Saviour of the World whose nature and titles had blasphemously been parodied by Caesar. The emperors had accepted from the East, as strengthening their position, adoration as divinities customary in the case of oriental kings. Temples had been established for their worship. Augustus had been addressed in an inscription as 'Caesar, who reigns over the seas and continents, Jupiter, who holds from Jupiter his father the title of Liberator, Master of Europe and Asia, Star of all Greece, who lifts himself up with the glory of great Jupiter, Saviour'. Son of God, *divi filius*, was now part of the imperial titles, and the mad Gaius Caligula, flattered by his sycophants, had taken the designation all too literally.

By accepting Jesus as the Christ the Christians gave their allegiance to another Imperium than that of Caesar, a government created by God and not by men. Thus even while remaining law-abiding they could be classed as enemies of the State, and were easily confounded with the Jewish Zealot-Messianists who believed that the Messiah would overthrow the Roman Empire and were not even waiting for his advent to begin the good work. 'They found in their sacred scriptures,' says Josephus, 'an ambiguous oracle that at this time one from their country would become ruler of the civilized world.'[2] The Emperor Claudius, who succeeded Caligula, found it imperative to write to the Jews of Alexandria warning them not to entertain itinerant Jews from Syria and Upper Egypt, if they did not wish to be treated as abettors of 'a pest which threatens the whole world'.[3] More drastically he ordered the expulsion of (foreign) Jews from Rome, 'who were continually making disturbances at the instigation of Chrestus'[4] (i.e. engaging in messianic agitation). Dio Cassius says that Claudius closed the synagogues at Rome,[5] where seditious meetings could take place. Many of the provincial Jews were themselves alarmed at the arrival of these nationalists, which imperilled their own

[1] *Acts of Paul and Thekla.*   [2] Jos. *Wars*, VI. v. 4.
[3] *Letter of Claudius to the Alexandrians.*   [4] Suet. *Claud.* xxv.
[5] *Hist.* lx. 6.

security, if they were believed to be parties to their plotting. Paul and his companion Silas were taken to be two of these agitators by the Jews of Thessalonica. In self-protection they denounced them, informing the politarches that 'these subverters of the civilized world (the Roman Empire) have now reached here . . . and they are all actively opposed to the imperial decrees, saying there is another king, one Jesus'.[6] Paul was later indicted before the procurator Felix at Caesarea as a 'plague-carrier, a fomentor of revolt among all the Jews of the Empire, a ringleader of the Nazarene sect'.[7]

The Christians throughout the Empire became a people apart, members, as were their fellows in Palestine, of the Community of God, the True Israel, distinguishing themselves both from the Jews and the Gentiles. They were credited by their opponents with horrible practices at their love-feasts, and stigmatized as 'enemies of the human race'.[8] They multiplied none the less, offering salvation from sin and hope of eternal life by association with Christ in his death, burial and resurrection, a mystery understandable by those acquainted with the mystery cults of the period, especially that of Mithras. Unlike other associations, no slave was barred from the Community: at least in Christ he became a free man with equal rights. And thus the slave and the social misfit, the pervert and the outcast, gravitated towards the Movement, causing a great deal of trouble within, and getting the Christians a bad name outside. Paul himself was terribly distressed by the unexpected interpretation of his principle of 'liberty from the Law in Christ'. It required the Neronian persecution, when the Christians were charged with having set fire to Rome, and the subsequent outlawing of Christianity by the Flavian emperors, to purge the Community of much of its dross. From the Jewish Nazarene side horror at the immorality among the Christians was expressed in open letters sent out in the names of Judas brother of James and Simon Peter (II. Peter).

In Judea, where few non-Jews had come into the Movement, there were no less considerable changes in its composition. There had been an influx of priests and Pharisees and persons belonging to various eclectic groups. This led to stricter practice of the Law, a considerable literary activity, and a developed messianic doctrine. In Jewish esoteric circles the Messiah had been regarded as a pre-existent being, the Heavenly Man created by God before the foundation of the world, the Pattern in whose likeness the universe was formed. It was now held by the Nazarenes that it was this archetypal Son of Man,[9] higher than angels and archangels, the divine Son of God, who had incarnated in Jesus at his baptism, or as some said at his birth, and in the resurrected and immortalized body of Jesus had reascended to heaven. This interpretation of the Messiah made

[6] Acts xvii. 6-7.   [7] Acts xxiv. 5.   [8] Tacitus, *Annals*, xv. 44.
[9] Cp. *Enoch*, xlvi-xlviii. The mystical books of Enoch were among the extra-canonical writings held to be inspired in early Christian circles.

a strong appeal to Paul, himself one who had mystical experiences, and he elaborated it in several of his letters. Moreover this 'Christ of glory' was regarded as present in spirit with believers, guiding and directing his Community. Visions of him, and revelations from him, were considered quite natural, though granted only to advanced and chosen persons. But all could share to some extent in the distribution from Above of spiritual gifts which were believed to be the direct result of Christ's ascension, and which included both lower and higher manifestations of psychic phenomena.

By the middle of the seventh decade of the first century A.D. the great lights had been extinguished. James the brother of Jesus at Jerusalem; Paul and Peter at Rome, had suffered for their convictions. The terrible conflagration at Rome in the summer of A.D. 64 had brought a tortured death to a multitude of Christians. In Palestine the misrule of the procurator Gessius Florus was forcing the Jews at last into open revolt. This must be, many held, the prophesied Time of the End, and soon the Messianic Era must dawn. Constancy became the watchword of the believers.

Just before the war broke out in Judea the Nazarenes of Jerusalem received a revelation, perhaps preserved in what is called the *Little Apocalypse* imbedded in the Synoptic Gospels. They were warned by Jesus to escape to the mountains, and a considerable exodus took place across the Jordan, many finding refuge in the region of Pella in the Decapolis. Possibly other communities of the Saints (Essenes) from the neighbourhood of the Dead Sea moved with them, or a little later, as the war developed.

When Jerusalem fell after a bitter siege and struggle in A.D. 70 and the sacred Temple went up in flames, the Nazarenes had lost the centre of their authority, and to a large extent contact with the Christians abroad had been temporarily severed. Nevertheless in their place of exile the surviving leaders and those of the kindred of Jesus met and elected as their head a cousin of Jesus called Simeon son of Clopas or Cleophas. The government of the Nazarenes remained chiefly in the hands of the messianic family until early in the following century. Among these 'Heirs' (*Desposynoi*) we hear in particular of James and Sokker, grandchildren of Judas a brother of Jesus. The family was proud of its Davidic descent, and was in no little danger from the Romans as furnishing possible leaders of another Jewish revolt. It is due to these Heirs that we have at least one of the genealogies of Jesus, and two or three of the Open Letters in our Collection may have come from them.

For many believers throughout the Roman Empire the period that followed A.D. 70 was one of despondency. The Antichrist had triumphed, and the expected Second Advent of Christ had not materialized. The communities in many lands were now on their own, and in their present mood were very ready to listen to new teachers with novel half-pagan doctrines. Christianity drew further away from Judaism, and among some sections views of the nature of Christ became more consistent with heathen concepts of the Deity. The Jews were held to have been abandoned by God, and there might have been a complete break with the historic origins of what was now a distinct religion had it not been for those who clung to as much of the truth as they knew and the collectors of traditions who produced the Gospels.

Towards the close of the century a new wave of persecution struck the Church. The Antichrist of this period was the Emperor Domitian, who required himself to be addressed as 'our Lord and God'. While many weak Christians fell away, the general effect was salutary. The prophetic vision was recaptured, and the *Apocalypse*, or *Revelation*, gave out its solemn message of warning and hope to the oppressed communities of Asia Minor. Only a little while, and Christ would surely come with the legions of heaven at his back to overthrow the oppressors. Suffering and martyrdom drew Christians together as never before. Communities made contact with one another, helped each other. As a result a common faith and practice gradually emerged, and a common collection of revered writings began to be acknowledged. In due course, though this was still a good way off, the New Testament would take its place beside the Old. The struggle with heresy, particularly the Gnostic systems, went on until well into the second century; but now there was a strength to meet and combat them which had not been there before. Christianity had come to stay.

The Nazarenes, or Jewish Christians, also enjoyed a period of revival in the second century. But by this time it was taken amiss by both Church and Synagogue that there should be any group occupying a halfway house between them. Christianity under the Church Fathers, Judaism under the Rabbis, tacitly agreed about the Nazarenes and Ebionites that, in the words of St. Jerome, 'while they will be both Jews and Christians, they are neither Jews nor Christians'.[10]

The last figure of note in the New Testament Collection is John the Elder of Ephesus, embodiment of the new orthodoxy, contender for the Faith against Jews and heretics, yet with a message of love for those regarded as true believers. With him, it may be, there passed away the last direct link with those who had actually seen and spoken to the historical Jesus of Nazareth.

2. *The Palestinian Background*

The Synoptic Gospels faithfully depict the social, political, religious and economic conditions prevailing in Palestine in the first half of the first century A.D. But they require to be read with attention, and in the light of other available information.

[10] *Ep. to Augustine.*

Sometimes it is from the sayings of Jesus and his parables, sometimes from incidental statements, that we obtain an insight into the situation. And what we read has to be associated with what we find in other works. In dwelling on the spiritual aspects of the Christian message we may easily overlook what the evangelists have preserved of the distressing state of Jewish affairs. This when understood, however, only makes that message more pertinent and intelligible.

Let us glance briefly at some of the things that are mentioned. A man who could not pay his lord the exorbitant dues demanded was liable to be sold with his wife and children to defray the debt (Mt. xviii. 25). The poor widow, whose little livelihood has been taken away, has to deal with an unjust judge who fears neither God nor man, and she has no other means of redress than her importunity (Lk. xviii. 1-5). Burglary and brigandage are common crimes (Mt. vi. 19, xxiv. 43; Lk. x. 30). State tax collectors extort excessive revenues (Lk. xix. 8), while the rich nobleman, hated for his hardness, goes off to enjoy himself abroad, leaving his underlings to amass money for him the best way they can in his absence (Lk. xix. 12-17). The self-satisfied capitalist decides to retire on his gains (Lk. xii. 16-21). The plutocrat feasts sumptuously in his villa, caring nothing for the beggar covered with sores lying at his gates (Lk. xvi. 19-31). In a mental stupor by reason of their privations the common people follow any benefactor about like dogs (Mt. ix. 35-38, xiv. 13, etc.), and bring their sick folk for healing (Mt. iv. 23-25, xv. 30-31, etc.). False prophets trade on the people's misery (Mt. vii. 15-16). On signs of open disaffection the forces of the Occupying Power cut down the people in cold blood, even when engaged in worship (Lk. xiii. 1-2). Reformers and patriotic preachers are arrested, and more often than not executed (Mt. x. 16-39). Faithful souls run grave risks in giving such persons shelter (Mt. x. 40-42). Spies and informers abound, and mingle with the crowds waiting to catch some word of antagonism to the authorities (Mt. xiii. 9-13, etc.), or ask pointed questions involving political issues (Mt. xv. 15-21). The authorities are in continual fear of popular risings (Mt. xxvi. 5).

These are only a few of the references to many aspects of the situation which the Gospels disclose. The picture may seem to be overdrawn; but this is not so when viewed from the standpoint of the Palestinian peasantry, and ample confirmation is obtainable from other contemporary sources. The interested reader should by all means study the pages of Josephus, the Jewish historian, whose works are readily available in Whiston's translation, though very much better represented in the edition of the Loeb Classical Library in the translation by H. St. J. Thackeray and Ralph Marcus. The books of the *Apocrypha* in the Revised Version are also important, especially the *Maccabees*. Then among essential documents are the Jewish Apocalyptic and Pseudepigraphic writings, English versions of which are largely provided in the series of *Translations of Early Documents* issued by the Society for the Promotion of Christian Knowledge. To this literature belong the *Books of Enoch*, the *Testaments of the XII Patriarchs*, the so-called *Assumption of Moses*, the *Book of Jubilees*, the *Psalms of Solomon*, the *Apocalypse of Ezra*, the *Apocalypse of Baruch*, the Jewish *Sibylline Oracles*, and several others. There are other Jewish books too, less accessible in English, notably the *Targumin* and *Midrashim*, and finally the Rabbinical *Mishnah*, of which there is an excellent English translation by Herbert Danby.

Since it is only possible in this General Introduction to touch upon a limited number of preparatory matters affecting the Palestinian background, it may be most useful if these are arranged under the following sub-heads: (a) A Short Historical Survey, (b) The Galilean Scene, and (c) The Sermon on the Mount. These sections are designed to set the stage so to speak for intelligent reading of the Gospels and *Acts*.

(a) *A Short Historical Survey*

Around the beginning of the second century B.C. the Jews were called upon to meet a most serious threat to their ancestral Faith and Institutions. This arose from the seductive character of the Greek way of life, with which the Jews had come increasingly into contact since the time of Alexander the Great. It became fashionable to take Greek names, adopt Greek dress, follow Greek customs, read Greek literature, and attend or take part in the Greek Games and displays. The upper classes were chiefly influenced, and these included members of the ruling Jewish hierarchy. Where such flirting with paganism was carried on by the officiating ministers of the One God of Israel it could not be long before all sections of the population were led away from strict attachment to monotheism. Among some of the priests and scribes protestant and puritan bodies of pietists, Chasidim, organized themselves to combat the peril. A 'New Covenant' with God was proclaimed, the covenant spoken of by Jeremiah the Prophet (xxxi. 31-34), and all the faithful were called upon to pledge their allegiance to it.

The Jewish Covenanters had not long begun their work when the situation further deteriorated. The Seleucid monarch Antiochus Epiphanes gave direct assistance to the Hellenizing process by attempting the conversion of the Temple at Jerusalem into a sanctuary of Zeus Olympius and seeking to enforce the abandonment of Judaism. A Resistance Movement came into being inspired by the priest Mattathias and his five sons, Judas, Jonathan, Simon, John and Eleazar. The Chasidim and other Zealots of the Law joined the Maccabees in the bloody struggle that followed. The Temple was cleansed and the worship of God restored.

Under the successful Maccabees a reaction against paganism set in. The Jews fought for and finally won their political independence. A new ruling dynasty combined with the high priesthood was established in the family of Mattathias (the Hasmoneans) through the line of the third son Simon. The Chasidim of the stricter sort did not support the new regime, and gave rise to a number of groups and communities, some of them strongly mystical, later classed as Essenes, who produced much of the Apocalyptic and Pseudepigraphic literature. Other pietists, remaining in close contact with national affairs, became distinguished in the reign of John Hyrcanus (135-103 B.C.) son of Simon, as Pharisees and Sadducees. The former, constituting a small but influential fraternity, were concerned with the sanctification of Jewish life through ordinances designed to assure freedom from contamination as required by the Mosaic Code. The latter were sticklers for the application of the Code in its explicit sense. They became bitter rivals and enemies, competing for power at Court and in the national Council (the Sanhedrin). They also in due course became representative of class distinctions, the Pharisees being regarded as champions of the people, while the Sadducees were identified with the hierarchy and aristocracy. Both parties had their extremists, who tended to exaggerate in teaching and practice the peculiarities of their respective positions, giving rise to mutual insult and exchange of harsh invectives and affording some real justification for charges of hypocrisy.

The Hasmonean dynasty lasted little more than a century and was brought to an end by the unhappy conflict between the two sons of Alexander Jannaeus (102-75 B.C.), the weak John Hyrcanus II and the ambitious Aristobulus. In its early stages this conflict brought the Romans on the scene in the person of Pompey, who subjugated Judea in 63 B.C. and earned the execration of the pious by daring to enter the inner holy place of the Temple at Jerusalem.

Judea became the vassal of Rome, with the powerful Antipater the Idumean, friend of Hyrcanus, made procurator, or governor, by Julius Caesar in 47 B.C. Antipater's son Herod became governor of Galilee, and ten years later by favour of Octavian and Marc Antony king of Judea. Transferring his support to the winning side in the struggle between these two for the mastery of the Roman world, Herod was confirmed in his government by Octavian, who himself in 27 B.C. became the Emperor Augustus.

Herod's reign was not one of peace. At its very beginning he had to suppress risings in Galilee in favour of Antigonus, last of the Hasmonean line. The Galileans had hated Herod ever since when governor of Galilee he had attacked their bands of guerillas who lived by plundering the neighbouring Syrians. Now the bands were again attacked and dispersed, but far from extinguished. They still had hide-outs in their highlands near the Sea of Galilee, and plenty of helpers among the fisher folk. In this region the torch of liberty from oppression burned brightest, liberty from the yoke of Rome and the Edomite.

Here were many who looked for the coming of the Messiah, the Deliverer of Israel.

The ambitious Herod went further out of his way to alienate his Jewish subjects by paganizing and Romanizing Palestine. He built theatres and staged costly games, while everywhere Caesar was honoured by inscriptions and the exhibition of trophies. New towns adorned with heathen statuary rose at his command, each testifying to his Roman loyalty. Strato's Tower became the port of Caesarea: Sebaste (Augustus) replaced the ancient Samaria. Only were Herod's building schemes halted for a time by prolonged droughts which forced him to purchase grain to feed his starving people. Galilee the fruitful became Galilee the barren, and thousands perished from want and disease.

In his domestic life Herod had continually to fear plots against his throne by members of his own family. He became a gloomy tyrant, even suspecting conspiracies when there were none. His officers had orders to see that the people were kept constantly at work. He prohibited public meetings and instituted an elaborate spy system. The grandiose plan to rebuild the Temple at Jerusalem as one of the wonders of the world could not endear him to his ill-used and offended subjects. He died miserably in 4 B.C. unmourned and unloved.

Herod was succeeded by his son Archelaus, who could not assume the title of king until confirmed on the throne by Caesar. His short term of rulership began in the worst possible way with a massacre of pilgrims assembled at Jerusalem for the Passover, who had dared to demand redress for their grievances. Forced to leave for Rome, Archelaus left the supervision of his affairs to Quinctilius Varus, governor of Syria. Almost immediately after his departure there was another outbreak at the Pentecost, due to the folly of Caesar's agent Sabinus, who had gone to Jerusalem to secure Herod's effects on his master's behalf, Herod having appointed Augustus executor of his will. The outbreak ended in a battle with the forces of Varus, who came hastily south with two legions and a host of auxiliaries. Around the walls of Jerusalem a forest of crosses was set up on which hung more than two thousand Jewish sufferers.

Archelaus returned from Rome with the title of ethnarch, with promise of kingship if his behaviour proved satisfactory. But in the tenth year of his government he was called to account at Rome for mismanagement of Jewish affairs and banished to Gaul. Judea now came under direct Roman rule with Coponius as procurator. At the same time (A.D. 6) Sulpicius Quirinius took over as legate of Syria, of which province Judea now formed a part. It was Quirinius who carried through the periodic census for taxation instituted by Augustus, such tax being the personal perquisite of the emperor. There was energetic protest by the Jews on the ground that the imposition was an infringement of their laws and liberties, and even a threat of revolt from a section of the Zealots led by Judas of Galilee.

Once again the Galileans were in the forefront of national opposition to foreign domination, with the watchword, 'No ruler but God'.

There had been too much suffering, however, for any general willingness to espouse the Zealot cause, though it had many sympathisers. It was about this time that Jesus of Nazareth attained the age of twelve, and paid his first and memorable visit to Jerusalem.

A period of comparative quiet was broken in A.D. 26 with the coming of Pontius Pilate as governor. In the meantime (A.D. 14) Augustus had died and was succeeded by Tiberius. There had been several intervening changes both in the governorship and in the high priesthood. The high priests were now appointed by the Roman governors, and were thus to an extent collaborators with the regime upon which their position depended. Notable among them had been Hanan, otherwise Annas or Ananus, son of Seth, five of whose sons became high priests. The present holder of the office was Annas's son-in-law Joseph Caiaphas. Beside the Hananites, there were other great hierarchical families, the most prominent being the Boethusians. These all controlled the Court of the Priests, and to a considerable extent the Sanhedrin, now shorn of much of its civil power. The Pharisees were well-represented in the Sanhedrin, but their principal external activities lay in the field of popular religious education through the synagogues, which combined the functions of places of worship and instruction.

The year A.D. 26-27 was a Sabbatical Year, and the cessation of agricultural activities not only gave the population more leisure to concern themselves with other matters, but particularly turned their thoughts towards release, the keynote of these septennial periods. This one was to prove specially significant, for at its commencement Pilate deeply offended Jewish religious sentiment by letting the legionaries carry their standards into Jerusalem bearing medallion portraits of the emperor. Crowds flocked to Caesarea to beg for the removal of the standards, and Pilate was most reluctantly forced to yield or risk insurrection. In the spring their appeared in the wilderness of Judea a prophet, John the son of Zechariah, proclaiming the near advent of the Kingdom of God, and calling on the people to repent and wash away their sins in the waters of Jordan. The country was stirred from end to end, and among those who responded to the call was Jesus, who after his immersion took up the Baptist's cry, and so commenced his own ministry. If one were to inquire what was chiefly present to the mind of the multitude at this period, one would receive a threefold answer: (1) food, for the people were often starving; (2) faith in God's miraculous intervention in their dire need; (3) assurance that the proud heathen would ere long be subject to a redeemed Israel. It was on these three counts that Jesus, having attained to full consciousness of his messiahship, was tempted in the wilderness.

About two years later Pilate again roused popular indignation by seizing the sacred *Qorban,* the Temple funds, in order to build an aqueduct to carry water into Jerusalem. This time many were killed in the tumult through the Roman troops exceeding their orders. Not long after, the exact year is uncertain, Jesus was secretly arrested outside Jerusalem just before the commencement of the spring festival of Unleavened Bread and crucified for his messianic pretensions.

The Samaritans, no less than the Jews, had suffered at Pilate's hands, and through their accusations he was recalled to Rome in A.D. 36 to answer the charges against his administration. Vitellius, legate of Syria, came personally to Jerusalem at the Passover of A.D. 37 to try to repair some of the damage done to the Roman cause, and he deprived Caiaphas of the high priesthood. It is not without significance that the two persons mainly responsible for the execution of Jesus—the Roman governor and the Jewish high priest—should have been removed from office within a few months of one another. News had now arrived of the death of Tiberius, who was succeeded by the weak-minded Gaius Caligula. Gaius, flattered by his sycophants, came to believe himself to be Jupiter incarnate, and brought a further calamity on the Jews by ordering his statue to be placed in the Temple at Jerusalem.

Not since the days of the Maccabees had there been such a threat to the very foundations of the Jewish Faith. Many took the view that it presaged the Time of the End, and that the Messiah would now be revealed to execute God's vengeance on the Romans. The more militant were for taking up arms, and a full-scale revolt might have developed had it not been for the decision of Petronius, then legate of Syria, to disobey the emperor's orders. Caligula dispatched a letter telling the legate to commit suicide for his disobedience; but this was providentially delayed in transit, and another letter arrived first with the information that Caligula had been assassinated. These events of A.D. 40-41 cannot have failed to exercise an influence on the Nazarenes, who had a powerful community at Antioch in Syria, the city which was the official seat of the legate. Incidentally, A.D. 40-41 was another Sabbatical Year.

Claudius now became emperor and appointed as king of Judea his friend Agrippa, a grandson of Herod I. Once again the Jewish people had a king, if only a puppet king. Agrippa did his utmost to please his subjects, and was scrupulous in the observance of Jewish customs; but he died suddenly in A.D. 44, and once more the country came under direct Roman rule. The response of the nationalists was to increase their activities, many subsisting largely by brigandage. The new governor Cuspius Fadus, and associated with him for a time a pro-Roman Jew Tiberius Alexander, carried out a ruthless policy of suppression. But by execution, imprisonment or banishment, they could bring about no more than a temporary pacification. Under the subsequent governors, Cumanus, Felix and Festus, the spirit of revolt steadily increased. As Josephus the contemporary Jewish historian described the situation: 'The imposters and brigands, banding together, incited numbers to revolt, exhorting them to assert their independence, and threatening to kill any who submitted to Roman domination and forcibly to suppress those who voluntarily accepted servitude. Distributing themselves in companies throughout the country, they looted the houses of the wealthy, murdered their owners, and set the villages on fire. The effects of their frenzy were thus felt throughout all Judea, and every day saw this war being fanned into fiercer flame.'[11]

It was under these conditions that the Nazarenes gained thousands of new adherents of Zealots for the Law. While others were forced to await a Messiah unknown, and were distracted with doubts and uncertainties, they had the strength of assured knowledge. Their aged and widely honoured leader, however, James the brother of Jesus, was murdered by the pro-Roman party about A.D. 62. Nothing now could stop the revolt, which developed fully four years later. Vespasian was sent by Nero to regain control of the country, and the conflict was a terrible one. The Jews ill-equipped and torn by faction nevertheless fought the greatest military machine of the age with fanatical courage. Finally Vespasian, made emperor in A.D. 70, left to his son Titus the siege and capture of Jerusalem, which fell in the summer of that year.

Such, in brief, were the grim circumstances in which Christianity was born and cradled, with no lullaby to still its infant cries, only the terrible sound of the echoing hoof-beats of the Four Horsemen of the *Apocalypse,* Pestilence, the Sword, Famine and Death.

(b) *The Galilean Scene*

The Galilean highlands, where Jesus spent the greater part of his life, differed not only in physical features from Judea: the people also were different. They were a ruder folk of mixed origin, Jews by religion, but many of their customs and practices were distinctive, and they were highly superstitious. In speech they employed a barbarous dialect of Aramaic, difficult for a stranger to follow because of the slurring of the gutturals. They were by no means inhospitable, but inclined to be puritanical. Their chief enemies were the heathen of the Syrian coastal plain, which explains their reaction to the speech of Jesus in the synagogue at Nazareth, as reported by Luke. They also had every reason to detest the Herodians, as we have to some extent seen, and had lost the flower of their manhood in the fighting which had established Herod on the throne. Many lived the lives of outlaws in the caves of the mountains, and at the time Jesus was born they had found a leader in Judas of Galilee, who upon the king's death had raided the armoury of

[11] *Wars*, II. xiii.

Sepphoris, chief city of Galilee, to equip his bands with weapons. Sepphoris lay only two hours' march to the north-west of Nazareth, and when the city was sacked and burnt by Varus in his southward advance to release Sabinus and his men trapped in Jerusalem, the mother of Jesus may well have known fear for herself and her offspring as the Arabian mercenaries ravaged the countryside.

When Herod Antipas became tetrarch of Galilee and Perea, the Zealots were still active and gave special trouble at the time of the taxing. Proud and independent, the Galileans would be slaves to no man, not even to Caesar himself.

Galilee, however fair and peaceful in outward seeming when Jesus knew it, was ever seething with unrest. Beggary had multiplied to an inconceivable extent even in a country where the mendicant was a familiar figure. Robbery with violence was so common that the courts had difficulty in dealing with the cases. Disease was rampant. A physician visiting the towns and villages could not hope to cope with the enormous number of nerve-cases, the blind, the deaf, the dumb, lepers, epileptics and paralytics, many of them owing their sufferings to the political and economic conditions. Women were hysterical, men frightened at shadows. The land was ridden by a great fear of the Evil One and his demons. Superstition and religiosity flourished. Many resorted to magical practices. Many made pilgrimages to the shrines of saints and to holy springs. There were those who gave themselves up to agonized prayer and severe fasting, and poor souls who ran wild and naked in the waste places and sheltered in tombs in the rocks.

It was in Galilee, perhaps more than anywhere else in Palestine, that the Deliverer was expected. The Messiah would come, and some were convinced it would be in Galilee. In the Vale of Arbel, scene of the great defeat at the hands of Herod, he would raise his standard of victory.

As Jesus knew it, the road from Nazareth, set on the slope of a hill, ran on to Kefar-Kenna, Cana of Galilee. On the mountainside opposite was a famed holy place to which there was a constant stream of pilgrims. It was the tomb of the Prophet Jonah, he who had brought the Ninevites to repentance. Further on, the road began to dip down, and between the hills could be glimpsed the Lake of Chinnereth, the Sea of Galilee, hundreds of feet beneath. There it lay, a sapphire jewel in a setting of old gold, one of the loveliest scenes upon which the eye of man could rest. As the road descended in a succession of bends so the temperature rose steadily to tropical heat. Lush vegetation flourished in profusion. The date palm reared its stately head. On either side of the road were to be seen plantations of olives, fig-trees and vines, while the increase of traffic and the distant prospect of buildings gave evidence of a populous area.

The road turned north along the lakeside, but a branch to the right led down to the town of Rakkath and the Hot Springs noted for their curative properties. Here Antipas built his city of Tiberias in the emperor's honour. The lake itself was dotted with craft, while on the strand fishermen repaired their boats and mended their nets. Much of the fish caught was landed at a place called Tarichea, there to be pickled in brine and sold for distribution to all parts of the country. The fishermen, like those of the same calling in many other lands, were simple direct folk with an assured faith in God and a no less assured belief in demons and malignant spirits, who could raise a sudden storm and keep the fish from their nets. It was they no doubt who carried momentous news and gossip to the various towns and villages bordering the lake, and sometimes acted as a link between the outlaws and their secret sympathizers.

On the far side of the lake the mountains of the Gaulan showed up harshly as a high plateau pouring itself into the water in plum-coloured lumps intersected by clefts and gorges. This too was Herod's territory, except for the free cities of the Decapolis. Over there, however, they were mainly foreigners and pig-breeders.

The road swung out from the shore and back again to industrious Magdala with its dye-works. The mountains on the left, seeming higher for the deep depression in which the blue lake glistened, were pierced with glens, notably that of Arbel, dark with foliage. But presently the highlands receded, and there spread out lay the Plain of Gennesareth, greatly favoured because of its temperate climate and extreme fertility. Here were the estates of the rich and noble; but the general state of affairs required them to be heavily fenced and guarded against thieves. Away to the north-west could be seen a city set on a hill, the fortified town of Zefat. Nearer at hand were the ravines which had often harboured the outlaws, while in the far distance to the north-east rose up the snow-clad glory of Mount Hermon.

Traversing the edge of the plain, threading its way through groves and orchards, the road turned again to the lake, and reached it near the busy mart and customs-station of Kefar-Nahum (Capernaum). A large foreign element was to be found here, and the Jews tended to be more lax in their religious observances. The poorer and, by contrast, more devout Jewish folk found a home in the adjacent fishing-village of Bethsaida.

The road was now joined by another coming across the hills from the Mediterranean coast at Syrian Acco (Ptolemais). It continued round the head of the lake to the frontier town of Bethsaida-Julias, and on eventually to ancient Damascus.

This was the land that Jesus knew intimately and loved greatly. From its hills and dales, its flowers and trees, fields and plantations, the life of its people in work and worship, home and farm, he drew inspiration for the stories with which he illustrated his teaching. Nothing escaped his observant notice, and certainly not the religious, political and economic conditions then prevailing. He was apt with a homely proverb, a telling quotation: his compassion reached out to help all who suffered. His consciousness of the unique and supremely responsible office to which he felt himself to have been called never made him aloof from his fellows. Only in mystical moments of prayer and meditation was he withdrawn and apart. The man who could speak, as we shall hear him speaking, had first-hand knowledge of men and affairs, and an acute perception of the implications of what he heard and saw. The evils of his time did not escape him: he evaded none of them, and addressed himself to their remedy.

(c) *The Sermon on the Mount*

For an understanding of the teaching of Jesus to his generation it is natural to turn to the so-called Sermon on the Mount. Here we have both a statement of his own policy and that of the Nazarenes in a collection of declarations on various issues which it may be useful and illuminating to bring into relationship with contemporary circumstances and ideas.

The opening benedictions and denunciations reflect the attitude of the Chasidic groups, as may be seen from the following quotations:

> 'They who have died in grief shall arise in joy,
> And they who were poor for the Lord's sake shall be
>   made rich,
> And they who have been in want shall be filled,
> And they who have been weak shall be strong,
> And they who are put to death for the Lord's sake shall
>   awake to life."[12]
> 'Woe to you rich! for you have trusted in your riches,
>   and from your riches you shall depart, because you
>   have not remembered the Most High in the days of
>   your riches. You have committed blasphemy and
>   unrighteousness and have become ready for the Day
>   of Slaughter and the Day of Darkness and the Day
>   of Judgment.
> Woe to you sinners! for you persecute the righteous; for
>   you will be delivered up and persecuted you people
>   of injustice, and heavy will their yoke be upon you.
> Woe to you! who devour the finest of the wheat and
>   drink the power of the source of the fountain, and
>   tread underfoot the lowly with your might."[13]

Attitude towards the Law (*the Torah*), (Mt. v. 17-20)

Since the heroic days of the Maccabees the Law had become the people's possession: they had died for it: it was the very foundation of their national existence. Loyalty to the Law was therefore a first essential of messianic policy. In the popular

[12] *Test. Judah,* xxv. 4.   [13] *Enoch,* xciv.

expositions of the prophetic writings Isa. ix. 6-7 had been interpreted messianically, and the expression 'the government shall be upon his shoulder' had been rendered 'he has taken the Law upon himself to keep it.'[14]

Weighty and light precepts were alike of God's giving. As one of the early rabbis said: 'Be heedful of a light precept as of a weighty one, for you do not know the grant of reward for each precept.'[15]

Three crimes might not be committed by a man, even if his life were in danger, those of idolatry, adultery and murder.[16] These three are dealt with in turn in the Matthean version of the Sermon on the Mount, though idolatry is considered under the aspect of oaths.

Concerning Murder (Mt. v. 21-24)

At this time life was held very cheaply and human relationships were strained to breaking point. The utterance of an angry or slanderous word was often followed by tragic consequences. Therefore even to be enraged with one's brother must be regarded as tantamount to the commission of the capital crime.

Consequently the Chasidim declared: 'Unless you keep yourselves from the spirit of lying and of anger, and love truth and long-suffering, you shall perish. For anger is blindness, and does not permit one to see the face of any man with truth.'[17] And again: 'For the spirit of hatred works with Satan, through hastiness of spirit, in all things to men's death; but the spirit of love works with the Law of God in long-suffering to the salvation of men.'[18]

'Be as eager to secure your fellow's honour as your own; and do not yield easily to anger.'[19]

Concerning Adultery (Mt. v. 27-28)

The plague of vice temporarily checked by the Maccabean reformation had broken out afresh in Israel. Territorial barriers could not stem the rising tide of corruption which was engulfing the pagan world. It was 'an evil and adulterous generation'. Morals were so lax that not so long after the time of Christ the Pharisee leader R. Jochanan ben Zaccai ordered the cessation of the ordeal by bitter waters (Num. v. 11-31), basing his action on Hosea iv. 14: 'I will not punish your daughters when they commit whoredom, nor your spouses when they commit adultery.' The well-to-do are described as 'committing adultery with their neighbours' wives, treading God's Sanctuary in all their pollutions, leaving no sin which they did not commit, even worse than the Gentiles.'[20]

Said the Chasidim: 'He who has a pure mind in love, does not

[14] Targ. Pal.   [15] Aboth. ii. 1.   [16] Sanhed. 64a.
[17] Test. Dan. ii. 1-2.   [18] Test. Gad, iv. 7.   [19] Aboth, ii. 15.
[20] Ps. Sol. viii. 8-14.

look at a woman with a view to fornication; for he has no defilement in his heart, because the Spirit of God rests upon him.'[21]

Concerning Oaths (Mt. v. 33-37)

With heathendom at the very gates it had become increasingly necessary to preserve the Name of God from profanation. The people continually hearing their Gentile neighbours swear by Zeus, by the Capitoline Jove, and by other divinities, might easily be led to use the name of the God of Israel as lightly. Pronunciation of the sacred Tetragrammaton JHVH was therefore restricted to the high priest in the Temple on the most solemn occasion, and elsewhere priests and people when engaged in worship substituted Adonai (the Lord). In ordinary intercourse even Adonai was not used, but such indirect expressions as 'Heaven', 'the Name', 'the Place'. Yet even if such a precautionary term for the Godhead was employed in an oath the vow was binding. This applied equally when a man vowed by anything dedicated to God. But the pious agreed that swearing was to be discouraged, though in deference to human weakness the Pharisees allowed the use of oaths to which no guilt of profanation of the Name attached, such as 'By Jerusalem!' or 'By the Temple!' or 'By the life of my head!'

The Chasidim insisted that oaths were not required, and that 'Yes' or 'No' should be as binding as any oath. All swearing indirectly countenanced idolatry.

Concerning Retaliation (Mt. v. 38-48; Lk. vi. 27-36)

Like many Chasidim and moderate Pharisees Jesus was opposed to armed revolt, since if the people were faithful to God he would intervene to save them. The Kingdom of God could not be hastened by violence. The policy of 'No Reprisals' was a difficult one to advocate since the people were largely at the mercy of the legionaries, many of them mercenaries who hated the Jews. The sufferings of the poor Jewish peasant were particularly severe. At any moment impost collectors might break into his hovel to impound his few possessions, brutally striking him if he resisted (Mt. v. 39). If he had nothing else worth taking they would even strip him of his tunic (Mt. v. 40). As he passed along the road with his donkey he might meet a company of soldiers who would compel him to carry their baggage for miles in the opposite direction to which he was going (Mt. v. 41). The very word for this forced service was hebraized from the Greek, so that the *angaria* (impressment) was spoken of with sullen hatred. Requests for money, with no intention to repay, was another affliction to be endured (Mt. v. 42; Lk. vi. 30); so that it is hardly surprising that there should be resistance. Yet it is noteworthy that Jewish tradition

[21] *Test.Benj.* viii. 2.

attributes the destruction of Jerusalem to initial acts of retaliation such as Jesus would fain have prevented.[22] Reprisals would only aggravate the people's unhappy condition.

At a later time, when the position had little changed, the rabbis inculcated the same lesson: 'Be rather an object of curses than curse yourself';[23] 'A man should always be among the persecuted rather than among the persecutors';[24] 'They who being reviled revile not again, who take no heed of insults, and act out of love, rejoicing in affliction, of them Scripture says, "Them that love him are as the sun when it goes forth in its strength".'[25]

The references we have now given, and they could be greatly multiplied, illustrate how relevant was the message of Jesus to the circumstances prevailing in Palestine at the time. He saw clearly as much as and more than other Jews of faith and insight, and he dared to announce his conclusions with all the weight of a personal and independent authority.

Jesus boldly called on his people for an 'excess' of love and well-doing that would make them mete for deliverance. But he hastened to explain that by 'doing more than others' he did not mean an ostentatious display of piety. Just as in the earlier part of his speech he had grouped his remarks concerning the Law around the fundamental commandments dealing with murder, adultery and idolatry, so he went on to speak of piety under the three forms in which Judaism enjoined its practice—almsgiving, prayer and penitence (fasting).[26] One can readily understand that there were many devout souls who gave themselves to prayer, fasting and charity, that God might remove the threatened perils. These persons would have been ashamed to confess their vicarious atonement. One can as readily appreciate the temptation of less single-minded individuals to let it be seen that they were interceding for the nation. The poor people in their desperate plight would follow such with their blessings, assured that there must be a response from heaven to the pleas of these presumed saints.

Jesus warned his hearers against three types of persons, the ostentatious pietist, the fault finder, and the false prophet. The tragedy was that behind each type there was the insistent anxiety for deliverance, a continual longing for the presence of God. In those days brother was looking on brother with a jaundiced eye, and with some the search for error in others amounted almost to a mania. It was 'a generation which judged its judges',[27] tradition records, and quotes the same proverb Jesus used about the splinter and the shaft. Such a generation inevitably made for schisms and factions. If the people would spend themselves in doing good to others they would have no time for fault-finding and witch-hunting.

Nevertheless the groups and the rival parties were there, the petty chiefs who had their hour, the religious enthusiasts who

[22] *Gitt.* 57a. [23] *Shabb.* 55a. [24] *Abod. Zara*, 93a. [25] *B. Kama*, 93a.
[26] *TJ. Taan.* 2a. [27] *B. Bathra*, 15b.

preached messages of hope, but did little to realize the hopes they raised. On the other hand there were the wolves in sheep's clothing, battening on the people's misery, those false prophets who, taking advantage of the distraught and helpless, promised to a longing and expectant nation, believers in the miraculous, signs and wonders which were to presage the Redemption. No miracle was too remarkable for the wretched and credulous multitudes to swallow, with the natural result that they became an easy prey of a host of charlatans.[28] 'By their fruits you will recognize them.'

Into the brief compass of the Sermon on the Mount is packed all that Jesus felt was of real import for the spiritual and material welfare of his people in their hour of crisis. He cleared away the shifting sands and got down to bed-rock, enunciating those abiding principles upon which alone the Community of the Kingdom of God could be securely founded. And he himself exemplified his own teaching, knowing clearly as the months went by that he would be, indeed must be, the victim of the forces governing 'this world', but remaining firm in his conviction that this was the way to attain 'that world', the coming Kingdom of God.

It is a Roman author, even if he may be guilty of some prejudice, who has supplied what may be regarded both as a justification of the Sermon on the Mount and as an illuminating commentary on the ultimate consequences for Jesus himself.

'Among the calamities of that black period,' writes Tacitus, 'the most trying grievance was the degenerate spirit, with which the first men in the senate submitted to the drudgery of becoming common informers; some without a blush, in the face of day; and others by clandestine artifices. The contagion was epidemic. Near relations, aliens in blood, friends and strangers, known and unknown, were, without distinction, all involved in one common danger. The fact recently committed, and the tale revived, were equally destructive. Words alone were sufficient; whether spoken in the forum, or amidst the pleasures of the table . . . Informers struggled, as it were in a race, who should be first to ruin his man; some to secure themselves; the greater part infected by the general corruption of the times.'[29] Only in A.D. 28, in the calends of January, Sabinus, an eminent Roman knight, had been seized in Rome, and dragged through the streets to summary execution on a feast day. The general murmur was, 'Will there never be a day unpolluted with blood? Amidst the rites and ceremonies of a season sacred to religion, when all business is at a standstill, and the use of profane words is by law prohibited, we hear the clank of chains; we see the halter, and the murder of a fellow-citizen. The innovation, monstrous as it is, is a deliberate act, the policy of Tiberius. He means to make cruelty systematic. By this unheard-of outrage, he gives public notice to the magistrates, that on the first

[28] Cp. Jos. *Antiq.* XX. v. 1; vii. 6.   [29] Tacit. *Annals,* Book VI. vii.

day of the year they are to open, not only the temples and the altars, but also the dungeons and the charnel-house.'[30]

What hope, then, was there for Jesus of Nazareth on the feast of the first month of the Jewish national year, if he were charged with 'blasphemy' before the arrogant Roman who administered Judea for his despotic master?

(3) *The Text and Translation*

In the foregoing pages we have endeavoured to show, mainly in the social and political sphere, how closely in touch are the writers of the New Testament with the thought and the circumstances of their time, and more particularly in relation to conditions in Palestine. These things, to borrow Paul's words, 'were not done in a corner'. The reporting of them, even in small details, gives evidence of reliable sources of information. To establish the truth of this in any way comprehensively would require a volume at least as long as the New Testament itself. A number of additional points, however, are touched upon in the prefaces to the various documents and in the footnotes to the translation. It may be that these will whet the reader's appetite rather than satisfy it; and nothing could be more desirable.

But is it not alone in references and allusions that the documents reflect their time and are of their time. They belong to it in atmosphere, and in the realm of ideas, though it is only in our day that knowledge has begun to pile up which discloses what were the precise elements in Judaism which gave rise to Christianity. We can now see relationships where previously it was assumed that there were antitheses. This should be salutary both for Jews and Christians, and in fact has already begun to promote a better understanding between them.

In language also, as we have learnt from an examination of remains of the period, many of the New Testament documents reflect the contemporary speech of ordinary people. And why should it be otherwise when they were meant for ordinary people? There was an everyday Greek which served the needs of a large part of the multi-racial population bordering the eastern Mediterranean, and translation of the New Testament in the present century has been considerably assisted by observing the sense of words and expressions as employed in private correspondence, in contracts, and in other non-literary material excavated in Egypt. Jesus himself spoke the Galilean dialect of Aramaic, a language having a kinship with Hebrew. In a few instances what may have been his actual words in that language have been preserved. Both Hebrew and to a lesser extent Aramaic were in use for literary purposes among the Palestinian Jews, and there is every reason to believe that parts of the New Testament depend on sources originally written in one of those languages. We now possess a number of post-

[30] *Ibid.* Book IV. lxx.

Biblical and pre-Talmudical Hebrew works, and these exhibit the changes that had taken place in the language in the intervening centuries. Direct translation of Semitic texts into Greek by any of the New Testament writers is not probable. It seems more likely that Greek versions of some of the original records were already available. But no modern translator can afford to neglect the intimations of underlying Semitic sources when he is dealing with portions of the Gospels, the *Acts*, and the *Revelation*.

The Jewishness that is almost everywhere present in the Greek New Testament is truly remarkable. It is seen in the midrashic method of teaching used by Jesus, notably in the parables, and in the rabbinical manner of argument employed by Paul. The Alexandrian school of Jewish thought is represented by the *Homily to the Hebrews,* while the mystical and visionary concepts and literary forms characteristic of Chasidic Judaism appear both in the writings of Paul and in the *Revelation.* But the Jewishness comes out in hundreds of small points, in proverbs and expressions, poetical passages and colloquialisms, and in sentiments and associations of all kinds. Many of these have been recognized by scholars; but there are some which previously have escaped notice. Of particular interest and significance are the liturgical elements, the Jewish construction of prayers, the delight in benedictions and doxologies. There are both direct and indirect references not only to rites and ceremonies connected with the Temple and Synagogue, but also to some of the most ancient Jewish prayers and praises which still find a place in the modern *Authorised Jewish Prayer Book.* It is essential for the translator of the New Testament to be fully informed on these matters, and a number of the references have been supplied in the footnotes to the present version. The reader wishing to make further study of the subject will be assisted by the following works: Oesterley, *The Jewish Background of the Christian Liturgy;* Gavin, *The Jewish Antecedents of the Christian Sacraments;* Abrahams, *Annotated Edition of the Authorised (Jewish) Daily Prayer Book;* De Sola Pool, *The Old Jewish-Aramaic Prayer the Kaddish;* and Edersheim, *The Temple, its Ministry and Service as they were at the time of Jesus Christ.* To give only a single instance of the importance of consulting the Jewish liturgical sources, we should never have had the expression 'and on earth peace' in the angelic doxology in Lk. ii. 14 had this been done by former translators. The 'glory' is to God above and below, in the highest and on earth, the 'peace' is to men of good will, or better, to men who please him.

There are some rectifications of the text itself suggested by a knowledge of Hebrew and Aramaic. These, of course, can only be made conjecturally. But in several cases the evidence is quite overwhelming that the original translator into Greek has misunderstood or made a slip in his rendering of the Hebrew, and in translation there have also been lost certain plays on words and poetic parallelisms. To check thoroughly and recover as much as possible all Hebraic elements have independently by the present translator been converted into Hebrew or Aramaic, as might be appropriate, during the early stages of his work. The results, insignificant as they may seem, have in his opinion justified this extra labour, and he has here followed in the steps of scholars who have treated in the same way the Greek and other versions of some of the Jewish apocalyptic and pseudepigraphic writings, and even the Gospels.

Unfortunately, we do not possess those Greek translations of the Hebrew documents which were employed by some of the New Testament writers, except in so far as they have reproduced them or show dependence on them.[81] We cannot even tell, as regards the Nazarene sources, exactly what was their nature and scope, though a good idea has been obtained by painstaking analysis and comparison of the Christian Scriptures as they now stand. Naturally such foundation material would tend to disappear and cease to be copied once the books we now have had found wide acceptance. But there is no justification for the view that an oral tradition predominated. Some of the lost literature of the early Judaeo-Christians, suited more particularly to Jewish circles, was probably never translated out of the original Hebrew at all, and largely perished or was hidden away during the calamitous period of the war with Rome and its aftermath. What remained available was primarily what had already gone out in Greek dress beyond the area of conflict, and what had been written elsewhere than in Palestine, principally letters like those of Paul.

The greater part of the present New Testament belongs to the second forty years of Christianity, the period roughly from A.D. 70-110. This, however, may represent only a fraction of the Apostolic literature that was produced. Both in the New Testament and elsewhere there is mention of books which have not survived, letters no longer extant. Of some ancient uncanonical Gospels fragments remain either in manuscript or in quotations in the writings of the Church Fathers; but those at present known seem rather to belong to the third forty years, A.D. 110-150. This is also true of certain writings which have descended to us virtually intact and which are commonly entitled *The Apostolic Fathers* in their collected form. We especially miss, however, the works of Papias and Hegesippus, known only from brief and tantalizing quotations.

The text of the New Testament on which we must base our translation is what is called a critical text, arrived at by a painstaking study of copies and versions of the different books made for the most part, but not exclusively, between the second and fifth centuries. No individual manuscript is followed completely, and there are some which have preserved venerable

---

[81] Cp., for instance, *Acts of Barnabas,* 'Barnabas had received documents from Matthew, a book of the voice (message?) of God, and a narrative of miracles and doctrines.'

and interesting readings which may reflect a genuine tradition, which yet have had to be discarded. In the present version a few of such readings have been included in the text within square brackets or quoted in the footnotes. Progress in textual matters steadily proceeds, and the present editor and translator has not rigidly adhered even to the most recent critical editions. Errors there still may be in numerous points of small detail, which will have to be corrected with greater knowledge, but no radical changes are now likely to be required. It may be accepted with confidence that we have at command the New Testament substantially as the writings contained in it could be read within a century of their composition.

We are to imagine our documents as written on one side of sheets of papyrus writing paper about five inches wide by ten inches deep, each sheet joined at the bottom to the top of the next, so making up a roll of whatever length was required. The handwriting would normally be rather small, possibly in the case of literary works in double-column, the words not separated and with occasional contractions, and arranged in even lines without punctuation. Occasionally a dot would mark a change of theme or a small space indicate a paragraph. A correction or short note might be inserted between the lines, or at top or bottom of a sheet. Margins being narrow offered little room for annotation. The title of a book, or destination of a letter, would be added at the back of the finished roll.

There were no chapters or verses in the manuscripts. The chapters now in use in ecclesiastical versions were adopted in the thirteenth century and the verse divisions as late as the sixteenth century. Their value was to assist reading and reference, but they are in no sense authoritative. In the present version they have been employed only in the footnotes, both for Old and New Testament references, for purposes of study and comparison. Otherwise, as regards the New Testament, the general reader will find where needful the page number in this volume given additionally. The absence in the originals of the divisions with which we are now familiar does not mean, however, that the documents had no structure. In several cases it has been possible to ascertain the plan upon which a book has been constructed by its author. In such cases, as far as was practicable, that plan has been reproduced. Thus the *Gospel of Mark* is made up of a series of short episodes, which have been numbered. The *Gospel of Matthew* is in five books with subsections, together with a Prologue and Epilogue. The *Gospel of John* exhibits remains of a series of clearly defined sections. The *Book of Revelation* consists of two books, with a Prologue and Epilogue, each book containing a group of visions to which the present translator has given descriptive titles. In other documents, e.g. *Luke-Acts*, chapters have been introduced according to the sense, while letters have only been broken up into suitable paragraphs.

In addition to these changes in presentation designed to

bring out the character of each work, elements of documents have wherever possible been distinguished, notably in the case of Paul's letters to the Corinthian community, where the original four letters have been restored partially and conjecturally out of the two into which they had become combined, probably for reasons of economy.

In the Gospels and the *Acts* author's or very early editor's notes are found in the text itself. Where they could reasonably be identified as such they have been extracted and printed at the foot of the page where nowadays we should expect to find them. To prevent confusion with the translator's own notes they have been set in slightly larger type and are indicated by letters of the alphabet instead of numerals. It is hoped that this arrangement will assist and increase understanding.

The order in which the books appear in the ecclesiastical versions is again a grouping of convenience, and is not authoritative. We have the Gospels, *Acts,* Epistles, and *Revelation.* But the New Testament is not a planned volume, and in arranging its elements for general and intelligent reading certain changes in order are obviously desirable, first to keep together those documents which are in some way associated, and second to give some consideration to chronological sequence. Commonsense requires that the *Gospel of John* should not be sandwiched between the two parts of Luke's work, the *Gospel* and the *Acts,* nor should the *Gospel of John* be separated from the letters of John. Equally a rational editing of the letters of Paul requires that they be placed as far as possible in chronological order.

In the present version, therefore, a slightly different arrangement has been adopted. The Synoptic ('common viewpoint') Gospels have as usual been placed at the beginning, because they tell the story of the life and work of Jesus, but with *Mark* put first, followed by *Matthew* and *Luke* which largely incorporate it, in that order. Then immediately after *Luke* comes the *Acts* by the same author, which describes the growth and expansion of the Christian Movement. Those who are reading the New Testament for the first time are recommended in the first instance to skip *Mark* and *Matthew* and start with *Luke,* so that they do not have to cover a good deal of the same ground three times over. Next come the letters of Paul, which are illuminated by the *Acts,* in chronological order, beginning with the letters to the community at Thessalonica. After these comes a *Homily to the Hebrews* by an unknown author, but related to the school of Pauline thought; then a group of letters standing in the names of Palestinian writers, but later in date, with the doubtful *II. Peter* last. Finally comes a collection of Johannine documents, the *Gospel,* Letters, and the *Revelation,* which in their present form are probably the latest works in the New Testament.

Before leaving the text there are certain other matters which call for comment. In the majority of cases the view taken of glosses is that of leading modern scholars. Some transpositions of material have been necessary, notably in the *Gospel of John,* which is in great confusion. The changes, and the reasons for them, are briefly explained in the prefaces and footnotes to the books concerned. Actual emendations of the text have been kept to a minimum, and only those have been made which in the editor's opinion had the very strongest justification.

To turn now to the translation itself. The reader of the Greek obviously enjoys many advantages. He can appreciate differences in style and literary quality. He can detect influences and the use of sources. He can grasp the mood and feelings of the writer, sympathize with his difficulties in expressing himself, or admire the facility and beauty of his composition. It is the responsibility of the translator to be the medium by which as much of the character and quality of the documents is transmitted as can be achieved in a readable and realistic manner. This is difficult enough where only a single author is concerned. It is manifestly much harder when the translator has to deal with a number of strongly individual writers. He may not, to do his job properly, employ a uniform style throughout. He must endeavour to vary it appropriately, as the actor his voice and gestures. He must not be afraid of the unliterary phrase and the colloquialism, when much of what he is translating is unliterary and colloquial; and he requires both wide knowledge and deep insight.

As to these qualifications, the present translator has been at infinite pains to attempt to measure up to them; it is not for him to say to what extent he has succeeded. He will only draw attention here to certain features, having already set down the guiding principles in the Preface to the volume. Yet perhaps it should be stated again with every possible emphasis that his is a non-ecclesiastical version, the work of an historian and man of letters, not of a theologian, and is not therefore binding on anyone's conscience.

The translator has felt it to be important for his purpose not to employ in his rendering familiar ecclesiastical terms where they could be avoided, since the use of them would give the impression that they were peculiarly Christian in origin and association. This relates to such words as baptism (immersion), church (community), apostle (envoy), bishop (supervisor), and deacon (administrator), but also sometimes to words like 'salvation', 'righteousness', 'faith', and 'grace', which occasionally do not accurately represent the sense of the original. Many Greek words have different meanings, according to the context in which they are placed, or are interpreting Hebrew words, and it would be quite wrong always to translate them by the same English expression. Some very telling composite words like *oligopistos* cannot effectively be rendered by a single word in English, and one has to do one's best with a phrase like 'feeble in faith'. While, in general, modern speech has been employed, the older English has been kept for the language of prayer, and here and there to retain the flavour of an orientalism. Finally, as regards proper names, these as a rule are given in their most familiar form, whether they relate to Old or New Testament characters, thus Isaiah and Elijah, not Esias and Elias. But there are exceptions, especially where the termination of the name either in Hebrew or Greek has direct reference to God, thus Zechariah, not Zacharias, father of John the Baptist, and Timotheus, not Timothy. Place names also have mostly been retained in the form best known, e.g. Capernaum instead of the more accurate Kefar-Nahum.

The references given in the Introduction and notes will chiefly be of interest and service to the serious student, though some of them may be found helpful to the general reader seeking further enlightenment. For this reason consideration of accessibility of reference material has been taken fully into account. A complete index of the ancient authorities mentioned, with an explanation of the abbreviations, will be found at the end of the volume. In two instances, however, modern sources of information have been cited both in the notes and index, (JE) *Jewish Encyclopaedia* (Funk and Wagnalls) and (AJP) *Authorised (Jewish) Daily Prayer Book* (Eyre and Spottiswoode). The writer is indebted to the works of a host of scholars; but it would have been out of place in a work primarily intended for popular reading to load the pages with the hundreds of acknowledgments that would have had to be listed, and with the discussion of various opinions which could hardly have been avoided.

Quite deliberately the notes have been restricted to furnishing such information as might be of material use and interest to the studious, without being too academic. There has been no intention to provide a full-scale commentary, only to convey an impression of the native atmosphere and climate of ideas. For parallel passages in the Gospels explanatory notes have not usually been repeated; but a minimum amount of cross-referencing has been supplied.

Perhaps sufficient has now been said to introduce a version of the New Testament which in some ways breaks new ground and represents a fresh and distinctive approach. It may be fitting in the special circumstances for the writer not to conclude with his own words, or with the words either of a Jewish or Christian scholar on the Christian Scriptures, when he might be accused either of prejudice or flattery, but rather with the words plain spoken and not particularly gracious of a Christian scholar, George Sale, presenting his English version of the Mohammedan Scriptures, the *Quran*. 'Having therefore undertaken a new translation, I have endeavoured to do the original impartial justice; not having, to the best of my knowledge, represented it, in any one instance, either better or worse than it really is.'

CHRONOLOGY OF NEW TESTAMENT TIMES

Date   Event

B.C.

c.5   Birth of Jesus of Nazareth.

4   Death of Herod. Archelaus becomes ruler of Judea, and
A.D.   Herod Antipas tetrarch of Galilee and Perea.

6   Archelaus deposed. Judea united to Roman province of Syria. Quirinius legate of Syria. Coponius procurator of Judea.

7   Roman census completed in Judea. Ananus son of Seth made high priest.

14   Death of Augustus Caesar. Accession of Tiberius.

25   Joseph Caiaphas made high priest.

26   Pontius Pilate becomes procurator of Judea in succession to Valerius Gratus.

27   John the Baptist proclaims Kingdom of God. Jesus immersed by John and begins his ministry.

c.29   Jesus arrested and crucified.

36   Pilate recalled.

36-37   Stephen the deacon martyred. Caiaphas deposed and Jonathan son of Ananus made high priest. Death of Tiberius and accession of Gaius Caligula. Saul of Tarsus becomes a Nazarene.

40   Caligula attempts to have his statue set up in Temple at Jerusalem. Saul and Barnabas at Antioch in Syria.

41   Caligula assassinated. Accession of Claudius. Herod Agrippa made king of Judea.

c.43   Martyrdom of James son of Zebedee.

44   Death of Agrippa. Cuspius Fadus made procurator of Judea.

46-48   Paul's first missionary journey with Barnabas.

49   Council at Jerusalem on terms of admission of Gentile converts.

50   Paul's second missionary journey begins.

51-52   Paul at Athens and Corinth.

53   Paul's third missionary journey begins.

54   Death of Claudius and accession of Nero.

55-56   Paul at Ephesus, then Macedonia and Corinth.

57-58   Paul returns from Asia and arrives at Jerusalem in the spring. There arrested.

58   Felix procurator of Judea. Ananias son of Nedebeus high priest.

60   Festus procurator of Judea. Paul sent to Rome.

61   Paul arrives at Rome.

c.62   James brother of Jesus martyred at Jerusalem.

64   Paul martyred at Rome. Great fire of Rome, and persecution of Christians.

c.65   Martyrdom of Peter.

66   Jewish revolt against Rome begins.

68   Death of Nero. Nazarenes leave Jerusalem (?)

70   Vespasian becomes emperor. Titus captures Jerusalem.

c.71   Simeon a cousin of Jesus becomes head of the Nazarenes.

79   Death of Vespasian. Accession of Titus.

81   Death of Titus. Accession of Domitian.

95   Domitian persecutes the Christians.

96   Domitian assassinated. Accession of Nerva.

98   Death of Nerva. Accession of Trajan.

NOTE: All dates of Christian events are approximate.

TABLE FOR COMPARISON WITH
THE AUTHORISED (KING JAMES) VERSION

xlv

TABLE FOR COMPARISON

	PAGE	A.V.	PAGE	A.V.
I. Jno.				
431	i. 1-ii. 7.	442-43	ii. 16-iii. 2.	456	xiii. 17-xiv. 7.
431-32	ii. 8-25.	443	iii. 3-15.	456-57	xiv. 8-19.
432-33	ii. 26-iii. 14.	444	iii. 16-22.	457-58	xiv. 20-xv. 7.
433-34	iii. 15-iv. 8.	444-45	iv. 1-10.	458-59	xv. 8-xvi. 11.
434-35	iv. 9-v. 8.	445	iv. 11-v. 10.	459	xvi. 12-21.
435	v. 9-21.	446	v. 11-vi. 6.	460	xvii. 1-10.
		446-47	vi. 7-17.	460-61	
II. Jno.		447-48	vii. 1-10.		xvii. 11-xviii. 8.
436	i. 1-13.	448	vii. 11-viii. 5.	461-62	xviii. 9-19.
		449	viii. 6-8.	462-63	
III. Jno.		449-50	viii. 9-ix. 6.		xviii. 20-xix. 4.
437	i. 1-14.	450-51	ix. 7-19.	463-64	xix. 5-16.
		451-52	ix. 20-x. 11.	464-65	xix. 17-xx. 5.
Rev.		452	xi. 1-12.	465	xx. 6-xxi. 4.
440	i. 1-11.	453	xi. 13-19.	466	xxi. 5-16.
441	i. 12-ii. 4.	453-54	xii. 1-10.	466-67	xxi. 17-xxii. 5.
441-42	ii. 5-15.	454-55	xii. 11-xiii. 4.	467-68	xxii. 6-18.
		455	xiii. 5-16.	468	xxii. 19-21.

MARK

THE RECOLLECTIONS OF PETER

Preface to *Mark*

THE OLDEST EXTANT ACCOUNT of the life and teaching of Jesus is that which is attributed to Mark, doubtless the John Mark of Jerusalem mentioned in the *Acts of the Envoys,* who is credited with evangelizing Egypt. By a second century writer, Papias of Hierapolis, he is said to have acted as Peter's interpreter, and to have written down afterwards as accurately as he could remember what Peter had related in his addresses of the things said and done by Jesus. Papias explains that Mark was not attempting 'an orderly narrative', that is to say to write a book in the ordinary sense.

The tradition agrees with the character of our work, which consists of a series of episodes set down with great economy of words and without literary polish. Often one feels that the writer is too abrupt and uncommunicative, which to some has suggested that he is abridging. He has an extraordinary fondness for the word *euthys,* 'at once', 'directly', 'immediately', often used like the colloquial *'next thing* he was running down the road', which conveys the sense of a spoken rather than a written story. It is this unaffectedness and conversational tone that constitutes so much of the charm of the book, and which leaves little room for doubt that it is in fact the reminiscences of Peter we are reading. Some words of Jesus are even left in the original Aramaic.

Section xxxvi (Mk. xiii) probably reflects a short document in the nature of a revelation by Jesus to the Jerusalem Christians, which tradition says was given shortly before the Jewish war with Rome, presumably therefore about A.D. 66. Its inclusion must mean that the book is subsequent to that date, though it need not be many years later, perhaps about A.D. 72-75.

The work is designed for the non-Jewish reader, as is evident from the text, though Jewish forms of expression often occur as one would expect from a Jewish writer reporting a Jewish speaker. The document also contains comments and a number of notes explaining Jewish customs or translating Aramaic and Hebrew words. It is impossible to say whether these were made by the writer, though this appears highly probable, or added by a very early copyist. In conformity with the plan of the present version such notes and comments are printed below the text and are indicated by letters of the alphabet, while the present translator's notes are printed in small type and are indicated by numerals.

The end of *Mark* is defective, which not only speaks for the antiquity of the work, because it was the ends of scrolls that suffered first, but also its scarcity, since at an early date no perfect copy was available. Thus *Mark* is a most impressive and valuable witness.

———◆———

THE GOOD NEWS OF JESUS CHRIST

Mark's Version

INTRODUCTION

The Good News of Jesus Christ began exactly as stated in Isaiah the prophet,

> *Lo, I send my messenger before you,*
> *To pave the way for you.*
> *A voice cries out in the wilderness,*
> *'Make ready the Lord's road!*
> *Put his highways in order!'*[1]

John the Baptist[2] appeared in the wilderness, announcing a penitential immersion for forgiveness of sins; and the whole Judean countryside and all the inhabitants of Jerusalem flocked to him, and were immersed by him in the River Jordan as they confessed their sins.

John wore camel-hair clothing with a leather girdle round his waist, and he lived on locusts and wild honey. He further announced, 'After me will come one who is mightier than I, whose sandal-straps I am not fit to stoop down and untie. I have immersed you in water, but he will immerse you in holy Spirit.'

I

Now it was at this time that Jesus came from Nazareth in Galilee, and was immersed by John in the Jordan. No sooner, however, had he come up from the water than he saw the skies part and the Spirit like a dove descending to him, while a voice came from the skies, 'You are my dear Son. With you I am well satisfied.'

At once the Spirit drove him out into the wilderness; and he remained in the wilderness for forty days, tempted there by Satan. He was among the wild beasts, and the angels took care of him.

[1] Mal. iii. 1 combined with Isa. xl. 3.   [2] I.e. the Immerser or Dipper.

II

After John had been arrested, Jesus went to Galilee, proclaiming God's News[3] and declaring, 'The appointed time has come, and the Kingdom of God[4] is at hand. Repent, and believe the News!'

As he passed along the shore of the Sea of Galilee he saw Simon, and Simon's brother Andrew, casting a net into the sea.[a]

Jesus said to them, 'Follow me, and I will make you fishers of men.'

At once they abandoned their nets and joined him.

A little further on Jesus saw James the son of Zebedee and his brother John. They were in the boat repairing their nets. Directly he called them they left their father Zebedee in the boat with the hired hands and set off with him.

III

They made their way to Capernaum,[5] and there on the sabbaths Jesus went into the synagogue and taught. They were astounded at his teaching; for he taught with authority and not like the scribes.

Now in their synagogue there was a man possessed by a foul spirit, and it screamed out, 'What do you want with us, Jesus the Nazarene? Have you come to destroy us? I know who you are, the Holy One of God!'[6]

'Be quiet!' Jesus rebuked it, 'and come out of him.'

Then the foul spirit convulsed the man, and with a sharp cry came out of him.

They were all amazed, so much so that they questioned one another, 'What does this mean? Is it a new teaching? He even commands the foul spirits with authority, and they obey him!'

At once the report of him spread in all directions throughout the whole district of Galilee.

IV

Jesus left the synagogue immediately and went with James and John to the home of Simon and Andrew. Simon's mother-in-law was laid up with a fever, and they at once told him about her. Going to her he raised her up, taking her by the hand; and the fever left her, and she waited on them.

---

[a] They were fishermen.

[3] Here, as in most other places, it seemed best to render *Evangelion* as 'News' *par excellence.*

[4] The time when God will be acknowledged by the world as the supreme Ruler.

[5] Kfar-Nahum, 'Village of Nahum.'

[6] Synonymous with Nazirite, a person consecrated to God, Judg. xvi. 17 (LXX). Here specifically the Messiah. There was early Christian play on the likeness of the words Nazarene and Nazirite.

When evening came, and the sun had set,[7] the people brought him all who were ill and those who were demon-possessed. Indeed, the whole town was congregated at the door. Jesus cured those who were troubled with various complaints and expelled many demons, but he would not let the demons speak because they knew him to be the Messiah.

Having risen early while it was still quite dark, Jesus went out and made for the open country, and there prayed. But Simon and his friends were close behind, and when they found him they said to him, 'Everyone is looking for you.'

'Let us go elsewhere,' he said, 'to the neighbouring towns, that I may speak there also. That is why I came away.'

So he set off, preaching in their synagogues all over Galilee, and expelling the demons.

V

Now a leper came to him begging him on his knees, 'If only you will you can make me clean.'

With deep pity Jesus put out his hand and touched him, saying, 'I do will it. Be cleansed!'

At once the leprosy was gone from him, and he was clean again.

Jesus sent him away immediately, giving him strict injunctions, 'Be sure you tell no one. Go instead and show yourself to the priest and offer for your cleansing what Moses prescribed as evidence to them.'[8]

But when the man left he blurted it all out and broadcast the fact, so that it became impossible for Jesus to enter a town openly. He was forced to stay outside in the open country; and there they came to him from every quarter.

VI

When Jesus again entered Capernaum some time afterwards the report went round, 'He is home again.' And so many people collected that there was no more room, not even at the door; and he gave them his message.

One party arrived bringing him a paralysed man carried by four bearers. Unable to get near him because of the crush they dismantled the roof directly above him, and when they had cleared a passage they let down the mattress on which the paralytic was lying. Seeing what faith they had, Jesus said to the paralytic, 'Son, your sins are forgiven you.'

There were some of the scribes there, sitting and debating in their minds. 'What is this he is saying? He blasphemes. Who but One, God himself, can forgive sins?'

Sensing at once that this was what they were arguing to

[7] Signifying the end of the sabbath.
[8] Lev. xiv: cp. Deut. iv. 44.

themselves, Jesus said to them, 'Why are you debating these things in your minds? Which is easier, to tell the paralytic, "Your sins are forgiven you," or to say to him, "Rise, pick up your mattress and walk"? But that you may know that the Son of Man[9] is entitled to forgive sins on earth'—he addressed the paralytic, 'To you I say, rise, pick up your mattress, and go to your home.'

He rose, and immediately picking up his mattress went out in sight of them all; so that they were all astounded and praised God,[10] for, said they, 'we have never seen the like of this'.

VII

Jesus went again to the seashore, and the whole crowd came to him there, and he taught them. As he went along he saw Levi the son of Alphaeus seated at the customs-station,[11] and said to him, 'Follow me!'

Levi got up and followed him, and then invited him to dinner at his house; and many tax-collectors and sinners[12] sat down to dine with Jesus and his disciples.[a]

The Pharisee scribes, observing that Jesus ate with sinners and tax-collectors, said to his disciples, 'How can he eat with tax-collectors and sinners?'

Jesus heard this and said to them, 'It is not the healthy who need a doctor, but those who are ill. I have not come to call religious people, but sinners.'

Now the disciples of John[13] and of the Pharisees were observing a fast.[14] Jesus was asked, 'Why is it that the disciples of John and the disciples of the Pharisees are fasting while your disciples are not fasting?'

Jesus replied, 'Is it customary for the bridal party[15] to fast while the bridegroom is with them?[b] The time will come when the bridegroom will have taken leave of them: that will be the time for them to fast.

'No one sews a patch of newly made cloth on an old cloak. If he does, it will drag the stuff apart—the new from the old—and

[a] A number of them had joined him.
[b] For the period the bridegroom is with them it is not customary to fast.

[9] Jesus customarily spoke of himself as the Son of Man. This usually meant simply 'a man'; but among the Jewish mystics it had come to mean the Heavenly Man, identified by some with the Messiah.
[10] Formulae of praise to God were prescribed suited to various occasions, such as on witnessing a marvel, as here. The actual form is given in *Matthew*. See p. 100; n. 59.
[11] As a trading port Capernaum had a customs-station.
[12] Sinners here means Jews who live like Gentiles not observing the dietary and other laws. They are regarded with Jewish collectors of the Roman taxes and certain other categories as outside the pale of decent society. Strict Jews would not eat with such persons.
[13] I.e. the Baptist.
[14] The Pharisees fasted on Mondays and Thursdays.
[15] Lit. 'Children of the bridal bower' (Heb. idiom). These included the groomsmen, bridesmaids, and the parents of the bridal pair.

the tear will be made worse. Nor does anyone pour new wine
into old wine-skins. If he does, the wine will burst the skins, and
both wine and skins will be lost.'

VIII

Jesus happened to take his way on the sabbath through the
standing corn, and his disciples plucked the ears as they went
along. 'Look!' the Pharisees said to him, 'Why are they doing
what is not permitted on the sabbath?'

'Have you never read,' Jesus answered, 'what David did when
need arose and he and his companions were hungry, how he
went into the house of God[a] and ate the loaves of the Presence[b],
and even gave some to his men? The sabbath was made for
man's sake,' he pointed out, 'not man for the sabbath's sake.'[c][16]

When next he went to the synagogue there was a man there
with a withered hand. They waited expectantly to see whether
he would cure him on the sabbath, so that they could bring a
charge against him.

'Come up to the front,' he invited the man with the withered
hand.

Then he said to them, 'Is it permitted on the sabbath to do
good or to do harm, to save life or to destroy it?'

They remained silent.

When he had looked angrily around at them, visibly hurt by
their callousness, he said to the man, 'Stretch out your hand!'

He stretched it out, and his hand was restored.

Thereupon the Pharisees left and immediately conferred with
the Herodians[17] about Jesus, how they could destroy him.

IX

Jesus with his disciples withdrew to the sea, and a vast concourse from Galilee followed him. From Judea and Jerusalem
too great numbers came to him when they learnt of his activities,
and from Idumea, from beyond Jordan, and from the region of
Tyre and Sidon.

He told his disciples to hurry forward the preparation of a
small ship for him because of the throng, in case they should

[a] Abiathar was then high priest. (According to I. Sam. xxi. the
priest was Ahimelech. *Tr.*)
[b] Which only the priests were allowed to eat.
[c] So the Son of Man is master even of the Sabbath.

[16] This was also the Rabbinical teaching of which perhaps Jesus is reminding the
Pharisees. There was another comparable saying, 'The world was made only for
the sake of Israel.'
[17] Herodians, the party supporting the regal pretensions of the Herodian family,
descendants of Herod the Great, who would be hostile to any Davidic claimant to
the throne. The Pharisees were bitterly opposed to the Herodians, and must have
been enraged indeed to be induced to associate themselves with them.

mob him.[e] Meanwhile he climbed the hill, and summoned those he wanted, and they came to him. Of these he appointed twelve, whom he termed envoys, to be associated with him, so that he could send them out to preach with power to expel demons.

He appointed as the twelve, Peter,[b] James the son of Zebedee and his brother John,[c] Andrew, Philip, Bartholomew, Matthew, Thomas, James the son of Alphaeus, Thaddaeus, Simon and Zealot,[19] and Judas Iscariot.[d]

X

When Jesus returned home the crowd reassembled, so that it became impossible for them even to take their meals.

On hearing what was going on, his relations came to take charge of him. 'He must be out of his mind,' they said. But when the scribes from Jerusalem came down their view was, 'He is possessed by Beelzebul. He expels demons by the chief of the demons.'

Calling the scribes to him Jesus addressed them in proverbs. 'How can Satan expel Satan?' he inquired. 'If a kingdom is at odds with itself that kingdom cannot endure. And if any household is at odds with itself that household cannot endure. So if Satan takes action against himself, and is divided, he cannot endure. That is the end of him. On the other hand no one can enter the Strong One's abode to loot his possessions before he has first bound the Strong One. Only then can he loot his abode.

'I tell you positively,[20] men will be forgiven everything, their crimes, and every slanderous thing they may have spoken; but there can never be forgiveness for the man who slanders the holy Spirit: he has committed a lasting crime.'[e]

At this juncture his mother and brothers arrived, and standing outside sent to call him. There was a crowd seated round him, but they managed to tell him, 'Please, your mother and brothers are outside inquiring for you.'

[a] For he had cured many, causing all those who were afflicted with diseases to fling themselves on him to touch him. And the foul spirits, when they detected him, assailed him with the cry, 'You are the Son of God,'[18] though he insisted that they should not reveal his identity.

[b] Meaning 'Rock', the name he gave Simon.

[c] He gave them the nickname *Boanerges,* which means 'Tempestuous'. (Lit. Aram. 'Sons of the storm-wind'. *Tr.*)

[d] Who actually betrayed him.[21]

[e] They had said, 'He is possessed by a foul spirit.'

[18] Son of God, a royal title like Messiah, see Ps. ii.: II. Sam. vii. 13-14, and cp. Mk. i. 24; Mt. xvi. 15-18, xxvi. 63; Jn. i. 49, xx. 31. The king was God's earthly representative. The title was borrowed from the East by the Caesars as *divi filius.*

[19] Lit. 'Kananean', Aram. *Qana,* a member of the Zealots, the extreme militant patriotic party: cp. Lk. vi. 15.

[20] Lit. 'Amen'. Jesus constantly employed this emphatic Hebrew word, which the Greek has not translated.

[21] 'Betrayed him.' Hed. *hisgir-otho* (or *hiskir-otho*), a very early word-play on the name Iscarioth, as it is spelt in the text.

'What do you mean, my mother and brothers?' he replied. Looking round the circle seated about him, he said, 'Here are my mother and brothers. Whoever does the will of God is my brother and sister and mother.'

XI

Once more Jesus taught beside the sea, and such a vast crowd collected that he went on board ship and sat there in the shallows, while all the crowd stood on shore at the water's edge.

He taught them a great many things by similes. 'Now listen,' he said as he taught. 'The sower went to sow. As he sowed some seed fell by the wayside and the birds came and ate it up. Other seed fell on stony ground where there was not much soil, and sprouted rapidly because the soil had little depth. But when the sun came up it was parched, and because it had no root it withered. Other seed fell among thistles, and the thistles sprang up and choked it, and it produced no fruit. Still other seed fell in good soil and produced fruit, having sprung up and grown tall, yielding thirtyfold, sixtyfold, and even a hundredfold.' He concluded, 'Let him who can catch my meaning do so.'[22]

When they were on their own, his associates, including the twelve, asked him to explain the simile.

Then he said to them, 'You are entitled to know the secret of the Kingdom of God, but for those outside[23] everything is expressed in similes, that

> They may see indeed, but not perceive,
> And hear indeed, yet not understand,
> Lest they turn again and be forgiven.[24]

'Does this simile convey nothing to you?' he asked. 'How then will you grasp the implication of my other similes?

'The sower sows the Message. There are those who are "by the wayside" where the Message is sown; and no sooner have they heard it than along comes Satan and pecks out the Message that is sown for them. Then there are those who are like the seed sown on stony ground. No sooner have they heard the Message than they accept it joyfully; but having no root in themselves they are short-lived, and so when trouble or persecution arises because of the Message they are immediately put off. Then there are the "sown among thistles" kind of people. These are they who really heed the Message; but the constant economic struggle, the lure of getting rich, and the cravings that come for all sorts of other things, choke the Message, and it becomes unfruitful. Finally there are the "sown in good soil" kind of people. These are they who hear the Message, welcome it, and produce fruit, thirtyfold, sixtyfold, and even a hundredfold.'

---

[22] Lit. 'Whoever has ears to hear let him hear.'
[23] 'Those outside', the generality of people, not belonging to the Elect, who are those 'on the inside'.
[24] Isa. vi. 9-10.

Then he said to them, 'Is a lamp brought in to be put under a measuring-bowl or beneath a bed? Is it not for setting on the lampstand? Nothing is hidden that is meant to be disclosed, neither is anything concealed that is meant to be brought to light. Whoever can catch my meaning let him do so.

'Mark this,' he added. 'It is the measure you give that will be measured out to you,[25] and added to you. He who has will get more, while he who has not will be deprived even of what he has.'

Then he said, 'The Kingdom of God is as if a man were to scatter grain on the ground, and to sleep and wake, day in and day out, with the grain sprouting and shooting up he knows not how. For the earth produces fruit by its own agency, first the blade, then the ear, and finally the full wheat in the ear. But when the grain is ripe, he at once employs the sickle; for it is harvest time.

'How can we best illustrate the Kingdom of God?' he continued. 'By what simile shall we depict it? As a grain of mustard seed, perhaps, which when it is sown is the most minute of seeds. Yet once sown it shoots up and becomes taller than any other herb, and produces great branches, so that the birds of the air nestle in its shade.'

By many such similes he gave his message to the people, so far as they were capable of grasping it. He did not address them, however, except by simile; but privately he made everything clear to his disciples.

XII

That same day when evening came Jesus said to them, 'Let us cross to the farther shore.'

So when they had dismissed the crowd they took him along in the ship on board which he was, while other ships accompanied him. But a severe squall of wind came on, and the waves flooded into the ship, so that it was already awash. He himself was asleep on the mat in the stern.

So they woke him, and said to him, 'Teacher, don't you care that we are perishing?'

When he was roused, he rebuked the wind and said to the sea, 'Hush! Be still!' Then the wind died away and there was a great calm. 'Why are you so cowardly?' he said to them. 'Have you no faith?'

Then they were terribly afraid, and said to one another, 'Who can he be, that both the wind and the sea obey him?'

XIII

So they came to the other side of the sea, to the land of the Gerasenes. As soon as he had landed from the ship there came

[25] A current proverb meaning here, 'You will be enlightened according to your lights'.

to meet him from the cemetery a man possessed by a foul spirit, who made his home in the tombs. It had been found impossible to confine him even with chains; for the man had often been confined with fetters and chains, and had torn off the chains and forced the fetters. No one now had the power to restrain him. Night and day he was in the tombs or in the hills shrieking and gashing himself with stones.

Seeing Jesus from a distance he ran and prostrated himself before him screaming out. 'What do you want with me, Jesus, Son of God Most High? Do you swear to God not to torture me?'[a]

Jesus asked the spirit, 'What is your name?'

'My name is Legion,' it replied. 'There are many of us.' And it begged him repeatedly not to send them out of the country.

Now on the hill there a large herd of swine was feeding. So the spirits begged, 'Send us into the swine. Please let us enter them.'

Jesus yielded to their entreaty,[26] and when the foul spirits had come out they entered the swine, and the herd, two thousand strong, dashed down the steep slope into the sea, and were drowned.

The herdsmen ran off and told their tale to town and farm, and everyone went to see what had happened. When they came to Jesus and looked at the demoniac, now seated clothed and sane, they took alarm. Those who had been witnesses described to them what had happened to the demoniac and about the swine, and they begged Jesus to leave their shores.

As he was going on board, the demoniac begged to come with him. He would not permit this, however, but told him, 'Go back to your own people, and tell them what the Lord has done for you, and how he has taken pity on you.'

But he went away and started to proclaim in the Decapolis[27] what Jesus had done for him; and everyone marvelled.

XIV

No sooner had Jesus recrossed by boat to the other side and set foot on shore than a great crowd gathered round him. The president of one of the synagogues came, a man called Jair, and when he saw him he fell at his feet with the moving entreaty, 'My small daughter is near her end, but if you will only come and lay your hand on her she will be spared and live.'

Jesus set off with him. The crowd followed pressing him closely.

There was a woman who had suffered twelve years with a flow

[a] He had said, 'Come out of the man, you foul spirit.'

[26] As swine were unclean animals among the Jews it was considered justifiable by Jesus that the unclean spirits should enter them.

[27] A self-governing confederacy of ten Greek cities mainly east of the Jordan: Gadara, Scythopolis, Hippos, Damascus, Canatha, Pella, Gerasa, Philadephia, Dium and Raphana (Pliny, *Nat. Hist.* v. 18).

of blood. She had undergone a variety of treatments from numerous doctors, and had exhausted her resources without obtaining any benefit: on the contrary, she had got worse. Having heard what was said about Jesus she came up behind him in the crowd and touched his cloak, for she said, 'If I can only touch his clothes I shall get better.'

At once her flow of blood stopped at its source, and she was physically conscious that she was cured of her complaint. Jesus also was immediately aware that power had been drawn from him, and turned round in the crowd and asked, 'Who touched my clothes?'

'You can see how the crowd has been pressing you,' said his disciples, 'and you ask, "Who touched me?" '

But he went on looking round to discover who had done it.

Then the woman, fearful and trembling, knowing what had happened to her, came forward and fell down before him and told him the whole truth.

'Daughter,' he said to her, 'your faith has cured you. Go in peace, and be free of your complaint.'

Hardly had he finished speaking when word came from the president's house, telling him, 'Your daughter has died, why trouble the teacher further?'

But Jesus hearing the message delivered said to the president, 'Don't be afraid, simply trust.'

He would not allow anyone to accompany him now except Peter and James, and James's brother John. When they reached the president's house he was confronted with a scene of uproar with much weeping and wailing, and as he went in he said to them,[28] 'What are you howling for and making such a din? The girl is not dead, only sleeping.' But they jeered at him.

When he had got rid of them all, he took the girl's father and mother and his companions and entered the girl's room. Taking her hand he said, '*Talitha, koum!*'[a]

The little girl rose directly and walked about.[b] At this the parents were quite overcome with emotion. Jesus gave them strict orders to keep the matter to themselves, and told them to give the child some nourishment.

XV

On leaving there Jesus went to his native place, and his disciples accompanied him. When the sabbath came he taught in the synagogue, and the congregation was astounded as they listened and said, 'Where does he get all this? How has he obtained this wisdom and these various powers manifested by him? Isn't he the carpenter, the son of Mary, brother of James,

---

[a] This means when translated, 'Wake up little girl, I tell you.'
[b] She was twelve years old.

[28] The professional mourners who attended on such occasions.

Joses, Juda and Simon? Aren't his sisters still resident here?'
And they were affronted at him.

Then Jesus said to them, 'Is it not the fact that a prophet is
only unhonoured in his native place, among his own kin, and in
his own home?'

He was unable to perform a single miracle there, except to
lay his hand on a few sick folk and cure them. He was amazed
at their lack of faith.

So he toured the surrounding villages teaching. Then summoning the twelve he sent them out in pairs, and gave them
authority over foul spirits. He instructed them to take nothing
on their journeys but a staff, no food, no wallet, no money, to
wear sandals and to carry no spare tunic.

'Wherever you lodge,' he told them, 'make that your quarters
until you leave again. Any place where they will not welcome
you, or even listen to you, when you resume your journey shake
the dust from your feet as evidence to them.'

Setting out, therefore, they called on the people to repent,
expelled many demons, and anointed with oil many sick folk
and cured them.

XVI

Now King Herod[29] heard of Jesus, for his name had become
famous, and he said, 'John the Baptist has risen from the dead;
that is why miracles are effected by him.' Others declared he
was Elijah, still others that he was a prophet like one of the
prophets of old. But when Herod heard of him he said, 'It is
John whom I beheaded: he has risen again.'

It was Herod who had been responsible for arresting John
and confining him in a fortress on account of Herodias, his
brother Philip's wife, because he had married her. John had told
Herod, 'It is illegal for you to have your brother's wife.' So
Herodias bore him a grudge, and wanted to have him executed.
But this she could not accomplish, for Herod was in awe of
John, knowing him to be a saintly and holy man. He observed
him closely, and was much affected by hearing him, and was
very ready to listen to him.

An opportune day came for Herodias when Herod gave his
anniversary banquet to his nobles, commanders, and the leading
Galileans. The daughter of this Herodias came in and danced
and charmed Herod and the assembled guests.

'Ask whatever you like and it is yours,' the king said to the
maiden. Indeed he swore to her, 'Whatever you ask is yours,
even if it is half my kingdom.'[30]

When she went out she said to her mother, 'What shall I ask
for?'

'The head of John the Baptist,' her mother replied.

[29] Herod Antipas was tetrarch of Galilee, and only by courtesy could be called king.
[30] See Esth. v. 3.

At once she hastened to the king and said, 'I want you to give me here and now on a platter the head of John the Baptist.'

The king was greatly upset, but because of his oaths and the guests he could not refuse her. So he immediately sent his executioner with orders to bring John's head. The man went off and beheaded John in the fortress, and brought his head on a platter and handed it to the maiden, and she gave it to her mother.

When John's disciples heard the news they came and fetched his body and laid it in a tomb.

XVII

Now the envoys rejoined Jesus and reported to him everything they had done and taught. And he said to them, 'Come away to the country by yourselves and rest awhile.'[a]

So they set off for the country by boat; but they were noticed and recognized by many, who ran round the lake in a body on foot from all the towns and arrived ahead of them.

On stepping ashore Jesus was confronted with a vast crowd, and was filled with compassion for them, for they were like shepherdless sheep; and he taught them at some length.

It was already getting late when his disciples approached him and said, 'This place is open country and it is now late. Dismiss the people that they may go off to the surrounding hamlets and villages and buy themselves something to eat.'

'Why do you not give them food yourselves?' he replied.

They protested, 'Are we to go off and buy two hundred dinars[81] worth of bread to feed them with?'

'How many loaves have you?' he inquired, 'Go and find out.'

'Five,' they said on investigating, 'and two fish.'

He told them to get all the people to sit down in parties, and they squatted in groups of hundreds and fifties. Taking the five loaves and the two fishes Jesus looked up to heaven, recited the blessing, broke the bread into small pieces, and gave them to his disciples to distribute, and shared out the two fishes to everyone. Then all ate and were satisfied, and they collected twelve basketfuls of crumbs and fragments of fish. No less than five thousand men had partaken of the loaves.

Jesus insisted next that his disciples embark in the boat and cross in advance to Bethsaida[82] while he dismissed the crowd. When he had said good-bye to them he went off to the hill to pray. The boat was well out to sea when evening came, while he was alone on shore. Observing them labouring at their oars, for they had the wind against them, he came to them towards dawn walking on the sea, and made as if to pass them by. But

[a] For there were many people coming and going, and not even a place to eat.

[81] A dinar (denarius) was worth about 9½d., so 200 would be about £8.
[82] Beth-saida, 'Place of Fishing Nets,' a fishing village near Capernaum.

seeing him walking on the sea they thought he was a ghost and cried out.[a] At once he spoke to them and said, 'It's all right! It is I. Don't be alarmed.'

When he got into the boat with them the wind died down. They were in a great state; for they gave no thought to what had happened in the case of the loaves: their minds were obtuse.

On completing the crossing they came to land at Gennesaret and moored there. But no sooner were they out of the boat than the people recognized Jesus and ran round the whole district, and started to bring those who were ill on mattresses to where they heard he was. And no matter where he went, into village, town, or hamlet, they laid the infirm in the open streets where they begged him to let them touch the tassel of his cloak,[33] and whoever succeeded in touching it recovered.

XVIII

Now the Pharisees betook themselves to Jesus with certain of the scribes coming from Jerusalem, and they observed some of his disciples eating their meal with soiled hands.[b] So they asked him, 'Why do your disciples not behave in accordance with the tradition of the elders? Why do they eat with soiled hands?'

Jesus replied, 'Well did Isaiah prophesy of you hypocrites as it is stated,

> *Here is a people that pays me lip-service,*
> *But their minds are far removed from me.*
> *It is useless for them to worship me*
> *While teaching as doctrine injunctions of men.*[34]

Neglecting God's commandments you cling to human tradition.

'No doubt you are right,' he went on, 'to set aside God's commandment if you must keep your own tradition. For Moses said, "Honour your father and mother,"[35] and "he who speaks ill of father or mother shall surely die."[36] But you declare, "If anyone says to father or mother, Whatever of mine might benefit you is *korban*,[c] he is released from obligation to provide for his father

---

[a] They all saw him and were terrified.
[b] That is to say, unwashed. The Pharisees, and indeed all Jews, adhering to the tradition of the elders, never eat before washing the whole hand. They do not eat what comes from the market until they have soused it in water, and there is a great deal more they have to do, rinsing cups, bowls and dishes.
[c] Meaning 'a votive gift'.

[33] Regarding the tassel of Jesus as of special sanctity (see Num. xv. 37-41). Every pious Jew wore the tassel on his cloak with a blue thread inserted in it. To-day it is worn on a special four-cornered undergarment and in synagogue on the prayer-shawl. It is a custom in synagogue to touch the scroll of the Law with it.
[34] Isa. xxix. 13.
[35] Exod. xx. 12.
[36] Exod. xxi. 17.

or mother."[37] Thus you nullify the word of God by the tradition you have transmitted. You do other things of the same sort.'

Summoning the crowd to him once more, he said to them, 'Listen to me, all of you, and mark what I say. Nothing external to a man can soil him by entering him: it is only what emanates from a man that soils him.'

When he had gone indoors away from the crowd his disciples questioned him about this saying.

'Are you so dense?' he said. 'Do you not realize that everything external that enters a man cannot soil him because it enters his stomach, not his mind, and is evacuated in the toilet.[a]

'It is what emanates from a man that soils him,' he continued. 'It is from inside, from a man's mind, that evil designs proceed, impurity, thieving, murder, adultery, covetousness, roguery, deceit, lewdness, envy, slander, arrogance and folly. All these evil things emanate from within and they soil a man.'

XIX

Setting out from there Jesus went away to the borders of Tyre and Sidon. Entering a house, he did not wish his presence to be known; but he could not escape notice. In fact at once a woman who had heard about him, and whose daughter was possessed by a foul spirit, came and threw herself at his feet,[b] and entreated him to expel the demon from her daughter.

'The children must be fed first,'[38] he told her. 'It is not fair to take the children's food and throw it to puppies.'

'Quite so, sir,' she replied. 'Yet the puppies under the table eat the scraps the children drop.'

'Because you have said that,' he said, 'go your way: you will find the demon has gone from your daughter.'

When she arrived home she found the child lying in bed and the demon gone.

XX

Leaving the borders of Tyre, Jesus made his way via Sidon to the Sea of Galilee, along the frontier of the Decapolis.

They brought to him a deaf man with an impediment in his speech, and begged him to lay his hand on him. So he took him aside out of the crowd and inserted his fingers in his ears. Then spitting, he touched his tongue, and looking up to heaven heaved a sigh, and said to the man, *'Ephphatha!'* [c] And his ears were opened, and the constriction on his tongue was freed, and he could speak properly.

[a] He thus pronounced every kind of food clean.
[b] The woman was a Greek, in origin a Syrophoenician.
[c] This means 'Open up!'

[37] A man was obligated to maintain his parents, and yet by a 'rash vow' of his property to God he might seem to escape the obligation, his vow of *korban* becoming in effect a cursing of his parents.
[38] The mission of Jesus was in the first place to the Jews.

He gave them orders to say nothing about it; but as explicitly as he had ordered them the more decidedly did they proclaim it. And the people were astonished beyond measure, and exclaimed, 'He[39] has done everything well', and, 'He makes the deaf hear and the dumb speak.'

XXI

At that time once again the crowd being so great and having nothing to eat Jesus summoned his disciples and said to them, 'I am deeply concerned about the people. For three days now they have remained with me with nothing to eat, and if I send them home starving they will collapse on the way; and some of them have come a long distance.'

His disciples answered, 'Where in this open country is anyone going to get bread enough to feed these people?'

'How many loaves have you?' he asked.

'Seven,' they said.

Jesus then instructed the crowd to sit down, and taking the seven loaves he gave thanks, broke the bread, and handed it to his disciples to distribute; and they distributed it to the people. They also had a few small fish, over which he recited the blessing and told them to distribute these as well. So the people ate and were satisfied, and they took up seven hampers of the fragments left over. There were about four thousand people.

After dismissing them Jesus went at once on board ship and left for the region of Dalmanutha.

XXII

The Pharisees here came forward to question him, trying to trap him, inviting him to furnish a sign from Heaven.

With a deep sigh Jesus said, 'Why does this generation require a sign? I say positively, this generation will get no sign.'

Upon this he left them, and re-embarking crossed to the other side.

Now the disciples had neglected to take bread, and had no more than a single loaf with them on board. Then he advised them, 'Be on your guard against the leaven of the Pharisees and of Herod!'

They argued among themselves, 'Is this because we have no bread?'

Realizing this he said to them, 'What are you arguing about, because you have no bread? Haven't you yet grasped or understood? Are your wits so dull? Have you lost the use of your eyes and ears? Don't you remember when I broke the five loaves for the five thousand? How many basketfuls of fragments did you take up?'

[39] 'He' would seem to refer to God. The people said the appropriate benedictions, the first being that customarily recited on hearing good news, 'Blessed is he who is good and the doer of good' (*Berach.* ix. 2). See above p. 54, n. 10.

'Twelve,' they told him.

'And the seven for the four thousand? How many hampers of fragments did you take up?'

'Seven,' they told him.

Then he said, 'Do you still not understand?'

XXIII

They came now to Bethsaida. There they brought to him a blind man and begged him to touch him. He took the blind man's hand and led him outside the village. And when he had spat on his eyes he laid his hands on him and inquired, 'Do you see anything?'

He screwed up his eyes and said, 'I can distinguish people now, because they look as if trees were walking about.'

Once more Jesus laid his hands on his eyes. The man stared, and his sight adjusted itself, and he could see everything distinctly. Then Jesus sent him home saying, 'Do not even go into the village.'

XXIV

Jesus with his disciples went next to the villages belonging to Caesarea-Philippi, and on the way he asked his disciples, 'Who do people say I am?'

'John the Baptist,' they replied. 'Though others say Elijah, or one of the other prophets.'

'And who do you say I am?' he asked them.

Peter answered, 'You are the Messiah.'

He gave them strict injunctions to tell this to no one.

Jesus now taught them that the Son of Man must undergo much suffering and be rejected by the elders, head priests and scribes, and be killed, and rise again three days later. He stated the fact plainly; but Peter took him up on it, and remonstrated with him. Then Jesus turned, and with his eye on his disciples reproved Peter, and said, 'Follow me, *satan!*[40] Yours is the human viewpoint, not God's.'

Then he summoned the crowd as well as his disciples and said to them, 'Whoever will follow me must be utterly reckless and ready for execution[41] in joining me; for whoever would preserve his life will lose it, while he who loses his life for me and the News will preserve it. How will it benefit a man to gain the whole world if his life is forfeited? What can a man offer in barter for his life? Whoever, therefore, is disdainful of me and of my words in this adulterous and reprobate generation will find the Son of Man disdainful of him when he comes in his Father's state with the holy angels.

[40] Peter was acting in opposition as a *satan*, an 'adversary'. Others render, 'Get behind me, Satan.'

[41] Lit. 'Let him disown himself and take up his own cross.' Death by crucifixion was for crimes against the State. The condemned often carried their cross to the place of execution.

'I tell you positively,' he continued, 'there are some standing here now who will not experience death before they see the Kingdom of God inaugurated.'[42]

XXV

Six days later Jesus took as companions Peter, James and John, and led them up a high mountain entirely by themselves. In their presence he was transformed, and his robes became more dazzlingly white than any fuller on earth could bleach them. Then Moses and Elijah appeared to them, and entered into conversation with Jesus. Peter could not help saying, 'Rabbi, how fortunate we are to be here! Now let us make three bowers, one for you, one for Moses, and one for Elijah.'[a]

Then a cloud came, casting a shadow over them, and a voice spoke out of the cloud, 'He is my dear Son. Listen to him.'

On looking about suddenly they no longer saw anyone with them but Jesus himself.

As they descended the mountain he gave them instructions not to relate what they had seen to anyone before the Son of Man had risen from the dead. So they kept the matter to themselves, only debating what this rising from the dead could mean. All they asked him was, 'Why do the scribes say, "First of all Elijah must come"?'

He answered, 'If Elijah is to come first to put everything right,[43] how comes it to be stated of the Son of Man that he is to undergo much suffering and be treated with contempt?[44] I am telling you differently, that Elijah has come, and they have done what they would with him, just as it is stated of him.'[45]

XXVI

When he came to his disciples he saw a great crowd round them, and scribes debating with them. At once the crowd, surprised to see him, rushed forward to greet him. So he inquired, 'What are you debating with my disciples?'

One of the crowd replied, 'Teacher, I have brought you my son, who is possessed by a dumb spirit. Wherever he is when the seizure takes him, it hurls him to the ground, and he foams and grinds his teeth. It is wearing him out. I tried to get your disciples to expel it, but they had not the power.'

'O faithless generation!' Jesus exclaimed. 'How long must I be with you? How long must I put up with you? Bring him to me.'

So they brought him to Jesus. On seeing him the spirit at once threw the boy into a fit, and falling to the ground he rolled about foaming.

[a] He had no idea what to say: they were all so frightened.

[42] Lit. 'instituted in power.'
[43] Mal. iv. 5-6.
[44] Cp. Ps. xxii; Isa. liii.
[45] Cp. I. Kings xix. 2, 10.

Jesus asked his father, 'How long has he been like this?'

'From infancy,' he said. 'It has often thrown him into fire and into water to make away with him. If there is anything you can do, please help us and take pity on us?'

'Anything you can do?' echoed Jesus. 'Everything can be done for one who believes.'

The child's father at once cried out, 'I do believe! Only assist my lack of faith.'

When Jesus saw the crowd swiftly converging he laid his injunctions on the foul spirit. 'You deaf and dumb spirit,' he said to it, 'I order you to come out of him and never enter him again.'

After shrieking and convulsing him violently it went out leaving the boy like a corpse. Indeed the majority of those present said, 'He's dead.' But Jesus taking him by the hand raised him, and he stood up.

When Jesus had gone indoors his disciples asked him privately, 'Why couldn't we expel it?'

Jesus told them, 'This type can be got out in no other way than by prayer.'

XXVII

On leaving there they travelled through Galilee, but Jesus did not want the fact publicized, since he was teaching his disciples and telling them, 'The Son of Man will be handed over to the authorities, and they will kill him; but three days after he has been killed he will rise again.'

They did not understand what he meant, however, and were afraid to ask him.

Then they reached Capernaum. As soon as he was inside the house Jesus asked them, 'What were you arguing about on the way?'

They were speechless; for what they had been arguing with one another on the way was which of them was greatest.

When he had sat down he called the twelve and said to them, 'Whoever wants to be chief must be the lowliest of all and the servant of all.'

Then taking a child he stood him before them, and putting his arm about him told them, 'Whoever receives a child like this on my behalf receives me, and whoever receives me does not so much receive me as him who sent me.'

John said to him, 'Teacher, we saw someone expelling demons in your name, but we stopped him because he does not belong to our company.'

'You did wrong to stop him,' Jesus told him, 'for no one who performs miracles in my name can readily revile me. For whoever is not against us is on our side.

'Whoever refreshes you with a cup of water because you belong to the Messiah, I tell you truly, he will not lose his reward. But whoever gives one of these humblest of believers grounds for complaint it would be much better for him to have a millstone hung round his neck and to be thrown into the sea. So if your hand gives grounds for complaint cut it off. It is better for you to enter Life[46] maimed than with two hands to have to go to Gehenna.[a] And if your foot gives you grounds for complaint cut it off. It is better for you to enter Life crippled than with two feet to be thrown into Gehenna. And if your eye gives you grounds for complaint pluck it out. It is better for you to enter the Kingdom of God one-eyed than with two eyes to be thrown into Gehenna.[b] Salt is an excellent thing, but if the salt becomes insipid how shall its tang be restored? Keep your keenness,[47] but be at peace with one another.'

XXVIII

When he left there Jesus went to the borders of Judea and Transjordan, and again the crowds resorted to him, and again as was his practice he taught them.

There were also Pharisees who came to trap him, asking him if it was right for a man to divorce his wife.

'What did Moses command you?' he answered.

They told him, 'Moses allowed a deed of severance to be written, and in this way to divorce her.'[48]

'Because of your callousness he wrote that commandment for you,' Jesus told them. 'But from the beginning of creation "He made them male and female—for this reason a man shall leave his father and mother—and the two will be one flesh."[49] So then they are two no longer, but one flesh. Therefore let no one sever what God has united.'

When they were indoors once more his disciples asked him about this, and he said to them, 'Whoever divorces his wife and marries another commits adultery against his true wife, and should she divorce her husband and marry another she too commits adultery.'

The people brought him their children to touch, but the disciples reproved them. Jesus was displeased when he saw it, and said to them, 'Let the children come to me. Do not stop them. The Kingdom of God is composed of such as they. I tell you positively, whoever does not accept the Kingdom of God like a child can never enter it.'

[a] To the unquenchable fire.
[b] Where their worm never dies and the fire never goes out (Isa. lxvi. 24. *Tr.*); for each will be preserved[50] by fire.

[46] Short for 'the life of the Messianic Era', the reign of Messiah when believers will have acquired immortality.
[47] Lit. 'Have salt in yourselves.'
[48] Deut. xxiv. 1.
[49] Gen. i. 27, ii. 24.
[50] Lit. 'salted' (cured), explaining the previous words. Some texts add, 'And every sacrifice shall be salted with salt' (Lev. ii. 13), finding difficulty with the sense and wrongly attributing the comment to Jesus because of what follows.

Gathering the children in his arms he blessed them, laying his hand on each.

XXIX

When Jesus again took the road there was one who ran forward and kneeling before him asked him, 'Good teacher, what must I do to share in the Messianic Era?'[51]

'Why do you address me as good?' Jesus said. 'None is good but One, God himself. Surely you know the commandments, "Commit no murder, commit no adultery, commit no theft, bear no false testimony, do not defraud, honour your father and mother"?'[52]

'I have truly kept all these from my youth, teacher,' he told him.

Jesus regarded him with affection, and said to him, 'You have one thing more to do. Go and sell all you possess and give it to the poor, and you shall have treasure in heaven. Then come and join me.'

He was dejected at this, and went away distressed, for he owned considerable property.

As Jesus gazed after him he said to his disciples, 'How difficult it is to get those with means to enter the Kingdom of God!'

The disciples were greatly surprised at his words, but Jesus repeated, 'Children,' he said, 'how difficult it is to enter the Kingdom of God! It is easier for a camel to pass through the eye of a needle [53] than for a rich man to enter the Kingdom of God.'

'How then can anyone be saved?' they said in amazement.

Jesus looked at them and replied, 'Humanly it is impossible, but not to God. To God everything is possible.'

Peter spoke up. 'What about us? We have given up everything to follow you.'

Jesus said, 'I tell you for a fact, there is not one who has given up house or brothers or sisters or mother or father or children or lands for my sake and the News without expecting, as well as persecution, to receive here and now a hundred times as much —houses, brothers, sisters, mothers, children and lands, and Eternal Life in the Messianic Era. But many who would be chief will be lowest, and the lowest will be chief.'

XXX

They were now on the way up to Jerusalem, and Jesus was preceding them, when they took alarm, and those who followed

---

[51] Lit. 'to inherit Eternal Life.' Cp. the saying of Hillel, 'He who has acquired for himself words of the Law has acquired for himself Life in the World to Come' (*Aboth*, ii. 8).

[52] Exod. xx.

[53] A proverbial expression, meaning to achieve the impossible. It is found elsewhere in Jewish literature with the substitution of elephant for camel.

became afraid. So once more Jesus called the twelve to his side and told them what was going to happen to him. 'Look,' he said, 'we are on the way up to Jerusalem, and the Son of Man will be handed over to the head priests and scribes. They will condemn him to death and hand him over to the Gentiles, who will make sport of him, flog him, and kill him; yet three days later he will be raised up.'

Then James and John, the two sons of Zebedee, came to him and said, 'Teacher, there is something we want you to do for us.'

'What is it you want me to do for you?' he inquired.

They told him, 'Grant us when you attain your state [54] to be seated one on your right and the other on your left.'

'You have no idea what you are asking,' Jesus said to them. 'Can you drink from the same cup as myself, or experience the immersion I shall undergo?'

'We can,' they replied.

Jesus told them, 'You shall drink the same cup as myself, and experience the immersion I undergo; but to sit on my right or on my left is not mine to grant: that is for those for whom it is reserved.'

When the ten heard of this they were furious with James and John. So Jesus summoned them to him and said to them, 'You know that those who are regarded as rulers among the Gentiles lord it over them, and their notables wield authority over them. It shall not be so with you. Rather if anyone would be of note among you let him be your servant, and if anyone would be chief among you let him be everyone's slave; for even the Son of Man did not come to be served, but to serve, and to give his life as a ransom for many.'

XXXI

So they came to Jericho. As Jesus was leaving Jericho with his disciples and a considerable crowd, Bar-Timaeus,[a] a blind beggar, was seated by the roadside. Hearing it was Jesus the Nazarene, he cried out, 'Pity me, Son of David,[55] Jesus!'

Many insisted he should be silent, but he only cried out the more, 'Pity me, Son of David!'

Jesus stopped. 'Call him,' he said.

So they called the blind man. 'Take heart,' they told him. 'Get up, he's calling you.'

He threw aside his cloak, leapt to his feet, and went to Jesus.

'What can I do for you?' Jesus inquired.

'Rabboni, if only I may see again,' said the blind man.

Jesus said to him, 'Go your way, your faith has cured you.'

At once he could see again, and joined Jesus on the road.

[a] The son of Timaeus.

[54] Lit. 'in your state, or glory'.
[55] By addressing Jesus as Son of David the beggar was identifying him publicly with the Messiah, a dangerous thing politically.

As they neared Jerusalem at Bethpage[56] and Bethany[57] by the Mount of Olives, Jesus sent two of his disciples with the instructions, 'Go to the village there, and as soon as you have entered it you will find a foal tethered, never previously ridden by anyone. Untie him and bring him here. Should anyone ask you, "What are you up to?" say, "The Master needs him." Then he will at once send him back here.'

They went off and found a foal tethered by a doorway in the open on the outskirts, and untied him. When some of those standing there said to them, 'What are you up to, untying the foal?' they replied as Jesus had told them, and they let them have him. They brought the foal to Jesus and laid their cloaks on him, and he mounted him. Many spread their cloaks on the road, others spread rushes cut from the fields, while those in front and those behind cried, '*Hosanna!*[58] Blessed is he who comes in the Lord's name! Blessed is the coming kingdom of our father David! *Hosanna* in the heavenly heights!' [59]

XXXII

So Jesus entered the Temple at Jerusalem. But after looking about at everything[a] he left for Bethany with the twelve.

The following day when they were coming away from Bethany Jesus was hungry. Seeing in the distance a fig tree in leaf he made for it in hope of finding fruit on it.[b] But when he reached it he found nothing but leaves. Thereupon he said to it, 'Let no one eat fruit of you again for ever!'[c]

Then they came to Jerusalem. On entering the Temple Jesus ejected those who bought and sold in the Temple, and overturned the tables of the moneychangers and the stalls of the pigeon-dealers, and would not allow anyone to carry gear through the Temple.[60] And he taught, 'Is it not stated, "My house shall be known as a place of prayer for all nations"?[61] You have turned it into a robbers' den.'[62]

This came to the attention of the head priests and scribes, and they discussed how to destroy him; for they were in fear of him, because all the people were greatly impressed by his teaching. But when evening came he and his disciples left the city.

As they passed by in the morning they saw the fig tree

[a] It was already late in the day.
[b] Actually it was not the season for figs.
[c] His disciples heard him say it.

[56] Beth-page, 'Place of Unripe Figs'.
[57] Beth-th'ena, 'Place of a figtree', or perhaps Beth-hine.
[58] A Hebrew expression, 'Aid us now!' taken with the words that immediately follow from Ps. cxviii. 25-6, last of the group of festival psalms (cxiii-cxviii) known as the *Hallel* (Praise).
[59] Cp. Job xxv. 2.
[60] The outer court of the Temple, known as the Court of the Gentiles, was used for the sale of sacrificial birds and beasts and for changing heathen coinage into that of the Sanctuary.
[61] Isa. lvi. 7.
[62] Jer. vii. 11.

withered from its roots. Recalling what had happened, Peter said to Jesus, 'Look, rabbi! The fig tree you cursed has withered.'

Jesus replied, 'Have faith in God. I tell you positively, if anyone should say to this hill, "Go and hurl yourself into the sea," and should have not the slightest doubt, but fully believe that what he says will happen, he will bring it about. That is why I tell you, whatever it may be you pray for or ask for, believe that you will obtain it and you will have it. And let all of you when you stand in prayer forgive, if you have something against anyone, that your heavenly Father may also forgive you your shortcomings.'

XXXIII

So they came once more to Jerusalem. While Jesus was walking in the Temple the head priests and scribes with the elders approached him and said, 'By what right are you acting in this way, and who gave you the right to do so?'

Jesus replied, 'Let me ask you one question, and when you have answered it I in turn will tell you by what right I am acting in this way. Was John's rite of immersion of divine or human origin? Answer me that.'

They debated among themselves, 'If we say, of divine origin, he will say, "Why then did you not believe him?" But if we say, of human origin ——.' There they feared the people, who all held John to be a prophet. So they answered Jesus, 'We cannot tell.'

'In that case,' said Jesus, 'I do not have to tell you by what right I am acting in this way.'

Then he proceeded to speak to them in similes. 'There was once a man who planted a vineyard,[63] and surrounded it with a hedge, excavating a vat, and erecting a watch-tower. Then he leased it to cultivators and went abroad. In due course he sent a servant to the cultivators to receive his share of the vineyard's produce. But they seized and beat him, and sent him away empty-handed. So he sent to them again, another servant this time. They set on this one and treated him shamefully. He sent yet another. Him they killed. So with many more, whom they either flogged or put to death.[64] There still remained his own dear son. Finally he sent him to them saying, "They must respect my son." But those cultivators said to themselves, "Here is the heir. Come on! We have only to kill him and the estate will be ours." So they did kill him, and threw him outside the vineyard. How will the owner of the vineyard act? He will come and destroy those cultivators and lease his vineyard to others. You do not seem to have read the Scripture,

The stone which the builders rejected
has become the coping-stone.

[63] Cp. Isa. v. 1-7.   [64] Cp. II. Chron. xxxvi. 15-16.

*This is the Lord's doing,
and is marvellous in our eyes.'* [65]

Then they considered arresting him, but feared the people; for they realized that he had directed the simile against themselves. So they left him and went away.

XXXIV

Now they sent some of the Pharisees and Herodians to trap him in speech. When they came they said to him, 'Teacher, we are aware of your sincerity and impartiality, for you are not influenced by outward appearance, but teach the way of God honestly. Is it right, or not, to pay the poll-tax to Caesar? Should we pay it, or not pay?'

Marking their dissimulation, however, Jesus said to them, 'Why do you try to catch me? Bring me a dinar to look at.'

They brought him one. Then he said to them, 'Whose is this portrait and inscription?'

'Caesar's,' they told him.

Jesus said, 'Render to Caesar what is Caesar's and to God what is God's.'

They were amazed at him.

Then Sadducees[a] came to him, and they put it to him, 'Teacher, Moses laid it down for us that if anyone's brother dies and leaves a wife but no children, he should marry his brother's wife to raise a family for his brother.[66] Once there were seven brothers. The first married and died childless. Then the second married his widow and also left no family. It was the same with the third. Indeed all the seven left no family, and finally the woman herself died.[67] In the resurrection of which of them will she be the wife, for all seven were married to her.'

Jesus said to them, 'Surely your error is due to ignorance of the Scriptures and of the power of God. For when the resurrection of the dead takes place there will be no marrying or giving in marriage: they will be like the angels in heaven. But in confirmation that the dead are raised, you must have read in the book of Moses about the bush, where God spoke to Moses saying, "I am the God of Abraham, and the God of Isaac, and the God of Jacob." [68] He is not the God of the dead, but of the living. You are greatly in error.'

Having listened to their questions one of the scribes approached him, appreciating how well Jesus had answered them. He asked him, 'Which is the supreme commandment?'

Jesus replied, 'The supreme commandment is, "Hear, O

---

[a] Those who say there is no resurrection.

[65] Ps. cxviii. 22-3.
[66] Deut. xxv. 5-6.
[67] Cp. the story of the seven brothers martyred with their mother in the Antiochian persecution (II. Macc. vii. 1-41), which concludes 'And finally after her sons the mother died.'
[68] Exod. iii. 2-6.

Israel, the Lord is our God, the Lord is One. You are to love the Lord your God with your whole heart, with your whole soul, with your whole mind, and your whole might." [69] The next is, "You are to love your neighbour as yourself." [70] No other commandment is greater than these.'

The scribe said to him, 'Excellent, teacher! As you truly say, he is One, and there is no other beside him, and to love him with all one's understanding and with all one's might, and to love one's neighbour as oneself, is of far more consequence than all the burnt-offerings and sacrifices.'

Then Jesus, finding him answer so intelligently, said to him, 'You are not far from the Kingdom of God.'

No one ventured to question him further.

XXXV

Now Jesus asked as he taught in the Temple, 'Why do the scribes declare the Messiah to be the son of David? Did not David himself say by inspiration,[71]

> The Lord said to my lord, "Sit on my right
> Till I set your enemies beneath your feet."[72]

David himself calls him lord. How then is he his son?'

The vast crowd listened to him with pleasure. In the course of his teaching he said, 'Beware of those scribes who love to parade in uniform, to be saluted in the market-places, to have the chief seats in the synagogues, and the best places at the festal banquets. They are the people who prey on widows, and for pretext pray at great length. There is a still longer sentence in store for them.'

As he sat opposite the treasury he watched how the crowd threw coins into the treasury,[73] and many rich people threw in a great deal. Then there came one poor widow and threw in two lepta.[a] On this he summoned his disciples and said to them, 'I tell you positively, that poor widow has thrown in more than all the others who have thrown money into the treasury. All of them have given out of their affluence, but she out of her penury has given all she has, her entire means.'

XXXVI

As Jesus was leaving the Temple one of his disciples said to him, 'Look, teacher, what magnificent stones and buildings these are!'

[a] Which amounts to a farthing.

[69] Deut. vi. 4-5.
[70] Lev. xix. 18.
[71] Lit. 'by the holy Spirit'.
[72] Ps. cx. 1.
[73] I.e. into the donations chests. There were 13 of these shaped like inverted trumpets, each labelled with the purpose for which the fund was employed.

Jesus replied, 'You see these vast buildings? There will not be left here one stone upon another that is not thrown down.'

As he sat on the Mount of Olives opposite the Temple, Peter, James, John and Andrew asked him privately, 'Tell us when this will happen, and what sign there will be when all this is to be consummated.'

Jesus proceeded to tell them. 'Take care,' he said, 'that no one misleads you. Many will come using my title, saying, "I am he," and will deceive many. But when you hear of wars and rumours of wars do not be perturbed. This is bound to happen; but it is not the End[74] yet. For nation will rise against nation and kingdom against kingdom. There will be earthquakes in various places; there will be famines. These are the beginnings of the Pangs.[75]

'But watch out for yourselves. They will hand you over to Sanhedrins, and flog you in synagogues, and you will be brought before governors and kings on my account as a testimony to them; for the News must first be proclaimed to all the Gentiles. Now when they bring you up for examination do not be concerned in advance with what you are going to say. Say what comes to you at the time; for it will not be you who speak but the holy Spirit. Brother will then betray brother to death, and the father his son, and children will rise up against their parents and cause their death. You will be universally detested on my account; but he who is steadfast to the end will be saved.

'When, however, you see the "Abomination of Desolation"[76] standing where it should not,[a] then let those who are in Judea fly to the hills. Let not him who is on the house-top go down or make his way in to fetch anything from his house; and let not him who is in the field turn back to fetch his cloak. Woe, indeed, to pregnant women and nursing mothers in those days! Pray that it may not be in winter; for those days will bring such misery as there has never been the like from the beginning of the world God created until that time, nor ever shall be again. If the Lord did not limit those days not a single human being would survive; but for the sake of his Elect, whom he has chosen, those days will be limited.

'Then should anyone say to you, "See, here is the Messiah!" or "There he is!" do not credit it, for false Messiahs and false prophets will arise, and will exhibit signs and wonders to lead astray the Elect if possible. Be on your guard! I have warned you beforehand. But when those days really come, after that misery, the sun will be eclipsed, the moon will not shed its lustre,

---

[a] Let the reader take note (or, 'work this out'. *Tr.*).

[74] The end of the present world order (Dan. xii. 13). Section xxxvi probably reflects a short document in Hebrew issued by the Jerusalem Community. Tradition tells of a revelation given to this Community prior to the Jewish war with Rome (A.D. 67-70). The document has become known as the 'Little Apocalypse'. A fuller version is given in *Matthew* (see pp. 126-128).
[75] Currently called 'The Pangs of Messiah' (the birth pangs of the Messianic Era).
[76] Dan. ix. 27, xii. 11.

the stars will fall from heaven, and the planets will reel.[77] Then the Son of Man will be seen coming in clouds[78] with great pomp and splendour, and then he will dispatch the angels to gather up the Elect from the four winds, from farthest earth to farthest heaven.[79]

'Take an illustration from the fig tree. When its branch has become tender and the leaves sprout you know that the summer[80] is near. So you, when you see all this happen, will know that it (the End) is near, at the very doors. I tell you positively, this generation will not pass away before all this transpires. Heaven and earth will pass away, but my words will never pass away.[a] Be watchful! Be vigilant! For you do not know when the time will be. It is like a man absent from home, who has vacated his house and left his servants in charge, assigning to each his duty, and has instructed the porter to keep on the alert. Be alert, therefore, for you do not know when the master of the house will come, in the evening, at midnight, at cock-crow, or in the morning,[81] in case coming suddenly he should find you sleeping. What I say to you I say to all, be alert!'

XXXVII

Now the Passover and the Feast of Unleavened Bread[82] were two days off, and the head priests and scribes were discussing how they could arrest Jesus by stealth and execute him. 'It can't be at the festival,' they said, 'or there may be a popular outbreak.'

While Jesus was at Bethany dining at the house of Simon the leper, there came a woman with an alabaster flask of pure oil of nard, a most costly perfume, which she opened and poured over his head. But there were some there who waxed indignant. 'What good has this waste of oil done? That oil could well have been sold for more than three hundred dinars[83] to be given to the poor.' And they stormed at her.

'Leave her alone,' said Jesus. 'Why do you scold her? She has done me a good turn. You always have the poor with you, and you can show them a kindness whenever you wish; but you will not always have me. She has done her best: she has anticipated the anointing of my body for burial. I tell you positively,

---

[a] But none can tell when that day or hour will be, neither the angels in heaven, nor the Son, only the Father.

[77] Lit. 'the powers (or influences) of heaven', Isa. xiii. 10, xxxiv. 4. See p. 127, n. 152.
[78] Dan. vii. 13.
[79] Zech. ii. 6; Deut. xxx. 4.
[80] In the Old Hebrew a play on the words qa'its (summer fruit) and qets (the end), cp. Amos viii. 1-2. Perhaps to imitate this the Greek has 'at the doors' (thyrais) following upon 'summer' (theros).
[81] Jewish day sunset to sunset, night divided into four watches, thus these times, 9 p.m., 12 p.m., 3 a.m. and 6 a.m.
[82] See Exod. xii.
[83] About £12.

wherever the News shall be proclaimed throughout the world, what she has done will also be related to commemorate her.'

Then Judas Iscariot, one of the twelve, went off to the head priests to betray Jesus to them. When they heard what he had to say they were delighted and promised him money. So he set himself to find out how he might conveniently betray him.

XXXVIII

On the first day of the Feast of Unleavened Bread, when they sacrificed the passover,[84] the disciples of Jesus said to him, 'Where do you wish us to make ready for you to eat the passover?'

He then dispatched two of his disciples and told them, 'Go into the city, where a man will meet you carrying a water-pot. Follow him, and wherever he enters say to the owner of the house, "The teacher says, which guest-room am I to have to eat the passover with my disciples?" He will then show you a large upstairs dining room ready laid out.[85] There prepare for us.'

So the disciples went off to the city and found everything turn out as he told them; and they made ready the passover.

When evening came he arrived with the twelve. As they reclined and ate Jesus said, 'I tell you positively, one of you eating with me will betray me.'

Deeply distressed one after the other said to him, 'Not me, surely?'

'It is one of the twelve[86] dipping in the dish with me,' he told them. 'Though the Son of Man goes the way that is written of him, woe, none the less, to the one by whom the Son of Man is betrayed. Better for him had he never been born.'

As they were eating he took the bread, and reciting the blessing broke it and gave it to them, and said, 'Take it: it signifies my body.' Then taking a cup and giving thanks he handed it to them and all of them drank from it, and he said to them, 'It signifies my "blood of the covenant" poured out for many. I tell you positively, I will not again drink of the fruit of the vine[87] till the day when I drink it new in the Kingdom of God.'

After the hymn-singing they went out to the Mount of Olives. Then Jesus said to them, 'All of you will waver in your loyalty, for it is stated, "I will strike at the shepherd, and the sheep will be scattered."[88] But after I have been raised up I will precede you to Galilee.'

Peter told him, 'Even if everyone else wavers, I shall not.'

---

[84] I.e. The paschal lamb.
[85] There is a mystery about these secret arrangements since the identity of the householder is not disclosed. But see Jn. xiii. 23, xix. 26-7, below pp. 416, 425.
[86] This could imply that there was at least one other present beside the twelve, namely the owner of the house.
[87] Jesus had just recited over the wine, 'Blessed art thou, O Lord our God, King of the universe, creator of the fruit of the vine'.
[88] Zech. xiii. 7.

Jesus replied, 'I tell you positively, to-day—this very night indeed—before the cock crows twice you yourself will disown me three times.'

But he insisted, 'Even if I have to die with you I will never disown you.'

So said they all.

XXXIX

When they came to a spot called Gethsemane Jesus said to his disciples, 'Stay here while I pray.' Then he took Peter, James and John along with him. He was restless and depressed, and said to them, 'I am in very low spirits.[89] Stay here and keep watch.'

Going on a step further Jesus fell upon the ground and prayed that if it were possible the crisis might pass him by. '*Abba*,'[a] he said, 'to thee everything is possible. Let this cup pass me by. Yet let it not be as I wish, but what thou wishest.'

When he came back he found them sleeping, and said to Peter, 'Are you asleep, Simon? Could you not manage to stay awake a single hour? Be vigilant and prayerful, or you may find yourself tempted. The spirit is willing enough, but the flesh is frail.'

He went away again and prayed the same prayer. Returning once more he again found them asleep; for their eyes were heavy and they could hardly speak to him. When he came the third time he said to them, 'Are you going on sleeping and taking your rest? That's enough! The time has come. Look, the Son of Man is betrayed into the hands of sinners! Come, let us be going. See, my betrayer approaches!'

He was still speaking when Judas, one of the twelve, came, and with him a force armed with swords and clubs dispatched by the head priests, scribes and elders. The betrayer of Jesus had arranged the following signal with them, 'The one I embrace is the man you want, seize him and take him away securely.' So directly he arrived he approached Jesus with 'Rabbi!' and embraced him warmly. Then they laid hands on Jesus and seized him; but one of the bystanders[90] drew his sword and struck the high priest's servant, severing his ear.

Jesus said to them, 'Have you come out as after a brigand with swords and clubs to apprehend me? I was with you daily in the Temple teaching, and you did not arrest me there, so that the Scriptures should be fulfilled.'

Everyone then deserted him and fled. One youth did follow close behind him clad only in a linen wrap. They seized him; but abandoning the linen wrap he fled away naked.

[a] 'Father.'

[89] Lit. 'My soul is very sad, even to death.'
[90] *John* says it was Peter.

XL

Now the head priests and the entire Sanhedrin sought evidence against Jesus on which to condemn him to death, but they failed to find it; for though many gave false evidence against him their testimonies did not agree. Then some came forward and testified falsely against him, 'We heard him say, "I will pull down this man-made Sanctuary, and in three days I will build another that is not man-made."[91] But even so their testimonies did not agree.

On this the high priest rose in person to ask Jesus, 'Have you no answer to make to these charges?'

But he was silent and made no reply.

So the high priest asked him again, 'Are you the Messiah, the Son of the Blessed One?'

'Yes I am,' Jesus replied. 'And you will all see the Son of Man installed in the place of authority,[92] and coming with the clouds of heaven.'

Then the high priest tore his tunic[93] and cried, 'What further evidence do we need? You have heard the traitorous[94] confession. What is your verdict?'

Unanimously they judged him deserving of the death-penalty. Some of them spat at him, and covered his face and struck him saying, 'Prophesy!' Even the attendants cuffed him.

Meanwhile as Peter was below in the hall one of the maidservants of the high priest came by, and noticing Peter warming himself she looked at him intently and said, 'Of course, you were with the Nazarene, with that Jesus.'

But he flatly denied it. 'I don't know him,' he said, 'and I don't know what you're talking about.'

He went outside to the forecourt. But the maid seeing him again said to the bystanders, 'There's one of them.'

Once more he denied it. But shortly after the bystanders said to Peter, 'You certainly are one of them. You're a Galilean.'

He cursed and swore, 'I don't know this man you're talking about.'

Immediately the cock crowed a second time. Then Peter recalled what Jesus had told him, 'Before the cock crows twice you will disown me three times.' As it came home to him he wept.

XLI

Directly morning came, after the head priests had conferred with the elders and scribes, the entire Sanhedrin in fact, they

[91] Accusing Jesus of the Jewish capital crime of being a wizard or magician. See Lev. xx. 27. Hostile writers held Jesus to have been a sorcerer.
[92] Lit. 'on the right hand of power' (cp. Dan. vii. 13-14).
[93] An action expressing grief, customary with mourners.
[94] The Greek *blasphemia* here denotes the capital crime in Roman law of lèse-majesty. The capital charges in Jewish religious law had failed. It was no blasphemy against God to claim to be the Messiah: it was high treason against Caesar. Cp. Lk. xxiii. 2; Tac. *Annals*, Bk. IV, lxx; Bk. VI, vii.

had Jesus manacled and led him away and handed him over to Pilate.[95]

Then Pilate asked him, 'Are you king of the Jews?'

'As you say,' he replied.

The head priests then indicted him in full.

'Have you no defence to make?' Pilate asked him again. 'You hear all these charges they bring against you.'

But to Pilate's surprise Jesus made no further response.

It was customary at this festival for Pilate to release to the people any one prisoner for whom they asked clemency. Now there was one called Bar-Abbas imprisoned with other insurgents who had committed murder during the rising.[96] So the crowd came round and requested him to follow his usual practice. Pilate replied, 'Do you want me to release the king of the Jews?'[a]

The head priests, however, persuaded the crowd to prefer Bar-Abbas to be released to them. Pilate put it to them again. 'What then am I to do with him you call king of the Jews?'

'Crucify him!' they cried.

'What crime has he committed?' Pilate asked.

But they only shouted the more, 'Crucify him!'

So Pilate anxious to appease the crowd released Bar-Abbas to them, and after having Jesus flogged handed him over to be crucified.

XLII

The soldiers marched Jesus outside the court,[b] and summoned the whole cohort. Then they arrayed him in scarlet, and when they had plaited it they invested him with a victor's wreath made of thorn, and saluted him with, 'Hail, king of the Jews!' They also struck him on the head with a cane, and spat at him, and bent their knees in homage to him.

After they had mocked him, they stripped off the scarlet and dressed him in his own clothes and marched him off to be crucified. They requisitioned a passer-by, one Simon the Cyrenian,[c][97] who was coming in from the country, to carry his cross. When they had brought Jesus to the place Golgotha[d] they offered him wine impregnated with myrrh; but he refused it. Then they crucified him, and shared out his clothes among themselves, throwing dice to decide who should have what.

It was nine o'clock in the morning when they crucified him.

[a] He realized it was out of malice that the head priests had handed him over.

[b] That is to say, the praetorium.

[c] He was the father of Alexander and Rufus.[98]

[d] This means when translated 'Place of a Skull'.

[95] Pontius Pilate, Roman governor of Judea, A.D. 26-36.

[96] Probably the rising which occurred when Pilate appropriated the sacred funds to build an aqueduct. See Jos. *Wars*, II. ix. 4 and cp. Lk. xiii. 1, below p. 169.

[97] West of Egypt, where there was a large Jewish community.

[98] Evidently persons well known in the church, perhaps at Alexandria.

The wording of the charge which had been written out was 'The King of the Jews'. With him they crucified two brigands, one on his right and the other on his left. And all who went that way vilified him, nodding their heads and saying, 'Hi, you, who can pull down the Sanctuary and build it in three days, save yourself and come down from the cross!'

The head priests also with the scribes derided him, and said, 'He delivered others, but cannot save himself. Let the Messiah the king of Israel come down now from the cross that we may see and believe.' Even those who were crucified with him reviled him.

When midday came there was darkness over the whole landscape until three o'clock. Then at three o'clock Jesus called out, *'Eloi, Eloi, lama sabachthani?'*[a]

Some of the bystanders hearing this said, 'Hark, he is calling Elijah!' Someone ran to saturate a sponge with vinegar, spiked it on a cane and offered it to him to drink, saying 'Quiet! Let us see if Elijah will come to take him down.'

But Jesus giving a piercing cry expired; and the curtain of the Sanctuary was ripped in two from top to bottom.

When the centurion who stood in front of him saw that he had expired, he said, 'Truly this man was God's Son!'[99]

There were also some women there looking on at a distance. Among them were Mary of Magdala, Mary the mother of the younger James and of Jose, and Salome. These had followed Jesus in Galilee and looked after him; but there were others as well who had come up with him to Jerusalem.

XLIII

When evening came, since it was the preparation day,[b] Joseph of Arimathea, a distinguished councillor, arrived, who was also himself awaiting the Kingdom of God. He ventured to go to Pilate and ask for the body of Jesus. Pilate was surprised that he had died so quickly, and having sent for the centurion asked if he was already dead. When the centurion confirmed it, Pilate granted Joseph the corpse. After purchasing a linen winding-sheet Joseph took Jesus down, swathed him in the linen, and laid him in a tomb quarried out of the rock: he then rolled a boulder against the entrance of the tomb. Mary of Magdala and Mary mother of Jose observed where he was laid.

After the sabbath was over, Mary of Magdala, Mary mother of James, and Salome, bought spices in order to go and anoint him. And very early in the morning of the day after the sabbath

[a] This means when translated 'My God, my God, why have you deserted me' (Ps. xxii. 1 in Aramaic. *Tr.*).
[b] That is to say, the day before the sabbath.
[99] The Caesars adopted the title *divi filius,* Son of God.

they came to the tomb as soon as the sun was up. 'Who is going to roll away the boulder for us from the entrance of the tomb?' they asked themselves. But when they came to look they saw that the boulder had been rolled aside.[a] On entering the tomb they were startled to see a young man sitting on the right clad in a flowing white robe. 'Do not be alarmed,' he said to them. 'You are looking for Jesus the Nazarene who was crucified. He has risen. He is not here. Look, this is the place where he was laid. Go now and tell his disciples, and Peter particularly, he is preceding you to Galilee. You will see him there just as he told you.'

They fled out of the tomb, for they were trembling and unnerved. And they said nothing to anyone, for they were afraid . . .

(Here the text breaks off abruptly. The standard ending[100] supplied by an early copyist reads as follows:)

[Having risen early on the morning after the sabbath Jesus appeared in the first instance to Mary of Magdala from whom he had expelled seven demons. She then went and informed those who had been with him, who were mourning and weeping. When they heard he was alive and that she had seen him they did not credit it. But later on he appeared to two of them in another guise while they were out walking on their way into the country. They too came and told the rest, yet still they did not credit it. Afterwards while they were dining he appeared to the eleven and reproached them for their disbelief and obtuseness in failing to credit those who had seen him when he had risen from the dead. 'Travel the world over,' he told them, 'and proclaim the News to all creation. Whoever believes and is immersed will be saved, but whoever does not believe will be condemned. And these signs shall attend those who have believed: they shall expel demons in my name; they shall speak in tongues; they shall take up snakes; if they drink anything poisonous it will not harm them; and they shall lay hands on the sick and cure them.'

So then the Lord Jesus, after he had spoken to them, was taken up to heaven and sat at God's right hand. But they set off and preached everywhere, the Master working with them and confirming the Message by the signs that authenticated it.]

[a] It was very massive.

[100] The standard ending largely reproduces information found in *Matthew* and *Luke-Acts*. Alternative endings are extant, but it is not known how much of the original text is missing.

MATTHEW
THE MAXIMS OF THE MASTER

Preface to *Matthew*

MATTHEW WAS A JEW employed as a tax-collector at Capernaum who became a follower of Jesus. He is otherwise called
Levi the son of Alphaeus. Also among the Twelve was a James
the son of Alphaeus. Matthew is said by Papias (early second
century) to have compiled 'the maxims' (*logia*) in Hebrew and
'everyone translated them to the best of his ability'. Our document may have been attributed to Matthew because it made
particular use of the 'Dominical Oracles' or 'Maxims of the
Master'. A feature of the work is the number of aphorisms, proverbs and similes it contain. Certain expressions, poetic forms
and word-plays, revealed by retranslation from Greek into Hebrew assisted by an old Hebrew version of the book, certainly
point to one major source that was originally written in that
language. This was possibly that same 'Teaching Source' which
scholars have called 'Q' (German *quelle,* source), and which
in Greek translations was employed by both *Matthew* and *Luke*.
It is not to be confounded with an ancient Aramaic version of
Matthew in use among Judaeo-Christian groups in Syria and
Palestine down to at least the fifth century, also known—if it
was the same—as the *Gospel according to the Hebrews*.

In common with *Luke, Matthew* also used *Mark* as another
major source, substantially in its present form. The whole work
suggests a skilful blending, perhaps with the intention of creating an 'authorised version' of the Gospel 'appointed to be read
in churches.' The document consists of Five Books, with a Prologue and Epilogue, and this structure—so far as it can roughly
be ascertained—is reproduced in the present translation. The
author may have had in mind the Five Books of Moses, though
there is reason to believe that the *Logia* were in five books. At
any rate Papias arranged his own exposition of the Dominical
Oracles in this form. Another feature of our document is the
inclusion of prophetic 'proofs' from the Old Testament held to
relate to Christ. Of particular interest in this connexion is the
account of the Nativity of Jesus, differing entirely from *Luke's*
version, reflecting stories currently told of the births of Abraham and Moses.

The style of the writing varies naturally with that of the
sources employed, but the consequent strong Hebraic tone can
be misleading. It requires close examination to determine that
the author was not himself a Jew. He is, however, no mere com-
piler, and has left his own impress on the book. Among his

contributions may be included not only the arrangement of material and improvements of *Mark's* style, but also a heightening of the miraculous elements, and in places doubling the number of persons cured, e.g., two Gadarene demoniacs and two blind men at Jericho. This last may be due to finding a similar story in *Mark* and the other main source. Also to be noted is the animus against Pharisaic Judaism, references to the status of the Church and to Church discipline, and evidences of persecution by the Roman authorities. Such features suggest a comparatively late date of composition, perhaps about A.D. 90-95.

———◆———

THE GOOD NEWS OF JESUS CHRIST

Matthew's Version

PROLOGUE

I

The ancestral scroll[1] of Jesus Christ, son of David, son of Abraham.

> Abraham begot Isaac:
> Isaac begot Jacob:
> Jacob begot Judah and his brothers:
> Judah begot Pharez and Zarah by Tamar:
> Pharez begot Hezron:
> Hezron begot Ram:
> Ram begot Amminadab:
> Amminadab begot Nahshon:
> Nahshon begot Salmon:
> Salmon begot Boaz by Rahab:
> Boaz begot Obed by Ruth:
> Obed begot Jesse:
> Jesse begot King David.
>
> David begot Solomon by Uriah's wife:
> Solomon begot Rehoboam:
> Rehoboam begot Abijam:

[1] This scroll may be based on records circulated by the *Desposynoi*, 'Heirs', as the surviving relations of Jesus were called. 'These coming from the Jewish villages of Nazara and Cochaba to other parts of the country set out the foregoing genealogy from the chronicle' (Jul. Afric., *Letter to Aristides*, quoted by Euseb. *Eccl. Hist.* Bk. I. ch. vii). The record was evidently originally in Hebrew.

PALESTINE in the time of JESUS CHRIST

Sidon
Sarepta
Tyre
Ptolemais
The Great Sea
Caesarea
Apollonia
Joppa
Jamnia
Azotus
Ascalon
Gaza
Beersheba

PHENICIA
SYRIA
ABILENE
Damascus
Caesarea Philippi
ITUREA
TRACHONITIS
Chorazin
Capernaum
Bethsaida
GALILEE
Magdala
Sepphoris
Tiberias
Cana
Nazareth
Nain
Scythopolis
SAMARIA
Aenon
Samaria
Shechem
Antipatris
Salim
Lydda
Ephraim
Nicopolis
Jericho
Emmaus
JERUSALEM
Bethlehem
Herodium
Hebron
Engedi
Masada
JUDEA
IDUMEA

BethsaidaJulias
SEA of GALILEE
Hippos
Gadara
DECAPOLIS
Pella
Dium
Gerasa
PEREA
Philadelphia
Bethany-beyond-Jordan
Machaerus

GAULANITIS
BATANEA
Raphana
Canatha
AURANITIS
Jordan
DEAD SEA
Plain of Sharon

Tetrarchy of Philip

Tetrarchy of Herod Antipas

J.F.H.

0   25   Miles   50   75

87

Abijam begot Asa:
Asa begot Jehoshaphat:
Jehoshaphat begot Joram:
Joram begot Uzziah:
Uzziah begot Jotham:
Jotham begot Ahaz:
Ahaz begot Hezekiah:
Hezekiah begot Menasseh:
Manesseh begot Ammon:
Ammon begot Josiah:
Josiah begot Jeconiah and his brothers
    about the time of the Babylonian Exile.

During the Babylonian Exile
Jeconiah begot Shealtiel:
Shealtiel begot Zerubbabel:
Zerubbabel begot Abiud:
Abiud begot [Abner:[2]
Abner begot] Eliakim:
Eliakim begot Azzur:
Azzur begot Zadok:
Zadok begot Achim:
Achim begot Elihud:
Elihud begot Eleazar:
Eleazar begot Matthan:
Matthan begot Jacob:
Jacob begot Joseph the husband of Mary,
    who begot[3] Jesus styled Christ.

Thus there were fourteen[4] generations in all from Abraham
to David, fourteen generations from David to the Babylonian
Exile, and fourteen generations from the Babylonian Exile to
the Messiah.

II

The birth of the Messiah came about in this way. His mother
Mary had become betrothed to Joseph; but before they could
be wed she was found to be with child by the holy Spirit. Joseph
her husband being a devout man, yet unwilling to disgrace her
in public, wanted to divorce her quietly. But while he was thinking the matter over an angel of the Lord appeared to him in a
dream and said, 'Joseph, son of David, do not be afraid to accept Mary as your wife, for the child she has conceived is by the

[2] Restored from an old Hebrew MS (Du Tillet) in the National Library at Paris.
   Likeness in Heb. of the name Abner (*Abiner,* I. Sam. xiv. 50) to the preceding
   name Abiud (*Abiur,* Sin. Syr.) doubtless caused the omission. Without it the
   third group has only thirteen names.
[3] Following Sin. Syr.
[4] The number is artificial and obtained by omissions. It has been suggested that
   the three groups correspond to the three letters of the name David in Heb.
   (DVD), the numerical value of which is 14.

holy Spirit. She will bear you[5] a son whom you are to name Jesus; for he will save[6] his people from their sins.'[a7]

When Joseph woke he acted as the angel of the Lord bade him, and accepted his wife; but he had no intercourse with her until she had borne a son, whom he named Jesus.

III

Now when Jesus was born in Judean Bethlehem in the reign of King Herod[8] magi[9] from the east arrived in Jerusalem inquiring, 'Where is he who is born to be king of the Jews, for we in the East have seen his star and have come to pay him homage?'

King Herod was greatly agitated[10] when he heard this, and all Jerusalem as well; and convening all the head priests and learned representatives of the people[11] he asked to be informed where the Messiah would be born.

'In Judean Bethlehem,' they told him, 'for it is so stated by the prophet,

> *And you, Bethlehem, country of Judah,*
> *are not least among the leaders of Judah;*
> *For from you shall arise the prince,*
> *who shall shepherd my people Israel.'*[12]

Then Herod sent for the magi privately, and obtained from them the exact date at which the star had appeared. Then he sent them to Bethlehem and said, 'Go and make exhaustive inquiries for the child; and directly you have discovered him send me word that I too may come and pay him homage.'

When they had heard the king they set out, and the star which they had seen in the East led them on until it came and stood still directly above where the child was. Seeing the star they rejoiced greatly, and entering the house they saw the child with his mother Mary. Prostrating themselves before him they opened their baggage and presented their gifts to him, gold, frankincense and myrrh. But being apprised in a dream that

---

[a] All this transpired to fulfil what the Lord had announced by the prophet saying, 'See, the maiden is with child, and shall bear a son, whom they shall name Immanuel',[13] which means when translated 'God is on our side'.

[5] Sin. Syr.
[6] Heb. *yoshia*, a play on the name *Yeshua* (Gr. Jesus).
[7] 'Sins'. The original source word was probably 'enemies' (cp. Lk. ii. p. 123). The nativity story in *Matthew* owes much to the contemporary legends of the birth of Moses. See Jos. *Antiq.* II, ix. 2-4.
[8] King of Judea 37-4 B.C.
[9] Magi, strictly Persian priests of the Zoroastrian faith, but also oriental sages in general, credited with astrological and occult knowledge.
[10] Heb. *y'cherad*, possibly playing on the name Herod. He was in great fear of plotters against his life and throne.
[11] Lit. 'scribes of the people'. Herod summoned the full Sanhedrin consisting of the Sadducean hierarchy and the Pharisean scribes.
[12] Mic. v. 2.
[13] Isa. vii. 14.

they should not return to Herod they journeyed back to their own country by a different route.

No sooner had they taken their departure than an angel of the Lord appeared in a dream to Joseph and said, 'Rouse yourself, and take the child and his mother and escape to Egypt, and stay there until I tell you; for Herod will attempt to kill the child.' On waking, therefore, he took the child and his mother by night and departed for Egypt, and remained there until Herod's death.[a]

When Herod realized that he had been duped by the magi he flew into a passion, and had all the boys killed in Bethlehem and its entire neighbourhood who were two years old or under, going by the date he had obtained from the magi.[b]

Once Herod was dead, however, the angel of the Lord appeared in a dream to Joseph in Egypt and said, 'Rouse yourself, and take the child and his mother and journey to the land of Israel; for those who tried to take the child's life are dead.' On waking, therefore, he took the child and his mother and went to the land of Israel. But learning that Archelaus was ruling Judea in his father Herod's stead he was afraid to go there; and being warned in a dream he travelled on to the district of Galilee, and settled in a town called Nazareth.[c]

BOOK I

I

At this period John the Baptist made his appearance, proclaiming in the wilderness of Judea, 'Repent, for the Kingdom of Heaven[17] is at hand!'

It was he whom the Prophet Isaiah announced when he said,

[a] This was to fulfil what the Lord had announced by the prophet saying, 'Out of Egypt have I called my son.'[14]

[b] Then was fulfilled what was announced by the Prophet Jeremiah saying,

> A sound was heard in Ramah,
> Lamentation and bitter weeping,
> Rachel weeping for her children,
> Inconsolable for their loss.[15]

[c] Thereby was fulfilled what was announced by the prophets, 'He shall be called Nazorean.'[16]

[14] Hos. xi. 1.

[15] Jer. xxxi. 15. Rachel, wife of the Patriarch Jacob, was buried near Bethlehem (Gen. xxxv. 19).

[16] There is no exact O.T. reference for this quotation. It may be that by a Hebrew word-play the town Nazara is linked with the word *zara* ('the seed' of promise, the Messiah) looking back to Gen. xxi. 12, lit. '(In Isaac) shall be called (to thee) seed (*zara*).' See Rom. ix. 7; Heb. xi. 18; Gal. iii. 16. The play is also on the word Nazirite, cp. Exod. xiii. 2 with Judg. xiii. 5 and I. Sam. i. 20. A Nazirite was one dedicated or under a special vow to God. Cp. also *netser* ('the branch'), Isa. xi. 1.

[17] In order not to risk taking God's name in vain the pious Jew used substitutes such as 'Heaven', or 'the Place'.

A voice cries out in the wilderness,
'Make ready the Lord's road!
Put his highways in order!' [18]

John wore camel-hair clothing with a leather girdle round his waist, and he lived on locusts and wild honey.

Then Jerusalem, and all Judea, and all the vicinity of Jordan flocked to him, and were immersed by him in the River Jordan as they confessed their sins.

Observing many of the Pharisees and Sadducees coming for immersion John said to them, 'Vipers' brood, who warned you to escape from the coming Wrath? Well then, produce fruit consistent with repentance, and content yourselves no longer with saying, "We have Abraham as our father," for I tell you that from these stones [19] God can supply Abraham with sons. Already the axe is laid to the root of the trees. Any tree that fails to produce good fruit will be cut down and cast into the fire. I am only immersing you in water in token of repentance, but after me comes one mightier than I whose sandals I am not fit to touch: he will immerse you in holy Spirit and fire. His winnowing-shovel is in his hand, and he will thoroughly cleanse his threshing-floor, gathering the wheat into his granary, but burning up the chaff with unquenchable fire.'

Then Jesus arrived at the Jordan from Galilee to be immersed by John. But John stopped him and said, 'I need to be immersed by you, and yet you come to me?'

Jesus replied, 'Never mind that. It is of more consequence that one should do one's whole duty.'

So John let him have his way.

[When Jesus was immersed a bright light played upon the water, so that all who had come there were afraid.] [20] After his immersion Jesus at once rose up from the water, and lo, the skies were parted, and he saw the Spirit of God descend like a dove alighting on him, while a voice from the skies declared, 'This is my dear Son with whom I am well satisfied.'

II

Then Jesus was led by the Spirit into the wilderness to be tempted by the Devil. After fasting for forty days and forty nights he was starving. So when the tempter came he said to him, 'If you are the Son of God tell these stones to become loaves.'

To this Jesus replied, 'It is stated, "Not by bread alone shall a man live, but by every utterance that proceeds from the mouth of God."' [21]

[18] Isa. xl. 3.
[19] 'Stones . . . sons'. Reproducing as nearly as possible the underlying Hebrew play on the words *abanim* and *banim*.
[20] This ancient reading of the *Gospel of the Hebrews* and some Old Latin MSS. is included here as worthy of preservation.
[21] Deut. viii. 3.

Then the Devil took him to the holy city and set him on a turret of the Temple, and said to him, 'If you are the Son of God throw yourself down, for it is stated,

> *"He shall charge his angels on your behalf,*
> *And with their hands they shall support you,*
> *Lest you strike your foot against a stone."* [22]

Jesus answered, 'It is further stated, "You are not to put the Lord your God to the proof." ' [23]

Next the Devil took him off to a lofty mountain, and showed him all the kingdoms of the world and their splendour, and said to him, 'I will give you all these if you will fall down and do me homage.'

Then Jesus said to him, 'Begone Satan! It is stated, "You are to do homage to the Lord your God, and be subject to him alone." ' [24]

Thereupon the Devil left him, and angels came and attended to his needs.

III

When Jesus learnt that John had been arrested he returned to Galilee, and abandoning Nazareth he made his home at Capernaum, which is beside the sea on the Zebulon-Naphtali border,ᵃ

From that time Jesus began to proclaim, 'Repent, for the Kingdom of Heaven is at hand!'

As he was walking by the Sea of Galilee Jesus saw two brothers who were fishermen, Simon called Peter and his brother Andrew. 'Follow me,' he said to them, 'and I will make you fishers of men.'

Forthwith they abandoned their nets and followed him.

Farther on he saw two other brothers, James the son of Zebedee and his brother John. They were in the boat with their father Zebedee mending their nets. When he called them they too at once left the boat and their father and followed him.

Then Jesus toured Galilee teaching in their synagogues, proclaiming the News of the Kingdom, and curing every kind of disease and ailment among the people. Report of him spread throughout Syria,[25] and they brought to him all who were ill,

ᵃ Thereby was fulfilled what was announced by the Prophet Isaiah,

> 'Lands of Zebulon and Naphtali,
> The sea road, beyond the Jordan,
> Galilee of the Gentiles.
> The people who sat in darkness
> Saw great light;
> And those who sat in deepest gloom,
> To them light has arisen.' [26]

[22] Ps. xci. 11-12.
[23] Deut. vi. 16.
[24] Deut. vi. 13.
[25] The Old Hebrew has the more likely reading 'among all the people (*haam*)', subsequently changed to *Aram* (Syria). See Euseb. *Eccl. Hist.* i. 13, *Letter of Abgar, Prince of Edessa*.
[26] Isa. ix. 1-2.

afflicted with various diseases and pains, or demon-possessed (epileptics and paralytics); and he cured them. And many people followed him from Galilee, the Decapolis, Jerusalem, Judea, and from beyond Jordan.

IV

Now when Jesus saw the crowds he ascended the hillside, and when he had sat down his disciples gathered round him, and he began to teach them.

'How fortunate are the oppressed in spirit,' he said, 'for theirs is the Kingdom of God!

'How fortunate are those who grieve, for they shall be comforted!

'How fortunate are the gentle, for they shall inherit the land!

'How fortunate are those who hunger and thirst for justice, for they shall be satisfied!

'How fortunate are those with pure minds, for they shall see God!

'How fortunate are the peacemakers, for they shall be called sons of God!

'How fortunate are those who are persecuted in the cause of justice, for theirs is the Kingdom of God!

'How fortunate are you when they revile you, and persecute you, and speak every kind of evil of you falsely because of me! Rejoice and be glad, for your heavenly reward is great; for so did they persecute the prophets who were before you.

'You are the salt of the earth. But if the salt becomes insipid by what means can its tang be restored? It is then good for nothing but to be thrown out for men to trample underfoot.

'You are the light of the world. A city cannot be hidden that is perched on the brow of a hill. A lamp is not lit to be placed under a measuring-bowl, but on a lampstand, to give light to all who are in the house. So let your light shine in the sight of men, that they may observe your good conduct and praise your heavenly Father.

'Do not imagine that I have come to abolish the Law and the Prophets: I have not come to abolish them but to give effect to them. I tell you positively, until heaven and earth pass away not one iota, not a single stroke, shall be removed from the Law till everything has come to pass. So whoever would relax the most insignificant of commandments, and teach men so, shall be treated as insignificant in the Kingdom of Heaven. But whoever both observes and teaches them shall be treated as of consequence in the Kingdom of Heaven. I tell you therefore, unless your devoutness exceeds that of the scribes and Pharisees you will never enter the Kingdom of Heaven.

'You have heard how those of old were told, "You shall not commit murder." [27] Those who commit murder are liable to the

[27] Exod. xx. 13. The reader is referred to the Introduction, for additional matter explanatory of the Sermon on the Mount.

death penalty. But I tell you that whoever is enraged against his brother is liable to the death penalty, whoever calls his brother "*Raka*"[28] is liable to punishment by the Sanhedrin, whoever calls him "*More*"[29] is liable to be doomed to blazing Gehenna. So if you bring your offering to the altar, and there recall that your brother has something against you, leave your offering before the altar, and first make your peace with your brother, then come and present your offering. Come to terms quickly with your opponent while you and he are on the way to court, in case your opponent turns you over to the judge, and the judge in turn to the executive officer, and you are thrown into jail. I tell you positively, you will not get out again until you have paid up the last farthing.

'You have heard how it was declared, "You shall not commit adultery."[30] But I tell you, whoever stares lustfully at a woman has already committed adultery with her in his mind. If therefore your right eye gives cause for complaint pluck it out and cast it from you. It is more advantageous for you to be disfigured than that your body intact should be cast into Gehenna. Or if your right hand gives cause for complaint cut it off and cast it from you. It is more advantageous for you to be maimed than that your body intact should go into Gehenna.

'It was also declared, "Whoever divorces his wife must give her a deed of severance."[31] But I tell you, whoever discards his wife, except on grounds of adultery, makes her commit adultery, and whoever then marries her commits adultery.

'Further you have heard how those of old were told, "You are not to swear falsely, but pay to the Lord what you vow."[32] But I tell you, use no oath at all, neither by heaven, since it is God's throne, nor by the earth, since it is his footstool, nor by Jerusalem, since it is the city of the Great King. Do not even swear by your head, since you are powerless to whiten a single hair or to turn it black again. Confine yourself, therefore, to plain "Yes" or "No". Anything beyond that is wrong.[33]

'You have heard how it was declared, "An eye for an eye, and a tooth for a tooth."[34] But I tell you, do not offer resistance to wrong.[35] Whoever hits you on the right side of the jaw, turn the other side to him. Whoever would go to law to take away your tunic, let him have your cloak as well. Whoever would compel you to go one mile, go with him even two. Give to him who asks you, and from him who would borrow from you do not turn away.

'You have heard how it was declared, "You are to love your

---

[28] Aram. meaning scoundrel.
[29] Aram. meaning rebel against God.
[30] Exod. xx. 14.
[31] Deut. xxiv. 1.
[32] Deut. v. 11 with xxiii. 23.
[33] This agrees with the Essenes. 'Any word of theirs has more force than an oath; swearing they avoid, regarding it as worse than perjury' (Jos. *Wars* II. viii 6).
[34] Exod. xxi. 24.
[35] Galilee was the headquarters of the Jewish resistance movement.

neighbour, but hate your enemy.'[36] But I tell you, love your enemies, pray for those who persecute you, that you may become sons of the heavenly Father, who makes his sun rise on the bad and good alike, and showers rain on the just and the unjust. For if you only love those who love you, what reward have you? Do not even tax-collectors[37] do this? And if you only give your regard to your brothers, what do you do more than others? Do not the Gentiles do the same? So you must be perfect as your heavenly Father is perfect.

'Be sure you do not let people see you perform your charitable actions. If you do you will have no reward from your heavenly Father. So when you bestow alms do not blare it out in advance like the hypocrites do in the synagogues and streets to court public esteem. I tell you for a fact, they are receiving their reward in full. But you, when you bestow alms, do not let your left hand know what your right hand is doing; so that your alms are in secret, and your Father who sees in secret will reward you.

'Similarly when you pray, do not be like the hypocrites, who love to stand praying in the synagogues and at street corners to be seen by people. I tell you positively, they are receiving their reward in full. But you, when you pray, enter your inner apartment and close the door, and pray to your Father who is in secret, and your Father who sees in secret will reward you. Further when you pray, do not uselessly repeat yourself as the Gentiles do;[38] for they imagine that by constant reiteration they will gain attention. Do not imitate them, therefore, since your Father knows what your needs are before you ask him.

'Pray rather in this way, "Our Heavenly Father, may thy name be sanctified, thy Kingdom established, thy will be obeyed on earth as it is in heaven. Give us to-day our needful food, and forgive us our failings,[39] as we too forgive those who have failed us. And do not put temptation in our way, but shield us from harm."[40] For if you forgive people their failures your heavenly Father will forgive you; but if you do not forgive people their failures neither will your heavenly Father forgive yours.

'And when you fast do not be like the long-faced hypocrites, who mar their looks so that it may be evident to people that they are fasting. I tell you positively, they are receiving their reward in full. But you, when you fast, anoint your head and bathe your face, so that you do not appear to people to be fasting, only to

---

[36] Lev. xix. 18. The second part of the saying is not in the O.T., but the 'Zadokites' vowed 'to love all the Children of Light and hate all the Children of Darkness' (*Manual of Discipline*).

[37] See above, p. 54, n. 12.

[38] Cp. I. Ki. xviii. 26.

[39] A formula of absolution from rash vows and promises (*Kol Nidrei*) is still recited by Jews on the eve of the Fast Day of Atonement. Failings, or obligations, is perhaps used in this sense. The reference to fasting would then follow naturally after the prayer.

[40] Or, 'Rescue us from the Evil One'. On the whole prayer cp. the Jewish liturgy (AJP pp. 7, 37).

your Father who is in secret, and your Father who sees in secret will reward you.

'Lay up no store for yourselves on earth, where locust-grub and moth destroy, and where thieves break in and steal. Rather lay up for yourselves store in heaven, where neither locust-grub nor moth destroys, and where no thieves break in and steal. For "where your hoard is your heart is."[41]

'The eye is the lamp of the body. If therefore your sight is sound your whole body will be radiant; but if your sight is bad your whole body will be in gloom.[42] If then the light that is in you is gloom, how deep the gloom!

'No one can serve two masters, for either he will hate the one and love the other, or else he will be devoted to the one and despise the other. You cannot serve both God and mammon.[43] Therefore I tell you, do not vex yourselves about what you are to eat or drink, or how your body is to be clad. Is not the soul of more consequence than food, and the body than clothing? Observe the birds of the air. They neither sow nor reap, nor gather into granaries, yet your heavenly Father feeds them. Are you not of more value than they? Which of you by mental effort can add a span to his height? Why then are you worried about clothing? Study the wild iris, how they shoot up. They neither toil nor spin, yet I tell you that not even Solomon in full regalia was arrayed like one of these. So if God thus attires the wild plant, which blooms to-day and to-morrow is thrown into the oven, shall he not much more clothe you, you feeble in faith? Be anxious then no longer, saying, "What are we to eat, or drink?" or "What are we to wear?" With such matters the Gentiles concern themselves. So make God's Kingdom and duty to him your first concern, and all these things will be added to you. Do not worry about to-morrow. Leave to-morrow to worry about itself. "One day's trouble at a time is enough."[44]

V

'Do not judge, and you will not be judged.
Do not condemn, and you will not be condemned.[45]
For the judgment you pass will be passed on you,
And the measure you use will be used for you.

'How is it you can see the splinter in your brother's eye but cannot detect the shaft that is in your own eye?[46] How can you say to your brother, "Allow me to extract the splinter from your eye," while all the time there is a shaft in your own? Hypocrite,

[41] 'Store on earth . . . in heaven,' current saying, as also the quotation.
[42] Double meaning. If your outlook is generous your whole personality will be radiant, if envious it will be gloomy.
[43] Mammon, i.e. wealth, commonly called 'the false mammon'.
[44] Current proverb.
[45] Restored from the Old Hebrew, and so restoring the parallelism of the 1st and 3rd, 2nd and 4th lines.
[46] Based on a current saying. See *Baba Bathra*, 15b; *Arachin*, 16b. Speck may be read instead of splinter.

first extract the shaft from your own eye, and then you will see clearly to extract the splinter from your brother's eye.

'Do not offer gems[47] to the dogs,
　or they may turn and rend you;
Nor strew your pearls before pigs,
　or they may trample them under foot.

'Ask and you will be given.
Seek, and you will find.
Knock, and you will be admitted.
For he who asks will receive,
And he who seeks will find.
And he who knocks will be admitted.

'Which of you will give his son a stone if he asks for bread, or a snake if he asks for fish?[48] If you then, bad as you are, know how to give good gifts to your children, how much more shall your heavenly Father give what is good to those who ask him. Therefore in whatever way you would have people treat you, treat them the same; for this sums up the Law and the Prophets.[49]

'Enter by the narrow gate; for wide is the gate and spacious the way that leads to Destruction,[50] and many there are who enter by it. But narrow is the gate and constricted the way that leads to Life, and few there are who find it.

'Beware of the false prophets, who come to you in sheep's fleeces,[51] but underneath they are ravening wolves. You will recognize them by their fruits. Are grape-clusters picked from thorns, or figs from brambles? So every good tree produces good fruit, while every harmful tree produces harmful fruit. A good tree cannot bear harmful fruit, neither can a harmful tree produce good fruit. Every tree that does not produce good fruit is cut down and cast into the fire.[52] So by their fruits you will recognize them.[53]

'Not everyone who hails me as "Master, Master!" will enter the Kingdom of Heaven, only those who do the will of my heavenly Father. Many will say to me at that time, "Master, Master, have we not prophesied in your name, expelled demons in your name, and in your name performed many miracles?" But then I shall tell them plainly, "I have never authorized you. Be off with you, you illegal practitioners!"

'Whoever, therefore, hears these sayings of mine and carries

---

[47] The Greek has 'a holy thing' due to a misunderstanding of the Hebrew word in the original source which equally means 'sparkling things', jewels, cp. Lam. iv. 1. The lost parallelism is further restored by a transposition of the lines.
[48] There is a certain similarity in shape between the contrasted objects.
[49] The famous Rabbi Hillel (died c. A.D. 10) taught to this effect, and his dictum may have been known to Jesus.
[50] Representing the Heb. *Abaddon* (the Abyss of Doom) opposed to Life (the resurrection life of the Messianic Era).
[51] Cp. Zech. xiii. 4.
[52] Cp. the words of John the Baptist, iii, 10, above, p. 90-91.
[53] Cp. current proverb, 'A gourd, a gourd, is known by its branch'.

them out will be like a prudent man who built his house on rock. The torrent poured down, the floods came, the tempest blew, and beat against that house; but it did not fall, for it was founded on rock. Everyone, however, who hears these sayings of mine and fails to carry them out will be like a stupid man who built his house on sand. The torrent poured down, the floods came, the tempest blew, and beat against that house; and down it fell, and mighty was its collapse.'

As Jesus came to the end of his discourse the people were amazed at his teaching, for he taught them as one with authority, and not as their scribes.

BOOK II

I

When Jesus came down the hill great crowds followed him. Now there came a leper and prostrated himself before him saying, 'Sir, if you will you can make me clean.'

Then Jesus put out his hand and touched him and said, 'I do will it. Be clean!'

At once he was cleansed of his leprosy, and Jesus said to him 'See that you tell no one, but go and show yourself to the priest, and present the offering Moses prescribed as evidence to them.'

As Jesus entered Capernaum a centurion approached him and said, 'Sir, my orderly is lying at home paralysed, suffering terribly.'

'I will come and cure him,' Jesus said to him.

But the centurion replied, 'Sir, I am no fit person for you to come under my roof. Simply command it and my orderly will recover. For I am a man under orders myself, and soldiers are under my own orders.[54] I have only to say to one "Go", and he goes, and to another "Come", and he comes, and to my servant "Do this", and he does it.'

When Jesus heard this he was astonished and said to those who were following him, 'Not in all Israel have I found faith like this. I tell you that many from the East and West shall come and recline[55] with Abraham, Isaac and Jacob in the Kingdom of Heaven, while the sons of the Kingdom[56] will be ejected into the darkness outside, where there will be wailing and grinding of teeth.'

[54] See note to corresponding passage in Lk. vii, below p. 155, n. 51.
[55] Recline, at the Messianic banquet of the righteous.
[56] The natural heirs, Israelites.

Then Jesus said to the centurion, 'Go! As you have believed so let it be to you.'

At that very hour the orderly was cured.

On entering Peter's house Jesus saw his mother-in-law who had been laid up with a fever. He took her by the hand and the fever left her, and she got up and waited on him.

When evening came many demoniacs were brought to him, and he expelled the spirits by an order, and cured all who were ill.[a]

II

When Jesus saw the crowd about him he gave orders to cross over to the farther shore. Then one of the scribes approached him and said, 'Teacher, I will follow you wherever you go.'

'The foxes have lairs,' Jesus replied, 'the birds of the air have nests, but the Son of Man has not a floor[57] where he may lay his head.'

Another disciple said to him, 'Sir, give me leave first to bury my father.'

'Follow me,' Jesus told him, 'and leave the dead to bury their dead.'

Then he went on board ship and his disciples accompanied him. While on the sea a great squall arose, so that the ship was swamped by the waves. But he lay sleeping. So his disciples came and roused him and said, 'Save us, sir, we are lost!'

'What cowards you are, you feeble in faith!' he answered.

Then he rose and rebuked the winds and the sea, and a great calm ensued. The men were amazed and said, 'Whoever is he, that even the winds and the sea obey him?'

When Jesus reached the Gadarene country on the farther shore he was met by two demoniacs coming out of the tombs. So highly dangerous were they that no one would venture to take that road.

'What do you want with us, Son of God?' they shrieked. 'Have you come to torture us before the time?'

Some way off from where they were a herd of many swine were feeding. So the demons in the men begged him, 'If you are going to expel us send us into the herd of swine.'

'Be gone!' he told them.

So on coming out of the men they went into the swine, and the whole herd made a wild dash down the bank into the sea, and perished in the water. The herdsmen fled and made off to the town, and told their tale, and also about the demoniacs. At this the entire city made for Jesus in a body, and when they

[a] Thereby was fulfilled what was announced by the Prophet Isaiah, 'Himself took our infirmities, and bore our diseases.'[58]

[57] Following the Old Hebrew. The 'floor' was the meanest form of lodging for travellers, a raised platform in the caravanserai above where the animals were tethered.
[58] Isa. liii. 4.

reached him they entreated him to leave their territory. So re-embarking he crossed over and came once more to his own town.

Now there was a paralytic brought to him prostrate on a mattress. Then Jesus, seeing the faith of the bearers, said to the paralytic, 'Courage, son! Your sins are forgiven you.'

Some of the scribes present said to themselves, 'He blasphemes.'

Reading their thoughts Jesus said, 'Why do your minds harbour evil thoughts? Which is easier, to say, "Your sins are forgiven you", or to say, "Rise and walk"? But so that you may know that the Son of Man is entitled on earth to forgive sins'— he said to the paralytic, 'Rise, pick up your mattress, and go to your home!'

Thereupon the paralytic rose and went home.

When the people saw this they were afraid, and praised God who had conferred such power on mortal men.[59]

III

As Jesus continued on his way he saw a man called Matthew seated at the customs-station, and said to him, 'Follow me!'

He rose and followed him.

When Jesus sat down to dine in the house many tax-collectors and sinners[60] also came and dined with Jesus and his disciples. Now when the Pharisees saw this they said to his disciples, 'How comes it that your teacher eats with tax-collectors and sinners?'

Jesus overheard this and replied, 'It is not the healthy who need a doctor, but those who are ill. So go and study what this means, "Compassion is what I desire, not sacrifice."[61] I have not come to call religious people, but sinners.'

Then the disciples of John approached him and asked, 'How comes it that we and the Pharisees fast while your disciples do not fast?'

Jesus replied, 'Does the bridal party[62] grieve while they have the bridegroom with them? The time will come when the bridegroom will have taken his leave: that will be the time for them to fast. No one sews a patch of new cloth on an old cloak, for he only drags the material from the cloak and the tear is made worse. Nor does anyone pour new wine into old wine-skins. If he does, the skins will be split, the wine will be spilt, and the skins spoilt. No, one pours new wine into new wine-skins, and both remain intact.'

While he was telling them these things a certain official approached and prostrated himself before him and said, 'My daughter has just passed away; but if you will come and lay your hand on her she will live.'

---

[59] Forms of benediction existed for recital on appropriate occasions. The form used here was probably, 'Blessed is he who has given of his power to flesh and blood'.
[60] See Mk. p. 54, n. 12.
[61] Hos. vi. 6.
[62] See Mk. p. 54, n. 15.

Jesus rose and followed him, accompanied by his disciples.

Now a woman who had suffered twelve years with a haemorrhage came up behind and touched the tassel[63] of his cloak, for she said to herself, 'If only I can touch his cloak I shall get well.'

But Jesus turned round and saw her and said, 'Courage, daughter! Your faith has cured you.'

From that moment the woman was cured.

When Jesus entered the official's residence and saw the pipers and professional dirge-makers he said, 'Be off! The little girl is not dead, only sleeping.'

They jeered at him. But when the crowd had been ejected he went in and took her by the hand, and the little girl rose up. And the tale of this spread throughout that country.

IV

When Jesus continued on his way two blind men followed crying, 'Pity us, Son of David!'

As he entered the house the blind men came up to him, and Jesus said, 'Do you believe I can do this?'

'Yes, sir,' they answered.

Then he touched their eyes and said, 'Let it be to you according to your faith.'

And their eyes were opened. 'No one is to know of this,' he warned them. But when they went away they spread the tale throughout that region.

As they left there was brought to him a dumb demoniac, and when the demon was expelled the mute spoke. The people were amazed and said, 'Nothing like this has been seen in Israel.'

So Jesus toured all the towns and villages, teaching in their synagogues and proclaiming the News of the Kingdom, and curing every kind of disease and infirmity.

V

When Jesus saw the crowds he was filled with compassion for them, for they were weary and dejected like sheep which have no shepherd. Then he said to his disciples, 'The harvest is indeed plentiful, but the labourers are few. Beseech the Harvest-master to send out labourers to gather in his harvest.'

Then summoning his twelve disciples he gave them power over foul spirits to enable them to expel them and to cure every kind of disease and infirmity.

These are the names of the twelve envoys. First there was Simon (called Peter) and his brother Andrew, then James the son of Zebedee and his brother John, Philip and Bartholomew, Thomas and the tax-collector Matthew, James the son of Alphaeus and Thaddaeus, Simon the Zealot and Judas the Iscariot, who in fact betrayed him.

These twelve Jesus dispatched with the following instruc-

[63] See Mk. p. 63, n. 33

tions: 'Keep away from Gentile centres, and do not enter any Samaritan town. Go instead to the lost sheep of the house of Israel. As you travel proclaim, "The Kingdom of Heaven is at hand." Cure the ailing, raise the dead, cleanse the lepers, expel the demons. You have received without payment, so give without payment. Take neither gold, nor silver, nor copper in your belts, nor a wallet for the road, nor two tunics, nor shoes, nor a staff; for "the labourer deserves his keep".[64] When you enter a town or village inquire first who in it is worthy, and stay there until you leave again. When you enter a household give it greeting,[65] and if the household is worthy let your peace come upon it; but if it is not worthy let your peace return to you. If anyone will not welcome you or listen to what you have to say, when you leave that house or town shake off the dust from your feet. I tell you for a fact, it will be more tolerable for the people of Sodom and Gomorrah in the Day of Judgment than for that town.

'See, I am sending you as sheep among wolves, so be as subtle as serpents yet simple as doves. Watch out for the authorities, for they will hand you over to the Sanhedrins and flog you in their synagogues, and you will be brought before governors and kings on my account, as a testimony to them and to the Gentiles. But when they hand you over do not concern yourselves with the manner or matter of your speech, for it will come to you at the time what you are to say; for it will not really be you speaking but the Spirit of your Father speaking through you. Then brother will betray brother to death, and the father his son, and children will rise up against their parents and bring about their death. You will be universally detested on my account. But he who is constant to the end will be preserved. So when they persecute you in one town escape to another. I tell you for a fact, you will not have exhausted the cities of Israel before the Son of Man arrives.

'The disciple is not superior to his teacher, nor the servant to his master. Let it suffice the disciple to be deemed the equal of his teacher, and the servant of his master. If they have called the owner of the house Beelzebul,[66] how much more those of his household? You have no cause to fear them therefore, for nothing is covered up that shall not be disclosed, nor hidden away that shall not be made known. What I tell you in the dark speak out in broad daylight, and what you hear in a whisper shout from the housetops. Have no fear of those who kill the body, but can by no means kill the soul. Fear him instead, who can destroy both soul and body in Gehenna. Are not two sparrows sold for an assar?[67] Yet not one of them shall fall to earth without

---

[64] Josephus says of the Essenes: 'They carry nothing whatever with them on their journeys, except arms as a protection against brigands. . . . They do not change their garments or shoes until they are torn to shreds or worn threadbare with age' (*Wars*, II. viii. 4).
[65] In the form, 'Peace be with this house'.
[66] Prince of the demons.
[67] Equal to about two-thirds of a penny.

your Father's consent. As for yourselves, every hair of your head is counted. So have no fear, you are of more consequence than many sparrows. Whoever therefore identifies himself with me before the authorities, I too will identify myself with him before my heavenly Father. But whoever repudiates me before the authorities, I too will repudiate him before my heavenly Father.

'Do not imagine I have come to bring peace to the earth.[68] I have not come to bring peace but a dagger. For I have come "to set a man against his father, and the daughter against her mother, and the daughter-in-law against her mother-in-law: a man's enemies will be those of his own household".[69] He who holds father or mother dearer than me is not worthy of me, and he who holds son or daughter dearer than me is not worthy of me. And he who does not shoulder his cross[70] and follow me is not worthy of me. He who gains his life will lose it; but he who is ready to lose his life will gain it. He who welcomes you welcomes me, and he who welcomes me welcomes him who sent me. He who welcomes a prophet as a prophet will reap a prophet's reward, and he who welcomes a just man as a just man will reap a just man's reward;[71] and he who refreshes the humblest believer, if only with a cup of cold water, as a disciple, I tell you truly, he shall not lack his reward.'

When Jesus had finished instructing his twelve disciples he went elsewhere to teach and preach in their various towns.

BOOK III

I

When John in prison came to hear of the Messiah's activities he sent by his disciples to ask Jesus, 'Are you the Destined One, or are we to expect someone else?'

Jesus answered, 'Go back and inform John of what you hear and see. The blind receive light, the lame walk, the lepers are cleansed, the dead are raised, and the poor are given the Good News.[72] Fortunate is he who has no misgivings about me.'

When they had left, Jesus spoke to the crowds about John, 'What did you go out into the wilderness to see, a cane[73] shaken by the wind? Or did you go out to see something else, a man clothed in soft draperies?[74] Surely those who wear soft draperies

---

[68] Cp. Isa. ix. 6-7; xi. 1-9. The Messiah was expected to bring peace.
[69] Mic. vii. 6.
[70] See Mk. p. 66, n. 41.
[71] There would be a reward for those who did not accept Jesus as the Messiah, but only as a prophet or just man.
[72] Cp. Isa. xxxv. 5; lxi. 1.
[73] Double meaning, playing on the Heb. *qaneh* (a reed) and *qana* (a Zealot), i.e. 'a Zealot swayed by passion'.
[74] Metaphorically, 'a man surrounded with flatteries', another double meaning.

are found in kings' palaces. What then did you go out for, to see a prophet? Yes, I tell you, and much more than a prophet. He it is of whom it was stated, "See, I will send my messenger before you, to pave the way for you."[75] I tell you truly, among all of women born there has never arisen a greater than John the Baptist,[76] yet the most insignificant in the Kingdom of Heaven is greater than he. From John the Baptist's time until now, however, the Kingdom of Heaven is under pressure, and the violent seize upon it; for all the Prophets and the Law prophesied up to John, and if you are willing to accept it, he is Elijah who was to come.[77] Whoever can catch my meaning let him do so.

'How shall I describe this generation? It is like children squatting in the market place, who call out to their playmates,

"We've played you a jig, but you haven't danced.
We've played a lament, but you haven't mourned."[78]

For John came neither eating nor drinking, and they say, "He is demon-possessed." The Son of Man came both eating and drinking, and they say, "There you are, a glutton and a drunkard, an associate of tax-collectors and sinners." Yet, "Wisdom is vindicated by her works." '[79]

Then Jesus began to reproach the towns in which his powers had been chiefly displayed, because they had failed to repent.

'Woe to you, Chorazin! Woe to you, Bethsaida! For had the miracles been performed in Tyre and Sidon that have been performed in you they would long since have repented in sackcloth and ashes. Further, I tell you, it will be more tolerable for Tyre and Sidon in the Day of Judgment than for you. As for you, Capernaum, are you not raised up to heaven? You will surely be razed to hell.[80] For had the miracles been performed in Sodom that have been performed in you it would have lasted to this day. Further, I tell you, it will be more tolerable for the land of Sodom in the Day of Judgment than for you.'

It was on this occasion that Jesus said, 'I bow to thy will, Father, Lord of heaven and earth, because thou hast hidden these things from the wise and prudent, and disclosed them to babes. Even so, Father, for so it seemed good in thy sight.

'Everything has been made over to me by my Father, yet no one esteems the Son except the Father. Neither does anyone esteem the Father except the Son, and he to whom the Son chooses to reveal him. Come to me, all you who are weary and overburdened, and I will relieve you. Take my yoke upon you, and learn from me; for I am gentle and of a quiet disposition,

[75] Mal. iii. 1.
[76] Cp. Deut. xxxiv. 10.
[77] Cp. Mal. iv. 5. The Elijah prophecy is the last word of the Heb. O.T. division of the Law and the Prophets.
[78] I.e. 'beaten your breasts'.
[79] Cp. Wisd. Sol. viii. 6-7.
[80] Cp. Isa. xiv. 15; 'raised . . . razed,' here preserving an alliteration in the Old Hebrew.

and you will get relief;[81] for my yoke does not chafe and my load is light.'[82]

II

At this time Jesus proceeded on the sabbath through the standing corn, and his disciples being hungry began to pick the ears of corn and eat. Observing this the Pharisees said to him, 'Look, your disciples are doing what is not allowed on the sabbath.'

'Have you not read,' Jesus replied, 'what David did when he was hungry, and his men as well, how he entered God's house and ate the loaves of the Presence, which were forbidden both to him and his men to eat[83] and were for the priests alone? Or have you not read in the Law that on the sabbath the priests in the Sanctuary violate the sabbath and are guiltless?[84] I tell you, something greater than the Sanctuary is here. If you had known what the text means, "Compassion is what I desire, not sacrifice",[85] you would not have condemned the guiltless; for the Son of Man is master of the sabbath.'

When he left there he went into their synagogue, and there was a man there with a withered hand. They asked him, so that they could bring a charge against him, 'Is it permissible to cure on the sabbath?'

Jesus replied, 'Which of you with a single sheep will not take hold of it and lift it out if it falls into a pit on the sabbath? Is not a man of more account than a sheep? Therefore it is entirely permissible to do good on the sabbath.'

Then he said to the man, 'Stretch out your hand!'

He stretched it out, and it was restored as sound as the other.

Then the Pharisees went out and consulted about him, how best to destroy him.

When Jesus knew of this he left there. Many followed him, and he cured them all, but insisted that they should not publicize him.[a]

[a] This was to fulfil what was announced by the Prophet Isaiah saying,

> Here is my servant, whom I have chosen,
> My dear one, of whom I am so proud!
> I have put my Spirit upon him:
> He shall dispense justice to the nations.
> He will neither wrangle nor shout;
> No one will hear his voice in the streets.
> A crushed reed he will not snap off;
> A smouldering wick he will not snuff out;
> Till he triumphantly vindicates justice,
> And nations confide in his name.[86]

[81] Jer. vi. 16.
[82] Cp. Ecclus. li. 23-27.
[83] I. Sam. xxi. 2-6.
[84] Num. xxviii. 9-10. Servile work in the Temple did not count as such.
[85] Hos. vi. 6.
[86] Isa. xlii. 1-4 (adapted).

III

Now there was brought to Jesus a blind and dumb demoniac, and he cured him, so that the dumb could both speak and see. And all the people were amazed and said, 'Surely he is the Son of David.'[87]

On hearing this the Pharisees said, 'He only expels demons with the aid of Beelzebul the chief of the demons.'

Knowing what was in their minds, Jesus said to them, 'Every kingdom in conflict with itself cannot endure. If then Satan expels Satan he is in conflict with himself. How then can his kingdom endure? So if I expel demons by Beelzebul, by whom do your sons expel them? So they shall be your judges. But if I expel demons by the Spirit of God then the Kingdom of God has caught you unawares. For how can anyone enter the Strong One's[88] abode and plunder his possessions without first binding the Strong One? Then he can loot his abode. Whoever is not with me is against me, and whoever does not gather with me scatters. I tell you therefore, every folly and insult will be forgiven men, but insult of the Spirit will not be forgiven. Anyone who says a word against the Son of Man will be forgiven, but if he speaks against the holy Spirit he will get no forgiveness either in this world or in the one to come. Either make the tree good and its fruit good, or make the tree harmful and its fruit harmful; for "the tree is known by its fruit".

'Vipers' brood! How, evil as you are, can you say anything good? For "what the mind is stored with the mouth speaks." The good man from his good store gives out good, while the evil man from his evil store gives out evil. I tell you, men will be called to account at the Day of Judgment for every idle remark they make, for "it will be your words that right you and your words that ruin you."'

Some of the scribes and Pharisees then said, 'Teacher, we want to see a sign from you.'

Jesus replied, 'An evil and adulterous generation requires a sign, does it! Well, it will get no sign except that of the Prophet Jonah. For just as Jonah was three days and nights in the maw of the sea-monster, so will the Son of Man be three days and nights in the heart of the earth. The men of Nineveh will rise up at the judgment, and this generation with them, and they will damn it; for they repented at the preaching of Jonah, and what is of more consequence than Jonah is here. The Queen of the South will rise up at the Judgment, and this generation with her, and she will damn it; for she came from the lower hemisphere to hear the wisdom of Solomon, and what is of more consequence than Solomon is here.

'As soon as the foul spirit has left a man it wanders through

[87] I.e. the Messiah.
[88] I.e. the Devil.

arid wastes seeking refreshment and finding none. Then it decides, "I'll go back to my old home." When it gets there it finds it untenanted, swept clean, and tidied up. Then it sets off and secures seven other spirits more noxious than itself, and in they go to live there. So the last state of that man is worse than the first. So will it be with this evil generation.'

He was still addressing the crowds when his mother and brothers stood outside wishing to speak to him. But he put it to the man who informed him, 'Who is my mother, and who are my brothers?' Then indicating his disciples he added, 'See, here are my mother and brothers. Whoever does the will of my heavenly Father is my brother and sister and mother.'

IV

That day Jesus left the house and sat down on the seashore; and great crowds gathered round him, so that he had to go on board a boat and sit in it while the crowds stood on the beach.

He spoke a great deal to them in similes, as for instance: 'The sower went out to sow; and as he sowed some seed fell by the wayside where the birds came and picked it up. Other seed fell on stony ground where there was not much soil; and at once it sprouted because the soil had little depth. But when the sun was up it was parched and withered away for lack of root. Other seed fell among thistles; and the thistles shot up and stifled it. Other seed fell on good soil, and yielded a crop, a hundredfold, sixtyfold, or thirtyfold. Let him who can catch my meaning do so.'

Then the disciples approached and said to him, 'Why are you speaking to them in similes?'

Jesus answered, 'Because you are entitled to know the secrets of the Kingdom of God, but they are not entitled; for whoever has will get more, and will have a surplus, while he who has not will be deprived even of what he has. That is why I am speaking to them in similes, so that though seeing they do not really see, and though hearing they do not really hear or comprehend. In them is fulfilled the prophesy of Isaiah.

> *You shall hear indeed, but fail to grasp.*
> *You shall see indeed, but fail to perceive,*
> *For the mind of this people is dense,*
> *And their ears are hard of hearing,*
> *And their eyes they have fast closed,*
> *In case they should see with their eyes,*
> *And hear with their ears,*
> *And comprehend with their minds,*
> *And turn again, and I must heal them.*[89]

But how fortunate are your eyes, because they do see, and your

[89] Isa. vi. 9-10.

ears, because they do hear! I tell you positively, many prophets and just men have longed to see what you are seeing, but have missed seeing it, and to hear what you are hearing, but have missed hearing it. Listen then to the simile of the sower.

'Whoever hears the Message of the Kingdom, and fails to comprehend, along comes the Evil One and promptly picks out what has been sown in his mind. This is he who had the wayside sowing. As for him who had the sowing in stony ground, he it is who hears the Message, and at once accepts it with joy; but having no root in himself he does not last long. So when trial or persecution comes on him on account of the Message he is at once put off. As for him who had the sowing among thistles, he it is who heeds the Message, but worldly cares and the lure of riches stifle the Message and he becomes unfruitful. But he who had the sowing in good soil is he who hears the Message and grasps it, and who bears fruit, and yields a hundredfold, or sixty-fold, or thirtyfold.'

He offered them a further simile. 'The Kingdom of Heaven may be represented as a man who sowed good seed in his field. But while the labourers slept his enemy came and sowed weeds[90] among the wheat and went away. So when the blade sprouted and bore fruit the weeds were revealed. Then the owner's servants approached and said, "Sir, didn't you sow good seed in your field? Where then do these weeds come from?"

' "Some enemy has done this," he told them.

' "Do you want us to go and root them out?" they asked him.

' "No," he replied, "for in rooting out the weeds you may up-root the wheat as well. Let both grow together until harvest, and at harvest time I will tell the reapers, Root out the weeds first and bind them in bundles for burning, but gather the wheat into my granary." '

He offered them a further simile. 'The Kingdom of Heaven may be represented as a grain of mustard-seed which a man took and planted in his field. It is indeed the smallest of seeds, but when it has grown it is taller than other plants, and reaches tree height,[91] so that the birds of the air come and nest in its branches.'

He added another simile. 'The Kingdom of Heaven may be represented as leaven which a woman took and buried in three seahs[92] of flour until the whole was leavened.'

Jesus addressed these things to the people in similes, and except by simile he said nothing to them.[a]

[a] Thereby was fulfilled what was announced by the prophet, I will open my mouth in proverbs: I will voice things concealed since Creation.[93]

[90] Wheatlike weeds (Heb. *zunin*, Gr. *zizania*), probably darnel.
[91] At times reaching ten feet.
[92] Three seahs made one ephah, rather more than a bushel.
[93] Ps. lxxviii. 2.

V

Then Jesus dismissed the people and went home. There his disciples approached him and said, 'Explain to us the simile of the weeds in the field.'

So he told them, 'He who sowed the good seed is the Son of Man. The field is the world. The good seed represents the sons of the Kingdom. The weeds represent the sons of the Evil One, while the enemy who sowed them is the Devil himself. The harvest is the Consummation of the Age, and the reapers are the angels. Just as the weeds were rooted out and burnt, so will it be at the Consummation of the Age. The Son of Man will send out his angels, and they will root out of his Kingdom all subversive elements, and those who behave lawlessly, and cast them into the fiery furnace, where there will be wailing and grinding of teeth. Then shall the just beam forth like the sun in their Father's Kingdom. Let him who can catch my meaning do so.

'The Kingdom of Heaven may be represented as a treasure buried in a field, which a man found there and hid. In his delight he goes and sells all he possesses to buy that field.

'Alternately the Kingdom of Heaven may be represented as a merchant seeking fine pearls. Finding one magnificent specimen, he goes off and disposes of all his stock and buys it.

'The Kingdom of Heaven may again be represented as a drag-net cast into the sea and gathering up fish of every kind, which when filled they hauled on to the beach, and sitting down sorted out the good into crates and threw the bad away. It will be like that at the Consummation of the Age. The angels will go out and separate the wicked from the just and cast them into the fiery furnace, where there will be wailing and grinding of teeth.

'Have you grasped all this?'

'Yes,' they told him.

Then he said to them, 'Thus every scribe well-versed in the Kingdom of Heaven may be represented as a householder who produces from his store things new and old.'

On concluding these similes Jesus left there, and coming to his native town he taught them in their synagogue. They were astounded, and said, 'How has he come by this wisdom and these powers? Isn't he the carpenter's son? Isn't his mother called Mary, and his brothers James, Joseph, Simon and Judas? Aren't all his sisters living here?' And they were affronted at him.

'No prophet is unhonoured,' Jesus told them, 'except in his native town and his own home.'

He did not perform many miracles there because of their disbelief.

BOOK IV

I

At this time Herod the tetrarch heard tell of Jesus, and said to his attendants. 'It is John the Baptist. He has risen from the dead. That is why miracles are effected by him.'

Herod had arrested John, bound and imprisoned him, on account of Herodias his brother Philip's wife. John had told him, 'It is illegal for you to have her.' But though ready to kill him, Herod feared the populace who regarded John as a prophet.

Now on the anniversary of Herod's accession the daughter of Herodias danced before the company, and so charmed Herod that he promised with an oath to give her whatever she asked. Prompted by her mother she said, 'Give me here and now on a platter the head of John the Baptist.'

Unhappy as the king was, because of his oaths and the assembled guests he ordered it to be given her, and sent to the prison and had John executed, and his head brought on a dish and given to the girl, and she took it to her mother.

John's disciples came and fetched his corpse and buried it, and then went and informed Jesus.

When Jesus heard the news he withdrew from there by ship to seclusion in the wilderness. But the people learning of this followed him on foot from the towns. So on arriving he found a vast crowd, and was moved with compassion for them, and cured their sick. When evening came his disciples approached him and said, 'This is open country, and it is already late. Dismiss the people that they may go off to the villages and buy themselves food.'

'There is no need for them to go,' Jesus told them. 'Give them something to eat yourselves.'

'All we have here,' they protested, 'is five loaves and two fish.'

'Bring them to me,' he said.

Then Jesus ordered the people to sit down on the grass, and taking the five loaves and the two fish he looked up to heaven, gave thanks, broke the bread and handed it to his disciples, and they to the people. Everyone ate and was satisfied; and they took up twelve basketfuls of the pieces left over. Of those who had partaken the men alone numbered about five thousand apart from women and children.

Then he insisted that his disciples take ship and precede him to the other side while he dismissed the people. Having done so, he made a solitary ascent of the mountain to pray. When it got late he was still there alone. The ship by now was a considerable distance[94] from land, lashed by the waves, for the wind was contrary.

In the fourth watch of the night[95] he came towards them walking on the sea. When the disciples saw him walking on the sea they were terrified and said, 'It's a malignant spirit!'[96] and cried out in fear.

But at once Jesus spoke to them. 'Courage!' he called out. 'It is I. There's nothing to be afraid of.'

Then Peter called back, 'If it really is you, Master, bid me come to you on the water.'

'Come!' he said.

So Peter climbed overboard, and walked on the water, and went towards Jesus. But facing the wind he was afraid, and beginning to sink cried out, 'Save me, Master!'

Jesus immediately stretched out his hand and caught hold of him, and said to him, 'Feeble in faith! Why did you doubt?'

When he got into the ship the wind dropped. Then those who were in the ship prostrated themselves to him and said, 'Truly you are the Son of God.'

Having crossed over they came to the Gennesaret country, and when the local populace became aware of his presence they sent round the whole vicinity, and brought him all who were ill, requesting him that they might simply touch the tassel of his cloak; and all those who did touch it recovered.

II

Then Pharisees and scribes from Jerusalem came to Jesus and asked, 'How is it that your disciples fail to conform to the tradition of the elders, for they do not wash their hands when they eat food?'

Jesus replied, 'And how is it that you fail to conform to the commandments of God through your tradition? For God said, "Honour your father and mother", and "he that curses father or mother shall surely die".[97] Yet you say, "Should a man say to father or mother, Let it be a votive gift whatever of mine may benefit you,[98] he is not to honour his father or mother." Thus you have nullified the word of God through your tradition. Hypocrites! Isaiah did well to prophesy of you,

> *Here is a people that pays me lip-service,*
> *But their minds are far removed from me.*
> *It is useless for them to worship me*
> *While teaching as doctrine instructions of men.*[99]

He summoned the people and said to them, 'Attend and un-

94 Gr. 'several furlongs'.
95 The fourth watch was from 3-6 a.m.
96 Heb. *mazziq*. The Greek has 'phantom' or 'apparition'.
97 Exod. xx 12: xxi. 17.
98 See above p. 64, n. 37.
99 Isa. xxix. 13.

derstand! It is not what enters the mouth that soils a man; it is what issues from the mouth that soils a man.'

Then the disciples approached and said to him, 'Do you realize that the Pharisees were affronted on hearing that pronouncement?'

Jesus answered, 'Every plant not watered by my heavenly Father will be uprooted. Never mind them, they are blind guides of the blind; and if one blind man guides another both of them will fall into the ditch.'

'Explain this simile to us,' urged Peter.

'Is it possible you still don't understand?' he said. 'Don't you realize that whatever enters the mouth finds its way into the stomach and is evacuated in the toilet? But what issues from the mouth emanates from the mind, and is this that soils a man. For from the mind spring evil suggestions, murders, adulteries, immoralities, robberies, false testimonies, slanders. These are the things that soil a man. But eating with unwashed hands does not soil a man.'

Leaving there Jesus departed for the district of Tyre and Sidon. A Canaanite woman belonging to those parts came out crying, 'Pity me, Son of David, sir! My daughter is terribly demon-possessed.'

But he gave her no reply.

So his disciples approached and begged him, 'Do get rid of her, for she keeps crying after us.'

'I have only been sent to the lost sheep of the house of Israel,' he answered.

Then she came forward and prostrated herself and said, 'Do help me, sir!'

He replied, 'It is not fair to take the children's food and throw it to puppies.'

'Quite so, sir,' she said. 'But even puppies may eat the scraps that fall from their masters' table.'

Then Jesus said to her, 'Madam, you have great faith. Let it be as you wish.'

From that moment her daughter was cured.

III

Crossing over from there Jesus proceeded along the shore of the Sea of Galilee, and climbed the hill and sat down there. And great crowds came to him bringing with them the lame, the blind, the dumb, and many others, and laid them at his feet, and he cured them; so that the people were amazed when they witnessed the dumb speaking, the lame walking, and the blind seeing, and they praised the God of Israel.

Then Jesus summoned his disciples and said, 'I am full of compassion for the people, for they have stayed with me three days and have nothing to eat. I would not dismiss them fasting or they may collapse on the way.'

His disciples said to him, 'Where in this open country are we to find enough bread to satisfy such a crowd?'

'How much bread have you?' he asked.

'Seven loaves,' they said, 'and some small fish.'

Then Jesus ordered the crowd to sit on the ground, and taking the seven loaves and the fish he gave thanks, broke and distributed the food to the disciples, and they to the people. And everyone ate and was satisfied; and they took up seven hampers full of what was left over of the pieces. No less than four thousand men had eaten apart from women and children.

Jesus then dismissed the people and went on board ship, and came to the borders of Magadan.

Now the Pharisees and Sadducees came to trap him with the request that he would show them a sign from Heaven. But he answered, 'An evil and adulterous generation wants a sign, does it? Well, it will get no sign except that of Jonah.'

With that he left them and went away.

When the disciples arrived at the farther shore they had forgotten to bring bread. So Jesus said to them, 'Be careful to avoid the leaven of the Pharisees and Sadducees.'

They argued among themselves, 'But we didn't bring any bread?'

Perceiving this Jesus said, 'What are you arguing about, you feeble in faith, that you have no bread? Have you no sense or recollection of the five loaves with the five thousand and how many baskets you took up, or of the seven loaves with the four thousand and how many hampers you took up? How can you possibly fail to understand that I was not referring to bread as such when I told you to avoid the leaven of the Pharisees and Sadducees?'

Then it dawned on them that he did not mean they should avoid leaven in the sense of bread, but the teaching of the Pharisees and Sadducees.

IV

On reaching the neighbourhood of Caesarea-Philippi[100] Jesus asked the disciples, 'Whom do people say the Son of Man is?'

'Some say John the Baptist,' they replied, 'others Elijah, others Jeremiah or some other prophet.'

'What about you?' he said to them. 'Whom do you say I am?'

Simon Peter answered, 'You are the Messiah, the Son of the Living God.'

'How fortunate you are, impulsive[101] Simon!' Jesus said to him. 'No mortal disclosed this to you: it was my heavenly Father. And so I tell you, since you are Peter, upon that rock

[100] Formerly Paneas, at the springs of the River Jordan. Herod Philip had enlarged it and changed its name in honour of the Emperor.
[101] Lit. 'Baryona', not perhaps 'Son of Jona' but Aram. word meaning unrestrained. Those who lost self-control and broke into open hostility against Rome were known as baryonim.

I will found my Community, and the gates of hell shall not prevail against it. To you I will give the keys of the Kingdom of Heaven. Whatever you prohibit[102] on earth shall be prohibited in heaven, and whatever you permit on earth shall be permitted in heaven.'[103]

Then he firmly impressed on the disciples that they should tell no one he was the Messiah.

From then onwards Jesus began to show his disciples how essential it was for him to go to Jerusalem, and there suffer many things at the hands of the elders, head priests and scribes, and be put to death, and rise again on the third day.

Peter caught hold of him and objected strongly, 'God forbid, Master! Nothing of the sort shall happen to you.'

But he turned on Peter and said, 'Get behind me, satan![104] You affront me; for yours is the human viewpoint, not God's.

Then Jesus said to his disciples, 'Whoever would follow me must be utterly reckless, and shoulder his cross[105] and follow me. For whoever would preserve his life will lose it, but whoever loses his life on my account will gain it. For what benefit has a man if he wins the whole world if his life is forfeited? What exchange can a man offer for his life? Very soon the Son of Man will come in his Father's state with his angels, and then he will reward each according to his deeds. I tell you for a fact, there are some standing here now who will not experience death before they see the Son of Man inaugurate his Kingdom.'

Six days later Jesus took as companions Peter, James and his brother John, and led them up a high mountain entirely by themselves. In their presence he was transformed, and his face shone like the sun and his robes became bright as the light. Suddenly Moses and Elijah appeared to them conversing with him.

Peter could not help saying, 'Master, how good it is that we should be here! If you wish I will make three bowers, one for you, one for Moses, and one for Elijah.'

He was still speaking when a bright cloud cast a shadow over them, and a voice spoke out of the cloud, 'This is my dear Son, with whom I am well-satisfied. Listen to him.'

When the disciples heard this they fell on their faces and were terribly afraid. But Jesus approached them and reassured them saying, 'Rise, there is nothing to fear.'

As they descended the mountain Jesus charged them, 'Say nothing of the vision to anyone until the Son of Man has risen from the dead.'

The disciples asked him, 'Why do the scribes say that first of all Elijah must come?'

'Elijah must indeed come,' Jesus replied, 'and effect a general

102 'Prohibit . . . permit', Lit. 'bind . . . loose', technical terms relating to rulings on the application of the religious code to conduct.
103 I.E. 'Your ruling (for or against) shall be the accepted ruling.'
104 See above, p. 66, n. 40.
105 See above, p. 66, n. 41.

1. Copper coin of Herod the Great

2. Jewish half-shekel

3. Denarius of Tiberius

reconciliation.[106] But I tell you, Elijah has already come, and they did not recognize him, but did what they would with him. So too will the Son of Man suffer at their hands.'

Then the disciples realized that he was speaking to them of John the Baptist.

When they reached the crowd a man approached him and fell on his knees before him and said, 'Take pity on my son, sir, he has bad attacks of epilepsy. Frequently he falls into the fire and into the water. So I brought him to your disciples, but they were quite unable to cure him.'

Jesus answered, 'Faithless and perverse generation! How long must I be with you? How long must I bear with you? Bring him here to me.'

Then Jesus reprimanded the demon and it came out of him. And the boy was cured from that hour.

Later the disciples approached Jesus privately and said, 'Why could we not expel it?'

[106] Mal. iv. 5-6.

'Because of your feeble faith,' Jesus told them. 'I tell you positively, had you but faith as minute as a grain of mustard seed you could say to this mountain, "Remove from here to there," and it would remove. Nothing would be beyond your capacity.'

V

While they were assembling in Galilee[107] Jesus said to them, 'The Son of Man is going to be betrayed into the hands of the authorities, and they will put him to death, but the third day he will be raised up.'

They were deeply distressed.

When they reached Capernaum collectors of the half-shekel[108] approached Peter and said, 'Your teacher pays the half-shekel, doesn't he?'

'Of course,' he replied.

But when they reached the house Jesus anticipated him, saying, 'What do you think, Simon? Upon whom do earthly kings levy tribute and poll-tax, their own sons or others?' When he replied, 'Upon others', Jesus rejoined, 'In that case sons are immune. But in case we should upset them go down to the sea, cast the baited-net, and take the first fish that is brought up. Open its mouth and you will find a shekel.[109] Take that and give it to them for us both.'

On that occasion the disciples approached Jesus and asked, 'Who will be greatest in the Kingdom of Heaven?'

He called a child to him and stood him in front of them and said, 'I tell you positively, unless you change and become child-like you will never enter the Kingdom of Heaven. Whoever therefore is as unassuming as this child will be the greatest in the Kingdom of Heaven. Whoever welcomes one such child on my account welcomes me. But whoever upsets any humble member who believes in me it would be better for him to have a millstone hung round his neck and to be thrown into the depth of the sea. Woe to the world because of grievances! Grievances are inevitable. Yet woe to the man responsible for the grievance! So if your hand or foot gives you grounds for complaint cut it off and cast it from you. It is better for you to enter Life maimed or crippled than with your two hands or feet to be flung into the Everlasting Fire. Or if it is your eye that gives you grounds for complaint pluck it out and cast it from you. It is better for you to enter Life one-eyed than with your two eyes to be flung into blazing Gehenna. So take care not to despise any humble members, for I tell you, their angels[110] in heaven are continually in the presence of my heavenly Father.

[107] For the pilgrimage to Jerusalem for the Passover.
[108] Gr. *didrachma*, the Temple tax obligatory for Jews, Exod. xxx. 11-16. On the 15th of Adar (twelfth month in the Jewish calendar, about March, 30 days before the Passover) the money-changers' tables were set up in the provinces, and on the 25th of Adar in the Temple. See *Shekal.* i. 3.
[109] Gr. *stater*.
[110] In Jewish belief every person had his own angel.

'What do you think? If a man has a hundred sheep and one of them strays, will he not leave the ninety-nine on the mountainside, and set off to seek the wanderer? And if he finds it, I tell you positively, he will rejoice over it more than over the ninety-nine that did not stray. So it is not my heavenly Father's will that one of these humble members should be lost.

'If then your brother errs, go and reprove him between him and you alone. If he listens to you, you have won back your brother. But if he fails to listen, take with you one witness[111] or two, for "by the confirmation of two or three witnesses every matter shall be decided".[112] If he pays no attention to them, speak to the community. If he pays no attention to the community, treat him as a Gentile or a tax-collector.[113] I tell you positively, whatever you prohibit on earth shall be prohibited in heaven.[114] I will go further and say, that if any two of you agree among yourselves on earth about anything for which you need to ask, my heavenly Father will undertake it for you, for "in every place where two or three are assembled in my name, I am there among them." '[115]

Then Peter approached and said, 'Master, how often should I forgive my brother when he wrongs me, seven times?'

Jesus replied, 'Not seven times, I tell you, but seventy-seven times. For this reason the Kingdom of God may be represented as a king who decided to go over his accounts with his servants. When he began to take account there was brought to him one who owed him ten thousand minas.[116] As he was unable to pay, his lord ordered that he be sold, with his wife and children and all his belongings, and that payment be made. Then the servant fell down and begged him, "Only be patient with me and I will repay everything." So the master of that servant took pity on him, released him, and remitted his debt. That servant, however, when he went out encountered one of his fellow servants who owed him a hundred dinars[117] and took him by the throat saying, "Pay what you owe me." Then his fellow servant fell down and appealed to him, "Only be patient with me and I will repay you." But he would not have it, and went instead and threw him into prison until he should repay the debt. When his fellow servants were aware of what had happened they were highly indignant, and reported the circumstances to their lord in detail. So his lord summoned him and said to him, "Vile slave! I remitted the whole of your debt to you because you begged me. It was your business to take pity on your fellow servant as I took

---

[111] Gr. 'one or two more', the original translator having misread the Heb. *ed* (witness) as *od* (more).

[112] Deut. xix. 15.

[113] See above p. 54, n. 12.

[114] See p. 114, n. 102.

[115] The quotation relates to the presence of God. The exact source is unknown, but cp. Exod. xx. 24 and I. Chron. vii. 14-16. The Jewish authorities express the same view (*Aboth*, iii. 2-6), where Mal. iii. 16 is cited to show that God's presence is with two, and Exod. xx. 24 to show that he is even with one person.

[116] Equal to about £40,000. The Gr. has 'talents'.

[117] About £4.

pity on you." Then his enraged lord handed him over to the tor-
turers until he should have paid back the whole debt. Just so
will my heavenly Father treat you if any of you does not freely
forgive his brother.'

When Jesus had concluded this discourse he crossed over
from Galilee and came to the borders of Judea beyond Jordan.[118]
Great crowds followed him, and he cured them there.

BOOK V

I

Now the Pharisees approached Jesus to trap him saying, 'Is
it permissible to divorce one's wife on every ground?'

'Have you never read,' Jesus replied, 'that he who created
mankind originally made them male and female,[119] and said,
"For this cause a man shall leave father and mother and cleave
to his wife, and the two shall become one flesh"?[120] So they are
no longer two but one flesh. Therefore, whom God has united
man cannot sever.'

They persisted, 'Why then did Moses instruct to give her a
deed of severance and so divorce her if she did not please
him?'[121]

'Moses gave you leave to divorce your wives because of your
callousness,' he told them, 'but that was not the original intention. Whoever divorces his wife, I tell you, except for adultery,
and marries another, himself commits adultery.'

The disciples put it to him, 'If that is how a man stands with
his wife it is not advisable to marry.'

'It is not everyone who can go as far as that,' he said, 'only
those to whom it is given. For there are eunuchs who have been
so from birth, and there are eunuchs who have been made so by
human agency, and there are eunuchs who have made themselves so for the sake of the Kingdom of Heaven. Whoever can
go so far let him do so.'

Then children were brought to him for him to lay his hand on
them and offer a prayer. But the disciples rebuked them. Jesus
said, 'Let the children alone, and do not hinder them from coming to me, for the Kingdom of Heaven is composed of such as
they.' And he laid his hand on them, and proceeded on his way.

Now a particular person came to him and said, 'Teacher,
what good must I do to acquire Eternal Life?'

Jesus said to him, 'Why do you ask me of the good? There is

[118] Taking the Perean route to Jerusalem, so avoiding Samaria, whose hostile inhabitants sometimes attacked Jewish pilgrim bands.
[119] Gen. i. 27.
[120] Ibid. ii. 24.
[121] Deut. xxiv. 1, following the Old Hebrew.

but One who is good. But if you desire to enter into Life keep the commandments.'

'Commandments to what effect?' he asked.

Jesus said, 'You are not to commit murder, you are not to commit adultery, you are not to steal, you are not to give false testimony, honour your father and mother,[122] and, you are to love your neighbour as yourself.[123]

The youth said to him, 'I have carefully observed all these. What else is there?'

'If you want to be complete,' Jesus replied, 'go and sell your property and distribute the proceeds to the poor. Then come and join me.[124]

When the youth heard this he went away dejected, for he had very considerable possessions.

Then Jesus said to his disciples, 'I tell you for a fact, the rich have a hard struggle to enter the Kingdom of Heaven. I would even say that a camel has an easier task to enter the eye of a needle than a rich man the Kingdom of God.'

The disciples were amazed at hearing this and said, 'Who then can be saved?'

Jesus regarded them intently and replied, 'Humanly speaking no one can, but to God everything is possible.'[125]

Peter spoke up, 'Here have we sacrificed everything to join you. How shall we fare?'

'I tell you positively,' Jesus replied, 'In the Reborn World,[126] when the Son of Man takes his seat on the throne of state, you too shall be seated on twelve thrones governing the twelve tribes of Israel. And everyone who has sacrificed home, or brother, or sister, or father, or mother, or children, or lands, on my account will receive ever so much more and inherit Eternal Life. But many first will be last and the last first.

'The Kingdom of Heaven may indeed be represented as a householder who went out very early in the morning to hire labourers for his vineyard. And when he had contracted with the labourers for a rate of a dinar[127] a day he sent them into his vineyard. He went out again at nine o'clock and saw others standing in the market place unemployed. To them he said, "You too go into my vineyard and I will treat you fairly." So they went along. He went out again at midday and about three o'clock and acted in the same way. Around five o'clock he again went out and found still others standing about and said to them, "How do you come to be standing the whole day unemployed?"

---

[122] Exod. xx. 12-16.
[123] Lev. xix. 18.
[124] The ancient *Gospel of the Hebrews* adds, 'But the rich man began to scratch his head, and it did not please him. So the Master said to him, "How can you say, I have carried out the Law and the Prophets, since it is stated in the Law, you are to love your neighbour as yourself, and there are many of your brethren, sons of Abraham, clad with dung, dying of hunger, and your house is full of many good things, and nothing at all goes out of it to them?" '
[125] Cp. Gen. xviii. 4; Jer. xxxii. 17.
[126] A current expression for the Messianic Era, see Isa. lxv. 17f.
[127] About 9½d.

They told him, "Because no one has hired us." He said to them, "You too go into my vineyard." When evening came the owner of the vineyard said to his steward, "Call the labourers and pay them their wages, starting with the last and ending with the first." When the five o'clock men came they each received a dinar. But when the first came they expected to receive more, but they equally received a dinar. So on getting it they grumbled at the householder, "These last have only worked an hour, and you gave them the same as us who have borne the burden of the day and the heat." He answered their spokesman, "I am not wronging you, my friend. Didn't you contract with me for a dinar rate? So take what is yours, and be off. I propose to give these last the same as you. Can't I do as I like with my own money? Or are you envious because I am generous?" So the last shall be first and the first last.'

II

As he was about to go up to Jerusalem Jesus drew his twelve disciples aside privately, and told them as they went along, 'See, we are going up to Jerusalem, and the Son of Man will be betrayed to the head priests and scribes, and they will sentence him to death, and hand him over to the Gentiles to be mocked and flogged and crucified, but the third day he will be raised up.'

Then the mother of Zebedee's sons approached him taking her sons with her, and having prostrated herself desired to make a request.

'What is your wish?' he said to her.

She answered, 'Declare that these two sons of mine shall sit the one on your right and the other on your left in your Kingdom.'

'You have no idea what you are all asking,' Jesus replied. 'Can you drink the cup I am going to drink?'

'We can,' they told him.

'You will certainly drink my cup,' he said to them, 'but as for sitting on my right and on my left that does not rest with me: it is for those designated by my Father.'

When the ten learnt of this they were highly indignant with the two brothers. So Jesus summoned them and said, 'You are aware that the rules of the nations lord it over them, and their officials tyrannize over them. It shall not be so with you. Whoever would be accounted great let him be your attendant, and whoever would be chief let him be your servant; just as the Son of Man did not come to be served but to serve, and to give his life in ransom for many.'

Now as they were leaving Jericho a great crowd followed him. And two blind men there sitting at the roadside, when they heard that Jesus was passing, cried out, 'Pity us, Son of David, sir!'

The crowd tried to silence them, but they only cried out all the more, 'Pity us, Son of David, sir!'

Then Jesus stopped, and called them saying, 'What can I do for you?'

'Sir,' they said, 'that our eyes may be opened.'

So Jesus had compassion on them and touched their eyes, and at once they regained their sight and followed him.

When they were close to Jerusalem, and had reached Bethphage by the Mount of Olives, Jesus sent forward two of his disciples and told them, 'Go to the village before you, and you will at once find an ass tethered with a foal at her side. Untie them, and bring them to me. If anyone questions you say, "The Master needs them," and he will send them forthwith.'[a]

So the disciples went forward and followed Jesus's instructions, and brought the ass and the foal. Then they placed their cloaks on them, and seated him on them, while the vast crowd spread their cloaks on the road, and others cut down branches from the trees and strewed them on the road. Then the people, both those who preceded him and those who followed, cried out,

'Hosanna, Son of David!
Blessed is he who comes in the name of the Lord.[129]
Hosanna in the heavenly heights!'

As he entered Jerusalem the whole city was in commotion saying, 'Who is it?'

To this the people responded, 'It is the Prophet Jesus from Nazareth in Galilee.'

Jesus went into the Temple, and drove out all who were buying and selling in the Temple, and overturned the tables of the moneychangers and the stalls of the pigeon-dealers, and told them, 'It is written, "My house shall be called a house of prayer",[130] but you have made it a robbers' den.'[131]

Blind and lame people came to him in the Temple and he cured them. Seeing the wonders he performed and the boys calling out in the Temple, 'Hosanna, Son of David!' the head priests and the scribes were indignant and said to him, 'Do you hear what they are saying?'

'Of course,' Jesus replied. 'Have you never read, "You have trained the lips of babes and sucklings to utter praise"?'[132]

At that he left them and went outside the city to Bethany and lodged there.

Early in the morning as Jesus was returning to the city he was

[a] This happened to fulfil what was announced by the prophet saying,

> Inform the daughter of Zion,
> 'See, your king comes to you,
> Gentle and mounted on an ass,
> And the foal of a beast of burden.'[128]

[128] Zech. ix. 9. The author misunderstanding the poetic reiteration provides two beasts and makes Jesus ride on both.
[129] Ps. cxviii. 25-26.
[130] Isa. lvi. 7.
[131] Jer. vii. 11.
[132] Ps. viii. 2.

hungry, and noticing a solitary fig tree by the roadside he went towards it; but finding nothing on it but leaves he said to it, 'Let there be no more fruit on you for ever!'

The fig tree withered away on the spot.

Seeing this the disciples were amazed and exclaimed, 'How has the fig tree withered away on the spot?'

'I tell you positively,' Jesus said, 'if you have faith and never doubt you will not only do what has been done to the fig tree, but if you say no less to this hill, "Be uprooted, and be cast into the sea!" it will take place. And indeed whatever you ask for in prayer you will receive if you believe.'

When he entered the Temple the head priests and elders of the people approached him as he was teaching and said, 'By what authority do you do this, and who furnished you with that authority?'

Jesus answered, 'Let me ask you one question myself, and if you answer me I too will tell you by what authority I do this. Was John's rite of immersion of divine or human inspiration?'

They discussed the question together saying, 'If we say, "of divine inspiration", he will say, "Why then did you not believe him?" But if we say, "of human inspiration", we are afraid of the crowd, for they all regard John as a prophet.' So they answered, 'We cannot tell.'

So Jesus in turn said, 'In that case neither will I tell you by what authority I do this. But give me your opinion. There was a man who had two sons. He approached the first and said, "My lad, go and work in my vineyard to-day." He replied, "All right, sir," but he did not go. Then he approached the second with the same request. "I don't want to," he answered, but later he changed his mind and went. Which of the two carried out his father's wishes?'

'The latter,' they replied.

Jesus said to them, 'I tell you for a fact, the tax-collectors and harlots will precede you into the Kingdom of God. For John came to you as in duty bound, and you did not believe him; but the tax-collectors and harlots believed him, and you when you saw it did not even change your minds later and believe in him.

'Now listen to another simile.[133] There was a householder who planted a vineyard, erected a fence round it, dug a wine-press in it, built a watch-tower, and let it out to growers to cultivate, and then went abroad. When the vintage season approached he dispatched his servants to the growers to receive his share of the produce. But the growers seized his servants, and beat one, killed another and stoned a third. So he sent another batch of servants more numerous than before; but they treated them the same way. Finally he sent his own son saying, "They are bound to respect my son." But when they saw the son the growers said to themselves, "Here is the heir! Come on, let us kill him and possess ourselves of his inheritance!" So they seized

[133] Inspired by Isa. v. 1-8.

him, dragged him outside the vineyard, and killed him. When the owner of the vineyard comes what will he do to those growers?'

They said to him, 'He will make a dreadful end of those wicked men, and let out the vineyard to growers who will render him the fruits in due season.'

'Have you never read in the Scriptures,' Jesus said, ' "The stone which the builders rejected has become the coping-stone. This is the Lord's doing and is marvellous in our eyes"?[134] Therefore I tell you, the Kingdom of God will be taken from you and given to a nation which yields its fruits. [Whoever falls on this stone will be crushed, and whoever it falls on will be pulverized.]'

When the head priests and Pharisees heard his similes they realized he was referring to them. They were anxious to arrest him, but they were afraid of the people who regarded him as a prophet.

One more simile Jesus addressed to them. 'The Kingdom of Heaven may be represented,' he said, 'as a king who gave a wedding for his son, and dispatched his servants to invite the guests to the wedding; but they would not come. So he dispatched more servants, saying, "Tell the guests my banquet[135] is fully prepared, my oxen and geese are roasted, everything is ready waiting. Please come to the wedding." But disregarding the invitation some went elsewhere, one to his farm, another to his trading, and others laid hold of his servants and ill-treated and killed them. So the king was enraged, and sent his troops, and exterminated those murderers, and set their city on fire.[136] Then he said to his servants, "Though the wedding is ready the guests were unworthy. Now go out into the thoroughfares, and invite to the wedding whoever you come across." So the servants went out into the roads and collected all the people they could find, good and bad alike, and the bridal banquet was supplied with company. When the king came in to view the company he noticed one man was not in wedding attire and said to him, "Friend, how did you gain admission without wedding attire?" He was speechless. Then the king said to the servants, "Bind him hand and foot and eject him into the darkness outside, where there will be wailing and grinding of teeth." For many are invited, but few are selected.'

III

Then the Pharisees went away and formulated a plan for trapping him in speech. They dispatched some of their disciples together with the Herodians to say, 'Teacher, we are well aware of your sincerity, and that you are not influenced by anyone, for you pay no regard to outward appearance. Give us your opinion

[134] Ps. cxviii. 22.
[135] The Messianic banquet.
[136] Language possibly influenced by the fall of Jerusalem. See Jos. *Wars*, II. xii. 2.

therefore, is it permissible to pay the poll-tax to Caesar or not?'

But Jesus detected their evil intention and replied, 'Why do you tempt me, you hypocrites? Show me a coin of the tax.'

They tendered him a dinar.

Then said he to them, 'Whose is this portrait and inscription?' 'Caesar's,' they answered.

'Render then to Caesar what is Caesar's,' he told them, 'and to God what is God's.'

They were amazed when they heard this, and left him and went away.

That same day Sadducees, who say there will be no resurrection, came to him and questioned him as follows: 'Teacher, Moses said, "If a man dies and leaves no children his brother shall take his widow in marriage and continue his brother's line."[137] Now there were seven brothers among us. The first married, and dying without issue left his wife to his brother. The same thing happened to the second and third, and to all the seven. Finally the woman herself died. In the resurrection to which of the seven will the woman belong, for they all had her in turn?'

Jesus replied, 'You are in error, knowing neither the Scriptures nor the power of God; for in the resurrection they do not marry or give in marriage: they are like the angels in heaven. As to the resurrection of the dead, have you not read what God announced to you saying, "I am the God of Abraham, the God of Isaac, and the God of Jacob?"[138] He is not God of the dead but God of the living.'

When the people heard this they marvelled at his teaching.

On hearing that Jesus had silenced the Sadducees the Pharisees took stock of the situation. Then one of them, a lawyer, posed a question to tempt him, 'Teacher, which is the supreme commandment in the Law?'

He told him, ' "You are to love the Lord your God with all your heart, and with all your soul, and with all your capacity."[139] This is the first and foremost commandment. There is a second that matches it, "You are to love your neighbour as yourself."[140] On these two commandments hinge the entire Law and the Prophets.'

While the Pharisees were assembled Jesus in turn asked them, 'What is your view of the Messiah? Whose son is he?'

'David's,' they replied.

'Why then,' he said, 'does David by inspiration call him lord, saying,

> *The Lord said to my lord, "Sit at my right hand*
> *Until I lay your enemies beneath your feet"?*[141]

If David calls him lord, how can he be his son?"

[137] See Deut. xxv. 5.
[138] Exod. iii. 6.
[139] Deut. vi. 5.
[140] Lev. xix. 18.
[141] Ps. cx. 1.

No one volunteered an answer, nor from that time forward did anyone venture to question him further.

Then Jesus addressed the people and his disciples. 'The scribes and Pharisees,' he said, 'sit in Moses's seat. Execute and observe, therefore, whatever they tell you; but do not act as they do, for they preach but fail to practise. They pack up heavy bales and load them on men's shoulders, but they have no wish to lift a finger to transport them themselves. And all their actions are performed for public notice; they broaden their phylacteries and enlarge their tassels.[142] They love the most prominent places at banquets, and the principal seats in the synagogues, to be greeted in the markets, and addressed by people as "Rabbi". But you are not to be called rabbi, for you have but one teacher, and all of you are brothers. Neither are you to call anyone father on earth, for you have but one heavenly Father. Nor are you to be called leader, for your only leader is the Messiah. The greatest of you shall be your servant; for whoever exalts himself shall be abased, while he who abases himself shall be exalted.

'Woe to you, hypocritical scribes and Pharisees! You obstruct people's way to the Kingdom of Heaven. You neither go in yourselves, nor allow those who are going to enter.

'Woe to you, hypocritical scribes and Pharisees! You traverse sea and land to make a single proselyte, and when he is gained you make him twice the son of Gehenna that you are.[143]

'Woe to you blind guides! You say, "Whoever swears by the Temple it does not signify, but whoever swears by the gold of the Temple is bound by his oath." You fools and blind! Which is superior, the gold or the Temple that consecrates the gold? You also say, "Whoever swears by the altar it does not signify, but whoever swears by the offering on it is bound by his oath." You blind! Which is superior, the offering or the altar which consecrates the offering? Whoever swears by the altar swears not only by it but by everything on it. And whoever swears by the Temple swears not only by it but by everything contained in it. And whoever swears by heaven swears not only by the throne of God but by him who sits upon it.

'Woe to you, hypocritical scribes and Pharisees! You tithe mint and dill and cummin, but overlook the graver matters of the Law, justice, mercy and honesty. These are the things you should have attended to without neglecting the others. You blind guides! You strain out a gnat and gulp down a camel.

'Woe to you, hypocritical scribes and Pharisees! You are much like whitewashed graves, which appear fair outside, but inside are full of dead men's bones and everything foul. So you too seem righteous to people outwardly, but inwardly you are saturated with hypocrisy and lawlessness.

'Woe to you, hypocritical scribes and Pharisees! You build

[142] See Deut. vi. 8; xxii. 12.
[143] I.e. as reprobate as you are.

the tombs of the prophets and ornament the monuments of the just, and say, "Had we lived in our fathers' time we should not have been their accomplices in shedding the blood of the prophets." So you testify of yourselves that you are the sons of those who slaughtered the prophets. Fill up, then, the measure of your fathers. Serpents, vipers' brood! How can you escape the doom of Gehenna? Therefore,

> *"See, I send you prophets, sages and scribes!*
> *Some of them you will kill and crucify,*
> *And some you will flog in your synagogues,*
> *And persecute from city to city;*
> *That on you may come all the just blood shed on earth*
> *From the blood of Abel the righteous*
> *To the blood of Zechariah the son of Berechiah,*
> *Whom you slew between the sanctuary and altar."*[144]

I tell you for a fact, all this shall befall this generation.[145]

> *"Jerusalem, Jerusalem! Killer of prophets,*
> *And stoner of those that are sent to her!*
> *How oft would I have gathered your children,*
> *As the mother bird her brood 'neath her wings?*
> *But you would not have it so.*
> *See, your house is left to you desolate!"*[146]

So I say to you, on no account will you see me from this time forward until you say, "Blessed is he who comes in the name of the Lord." '

Leaving the Temple Jesus went his way. But his disciples approached to point out to him the buildings of the Temple. 'Do you see all these?' he said to them. 'I tell you positively, there will not be left here one stone upon another that will not be thrown down.'

IV[147]

As Jesus sat on the Mount of Olives his disciples approached him privately and said, 'Tell us when these things will happen, and what will be the sign of your advent and of the Consummation of the Age?'

Jesus answered them, 'Take care that no one deceives you. For many claiming to be me will come saying, "I am the Messiah", and will deceive many. Inevitably you will hear of wars and rumours of wars. Do not be alarmed. This is bound to happen, but it does not mean that the End has come. For nation

---

[144] The exact source of the quotation is unknown, perhaps the lost ending of the *Wisdom of Solomon* (see *Enoch*, ix. 1). A shorter version in Lk. xi. 49-50 (below p. 166) is attributed to the 'Wisdom of God', cp. II. Chron. xxxvi. 14-16 and TJ, *Taanith*, 69a-b. The text as it stands seems to have been influenced by Mt. x. 17-18 (above p. 102).
[145] Cp. *Jubilees*, xxiii. 14.
[146] Probably same source as above.
[147] See Mk. xiii, and p. 76, n. 74.

will be aroused against nation, and kingdom against kingdom, and there will be famines and earthquakes in various places; but these are only the beginning of the Pangs.[148] Later they will subject you to torture and will kill you, and you will be detested by all nations on my account. Then many will turn traitor and betray one another and hate one another, and many false prophets will arise and mislead the multitude, and through the increase of lawlessness many will cool in their attachment.[149] But he that is constant to the end will be saved. And this News of the Kingdom shall be proclaimed world-wide as a testimony to all nations. Only then will the End come.

'When, therefore, you see the "Abomination of Desolation" announced by the Prophet Daniel[150] stand in the holy place,[a] then let those who are in Judea escape to the mountains, and let him who is on the housetop not go down to remove anything from his house, and let him who is in the field not turn back to fetch his coat. Woe to pregnant women and nursing mothers in those days! You must pray that your flight will not be in winter or on the sabbath, for there will be great affliction then such as there has never been since the world began down to the present time, nor ever will be again. If that period had not been shortened not a single human being would be preserved; but for the Elect's sake that period will be shortened.

'Then if anyone tells you, "Look, here is the Messiah!" or "There he is!" do not credit it, for false messiahs and false prophets will arise and exhibit great signs and wonders, so as to deceive even the Elect if possible. See, I have told you beforehand. So if anyone says to you, "He is in the wilderness", do not go out. If he says, "He is behind closed doors", do not credit it. For as the lightning flashes from the East and is visible to the bounds of the West so will be the advent of the Son of Man. "Where the carcase is, there the vultures flock."[151]

'Immediately after the affliction of those days,

> Eclipsed shall be the sun
> And the moon shall no more her lustre shed,
> Out of heaven the stars shall fall:
> The heavenly bodies shall be shaken.[152]

And then shall appear in heaven the sign of the Son of Man, and then shall all the tribes of earth mourn,[153] when they see the Son of Man coming in the clouds of heaven[154] with great pomp and state. And he will dispatch his angels with a loud trumpet blast

[a] Let the reader understand the allusion.

[148] See above p. 76, n. 75.
[149] Cp. Jos. *Wars*, II, xiii. 4-6.
[150] Dan. ix. 27; xii. 11.
[151] Cp. Job xxxix. 30.
[152] Isa. xiii. 10; xxxiv. 4, but here probably taken from a lost apocalyptic source used also by the author of the *Assumption of Moses*, x. 5.
[153] Zech. xii, 10.
[154] Dan. vii. 13.

to gather up his Elect from the four winds,[155] from one extremity of heaven to the other.[156]

'Now learn a lesson from the fig tree. When its branch has become tender and the leaves sprout you know that summer is at hand. So you, when you see all this, will know that it[157] is at hand, at the very doors. I tell you truly, this generation will by no means pass away before all these things take place. Heaven and earth will pass away, but my words will not pass away. Yet no one knows the exact day and hour, neither the angels in heaven, nor the Son, only the Father. For as it was in the time of Noah so will be the advent of the Son of Man. Just as at that time before the Flood they were eating and drinking, marrying and giving in marriage, until the day Noah entered the ark, and knew nothing until the deluge came and swept them all away; so will be the advent of the Son of Man. Then two men will be in a field, one will be taken and one left behind. Two women will be grinding at the mill, one will be taken and one left behind. So be alert, for you do not know on what day your Master will come. But realize this, if the householder had known in which watch the thief would come he would have been on the alert and not allowed his house to be broken into. So you too be ready, for at an unexpected hour the Son of Man will come.

'Who, then, is that loyal and prudent servant whom his master has put in charge of his staff to cater for them regularly? Fortunate is that servant whom his master at his coming finds so engaged. I tell you truly, he will entrust him with all his possessions. But if he is a bad servant, who says to himself, "My master is detained", and begins to strike his fellow servants and to eat and drink with drunkards, the master of that servant will arrive on a day he does not expect, and at an hour he does not anticipate, and will take him by surprise and assign his place with the hypocrites. There will be wailing and grinding of teeth.

V

'The Kingdom of Heaven may then be compared to ten maidens, who took their lamps[158] and went out to meet the bridegroom. Five of them were foolish and five were prudent. The foolish ones took their lamps, but took no oil with them, while the prudent took oil in the containers with their lamps. When the bridegroom was detained all of them dozed off and fell asleep. In the middle of the night, however, there came a shout, "The bridegroom is coming! Go out to meet him." Then all those maidens rose and trimmed their lamps. The foolish then said to the prudent, "Give us some of your oil, for our lamps are going out." But the prudent replied, "We cannot, or there may not be enough for us and you. You had better go to the

155 Zech. ii. 6.
156 Deut. xxx. 4.
157 I.e. the End. For the play on words see above p. 77, n. 80.
158 These were set on the top of poles.

dealers and buy what you need." But while they were away buying the bridegroom arrived, and those who were ready went in with him to the wedding, and the doors were shut. Later the rest of the maidens came and said, "Sir, sir, let us in!" But he answered, "I tell you truly, I don't know you." Be alert, therefore, for you do not know either the day or the hour.

'It is like a man travelling abroad, who summoned his personal servants and entrusted them with his property. To one he gave five talents,[159] to another two, and to another one, to each according to his individual capacity, and so went abroad. Forthwith he who had received the five talents went and traded with them and made a further five talents profit. He who had received two made a profit of two talents. But he who had received one talent went and dug a hole and buried his master's money.

'A long time after, the master of those servants returned and went over the accounts with them. Then he who had received the five talents presented himself and produced the additional five talents and said, "Master, you entrusted me with five talents, see, I have gained a further five talents." His master said to him, "Fine, my worthy and loyal servant! You have been reliable in minor matters, I will put you in charge of major affairs. Enjoy your master's prosperity." Then he who had the two talents presented himself and said, "Master, you entrusted me with two talents, see, I have gained a further two talents." His master said to him, "Fine, my worthy and loyal servant! You have been reliable in minor matters. I will put you in charge of major affairs. Enjoy your master's prosperity." Then he who had received the one talent presented himself and said, "Master, I knew you to be a hard man, reaping where you have not sown, and gathering where you have not scattered; so I was afraid and went and buried your talent in the ground. See, here is what is yours." Then his master replied, "You worthless and unenterprising servant! You knew that I reap where I have not sown, and gather where I have not scattered. You ought to have placed my money on the exchange, so that on my return I should have had back my capital with interest. Take the talent from him and give it to the one with ten talents. For to him who has more shall be given, and he shall have a surplus, but from him who has not even what he has shall be taken away. As for the unprofitable servant, throw him into the darkness outside, where there will be wailing and grinding of teeth."

'When the Son of Man comes in state with all the angels with him he will sit on his throne of state, and all nations will be ranged before him. And he will separate one from another as a shepherd separates the sheep from the goats. The sheep he will place on his right and the goats on his left. Then the king will say to those on his right, "Come, favourites of my Father, inherit the kingdom prepared for you from the creation of the world. For I was hungry and you fed me, thirsty and you refreshed me,

[159] A talent equals about £240.

a stranger and you entertained me, naked and you clothed me, ailing and you cared for me, in prison and you visited me."[160] Then the just nations will reply, "Lord, when did we see you hungry and fed you, or thirsty and refreshed you; when did we see you a stranger and entertained you, or naked and clothed you; when did we see you ailing, or in prison, and visited you?" Then the king will answer them, "I tell you truly, in so far as you did it to one of these humble brothers of mine you did it to me." Then he will say to those on the left, "Depart from me, you cursed ones, to the Everlasting Fire prepared for the Devil and his angels. For I was hungry and you did not feed me, thirsty and you did not refresh me, a stranger and you did not entertain me, naked and you did not clothe me, ailing and in prison and you did not care for me." Then they in turn will reply, "Lord when did we see you hungry, or thirsty, or a stranger, or naked, or ailing, or in prison, and did not serve your need?" He will answer, "I tell you truly, in so far as you did not do it to one of these lowliest ones you did not do it to me." So these nations will go away to Eternal Punishment, but the just nations to Eternal Life.'

When Jesus had concluded this discourse he said to his disciples, 'You know that the Passover is in two days' time, and the Son of Man will be handed over for crucifixion.'

EPILOGUE

I

Now the head priests and elders of the people assembled at the residence of the high priest, who was called Caiaphas, and they deliberated how they might secure Jesus by trickery and execute him. But they decided, 'Not at the festival, or there may be a popular outbreak.'

While Jesus was at Bethany at the house of Simon the leper a woman approached him with an alabaster flask of costly oil which she poured on his head as he reclined at table. But when the disciples saw this they were indignant and said, 'What sense is there in such waste? It could have been sold for a considerable sum and the money distributed to the poor.'

When Jesus was aware of this he said to them, 'Why do you upbraid the woman? It is a very kind action she has performed for me. You have the poor always with you, but you will not have me always. By diffusing this oil over my body she has carried out my burial rites. I tell you positively, wherever this News is proclaimed throughout the world what she has done will also be related to commemorate her.'

---

[160] Cp. *Test. Joseph*, i. 3-7, where Joseph expresses in similar terms God's dealings with him in Egypt.

Then one of the twelve, called Judas Iscariot, went off to the head priests and said, 'How much will you give me to hand him over to you.'

They allotted him thirty pieces of silver, and from then on he sought a convenient opportunity to betray him.

II

On the first day of the Feast of Unleavened Bread the disciples approached Jesus and said, 'Where do you wish us to prepare for you to eat the Passover?'

'Go into the city,' he told them, 'to so-and-so, and say to him, "The Teacher says, my time is at hand. I and my disciples will keep the Passover at your house." '

So the disciples carried out Jesus's instructions, and prepared the Passover.

When evening came he reclined at table with the twelve. As they were eating he said, 'I tell you for a fact, one of you will betray me.'

They were deeply distressed, and each of them started to protest, 'Surely it is not me, Master?'

'He who dips his hand in the dish with me,' he replied, 'is the one who will betray me. The Son of Man is certainly going the way that was written of him, yet woe to that man by whom the Son of Man is betrayed. Better for that man had he never been born.'

Then Judas, who did betray him, answered, 'Surely it is not me, Rabbi?'

He said to him, 'So you have said.'

As they were eating Jesus took bread, recited the blessing, broke it, and gave it to his disciples, and said, 'Take, eat; this signifies my body.'

Then he took the cup, gave thanks, and passed it to them saying, 'Drink from it all of you, for this signifies my "blood of the covenant"[161] poured out for many in forgiveness of sins. I tell you, from now on I will by no means drink of this fruit of the vine[162] until the day comes when I drink it new with you in my Father's Kingdom.'

After the hymn-singing they went to the Mount of Olives. Then Jesus said to them, 'All of you will waver in your loyalty to me to-night, for it is stated, "Strike at the shepherd and the sheep of the flock will be scattered."[163] But when I have been raised up I will precede you to Galilee.'

Peter replied, 'If they all waver in their loyalty to you, I will never waver.'

[161] Exod. xxiv. 8.
[162] A phrase from the blessing over the fourth obligatory cup of wine in the Passover service, where mention is also made of the consolation of Israel in the Messianic Era. See above p. 78, n. 87.
[163] Zech. xiii. 7.

'I tell you for a fact,' Jesus said to him, 'this very night before cock-crow you will disown me three times.'

'Even if it means dying with you,' declared Peter, 'I will never disown you.'

So said all the disciples.

Then Jesus arrived with them at a place called Gethsemane and said to the disciples, 'You stay here while I go over there to pray.' He took with him Peter and the two sons of Zebedee: he felt miserable and depressed. 'I am in very low spirits,'[164] he said to them. 'Stay here and keep watch with me.'

Then he went on a little way and fell on his face in prayer saying, 'Father, if possible let this cup pass me by, though not as I will, but as thou wilt.'

He returned to his disciples and found them sleeping, and said to Peter, 'Could you not manage to watch with me for a single hour? Be vigilant and prayerful, or you may find yourselves tempted. The spirit is willing enough but the flesh is frail.'

He went away a second time and prayed, 'Father, if it is not possible for this cup to pass by without my drinking it, be it as thou wilt.'

Coming once more to his disciples he found them asleep, for their eyes were heavy. So he left them again and went away, and prayed a third time repeating the same prayer. Then he came back to his disciples and said to them, 'Are you going on sleeping and taking your rest? See, the hour is at hand for the Son of Man to be delivered into the hands of sinners. Rise and let us be going. My betrayer approaches.'

He was still speaking when Judas, one of the twelve, came, and with him a large crowd armed with swords and clubs dispatched by the head priests and elders of the people. His betrayer had given them a signal saying, 'The one I embrace, that is he. Seize him.' At once he approached Jesus and cried, 'Greetings, Rabbi!' and embraced him.

'Friend, attend to your business,' Jesus said to him.

Then they approached and laid hold of Jesus and seized him. At this, one of those with Jesus dropped his hand to his sword, drew it, and struck the high priest's servant, severing his ear. Jesus said to him, 'Put up your sword, for all who draw the sword shall die by the sword. Do you imagine that I could not appeal to my Father and he would immediately send to my aid full twelve legions of angels? But then how would the Scriptures be fulfilled that this is what must happen?'

Thereupon Jesus said to the crowd, 'Have you come out with swords and clubs to capture me as if I were a brigand? I sat daily in the Temple teaching and you never arrested me; but all this has come about that the writings of the Prophets should be fulfilled.'

Then all the disciples deserted him and fled. Those who had arrested Jesus marched him off to the high priest Caiaphas,

164 See above p. 79, n. 89.

where the scribes and elders were assembled. Peter had followed him at a distance as far as the high priest's courtyard, and going inside he sat down with the retainers to await the outcome.

Now the high priest and the whole Sanhedrin sought false evidence against Jesus on which they could condemn him to death; but they failed to obtain it, though many false witnesses came forward who said, 'He stated, "I can pull down God's Sanctuary, and rebuild it in three days." '

Then the high priest rose and said to him, 'Do you make no defence to these charges they bring against you?'

But Jesus was silent.

Then the high priest said to him, 'I put you on oath by the Living God to tell us whether you are the Messiah, the Son of God.'

'So you have said,' Jesus replied. 'I will only tell you this, hereafter you will see the Son of Man seated at the right hand of power and coming with the clouds of heaven.'[165]

Then the high priest tore his tunic and cried, 'He has blasphemed.[166] What further need have we of witnesses? You have just heard the traitorous confession. What is your verdict?'

'He is liable to the death penalty,' they answered. Then they spat in his face and struck him, crying as they cuffed him, 'Prophesy to us, you Messiah! Who hit you?'

Meanwhile Peter had been sitting outside in the courtyard. One of the maidservants approached him and said, 'Surely you were with Jesus the Galilean?'

But he denied it before them all and said, 'I don't know what you are talking about.'

As he was going out to the gateway, however, another girl saw him and said to those who were there, 'He was with Jesus the Nazarene.'

Again he denied with an oath, 'I don't know the man.'

A little later the bystanders approached and said to Peter, 'Of course you're one of them. Your accent gives you away completely.'

Then he began to curse and swear, 'I don't know the man.'

Immediately the cock crowed and Peter recalled how Jesus had said, 'Before cock-crow you will disown me three times.' And he went outside and wept bitterly.

III

When morning came all the head priests and elders of the people deliberated how to contrive Jesus's death. Having manacled him they marched him off and handed him over to the governor Pilate.

Then Judas the betrayer, seeing him condemned, was filled

[165] Cp. Ps. cx. 1, Dan. vii. 13.
[166] See above p. 80, n. 94.

with remorse and returned the thirty pieces of silver to the head priests and elders saying, 'I have sinned in betraying innocent blood.'

'How does that affect us?' they said. 'It is your concern.'

So he flung the silver into the Temple,[167] and withdrew, and went away and hanged himself. But the head priests took out the silver and said, 'It is not proper for it to be cast into the sacred funds:[108] it is blood money.' After consultation they bought Potter's Field with it as a burial place for aliens, and this is how it got the name of Bloody Field, which it still bears.[a]

Now Jesus stood before the governor, and the governor interrogated him. 'Are you king of the Jews?' he asked.

'As you say,' Jesus replied.

But when he was indicted by the head priests and elders he made no reply.

Then Pilate said to him, 'Do you not hear how many things they are charging you with?'

But he gave him no reply whatever, so that the governor was greatly astonished.

At the festival it was the governor's practice to release to the public any one prisoner they might choose. There was at this time in custody a noted prisoner called Bar-Abbas. So when the people assembled for the purpose Pilate said to them, 'Whom do you wish me to release to you, Bar-Abbas or Jesus styled Christ?' He knew they had handed him over out of malice.

When he tad taken his place on the tribunal his wife sent him a message saying, 'Do nothing to that good man, for I have had a very bad time to-day dreaming about him.' But the head priests and elders won over the people to ask for Bar-Abbas and destroy Jesus. So when the governor said to them, 'Which of the two do you want me to release to you?' they answered, 'Bar-Abbas.'

Pilate then said to them, 'And what shall I do with Jesus styled Christ?'

Unanimously they cried, 'Let him be crucified!'

'But what crime has he committed?' he asked.

But they shouted persistently, 'Let him be crucified!'

When Pilate saw there was nothing further he could do without exciting even more of a tumult, he took water and rinsed his hands in the sight of the people saying, 'I am innocent of this man's blood. It is your concern.'

[a] This was to fulfil what was announced by the Prophet Jeremiah saying,

> So they took the thirty pieces of silver,
> The price of him who was valued,
> Whom they assessed of the children of Israel,
> And gave them for the potter's field
> As the Lord had instructed me.[169]

[167] I.e. the offertory chests, one of which was for the purchase of sin-offerings.
[108] Lit. 'the Qorban.'
[169] Jer. xxxii. 6f and Zech. xi. 12-13.

SPQR

J.F.H.

A Roman Judgment

To this all the people responded, 'His blood be on us and our children!'

So he released Bar-Abbas to them, and had Jesus flogged and handed him over for crucifixion.

Then the governor's soldiers took Jesus into the praetorium and gathered the whole cohort round him. Having stripped him they draped him in a scarlet cloak, and when they had plaited a victor's wreath out of thorns they set it on his head, and put a cane in his right hand, and bending the knee to him they mocked him saying, 'Hail, king of the Jews!' Then spitting on him they took the cane and struck him on the head. When they had sufficiently derided him they stripped him of the cloak and re-clad him in his own clothes and marched him off to be crucified.

As they went out they found a man of Cyrene called Simon and forced him to carry the cross. When they came to the place called Golgotha—which is to say 'Skull Place'—they gave him a drink of wine mixed with gall; but when he had tasted it he refused to drink it. After crucifying him they portioned out his clothes and threw dice for them, and sitting down they kept guard over him there. They also set over his head the charge against him in these terms: 'This is Jesus the King of the Jews.'

Then two brigands were crucified with him, one on his right and the other on his left. And all who passed by vilified him, shaking their heads and saying, 'You who can pull down the Temple and rebuild it in three days, save yourself. If you are the Son of God come down from the cross.'

The head priests with the scribes and elders similarly derided him and said, 'He saved others, but cannot save himself. He is

135

king of Israel, so let him come down from the cross and we will believe in him. He relied on God: let him rescue him if he wants him,[170] for he said, "I am the Son of God." '

Even the brigands, who were crucified with him, reviled him.

Now from noon there was darkness over the whole land until three o'clock. Then about three o'clock Jesus uttered a loud cry saying, '*Eloi, Eloi, lema sabachthani!*'—which means, 'My God, my God, why have you deserted me.'[171] Some of those standing there, hearing this, said, 'He is calling Elijah.'

At once one of them ran and fetched a sponge, saturated it with vinegar, and spiking it on a cane, held it out to him to drink. But the rest said, 'Leave him alone, and we shall see if Elijah will come to save him.'

But Jesus gave another loud cry, and expired.

At this, the curtain of the Sanctuary was ripped in two from top to bottom, the earth shook, the rocks were riven, the tombs sprang open and many bodies of the saints laid to rest were raised, and issuing from their tombs after his resurrection entered the holy city and were plainly seen by many people.[172]

The centurion and his men who had been guarding Jesus, seeing the earthquake and other disturbances, were greatly frightened and exclaimed, 'Undoubtedly he was God's Son!' Many women were also there looking on from a distance. They were those who had followed Jesus from Galilee attending to his needs. Among them was Mary of Magdala, Mary the mother of James and Joseph, and the mother of Zebedee's sons.

When evening came a wealthy man from Arimathea called Joseph, himself a disciple of Jesus, personally approached Pilate and asked for the body of Jesus. Then Pilate gave orders for it to be given to him. So Joseph received the body, wrapped it in a clean linen sheet, deposited it in his new rock-cut tomb, and after rolling a heavy boulder across the mouth of the tomb went away. But Mary of Magdala and the other Mary were there sitting opposite the burial place.

IV

Next day, which was the day following the preparation day, the head priests and Pharisees went together to Pilate and said, 'Sir, we recall how that imposter while alive said, "After three days I shall be raised up." Give orders, therefore, for the burial place to be secured until the third day has passed, in case his disciples should come and steal him and then tell the people he has risen from the dead. The final imposture would then be worse than the original one.'

---

[170] Cp. Ps. xxii. 7-8, and above previous paragraph.
[171] Ps. xxii. 1 in Aramaic. The old Hebrew has '*Lama shekachtani*' ('why have you forgotten me' Ps. xlii. 9).
[172] These signs are drawn from the current expositions of what would happen at the Day of Judgment as foreshadowed in what took place at the giving of the Law on Sinai.

Pilate said to them, 'You have your force.[173] Maintain as much security as you like.'

So they went away and secured the tomb, and placed a police cordon round the boulder.

When the sabbath was over, as the day after the sabbath began to dawn, Mary of Magdala and the other Mary came to inspect the burial place. Now a great earthquake had taken place, for an angel of the Lord descended from heaven, and approached and rolled aside the boulder and sat on it. His appearance was like lightning and his clothing white as snow. The guards shook with terror at him and became as dead men. Then the angel addressed the women and said, 'Do not be alarmed. I know you are looking for Jesus who was crucified. He is no longer here. He has been raised up exactly as he said. Come and look at the place where he lay. Now go quickly and tell his disciples, "He has been raised from the dead, and is preceding you to Galilee. You will see him there." My message is delivered.'

So they left the tomb quickly with mingled fear and excessive joy, and ran to inform his disciples. Just then Jesus came to meet them and said 'Peace be with you.'[174]

They approached and grasped his feet, and prostrated themselves before him. 'Do not be alarmed,' Jesus said. 'Go and tell my brothers that they are to go to Galilee and will see me there.'

As they resumed their way, some of the police went into the city to inform the head priests of everything that had happened. And when these had consulted with the elders they gave the guards a considerable sum of money telling them, 'You are to say, "His disciples came by night and stole him while we were asleep." And if the governor hears of it, we will win him over and exonerate you.'

So they took the money and acted as they had been primed. And this is the version that is still current among the Jews.

V

The eleven disciples went away to Galilee to the mountain which Jesus had arranged with them. When they saw him they prostrated themselves, though they were somewhat uncertain. But Jesus approached and spoke to them and said, 'I have received complete authority in heaven and on earth. Go, therefore, and make disciples of all the Gentiles, immersing them in the name of the Father, and the Son, and the holy Spirit, teaching them to observe whatever I have commanded you. I shall indeed be constantly at your side until the Consummation of the Age.'[175]

[173] The civil force under the authority of the Sanhedrin, Gr. custodia.
[174] Following the Old Hebrew, the Greek has 'Hail!'
[175] See Mt. xxiv. 14, above p. 126, the end of the present order and the commencement of the Kingdom of God.

LUKE

A HISTORY OF
CHRISTIAN BEGINNINGS

PART I

How the Good News came to Israel

Preface to *Luke*

THIS GOSPEL and its sequel the *Acts of the Envoys* were in all probability written in their original form by the companion of Paul of Tarsus whom he affectionately calls 'Dear Doctor Luke'. The author's knowledge of Jewish customs makes it likely that he was a Gentile monotheist in close touch with Hellenistic Judaism. He was a medical man, and tradition makes him a native of Antioch in Syria. Irenaeus (c. A.D. 180) states that Luke has given us the version of the Gospel that Paul proclaimed, and it may owe a good deal to Paul's influence and information.

When these books were written Christianity was already branded by the Romans as a hostile and subversive faith, and an important part of Luke's purpose appears to have been to present its origin and development in the most favourable light to the imperial authorities. They thus represent both the first Christian *Apology* and the first 'History of Christian Beginnings'. As far as his sources permit the author dissociates Jesus and his teaching from preoccupation with the Jews and Judaism, and depicts him as the ideal virtuous man. The injunction to the Twelve not to go to Gentiles and Samaritans is dropped, and Syrian and Samaritan are well spoken of. The Roman personalities, including Pilate, are set in an even better light than in *Matthew*. The Theophilus to whom the books are inscribed may have been a high imperial official, or a fictitious 'Lover of God' who is supposedly such an official.

The Christian sources employed by Luke in the Gospel are largely the same as used by *Matthew*, though they have been treated with slightly more liberty in the interests of style and overall purpose. As compared with *Matthew* Luke does not go in for a wholesale rearrangement of source material: he prefers to incorporate it in blocks, and he often interjects a question from someone or a brief incident to serve as a link between teachings of Jesus not really connected. *Mark* and 'Q' are again the main sources. The chief new material, apart from certain additional parables, deals with the birth of John the Baptist and of Jesus. For the former, Luke probably employed a Christianized version of a lost book of the 'Nativity of John', published originally by the Baptist's disciples in support of their claim that he was the Messiah. Other written sources have not yet been traced, but the writer's assertion is fully borne out that he has been at great pains to obtain accurate information.

Allowing for faithfulness to those sources which closely followed their Hebrew originals, *Luke* is written in very readable Greek. The author has a great liking for people, and reveals

139

himself as a sympathetic character with an eager curiosity and zest for life. As an amateur historian he is guilty of some errors in chronology, but these do not detract from the general reliability of his work. If the view is correct that he used Josephus's *Antiquities of the Jews* (published in A.D. 94) his books would date from the closing years of the first century. They could, of course, have been written somewhat earlier and afterwards revised.

THE GOOD NEWS OF JESUS CHRIST

Luke's Version

FOREWORD

SINCE it is the case that many have endeavoured to draw up an account of those matters held by us to be fact, exactly as they transmitted them to us who initially were the eyewitnesses and bearers of the Message, I have thought fit myself, as I have carried out a thorough investigation of all the circumstances from their beginnings, to set them down for you consecutively, Your Excellency[1] Theophilus, that you may realize how well-founded are the things of which you have been informed.

CHAPTER I[2]

In the reign of Herod king of Judea there was a priest called Zechariah, of the course of Abijah,[3] who had a wife of the daughters of Aaron called Elizabeth. They were both devout people before God, carrying out all the Lord's commandments and enactments scrupulously. They were childless, however, as Elizabeth was barren, and they were now both of them well advanced in years.

An incident occurred while he was officiating as priest before God during the turn of his course. In accordance with priestly custom the duty fell to him of burning incense on going into the Lord's Sanctuary, and the great mass of the people were outside praying at the time of the incense-burning. It was then that there appeared to him an angel of the Lord standing on the right of

---

[1] The title would indicate a high imperial official.
[2] This chapter appears to be derived from a Baptist messianic source, used later to compose the apocryphal *Gospel of the Nativity of Mary*.
[3] I. Chron. xxiv. 10. The course of Abijah was the eighth course of the priests.

Plan of JERUSALEM before 70 A.D.

the altar of incense. Zechariah was greatly startled at seeing
him, and overcome with fear. But the angel said to him, 'Do not
be afraid, Zechariah, for your petition has been granted, and
your wife Elizabeth will bear you a son. You must call him
John. He will be your joy and delight, and many will rejoice at
his birth. He will be a great man before the Lord, and must not
drink wine or intoxicants,[4] and will be filled with holy Spirit
from the moment he leaves his mother's womb. Many of the
children of Israel will he turn to the Lord their God. He will
precede him in the spirit and capacity of Elijah, "to turn the
hearts of the fathers to the children",[5] and the disobedient into
exemplary characters, to provide the Lord with a people fully
prepared.'

'How am I to know this?' Zechariah said to the angel. 'I am
myself an old man, and my wife is well advanced in years.'

'I am Gabriel,'[a] the angel replied, 'and have been sent to speak
to you and convey this news to you. But now you will be dumb
and unable to speak until the time when all this comes about,
because you have failed to believe my words which will be
accomplished in due course.'

In the meantime the people were waiting for Zechariah, and
were surprised at the length of time he remained in the Sanctuary. When he did come out he could not speak to them, and
they realized that he had seen a vision in the Sanctuary by the
way he was gesticulating to them while remaining speechless.

He went home as soon as his term of duty was over, and it
was after this that his wife Elizabeth conceived. She kept herself
in seclusion for five months saying, 'This is what the Lord has
done for me when he determined to remove my disgrace among
men.'

During her sixth month the angel Gabriel was sent by God to
a town of Galilee called Nazareth, to a maiden betrothed to a
man named Joseph, of the house of David. The maiden's name
was Mary. On entering her home he said, 'Greeting, highly
favoured one![6] The Lord be with you.'

She was greatly perturbed by his language, and concerned at
what this greeting might imply. But the angel said to her, 'Do
not be alarmed, Mary. You have found favour with God. You
will conceive in your womb and have a son,[7] whom you are to
call Jesus. He will be a great man, and be termed "Son of the
Most High", and the Lord God will give him the throne of his
ancestor David: he will reign over the house of Jacob for ever,
and his sovereignty shall be without end.'[8]

[a] The one who stands before God, (Explaining the Hebrew name
    Gabriel as 'God's man of valour'. *Tr.*)

[4] John was to be a Nazirite.
[5] Mal. iv. 6.
[6] The expression can be taken in rather a coarse sense, which would explain Mary's
    alarm.
[7] Cp. Judg. xiii. 3-5 (LXX).
[8] Isa. ix. 7.

Mary said to the angel, 'How can this come about, since I am unwed?'

'The holy Spirit will pass over you, and the power of the Most High will overshadow you,' replied the angel. 'That is why the child that is born will be called "Holy", "Son of God". See, there is your relative Elizabeth, even she has conceived a son in her old age, and the one who was barren is in her sixth month; for nothing whatever is impossible to God.'

'I am the Lord's maidservant,' said Mary. 'Let it be to me as you say.'

Then the angel left her.

Mary made immediate preparations, and travelled in haste to a town in Judah, where she visited Zechariah's house and greeted Elizabeth. No sooner did Elizabeth hear Mary's greeting than the unborn babe jumped in her womb; and Elizabeth was inspired by the holy Spirit and cried out, 'Blest are you among women, and blessed is the fruit of your womb! How comes it that I am honoured by a visit from the mother of my Lord? For as soon as ever your greeting sounded in my ears the unborn babe in my womb jumped for joy. And happy is she who has believed that what has been told her by the Lord will be accomplished.'

Then she sang:[9]

> *'My soul magnifies the Lord,*
> *My spirit exults in God my saviour;*
> *For he has marked his servant's disgrace.*
> *All ages will call me happy henceforward;*
> *For the Mighty One has wrought marvels for me,*
> *And holy is his name.*
> *Generation by generation his mercy is shown*
> *To those who revere him.*
> *He has employed the power of his arm;*
> *He has scattered the proud in their purpose:*
> *He has deposed tyrants from their thrones,*
> *And exalted those of low degree.*
> *He has filled the hungry with good fare,*
> *And men of means he has sent away empty.*
> *He has aided his servant Israel,*
> *Mindful of mercy*
> *(As he told our fathers he would be)*
> *To Abraham and his offspring for ever.'*[10]

Mary stayed with her about three months and then returned home.

When the time came for Elizabeth's delivery she gave birth to a son. And when her neighbours and relations heard that the

[9] The poem was subsequently transferred to Mary by simply adding her name, though the text makes it clear that the singer is Elizabeth.

[10] Cp. *Jubilees* xxv. 17. In this ancient work songs are put into the mouths of Rebecca and Isaac of the same order as those attributed here to Elizabeth and Zechariah. See *Jub.* xxv. 15-23; xxxi. 15-20.

Lord had magnified his mercy to her they rejoiced with her, and on the eighth day they duly attended the boy's circumcision, proposing to name him Zechariah after his father. But the mother intervened. 'No,' she said, 'he is to be called John.'

'None of your relations bears that name,' they said to her.

They invited his father by signs to indicate what he wanted him called. Having motioned for a tablet he wrote, 'His name is John.' They were all amazed. Instantly his mouth and tongue were freed of impediment and he spoke, blessing God. Fear fell on all his neighbours, and all these events were widely reported throughout the Judean highlands. Everyone who heard kept them in mind saying, 'What is this child going to be, for evidently the Lord's hand is with him?'

Now his father Zechariah was inspired by the holy Spirit and prophesied as follows:

> 'Blessed be the Lord God of Israel,
> For he has visited and ransomed his people,
> And raised up for us a means of deliverance[11]
> From the house of his servant David,
> As he said by his holy prophets of old;
> Deliverance from our foes and all who hate us,
> To maintain his mercy to our fathers,
> And to call to mind his holy covenant,
> The oath which he swore to our father Abraham,
> Assuring that fearlessly, freed from foes,
> We should worship him all our days
> Purely and piously in his presence.
> And you, child, shall be called "Prophet of the Highest";
> For you shall precede the Lord to pave his road,
> To give intelligence of deliverance to his people,
> Through the tender mercies of our God
> Whereby a sunbeam from above has penetrated to us,
> Lighting those in gloom and grim shadow,[12]
> Directing our feet to a path of safety.'

The child grew and developed strength of character, and lived in the wilderness until the time of his appearance to Israel.

[11] Lit. 'a horn of deliverance'.
[12] See Isa. ix. 2.

CHAPTER II

At that time a decree was issued by Augustus Caesar to conduct a census of the whole Empire.[a] Everyone went to be
registered, each to his own town. So Joseph went up from
Galilee, from the town of Nazareth, to Judea, to David's town
called Bethlehem, because he was of the family and lineage of
David, there to be registered with Mary his betrothed, who was
in an advanced state of pregnancy. The time for her delivery
actually arrived while they were there, and she bore her first-
born son, wrapped him round and laid him in a cattle-trough
as they had no place in the inn.

There were shepherds in the same district camped out in the
open keeping watch over their flock by night. And an angel of
the Lord appeared to them, and the glory of the Lord shone
around them; and they were terrified. But the angel said, 'Do not
be afraid. I bring you news of a great joy which will be shared
by all the people, that to-day in David's town a deliverer has
been born to you, none other than the Lord Messiah. Here is
your proof. You will find a baby wrapped round and lying in a
cattle-trough.'

Suddenly there was with the angel a concourse of the heavenly host praising God, and singing,

> *'Glory be to God on high and on earth:*
> *Peace be to men who please him.'*[13]

No sooner had the angels left them and returned to heaven
than the shepherds said to one another, 'Let us by all means go
to Bethlehem and see this thing that has happened, of which the
Lord has told us.'

Hurrying off, they came and found Mary and Joseph, and the
baby lying in the cattle-trough. Having seen them, they made
known what had been told them about the boy, and all those
who heard were amazed at what was told them by the shepherds.
But Mary took note of these things, turning them over in her
mind. Then the shepherds went back where they came from,
glorifying and praising God for everything they had heard and
seen, which was exactly as they had been told.

When the requisite eight days had elapsed for circumcising
him the boy was given the name Jesus, as called by the angel
before he was conceived in the womb.

[a] This census was first carried out when Quirinius[14] was legate of
Syria.[15]

[13] In the Temple liturgy the *Kedushah* ('Sanctification') expressed the song of the
heavenly host in the words of Isa. vi. 3 and Ezek. iii. 12. See also the close of
the ancient meditation: 'He who makes peace in his high places, may he bestow
peace on us and on all Israel' (AJP, p. 54), also included in the *Kaddish*, AJP,
p. 78.

[14] Publius Sulpicius Quirinius, d. A.D. 21. See Tacit. *Annals* III. 48.

[15] In A.D. 6-7. See Jos. *Antiq.* XVIII. i. 1.

Later, when the days of their purification were over in accordance with the Law of Moses, they took him to Jerusalem to present him to the Lord,[a] and to offer sacrifice as stated in the Law of the Lord, 'a pair of turtle-doves or two young pigeons'.[16]

Now there was a man in Jerusalem named Simeon, a devout man, who awaited the Consolation of Israel,[17] one on whom the holy Spirit rested. It had been conveyed to him by the holy Spirit that he would not die before he had seen the Lord's Anointed. He was led by the Spirit to the Temple; and when the parents brought in the child Jesus to follow the practice of the Law with regard to him, he took him in his own arms and blessed God, saying, 'Now dismiss thy servant in peace, O Lord, according to thy word; for mine eyes have seen thy deliverance, which thou hast provided in the presence of all peoples, a beacon-light to the Gentiles,[18] a glory to thy people of Israel.'

Both the father and mother of Jesus were amazed at this statement about him. Simeon blessed them, and said to his mother Mary, 'He is put here for the fall and rising again of many in Israel, as a disputed proof—even you will be torn with uncertainty[19]—by which the reasoning of many minds will be disclosed.'

Then there was Hannah a prophetess, daughter of Phanuel, of the tribe of Asher. She had attained a great age, having had seven years of married life from maidenhood, and then had remained a widow for eighty-four years. She never left the Temple now, worshipping there with fasting and prayer night and day. Happening to be by at that moment she praised God aloud, and spoke about the child to all who awaited the liberation of Jerusalem.

When the parents of Jesus had carried out everything required by the Law of the Lord, they returned to Galilee to their own town of Nazareth. There the child grew and developed a keen intellect, being gifted by God.

Now his parents made an annual journey to Jerusalem for the Passover festival. When he was twelve they had gone up as usual for the festival; but when they were on the point of returning, having completed the prescribed period,[21] the boy Jesus lingered in Jerusalem, and his parents were unaware of it. Assuming him to be with the party they had completed a day's journey before they searched for him among their relations and acquaintances. Failing to find him they turned back to Jerusalem to hunt for him there. It was three days later that they discovered him in the Temple, sitting among the teachers, listening to

[a] As it is written in the Law of the Lord, 'Every male child that is the beginning of motherhood shall be consecrated to the Lord'.[20]

[16] Lev. xii. 8.
[17] The deliverance of Israel at the coming of the Messiah.
[18] Cp. Isa. xi. 10.
[19] Lit. 'a sword shall divide your soul' (cp. Mark iii. 21, 31, above p. 56).
[20] Cp. Exod. xiii. 2.
[21] The seven days of the festival.

them and asking them questions, with everyone who heard him amazed at his comprehension and by his answers.[22] They had a shock when they saw him, and his mother said to him, 'Why have you treated us like this, boy? Here have your father and I been searching anxiously for you.'

'Why did you search for me?' he said to them. 'Didn't you know I was bound to be occupied with my Father's affairs?'

They could not make sense of what he said to them. However, he came away with them and went back to Nazareth, and behaved obediently towards them; but his mother stored all these things in her mind.

So Jesus advanced in age and intelligence, in favour with God and man.[23]

CHAPTER III

During the fifteenth year of the reign of Tiberius Caesar,[24] when Pontius Pilate was governor of Judea and Herod was tetrarch of Galilee, while his brother Philip was tetrarch of the Iturean Trachonitis region, and Lysanias was tetrarch of Abilene, in the course of the high priesthood of Annas and Caiaphas, divine utterance took possession of John the son of Zechariah in the wilderness. He went over the whole Jordan district proclaiming an immersion in penitence, for the forgiveness of sins, as it is stated in the book of the sayings of the Prophet Isaiah,

> *A voice cries out in the wilderness,*
> *'Make ready the Lord's road:*
> *Put his highways in order!*
> *Let every crevasse be filled in,*
> *And every hill and hump reduced.*
> *Let the twists be straightened,*
> *And the rough places smoothed;*
> *That all flesh may see God's deliverance.'* [25]

Accordingly, he said to the crowds coming to him for immersion, 'Vipers' brood! Who warned you to flee from the coming Wrath? Produce fruit, then, consistent with repentance, and refrain from saying to yourselves, "We have Abraham as our father", for I tell you that from these stones God can supply Abraham with sons. Already the axe is laid to the root of the trees. Any tree, therefore, that fails to produce good fruit will be cut down and cast into the fire.'

The crowds asked him, 'What are we to do then?'

---

[22] Cp. Josephus, *Life*, ii.
[23] Cp. I. Samuel ii. 26.
[24] If of Tiberius's independent reign this would be A.D. 29. But Tiberius was associated in the government of the Empire before the death of Augustus, which would make the 15th year either A.D. 26 or 28. From other indications A.D. 26 appears to have been intended.
[25] Isa. xl. 3-5. The physical alterations described seem here to be understood as applying to human character.

'Whoever has two coats,' he replied, 'let him share with the man who has none. And whoever has a store of food let him do likewise.'

Even tax-collectors came to be immersed, and said to him, 'What should we do, master?'

He told them, 'Exact no more than the amount fixed for you.'[26]

Men in the army also asked him, 'What about us? What are we to do?'

'Never use brutality or threats of false charges,'[27] he told them, 'but be content with your pay and keep.'

As the people were agog, with everyone wondering about John in their minds, whether he could be the Messiah, John settled the matter for all by saying, 'I am certainly immersing you in water, but a mightier than I is coming, whose sandal-strap I am not fit to untie: he will immerse you in holy Spirit and fire. His winnowing-shovel is in his hand to thoroughly cleanse his floor, and gather the wheat into his granary; but he will burn up the chaff with unquenchable fire.'

Thus with many another appeal did he give his message to the people. But Herod the tetrarch, because he was reproved by John about his brother's wife Herodias, and for all the misdeeds Herod had committed, crowned all his other wrongs by imprisoning him in a fortress.

Now when all the people had been immersed and Jesus too had been immersed and was praying, the sky opened and the holy Spirit descended upon him in bodily form like a dove, while there came a voice from heaven, 'You are my dear Son: to-day I have begotten you.'[28]

(At the outset of his career Jesus himself was about thirty years of age, being, as was understood, the son of Joseph—the son of Eli—the son of Matthat—the son of Levi—the son of Melchi[29]—the son of Jannai—the son of Joseph—the son of Mattathias—the son of Amos—the son of Nahum—the son of Chesli—the son of Naggai—the son of Mahath—the son of Mattathias—the son of Shimei—the son of Josech—the son of Jodah—the son of Johanan—the son of Resa[30]—the son of Zerubbabel—the son of Shealtiel[31]—the son of Neri—the son of Melchi—the son of Addi—the son of Kosam—the son of Elmadan—the son of Er—the son of Jesus

[26] Tax collectors were allowed to retain any sums they could extort in excess of the amount due under the assessment.
[27] Soldiers, especially mercenaries, were given to terrorism as a means of supplementing their pay.
[28] Ps. ii. 7. This seems to be the original reading here.
[29] There is some evidence that the names of Matthat and Melchi have been transposed. Julius Africanus (third cent.) makes Melchi the half-brother of Matthan of *Matthew's* genealogy, married to his widow Estha. Ancient Jewish and Christian traditions suggest that Mary was the granddaughter of Matthan on the side of her father Joachim, and they agree that Matthan and Melchi were brothers.
[30] Or Rephaiah.
[31] Or Salathiel.

—the son of Eliezer—the son of Jorim[32]—the son of Maththat—the son of Levi—the son of Simeon—the son of Judah
—the son of Joseph—the son of Onan—the son of Eliakim—the son of Melea—the son of Menna[33]—the son of Mattatha
—the son of Nathan—the son of David—the son of Jesse—the son of Obed—the son of Boaz—the son of Salmon—the
son of Nahshon—the son of Aminadab—the son of Aram—the son of Hezron—the son of Perez—the son of Judah—the
son of Jacob—the son of Isaac—the son of Abraham—the son of Terah—the son of Nahor—the son of Serug—the son
of Reu—the son of Peleg—the son of Eber—the son of Shelah—the son of Cainan—the son of Arphaxad—the son of
Shem—the son of Noah—the son of Lemech—the son of Methuselah—the son of Enoch—the son of Jared—the son
of Mehalalel—the son of Kenan—the son of Enosh—the son of Seth—the son of Adam—the son of GOD.)[34]

Jesus returned from the Jordan inspired, and was led by the Spirit into the wilderness where he was tempted by the Devil for forty days. He ate nothing during this period, and when it was finished he was starving. So the Devil said to him, 'If you are the Son of God, why don't you tell this stone to become bread?'

Jesus replied, 'Because it is stated, "Man is not to live by bread alone."'[35]

Then he carried him off to show him all the kingdoms of the Empire[36] in an instant of time. 'I will make you master of all this, with all their resources,' said the Devil, 'because it is given wholly into my power, and I can confer it on whom I please. You have only to pay me homage and it shall be yours.'

'It is stated,' Jesus replied, ' "You are to pay homage to the Lord your God and to worship him alone."'[37]

Next he took him to Jerusalem, and stationed him on a turret of the Temple, and said to him, 'If you are the Son of God, throw yourself down from here. For it is stated, "He will instruct his angels about you to take care of you. They shall cradle you on their hands in case you should strike your foot against a stone."'[38]

Jesus replied, 'It is said, "You are not to put the Lord your God to the proof."'[39]

Having fully completed his tempting the Devil left him for the time being.

Jesus returned to Galilee as a powerful preacher, and was the talk of the whole district. When he taught in their synagogues everyone applauded him.[40]

[32] Or Jehoram.　　　　[33] Or Menahem.
[34] This genealogy traces the descent of Jesus from David through Nathan, while that in *Matthew* is through Solomon.
[35] Deut. viii. 3.
[36] Lit. 'the inhabited world', often used of the Roman Empire.
[37] Deut. vi. 13.　　　　[38] Ps. xci. 11-12.　　　　[39] Deut. vi. 16.
[40] The Hebrew equivalent of 'Bravo!' was used by the congregation at the end of a good preacher's discourse.

Then he came to Nazareth where he had grown up, and went into the synagogue, as he habitually did on the sabbath days, and stood up to read. The scroll of the Prophet Isaiah was handed to him, and having opened the book he found the place where it was written,

> 'The Spirit of the Lord is on me,
> By which means he has anointed me,
> To give good news to the wretched.
> He has sent me to proclaim
> Release to the prisoners,
> The light of day for those denied it;
> To set broken men at liberty,
> To proclaim the Lord's amnesty year.'[41]

After reading this passage he rolled up the scroll, returned it to the assistant, and sat down. The eyes of everyone in the synagogue were turned on him.

'To-day in your hearing this Scripture is accomplished,' he began his address.

He carried his audience with him, spellbound by the cheering words that fell from his lips. 'Can this be Joseph's son?' they said.

He went on, 'No doubt you will quote to me the proverb "Doctor cure yourself!" All that we have heard you have done at Capernaum do here in your native town. I tell you truly, no prophet is accepted in his native place. I must plainly point out to you that there were many widows in Israel in Elijah's time, when heaven was shut for three-and-a-half years and the whole land suffered a severe famine, but Elijah was sent to none of them except a widow woman of Sidonian Sarepta. There were also many lepers in Israel when Elisha was prophet, but none of them was cleansed except Naaman the Syrian.'

On hearing this everyone in the synagogue was outraged,[42] and rose up to eject him from the town. They hustled him to the brow of the hill on which their town was built with the intention of throwing him down. But he extricated himself from them and went away.

He came down to the Galilean town of Capernaum, and taught there on the sabbaths; and they were astonished at his teaching because his message had the force of authority.

In that synagogue there was a man possessed by a foul demon, which screamed out, 'Ai! What do you want with us, Jesus the Nazarene? Have you come to destroy us? I know who you are, the Holy One of God!'[43]

[41] Isa. lxi. 1-2. The year A.D. 26-27 was a Sabbatical Year, the year of release.
[42] The Syrians at this time were mortal enemies of the Galileans. It was therefore most offensive to them that Jesus should instance how two Syrians had been preferred to all Israel. See Jos. *Antiq.* XIV. ix. 2.
[43] See above p. 52, n. 6.

Jesus rebuked it. 'Be quiet,' he said, 'and come out of him.'

When the demon had hurled the man out in front it went out of him without doing him any injury.

They were all overcome with amazement, and turned to one another saying, 'What can it mean? He commands foul spirits with power and authority, and they come out!' The whole district was set talking about him.

Rising from the synagogue he went to Simon's house. Simon's mother-in-law was in a high fever, and they told him about her. Standing over her he rebuked the fever and it left her. So she got up at once and waited on them.

As the sun set all who had those who were ailing with various complaints brought them to him, and he laid his hands on each of them and cured them. From many of them demons came out crying, 'You are the Son of God!' But rebuking them he would not let them speak, because they knew him to be the Messiah. Going out at daybreak he set off into the country. But the crowds went in search of him, and when they came up with him they hemmed him in so that he should not leave them.

'There are other towns as well,' he told them, 'to which I must proclaim the Kingdom of God. It was for that purpose I was sent.'

So he preached in the various synagogues of Judea.[44]

CHAPTER IV

At one time, with the crowd pressing heavily upon him to hear God's Message, Jesus stood beside Lake Gennesaret. Then he noticed two boats drawn up by the lake, but the fishermen had got out of them to clean their nets. Going on board one of them—it was Simon's—he asked him to put out a little from the land, and sitting down he taught the crowd from the boat.

When he had finished speaking, he said to Simon, 'Now put out into deep water, and let down your nets for a catch.'

'We've toiled all night long, chief, and caught nothing,' Simon replied, 'but if you say so I will lower the nets.'

Having done this they enclosed a large shoal of fish, and their nets broke. They made signs to their partners in the other boat to come to their assistance. So they came and filled both the boats to sinking point.

When he saw this Simon Peter fell at Jesus's knees saying, 'Leave me, sir, for I am a sinful man!'[a]

James and John, the sons of Zebedee, who were Simon's associates, echoed his words.

'Don't be afraid,' Jesus told Simon. 'From now on your job will be catching men alive.'

[a] He was overcome with amazement, as were those with him, at the haul of fish they had caught.

[44] Judea is incorrectly put for Galilee, Mk. i. 39, above p. 53. Lk. appears to think of all Jewish territory in Palestine as Judea, reflecting the administrative position after A.D. 40. See again below pp. 187, 193.

When they had brought their boats to land they abandoned everything and followed him.

In one of the towns he visited there was a man covered with leprosy. When he saw Jesus he fell on his face entreating him, 'Sir, you can cleanse me if only you will.'

Stretching out his hand he touched him saying, 'I do will it. Be cleansed!'

At once his leprosy left him. He ordered him to tell no one, but to go and show himself to the priest, and offer for his cleansing what Moses prescribed as evidence to them. Yet more than ever the word got about concerning him, and crowds gathered to hear him and to be cured of their complaints. But Jesus retired to the open country to engage in prayer.

It happened one day when he was teaching that there were Pharisees and doctors of the Law sitting there, who had come from various Galilean villages, and from Judea and Jerusalem. He was exercising the Lord's curative power. Just then some men arrived bringing on a mattress a man who was paralysed. They tried to bring him in to lay him before Jesus; but unable to find a way to get him through the crowd they mounted to the top of the house and lowered him on a mattress through the tiling directly in front of Jesus. Seeing what faith they had he said, 'Man, your sins are forgiven.'

The scribes and Pharisees started arguing, 'Who is this who talks blasphemously? Who but God alone can forgive sins?'

Jesus was aware of their discussion and said to them, 'What are you debating in your minds? Which is easier, to say "Your sins are forgiven," or to say, "Rise and walk?" But that you may know that the Son of Man is entitled to forgive sins on earth'— he addressed the paralytic, 'To you I say, "Rise, pick up your mattress, and go to your home!"'

At once he stood up before them, picked up his bed, and went to his home praising God. They were all astounded, and praised God, murmuring fearfully, 'We have seen extraordinary things to-day.'

When he went out later he observed a tax-collector called Levi seated at the customs-station, and said to him, 'Follow me!' Leaving everything he got up and followed him.

Then Levi gave a big reception for him at his house, with a large company of tax-collectors and others dining with them. The Pharisees and their scribes voiced their protests to Jesus's disciples. 'Why do you eat and drink with tax-collectors and sinners?' they said.

It was Jesus who answered them, 'It is not the healthy who need a doctor, but those who are ill. I have not come to summon religious people, but sinners, to repentance.'

They said, 'John's disciples fast regularly and say the prescribed prayers, exactly like the Pharisees, but yours eat and drink.'

'You cannot expect the bridal party to fast while the bridegroom is with them,' Jesus told them. 'The time will come when the bridegroom will have taken leave of them: that will be the time for them to fast.'

He added this illustration. 'No one puts a piece rent from a new cloak on an old one. If he does, not only does he tear the new, but the piece from the new is out of keeping with the old. Neither does anyone pour new wine into old wine-skins. If he does, the new wine splits the wine-skins, and is spilt itself, and the skins are destroyed. No, new wine is poured into new skins. Nor does anyone want new wine after drinking the old. "You can't beat the old," he says.'[45]

Now on the sabbath he happened to take his way through the standing corn, and his disciples picked and ate the ears, rubbing them between their hands. But some of the Pharisees said, 'Why are you doing what is not allowed on the sabbath?'

Jesus answered them, 'Have you never read what David did when he and his companions were hungry, how he went into the house of God and took the loaves of the Presence and ate them, and shared them with his companions, loaves which only the priests were allowed to eat?' Then he added, 'The Son of Man is master of the sabbath.'[46]

When he went to the synagogue to teach on another sabbath there was a man there whose right hand was withered. The scribes and the Pharisees watched him closely to see whether he would cure on the sabbath, so that they could obtain evidence on which to charge him. Knowing what was in their minds, he said to the man with the withered hand, 'Rise, and come up in front.'

He stood up and came forward.

Then Jesus said to them, 'I put it to you, which is the right thing on the sabbath, well-doing or evil-doing, saving life or destroying it?' Having looked around at them all, he said to the man, 'Stretch out your hand.' He did so, and his hand was restored. They were furious and talked together of what they could do to Jesus.

CHAPTER V

Now at that time Jesus went off to the hill to pray, and was all night long in prayer to God. When it was day he called his disciples, and chose twelve of them, whom he termed envoys. There was Simon, whom he named Peter, and his brother Andrew, James and John, Philip and Bartholomew, Matthew and Thomas, James son of Alphaeus and Simon called the Zealot, Judas son of James and Judas Iscariot, who turned traitor.

[45] Both the form and point of the illustration differ from *Mark's* version (Mk. ii. 21-22, above p. 54-55).

[46] Codex D. inserts: 'The same day, observing someone working on the sabbath, he told him, "My man, if you know what you are about you are blessed, but if you do not know, you are accursed and a violater of the Law."'

Descending with them he stood on a level space with a large body of his disciples, and a mass of the people drawn from all over Judea, from Jerusalem, and from the seaboard of Tyre and Sidon, who had come to hear him and to be cured of their diseases; and those who were troubled with foul spirits were given relief. Indeed the whole crowd tried to touch him, because power emanated from him and cured everyone.

Then looking at his disciples he said, 'How fortunate are you poor! Yours is the Kingdom of God. How fortunate are you who hunger now! You shall be satisfied. How fortunate are you who weep now! You shall laugh. How fortunate are you when men detest you, and when they ostracize you, vilify you, and stigmatize all of your kind as bad on the Son of Man's account![47] Rejoice when that happens, and jump for joy, for rich is your recompense in heaven. Their forefathers treated the prophets exactly the same.

'But woe to you rich! You have had your good cheer. Woe to you who have had your fill now! You shall go hungry. Woe to you who laugh now! You shall mourn and weep.[48] Woe to you when all men speak well of you! Their forefathers treated the false prophets exactly the same.

'To all of you who are listening I say, love your enemies, treat well those who hate you, bless those who curse you, pray for those who abuse you. To him who hits you on the right side of the jaw offer him the other as well, and from him who takes your tunic do not withhold your cloak also. Give to all who ask you, and from him who takes your belongings do not demand them back. As you would have people treat you, treat them the same way.

'If you only love those who love you, what virtue is that of yours? Even the sinners love those who love them. And if you treat well those who treat you well, what virtue is that of yours? Even the sinners do that. And if you lend to those from whom you expect to receive, what virtue is that of yours? Sinners lend to sinners on a reciprocal basis. Rather love your enemies and treat them well, and lend without expectation of return. Then you will have a rich recompense, and be sons of the Most High, who is kind to the ungrateful and evil. Be as compassionate as your Father is compassionate.

'Refrain from judging, and you will not be judged. Refrain from condemning, and you will not be condemned. Acquit, and you will be acquitted. Give, and it will be given you. Good measure, pressed down, shaken together, and brimming over, they will tip into your lap: for the measure you will use will be used for you.'

He also addressed them in proverbs.[49]

'Can a blind man guide a blind man? Will not both tumble into the ditch?

[47] See *Test. Judah*, xxv. 4. [48] See *Enoch*, xciv.
[49] See notes to pp. 96-97.

'The disciple is not superior to his teacher; but when fully trained he has the standing of his teacher.

'How is it you can see the splinter in your brother's eye, but cannot detect the shaft in your own eye? How can you say to your brother, "Allow me to extract the splinter from your eye," when you fail to see the shaft in your own? Hypocrite! First extract the shaft from your own eye, and then you will see clearly to extract the splinter from your brother's eye.

'No good tree produces harmful fruit, nor yet does a harmful tree produce good fruit. By its own fruit, therefore, will each tree be recognized.

'They do not pick figs from thorns, nor do they gather grape-clusters from brambles. The good man from his mind's good store gives out good, while the evil man from his evil store gives out evil; for what his mind is stocked with his mouth speaks.

'Why do you call me "Master, Master!" and do not do what I say? I will show you what a man is like who comes to me and hears my sayings and carries them out. He is like a man building a house, who dug deep down and laid his foundation on rock. When a flood came and the torrent dashed against that house, it failed to shake it because it was well-built. But whoever has heard my sayings and has not carried them out is like a man who built his house on the surface without a foundation.[50] When the torrent dashed against it it immediately collapsed, and great was the ruin of that house.'

When he had completed all he had to say for the benefit of the people he went to Capernaum. There a centurion's servant, whom he greatly prized, had reached the crisis of a serious illness. Having heard about Jesus he dispatched elders of the Jews to him, begging him to come and see his servant safely through. When they reached Jesus they earnestly entreated him saying, 'He deserves to be granted this request; for he loves our people, and had the synagogue built for us himself.'

So Jesus went with them. But he had not gone far, being still some distance from the house, when the centurion sent friends to him to say, 'Sir, do not inconvenience yourself. I am no fit person for you to come under my roof. Neither for the same reason did I regard myself as worthy to come and see you. Simply command it, and my orderly will be cured. For even I am a man subject to authority,[51] with soldiers under me. I say to one, "Go," and he goes, and to another, "Do this," and he does it.'

Jesus was amazed at hearing this, and turning to the crowd that followed him he said, 'I tell you, not even in Israel have I found faith like this.'

[50] It is to be observed here and elsewhere that Luke sometimes adapts the wording of his source to suit conditions more familiar to his readers. In this instance he changes the comparison with a house built on sand.

[51] Cp. the words used by the Roman legate Petronius to the Jews gathered at Tiberias in Galilee in trying to persuade them to accept the erection of Caligula's statue in the Temple. Josephus quotes him as saying, 'For I am subject to authority as well as you' (*Wars*, II. x. 4).

When those who had been sent had returned to the house they found the servant better.

The next day he went to a town called Nain,[52] and his disciples with a large crowd accompanied him. As he approached the gate of the town a dead man was being carried out, the only child of his widowed mother; and a crowd from the town was with her. On seeing her the Master took pity on her, and said to her, 'Please don't weep.'

Advancing, he touched the coffin, and the bearers halted. Then he said, 'Young man, I bid you wake!'

The young man sat up and began to speak; and he restored him to his mother.[53]

Everyone was seized with fear, and praised God saying, 'A great prophet has risen among us, and God has visited his people.'

This saying about him was spread everywhere in Judea as well as throughout the vicinity.

CHAPTER VII

To John his disciples brought word of all these events, and calling to him a certain two of his disciples he sent them to the Master to ask, 'Are you the Destined One, or should we expect someone else?'

When they reached him the men said, 'John the Baptist has sent us to you to ask, "Are you the Destined One, or should we expect someone else?" '

He was engaged at the time in curing many of diseases, plagues, and evil spirits, and blessing with sight many who were blind. This was the answer he gave them, 'Go and tell John what you have seen and heard, the blind see again, the lame walk, the lepers are cleansed, the deaf hear, the dead are awakened, the poor are given good news; and fortunate is he who has no misgivings about me.'

When John's messengers had left he began to speak to the crowds about John. 'What did you go out into the wilderness to look at, a cane shaken by the wind?[54] Or did you go out to see something else, a man enveloped in soft draperies?[55] Surely those who possess fine and delicate clothing are to be found in palaces. What then did you go out to see, a prophet? Yes, I tell you, and much more than a prophet. He it is of whom it was stated, "See, I will send my messenger before you, to pave the way for you."[56] I tell you, none born of women is greater than John, yet the most insignificant in the Kingdom of God is greater than he.'

All the people, even the tax-collectors, as they listened declared God just, having undergone John's rite of immersion.

---

[52] More correctly Naim.
[53] Cp. I. Kings xvii. 23.
[54] See above p. 103, n. 73.
[55] Above p. 103, n. 74.
[56] Mal. iii. 1.

But the Pharisees and doctors of the Law had disregarded God's wishes as it affected themselves in not being immersed by him.

'To what shall I compare the men of this generation?' Jesus continued. 'What are they like? They are like children squatting in the market-place calling out to each other,

"We've played you a jig, but you haven't danced.
We've played a lament, but you haven't mourned."

For John the Baptist came neither eating bread nor drinking wine and you say, "He is demon-possessed." The Son of Man came both eating and drinking and you say, "There you are, a glutton and a drunkard, an associate of tax-collectors and sinners." Yet "Wisdom is vindicated by all her children." '[57]

One of the Pharisees was anxious for him to dine with him. So he entered the Pharisee's house and reclined at table. Now there was a woman in the town known to be a sinner. When she learnt that he was a guest at the Pharisee's house she brought an alabaster flask of perfume and stood behind at his feet weeping, bathing his feet with her tears, and drying them with her hair. Then she caressed his feet and anointed them with the perfume. Seeing this, the Pharisee who was entertaining Jesus said to himself, 'If he were a prophet he would be aware what kind of woman she is who is touching him: he would know she is a sinner.'

Then Jesus turned to him and said, 'There is something I wish to say to you, Simon.'

'By all means, teacher,' he replied.

'There were two debtors of a certain moneylender. One owed him five hundred dinars[58] and the other fifty. Neither of them being able to pay he showed them both consideration. Which of them, then, will have most regard for him?'

'I assume,' answered Simon, 'the one to whom he showed most consideration.'

'You have judged correctly,' he told him.

Then turning to the woman he said to Simon, 'You see this woman? When I entered your house you gave me no water for my feet, but she has bathed my feet with her tears, and dried them with her hair. You gave me no kiss, but she, ever since she came in, has not left off caressing my feet. You did not anoint my head with oil, but she has anointed my feet with perfume. For that very reason, I tell you, her many sins are forgiven, because she showed respect. But one to whom there has been little to be forgiven shows slight respect.

'Your sins are forgiven,' he told her.

The other guests said to themselves, 'Who does he think he is that he even forgives sins?'

But he told the woman, 'Your faith has saved you. Go in peace.'

Thereafter he made a personal tour of every town and village,

[57] Exact source unknown, see p. 104, n. 79.
[58] A dinar is equal to about 9½d.

preaching and giving out the news of the Kingdom of God. The twelve went with him, and certain women whom he had cured of evil spirits and various ailments. There was Mary, called Magdalene, from whom seven demons had come out, and Johanna wife of Chuza, Herod's chancellor, Susanna, and many others, who attended to his needs from their means.

When a large crowd had gathered, drawn to him from the various towns, he addressed them in similes.

'The sower went out to sow his seed, and as he sowed some fell by the roadside and was trampled on, and the birds of the air ate it up. Other seed fell on the rock, and when it sprouted withered away from lack of moisture. Other seed fell among thistles, and the thistles sprang up with it and stifled it. Other seed fell on good soil, sprouted, and yielded a hundredfold crop.' When he had said this he added distinctly, 'Let him who can catch my meaning do so.'

His disciples, however, asked him what the simile meant.

'It is your privilege to know the secrets of the Kingdom of God,' he said, 'but for the others they are expressed in similes, that "while they see they may not perceive, and while they hear they may not understand." [59]

'Here is the meaning of this simile. The seed is God's Message, and those by the roadside are those who having heard it along comes the Devil and picks the Message out of their hearts, in case they should believe it and be saved. Those on the rock are those who welcome the Message with joy when they hear it; but these have no root: they believe for a while, but when the testing time comes they shrink away. What fell among thistles means those who have heard, but get themselves stifled with cares and riches and the pleasures of life, and never ripen. What fell on good soil means those who have heard the Message with a good and honest heart, possess themselves of it and bear fruit sturdily.

'No one lights a lamp to conceal it in a jar or put it under a bed: he sets it on a lampstand that those who enter may see the light. All this, then, is not concealed to remain undetected, nor hidden away that it should not be known and brought into the open. So listen very carefully; for to him who has shall be given, but from him who has not even what he seems to have shall be taken away.'

Then his mother and brothers came to him, but they could not get to him because of the crowd. He was informed, 'Your mother and brothers are standing outside wishing to see you.'

'My mother and brothers,' he replied, 'are those who hear God's Message and carry it out.'

One day both he and his disciples went on board ship, and he said to them, 'Let us cross to the other side of the lake.'

So they put to sea. But as they sailed he fell asleep.

Then a heavy squall of wind swept down on the lake, so that

[59] Isa vi. 9.

they were being swamped and in great danger. They went and woke him crying, 'Chief, chief, we are lost!'

When he was awake he rebuked wind and wave, and they ceased and were calm. 'Where is your faith?' he said to them.

Fearful and astounded they said to one another, 'Who can he be that he commands both the winds and the water and they obey him?'

They came to shore in the country of the Gerasenes, which lies opposite Galilee. No sooner had he landed than he was met by a man of their city who was demon-possessed. For a considerable time he had worn no clothes, and lived not in a house but in the tombs. Shrieking out directly he saw Jesus he fell down before him crying loudly, 'What do you want with me, Jesus, Son of the Most High God? Please do not torture me!'

That was because he had ordered the foul spirit to leave the man; for it had frequently seized him in its clutches, and he had been bound protectively with chains and fetters. But he had snapped his bonds, and had been driven by the demon into the wilderness.

Jesus asked him, 'What is your name?'

'Legion,' he replied, for a horde of demons had entered him. They begged him not to order them off to the Abyss.

Now there was a herd of a sufficient number of swine feeding on the hillside; and they begged him to give them permission to enter these. So he gave them permission. Abandoning the man the demons entered the swine and the herd made a wild dash down the slope into the lake and were drowned.

When they saw what had happened the herdsmen ran off and told their tale to town and farm; and the people went to see what had happened and came to Jesus. There they found the man from whom the demons had gone out seated clothed and sane at Jesus's feet, and they were afraid. But those who had been on-lookers informed them how the demon-possessed man had been cured. Nevertheless the entire population of the Gerasene district asked him to leave them, for they were in the grip of mortal fear. So going on board ship he took his departure, though the man from whom the demons had gone out begged to come with him. He sent him away, however, saying, 'Return home, and relate all that God has done for you.'

But he went away and proclaimed all over the city all that Jesus had done for him.

On Jesus's return the crowd gave him a hearty welcome, for they were all on the look-out for him. Then came a man called Jair, president of the synagogue, and fell at Jesus's feet begging him to come to his house as his only daughter, aged about twelve, was dying. As he was taking him there the crowds hemmed him in tightly. One woman, who had had a haemorrhage for twelve years which no one had been able to cure, managed to reach him from behind and touch the tassel of his cloak, and instantly her haemorrhage ceased.

'Who touched me?' exclaimed Jesus.

When everyone disclaimed responsibility Peter said, 'The whole crowd is pressing and crushing you.'

'Someone did touch me,' Jesus persisted, 'for I can feel that power has been drawn from me.'

Seeing that she had not escaped notice the woman came forward trembling, and prostrating herself before him declared in front of all the people why she had touched him and how she was instantly cured.

'Daughter,' he told her, 'your faith has cured you. Go in peace.'

While he was speaking someone came for the president of the synagogue to say, 'Your daughter has died. Do not trouble the teacher further.'

But Jesus overhearing told him, 'Don't be afraid. Simply believe, and she will be spared.'

On reaching the house he would allow none to enter but Peter, John and James, and the child's father and mother. Everyone was weeping and mourning for her. 'Do not weep,' he said. 'She is not dead, only asleep.'

But they jeered at him, aware that she was dead. He, however, took her by the hand and cried out, 'Wake up, child!' And her spirit returned, and she rose instantly; and he ordered food to be given her. Her parents were transported with joy; but he insisted that they should tell no one what had happened.

CHAPTER VII

When Jesus had called the twelve together he gave them power and authority over all demons, as well as to cure diseases. Then he dispatched them to proclaim the Kingdom of God and to heal. 'Take nothing with you on your journeys,' he told them, 'neither staff, nor wallet, nor food, nor money, not even two tunics. At whatever house you enter stay there until you have to leave again. Where they will not receive you, when you leave that town shake off the dust from your feet as a testimony to them.'

So on their departure they went from village to village proclaiming the News and effecting cures everywhere.

Now Herod the tetrarch heard of all these occurrences and was quite at a loss, as it was being said by some that John had risen from the dead, by others that Elijah had appeared, and by others that one of the prophets of old had come to life. Said Herod, 'I have beheaded John. Who then can this be of whom I hear such things?' And he endeavoured to see him.

When the envoys returned they related to Jesus everything they had done. Receiving them back he quietly withdrew to a town called Bethsaida. But the populace becoming aware of it followed him, and welcoming them he spoke to them of the

Kingdom of God and cured those who stood in need of healing.

As the day declined the twelve approached him and said, 'Dismiss the crowd that they may go to the neighbouring villages and farms and get accommodation and procure provisions, for here we are in open country.'

'You feed them yourselves,' he replied.

'But we have no more than five loaves and two fish,' they said. 'Unless you expect us to go and buy food for all these people?'[a]

'Get them seated in parties of about fifty,' he told his disciples.

So they did this and sat everybody down. Then taking the five loaves and two fish he looked up to heaven, said a blessing for them, broke, and handed them to his disciples to give out to the people. They all ate and were satisfied, and twelve basketfuls were picked up of the fragments they left over.

Once when he was praying alone his disciples joined him, and he asked them, 'Who do people say I am?'

'John the Baptist,' they replied, 'though others say Elijah, and others one of the prophets of old come to life.'

'And you,' he said, 'who do you say I am?'

'You are God's Anointed,' Peter answered.

He gave them strict instructions to tell no one this, declaring that the Son of Man must endure such suffering, and be rejected by the elders, head priests and scribes, and be killed, and be raised again on the third day.

Publicly he said, 'Whoever would follow me must be truly reckless, and take up his cross daily and follow me. For whoever would preserve his life will lose it; but whoever loses his life for me will preserve it. For how will it benefit a man to have gained the whole world and to perish or forfeit himself? Whoever, therefore, is disdainful of me and of my words will find the Son of Man disdainful of him when he comes in his own and the Father's splendour, and that of the holy angels. I tell you positively, there are some standing here now who will not experience death before they see the Kingdom of God.'

Some eight days after he had said this he took with him Peter, John and James, and ascended the mountain to pray. As he was praying the appearance of his face changed and his clothing turned a dazzling white. And now two men were conversing with him. These were Moses and Elijah, who appeared in glory and discussed his exodus[60] which he was soon to solemnize at Jerusalem. Peter and his companions were weighed down with sleep, but they became wide awake when they saw his splendour and the two men standing with him. Then as these were vanishing Peter said to Jesus, 'Chief, how fortunate

[a] There were about five thousand men.

[60] The Passover commemorated the Exodus of Israel from Egypt. It appears that the Crucifixion was interpreted as the Exodus of Israel (Jesus) from Egypt (Jerusalem), see Rev. xi. 6, where again the Two Witnesses seem to represent Moses and Elijah, below p. 452.

we are to be here! Now let us put up three bowers, one for you, one for Moses, and one for Elijah,' not realizing what he was saying.

As he was speaking there came a cloud, and cast a shadow over them, and they grew fearful as they entered the cloud. Then a voice spoke out of the cloud, 'He is my chosen Son. Listen to him.'

When the voice finished Jesus was found to be alone.

They kept silent at the time, and said nothing to anyone of what they had seen.

The next day a considerable crowd met him when they came down from the mountain. One man in the crowd cried out, 'Do take a look at my son, teacher. He is all I have, and there is a spirit that seizes him, and he will suddenly cry out; and it convulses him accompanied by foaming at the mouth, and leaves him with such difficulty as to shatter him completely. I begged your disciples to expel it, but they were quite unable to do so.'

'O faithless and perverse generation!' Jesus replied. 'How long must I be with you? How long must I bear with you? Bring your son here.'

But even as he came forward the demon threw him down and convulsed him. Jesus, however, rebuked the foul spirit, and cured the lad, and restored him to his father. All were amazed at God's superlative power.

While everyone was wondering about all he was doing, he said to his disciples, 'Get this clear, the Son of Man is to be delivered into the hands of the authorities.' But they did not catch his meaning, and were prevented from grasping it; and they were afraid to ask him for an explanation. A dispute, however, arose between them as to which of them would be greatest. Then Jesus, realizing what was going on in their minds, took a little boy and placing him at his side said to them, 'Whoever accepts this little boy for my sake accepts me, and whoever accepts me accepts him who sent me. So it is the most unassuming of you all who will be great.'

John said, 'Chief, we saw someone expelling demons in your name, but we stopped him because he does not belong to our company.'

'Do not stop him,' Jesus told him, 'for he who is not against you is on your side.'

CHAPTER VIII

Now when the time was due for him to be taken up, Jesus turned firmly towards Jerusalem, and dispatched messengers ahead of him. As they went forward they entered a Samaritan village to make preparations for him. But the people would not give him welcome because he was bent on going to Jerusalem. When his disciples James and John saw this they said, 'Master, will you have us invoke fire to descend from heaven to consume them, as Elijah did?' But he turned and rebuked them,[61] and they went on to another village.

As they were travelling along the road a man said to them, 'I will follow you wherever you go.'

'The foxes have their lairs,' Jesus told him, 'and the birds of the air their nests, but the Son of Man has no place where he may lay his head.'

To another he said, 'Follow me.' But he answered, 'First give me leave to go and bury my father.'

'Leave the dead to bury their own dead,' said Jesus, 'while you go and proclaim the Kingdom of God.'

There was still another who said, 'I will join you, sir, but first give me leave to say good-bye to those at home.'

'No one who sets his hand to the plough and looks backward is of any use to the Kingdom of God,' Jesus told him.

Later the Master nominated seventy others, and sent them ahead of him in pairs to every town and village he intended to visit. 'The harvest is plentiful,' he advised them, 'but the labourers are few. Entreat the Harvest-master to furnish adequate labour for his harvest.

'Now go! I am sending you like lambs into the midst of wolves. Carry no purse, no pack, no shoes. Do not stop to talk to anyone on the road. When you are about to enter a house first say, "Peace be on this house." If the occupant is peaceable your peace will rest upon him; but if he is otherwise it will revert to you. Stay in the one house, eating and drinking what they provide; for "the workman is entitled to his wages". Don't go wandering from house to house. Equally, when you have entered a town where you are welcomed, eat what they offer you and cure the sick people in it, and tell them, "For you the Kingdom of God is at hand." But when you enter a town where you are not welcomed announce in its public highways, "We will take nothing from your town. We wipe ourselves clean even of the particles of dust that stick to our feet. But you may as well know that the Kingdom of God is at hand." I tell you, when that day comes it will be more tolerable for Sodom than for that town.

'Woe to you, Chorazin! Woe to you, Bethsaida! For if the miracles had been performed in Tyre and Sidon that have been performed in you they would long since have repented in sack-cloth and ashes. However, when the Judgment comes it will be more tolerable for Tyre and Sidon than for you. You too, Capernaum! Will you be raised to heaven? No, you will be brought down to hell.

'Whoever gives heed to you gives heed to me, and whoever ignores you ignores me. And whoever ignores me ignores him who sent me.'

[61] II. Kings i. 10. Some MSS. add, 'And said, "You do not realize the kind of spirit you represent. The Son of Man has not come to destroy men's lives but to preserve them." '

The seventy returned delighted. 'Master,' they said, 'in your name even the demons obey us.'

Jesus told them, 'I saw Satan fall like lightning from heaven. I have indeed invested you with power to stamp on snakes and scorpions, and on every minion of the Enemy; and nothing whatever shall harm you. Nevertheless, do not rejoice simply because the spirits are subject to you: rather rejoice that your names are registered in heaven.'

Moved to ecstasy by the holy Spirit at that moment, he exclaimed, 'I acknowledge unto thee, Father, Lord of heaven and earth, that thou hast hidden these matters from the sage and prudent and hast disclosed them to babes. Even so, Father, for so it seemed good in thy sight.

'Everything has been made over to me by my Father, yet no one esteems the Son except the Father, nor the Father except the Son, and he to whom the Son chooses to reveal him.'

Then turning to his disciples exclusively he said, 'How fortunate are the eyes that see what you see! I can tell you that many prophets and kings have wanted to see what you see, but have not seen it, and to hear what you hear, but have not heard it.'

Now a certain lawyer rose to test him saying, 'Teacher, what am I to do to inherit Eternal Life?'

Jesus replied, 'What is stated in the Law? What do you read there?'

He said, 'You are to love the Lord your God with your whole heart, and your whole soul, with your whole strength, and with your whole mind, and your neighbour as yourself.'[62]

'You have answered correctly,' Jesus told him. 'Do that, and you will live.'

But wanting to make quite certain he said to Jesus, 'But what is meant by "my neighbour"?'

In answer Jesus said, 'A man went down from Jerusalem to Jericho and was waylaid by robbers,[63] who stripped him and beat him and made off, leaving him half dead. Now a priest happened to be taking that road, and seeing him there gave him a wide berth.[64] It was the same with a Levite who came to the place, and seeing him gave him a wide berth. But a travelling Samaritan came upon him, and moved to pity at seeing him, approached him and bandaged his injuries, pouring on oil and wine. Then laying him across his own beast he conveyed him to a hostelry and took care of him. When departing on the morrow he gave two dinars to the host with the injunction, "Look after him well, and I will reimburse you for any additional expense on my return journey." Which of these three, do you think, acted as neighbour to the man waylaid by robbers?'

'The one who treated him compassionately,' he replied.

[62] Deut. vi. 5, with Lev. xix. 18.
[63] Travellers were very liable to be attacked in the wild and precipitous country through which the Jerusalem-Jericho road passed.
[64] To avoid the ritual defilement caused by contact with a corpse.

'Go, then,' said Jesus, 'and act in the same way.'

As they journeyed on he entered a certain village, and a woman there called Martha welcomed him to her home. She had a sister called Mary, who seated herself at the Master's feet to listen to his discourse. But Martha was preoccupied with her various duties. Pausing beside him she said, 'Master, aren't you concerned that my sister should let me do all the waiting myself? Please tell her to give me a hand.'

'Martha, Martha,' the Master replied, 'you are anxious and distracted about many things, when only one is essential. Mary has selected that important function, and she shall not be deprived of it.'

When he was engaged in prayer at one place, one of his disciples said to him as he finished, 'Master, teach us a prayer just as John taught his disciples.'

'Whenever you pray,' he told them, 'say, "Father, let thy name be sanctified, let thy Kingdom be inaugurated. Give us daily our needful food; and forgive us our sins, for we ourselves forgive everyone obligated to us. And do not bring us into temptation."

'Take any one of you who have a friend,' he continued, 'and you go to him in the middle of the night and say, "Please lend me three loaves, for a friend of mine has arrived unexpectedly at my place, and I have nothing to offer him." But his friend answers from inside, "Don't bother me. The door is already bolted, and my family and I are all in bed. I cannot get up and give you anything." I tell you, if he will not get up to give him anything because he is his friend, yet because of his very effrontery he will bestir himself to give him as much as ever he wants. So I say to you, ask and you will be given, seek and you will find, knock and you will obtain entry; for whoever asks receives, the seeker finds, and for the knocker the door is opened.

'Take any father among you, if his son asks for fish will he give him a snake instead of a fish? Or if he asks for an egg will he give him a scorpion? If you then, bad as you are, know you must give good gifts to your children, how much more will your heavenly Father give holy Spirit to those who ask him?'

He was once expelling a dumb demon; and when the demon had gone out the dumb man spoke. The crowds were amazed, but some of them said, 'It is by Beelzebul the chief of the demons he expels the demons.' Others, to tempt him, wanted him to furnish a sign from heaven. But knowing their thoughts he told them, 'Every kingdom divided against itself is brought to ruin, and house topples on house. So if Satan is divided against himself, how will his kingdom endure? For you say it is by Beelzebul I expel the demons. If then it is by Beelzebul I expel the demons, by whom do your children expel them? Therefore they shall be your judges. But if I expel the demons by the finger of God then the Kingdom of God has caught you unawares.

'When the Strong One fully armed guards his own place his

property is safe. But when a mightier than he comes along and conquers him, he secures the armour on which he relied and distributes his spoils. Whoever is not on my side opposes me, and whoever is not gathering with me scatters. When the foul spirit leaves a man it traverses arid zones seeking relief and finding none. Then it decides, "I will go back to my old home." When it gets there it finds it swept clean and tidied up. Then it sets off and procures seven other spirits more noxious than itself, and in they go and live there; so the last state of that man is worse than the first.'

As he said this a woman in the crowd raised her voice and cried out, 'Blessed is the womb that bore you and the breasts you have sucked!'

'No,' he said. 'Blessed are those who listen to God's Message and obey it.'

To the crowd now grown thick he said, 'This present generation is an evil generation. It requires proof, but no proof will be given it except that of Jonah; for just as Jonah was a proof to the Ninevites, so will the Son of Man be to this generation. The Queen of the South will rise up at the Judgment with the men of this generation, and will damn them; for she came from the lower hemisphere to listen to the wisdom of Solomon, and what is of more consequence than Solomon is here.

'No one lights a lamp to put it in a cupboard or under a measuring-bowl, but on a lampstand, so that those who come in may see the light. Your eye is the lamp of your body. When your sight is sound your whole body will be radiant; but when it is bad your whole body will be in gloom. See to it, then, that the light that is in you does not become darkness. So if your whole body is radiant, with no trace of gloom, it will be lit up as completely as when the lamp illumines you with its light.'

When he had spoken so far, a Pharisee invited him to lunch with him. He accepted, and took his place at table. The Pharisee was rather surprised when he observed that he did not wash first before lunch. But the Master said to him, 'You know, you Pharisees are at pains to clean the outside of cups and plates, while your insides are full of rapacity and chicanery. What stupid people you are! Did not he who made the outside also make the inside? Bestow what you have hoarded in charity, and then you will have everything clean right through.

'But woe to you Pharisees! You tithe mint and rue and all kinds of herbs, and pass over justice and the love of God. These are the things you should have attended to without neglecting the others.

'Woe to you Pharisees! You love the chief stall in the synagogues, and salutations in the market-places. Woe to you, because you are like hidden graves, of which those who walk over them are unaware.'[65]

[65] So becoming defiled by contact.

One of the lawyers broke in here. 'Teacher,' he said to him, 'by talking like that you are castigating us as well.'

'Yes, and woe to you too, you lawyers!' Jesus replied. 'You load men with insupportable burdens, but you will not lift a finger to move these burdens yourselves. Woe to you, because you build tombs for the prophets your ancestors killed. Thus you both testify to and express your approval of the deeds of your ancestors, because they did the killing while you do the tomb-building. That is why the Wisdom of God states, "I will send them prophets and envoys, and some of them they will kill, and persecute others, that this generation may be answerable for the blood of all the prophets which has been shed since the foundation of the world, from the blood of Abel to the blood of Zechariah who perished between the altar and the house."[66] Yes, I tell you, this generation shall be answerable for it.

'Woe to you lawyers! You have taken away the key to knowledge. You will not enter yourselves, and you prevent others entering.'

As he was about to leave, the scribes and Pharisees badgered and plied him with questions on many issues, lying in wait to pounce on something he might say.

Meanwhile as the crowd massed in its thousands, so that they trod on one another, he had this to say to his disciples first of all. 'Be on your guard against the leaven of the Pharisees, namely their hypocrisy; for there is nothing covered up that shall not be revealed, or secret that shall not be known. Whatever you may say under the cloak of darkness will be heard in broad daylight, and whatever you may whisper behind closed doors will be shouted from the housetops.

'To you my friends I say, don't be afraid of those who can do no more than kill the body. If you would know whom to fear, fear him who after killing can cast into Gehenna. Are not five sparrows sold for two assars?[67] Yet not one of them escapes God's memory. The very hairs of your head are all counted. You have nothing to fear. You are of more consequence than many sparrows.

'I tell you, whoever identifies himself with me before men, the Son of Man will also identify himself with him before God's angels. But whoever repudiates me before men will be repudiated before God's angels. Whoever says a word against the Son of Man will be forgiven, but slander of the holy Spirit will not be forgiven. And when they bring you before synagogues, rulers and authorities, do not concern yourselves with the manner of your defence, or what you are to say; for the holy Spirit will instruct you at the time what you should say.'

Here one of the crowd called out to him, 'Teacher, tell my brother he must share our inheritance with me.'

[66] See above p. 126, n. 144.
[67] About 1¼d.

'Man,' he replied, 'who constituted me a judge or arbitrator over you?'

Then he addressed them all. 'Be sure you guard yourselves from greed of every kind, because one's life is not assured by the extent of what one possesses.'

He told a story to explain this to them. 'A certain rich man's lands were very productive. So he debated with himself, "What am I going to do, with insufficient space to store my crops? I have it," he said, "I will pull down my barns and build larger ones. There I can store my grain and all other fruits of my good fortune. Then I can say to my soul, Soul, you have an ample fortune laid by for many a year. Now take your ease, eat, drink, and enjoy yourself." But God said to him, "You foolish fellow, this very night your soul will be demanded from you. Whose, then, will be all you have accumulated?" That is the position of the man who hoards for himself but fails to become rich where God is concerned.'

Then he spoke directly to his disciples. 'That is why I tell you, do not vex your souls about what you are to eat, nor how your bodies are to be clothed; for the soul is more important than food, and the body than clothing. Look at the crows. They neither sow nor reap: they have neither storehouse nor barn. Yet God feeds them. Of how much greater consequence are you than birds? And which of you by mental effort can add an ell to his height? If you cannot do what is least, why worry about the rest? Study the wild irises, how they shoot up. They neither toil nor spin. Yet I tell you that not even Solomon in full regalia was arrayed like one of these. If God thus attires the wild plant that blooms to-day and to-morrow is thrown into the oven, shall he not much more clothe you, you feeble in faith? So do not be concerned with what you are to eat and drink, or get yourselves in a state, for with all these matters the nations of the world concern themselves. Your Father knows perfectly well that you need them. Concern yourselves with his Kingdom, and all these things will be added to you.

'Never fear, little flock. Your Father is glad to give you the Kingdom. Sell your possessions, and bestow the proceeds in charity. Provide yourselves with purses that never wear out, treasure never failing in heaven, where the thief never comes nor locust-grub ruins; for "where your hoard is your heart is".

'Let your belts be on and your lamps lit, and you yourselves like men awaiting their master's return from his wedding; so that when he arrives and knocks they may open the door to him immediately. Fortunate are those servants whom their master finds on the alert when he arrives! I tell you for a fact, he will put on an apron, seat them at table, and come forward himself to serve them. And whether it is in the second or the third watch he comes and finds them thus alert, fortunate are they. But you can appreciate this, if the householder had known the time the thief would come, he would have been on the alert and not allowed his house to be broken into. So be ready yourselves, for the Son of Man will come when you least expect him.'

Then Peter asked, 'Master, are you employing this illustration for our benefit, or does it apply to everybody?'

The Master replied, 'Who can be meant by the faithful and prudent steward whom his master puts in charge of his staff to distribute their rations regularly? Fortunate is that servant whom his master on arrival finds so engaged! I tell you for a fact, he will give him charge of all his possessions. If, however, that servant should say to himself, "My master is postponing coming," and begins to beat the men and women servants and to eat and drink, and get drunk, the master of that servant will turn up one day when least expected, at a time he does not dream of, and surprise him suddenly, and treat him as a disloyal person. That servant who knew his master's wishes will be flogged heavily, while the servant who was ignorant, but acted in a way that deserved a beating, will be flogged lightly. From him to whom much is given much is expected, and from him to whom much is entrusted even more is required.

'I have come to start a fire on earth, and how I wish it were already blazing! I have an immersion to undergo, and how anxious I am to get it over! You think I have come to give the earth peace. That is not so, I tell you. It is dissension I bring; for from now on five people in a single house will be at odds, three ranged against two, and two against three, father opposed to son, and son to father, mother against daughter, and daughter against mother, mother-in-law against her daughter-in-law, and daughter-in-law against her mother-in-law.'

Then he spoke to the crowds. 'When you see it clouding over from the west you say at once, "There is rain on the way," and so it proves. And when the south wind blows you say, "There's a hot spell coming," and so it proves. Well, you expositors, you can assess the aspects of earth and sky, how is it you fail to assess the present situation?

'Why do you not judge what is the best course for yourselves? Thus when you go with your opponent before the magistrate, you should be at pains to get free of his clutches on the way, in case he hauls you before the judge, and the judge hands you over to the debt-collector, and the debt-collector throws you into jail. I tell you, you won't get out again until you have paid up the last lepton.'[68]

At this juncture some people arrived to inform him about the Galileans whose blood Pilate had mingled with that of their sacrifices.[69]

'Do you imagine,' he replied, 'that these Galileans were worse sinners than all the other Galileans because they suffered in this way? That is not so, I tell you, but unless you repent you

[68] Equal to about one-twelfth of a penny.
[69] See p. 81, n. 96.

will all similarly perish. Or those eighteen who were killed when the tower at Siloam fell on them, do you imagine that they deserved this fate more than all the other inhabitants of Jerusalem? That is not so, I tell you, but unless you repent you will all perish as they did.'

Then he told this story. 'A man had a fig tree growing in his vineyard, and he came in quest of fruit on it, but found none. "For three years now," he told the gardener, "I have come in quest of fruit on this fig tree, but I have never found any. Cut it down. Why should it take up ground-space?"

' "Let it be for this year, sir," replied the gardener, "to give me a chance to dig round it and manure it. If it should bear fruit next year—well, you can still cut it down if it doesn't." '

When he was teaching in one of the synagogues on the sabbath there was a woman there who had been possessed by a spirit of infirmity for eighteen years. She was bent double, and without power to draw herself upright. On seeing her, Jesus called her to him and said to her, 'Madam, you are freed from your infirmity,' and laid his hand on her. At once she became erect, and praised God.

Displeased that Jesus cured on the sabbath, the president of the synagogue said to the congregation, "There are six days set aside for work, so come and be cured on those, but not on the sabbath day.'

'You hypocrites!' Jesus said to him. 'Does not each of you on the sabbath loose his ox or his ass from its stall and lead it away to drink? But this woman, apparently, because she is a daughter of Abraham, whom Satan has bound all these eighteen years, ought not to be loosed from her bonds on the sabbath day?'

When he put it this way all who opposed him were heartily ashamed, and the whole congregation rejoiced at his remarkable accomplishments. He said therefore, 'How shall I represent the Kingdom of God, and to what shall I compare it? It is like a grain of mustard-seed which a man took and put in his garden. There it grew and became a tree, and the birds of the air nested in its branches.

'To what shall I compare the Kingdom of God? It is like leaven, which a woman took and buried in three measures of flour until the whole was leavened.'

Thus teaching as he went Jesus passed through town after town and village after village, ever progressing steadily towards Jerusalem.

One man said to him, 'Sir, will there be only a few saved?'

'Strive to enter by the narrow gate,' he answered. 'Many, I tell you, will attempt to enter but will not succeed. Once the master of the house has got up and closed the door, you will be left standing outside banging at the door crying, "Sir, let us in!" But he will reply, "I'm sorry, but you are complete strangers to me." Then you will protest, "We have eaten and drunk with you, and you have taught in our streets." But he will repeat, "You are complete strangers to me. Be off, you rogues!" There will be howling and grinding of teeth then, when you see Abraham, Isaac and Jacob, and all the prophets, in the Kingdom of God, while you are thrown outside. They will arrive from East and West, North and South, and banquet in the Kingdom of God, though some who are in the lowest place will be foremost and some of the foremost will be lowest.'

Just then some Pharisees came to warn him, 'Leave here and get away, for Herod is out to kill you.'

'Go and tell that fox,' he replied, 'I propose to expel demons and perform cures to-day and to-morrow, and conclude my work on the third day. But it is essential that I continue to-day, to-morrow, and the day following, for it will never do for a prophet to perish outside Jerusalem.

'Jerusalem, Jerusalem, slayer of prophets and stoner of those sent to her! How often would I have gathered your children together like a bird her brood 'neath her wings! But you would not have it. Your house is now left to yourselves; for you will not see me again, I tell you, until you say, "Blessed is he who comes in the name of the Lord".'[70]

CHAPTER IX

One Sabbath when Jesus went to dine at the house of one of the leading Pharisees the company watched him intently. Just in front of him was a man suffering from dropsy. So Jesus asked the lawyers and Pharisees present, 'Do you permit curing on the sabbath, or not?'

They made no response. So he cured the man and dismissed him. Then he said to them, 'Should an ass or an ox fall into a cistern,[71] which of you will not at once extricate it on the sabbath day?' They were quite unable to dispute this.

Then he pointed a moral for the company in general, having noted how they chose the best places at table. 'When you are invited by someone to a wedding,' he told them, 'don't take the best seat, in case the host has invited a more esteemed guest than yourself, and having asked both you and him has to come to you and say, "Would you mind giving up this place?" Then, to your discomfiture, you will have to move lower down. Instead, when you are invited, occupy a low place; so that when your host comes he may say to you, "Do go up higher, friend." That will confer a distinction on you in the eyes of your fellow-guests. For everyone who elevates himself will be abased, while he who abases himself will be elevated.'

Then he addressed himself to his host. 'When you give a

[70] Ps. cxviii. 26, and see about p. 126.
[71] The illustration is purposely chosen to link up with the nature of dropsy, a gathering of watery fluid.

luncheon or dinner, do not ask either your friends, your broth-ers, your relations, or your rich neighbours, in case they too invite you back, and you get your favour returned. Rather, when you give a reception, invite the poor, the crippled, the lame, and the blind. Then you will be blessed, because they cannot return your favour, and you will be repaid at the resur-rection of the righteous.'

On hearing this one of the guests said to him, 'He will be a most fortunate man who banquets in the Kingdom of God.'

'There was once a man,' Jesus told him, 'who gave a great banquet, and invited many people. At the time fixed for the banquet he dispatched his servant to the guests with the mes-sage, "Your presence is requested, as all preparations are com-plete." But they all excused themselves. "I have bought a piece of land," the first replied, "and it is essential that I should inspect it. I do beg you to excuse me." Another said, "I have bought five yoke of oxen, and I am about to try them out. I do beg you to excuse me." Another said, "I have just got married, so am unable to come." So the servant presented himself and reported all this to his master. Then the master of the house was furious, and said to his servant, "Go out at once into the streets and lanes of the town and bring in the poor, the crippled, the blind, and the lame." The servant reported, "Master, your in-structions have been followed, and there is still room." So the master told his servant, "Go out into the highways and suburbs, and compel the people to come, that my house may be filled. I tell you, not a man of those who were invited will even taste my banquet." '

Now there was a vast crowd travelling along with him, and turning to them he said, 'If anyone comes to me and does not hate his father and mother, wife and children, brothers and sis-ters, yes and himself as well, he cannot be a disciple of mine. Anyone who does not shoulder his own cross and follow me cannot be a disciple of mine. For which of you desiring to build a tower does not sit down first and work out the cost to make sure he has enough to complete it, in case having laid the foun-dation, and being powerless to complete the work, all the on-lookers should jeer at him and say, "He started to build, but was powerless to complete?" Or what king on his way to engage in battle with another king does not sit down first and take counsel, whether with a force of ten thousand it is practicable to encounter one who is advancing against him with twenty thou-sand? Or whether, if it is not, while he is still at a distance, he should send an embassy to sue for peace? So then whoever of you does not turn his back on all he calls his own cannot be a disciple of mine. Salt is indeed good, but if the salt becomes insipid, how may its tang be restored? As soil or manure it is useless. They can only throw it outside. Let him who can catch my meaning do so.'

The tax-collectors and sinners habitually drew near to listen to him. This led the Pharisees and scribes to complain, 'He entertains sinners and eats with them.'

So Jesus used this illustration to them, 'Which of you men with a hundred sheep, if he loses one of them, will not leave the ninety-nine in the open and go after the lost one until he finds it? And when he does find it, will he not joyfully lay it across his shoulders, and reaching home call together his friends and neighbours crying, "Congratulate me, I have found my lost sheep?" Just so, I tell you, there will be more joy in heaven over one repentant sinner than over ninety-nine righteous people who have no need of repentance. Or which of you women with ten drachmas, if she loses a single drachma,[72] will not light a lamp and search diligently till she finds it? And when she does find it, will she not call together her friends and neighbours crying, "Congratulate me, I have found my lost drachma?" Just so, I tell you, there will be joy in the presence of God's angels over one repentant sinner.

'There was once a man who had two sons,' he continued. 'The younger of them said to his father, "Father, please give me the share of your fortune that will come to me." So he divided his estate between them.

'Some time afterwards the younger son sold up and travelled to a distant land, and there dissipated his fortune in loose living. When he had run through the lot a severe famine afflicted that country, and he began to feel the pinch. So he took service with a citizen of that country, who gave him a job on his farm feeding swine; and he longed to cram himself with the pods the pigs were eating, but no one gave him any. Then it came over him, "There are all those employees of my father's with more food than they can possibly eat, while here I am starving to death. I will get up and go to my father and tell him, Father, I have sinned against Heaven and in your sight, and no longer deserve to be called your son. Treat me as one of your employees." So he got up and went to his father.

'But while he was still a good way off his father saw him, and yearning with pity ran and threw himself on his neck and kissed him. Then the son said to him, "Father, I have sinned against Heaven and in your sight, and no longer deserve to be called your son. . . ."

'But his father called to his servants, "Hurry! Fetch my best robe and put it on him, and give him a ring for his hand, and shoes for his feet. Have the fattened calf slaughtered, and let us eat it up and enjoy ourselves; for this son of mine was dead and is alive again, he was lost and is found." So they set about merrymaking.

'Now his elder brother was in the field at the time; and as he approached the house on his way back he heard music and dancing, and called to one of the lads to inquire what it was all about. "Your brother has come," he told him, "and your father

[72] A silver coin equal, like a dinar, to about 9½d.

has slaughtered the fattened calf, because he has got him home safe and sound." He was so angry he would not go in. His father came out to beseech him, but he answered, "Here have I served you all these years and never once disobeyed your orders, and you have never given me even a kid to enjoy myself with my friends. But no sooner does this son of yours come, having squandered your estate with harlots, than you slaughter the fattened calf for him."

' "But son," he said to him, "you are constantly with me, and all that I have is yours. Surely we should make merry and rejoice because this brother of yours was dead and is alive again, and was lost and is found?" '

Jesus also told his disciples, 'There was once a wealthy man who had an agent who was accused to him of dissipating his resources. So he sent for him and said to him, "What is all this I hear about you? Give in the account of your management, for it is out of the question to keep you on as agent."

' "Whatever am I going to do," the agent said to himself, "now that my master is discharging me from my position? I am quite unfit for manual labour, and I am ashamed to beg. I know what I'll do, so that when I am deprived of the management the tenants will welcome me to their homes."

'So he sent for every single one of those who stood in his master's debt.

' "How much do you owe my master?" he asked the first.

' "A hundred baths[73] of oil," he replied.

' "Take the contract," he told him, "and sit down quickly and substitute fifty."

' "And how much do you owe?" he asked another.

' "A hundred kors[74] of wheat," he replied.

' "Take the contract and substitute eighty," he told him.

'The master applauded the unsatisfactory agent for his smartness; for the children of This World[75] in their generation are smarter than the children of Light.[76] So secure yourselves friends, independent of the false mammon,[77] so that when this fails[78] they will welcome you to the Eternal Abodes.

'He who is reliable with a little is equally reliable with a great deal, but he who is unsatisfactory in minor matters is unsatisfactory in major ones. If, therefore, you have not proved reliable with the false mammon, who will entrust you with the true? And if you have not proved reliable with what is another's, who will give you what is your own? No manservant can serve two masters. Either he will detest the one and love the other, or he will be devoted to the one and despise the other. You cannot serve both God and mammon.'

Listening to all this, the Pharisees being avaricious sneered at

[73] One bath equals nine gallons.
[74] One kor equals about ten bushels.
[75] The generality of people, not the Elect.
[76] See p. 95, n. 36.
[77] Delusive material wealth.
[78] Or, 'when you quit (this life),' following an alternative reading.

him. 'You are the people who vindicate yourselves in the sight of men,' Jesus told them, 'but God knows your hearts. For what ranks high with men is an abomination in the sight of God. Until John's time there were the Law and the Prophets; but since then the Kingdom of God is proclaimed and everyone forces his way into it. Yet it is easier for heaven and earth to pass away than for a single item of the Law to lapse.

'Everyone who divorces his wife and marries another commits adultery, and whoever marries a divorced woman commits adultery.[79]

'There was once a rich man, who entertained lavishly every day robed in purple and fine linen. There was also a beggar named Lazarus, who was covered with ulcers, laid at his door and longing to make a meal of the scraps from the rich man's table. Instead of that the dogs came and licked his sores.

'In due course the beggar died and was borne by the angels to the lap of Abraham.[80] The rich man also died and was buried. And in Hades, being in torment, he raised his eyes and from a distance saw Abraham with Lazarus in his lap, and cried out, "Father Abraham, take pity on me and send Lazarus to dip the tip of his finger in water and cool my tongue, for I am suffering agonies in this flame."

' "My child," replied Abraham, "recollect that you received your good fortune during your lifetime, while Lazarus similarly had evil fortune. But here and now he is comforted while you suffer agonies. And quite apart from that a huge chasm yawns between us and all of you, which prevents those who may wish to do so from crossing to you from this side, or crossing from your side to us."

' "I beg you then, father," he said, "to send him to my father's house—for I have five[81] brothers—that he may give them solemn warning, in case they too should come to this place of torment."

' "They have Moses and the Prophets," said Abraham. "Let them heed them."

' "Oh no, Father Abraham," he replied. "But if someone should come to them from the dead they will repent."

' "If they will not heed Moses and the Prophets," he told him, "neither will they be convinced if someone should rise from the dead." '

Then he said to his disciples, 'Causes of stumbling are bound to come, yet woe to him by whom they come. It would be better for him to have an upper millstone hung round his neck and to be flung into the sea than to upset one of these little ones. Be on your guard. If your brother sins, admonish him; and if he is contrite, forgive him. Even if he wrongs you seven times in a

[79] This saying, though evidently not far removed from the immediately preceding words in the author's source (cp. Mt. v. 18, 32), does not come in very aptly here.
[80] I.e. to Paradise.
[81] 'Five' perhaps because of the Five Books of Moses.

day, and seven times makes amends to you and says, "I'm sorry," forgive him.'

'Give us faith,' said the envoys to the Master.

'If you have faith no bigger than a grain of mustard-seed,' the Master told them, 'you could say to this mulberry tree, "Be uprooted and replanted in the sea!" and it would obey you.

'Which of you with a man doing the ploughing or herding says to him when he returns from the field, "Come along and sit down"? Doesn't he say to him instead, "Get my dinner ready and tidy yourself up, and wait on me until I have eaten and drunk. You can eat and drink yourself later"? Is he grateful to his servant for carrying out his orders? So with you, when you have carried out all your instructions, say, "We are mere menials. We have simply done our duty." '

CHAPTER X

In the course of his journey to Jerusalem Jesus had to pass through Samaria and Galilee.[82] As he entered one village he was met by ten men who were lepers. They stood at a distance and hailed him, 'Your lordship Jesus, take pity on us!'

When he saw their condition he said to them, 'Go and show yourselves to the priests.' And as they went on their way they were cleansed.

One of them, finding himself cured, turned back praising God aloud, and fell on his face at Jesus's feet thanking him; and he was a Samaritan.

'Surely there were ten cleansed,' Jesus commented. 'Where are the other nine? Have none of them come back to give God praise except this foreigner? Rise and go your way,' he told him. 'Your faith has saved you.'

Now being asked by the Pharisees when the Kingdom of God would be inaugurated, he replied, 'The Kingdom of God will not come by keeping a sharp look-out for it. Nor is it going to be said, "Here it is!" or "There it is!"—for the Kingdom of God is right beside you.'

To his disciples he said, 'The time will come when you will passionately long to see a single day of the Era of the Son of Man, and will not see it. They will tell you, "There he is!" or "Here he is!" But do not stir or hurry off; for as the lightning flashes across the sky so will be the Son of Man when his day comes. First, however, he must suffer greatly and be rejected by this generation.

'And just as it was in Noah's time, so will it be in the time of the Son of Man. They ate, they drank, they married, and were given in marriage, until the day Noah entered the ark and the deluge came and destroyed them all. Similarly, just as it was in

---

[82] Geographically this reference to Galilee is out of place in the author's arrangement of events, but his Markan source had located the healing of a leper in Galilee (Mk. i. 44).

Lot's time, they ate, they drank, they bought and sold, planted and built; but on the very day Lot left Sodom it rained fire and sulphur from heaven and destroyed them all. So will it be the day the Son of Man is revealed.

'That day let no one who is on the housetop with his things in the house go down to fetch anything, and let no one who is in the field turn to glance back. Remember Lot's wife. Whoever attempts to preserve his life will lose it, and whoever loses it will assure its survival. I tell you, there will be two men in one bed; the one will be taken and the other left behind. There will be two women together grinding; the one will be taken and the other left behind.'

'Where, Master?' they asked him.

'Wherever the carcase is the vultures will flock,' he replied.

Then he told them a story to illustrate how essential it was to be constant in prayer and not to slacken. 'There was once a judge in a certain town, who neither reverenced God nor respected man. And there was a widow in the same town who was always coming before him crying, "Protect me from my persecutor!" For some time he would not, but later he said to himself, "Though I neither reverence God nor respect man, yet because this widow keeps pestering me I will give her protection, or eventually with her coming she will completely wear me out."

'Listen,' said the Master, 'to what this false judge says. And shall not God give satisfaction to his Elect, who cry to him day and night? Will he forbear in their case? I tell you he will give them satisfaction speedily. Nevertheless, when the Son of Man comes will he find faith on earth?'

He also told the following story to some who were convinced of their own righteousness and were contemptuous of others.

'Two men went up to the Temple to pray, one was a Pharisee and the other a tax-collector. The Pharisee stood and prayed for his own gratification to this effect, "I give thee thanks, O God, that I am not like the generality of man, grasping, dishonest, adulterers, or even like this tax-collector here. I fast twice a week.[83] I pay tithe on all my increase."[84] But the tax-collector stood at a distance unwilling even to raise his eyes to heaven, and beat his breast saying, "O God, be reconciled to me a sinner!" I tell you this man went down to his house exonerated rather than the other. For everyone who exalts himself shall be abased, while he who abases himself will be exalted.'

When they also brought their infants to him to fondle the disciples observing this reproved them. But Jesus summoned them and said, 'Let the little children come to me, do not prevent them; for the Kingdom of God is composed of such as they. I tell you for a fact, whoever does not accept the Kingdom of God like a little child will never enter it.'

---

[83] On Mondays and Thursdays.
[84] It is believed that the Pharisees came into existence originally as a voluntary association pledged to separate the tithes required by the Mosaic Law.

One of the rulers then asked him, 'Good teacher, what must I do to inherit Eternal Life?'[85]

'Why do you call me good?' said Jesus. 'There is none good but One, God. You know the commandments: "Do not commit adultery, do not murder, do not steal, do not bear false witness, honour your father and mother." '[86]

'I have kept all these from my youth,' he replied.

When Jesus heard this he told him, 'That leaves only one thing more for you to do: sell everything you possess and distribute the proceeds to the poor and you will have treasure in heaven. Then come and join me.'

He became very dejected at hearing this, for he was extremely wealthy.

When Jesus saw it he said, 'What a hard struggle it is for those with means to get into the Kingdom of God! It is easier for a camel to pass through the eye of a needle than for a rich man to enter the Kingdom of God.'

Those who were listening said, 'Who then can be saved?'

'What is impossible to man is possible to God,' he replied.

'Here we are,' said Peter, 'we have left all we possess to follow you.'

'I tell you for a fact,' he said to them, 'there is no one who has left house, or wife, or brothers, or parents, or children, for the sake of the Kingdom of God, who will not receive many times more in the present time and Eternal Life in the Age to Come.'

Getting the twelve together, he said to them, 'Look, we are now going up to Jerusalem, and all those things which have been written by the Prophets of the Son of Man will have their fulfilment; for he will be handed over to the Gentiles, mocked, illused and spat upon, and when they have flogged him they will kill him; but the third day he will be raised up.'

But they understood nothing of this. The matter was hidden from them, and they failed to grasp the purport of what was said.

Now as Jesus approached Jericho a certain blind man sat by the roadside begging. Hearing the crowd go by he asked what was going on. They told him that Jesus the Nazarene was passing. So he cried out, 'Jesus, Son of David, pity me!'

Those who were in front insisted that he be silent. But he only cried out the more, 'Son of David, pity me!'

Jesus stopped, and ordered him to be brought to him. When he had approached he asked him, 'What can I do for you?'

'Sir, I want to see again,' he said.

'Then regain your sight,' Jesus told him. 'Your faith has saved you.'

Instantly he recovered his sight and followed him praising God. And all the people who saw it extolled God.

On entering the town Jesus passed through Jericho. Now there was a man there called Zacchaeus, who was chief tax-col-

[85] See above p. 70, n. 51.   [86] Exod. xx. 12-16.

lector and extremely well off. He was most anxious to catch a glimpse of Jesus, but being of small stature he could not manage it on account of the crowd. So running on ahead he clambered up a sycamore-fig tree so that he could see Jesus; for he was bound to pass that way.

As he reached the spot Jesus looked up and said to him, 'Hurry up and come down, Zacchaeus. I have to stay at your house to-day.'

Descending hastily he welcomed Jesus with joy; but all the onlookers murmured, 'He's gone to be the guest of a man well known to be a sinner.'

But standing there Zacchaeus told the Master, 'Half of my possessions, sir, I will give to the poor, and if I have extorted anything from anyone I will repay four times as much.'

'Salvation has come to this house to-day,' Jesus said to him, 'since here too is a son of Abraham. For the Son of Man came to seek and to save what was lost.'

To everything they had already heard Jesus added this simile, because of his proximity to Jerusalem, and because they had the idea that the Kingdom of God would be instituted forthwith. So he said, 'There was a certain exalted personage, who set off for a distant land to obtain for himself a crown, and return. Calling ten of his servants he gave them ten minas[87] and said to them, "Look after my interests until I return."

'But his countrymen hated him, and sent a deputation after him to say, "We do not want this man to reign over us."[88]

'When he had returned, having gained the crown, he directed that those servants to whom he had given the money should be summoned to his presence that he might learn the result of their transactions. Then came the first and said, "Sir, your mina has earned ten minas."

' "Fine, you excellent servant," he replied. "Since you have proved trustworthy in a small matter, take charge of ten cities."

'Then came the second and said, "Your mina, sir, has made five minas." He told him as well, "You take charge of five cities."

'Then another came and said, "Sir, here is your mina, which I have kept tucked away in a handkerchief. I was afraid of you, because you are a harsh man, lifting what you never laid down, and reaping what you never sowed."

' "I will convict you out of your own mouth, you rascally servant," he exclaimed. "You knew I was a harsh man, lifting what I never laid down, and reaping what I never sowed. Why then did you not invest my money, so that when I came I could get it back with interest?" Then he said to his henchman, "Take the mina from him and give it to the one who has ten minas."

[87] A mina is equal to about £4.
[88] Lk.'s version of the story told in Mt. xxv. 14-30, above p. 129, seems partly to have been influenced by the history of Archelaus, Herod the Great's successor, who went to Rome to be confirmed in the kingship by Augustus. His people also sent a deputation to oppose him. See Jos. *Wars*, II. vi. 1.

‘ "But sir," they said, "he already has ten minas."

‘ "I tell you," he replied, "that to everyone who has more shall be given; but from him who has not, even what he has shall be taken away. As for those enemies of mine, who did not want me to reign over them, bring them here and slay them in my presence." ’

Having told this story Jesus resumed his progress, ascending towards Jerusalem.[89]

As he approached Bethphage and Bethany towards the hill called the Mount of Olives he dispatched two of his disciples saying, 'Go to the village ahead of you, and as you enter it you will find a colt tethered which no one has ridden previously. Untie him and lead him here. And if anyone says to you, "Why are you untying him?" just say, "The Master needs him." ’

Going off, those who had been sent found it turn out exactly as they had been told. As they were untying the colt his owners said to them, 'Why are you untying the colt?' And they replied, 'The Master needs him.' So they brought the colt to Jesus, and throwing their cloaks across its back mounted Jesus on it; and as he moved off they spread their cloaks on the road.

When Jesus reached the descent of the Mount of Olives the whole company of his disciples broke into joyful cries of praise to God for all the wonders they had witnessed, saying,

'Blessed be the king, who comes in the name of the Lord.

Peace be in heaven, and glory be on high.'[90]

Some of the Pharisees in the crowd said to him, 'Teacher, reprimand your disciples.'

But he answered, 'I tell you, if they are silent the stones will cry out.'

Viewing the city as he approached, Jesus wept over it, saying, 'Oh, if only you realized at this moment what is for your welfare! But, alas, it is concealed from your sight. For a time is coming for you when your enemies will surround you with palisades, encircle and hem you in on all sides, and stamp you into the dust and your children within you.[91] They will not leave in you one stone upon another, because you failed to realize the time of your visitation.'

Then he entered the Temple, and began to eject those who sold there, telling them, 'It is stated, "My house shall be called a house of prayer,"[92] but you have made it a robbers' den.'[93]

He taught daily in the Temple, while the head priests and scribes sought to destroy him, and even the leaders of the people. But they could not determine how to effect this because the people stuck close to him to listen to him.

[89] The road ascends very steeply from Jericho, which lies about 1,200 ft. below sea-level, to Jerusalem, 2,900 ft. above sea-level.
[90] Lk. has altered the wording here, apparently to relate it to the song of the heavenly host at the Nativity, cp. above p. 145.
[91] The words attributed to Jesus here reflect the circumstances of the siege and capture of Jerusalem in A.D. 70.
[92] Isa. lvi. 7.
[93] Jer. vii. 11.

One day while Jesus was teaching in the Temple and proclaiming the News, the head priests and scribes accompanied by the elders came up to him and said, 'Tell us by what authority you are acting in this way, and who gave you this authority?'

He replied, 'I too have something to ask you. Will you tell me, was John's rite of immersion of divine or human inspiration?'

They discussed the matter among themselves to the effect that, 'If we say, "of divine inspiration", he will say, "Why then did you not believe him?" But if we say, "of human inspiration", all the people will stone us, for they are convinced that John was a prophet.' So they answered that they did not know its source.

So Jesus said to them, 'Neither will I tell you what authority I have for acting as I do.'

He then told the people the following story.[94] 'A man planted a vineyard and let it out to cultivators, and went abroad for some time. But when the vintage season came he dispatched a servant to the cultivators for them to give him his share of the vineyard's produce. But the cultivators thrashed him and sent him away empty-handed. The owner then sent another servant; but they thrashed him as well, and after treating him shamefully sent him away. He sent yet a third; and they went so far as to wound this one, and threw him out. Then the owner of the vineyard said, "What am I to do? I will send my dear son. Perhaps they will respect him." But when the cultivators saw him they argued to themselves, "Here is the heir. Let us kill him, that the inheritance may be ours." So they threw him outside the vineyard and killed him. What then will the owner of the vineyard do to them? He will come and destroy those cultivators and give the vineyard to others.'

When they heard this they said, 'God forbid!'

Looking straight at them he inquired, 'What then does this scripture mean, "The stone which the builders rejected has become the coping stone?"[95] Whoever falls on that stone will be crushed, while whoever it falls upon will be pulverized.'

The scribes and head priests dearly wished they could lay hands on him at that moment, but they were afraid of the people; for they knew perfectly well that this illustration was directed at them. Keeping him under close observation, however, they planted spies masquerading as pious persons to catch him out on some expression of his, so that they could obtain grounds for handing him over to the secular power and the governor's authority. These men questioned him. 'Teacher,' they said, 'we are aware that you speak and teach with complete candour and make no personal distinctions, but teach the

[94] Inspired by Isa. v. 1-8.   [95] Ps. cxviii. 22.

way of God in sincerity. Is it permissible or not to pay tribute to Caesar?'

Detecting their trickery, he said to them, 'Show me a dinar. Whose portrait and inscription does it bear?'

'Caesar's,' they answered.

'In that case render to Caesar what is Caesar's and to God what is God's.'

So they failed to catch him out before the people on this point, and being amazed at his reply they were silent.

Then some of the Sadducees came to him, those who say there will be no resurrection, and questioned him as follows. 'Teacher, Moses laid it down for us that should a man's married brother die childless he should marry his brother's wife so as to continue his brother's line.[96] Now there were seven brothers. The first took a wife and died childless, then the second and the third, and similarly all seven married her, but died and left no children. Finally the woman herself died. In the resurrection, then, of which of them will the woman be the wife, for all seven were married to her?'

Jesus answered, 'The children of This World marry and are given in marriage, but those who are deemed worthy to attain That World [97] and the resurrection of the dead neither marry nor are given in marriage. Neither are they any longer subject to death: they are equal to the angels and are sons of God, having become so by resurrection. But that the dead will be raised Moses indicates quite clearly at the bush, where he calls the Lord "the God of Abraham, of Isaac, and of Jacob".[98] He is not God of the dead, but of the living; for all are alive to God.'[99]

Some of the scribes then remarked, 'Teacher, you have put that very well.' They did not venture to ask him anything further.

But he said to them, 'Why is the Messiah said to be the son of David? For David himself says in the Book of Psalms,

> *The Lord said to my lord, "Sit at my right hand*
> *Until I make your enemies your footstool."*[100]

Since David calls him lord, how can he be his son?'

Then in the hearing of all the people he said to his disciples, 'Beware of those scribes who like to parade in uniform, and love to be saluted in the markets, to have the chief stalls in the synagogues, and the best places at the festal banquets. They are the people who prey on widows, and for pretext pray at great length. There is a still longer sentence in store for them.'

Glancing up he saw the rich throwing their gifts into the treasury-chest.[101] He also saw one very poor widow throw in two lepta,[102] and said, 'I tell you truly, that poor widow has thrown in more than all the others; for all of them have thrown in their

---

[96] Deut. xxv. 5-6.   [97] I.e. the Messianic Era.   [98] Exod. iii. 2-6.
[99] The explanation may be a note by the author, cp. Rom. vi. 10.
[100] Ps. cx.1.   [101] See above p. 75, n. 73.
[102] A lepton equals about one-twelfth of a penny.

gifts out of their affluence, while she out of her penury has thrown in all the means she possessed.'

When some spoke of the Temple, how it was adorned with magnificent stones and votive gifts, he said, 'You see all this? The time will come when there will not be left here one stone on another that is not thrown down.'

Then they asked him, 'Teacher, when will this actually happen, and what indication will there be when it is going to happen?'

'Take care that you are not deceived,' he replied, 'for many will come claiming to be me, saying, "I am he," and "The time has come." Do not go after them. Then when you hear of wars and disorders do not get excited, for these have to come first, but the End will not follow immediately.[103] Nation will be roused against nation, and kingdom against kingdom,' he informed them. 'There will be great earthquakes with famine and pestilence in various places, appalling spectacles also, and awful signs from heaven.[104] But before all this they will lay hands on you and persecute you, handing you over to synagogues and prisons, dragging you before kings and governors on my account. This will serve you as evidence. Fix in your minds, therefore, not to rehearse beforehand what you will say in your defence, for I will give you words and wisdom which none of your persecutors will be able to resist or refute. You will be betrayed by parents and brothers, relations and friends: they will be responsible for the death of some of you, and you will be universally detested on my account. Yet not a hair of your heads shall perish. By your constancy win your lives.

'Then when you see Jerusalem ringed with armies be certain that its devastation is at hand. Then let those who are in Judea flee to the hills, and those who are inside the city take their departure, and let those who are in the country not enter it; for these are the Days of Retribution in fulfilment of all that the Scriptures have stated.[105] Alas for pregnant women and nursing mothers in those days, for there will be great distress on earth and terror for this people! They will fall by the edge of the sword and be carried away captive to all nations, and Jerusalem will remain under Gentile domination until the Era of the Gentiles has ended.[106] That moment will be marked by signs in the sun, the moon and the stars, and on earth by nations haggard with utter helplessness at the pounding of sea and billow, men chill with fear and foreboding of what is overtaking the existing order; for the planets will totter. And then they shall see the Son of Man coming in cloud with great pomp and splendour.

[103] See above, p. 76, n. 74.
[104] For an account of such portents see Jos. *Wars*, VI. v. 3, and the Jewish *Sibylline Oracles*. The circumstances of the Jewish war with Rome are continually present in the writer's mind.
[105] Cp. Hos. ix. 7; Dan. ix. 26. In obedience to a revelation they had received the Jewish Christians are said to have fled from Jerusalem and to have taken refuge across the Jordan near Pella. Cp. Rev. xii. 14.
[106] Cp. Rev. xi. 2, and see above n. 104.

When these things begin to happen emerge from your retreat and lift up your heads for your deliverance is at hand.'

Then he gave them an illustration. 'Take the fig tree and all the trees. Once you see they have sprouted you are well aware that summer is close at hand. So when you see these things happen you will be no less aware that the Kingdom of God is at hand. I tell you positively, this generation will not pass away before all this takes place. Heaven and earth will pass away, but my words shall not pass away.

'But take care that your minds are not enfeebled by over-indulgence, drunkenness, or worldly pleasures, so that that day catches you unexpectedly like a trap; for inevitably it will spring upon all who dwell on the face of the earth.[107] So keep awake, pray constantly, that you may succeed in escaping all those things that are about to happen, and to stand in the presence of the Son of Man.'

Now during the day Jesus was in the Temple teaching, but at night he went out and camped on the hill called the Mount of Olives; and all the people came early to the Temple to listen to him.

·

CHAPTER XII

The Feast of Unleavened Bread, called Passover, was at hand, and the head priests and scribes were seeking a way to kill Jesus, for they feared the people. Then Satan entered Judas called Iscariot, who was one of the twelve, and he went off to confer with the head priests and officers on the best way of handing him over to them. They were overjoyed and agreed to give him money, while he gave his solemn assurances and sought a convenient opportunity to deliver him to them when away from the crowd.

Then came the day of unleavened bread when the passover has to be sacrificed, and Jesus sent Peter and John saying, 'Go and prepare for us to eat the passover.'

'Where do you wish us to make preparation?' they inquired.

'As you enter the city,' he told them, 'a man will meet you carrying a water-pot. Follow him into the house he enters, and say to the master of the house, "The Teacher asks you, which guest-room am I to have to eat the passover with my disciples?" He will then show you a large upstairs dining-room ready laid out. There prepare.'

Setting off they found everything turn out just as he told them, and they prepared the passover. Then when the time came he took his place in company with the envoys. 'I have greatly longed to eat this passover with you before I suffer,' he said to them, 'for I tell you I will not eat another until its fulfilment in the Kingdom of God.'

[107] Isa. xxiv. 17, and see I. Thess. v. 2-8.

Taking the cup, he said after giving thanks, 'Take it, and share it between you. I tell you, from now on I will not drink of the fruit of the vine till the Kingdom of God is inaugurated.'

Then taking bread, after giving thanks he broke and gave it to them saying, 'This signifies my body [which is given for you. Do this in commemoration of me.' Similarly he gave them the cup after the meal saying, 'This is the new covenant in my blood, which is poured out for you.][108] Moreover, the hand of my betrayer lies here on the table with mine. The Son of Man indeed goes his appointed way, yet alas for that man by whom he is betrayed.'

They began to speculate as to which of them would be likely to do such a thing. They also began to argue over which of them should be considered greatest.

But Jesus intervened. 'The kings of the Gentiles lord it over them,' he said, 'and their high authorities are termed Benefactors. It is otherwise with you. Let the greatest among you be as the inferior, and the one who issues orders as the one who receives them. Which is greater, the one who sits at table or the one who serves? Surely it is the one who is seated. Yet I am among you as one who serves. You are those who have stayed with me through all my trials, and just as my Father has promised me his Kingdom, so do I now promise you that you shall eat and drink at my table in my Kingdom; and you shall sit on thrones governing the twelve tribes of Israel.

'Simon, Simon, Satan has begged to have you that he may prize you loose like husks from the grain. But I have prayed that your loyalty may not fail, and on your restoration you must confirm your brothers.'

'In your cause, Master,' he replied, 'I am ready to go to prison and to death too.'

But he said, 'I tell you for a fact, Peter, the cock will not crow to-day before you have denied three times that you know me.'

Then to all of them he said, 'When I sent you out without purse, or wallet, or sandals, did you go short of anything?'

'No, nothing,' they answered.

'Yet now,' he said, 'whoever has a purse let him take it, and a wallet as well, and whoever has no dagger let him sell his cloak and buy one. For I tell you that this scripture will have its accomplishment in me, "He was classed with outlaws".[109] Yes, indeed, whatever has reference to me will have its fulfilment.'

'Here are two daggers, Master,' they said.

'That will do,' he told them.

Taking his departure he went as usual to the Mount of Olives, and his disciples followed him. When he reached the spot he said to them, 'Pray that you are not put to the test.' Then he withdrew about a stone's throw from them, and knelt down

[108] With this interpolated passage cp. I. Cor. xi. 24-25, below p. 277.
[109] Isa. liii. 12.

and prayed, 'O Father, if it be thy will let this cup pass me by. Yet not my will but thine be done.'

Then an angel appeared to him strengthening him. And being in agony he prayed more fervently, his sweat dropping to the ground like splashes of blood.

On rising from prayer he came to his disciples and found them sleeping from grief, and said to them, 'Why are you sleeping? Be up, and at your prayers, or you may find yourselves tempted.'

He was still speaking when a crowd came in sight, with the one of the twelve called Judas at their head. Approaching Jesus he embraced him. Jesus said to him, 'Judas, do you betray the Son of Man with a kiss?'

Those surrounding Jesus, seeing what was going to happen, cried, 'Master, shall we strike the sword?' One of them did strike the high priest's servant and severed his right ear.

'Leave this to me,' Jesus replied, and touching the ear healed him.

Then Jesus addressed those who had taken action against him, the head priests, officers of the Temple, and elders. 'Have you come out as against a brigand with swords and clubs? While I was with you daily in the Temple you never laid hands on me. But now is your time, when darkness reigns.'

Seizing him they conveyed him to the high priest's residence, while Peter followed at a distance. There they made up a fire in the courtyard, and when they sat down Peter sat with them. One of the servant girls seeing him seated there before the blaze gave him a keen look, and then announced, 'This man was with them too.'

But he denied it, 'I don't know him, woman.'

After a while someone else who saw him declared, 'Of course you are one of them.'

'I am not,' Peter declared.

When about another hour had elapsed another man stated with conviction, 'Certainly he was with them. He's a Galilean.'

'I don't know what you are talking about,' replied Peter.

Just then, before he had finished speaking, the cock crowed. The Master turned and looked at Peter; and Peter recalled the remark the Master had made to him, 'This very day before the cock crows you will deny me three times.' Going outside he wept bitterly.

Now the men who had charge of Jesus made sport of him, striking him while blindfolded, and then demanding, 'Come on, prophesy! Who was it hit you?' And many other insulting remarks they addressed to him.

When it was daylight, the senate of the people, head priests and scribes, assembled and conducted him to their Sanhedrin, urging him, 'If you are the Messiah, tell us.'

But he replied, 'Even if I do tell you, you will not believe, nor will you answer if I ask you a question. But hereafter the Son of Man will be seated at the right hand of the power of God.'

'Are you then the Son of God?' they all inquired.

'I am, as you say,' he told them.

Then they said, 'What further evidence do we need? We have heard his own confession.'

With that the whole assembly rose and brought him before Pilate, and proceeded to accuse him as follows: 'We have found this man subverting our nation, forbidding the payment of tribute to Caesar, and claiming to be Messiah, a king.'

'Are you the king of the Jews?' Pilate asked him.

'As you say,' he replied.

Pilate told the head priests and the crowd, 'I can find nothing criminal in this man.'

But they pressed their charges saying, 'He rouses the people, teaching all over Judea,[110] beginning with Galilee and ending up here.'

When Pilate heard that, he inquired whether the man was a Galilean, and learning that he belonged to Herod's [111] jurisdiction turned him over to Herod; who was in Jerusalem at this time. Herod was greatly delighted at seeing Jesus, for he had wanted to see him for a long time. From reports about him he hoped to witness some miracle performed by him. So he interrogated him at considerable length. Jesus, however, made no response. But the head priests and scribes stood there and vehemently accused him.

Once Herod with his men had had their sport with him and mocked him, he returned him to Pilate after arraying him in magnificent robes. That day Herod and Pilate became friends with one another; for previously they had been at enmity.

Pilate now summoned the head priests, rulers and people, and said to them, 'You have brought this man to me accused of subverting the people. After examining him in your presence I found nothing criminal such as you charged him with. Neither did Herod, for he has sent him back to us. You see, therefore, that he has done nothing to deserve death. Consequently I shall chastise him and release him.'

But the entire concourse yelled, 'Away with him! Release Bar-Abbas[a] to us!'

Once more Pilate, wanting to release Jesus, addressed them. But they only clamoured the more, 'Crucify him, crucify him!'

A third time he spoke to them. 'But what crime has he committed? I have found nothing in him to merit death. Consequently I shall chastise him and release him.'

But they bellowed their insistent demand for him to be crucified, and their clamour prevailed. Pilate gave the judgment they called for. He released the man thrown into prison for riot

---

[a] This was a man who had been thrown into prison for participation in a riot in the city and for murder.

[110] See p. 151, n. 44.
[111] Herod Antipas, tetrarch of Galilee and Perea.

and murder, for whom they had asked, and surrendered Jesus to their will.

As they marched him off they seized a certain Simon, a Cyrenian, coming from the country, and laid the cross on him for him to carry it behind Jesus. A great concourse of people followed him, and women who beat their breasts and bewailed him. Turning to them Jesus said, 'Daughters of Jerusalem, do not weep for me, but rather for yourselves and your children; for the time is coming when they will say, "Fortunate are the barren, and the wombs that have never borne, and the breasts that have never suckled!" Then will they cry to the mountains, "Topple on us," and to the hills, "Cover us." [112] For if this is what they do with green wood, what will happen to the dry?'

They brought two other malefactors to be executed with him. When they reached the place called Skull they crucified him there, with the malefactors one on his right and the other on his left. [But Jesus said, 'O Father, forgive them. They do not know what they are doing.'] [113] And they distributed his clothes by drawing lots.

The people stood there looking on, while their rulers sneered, 'He saved others, let him save himself if he is God's Anointed, the Chosen One.' The soldiers also mocked him, coming to him and offering him vinegar with the jeer, 'Save yourself, if you are the king of the Jews.'[a] Even one of the hanger malefactors reviled him, 'Aren't you the Messiah? Then save yourself and us.'

But the other malefactor rebuked him, 'Have you lost all fear of God because you have been given an identical sentence? In our case it was justified, for we have only got our deserts, but he has committed no felony.' Then he said, 'Spare me a thought, Jesus, when you inaugurate your kingdom.'

'I tell you for a fact,' Jesus replied, 'this very day you will be with me in Paradise.'

By this time it was about noon, and there was darkness over the whole land until three o'clock due to an eclipse of the sun, and the curtain of the Sanctuary was split down the middle. Then Jesus cried out in a loud voice, 'Father, into thy hands I commit my spirit',[114] and so saying he expired.

When the centurion saw what had happened he praised God saying, 'A true man if ever there was one!' And all the people who had gathered for the spectacle when they observed what had happened turned away beating their breasts [saying, 'Woe to us! What has been done to-day? Woe for our sins, for the desolation of Jerusalem has drawn near.'] [115]

All the acquaintances of Jesus and the women who had followed him from Galilee were standing at a distance looking on.

[a] The notice over him was in these terms, 'The King of the Jews'.
[112] Hos. x. 8, and cp. Rev. vi. 16.   [113] Cp. Acts vii. 60.   [114] Ps. xxxi. 5.
[115] Reading preserved in the Old Latin and partly in the Curetonian Syriac text.

Now there was a man called Joseph, a member of the Council, a good man and true,[a] from Arimathea, a town of Judea, one who awaited the Kingdom of God. Approaching Pilate he requested the body of Jesus, and taking it down, wrapped it in linen, and deposited it in a rock-cut tomb where no one had previously been buried. It was the day of preparation, and the sabbath had almost begun. The women, those who had come from Galilee with Jesus, followed behind, took note of the tomb and how the body was laid, and went away to prepare spices and ointments.

They were inactive on the sabbath as the commandment required; but at early dawn of the day after the sabbath they went to the tomb carrying the spices they had prepared. There they found the boulder rolled aside from the tomb, but when they entered it they did not find the body. While they were puzzling over this, suddenly two men stood beside them in dazzling robes. As the women bent their faces to the ground with fear, they said to them, 'Why do you seek the living among the dead? Remember how he told you while still in Galilee that the Son of Man must be betrayed into the hands of sinful men, and be crucified, and he raised up on the third day.' Then they recalled those words of his, and returning from the tomb reported all this to the eleven and the others.

They were Mary of Magdala, Johanna, Mary mother of James, and the other women with them, who told this to the envoys. But what they said seemed to them completely fantastic, and they refused to believe them. [But Peter got up and ran to the tomb, and peering in saw only the linen wrappings; and he went home wondering what had happened.]

That same day, however, two of the envoys were making their way to a village nearly seven miles from Jerusalem called Emmaus, and talking to each other of all these circumstances. They were deep in conversation and discussion when Jesus himself came up with them and walked beside them; but their eyes were kept from recognizing him.

'What is all this you are debating with each other as you walk?' he said to them.

They stood abashed.

Then one of them called Cleopas answered, 'Are you such an isolated stranger in Jerusalem that you do not know what has been going on there these days?'

'What, for instance?' he inquired.

'Why, about Jesus the Nazarene,' they said, 'a prophet mighty in word and deed in the sight of God and all the people, and how our head priests and rulers had sentence of death passed on him and crucified him. We were expecting him to be the one destined to deliver Israel. But there it is, it is now the third day since all this happened, though some women connected with us gave us a shock. They were at the tomb very

[a] He had been no party to their design and action.

early, and not only did not find his body, but came and told us also that they had seen a vision of angels, who declared he was alive. So some of our company went to the tomb, and found it just as the women said, but they did not see him.'

Then Jesus said to them, 'You fools, so slow-witted in grasping all that the Prophets have declared! Did not the Messiah have to suffer in this way before entering his glory?' And he proceeded from Moses and the various Prophets to explain to them in all the Scriptures what related to himself.

They were now approaching the village for which they were bound, and he gave the impression he was going farther. But they pressed him saying. 'Do stay with us. It is getting towards evening and daylight is going fast.' So he stayed with them.

Then when he sat down with them to eat he took the bread, recited the blessing, broke it, and handed it to them. Now their eyes were opened and they recognized him; and he vanished from their sight. Then they said to each other, 'Did not our hearts glow as he talked to us on the road, and as he expounded the Scriptures to us?'

Instantly they rose to return to Jerusalem, and found the eleven and their associates gathered there, who informed them that the Master had indeed risen and had appeared to Simon. Then they described their own experiences on the road, and how they recognized him when he broke the bread.

No sooner had they told their story than Jesus stood before them [and said to them, 'Peace be with you']. Startled and terrified, they believed they were seeing a ghost. But he said to them, 'Why are you alarmed, and what puts this idea into your heads? See my hands and my feet, that it is indeed I myself. Feel me and see. A ghost does not have flesh and bones as you see I have.' [So saying, he showed them his hands and feet.]

As they were still incredulous from joy and amazement, he said to them, 'Have you anything to eat handy?'

They offered him a piece of grilled fish. He accepted it and ate it in front of them. Then he said to them, 'I used these very words to you when I was with you, "Everything that is written of me in the Law of Moses, and in the Prophets and Psalms, must be fulfilled." '

Then he explained to them the implication of the Scriptures, and told them, 'Thus it is written, for the Messiah to suffer and be raised from the dead the third day, and for repentance to be proclaimed in his name to all nations for the forgiveness of their sins. Starting with Jerusalem, you are to testify to these matters. Be sure I shall send what the Father promised you. Stay in the city until you are invested with power from on high.'

Then he led them as far as Bethany, and lifting his hands blessed them. And as he blessed them he parted from them [and was borne up to heaven]. And they [when they had paid him homage] returned to Jerusalem full of joy, and were habitually in the Temple, blessing God.

LUKE

A HISTORY OF

CHRISTIAN BEGINNINGS

PART II

HOW THE GOOD NEWS CAME TO THE GENTILES

(Acts of the Envoys)

Preface to the *Acts*

IN THIS SEQUEL to his account of the life and teaching of Jesus, the author—who there is reason to believe was Luke—tells the story of the growth and expansion of the Christian Community. His task was twofold, to show how it came about that so many non-Jews throughout the Empire had become believers in Jesus, and to placate the authorities on behalf of the Christians by a narrative that makes clear they have no political or subversive designs and in general have been treated with fairness and friendliness by Roman officials. It is important to remember that at the time the author was writing Christianity was not a religion or association authorized by the Romans, as was Judaism, and was regarded and treated as hostile to the State and Empire. To profess Christianity was a capital crime.

The hero of the book is Paul, envoy to the Gentiles, himself a Roman citizen. Luke his friend, admirer, and companion for a considerable period, brings him at the end to Rome, after he had appealed to Caesar in order to escape certain death at the hands of the Sadducean hierarchy at Jerusalem. In the book Paul is left with that appeal still to be heard, enjoying full liberty of speech and access to his friends while under house arrest. It has been suggested that the author projected a third volume completing Paul's life, but it seems more probable that the outcome of the appeal was omitted deliberately, since Paul's execution at Roman hands would have helped to destroy the very impression Luke had laboured so carefully to create. 'And so we came to Rome' rather marks the climax of achievement, the arrival of Paul at the heart of the Empire he had so largely evangelized.

The title *Acts of the Envoys,* not original, is therefore somewhat misleading. Of the Twelve only Peter plays any considerable part in the story, and chiefly in connexion with the 'opening of the door of faith to the Gentiles'. The early scenes and events in Palestine are carefully chosen and arranged with an eye to the main object of the work, and leave great and tantalizing gaps which other available sources permit us as yet to cover only very sketchily. The Judaeo-Christian side of the story remains largely unknown, and a balanced judgment is therefore almost impossible. But what we are given is of much historical importance and interest, affording us an intimate and often dramatic glimpse of life and conditions in many lands in the first century A.D. Some minor errors which can be detected serve to bring more strongly into relief the general and even detailed authenticity of the descriptions. Of particular worth is a contemporary record written in the first person plural, either by the author or another, perhaps Silas, long extracts from which are reproduced.

The style and phraseology of much of the first half of the book reveal dependence on Hebrew or Aramaic material, at least indirectly. The Hebrew idiom here is not merely imitated, and indicates a written source or sources.

———◆———

THE ACTS OF THE ENVOYS

Luke (Part Two)

FOREWORD

In my previous treatise, Theophilus,[1] I covered everything that Jesus did and taught down to the time when, having instructed by the holy Spirit the envoys he had chosen, he was taken on high. To those envoys he had shown himself alive after he had suffered by many conclusive proofs, being seen by them over a period of forty days, during which he spoke of matters relating to the Kingdom of God. While in their company he ordered them not to leave Jerusalem, but to await 'what the Father promised, which you have heard from me. For John immersed in water, but you shall be immersed in holy Spirit very shortly.'

As they were going along together they asked him, 'Master, are you going to restore the kingdom to Israel at this time?'

'It is not for you to know times and seasons,' he replied. 'These are matters which the Father has reserved exclusively for himself. But you will be given power when the holy Spirit comes upon you, and will be my witnesses in Jerusalem, and throughout Judea and Samaria, and to the ends of the earth.'

When he had said this, while they looked on, he was borne on high, and a cloud blotted him from view. As they strained their eyes skywards after his going, two men in white robes appeared suddenly beside them, who said, 'Why are you Galileans staring at the sky? This Jesus who has been taken from you to heaven will return in exactly the same way as you have seen him go.'

Then they returned to Jerusalem from the hill called the Mount of Olives.[a]

_____

[a] It is close to Jerusalem, only a sabbath day's walk away. (About a mile. Tr.)

[1] Cp. the similar opening of Josephus's 2nd treatise *Against Apion*, dedicated to his patron Epaphroditus.

When they got back they went upstairs to the upper part of the house where they were staying, they being Peter, John, James and Andrew, Philip and Thomas, Bartholomew and Matthew, James son of Alphaeus, Simon the Zealot, and Judas son of James. These all by common consent were regular in attendance at prayers,[2] with the women, with Mary mother of Jesus, and with his brothers.

CHAPTER I

At this time Peter stood up before the brothers[a] and said, Brothers, it was inevitable that the scripture should be fulfilled which the holy Spirit declared beforehand by the mouth of David, regarding Judas who acted as guide to those who arrested Jesus; for he was of our number and appointed by choice to our ministry.[b] For it is written in the Book of Psalms, "Let his villa be desolate, and let no one dwell in it,"[3] and, "Let another take over his charge."[4] It is therefore essential that of the men associated with us during the whole course of the coming and going of the Lord Jesus among us, from the immersion by John to the day he was taken from us, one of them should be a witness with us to his resurrection.'

There were two nominations, Joseph surnamed Bar-Sabbas, called Justus,[5] and Matthias.

Then they prayed, 'Thou, O Lord, who knowest the hearts of all, do thou declare which of these two thou hast chosen to take the place in this ministry and envoyship left vacant by Judas when he went to his own place.'

So they held a ballot, and the vote went to Matthias; and he was elected to office in association with the eleven envoys.

At the completion of the Pentecostal period[7] they were all together at the same place, when suddenly there came a whistling out of the sky as of a tearing furious blast of wind that filled the whole house where they were sitting, and forking tongues as if of fire were seen by them which settled on each of them.[8] And all of them became ecstatic,[9] and began speaking in various tongues as the Spirit gave them articulation.

[a] There was a gathering of about a hundred and twenty individuals in all.
[b] This Judas acquired a plot of ground with his ill-gotten gains, and having pitched forward gashed open his middle and his intestines gushed out.[6] The fact became known to all the inhabitants of Jerusalem, so that that plot got the name in their language of *Hacel-dama* (Aram. *Chaqel-dema. Tr.*), which means 'Bloody Patch'.

[2] I.e. the three sessions of morning, afternoon and evening prayers.
[3] Ps. lxix. 25.   [4] Ps. cix. 8.   [5] An honorific title 'the Pious'.
[6] Cp. *Book of Ahikar* viii. 38; Papias, *Exposition of the Dominical Oracles.* Bk. iv., quoted by Apollinarius.
[7] When they had counted to the 50th day after Passover (Lev. xxiii. 15).
[8] The description answers to the wind called *khamsin*, which blows at this season of the year, see Ps. xxix. 5-8, though the manifestation here is of a psychic rather than a physical order.
[9] Lit. 'filled with Holy Spirit.'

Now there were resident in Jerusalem pious Jews from every nation under the skies. When this noise came the greater part gathered together and could not make it out, because each one heard them speaking his own language. Mystified and amazed they said, 'Aren't all these speakers Galileans? How is it then that we each hear our native language? Parthians, Medes, Elamites, natives of Mesopotamia, Edessa[10] and Cappadocia, Pontus, Asia, Phrygia and Pamphylia. Egypt and the parts of Libya round Cyrene, foreigners domiciled in Rome (both Jews and proselytes), Cretans, and Arabians,[11] we hear them proclaiming in our own tongues the great attributes[12] of God!'

They were indeed mystified and bewildered, asking each other, 'What can this possibly mean?' But some said scornfully, 'They're full of new wine.'

Then Peter, standing up with the eleven, raised his voice and bluntly told them, 'Jews and residents in Jerusalem all, get this clear, and heed what I say. These men are not drunk as you suspect: it is only nine in the morning. On the contrary, this represents what was stated by the Prophet Joel:

"Then in those Closing Days," God says,
"I will pour out my Spirit on all flesh,
And your sons and daughters will prophesy;
Your young men shall see visions,
And your old men dream dreams.
Even on my menservants and maidservants
Will I pour out my Spirit,
And they will prophesy.
I will show portents in the skies above,
And signs on the earth beneath,
Blood and fire and fumes of smoke."
The sun will be turned to darkness,
And the moon will become blood red,
Ere that great and awful Day of the Lord comes.
Then all who invoke the Lord's name will be saved.[13]

'Listen to this, Israelites! It concerns Jesus the Nazarene, a man proved to you to be from God by the miracles, signs and wonders, which God performed by him among you, as you yourselves know. This man, delivered up by God's deliberate intention and foreknowledge, you killed by having non-Jews[14] nail him up. But God raised him, having loosed the grip of

---

[10] Both context and sense show that the reading 'Judea' here must be wrong. On the evidence of an underlying Semitic source for this section I have assumed a scribal misreading of the original *Hadditha* (Edessa), which comes in most suitably geographically between Mesopotamia and Cappadocia. On the evangelization of Edessa see Euscb. *Eccl. Hist.* i. 13.

[11] The list contains 12 divisions, those associated between commas counting as one, corresponding to the 12 envoys.

[12] Lit. 'greatnesses' (cp. Ps. cxlv. 7; I. Chron. xvii. 19), i.e., God's holiness, sovereignty, glory, might, etc.

[13] Joel. ii. 28-32.

[14] Lit. 'the hands of those without law' (the Law of Moses).

death; for it was not possible for him to be held by it. David indeed, personating him, says,

> *"I kept the Lord steadfastly in view;*
> *For he is at my right hand lest I be shaken.*
> *So my heart is cheered and my tongue is glad:*
> *My very flesh will continue confident.*
> *For you will not relinquish my soul to Hell,*[15]
> *Nor will you allow your holy one to see decay.*
> *You have acquainted me with the ways of life:*
> *You will fill me with joy by your presence."*[16]

'Brothers, one can speak to you quite frankly about the Patriarch David. There is no question that he died and was buried, and we have his tomb with us to this very day.[17] Being then a prophet, and knowing that God had sworn to him by oath that he would seat one of his descendants on his throne,[18] he spoke with foresight of the Messiah's resurrection, that neither would he be relinquished to Hell, nor would his flesh see decay. God has raised this Jesus, a fact of which we are all witnesses. Being then exalted to God's right hand, and obtaining from the Father the promise of the holy Spirit, he has poured out what you now see and hear. David did not ascend to heaven, for he says himself,

> *The Lord said to my lord, "Sit at my right hand*
> *Till I make your foes a footstool 'neath your feet."*[19]

Let the whole house of Israel know positively that God has made this Jesus whom you have crucified both Lord and Messiah.'

As they listened they were cut to the quick, and said to Peter and the rest of the envoys, 'Oh, brothers, what are we to do?'

'Repent,' Peter told them, 'and let each of you be immersed for the forgiveness of your sins in the name of Jesus Christ, and you will receive the gift of the holy Spirit. For the promise is for you and your children, and for as many of those outside Israel[20] as the Lord our God shall call.'

In many other ways did he beg and entreat them, 'Save yourselves from this perverse generation.'

Then all those who accepted his message were immersed; and that day about three thousand persons were recruited. They were regular in attending the instruction of the envoys and the communal gathering with the breaking of bread and prayers. Every individual was awed, and many signs and wonders occurred through the envoys. All the believers collectively held everything in common. They sold their goods and possessions,

---

[15] Hades. *Sheol*, here personifying the grave.
[16] Ps. xvi, 8-11.
[17] See Jos. *Antiq* XVI. vii. 1.
[18] Ps. cxxxii. 11.
[19] Ps. cx. 1.
[20] Lit. 'those far off' (Isa. lvii. 19). Cp. below p. 326.

and distributed the proceeds to all according to individual need. By common consent also they were regular in daily attendance at the Temple, and breaking their bread at home took their meals with gladness and simplicity of mind, praising God and enjoying popular favour. Every single day the Lord added to those who were being saved.

CHAPTER II

Once when Peter and John were going up to the Temple for the afternoon service at three o'clock a man lame from birth was carried there. He was deposited daily by the entrance of the Temple called the Golden[21] Gate to solicit alms from those passing into the Temple. Seeing Peter and John about to enter the Temple he asked for alms from them. Peter looked at him, and so did John, and said, 'Rely on us.' So he reached out to them, expecting to receive something from them.

'I have no silver or gold,' Peter told him, 'but what I have I will give you. In the name of Jesus Christ the Nazarene, walk!' And he took him by the hand and raised him up.

Immediately his feet and ankles acquired strength, and he sprang upright and walked about, and entered the Temple with them walking and skipping and praising God.

All the people saw him walking and praising God, and recognizing him as the man who used to sit begging at the Golden Gate of the Temple, they were amazed and greatly excited at what had happened to him. As he kept close to Peter and John, all the people rushed to them in the portico called after Solomon.[22] There Peter addressed them as follows:

'Israelites, why are you surprised at this? Why do you stare at us as if by our own power or piety we had made this man walk? The God of Abraham, Isaac and Jacob, the God of our fathers, has honoured his servant Jesus, whom you handed over and disowned before Pilate when he had decided to release him. Yes, you disowned the Holy and Just One, and demanded that a murderer be granted you. You put to death the Fount[23] of Life, whom God raised from the dead, as we are witnesses; and by virtue of his name this man whom you see and know has been set on his feet. It is his name and the confidence it inspires which have given him his soundness of limb in the presence of you all.

'Well, brothers, I know you acted in ignorance, just as your rulers did, and God thus fulfilled what he had previously announced by the mouth of all his prophets, that the Messiah should suffer. Repent then, and turn again, that your sins may

---

[21] Golden in the sense of the colour of ripe corn, the eastern gate of polished Corinthian bronze which was exceptionally magnificent (Jos. *Wars*, V. v. 3). It is not certain whether it was the same as the Gate of Nicanor.

[22] On the porticoes see Jos. *Wars*, V. v. 2. These surrounded the Court of the Gentiles which lay outside the Temple proper.

[23] Or 'Founder'. A comparable title 'Founder of Justice' was given by the Jewish pietists (Zaddokites) to their leader (*Hab. Comm.*).

Approximate plan of the TEMPLE area.

Castle of Antonia

TADI GATE

Cloister

Herod's extension

Cloister

Antonia courtyard

TOWER

GOLDEN GATE

SOREG

Northern Cloister

CHEL

SOREG

CHEL

1

4

3

Court of the Women

2

SOREG

SOREG

KIPONUS GATE

The Mountain of the House or Sanctuary

Solomon's Portico

SOREG

SOREG

Court of the Gentiles

1 THE HOLY PLACE
2 HOLY OF HOLIES
3 ALTAR OF SACRIFICE
4 COURT OF THE PRIESTS

J.F.H.

WEST HULDAH GATE

EAST HULDAH GATE

be obliterated, and that times of relief[24] may come from the presence of the Lord, and he may send Jesus your foreordained Messiah, whom heaven must harbour till the Era of Restoration of which God spoke by the mouth of his holy prophets of old. Moses truly said, "The Lord God will raise up for you from your brothers a prophet like myself. You must heed whatever he tells you, and whoever fails to attend to that prophet will be cut off from the people.[25] In fact all the prophets, from Samuel onwards, who have at any time spoken, have announced these times.

'You are the sons of the prophets and of the covenant[26] which God made with our fathers, saying to Abraham, "In your off-spring all families of the earth shall be blest."[27] To you first, God, having raised up his servant, has sent him to bless you by turning every one of you from your evil ways.'

While they were addressing the people, the head priests, the captain of the Temple guard, and the Sadducees, came upon them, incensed at their teaching the people and proclaiming with reference to Jesus the resurrection of the dead. They arrested them and remanded them in custody until the following day; for it was already evening. But many of those who heard the Message believed, and the number of men now totalled about five thousand.

Next day their[28] rulers, with the elders and scribes, met in Jerusalem,[a] and having called the prisoners before them, de-manded, 'By what kind of power or name have you done this?'

Then Peter under inspiration replied, 'Rulers of the people and elders, if we are being interrogated to-day regarding the benefit conferred on a cripple, by what means he has been made sound, let it be known to you all, and to the whole house of Israel, that it is by the name of Jesus Christ the Nazarene whom you crucified, whom God raised from the dead. It is by this means that this man stands before you well and strong. This is the stone rejected by you builders, which has become the cop-ing-stone.[29] Deliverance by any other name there is none; for in all the world no other name has been provided by which we should be delivered.'

Remarking the eloquence of Peter and John, and noting that they were common uneducated men, they were amazed. As they recognized them for associates of Jesus, and seeing the man who had been cured standing there with them, they could make no rejoinder. Having ordered them to withdraw from the San-hedrin they put their heads together saying, 'What are we going

[a] Those who attended included the high priest Annas, Caiaphas, John, Alexander, and as many as were of the rank of head priests.

[24] Cp. Esth. iv. 14.
[25] Deut. xviii. 15, 18-19.
[26] Heb. idiom. 'Son of the Covenant', i.e., a Jew.
[27] Gen. xii. 3 · xii. 18.
[28] The author writes as a foreigner.
[29] See Ps. cxviii. 22.

to do with these men? It is patent that a significant sign has occurred through them for all the inhabitants of Jerusalem, and there is no denying it. But that it may not obtain even wider circulation among the people let us intimidate them by threats never to use his name again to anyone.' So calling them in they gave them stringent orders neither to mention Jesus nor to teach in his name.

Peter and John replied, however, 'You must be the judges whether it is right in God's sight to heed you in preference to God. So far as we are concerned we cannot refrain from speaking of what we have seen and heard.'

After subjecting them to further threats they let them go, finding no safe way of punishing them on account of the people, because they all praised God for what had happened; for the man was over forty years of age on whom this curative sign had been performed.

On their release they went to their own friends and reported to them what the head priests and elders had said. When they heard it they cried aloud to God with one accord, 'Lord of the universe, thou who didst make heaven and earth, the sea and all that is therein, thou art he who didst say through the holy Spirit by the mouth of our father David thy servant,

> *Wherefore did the heathen rage,*
> *And the peoples meditate vain things?*
> *The kings of the earth ranged themselves,*
> *And the rulers joined forces together,*
> *Against the Lord and his Anointed.*[30]

For assuredly in this city they joined forces together against thy devoted servant Jesus, whom thou didst anoint, both Herod and Pontius Pilate, with the Gentiles and people of Israel, to accomplish whatever thy hand and will had determined beforehand should be done.

'And now, Lord, regard their threatenings, and grant to thy servants to declare thy Message with all eloquence, with the stretching forth of thy hand to heal, and with signs and wonders to be performed through the name of thy devoted servant Jesus.' were assembled was shaken, and they all became ecstatic and When they had offered their petition the place where they declared God's Message eloquently.

CHAPTER III

The mass of believers were united heart and soul, and not one claimed any of his possessions as his own. Everything to them was common property. With telling effect the envoys of the Lord Jesus recounted the evidence of his resurrection, and indeed intense fervour animated them all. Neither was any of

[30] Ps. ii. 1-2.

them in want; for all those who owned lands or houses sold them and brought the price they realized and laid it at the feet of the envoys: it was then distributed to each according to need. For instance, Joseph a Levite, by birth a Cypriot, who was given the name of Barnabas[a] by the envoys, sold a farm he had and brought the money and laid it at the feet of the envoys. On the other hand, a man called Ananias with his wife Sapphira sold a property and kept back part of the proceeds with his wife's connivance, and bringing only a proportion laid that at the feet of the envoys.

'Ananias,' Peter said to him, 'however did Satan possess you to make you play the holy Spirit false and keep back part of the proceeds of the land? While you had it wasn't it your own? And when you disposed of it wasn't the money under your own control? Whatever made you do it? You have not lied to men, but to God.'

On hearing this Ananias fell dead, and great fear took hold of all who had listened. The young men rose and covered him up, and carried him out and buried him.

Some three hours later his wife came in unaware of what had happened. 'Tell me,' Peter said to her, 'did you sell the land for such a figure?'

'Yes,' she replied, 'that was the figure.'

'Whatever made you conspire together to try the Lord's Spirit?' Peter demanded. 'There at the door are the footsteps of those who have been burying your husband: they will carry you out too.'

Instantly she fell at his feet and expired. When the young men entered they found her dead, and carrying her out buried her beside her husband.

Great awe seized the whole community as well as those who had heard all this.[b]

Now by the hands of the envoys many signs and wonders were performed among the people, so that they even brought the ailing out into the streets and laid them on couches and mattresses, that when Peter came by at least his shadow might fall across some of them. The concourse of those bringing the ailing and people afflicted by foul spirits even came from towns all round Jerusalem, and every one of them was cured.

Then the high priest rose in a towering passion with all his associates,[c] and arrested the envoys and lodged them in the public jail. But during the night an angel of the Lord opened the prison doors, led them out, and said, 'Go and stand in the

[a] Translated it means 'Son of Encouragement'.[31]
[b] They were all by common consent in Solomon's portico. But none of the others dared adhere to them, though the people extolled them. Yet more believers did come over to the Master, a number both of men and women.
[c] They were of the Sadducean party.
[31] Bar-Nabas, i.e. the Encourager.

Temple, and declare to the people everything that concerns this Life.'[32]

On hearing this the envoys entered the Temple first thing in the morning and taught there.

When the high priest and his associates arrived they convened the Sanhedrin and the entire Senate[33] of the children of Israel, and sent to the jail to fetch the envoys. But when the officers got there they did not find them in the prison. So they returned and reported, 'We found the jail securely shut and the warders on duty at the doors, but on gaining admittance we found no one inside.'

When the captain of the Temple guard and the head priests heard this they were quite at a loss how it could have happened. Then someone came and informed them, 'The men you put in prison are actually standing in the Temple teaching the people.'

So the captain of the Temple guard went with his officers and brought them, but without using force, for they were afraid they might be stoned by the people.

When the envoys were before the Sanhedrin the high priest asked them, 'Did we not give you strict orders not to teach in this name? Yet here have you filled Jerusalem with your teaching, and want to make us answerable for this man's blood.'

Peter replied for the envoys, 'We owe a higher obedience to God than to man. The God of our fathers raised Jesus, for whose hanging on a gibbet[34] you were directly responsible. God has elevated him to his right hand as Founder[35] and Deliverer to afford Israel repentance and forgiveness of sins. We are witnesses to this fact, and so is the holy Spirit which God has bestowed on those who obey him.'

When they heard this they were cut to the quick and wanted to execute them. But a Pharisee called Gamaliel,[36] a teacher of the Law respected by the entire people, rose in the Sanhedrin and ordered the men to be taken outside for a while.

Then he said to the assembly, 'Israelites, be very careful before you carry out your intentions regarding these men. Some time ago Theudas started up,[37] claiming to be someone of consequence. To him about four hundred men attached themselves. He was killed, and all his followers scattered and brought to nothing. Later, Judas the Galilean started up at the time of the census,[38] and drew people after him. He too was killed, and all his followers dispersed. So I say to you, therefore, stand aside

[32] A Hebraism, lit. 'all the words of this Life', how to obtain the promise of Eternal Life in the Messianic Era.
[33] The Great Sanhedrin, not merely the council of the hierarchy, the lesser Sanhedrin, which dealt only with religious issues.
[34] Crucifixion not being a Jewish form of punishment there was no Hebrew or Aramaic word for it.
[35] See above p. 197, n. 23.
[36] Rabban Gamaliel, grandson of the famous Hillel, at this time a high officer of the Sanhedrin.
[37] Josephus (Antiq. XX. v. 1) dates the activity of Theudas much later than Judas of Galilee, later even than the time (33 or 34 A.D.) at which Gamaliel here makes this speech.
[38] See Lk. ii. 1, above p. 145; Jos. Wars, viii. 1, etc.

from these men and leave them alone, in case you may be found in conflict with God. If their design or action is of human inspiration it will fizzle out, but if it is of divine inspiration you cannot suppress them.'

Persuaded by him, they recalled the envoys, had them flogged, and after ordering them not to speak in the name of Jesus set them at liberty.

They left the presence of the Sanhedrin rejoicing that they had been thought worthy to suffer dishonour for the name; and daily in the Temple and at home they never ceased to teach and to proclaim Jesus as Messiah.

CHAPTER IV

At that period, when the number of disciples had substantially increased, there was a murmuring of the foreign Jews against the native Jews[39] because their widows were discriminated against in the daily distribution. So the twelve called a general meeting of the disciples and said, 'It is not satisfactory that we should neglect God's Message to look after tables.[40] So, brothers, recommend from among yourselves seven men of sympathy and sense who have your confidence, and we will appoint them for this function, while we concentrate on prayer and the requirements of the Message.'

The suggestion met with the approval of the entire company, and they selected Stephen, a man of great faith and insight, together with Philip, Prochorus, Nikanor, Timon, Parmenas,[41] and Nikolaus a proselyte from Antioch. These they presented to the envoys, who after prayer ordained them.

God's Message spread, and the number of disciples in Jerusalem was greatly augmented. Quite a considerable body of the priests gave their allegiance.

Stephen, full of fervour and power, performed great signs and wonders among the people. However, some persons arose belonging to the synagogue known as that of the Libyans,[42] Cyrenians and Alexandrians, and to the synagogue of those from Cilicia and Asia, and debated with Stephen. But they were unable to resist the sense and conviction with which he spoke. So they primed men to say, 'We have heard him use insulting language about Moses, and even God,' and they roused both the people and the elders and scribes. Then setting upon him they seized him and brought him before the Sanhedrin, and produced false witnesses who stated, 'This man never stops denouncing this Holy Place[43] and the Law; for we have heard him say that

---

[39] Gr. 'Hellenists against the Hebrews'.
[40] Or perhaps 'act as bankers'. The envoys had been receiving and distributing funds. Moneychangers were called 'table-men'.
[41] These were Hellenistic Jews as their names show.
[42] Accepting the emendation *Libystinon* for *Libertinon* (freedmen). Jews from different parts and different trades had their own synagogues in Jerusalem. Here those from N. Africa and Asia Minor are distinguished.
[43] I.e. the Temple.

Jesus the Nazarene will destroy this Place and change the customs handed down to us by Moses.'

Then all who sat in the Sanhedrin bent their gaze on him, and saw a countenance as open as that of an angel. 'Is all this true?' asked the high priest.

'Listen, brothers and fathers,' Stephen replied. 'The God of glory appeared to our father Abraham when he was in Mesopotamia, prior to his residence in Harran, and said to him, "Leave your country and kindred, and go to the land I will show you."[44] So he left the country of the Chaldeans and made his home in Harran. Later, after his father's death, God removed him to this land in which you now live. But he gave him no inheritance in it, not even a foot[45] of territory, though he had promised, when he had no child, to give it him as a possession and his descendants after him.[46] God also declared that his descendants would be aliens in a foreign land, where they would be enslaved and ill-treated for four hundred years; but "the nation to which they are enslaved I will judge."[47] God said, "and afterwards they shall go out and worship me in this place."[48] And God gave him the covenant of circumcision.

'So Abraham begot Isaac, and circumcised him on the eighth day, and Isaac begot Jacob, and Jacob the twelve Patriarchs. And the Patriarchs out of jealousy sold Joseph to Egypt; but God was with him, and brought him out of all his troubles, and gave him wit and wisdom in audience with Pharaoh king of Egypt, who appointed him controller of Egypt and of all his household.

'Now a famine and great affliction affected the whole of Egypt and Canaan, and our fathers could find no fodder. But Jacob having heard there was corn in Egypt dispatched our fathers on a first mission. On the second occasion Joseph made himself known to his brothers, and Joseph's kinship was disclosed to Pharaoh. Then Joseph sent and invited his father Jacob and all his relations to come to him, seventy-five persons in all; and Jacob went down to Egypt. There he and our fathers ended their days, and were carried to Shechem, and laid to rest in the sepulchre which Abraham had purchased for a sum of money from the sons of Hamor at Shechem.

'As the promised time approached which God had sworn to Abraham, the people increased and multiplied in Egypt until another king reigned over Egypt, who had no knowledge of Joseph. He got the better of our race, and ill-used our fathers, by forcing them to expose their infants so as to cause the race to die out. It was at this period Moses was born, a lovely child, who was nurtured for three months in his father's house. And when he was exposed, Pharaoh's daughter picked him up and reared

44 Gen. xii. 1.
45 Lit. 'step of a foot', Deut. ii. 5.
46 Gen. xvii. 8.
47 Gen. xv. 13-14.
48 Exod iii. 12.

him as her own son. Moses was trained in all the wisdom of the Egyptians and was mighty in speech and action.

'When he had reached the age of forty he had an inclination to take a look at his brothers of the children of Israel. Seeing one of them being injured, he defended him, and avenged the man who had been bludgeoned by striking down the Egyptian. He imagined that his brothers would realize that God was going to deliver them through his instrumentality; but they did not realize it. The next day, indeed, coming across two of them fighting, he intervened to make peace saying, "You are brothers. Why do you harm each other?" But the one who was injuring his fellow pushed him aside and said, "Who constituted you our ruler and adjudicator? Perhaps you would like to kill me as you did the Egyptian yesterday?"[49] Upon this Moses fled, and became an alien in the land of Midian, where he begot two sons.

'At the expiry of forty years an angel appeared to him in the wilderness of Mount Sinai in the flame of a burning thorn-bush, and Moses was amazed at the spectacle. As he went forward to inspect it the voice of the Lord came, "I am the God of your fathers, the God of Abraham, Isaac and Jacob." Then Moses trembled and dared not investigate. And the Lord said to him, "Remove your sandals, for the spot on which you stand is holy ground. I have indeed seen the ill-treatment of my people in Egypt, and I have heard their groans, and have come down to set them free. So now come, I am going to send you to Egypt."[50] This Moses whom they rejected saying, "Who constituted you ruler and adjudicator?" God sent to them as ruler and redeemer with the aid of the angel who appeared to him in the bush. He brought them out, performing signs and wonders in Egypt, and at the Red Sea, and in the wilderness for forty years.[51]

'It was this Moses who said to the children of Israel, "God will raise up for you from your brothers a prophet like myself."[52] He it was who at the assembly in the wilderness acted as intermediary between the angel who spoke to him on Mount Sinai and our fathers, and who received vital pronouncements[53] to give us. But our fathers did not want to submit to him, and put him from them, turning back in their minds to Egypt, telling Aaron, "Make us gods to march at our head, for we do not know what has become of this Moses who brought us out of the land of Egypt."[54] They made themselves a calf at that time, and celebrated a sacrifice to an idol, and rejoiced over what their hands had made. So God turned from them and gave them over to the worship of the host of heaven, as it is stated in the Book of the Prophets,[55]

49 Exod. ii. 13-14.
50 Exod. iii. 6-10.
51 Cp. *Assumpt. Mos.* iii. 11. To this point the speech follows the lines of the recital of the Exodus given at the *Seder* (Passover Eve Service).
52 Deut. xviii. 15.
53 Or 'Oracles' (*Logia*).
54 Exod. xxxii. 1.
55 The 12 Minor Prophets (Hosea to Malachi) forming one book.

> *"Was it to me you offered victims and sacrifices*
> *Those forty years in the desert, house of Israel?*
> *It was the shrine of Moloch you bore along,*
> *And the star of the god Rompha,*
> *Those images you made for your worship:*
> *So will I remove you beyond Babylon."*[56]

Yet our fathers had the Tent of Testimony in the wilderness, as God had ordained, telling Moses to make it according to the pattern[57] he had seen. Our fathers who succeeded them brought it in with Joshua to the territory possessed by the nations whom God drove out before our fathers. So it remained to the time of David, who found favour in God's sight, and promised to find a habitation for the God of Jacob. It was Solomon who built a house for God; though the Most High does not dwell in edifices, as the prophet says,

> *"The heaven is my throne,*
> *And the earth my footstool.*
> *What sort of house will you build me?"*
> *Says the Lord,*
> *"Or on what spot am I to rest?*
> *Did not my hand make all these things?"*[58]

'You stiffnecked and uncircumcised in heart and ears, you are always in opposition to the holy Spirit! As it was with your[59] fathers, so it is with you. Which of the prophets did your fathers not persecute? And which of those did they not kill, who proclaimed in advance the coming of that Just One whose betrayers and murderers you have now become, you who received the Law as an angelic compact, but have not kept it?'

When the members of the court heard this they were cut to the quick and ground their teeth at him. Stephen, inspired, gazed fixedly heavenwards and saw the divine glory, and Jesus stationed at God's right hand. 'Look!' he cried. 'I see heaven wide open, and the Son of Man standing at God's right hand.'

Shouting out, they stopped their ears, and rushing at Stephen by common consent they hustled him outside the city and stoned him. The witnesses[60] deposited their cloaks at the feet of a young man called Saul, and Stephen's execution had Saul's full approval.[a]

That same day there broke out a violent persecution of the community at Jerusalem, and except for the envoys they were all dispersed over the countries of Judea and Samaria. Pious

[a] So they stoned Stephen, while he appealed, 'Lord Jesus, receive my spirit.' Bending his knees he cried aloud, 'Lord, count not this sin against them,' and so saying fell asleep.

[56] Amos v. 25-27.
[57] The same words are used for 'Tent' and 'pattern' as for 'shrine' and 'images' in the quotation from Amos.
[58] Isa. lxvi. 1-2.
[59] Note the change in this paragraph from first to second person.
[60] Who were obliged to cast the first stones.

men interred Stephen, and made great lamentation for him.
Meanwhile Saul ravaged the community, entering house after
house and dragging off both men and women to prison.

CHAPTER V

Those who were dispersed went far afield[61] proclaiming the
Message. Philip, however, went down to the capital of Samaria[62]
and proclaimed the Messiah to them. The populace paid the
closest attention to what Philip had to say, listening with one
accord to his words, and noting the signs he performed.[a] There
was indeed much rejoicing in that city.

Now a man called Simon had been in that city previously,
practising magic and turning the heads of the Samaritan people,
claiming to be someone of consequence. High and low alike had
given heed to him saying, 'He is that divine power called the
Great Power.' He had so taken them in with his magical arts
that they had adhered to him for quite a time. But when they
believed Philip's preaching about the Kingdom of God and the
name of Jesus Christ they underwent immersion, both men and
women. Even Simon himself believed, and after his immersion
dogged the steps of Philip, observing with utter astonishment
both the signs and the remarkable miracles that took place.

When the envoys at Jerusalem heard that Samaria had welcomed God's Message they sent Peter and John to them. On
coming down these prayed that they might receive holy Spirit.[b]
Then they laid their hands on them and they received holy
Spirit.

When Simon saw that the Spirit was bestowed through the
imposition of hands by the envoys he offered them money saying, 'Give me this power too, so that whoever I place my hands
on may receive holy Spirit.'

'May your silver and yourself go to perdition!' Peter said to
him, 'for imagining that God's gift could be acquired for
money. You have no part or lot in this business, for your heart
is not right in God's sight. So repent of your wickedness, and
beg God that what your brain has hatched may be forgiven you;
for I perceive you are a sac of venom and the essence of
malevolence.'

'Do please entreat the Lord for me,' Simon replied, 'that not
a thing of what you have said may befall me!'

When the envoys had testified and given the Master's Message they returned to Jerusalem after proclaiming the News to
many Samaritan villages. But an angel of the Lord spoke to

---

[a] For many possessed by foul spirits had them come out of them
shrieking, and many paralytics and lame people were cured.
[b] So far it had not fallen on any of them: they had only reached
the stage of being immersed in the name of the Lord Jesus.
[61] See xi. 19, below p. 213.   [62] Then called Sebaste.

Philip saying, 'Rise and go south along the road that runs from Jerusalem to Gaza.'[a]

So he rose and set off, and thus came upon an Ethiopian eunuch holding high office under Kandace queen of the Ethiopians,[b] who had been to worship at Jerusalem and was now returning seated in his chariot reading the Prophet Isaiah.

'Go and join that chariot,' the Spirit prompted Philip.

When he ran forward he heard him reading the Prophet Isaiah, and said, 'Do you understand what you are reading?'

'However can I,' he replied, 'unless someone explains it to me?' He begged Philip to get up and sit beside him. The portion of Scripture he was reading was this,

> He was led as a sheep to the slaughter,
> And as a lamb before its shearer is mute,
> So he opens not his mouth.
> In his humility his judgment is taken away.
> His generation who shall describe;
> For his life is taken from the earth?[63]

So the eunuch said to Philip, 'Of whom, may I ask, is the prophet saying this, of himself or someone else?'

Speaking up, Philip began from the scripture to proclaim Jesus to him.

As they continued along the road they came to water. 'Look, water!' cried the eunuch. 'What is to prevent my being immersed?'

He ordered the chariot to stop, and they both stepped down into the water, Philip and the eunuch, and he immersed him. When they rose from the water the Spirit of the Lord snatched Philip away, and the eunuch joyfully resuming his journey never saw him again. But Philip found himself at Azotus,[64] and passing through proclaimed the News in every town until he reached Caesarea.[65]

CHAPTER VI

In the meantime Saul, still giving vent to dire threats against the disciples of the Master, went to the high priest and begged him for letters to Damascus, for the synagogues there; so that should he find any of this persuasion, whether men or women, he could bring them in bonds to Jerusalem as prisoners.

As he neared Damascus in the course of his journey, suddenly a light from heaven blinded him, and falling to the ground he heard a voice saying to him, 'Saul, Saul, why are you hunting me?'

---

[a] That road is desert.
[b] He was actually her Lord Treasurer.
[63] Isa. liii. 7-8 (LXX).   [64] Otherwise Ashdod on the coastal plain.
[65] Travelling north touching Lydda, Joppa, and other places where Peter afterwards visited the believers (ix. 32, below Ch. VII). Caesarea was the seat of the Roman governor of Judea and Samaria.

'Who are you, lord?' he asked.

'I am Jesus, whom you are hunting. Now rise, and go into the city, and you will be told what to do.'

Saul's companions stood there speechless, hearing the voice but seeing no one.

When Saul rose from the ground, and had opened his eyes, his sight had gone. So they led him by the hand, and conducted him to Damascus.

Now there was a disciple in Damascus called Ananias, and the Master said to him in a vision, 'Ananias!'

'Here I am, Master,' he replied.

'Rise,' said the Master, 'and go to the street called Straight Cut, and inquire at the house of Judas for Saul called the Tarsian. He is praying there, and has beheld a man called Ananias coming and laying his hands on him so that he may regain his sight.'

'But Master,' Ananias answered, 'I have heard of this man from many people, how much harm he has done your saints at Jerusalem. And now he is here with authority from the head priests to apprehend all who invoke your name.'

'Go nevertheless,' the Master told him, 'for he is my chosen instrument to uphold my name before nations and kings and the children of Israel. I will give him to understand how much he must suffer for my sake.'

So Ananias set off and went to the house, and laying his hands upon him said, 'Brother Saul, the Master—Jesus who appeared to you on the road as you came—has sent me, that you may regain your sight and receive spirtual illumination.'

At once something like scales fell from his eyes, and he could see again. Rising, he was immersed, and taking nourishment was strengthened.

Saul remained some time with the Damascus disciples[66] and forthwith proclaimed Jesus in the synagogues as Son of God. All who listened were amazed and said, 'Isn't he the man who at Jerusalem was so bent on the destruction of those who invoked this name that he came here expressly to conduct them as prisoners to the head priests?'

But Saul became increasingly skilful, and completely discomfited the Jewish inhabitants of Damascus, proving that here is the Messiah.

When things had gone on like this for some time the Jews plotted to kill him; but the plot was disclosed to Saul. They even kept a close watch on the gates day and night to kill him. The disciples, however, took him by night and lowered him down the city wall in a crate.

On arriving at Jerusalem Saul attempted to join the disciples. But they were all afraid of him and refused to credit that he

[66] Saul (Paul) says he went away to Arabia and then returned to Damascus. For his own version of the course of events see his letter to the Galatian communities, below pp. 257-258.

was a disciple. Barnabas got in touch with him, however, and brought him to the envoys, and described to them how Saul had seen the Master on the road, and how he had spoken to him, and how at Damascus he had argued eloquently on behalf of Jesus. So then he was free to come and go with them at Jerusalem, and spoke eloquently on behalf of the Master, particularly engaging the foreign Jews in debate. But when the brothers became aware that these had designs on his life they brought him down to Caesarea and sent him away to Tarsus.

The Community throughout Judea, Galilee, and Samaria now enjoyed peace. Founded upon and motivated by the fear of the Lord and the exhortation of the holy Spirit it grew ever larger.

CHAPTER VII

In the course of his visits to every section of the Community Peter duly came down to the saints living at Lydda. There he found a man called Aeneas, who had been bed-ridden with paralysis for eight years.

'Jesus Christ cures you, Aeneas,' Peter said to him. 'Rise, and make your bed.'

At once he got up; and all who lived at Lydda and Sharon saw him, and they came over to the Master.

In Joppa there was a female disciple called Tabitha.[a] She was noted for her charitable actions and gifts. At this time she was taken ill and died, and having washed her corpse they laid her in the women's apartment upstairs. Lydda was close to Joppa, so the disciples learning that Peter was there sent two men to him with the request, 'Please come to us as quickly as you can.'

So Peter rose and accompanied them. When he arrived at Joppa they took him upstairs, and all the widows stood there with him weeping and displaying the tunics and cloaks Dorcas had made while she was with them. Putting them all outside, Peter went down on his knees and prayed. Then turning to the corpse he said, 'Tabitha, rise!'

She opened her eyes, and seeing Peter sat up. After assisting her to rise he called in the saints and widows and presented her to them alive. This became known throughout Joppa, and many believed in the Master.

Peter stayed on for some time at Joppa with a certain Simon the tanner.

Now at Caesarea there was a man called Cornelius, a centurion of the cohort known as *Italica*,[67] pious and revering God[68] with all his family, one who gave a great deal in charity to the people and looked continually to God.

[a] Known as Dorcas by translation.[69]

[67] I.e. the Italian Cohort.
[68] A Gentile who accepted the One God, but was not a full proselyte to Judaism.
[69] Tabitha is Aramaic and Dorcas is the Greek translation of the name which means Gazelle.

About three o'clock[70] one afternoon he saw distinctly in a vision an angel of God coming and saying to him, 'Cornelius!'

Staring at him fearfully he replied, 'What is it, Lord?'

'Your prayers and charitable actions have come up for remembrance before God,' he told him. 'So now send to Joppa with an invitation to one Simon surnamed Peter. He is lodging with Simon the tanner, whose house is by the sea.'

When the angel who spoke to him had vanished, Cornelius summoned two of his retainers and a pious soldier who was devoted to him, explained everything to them, and dispatched them to Joppa.

Next day, while they were still on the road and approaching the city, Peter went up on the roof about noon to pray. He was feeling rather hungry and wanted his meal. While they were preparing it he fell into a trance, and saw heaven opened and a kind of bag let down like a huge sail-cloth, lowered to the ground by the four corners.[71] In this were a variety of quad-rupeds, creeping things of the earth and birds of the air. 'Rise, Peter, kill and eat!' came a voice to him. 'On no account, lord,' said Peter. 'I have never eaten anything impure[72] or unclean.' A second time the voice came to him, 'What God has cleansed you are not to treat as impure.' This happened three times, and then the bag was drawn up to heaven.

While Peter was struggling in his own mind for an explana-tion of the vision he had seen, the men sent by Cornelius had been inquiring for Simon's house, and now stood at the gate calling out to learn if the Simon surnamed Peter lodged there.

Peter was still pondering over the vision when the Spirit said, 'There are three men looking for you. Rise and go down and set off with them without hesitation, for I have sent them.'

Then Peter went down and told the men, 'I am the one you want. What can I do for you?'

They told him, 'Centurion Cornelius, a religious and god-fearing man, well-respected by the whole Jewish nation, was advised by a holy angel to send for you to come to his house to hear things you would have to say.'

So he invited them in and put them up, and the next day he rose and went with them accompanied by some of the brothers from Joppa. The following day they reached Caesarea. There Cornelius was awaiting them, and had invited his relations and intimate friends. Directly Peter entered he came forward and prostrated himself at his feet. But Peter raised him and said, 'Please stand up. I am just an ordinary human being.'

Conversing with him he went in, and found a number of people assembled. 'You are well aware,' Peter said to them, 'that it is quite against the rules for a Jew to associate with or visit

[70] The time of afternoon prayer.
[71] The version may have assumed this from the scene of loading and unloading in Joppa harbour no doubt visible to Peter from where he was on the roof of the house by the sea.
[72] See Lev. v. 2; xi. 46-7.

someone of another race. But God has shown me that I must not regard any man as impure or unclean. That is why I came when I was sent for without raising any objection. Please tell me, then, the reason you sent for me.'

'About this time four days ago,' Cornelius replied, 'about three in the afternoon, I was praying in my house, when a man stood beside me in shining robes and said, "Cornelius, your prayer has been heard, and your charitable actions have been mentioned before God. Send therefore to Joppa, and call for Simon surnamed Peter who lodges at the house of Simon the tanner by the sea." Now here we all are in God's presence to listen to everything the Lord has bid you say.'

Then Peter proceeded to speak as follows. 'Now indeed I realize that God makes no distinctions, but in every race the man who reveres him and acts charitably is accepted by him.

'You know the Message that God, who is Lord of all, sent to the children of Israel, proclaiming peace by Jesus Christ. That announcement, taking its rise from Galilee after the immersion which John proclaimed, spread throughout Judea, telling of Jesus of Nazareth, whom God anointed with holy Spirit and power, who went about doing good and curing all who were in the Devil's clutches; for God was with him. We are witnesses to everything he did in the land of the Jews and in Jerusalem. But they killed him and hanged him on a gibbet. This man God raised on the third day, and granted a sight of him, not to all the people but to witnesses previously selected by God, namely ourselves, who ate and drank with him after his resurrection from the dead. He then commanded us to preach to the people and solemnly declare that he is the man appointed by God as judge of the living and the dead. All the prophets testify to this, that everyone who puts his trust in him will receive forgiveness of sins for his sake.'

While he was delivering this speech the holy Spirit fell on all those who were listening to the Message. The believers from the Circumcision[73] who had accompanied Peter were amazed that the gift of the holy Spirit was poured out on Gentiles as well; for they heard them speaking in tongues and magnifying God.

Then Peter challenged, 'Dare anyone refuse water for the immersion of these people, who have received the holy Spirit just as we did?'

So he ordered that they should be immersed in the name of Jesus Christ. Afterwards they begged him to stay a few days.

Now the envoys and brothers resident throughout Judea heard that the Gentiles had also accepted God's Message. So when Peter went up to Jerusalem the believers of the Circumcision joined issue with him saying, 'You visited men who were uncircumcised and ate with them.'

Then Peter related to them the whole sequence of events. 'I

[73] Jews are thus distinguished from Gentiles (the Uncircumcision), corresponding to the Hebrew 'a son of the Covenant' and 'a non-son of the Covenant'.

was in the town of Joppa,' he told them, 'engaged in prayer, when in trance I saw a vision, a kind of bag let down like a huge sail-cloth, lowered from heaven by the four corners right to me. Peering into it, I clearly distinguished and saw the quadrupeds of the earth, wild beasts, creeping things, and the birds of the air. I also heard a voice saying to me, "Rise, Peter, kill and eat." I replied, "On no account, lord, for nothing impure or unclean has ever passed my lips." The voice came from heaven a second time, "What God has cleansed you are not to treat as impure." Three times this happened, and then the whole was drawn up again to heaven. At that very moment three men had arrived at the house where I was staying, sent to me from Caesarea; and the Spirit told me to accompany them without hesitation.

'These six brothers went with me, and we entered the man's house. He informed me that he had seen an angel in his house, standing there telling him, "Send to Joppa to Simon surnamed Peter, who has that to tell you by which you will be saved, you and all your house." As I proceeded to speak, the holy Spirit fell on them just as it did on us in the first place, and I was reminded of the Master's words, "John immersed in water, but you will be immersed in holy Spirit."[74] If, therefore, God was giving them the identical gift he gave us when we believed in the Lord Jesus Christ, was I someone who could impede God?'

When they had listened to this explanation they were satisfied, and praised God saying, 'So to the Gentiles too God has granted repentance that they should live.'[75]

CHAPTER VIII

Now those who were dispersed as a result of the persecution that broke out over Stephen travelled as far as Phoenicia, Cyprus and Antioch,[76] proclaiming the Message to none but Jews. Some of them were Cypriots and Cyrenians, who when they came to Antioch declared the Message to Greeks as well, proclaiming the Lord Jesus. The Lord's hand was with them, and a great number believed and came over to the Master.

When the news about them reached the ears of the Jerusalem Community they dispatched Barnabas[77] to Antioch. Having arrived and seen the evidence of God's mercy he was delighted, and encouraged them all with firm resolve to remain loyal to the Master; for he was a good man, of great spirituality and faith. A substantial body was now associated with the Master; so Barnabas set off for Tarsus in quest of Saul, and when he had found him he brought him to Antioch. For a whole year they

[74] See above p. 193.
[75] Lit. 'to Life', a Hebraism. They recited a benediction of God for bestowing on Gentiles also a share in the Messianic Kingdom. Cp. the dictum of R. Joshua ben Hananiah (c. A.D. 100), 'The righteous of all nations have a share in the World to Come (the Messianic Era).'
[76] In Syria on the Orontes, seat of the Roman legate of the province. See Jos. *Wars*, VII. iii. 3.
[77] Himself a Cypriot, above p. 201.

were jointly entertained by the community and instructed a considerable number of people. It was at Antioch too that the disciples first received[78] the designation of *Christians*.[79]

Now at this period prophets came down from Jerusalem to Antioch. One of them called Agabus rose and indicated[80] under inspiration that a severe famine would soon afflict the whole Empire.[a] Thereupon the disciples determined, as the means of each of them permitted, to send a contribution for the benefit of the brothers resident in Judea. This they carried out, forwarding it to the elders by Barnabas and Saul.

It was about this time that King Herod[81] launched a savage attack on certain members of the Community. He beheaded James the brother of John, and finding that this pleased the Jews he proceeded to apprehend Peter, whom he imprisoned on arrest,[b] setting four squads of four soldiers to guard him, purposing to bring him before the people after the Passover.

So Peter was held in custody, while prayer to God on his behalf was offered assiduously by the Community.

The very night before Herod was going to bring him up for trial, Peter was sleeping between two soldiers chained to them both,[82] while warders posted at the door guarded the prison. Suddenly, however, an angel of the Lord stood by him, and a light shone in the cell. Tapping Peter on the side, he roused him and said, 'Get up quickly!' And his chains fell away from his wrists.

'Fasten your girdle, and strap on your sandals,' said the angel. And Peter obeyed.

'Now throw your cloak round you and follow me,' he told him.

He followed him out, and had no idea that what the angel had done had really happened: he imagined he was seeing a vision. When they had passed through the inner and outer prison[83] they came to the iron gate leading to the city, which opened for them of its own accord. They went out, and had gone the length of one street when the angel suddenly left him.

'Now,' said Peter when he had recovered himself, 'I know for certain that the Lord has sent his angel to extricate me from Herod's clutches and every expectation of the Jewish people.'

Convinced of this, he went to the house of Mary mother of John surnamed Mark, where a number were assembled at prayer. Knocking at the street door, a maid called Rhoda came to answer it. Recognizing Peter's voice, she was too excited to

[a] It came in the reign of Claudius. (In A.D. 46. *Tr.*)
[b] The festival of Unleavened Bread was then in progress.

[78] Or 'first gave themselves'.
[79] I.e. Messianists, a coined Greek word with a Latin ending.
[80] By some symbolic action. See below p. 232.
[81] Herod Agrippa I, a grandson of Herod the Great, made king of Judea by Claudius in A.D. 41. He did everything possible to cultivate Jewish good opinion in religious matters, but died in A.D. 44.
[82] Lit. 'bound with two chains'.
[83] Lit. 'the first guard, then the second'.

open the gate, and ran in to tell them that Peter was standing at the gate.

'Nonsense,' they said. But she insisted it was true. 'It must be his angel[84] then,' they said.

Peter meanwhile kept on knocking. And when they did open up and saw him they were astounded. Waving his hand for silence, he described to them how the Lord had brought him out of the prison, and added, 'Give James[85] and the brothers the news.' Then he left and went elsewhere.

When morning came there was no little commotion among the soldiers as to what had become of Peter. When Herod sent for him, and he was not to be found, after interrogating the guards he ordered their execution. Then he went down from Judea to Caesarea and took up his residence there.

Now Herod was greatly incensed with the Tyrians and Sidonians. So they waited on him by common consent, and having secured the good offices of Blastus the king's chamberlain they sued for peace, dependant as their country was on the royal domains for food supplies. So on a day appointed Herod in full regalia seated himself in state and made them a speech.

The deputation greeted this with acclamation. 'It is the voice of a god, not of a man!' they cried.

Instantly an angel of the Lord struck him down, because he did not give God the praise, and being eaten by worms he expired.

But God's Message progressed and spread widely.

CHAPTER IX

Meanwhile Barnabas and Saul, having fulfilled their mission, returned from Jerusalem taking John surnamed Mark with them.

Now there were at Antioch with the community there both prophets and teachers. There was Barnabas, and Simeon nicknamed Niger,[86] Lucius a Cyrenian, Menahem a foster-brother of Herod the tetrarch, and Saul. As they were carrying out their sacred duties and fasting, the holy Spirit said, 'Set apart for me Barnabas and Saul for the task I have assigned to them.'

So when they had all fasted and prayed they laid their hands upon them and let them go. Thus commissioned by the holy Spirit they came down to Seleucia,[87] and from there sailed to Cyprus. Landing at Salamis they proclaimed God's Message in the Jewish synagogues, with John acting as their attendant.

Having traversed the whole island to Paphos, they encountered a magus, a Jewish false prophet called Bar-Jesus, who was in the retinue of the proconsul Sergius Paulus, a man of insight. The proconsul summoned Barnabas and Saul de-

---

[84] In Jewish belief each person had his own angel.
[85] Brother of Jesus, now head of the Jerusalem Community.
[86] I.e. 'the Black'.
[87] The port of Antioch.

siring to hear God's Message. But Elymas, the magus,^a opposed
them, trying to divert the proconsul from the faith. But Saul,
otherwise Paul,[88] in an inspired state, glared at him and said,
'You crafty parasite, Devil's spawn, enemy of everything
straightforward! Must you for ever be making crooked the
direct ways of the Lord? See, the Lord's hand is upon you.
Blind shall you be, getting no sight of the sun for a season.'

At once there fell on him a mist and a darkness, and he
groped about for someone to lead him by the hand. Then the
proconsul, seeing what had happened, believed, overwhelm-
ingly impressed by the Master's teaching.

Taking passage from Paphos those associated with Paul
reached Perga in Pamphylia. There John parted company with
them and returned to Jerusalem, while they travelled on from
Perga and arrived at Pisidian Antioch, where they attended the
synagogue on the sabbath day and took their seats. After the
reading of the Law and the Prophets the wardens of the synagogue sent them a message, 'Brothers, if there is any word of
encouragement you would like to address to the congregation,
please speak.'

Then Paul rose, and waving his hand for silence said, 'Fellow
Israelites and you who revere God,[90] give me your attention.

'The God of this people Israel chose our fathers and raised up
the people when they sojourned in Egypt, and brought them out
with a high arm,[91] and sustained[92] them for some forty years in
the wilderness. Having subjugated seven nations in the land of
Canaan, he gave Israel possession of their land for about four
hundred and fifty years. After the subjugation he gave them
judges down to the Prophet Samuel. Then they asked for a king,
and God gave them Saul the son of Kish, a man of the tribe
of Benjamin, for forty years. Then in his stead he raised up
David as their king, of whom he testified, "I have found David
the son of Jesse a man after my own heart, who will carry out
my wishes."[93] From his descendants, as he promised, "he raised
up for Israel a deliverer,"[94] namely Jesus, John having first proclaimed to all the people of Israel an immersion in penitence
before Jesus came on the scene. Towards the end of his public
career John declared, "I am not the one you suppose me to be.
But after me there will come one whose sandals I am unworthy
to untie."[95]

^a For so his appellation is to be translated.[89]

[88] Saul was a Roman citizen. Paulus was possibly his Roman cognomen, which in
his missionary work in the Roman Empire he now began to use after his meeting
with the proconsul L. Sergius Paulus.

[89] The author understands the Greek *magos* to be a translation of Elymas. Cp. *Alim*,
a sage (Arab.).

[90] Gentile monotheists who attended Jewish worship.

[91] Deut. xxvi 8.

[92] Deut. i. 31 (LXX), reading *trophophoreo* for *tropophoreo*.

[93] I. Sam. xiii. 14.

[94] Cp. the *Amidah* (Benediction 1), 'Who rememberest the pious deeds of the
fathers, and in love wilt bring a redeemer to their children's children' (AJP p.
44). This prayer formed part of the service.

[95] See Lk. 15-16, above p. 148.

'Brothers, sons of Abraham's race and those here with you who revere God, to us now comes the Message of deliverance. For the inhabitants of Jerusalem and their rulers, having failed to appreciate it and the utterances of the Prophets read every sabbath, by condemning him have fulfilled them. Having discovered nothing that merited death, they none the less begged Pilate that he should be killed. After completing everything written of him, they took him down from the gibbet and laid him in a tomb. But God raised him from the dead, when he was seen on a number of occasions by those who had come with him from Galilee to Jerusalem, who are now his witnesses to the people.

'Thus we are able to announce to you that the promise God made to the fathers he has carried out for us their children[96] by having raised up Jesus, just as in the second Psalm it is stated, "You are my son, to-day I have begotten you."[97] As to God's raising him from the dead, never more to return to decay, he has stated this, "I will bestow on you the benefits assured to David,"[98] relating to what he said elsewhere, "You will not let your beneficiary see decay."[99] David, indeed, having complied with God's wishes in his own generation, slept and was gathered to his fathers, and experienced decay. But he whom God raised up did not experience decay.

'Be it known to you, therefore, brothers, that through this man forgiveness of sins is proffered you, and by him all who believe are exonerated from everything in respect of which you could not be exonerated by the Law of Moses. Take heed, then, that there does not befall you what was stated in the Prophets,[100]

> *Look, you despisers, marvel and vanish away;*
> *For I will perform a miracle in your days*
> *You will never credit if one relates it to you.*[101]

As Paul and Barnabas were leaving, the wardens invited them to address the congregation on the same subject the following sabbath. When the people came out of the synagogue, many of the Jews and god-fearing Gentiles followed the envoys, who conversed with them and urged them to retain God's favour.

On the ensuing sabbath the whole town was assembled to hear God's Message. When the Jews saw the crowds, however, they were filled with envy and spoke in opposition to Paul's statements, and became abusive. So Paul and Barnabas bluntly told them, 'It was essential initially to proclaim God's Message to you; but since you spurn it and do not deem yourselves

[96] See note 94, above p. 216.
[97] Ps. ii. 7.
[98] Isa. lv. 3 (LXX).
[99] Ps. xvi. 10 (LXX), 'benefits . . . beneficiary' playing on the Greek *'ta hosia . . . ton hosion.'*
[100] The Book of the 12 Minor Prophets.
[101] Hab. i. 5.

worthy of Eternal Life, perforce we turn to the Gentiles. The Lord has instructed us to this effect,

> *I have set you as a light for the Gentiles,*
> *To be as deliverance to the ends of the earth.*[102]

When the Gentiles heard this they rejoiced and praised God's word, and those who were meant for Eternal Life believed.[103] So the Lord's Message was spread throughout the region. But the Jews worked upon the proselytes among the influential ladies[104] and upon the leading townsmen, and roused hostility against Paul and Barnabas; and they expelled them from their territory. The envoys shook the dust from their feet in protest, and went to Iconium; but they left the disciples joyful and inspired.

In Iconium similarly they went into the Jewish synagogue and spoke to the same effect, with the result that both Jews and a considerable number of Greeks believed.[a] But the unconvinced Jews agitated and poisoned the minds of the Gentiles against the brothers. The townsfolk were divided, some taking the side of the Jews, others siding with the envoys. So when a concerted attack was made by the Gentiles and the Jews with their rulers to mob and stone the envoys, they were apprised of it, and escaped to the cities of Lycaonia, to Lystra and Derbe and the neighbouring district, where they resumed their preaching.

At Lystra there sat a man impotent in his feet. Lame from birth, he had never been able to walk. He was one of those who listened to Paul speaking. Paul noticed him, and observing that he had the faith to be cured he said to him sharply, 'Get to your feet!' The man sprang up and walked.

When the populace saw what Paul had done they shouted in the Lycaonian tongue, 'The gods have come down to us in human form.' Barnabas they called Zeus, and Paul Hermes, because he was the spokesman. Thereupon the priest of Zeus-more-ancient-than-the-city[105] brought oxen and garlands to the gates, proposing with the populace to offer sacrifice. But learning of this the envoys Barnabas and Paul, rending their garments, rushed into the crowd crying, 'What are you about? We are the same kind of human beings as yourselves, preaching to you to turn from these errors to the Living God, who made heaven and earth, and the sea, and all they contain. In bygone ages he let all the nations go their own way. Yet even so, by his beneficence, he did not leave himself unattested, giving you

---

[a] They therefore spent some time there, speaking boldly for the Lord, who confirmed his gracious Message by permitting signs and wonders to be performed through their instrumentality.

[102] Isa. xlix. 6.
[103] Only a predestined number of Gentiles, it was believed, would share in the Messianic Kingdom.
[104] Judaism is known to have made a great appeal to these.
[105] Lit. 'Zeus (in being) before the city', his temple having been there prior to the city's foundation.

rain from heaven and fruitful seasons, satisfying your hearts with food and good cheer.'[106] But even by saying this they with difficulty prevented the people from sacrificing to them.

Then there came Jews from Antioch and Iconium, and incited the populace to violence; and having stoned Paul they dragged him outside the town believing him to be dead. But when the disciples had surrounded him he picked himself up and went into the town. The next day he set off with Barnabas for Derbe. After giving that town the News, and making a number of disciples, they turned back to Lystra, Iconium and Antioch, confirming the disciples, encouraging them to maintain their allegiance, and telling them, 'We have to enter the Kingdom of Heaven by the hard road.'[107]

When they had ordained elders for them in each community, and had prayed with fasting, they committed them to the keeping of the Lord in whom they had put their trust.

Traversing Pisidia, they reached Pamphylia, and after delivering the Message at Perga came down to Attaleia. From there they sailed for Antioch, from which city they had been commended to God's mercy for the mission they had now accomplished. Calling the community together on their arrival, they reported all that God had done for them, and how he had opened the door of faith to the Gentile. They stayed on there with the disciples for a considerable time.

CHAPTER X

Now certain persons came down from Judea and instructed the brothers, 'Unless you are circumcised in conformity with the Mosaic ordinance you cannot be saved.' And when there arose no small conflict and controversy with them on the part of Paul and Barnabas, it was decided that Paul and Barnabas with some others of the community should go up to the envoys and elders at Jerusalem about this question. Forwarded on their way by the community, they went through Phoenicia and Samaria giving out the news of the turning of the Gentiles to God to the great joy of the brothers.

On arrival at Jerusalem they were welcomed by the community, and by the envoys and elders, and reported all that God had done for them. But some of the Pharisean party raised objections and said, 'It is essential to circumcise them and charge them to observe the Mosaic Law.' The envoys and elders duly met to deliberate on the matter. After there had been much argument, Peter rose and addressed them.

'You are aware, brothers,' he said, 'that in the early days of our association God chose that through my agency the Gentiles should hear the Message of the Good News and believe it. God,

---

[106] Cp. Deut. xi. Paul's words here reflect passages in the Jewish festival grace before and after meals, where God is praised as 'the doer of good to all'.
[107] Lit. 'through many trials.' Quote by Prochorus, *Acts of John,* as a saying of Jesus.

who knows the heart, testified to their sincerity, giving them the holy Spirit equally with ourselves, and making no distinction of allegiance between us and them when purifying their hearts. Why then do you now try God, clamping a yoke on the necks of these disciples which neither our ancestors nor ourselves could manage to bear? Rather is it by the mercy of the Lord Jesus that we trust to be saved, as they do.'

The entire company preserved silence, and listened while Barnabas and Saul described the signs and wonders God had performed through them among the Gentiles.

When they had finished James[108] summed up. 'Brothers,' he said, 'please give me your attention. Symeon has narrated exactly what God contemplated originally, the taking from among the Gentiles of a people to bear his name. With this the sayings of the Prophets are in complete accord, as it is stated,

> *"Thereafter I will return*
> *And re-erect the fallen tent of David.*
> *I will re-erect its ruins and set it upright;*
> *That the rest of mankind may seek the Lord,*
> *Even all the Gentiles by whom my name is invoked,"*
> *Says the Lord, who makes this known from of old.*[109]

'My verdict is, therefore, that those of the Gentiles who turn to God be not molested, but that we write to them to abstain from whatever is polluted by idols, from sexual impurity, from eating strangled animals, and from blood.[110] For Moses from ancient times has had his preachers in every town, being publicly read in the synagogues every sabbath.'

Then the envoys and elders, and the entire convocation, resolved to select certain of their number and send them to Antioch with Paul and Barnabas, namely Judas called Bar-Sabbas and Silas, prominent men among the brothers, to convey the following letter:

'The envoys and elders, your brothers, present their compliments to the brothers from the Gentiles in Antioch, Syria and Cilicia.

Since it has come to our attention that some of our number, to whom we gave no such instructions, have been confusing you with their statements, unsettling your minds, it was unanimously resolved to send you special delegates along with our good friends Barnabas and Paul who have so devoted themselves to the cause of our Lord Jesus Christ. Accordingly we have commissioned Judas and Silas, who will confirm our decision verbally.

It was resolved by the holy Spirit and ourselves to impose on you no greater burden than these essential things, to abstain from what is dedicated to idols, from blood, from

---

[108] See above p. 215, n. 85.
[109] Amos ix. 11-12 (loosely quoted).
[110] With reference to diet.

eating strangled animals, and from sexual impurity. If you keep strictly to this you will be quite in order.

Farewell.'

When the envoys were dismissed they went down to Antioch, and having called the membership together they handed over the letter. On reading it they rejoiced at the cheering news. Judas and Silas also, both of whom were prophets, greatly encouraged the brothers by their words and gave them confidence.

In due course the brothers let them go with their good wishes to those who had sent them. But Paul and Barnabas stayed on at Antioch teaching and preaching the Lord's Message in association with many others.

CHAPTER XI

After some time Paul said to Barnabas, 'Let us go back and see how the brothers are faring in all those cities where we proclaimed the Lord's Message.'

Barnabas was anxious to take John called Mark too. But Paul did not think fit to take along one who had deserted them on reaching Pamphylia, and had not shared in the mission. Friction resulted, so that they parted company. Barnabas, taking Mark with him, sailed for Cyprus, while Paul, choosing Silas, left with the brothers' commendation to the Lord's favour, and travelled through Syria and Cilicia confirming the communities.

In due course they reached Derbe and Lystra. There they met a disciple called Timotheus, son of a believing Jewish woman and a Greek father, very well spoken of by the brothers at Lystra and Iconium. Paul wanted him to go with him, and had him circumcised because of the Jews in those parts; for they all knew his father was a Greek.

As they passed through the cities they delivered the stipulations for the communities to observe which had been decided upon by the envoys and elders at Jerusalem. Thus the communities were strengthened in their allegiance and increased in membership daily.

The envoys now traversed Phrygia and the Galatian region, being debarred by the holy Spirit from delivering the Message in Asia. Coming then in line with Mysia they attempted to journey into Bithynia;[111] but the spirit of Jesus did not permit them. So on reaching Mysia they came down to Troas.[112] There a vision appeared to Paul by night: it was a certain man of Macedon,[113] standing and appealing to him, 'Cross over to Macedonia and aid us.'

[111] Mysia lay to their west, Bithynia north and north-east (see map p. 222).
[112] The port Alexandria-Troas (Trojan Alexandria).
[113] Some definite person seems to be indicated, the most probable being the famous Philip of Macedon, father of Alexander the Great, known as 'the Man of Macedon' (Horace, Bk. III, Ode 16).

Map showing
the SPHERE of PAUL'S
ACTIVITIES

0   100   200   300 Miles

J.F.H.

[114] In accordance with the vision Paul had seen we at once endeavoured to get to Macedonia, deducing that God had summoned us to proclaim the News to them. Putting to sea from Troas, therefore, we ran a straight course to Samothrace, and the day following to Neapolis, and thence to Philippi, which is the top-ranking city of Macedonia, a Roman colony. We spent some time in the city, and on the sabbath day we went outside the gate to the river bank where we had reason to believe there was a Jewish oratory.[115] There we sat down and spoke to the women who attended it. There was one woman who listened called Lydia, a worshipper of God, of the city of Thyatira, who was in the purple cloth trade. The Lord opened her mind to receive what Paul said, and when she was immersed with her household she begged, 'If you are satisfied of my loyalty to the Master you must come stay with me.' We were absolutely forced to accept.

Once as we were going to the oratory a slave-girl possessed by an oracular spirit[116] met us, who made her masters a good living by fortune-telling. She persisted in following Paul and ourselves crying, 'These men are servants of the Most High God, who tell you the way to salvation.' For several days she carried on like this, until in desperation Paul turned round and told the spirit, 'In the name of Jesus Christ I order you to leave her!' Out it went that very instant.[117]

When her masters saw that their prospect of gain was gone, they seized Paul and Silas and dragged them to the magistrates' court, and brought them before the praetors. 'These men,' they said, 'Jews of course, are making serious trouble for this city of ours, advocating practices which as Romans we are not permitted to entertain, much less engage in.'

The crowd was solidly against the envoys; so the praetors gave orders to have them stripped and beaten with rods. When numerous strokes had been given them, they threw them into prison, cautioning the jailer to guard them securely. Having had a warning like that, he threw them into the inner prison, and secured their feet in stocks.

Around midnight Paul and Silas were at prayer praising God, with the other prisoners listening to them, when all of a sudden there was such a great earthquake as to shake the foundations of the jail. Immediately all the doors sprang ajar, and the fetters of all the prisoners were freed. Roused from his sleep, and seeing the doors of the prison standing open, the jailer drew his sword, and was about to kill himself thinking the prisoners had escaped, when Paul shouted, 'Don't harm yourself! Here

---

[114] Here begins the first of the notebook extracts used by the author. If they were written by Luke this would suggest that he joined the envoys at Troas.

[115] In Hebrew *Bet-tefilah* (Gr. *Proseuche*), a prayer centre.

[116] Lit. 'a pythonic spirit', associated with ventriloquism.

[117] As it is not clear how far the extract extends the indentation has been confined to passages written in the first person plural.

we all are.' Calling for lights he burst in, and all of a tremble fell down before Paul and Silas. Taking them outside he said, 'O sirs, what must I do to assure my safety?'

'Put your trust in the Lord Jesus,' they said, 'and both you and your family will be preserved.'

Then they gave him and his family God's Message. He took immediate care of them at that time of night, bathed their stripes, and was himself immersed and all connected with him. Conducting them to his house he set food before them, and rejoiced with all his family in their new found faith in God.

When morning came the praetors sent lictors with the message, 'Release those men.' The jailer broke this news to Paul. 'The praetors have sent word that you are to be released. So now you are quite free to go.'

But Paul sent word back to them, 'After flogging us in public uncondemned, men who are Romans of course,[118] they threw us into prison. Now they are throwing us out again secretly. Oh no! Let them come officially and fetch us out.'

The lictors reported these words to the praetors, who were dismayed when they heard they were Romans. Hurrying to the prison, they entreated them, and bringing them out begged them to leave the city. On coming out of the prison they went to Lydia's house, and having seen and encouraged the brothers they took their departure.

Following the road through Amphipolis and Apollonia they came to Thessalonica, where there was a Jewish synagogue. As was Paul's custom they went in, and for three successive sabbaths they discoursed from the scriptures, expounding them, and explaining how the Messiah had to suffer and to rise again from the dead, and that, 'this Jesus I am telling you about is the Messiah.'[119]

Some of them were convinced and adhered to Paul and Silas, with a large number of Greek proselytes and not a few influential ladies. But the Jews in their jealousy got hold of some worthless loafers, and forming a mob set the town in an uproar. They concentrated on Jason's house with the intention of bringing the envoys before the court; but failing to find them they dragged Jason and some other brothers before the politarchs,[120] clamouring that 'these subverters of the Empire have now reached here, and Jason has harboured them. All of them are violators of Caesar's decrees, and declare there is another emperor, Jesus,'[121] they alarmed the people and the politarchs when they heard this; but after taking surcties from Jason and the others they let them go.

At once the brothers sent away Paul and Silas by night to

---

[118] Echoing the sneer 'Jews of course' of the accusation in court.
[119] See I. Thess. ii. 2, below p. 251.   [120] The city prefects.
[121] The envoys were ignorantly or deliberately identified with the Jewish nationalist agitators, who at this time were visiting the Jewish communities in various parts of the Empire in order to foster revolt against Rome. See Suetonius, *Claud.* xxv; Dio Cass. *Rom. Hist.* lx. 6; and the *Letter of Claudius to the Alexandrians.*

Beroea, where on arrival they went straight to the Jewish synagogue. The Jews there were more civil than those at Thessalonica: they received the Message with every consideration,
examining the Scriptures daily to ascertain whether it was correct. Consequently many of them believed, and not a few Greek
ladies and gentlemen of quality.

When the Jews of Thessalonica were aware that God's Message was being proclaimed by Paul at Beroea as well, they came
there too to sway and stir up the populace. At once the brothers
sent Paul away to the coast, though Silas and Timotheus stayed
on at Beroea. Those who were escorting Paul accompanied him
as far as Athens, and there left him, taking back his instructions
to Silas and Timotheus to rejoin him as quickly as they could.

While Paul waited for them at Athens his spirit flared up
within him when he saw how the city was idol-ridden. Therefore he held forth in the synagogue to the Jews and proselytes,
and daily in the market-place to those who happened to be by.
There certain of the Epicurean and Stoic philosophers encountered him. 'What is this garbage-picker driving at?' said
some. To which others replied, 'He seems to be a propagator of
foreign divinities.'[a] So they took him along and brought him
before the Areopagus[122] with the request, 'May we be informed
of the nature of the new doctrine you are preaching? You are
bringing some queer notions to our attention, and consequently
we should like to know precisely what they mean.[b]

So Paul, standing before the Areopagus, spoke as follows:

'Athenians, I cannot help but notice how intensely religious
you are. For as I went about and looked at your various objects
of worship I even came across a pedestal[123] on which was inscribed, "To a God Unknown." It is he with whom I am
acquainting you, the One you unwittingly revere.

'The God who made the universe and everything in it, being
as he is Lord of heaven and earth, does not reside in artificial
temples, nor is he tended by human hands as though he stood
in need of anything, since he is the giver of life, breath and
substance to all.[124] From one man he produced every section of
the human race which occupies the entire surface of the earth,
and fixed the exact dimensions and boundaries of their settlement,[125] that they should seek after God; for if they would grope
for him they would find him, for in fact he is not far from each
one of us. Indeed, "by him we live, and move, and have our
being," as some of your own poets have also stated, "for we are
truly his offspring."[126] Being therefore God's offspring, we ought

[a] This was because he was proclaiming Jesus and the resurrection.[127]
[b] All Athenians and the foreign residents enjoy nothing better than
retailing or listening to the latest idea.

[122] The Council of Public Morals and Welfare.   [123] Or 'altar'.
[124] Cp. Jewish Grace after meals (AJP).   [125] Cp. Deut. xxxii. 8.
[126] From the opening lines of the *Phenomena* of Aratus of Cilicia. See also Cleanthes,
Hymn to Zeus.
[127] They took 'the resurrection' (*Anastasis*) to be a female divinity.

not to conceive the divine nature as capable of representation in gold, silver, or stone, modelled by art and human ingenuity.

'The ages of ignorance, however, God overlooked; but now he calls upon all mankind everywhere to repent, since he has set a day on which he will judge the world with justice by the man he has appointed, furnishing everyone with concrete proof of this by raising him from the dead.'

When they heard of the resurrection of the dead some scoffed, while others said, 'Perhaps you will tell us about this some other time.'

So Paul left their presence. But some joined him and believed, including Dionysius the Areopagite, a woman called Damaris, and a few others.

CHAPTER XII

After this Paul left Athens and went to Corinth. There he came across a Jew called Aquila, a native of Pontus, who had recently come from Rome with his wife Priscilla because Claudius had decreed the banishment of all Jews from Rome.[128] Paul got to know them, and because he was of the same trade he stayed with them and they worked together.[a] Every sabbath he discoursed in the synagogue, and convinced both Jews and Greeks.

When Silas and Timotheus came down from Macedonia Paul was deeply engaged with the Message, adducing evidence to the Jews that Jesus was the Messiah. But when they ranged themselves against him, and became abusive, he shook out his clothes, and told them, 'Your blood be on your own heads! I am guiltless. From now on I go to the Gentiles.'

So he changed his venue, and went to the house of a proselyte called Titus Justus,[129] which adjoined the synagogue. But Crispus,[130] president of the synagogue, believed in the Master, as did his whole family, and many of the Corinthians who listened believed and were immersed. The Master told Paul in a vision of the night, 'Do not be afraid. Speak out and do not be silent; for I am with you, and no one shall inflict any injury on you; for I have many people in this city.' So he settled down for a year and a half, teaching them God's Message.

During Gallio's[131] term as proconsul of Achaia, however, the Jews took common action against Paul, and brought him before the tribunal saying, 'This man is seducing the people to become proselytes irrespective of[132] the Jewish Law.'

[a] They were tentmakers by trade.

[128] See p. 224, n. 121.
[129] Gentiles who became full proselytes to Judaism, *Ger-zedek*, often on conversion took the appellation Zedek (Lat. Justus).
[130] See I. Cor. i. 14, below p. 268.
[131] L. Junius Gallio, brother of Seneca, proconsul of Achaia, July 51-June A.D. 52.
[132] Or 'contrary to'.

As Paul was about to reply, Gallio said to the Jews, 'If this were a matter of misdemeanour or criminal offence, Jews, I should properly sustain your cause.[133] But if it is a question of esteem and reputations, and of law as it concerns yourselves, that is your affair. I would rather not be a judge of such things.' And he barred them from the tribunal.[134]

Then all those present seized Sosthenes, president of the synagogue, and beat him in front of the tribunal; but Gallio had no responsibility for this.

Paul stayed on for some time, and then saying good-bye to the brothers sailed for Syria accompanied by Priscilla and Aquila, having his head shaved at Cenchreae as he was under a vow.[135] When they reached Ephesus Paul left them there, and going by himself into the synagogue he discoursed to the Jews. They begged him to make a longer stay, but he declined. Only as he took leave of them he said, 'God willing, I will return to you.'

He set sail from Ephesus, and on arrival at Caesarea went up to Jerusalem to pay his respects to the Community. Then he went down to Antioch, and after allowing himself a certain time there[136] he left again, covering successively the Galatian region and Phrygia, confirming all the disciples.

Meanwhile there arrived at Ephesus a Jew called Apollos, a native of Alexandria, a learned man well-versed in the Scriptures. He had some knowledge of the Faith of the Master, and being an enthusiast he spoke and taught very much to the point the matters relating to Jesus,[137] though acquainted only with John's immersion. He spoke very boldly in the synagogue, and Priscilla and Aquila having listened to him made friends with him and explained God's way to him more exactly. And when he wished to cross over to Achaia, the brothers, who were very taken with him, wrote to the disciples to make him welcome. On his coming he proved a valuable ally to those who by God's mercy had believed, for he confuted the Jews most forcefully by common consent, demonstrating from the Scriptures that Jesus was the Messiah.

Now while Apollos was at Corinth Paul came to Ephesus[138] by the up-country route and found some disciples there. 'Did you receive holy Spirit when you believed?" he asked them.

'We have heard nothing of any holy Spirit,' they told him.

'In what connexion, then, were you immersed?' he said.

'In connexion with John's immersion.'

'John carried out an immersion as an indication of repent-

[133] I.e. allow you to plead.
[134] I.e. refused their case a hearing.
[135] Some hold that it was Aquila who was under the vow.
[136] It is considered probable that Paul's letter to the Galatian communities was written at this time.
[137] Presumably the Messianic interpretation of the Scriptures.
[138] Ephesus was the capital of the Roman province of Asia. Its temple of Artemis was one of the wonders of the world (see below p. 229).

ance,' said Paul, 'telling the people they were to put their trust in the one who would come after him, namely in Jesus.'

On hearing this they were immersed in the name of the Lord Jesus. And when Paul had laid his hands on them the holy Spirit took possession of them, and they spoke in tongues and prophesied.[a]

Then Paul entered the synagogue, and over a period of three months he spoke out boldly, arguing and persuading about the Kingdom of God. But when some remained obstinate and unconvinced, disparaging the Faith before the congregation, he parted company with them and took the disciples away, continuing his discourses daily in the lecture hall of Tyrannus.[139] This went on for two years; so that all who lived in Asia, Jews and Greeks alike, heard the Master's Message. God effected extraordinary miracles through Paul's instrumentality, so that even handkerchiefs and loincloths[140] were taken away for the sick after physical contact with him, and by this means they were freed from their diseases and the evil spirits left them.

Then certain Jewish travelling exorcists attempted to use the name of the Lord Jesus on those possessed by evil spirits, saying, 'I adjure you by Jesus whom Paul proclaims!'[b] But the evil spirit replied, 'I know Jesus and I am familiar with Paul, but who do you think you are?' And the man in whom the evil spirit dwelt leapt on them and overpowered them both, so that they fled from that house lacerated and with their clothes in ribbons. This became known to all the inhabitants of Ephesus, Jews and Greeks alike, and they were seized with fear, and the name of the Lord Jesus was magnified. Many of those who believed came and confessed, and made a clean breast of their practices. Several who were practitioners of magic made a bonfire of their books in the sight of all. The value was computed, and was found to come to fifty thousand pieces of silver.[141]

Thus did the Master's Message powerfully extend and prevail.

CHAPTER XIII

At this stage of affairs Paul formed the intention of travelling to Jerusalem via Macedonia and Achaia, saying, 'When I have been there I must also visit Rome.' So he dispatched two of his assistants, Timotheus and Erastus, to Macedonia, while he stayed on for a time in Asia.

[a] There were about twelve men in all.
[b] They were[142] sons of a certain Skeva, a Jewish head priest, who did this.

[139] Cod. D. adds, 'from eleven to four'.
[140] Words of Latin origin, 'sudaria and semicinctia'.
[141] About £2,000.
[142] Omitting 'seven' before 'sons' since there were evidently only two. The name Skeva may have given rise to the number seven (Heb. sheva).

Just at that period there was a serious disturbance over the Faith. It was due to a certain Demetrius, a silversmith, who provided a good living for his craftsmen making shrines of Artemis. Calling them together and others engaged in similar employment, he addressed them as follows:

'Men, you fully appreciate that our livelihood depends on this employment. You will also have observed and noted that this fellow Paul with his persuasions has affected a whole lot of people, not only of Ephesus but of pretty well all Asia, saying that what human hands have made are no gods at all. This means not only that we run a grave risk of loss of reputation, but also that the temple of the great goddess Artemis, whom all Asia and the Empire reveres, will count for nothing, and her sway will be ended.'

When they heard this they got wildly excited and yelled, 'Up with Artemis of the Ephesians!'

The city was filled with confusion, and by common consent they rushed to the theatre, carrying along with them the Macedonians Gaius and Aristarchus, Paul's travelling companions. Paul would have gone in there to the people, but the disciples would not let him. Some of the Asiarchs [143] too, who were his friends, sent him word begging him to keep out of the theatre. Some there were shouting one thing and some another; for the assembly was completely confused, the majority not having the slightest idea for what cause they had congregated. Among all the crowd they decided it must have to do with Alexander, because the Jews were pushing him forward. Alexander then waved his hand for silence, anxious to defend himself to the people. But no sooner were they aware he was a Jew than they broke into a chorus of yelling for some two hours on end, 'Up with Artemis of the Ephesians!'

When the city recorder had got the crowd calmed down he said, 'Ephesians, where is there a single individual who does not know the city of the Ephesians as custodian of the temple of mighty Artemis, and of the heaven-sent statue? [144] Since these facts are indisputable, you ought to keep calm and do nothing outrageous; for you have brought these men here who are neither sacrilegious nor insulters of your goddess. If therefore Demetrius and the craftsmen with him have a grievance against anyone, the courts are open and there are proconsuls: let them mutually prefer their charges. If you wish to take the matter further, it will be dealt with in the assembly provided by law. We run the risk of being accused of riot over to-day's uncalled for proceedings; for we cannot offer the slightest justification for this concourse.' [145] With this he dismissed the assembly.

When the general commotion had subsided, Paul sent for the

---

[143] Prominent men elected to office as presidents and patrons of the festivals and games, also exercising some priestly functions in connexion with the cult of Rome and the Emperor.
[144] Apparently a meteoric stone bearing some resemblance to a woman.
[145] Or 'mass meeting'.

disciples, and having exhorted them and said farewell left for Macedonia. Travelling through those districts he addressed to the brothers many words of cheer, and so reached Greece, where he spent three months. But when a treacherous design was formed against him by the Jews as he was about to embark for Syria, he decided to return via Macedonia.

[146] In attendance on Paul were Sopater son of Pyrrhus of Beroea, Aristarchus and Secundus of the Thessalonians, Gaius of Derbe and Timotheus, and Tychicus and Trophimus of Asia. These going on head awaited us at Troas.

After the festival of Unleavened Bread we sailed from Philippi, and in five weeks' time we reached them at Troas, where we spent a week. Then on the day after the sabbath, when we were united for the communal meal, Paul discoursed to them prior to setting off on the morrow, and prolonged his address until midnight.

There were a number of lamps burning in the upstairs room where we were gathered, so a youth called Eutychus sat in the window.[147] As Paul's discourse went on and on, he grew drowsy and fell fast asleep. Drooping in his sleep he fell three floors down, and was picked up for dead. Paul went down, and threw himself upon him, and taking him in his embrace said, 'Do not lament. He is still alive.' He went upstairs again, broke bread, ate, carried on conversation for quite a time until dawn, and was then leaving, when the lad was carried in conscious, and they were enormously relieved.

We ourselves having gone on ahead to the ship sailed for Assos, with the intention of taking Paul on board there in accordance with his instructions. He proposed himself to travel overland. When he met us at Assos we embarked him and came on to Mitylene, and from there set sail and arrived the following day off Chios. The day after we hove to at Samos, and on the next reached Miletus [after a stop at Trogyllia]. This was because Paul had decided to sail past Ephesus, so that he would not have to linger in Asia; for he was anxious if at all possible to reach Jerusalem by Pentecost. From Miletus he sent to Ephesus, however, to summon the elders of the community. When they arrived he addressed them as follows:

'You are well aware how I have constantly acted in your interest ever since I first set foot in Asia, serving the Master with all humility and tears, and with the trials that came my way through the hostile schemes of the Jews. I have never concealed anything that might be of benefit to you, whether in preaching to you or teaching you, both in public and private, most earnestly entreating Jews and Greeks alike to turn to God and have faith in Jesus our Master.

[146] The notebook extracts are resumed here at Philippi, the city where the previous extract ended (above p. 223).
[147] Because of the smoke and fumes from the oil lamps. Windows were unglazed.

'Well, now I feel constrained to go to Jerusalem, not knowing what I shall have to face there. I only know that in city after city the holy Spirit has solemnly assured me that imprisonment and severe trials await me. But I set no value whatever on life for myself, only that I may finish my course and the commission I received from the Lord Jesus to witness expressly to the News of God's mercy.

'I know full well that all of you among whom I have gone proclaiming the Kingdom of God will never see my face again. Accordingly, I affirm to you here and now that I am clear of responsibility for the blood of all concerned, for I have not hesitated to declare to you God's whole purpose. Take heed to yourselves, therefore, and the entire flock of which the holy Spirit has appointed you supervisors. See to it that you tend God's community, which he has acquired with the blood of his own [Son]. I know that after I have gone home grievous[148] wolves will get in among you who will not spare the flock; and even from yourselves men will arise talking twistedly to draw away disciples. So be on your guard, remembering that night and day for three years on end I never ceased tearfully warning each one of you.

'Now I commit you to God, and to the Message of his mercy, which can fortify you and give you inheritance among all who are sanctified. I have coveted no one's silver, gold, or belongings. You are well aware that these hands have provided for my own needs and those of my associates. I have given you a complete demonstration how thus by your toil you should assist the incapacitated, bearing in mind those words uttered by the Lord Jesus, "It is a finer thing to give than to get." '[149]

When he finished speaking he knelt down with them all and prayed. A fit of weeping seized them, and they fell on Paul's neck and embraced him, grieving most over what he had said, that they were never going to see his face again. Then they escorted him to the ship.

When we sailed, after tearing ourselves away from them, we came on a straight course to Cos, the next day to Rhodes, and then to Patara. Finding a ship bound for Phoenicia, we went on board and sailed with her. After sighting Cyprus, and leaving it on our left, we sailed on to Syria and coasted down to Tyre; for there the ship was to discharge her cargo. Having located the disciples we stayed there a week; though they warned Paul by the Spirit not to go on to Jerusalem. We left, however, when our time was up, and were escorted on our way by them all, with their wives and children, until we were outside the town. Then after kneeling in prayer on the beach we said good-bye to one another; and we went on board while they returned home.

---

[148] *Baris,* also meaning influential.
[149] One of the 'Maxims of the Master' not in our present Gospels.

Completing the voyage from Tyre we arrived at Ptolemais. We paid our respects to the brothers and remained a day with them; but on the next we left for Caesarea, where we went to the house of the evangelist Philip[a] and stayed with him. He had four maiden daughters who were prophetesses. In the course of our lengthy stay a prophet called Agabus[150] came down from Judea and visited us. Taking Paul's girdle he bound his own hands and feet and declared, 'Thus says the holy Spirit, "The man to whom this girdle belongs the Jews in Jerusalem will bind and deliver him into the hands of the Gentiles." '

When we heard this, both we and the local disciples begged Paul not to go up to Jerusalem. But he replied, 'Why do you cry so, and weaken my resolve? For the sake of the Lord Jesus I am quite ready not only to be bound but even to die at Jerusalem.'

Failing to persuade him, we gave it up and said, 'The Lord's will be done.'

Some days later we made our arrangements to go up to Jerusalem. Several of the disciples from Caesarea went along with us to conduct us to Mnason, a Cypriot, one of the earliest disciples, with whom we would obtain lodging. Having duly reached Jerusalem, the brothers gave us a most friendly welcome. The next day Paul and ourselves had an audience with James. All the elders were present. And when we had paid our respects to them, Paul gave us a full description of all God had done among the Gentiles by his agency.[151]

CHAPTER XIV

When the elders had listened to what Paul had to say they praised God, and then said to him, 'You must take into consideration, brother, how many myriads there are among the Jews who have believed. Naturally they are staunch upholders of the Law, and they have been informed about you that you teach all the Jews in Gentile lands to apostatize from Moses, telling them not to circumcise their children or conform to the customs. What is this going to mean? They are bound to learn of your arrival. Here, then, is what you must do. We have four men under a mutual vow. Take over these men and undergo purification with them, and pay their offering costs so that they can shave their heads.[152] Everyone will then realize that there is no foundation whatever for what they have been informed about you, and that on the contrary you yourself conform and observe the Law. So far as Gentiles who have believed are con-

[a] One of the seven (i.e. the seven administrators, above p. 203, *Tr.*)

150 He predicted the great famine. See above p. 214.
151 The use of the first person ends at this point and is resumed on p. 243.
152 The men had taken a Nazirite vow. Paul had only to declare himself a Nazirite, and pledge himself to bring the offering for the four others. See Num. vi. 18; Mishnah, *Naz.* ii. 5.

cerned, we have communicated our decision that they should avoid what is dedicated to idols, blood, eating strangled animals, and sexual 'impurity.'[153]

Then Paul the very next day took over the men, and as being purified with them entered the Sanctuary, giving notice of when the completion of the purificatory period would take place on which the sacrifice should be offered for each one of them.[154]

When the seven days were almost up some Jews of Asia caught sight of him in the Sanctuary and roused all the people, crying as they seized him, 'Help, Israelites! Here is the fellow who goes around turning everyone everywhere against our people, and the Law, and this Place. He has even brought Greeks into the Sanctuary and desecrated this Holy place.'[a][155]

The whole city was set in uproar, and the people came rushing together. Those who had seized Paul dragged him outside the Sanctuary, and at once the gates were closed. They were attempting to kill him when word reached the military tribune that all Jerusalem was seething. Instantly he took troops and centurions and ran down to them,[156] and as soon as they saw the tribune and the troops they stopped striking Paul.

Warning inscription in Greek forbidding strangers to enter the Sanctuary at Jerusalem

Translation of the Greek text: 'No stranger is to enter within the balustrade round the Temple and enclosure. Whoever is caught will be responsible for his own death, which will ensue.'
(This notice was also exhibited in Latin and Hebrew.)

[a] They had previously seen Trophimus the Ephesian in the city with him, and imagined Paul had brought him into the Sanctuary.

[153] See above p. 220.   [154] Num. vi. 9, 13.
[155] Gentiles were forbidden to enter the Temple proper on pain of death. See illustration on this page.
[156] The Roman garrison was in Fort Antonia with direct access to the Temple area. See plan, p. 198.

Coming up, the tribune took him in charge, and ordered him to be bound with two chains, and inquired who he was and what he had been up to. Some of the crowd said one thing and some another; and as he could not discover the truth because of the commotion he ordered Paul to be conveyed into the fort. When the steps were reached it was found that he had to be lifted up them by the soldiers because of the pressure of the crowd; for the mass of the people surged close behind yelling, 'Away with him!'

When they were about to enter the fort, Paul said to the tribune, 'May I have a word with you?'

'Do you speak Greek?' he replied. 'Aren't you then the Egyptian who recently started an insurrection[157] and led those four thousand sicarii[158] out into the wilderness?'

'I am actually a Jew,' said Paul, 'from Tarsus in Cilicia, a citizen of no insignificant city. Please allow me to address the people.'

Receiving permission, Paul stood at the top of the steps and waved his hand for silence. When there was sufficient quiet he addressed them in the Hebrew language, 'Brothers and fathers, give me a chance to explain myself to you.' Hearing him speak to them in Hebrew they quietened down still more.

'I am a Jew born in Tarsus of Cilicia,' Paul continued, 'but brought up in this city at the feet of Gamaliel, strictly trained in our ancestral Law, being zealous on God's behalf, just as all of you here are. I was one who hunted down this Faith to the death, binding and delivering to prison men and women alike, as the high priest and the whole Senate can bear me out; for they furnished me with the letters to the brothers at Damascus with which I travelled to bring those who had gone there in bonds to Jerusalem for punishment.

'Now on my journey, when I was nearing Damascus, suddenly about noon a dazzling light from heaven flashed around me. I fell prone, and heard a voice saying to me, "Saul, Saul, why are you hunting me?" "Who are you, lord?" I answered. "I am Jesus the Nazarene whom you are hunting," he replied. Those who accompanied me saw the light, but they did not hear the voice of the one who spoke to me. Then I said, "What am I to do, lord?" The Master told me, "Rise, and go to Damascus, and there you will be told exactly what has been assigned you to do."

'As I was sightless from the brilliance of that light, I had to be led by the hand into Damascus by those who were with me. But Ananias, a man meticulous according to the Law and highly respected by all the local Jews, came to me, and standing there said, "Brother Saul, regain your sight!" And there was I looking

---

157 See Jos. *Wars*, II. xiii. 5, where he is credited with 30,000 followers. He planned to enter Jerusalem and overpower the Roman garrison, but was defeated and escaped with a few of his men.

158 'Dagger-men', militant Jewish nationalists who acted as assassins. See Jos. *Wars*, II. xiii. 3.

at him that very instant. Then he said. "The God of our fathers has designated you to know his will, to see that Just One, and to hear his very voice, that you may be a witness to all mankind of what you have seen and heard. So now what keeps you? Rise, and be immersed, and wash away your sins as you invoke his name!"

'When I had returned to Jerusalem, and was engaged in prayer in the Sanctuary, in trance I saw Jesus saying to me, "Hurry, get out of Jerusalem quickly, for they will not tolerate your testimony to me!" "But Master," I protested, "they know for a fact that it was I who in synagogue after synagogue imprisoned and bound those who believed in you; and when the blood of your witness Stephen was shed, I was the one who stood there approvingly and took charge of the cloaks of those who killed him." But his answer was, "Go, for I am sending you to the benighted Gentiles." '[159]

Up to this point they listened to him, but then they cried out, 'Away with the fellow from the earth! He's not fit to live.'

As they shouted, and tore their clothes, and flung dust in the air,[160] the tribune ordered him to be taken into the fort and examined by flogging, to discover the reason why they were so vociferous against him. As they were making him fast with straps, Paul said to the centurion in charge, 'Is it right for you to flog one who is a Roman and uncondemned?'

When he heard this the centurion went to the tribune and reported it. 'What do you propose to do?' he asked. 'The man is a Roman citizen.'

Going along, the tribune said to Paul, 'Tell me, are you a Roman?'

'Yes,' he replied.

'I had to pay a pretty penny for my citizenship,' said the tribune.

'But I had it by birth,' said Paul.

Those who were going to interrogate him at once stood away from him, and even the tribune was uneasy when he was aware he was a Roman, and that he had been responsible for binding him.

The next day, concerned to get at the truth of why Paul was denounced by the Jews, the tribune freed him, and requested the high priest and the full Sanhedrin to meet, and brought Paul down to confront them. Paul peered at[161] the Sanhedrin and said, 'Brothers, I have lived with a perfectly clear conscience before God to this day.'

Here, the High Priest Ananias[162] ordered those who stood beside Paul to strike him on the mouth.

[159] Or 'the Gentiles afar off'.
[160] As a mourning for the dead.
[161] Or 'looked straight at'. Peering has been used because the context suggests that Paul had only a blurred impression of the person addressing him and suffered from defective vision.
[162] Ananias, son of Nedebeus (Jos. *Antiq.* XX. v. 2.).

Then Paul said to him, 'God will strike you, you whitewashed wall. Do you sit there to judge me in accordance with the Law, and illegally order me to be struck?'

Those who stood beside him cried, 'Do you abuse God's high priest?'

'I did not know he was the high priest, brothers,' Paul said, 'for it is stated, "You must not speak evil of the ruler of your people."' [163]

When Paul was aware that one part of the Sanhedrin were Sadducees and the others were Pharisees, he cried out, 'Brothers, I am a Pharisee of Pharisee stock. I am being judged for the expectation of the resurrection of the dead.'

By saying this he set the Pharisees at loggerheads with the Sadducees, and there was a split in the assembly. For the Sadducees say there is no resurrection, nor any angel or spirit, but the Pharisees affirm both propositions. A first-class row ensued, with some of the Pharisee scribes hotly contending, 'We find nothing criminal in this man. If a spirit has spoken to him, or an angel—.' The conflict here became so furious that the tribune, afraid that Paul would get torn to pieces, ordered a company down to extricate him from them and escort him back into the fort.

The following night the Master stood beside him and said, 'Courage! As you have pleaded my cause in Jerusalem, so must you testify in Rome also.'

When day came some of the Jews made a compact, and took an oath neither to eat nor drink until they had killed Paul. There were more than forty who were parties to this conspiracy. These going to the high priest and elders said, 'We have taken a most solemn oath to taste nothing until we have killed Paul. You should therefore, with the Sanhedrin, represent to the tribune that he should bring him down to you as you propose to investigate his case more thoroughly, while we will be in wait to kill him before he reaches here.'

Paul's sister's son, who was close by, heard about the ambush, and went into the fort and informed Paul. Paul then summoned one of the centurions and said, 'Take this young man to the tribune. He has something to tell him.' So he took him along to the tribune and said, 'The prisoner Paul summoned me, and asked me to bring this young man to you as he has something to say to you.'

The tribune then took him by the arm, and retiring with him in private inquired, 'What is it you have to tell me?'

'Some of the Jews,' he said, 'have agreed to ask you to bring Paul down to the Sanhedrin to-morrow as they propose to go into his case more thoroughly. But you must not consent, for more than forty of their men will be lying in wait for him. They have taken an oath not to eat or drink till they have killed him. And now they are in readiness awaiting your assurances.'

[163] Exod. xxii. 28.

The tribune then dismissed the youth, cautioning him 'not to tell a soul what you have disclosed to me.' Next, having summoned two of his centurions, he issued instructions, 'Have two hundred men ready to go to Caesarea, also seventy cavalry and two hundred light infantry, this evening at nine o'clock sharp. And have a baggage train brought round to convey Paul safely to the Governor Felix.' He also wrote a letter to this effect:

'Claudius Lysias presents his compliments to His Excellency the Governor Felix.

'This man had been apprehended by the Jews, and they were about to kill him, when I arrived with a force and extricated him. On learning he was a Roman, and wishing to ascertain the reason he was being accused by them, I brought him down to their Sanhedrin. There I found him to be accused of questions affecting their law, but not of anything meriting death or imprisonment. On information received of there being a plot against this man, I have at once sent him to you, and likewise advised his accusers to lay before you their charges against him.'

Then in accordance with their instructions the soldiers took Paul and escorted him by night to Antipatris. But the next day they returned to the fort, leaving the cavalry to go forward with Paul. On reaching Caesarea they delivered the letter to the governor, and also surrendered Paul to him. When the governor had read the letter he asked Paul from what Province he came, and being told it was Cilicia he said, 'I will hear you as soon as your accusers arrive,' and remanded him in custody in Herod's praetorium.

Five days later the High Priest Ananias came down with some of the elders and an advocate Tertullus. These laid information against Paul with the governor.

When Paul had been summoned, Tertullus opened the case for his accusers as follows:

'Thanks to you, Your Excellency Felix, profound peace is our lot and law and order has been restored to our nation under your wise guidance.[164] This we freely and fully acknowledge with deep gratitude. In order not to weary you unduly, therefore, I beg for your consideration in putting our case with the utmost brevity.

'We have found this man a plague-carrier, a fomentor of revolt among all the Jews of the Empire, a ringleader of the Nazarene sect. When we apprehended him he was also attempting to desecrate the Sanctuary, as you can ascertain for yourself by investigating these several charges we bring against him.'

The Jews concurred, affirming that the facts were as stated. Then at a nod from the governor Paul made his reply.

'Knowing that you have had many years' experience in

---

[164] Felix had ruthlessly suppressed the Jewish patriotic revolutionaries. On his character and activities see Jos. *Antiq.* XX. viii; Tacit. *Annals*, XII. liv.

governing our nation I speak in my own defence with every confidence, since you can ascertain that barely twelve days have elapsed since I went up to worship at Jerusalem. They neither found me in the Sanctuary arguing with anyone, nor haranguing a crowd either in the synagogues or up and down the city. They can offer no shred of evidence to support the charges they now bring against me.

'I will admit to you that I serve the God of our fathers in accordance with the persuasion which they term a sect, believing whatever has been recorded in the Law and the Prophets, and having that hope in God—which indeed they themselves share—that there will be a resurrection of the just and also of the unjust. Because of this I am personally at pains always to have a clear conscience towards God and man.

'Now after an interval of several years I arrived to make charitable gifts to my nation, and also to offer sacrifices, engaged in which activities some Jews of Asia found me in the Sanctuary when I had undergone purification, with no sign of a crowd or commotion. They should have been here before you to accuse me if there had been anything against me. As they are not, let those who are here speak of what wrongdoing they discovered when I stood before the Sanhedrin, or about the one thing I cried out as I stood among them, "Concerning the resurrection of the dead I am being judged by you to-day!"'

Here Felix, who had very accurate knowledge of the Faith, adjourned the proceedings, saying, 'When Tribune Lysias gets down I will decide your case.'

While instructing the centurion to hold Paul, he was to permit him his liberty, and not to prevent his own people looking after him.

Shortly after this Felix was again in Caesarea with his wife Drusilla,[165] who was a Jewess, and sending for Paul listened to him on the subject of faith in Christ Jesus. As he discoursed about righteousness, self-control, and the coming Judgment, Felix became uncomfortable and said, 'You had better go now. When I have time to spare I'll call for you again.'

He rather hoped that Paul would make him a gift of money, which was why he sent for him fairly frequently and conversed with him. But when two years had passed Felix was succeeded by Porcius Festus. Anxious to stand well with the Jews, Felix left Paul still a prisoner.

CHAPTER XV

Three days after his entry into the Province Festus went up from Caesarea to Jerusalem. There the head priests and leading Jews made representations to him against Paul, and begged the favour of having him sent to Jerusalem, intending to am-

[165] She was a sister of Agrippa II, and left her husband Azizus, king of Emesa to marry Felix. She was noted for her beauty. See Jos. *Antiq.* XX. vii. 2.

bush and kill him on the way. But Festus replied that he was having Paul kept at Caesarea as he himself would very soon be going there. 'Any of you who care to do so,' he said, 'can accompany me down and bring your charges against him if the man has done something monstrous.'

When Festus had spent some eight or ten days with them he went down to Caesarea, and the day following took his seat on the tribunal and ordered Paul to be brought in. As soon as he was present, the Jews who had come down from Jerusalem surrounded him, preferring many serious charges which they could not substantiate. Paul's reply was, 'I have committed no offence against Jewish law, nor against the Sanctuary, nor against Caesar.'

Festus, anxious to stand well with the Jews, said to Paul, 'Are you willing to go up to Jerusalem to be tried before me there regarding these matters?'

Paul replied, 'I am standing now at Caesar's tribunal, where I should be tried. I have not injured Jews, as you can see quite plainly. If I am at fault and have done something that merits death I am not trying to beg myself off from dying. But if there is no foundation for these charges they bring against me, no one is entitled to gratify them. I appeal to Caesar.'

Then Festus, after conferring with the Council, answered, 'You have appealed to Caesar. To Caesar you must go.'

Shortly after, King Agrippa[166] and Berenice arrived at Caesarea to pay their respects to Festus. When they had been there a few days Festus broached the subject of Paul to the king.

'We have a man here,' he said, 'left a prisoner by Felix, against whom the head priests and elders made representations to me when I was in Jerusalem. They asked for his condemnation; but I told them it was not customary in the case of Roman citizens to grant any individual such a favour before the accused had had an opportunity to face his accusers and offer his defence to the charge. Consequently, when they came here with me, without any delay I took my seat next day on the tribunal, and ordered the man to be produced. But when his accusers stood forward they did not bring against him a single charge of any of the crimes I had supposed. They only had against him certain questions affecting their own religion, and a certain Jesus who had died, and whom Paul affirmed was alive. As I was quite out of my depth with an investigation dealing with such matters, I asked him whether he would go to Jerusalem and be tried there. But when Paul appealed for his case to be reserved for the verdict of Augustus,[167] I ordered his remand until I could send him to Caesar.'

'I should rather like to hear the man myself,' said Agrippa to Festus.

166 Son of Agrippa I, given the kingdom of Chalcis by Claudius. Berenice was his sister, afterwards mistress of Titus, son of the Emperor Vespasian.
167 A title of the emperor like 'His Majesty'.

'You shall hear him to-morrow,' he replied.

The next day Agrippa and Berenice came in full state, and entered the audience chamber accompanied by the military commanders and city notables. Festus ordered Paul to be brought in.

Festus then spoke. 'King Agrippa, and all who have honoured us with their presence, here you find a man over whom I have had the whole pack of Jews down on me both in Jerusalem and here, yelping that he ought not to live any longer. But when I was aware that he had really done nothing meriting death, and when he appealed to Augustus, I decided to send him. I find myself, however, with nothing definite to write to our Lord. I have therefore brought him before you, and especially before you King Agrippa, so that after this examination I might know what to write; for it seems senseless to me to be sending a prisoner without at the same time specifying the charge against him.'

Then Agrippa said to Paul, 'You have our leave to speak for yourself.'

So Paul extended him arm and began his defence.

'I count myself fortunate, King Agrippa, that it is before you here to-day that I am to answer all the charges Jews have brought against me, particularly because I know you to be so well-versed in all Jewish customs and questions. I beg you, therefore, to accord me a patient hearing.

'With my early life, which was spent entirely among my own nation at Jerusalem, Jews are fully familiar. Being acquainted with my antecedents they could testify, if they would, that I lived in accordance with the strictest section of our Faith, as a Pharisee.[168]

'So here I stand trial for that Hope, which was God's own promise to our fathers, and to which by their devotional zeal night and day our twelve tribes expect to attain. It is for harbouring this very Hope, Sire, that Jews are accusing me. Why should one regard it as incredible that God raises the dead? I used myself to think it necessary to act in utmost opposition to the authority of Jesus the Nazarene, which moreover I did in Jerusalem, and locked up many of the saints in prison with the warrant I had from the head priests. When they were sent to their death I pressed the vote against them, and had them punished repeatedly in all the synagogues, and compelled them to revile Jesus. Being mad with them beyond measure I even hunted them to towns across the border.

'Travelling while so engaged to Damascus, with a warrant and commission from the head priests, I saw, Sire, while on the road at midday, a light from heaven stronger than the sun's glare shining about me and those who accompanied me. We all fell to the ground, and then I heard a voice saying to me in Hebrew, "Saul, Saul, why do you hunt me? You only hurt

[168] Cp. Jos. *Life*, ii, on his early training as a Pharisee.

yourself kicking against the goad." "Who are you, lord?" I asked. The Master said, "I am Jesus whom you are hunting. Get up now, and stand on your feet. I have appeared to you personally to take you in training as my assistant, and as witness that you have seen me, and of what I shall make clear to you later. I am setting you apart from your people, and from the Gentiles to whom I am going to send you, to give them the power of distinction, that they may turn from darkness towards the light, and from the authority of Satan to God; that they may receive forgiveness of their sins, and inheritance with the sanctified by their loyalty to me."

'There could be no question, King Agrippa, of disobeying the heavenly vision, and accordingly, to those in Damascus first, then to the inhabitants of Jerusalem, the whole country of Judea, and afterwards to the Gentiles, I preached repentance and turning to God, and the performance of deeds indicative of repentance. As a consequence the Jews seized me in the Sanctuary and attempted to murder me. Aided, however, by God's providence, I continue to stand—just as I am doing at this moment—witnessing to high and low, uttering no single word beyond what the Prophets foretold would happen, yes, and Moses himself, that the Messiah would suffer, that he would be the first to rise from the dead, and thereafter bring light to our people and to the Gentiles.'

When he had reached this part of his defence, Festus interjected, 'You are raving, Paul! All this study has disturbed your reason.'

'I am not mad, Your Excellency Festus,' Paul rejoined. 'I am speaking plainly matters of fact and sense; for the king, before whom I can express myself freely, well understands these things. I am persuaded that none of them has escaped his notice, for they were not done in a corner.

'King Agrippa, do you believe the Prophets? Of course you do.'

Said Agrippa to Paul, 'In next-to-no-time you will be persuading me to turn Christian.'

'I pray God,' Paul replied, 'that whether in next-to-no-time or a long time, not only you but all who hear me to-day will become as I am, except for these chains.'

Then the king rose, followed by the governor, Berenice, and the assembled company. When they had withdrawn they discussed the matter among themselves. 'The man has done nothing,' they agreed, 'to deserve death or imprisonment.'

'He could have been released,' said Agrippa to Festus, 'had he not appealed to Caesar.'

Map of
PAUL'S JOURNEY
to ROME

J.F.H.

When it was decided we should sail for Italy, they entrusted Paul and some other prisoners to a centurion called Julius, of the Augustan[170] cohort. Going on board a ship of Adramyttium which was due to sail, calling at the Asiatic ports, we put to sea. Aristarchus,[171] a Macedonian of Thessalonica, accompanied us.

The next day but one we touched at Sidon, Julius treating Paul very decently, liberating him on parole to visit his friends to benefit by their attentions. Putting to sea again, we ran under the lee of Cyprus because of adverse winds, and driving on through the sea off Cilicia and Pamphylia we made the port of Myra in Lycia. There our centurion found an Alexandrian boat[172] bound for Italy, and transferred us to her. For some days, battling against the wind, we made poor progress, and with difficulty reached a point off Cnidus; and had to sail under the lee of Crete off Cape Salmone. We had a hard job to weather it and reach a place called Fair Havens, near which was the town of Lasea.

After being held up here for a considerable time, and navigation having become very risky because the Fast Day[173] had already gone by, Paul advised them, 'Gentlemen, it is my conviction that the voyage will bring strain and stress not only to cargo and vessel but to ourselves as well.' But the centurion preferred to follow the advice of the navigator and the captain rather than Paul's recommendations. The harbour was by nature unsuitable for lying up, so the majority favoured putting to sea again and having a good try to reach and lie up at Phoenix, a harbour of Crete facing south-west and north-west. So when a moderate wind from the south sprang up they weighed anchor hugging the coast of Crete, thinking they would achieve their object.

But not long after there swept down from the island a violent norther[174] known as Euraclyon. When it caught the ship, and finding ourselves unable to turn her into the wind, we let her drive along. Running under the lee of a small island called Clauda, we struggled hard to haul in the ship's boat; and when it was aboard they brought into commission their cable supports to undergird the vessel. Then apprehensive of being thrown on the Syrtis quicksands,[175] they let down sail and drifted.

---

[169] The greater part of this chapter is from the notebook source.
[170] Or 'Samaritan' (Gr. *Sebastes*). The name of Samaria had been changed to Sebaste (August) in honour of Augustus Caesar.
[171] He had come with Paul from Philippi. See above p. 230.
[172] One of the Alexandrian grain ships, as appears further on.
[173] The Day of Atonement, 10th of the 7th month Tishri of the Jewish year, falling in October.
[174] Lit. 'a typhonic wind'.
[175] North of Libya.

Next day, as we were in great distress, they cleared the decks, and the day following we threw the ship's gear overboard with our own hands. For days on end neither sun nor stars were visible, while the storm raged with unabated fury and all remaining hope that we should be saved was abandoned. Then, when food was running short, Paul stood before them and said, 'You should have taken my advice, gentlemen, and never put out from Crete, and let yourselves in for this storm and stress. But as things are now, my advice to you is to take heart, for not one life will be lost, only the ship. For last night there stood by me an angel of the God whose I am—and whom I serve, saying, "Never fear, Paul, you must stand before Caesar. And see, God has given you all those who sail with you." So courage, gentlemen, for I have faith in God that it will turn out exactly as I have been told. But we are to be cast on an island.'

The fourteenth night of our drift across the Adriatic,[176] around midnight, the sailors had the impression they were approaching land. When they took soundings they found twenty fathoms, and sounding again after a short interval they found fifteen fathoms. Fearing we should be cast on a rocky coast, they let go four anchors by the stern, and longed for daylight. But some of the sailors tried to abandon ship, and they were lowering a boat into the sea, on the pretext that they were going to lay anchors from the bow, when Paul said to the centurion and his men, 'If they don't stay in the ship there is no chance of your being saved.' Then the soldiers hacked away the boat's hawsers, and let her fall away.

While they waited for daybreak Paul encouraged them to take some food, saying, 'This will be the fourteenth day you have been constantly on the watch and gone without your meals, never taking a bite. I beg you, therefore, to take some nourishment, for this will contribute to your preservation. In no case will a hair of your heads be lost.'

Having said this, he took bread and gave thanks to God before them all, broke it and began to eat. At this they all cheered up and followed his example. All told we were about seventy-six souls on board. Then when they had eaten sufficient food they lightened ship by throwing out the grain into the sea.

When day came they did not recognize the coast; but they perceived a creek with a sandy shore on which they determined if they could to beach the vessel. Casting off the anchors fore and aft, they left them in the sea, and at the same time loosing the lashings of the rudders and hoisting the foresail to the breeze they held for the shore. Chancing on a place where two seas met, they ran the ship aground. Here

176 Then including the central Mediterranean.

Ship anchored by the stern

the forepart stuck fast and held firm, while the stern went to pieces under the shock.

The soldiers were for killing the prisoners in case any of them should swim off and escape. But the centurion, determined to save Paul, vetoed their suggestion, and ordered those who could swim to jump for it first and get to land, while the rest followed, some on planks and others on any other pieces of the ship that were handy. In this way all came safely to shore.

It was not until we had recovered that we found out that the island was called Melita.[177] The natives treated us with uncommon civility; for they kindled a fire and made us comfortable because of the drenching and the cold. Paul had been collecting an armful of sticks, and was engaged in laying them on the fire, when a viper drawn out by the heat fastened itself on his hand. Seeing the creature hanging from his hand, the natives said to one another, 'He must be a murderer, whom Justice will not allow to live, though he has come safely out of the sea.' However, he shook off the creature into the fire and suffered no ill effects, though they fully expected him to swell up or suddenly drop dead. After waiting for some time and seeing nothing out of the ordinary happen to him they changed their minds and said he must be a god.

Hereabouts was the estate of the chief commissioner of

[177] Now Malta.

the island called Poplius,[178] who received us and very kindly provided lodging for three days. The father of Poplius was laid up with an attack of fever and dysentery. Paul went to his room, and after praying laid his hands on him and cured him. The consequence was that others on the island who had ailments came and were cured. They not only loaded us with handsome presents, but furnished the requisite stores.

Three months later we embarked in an Alexandrian ship displaying the emblem of the Dioscuri[179] that had wintered at the island. Putting in at Syracuse we stayed there three days, and from there by tacking we reached Rhegium. A day later we had the advantage of a south wind which wafted us in two more days to Puteoli,[180] where we found brothers who invited us to spend a week with them.

And so we came to Rome. From there the brothers, who had heard all about us, had come to meet us as far as Market Appii and Three Taverns, and Paul when he saw them thanked God and took courage. When we had entered Rome[181] Paul was allowed to occupy a private lodging with the soldier who acted as his guard.[182]

When three days had passed Paul summoned the heads of the Jewish community, and when they had assembled he addressed them as follows:

'You see in me, brothers, a prisoner from Jerusalem, who though he has done nothing against our people or our ancestral customs was handed over to the Romans. When they had examined me they proposed to set me free, as there was nothing whatever against me to justify a death sentence. But when some of the Jews opposed this I was forced to appeal to Caesar, though not because I have any grounds of complaint against my nation. My reason for asking you here is to see you and speak to you, because it is for the sake of the Hope of Israel I wear this chain.'

'We have received no communication about you from Judea,' they told him, 'neither have any of the brothers arrived to report to us or advise us of anything to your detriment. But we should appreciate hearing from you what your opinions are, for all we know for certain about this sect is that everywhere it is disparaged.'

Having fixed a date with him, most of them turned up at his lodging. To these he earnestly expounded the Kingdom of God, persuading them about Jesus from the Law of Moses and from the Prophets from early morning until evening. Some were convinced by what he said, but others did not credit it.

---

[178] Possibly the Greek name Popilius, but more likely the Roman Publius.
[179] Castor and Pollux.
[180] Cp. the somewhat similar voyage of Josephus, *Life*, iii.
[181] Omitting the gloss, 'the centurion handed the prisoners over to the camp commander, but . . .'
[182] The notebook extracts end here.

On this note of discord among themselves they took their leave, with Paul saying this parting word, 'Rightly did the holy Spirit say to your fathers by the Prophet Isaiah,

> *Go to this people, and tell them,*
> *"You will hear indeed, but not comprehend.*
> *You will see indeed, but not perceive."*
> *For the mind of this people is obtuse;*
> *Their ears have grown hard of hearing,*
> *And their eyes they have fast closed,*
> *In case they should see with their eyes,*
> *And hear with their ears,*
> *And turn again, and I should heal them.*[183]

'You had better know this, that God's salvation has been sent to the Gentiles. They certainly will listen to it.'

Paul resided two full years in his own rented apartment, and welcomed all who visited him there, proclaiming the Kingdom of God, and teaching all about the Lord Jesus Christ with unrestricted freedom of speech.[184]

[183] Isa. vi. 9-10.
[184] The last paragraph may be a copyist's addition to compensate for the worn and defective end of the original scroll.

THE LETTERS OF PAUL OF TARSUS

FIRST SERIES

LETTERS ON ACTIVE SERVICE

Preface to *Paul's Letters (First Series)*

THE *Acts of the Envoys* is itself the indispensable introduction to the letters of Paul. Without the outline of Paul's career which it provides we should largely be unaware when or under what circumstances the Envoy to the Gentiles visited various cities and countries. Many passages in the correspondence would be obscure, and we should find great difficulty in arranging the letters in chronological order and determining their approximate dates. As it is, we can be fairly sure of our ground in editing the letters, and this is of the utmost importance, since the letters in turn, as the earliest known Christian records, enable us to test the general historical accuracy of the *Acts*. We can see that much has been passed over and toned down by Luke, and the inside story as given by Paul is singularly revealing of the actual state of the early Christian communities in the eastern part of the Roman Empire. Here is no idealized picture, but a frank and sometimes scathing disclosure of situations and conditions.

As we discover the unpromising human material of which the communities were often composed, and apprehend what pain and anxiety were given to the man chiefly responsible for their foundation, we cannot but feel tremendous admiration for his vision and courage, organizing ability and concentration of purpose. Paul lives in his letters, and from them we get to know him more intimately than any other New Testament writer. We may not always be in sympathy with him. We may find him rather puritanical, his ideas often strange, his illustrations far-fetched, his arguments involved and hard to follow; but in every mood he is stimulating and challenging.

Paul's correspondence is admittedly difficult to translate. There are several reasons for this. For the most part he dictated to secretaries, and probably at odd times, and this allowed him to let his thoughts follow bypaths occasionally before returning to his main theme, or alternatively to proceed at a great pace piling clause on clause of a sentence which seemed as if it would be interminable. The different amanuenses have some responsibility for the uneven result and construction; but Paul was often dictating under strong emotion. He had the further difficulty of trying to convert Jewish ideas into Greek terms, which sometimes meant using Greek words in other than their normal connotation, thus creating a kind of *lingua Christiana*. His mind was cast in a rabbinical mould, and filled with expressions and phrases, Biblical, liturgical and mystical, which were alien to the majority of his readers. Without Paul's equipment one may easily misunderstand and misrepresent him. His language is rich in imagery, drawn as much from the Graeco-Roman world as the Jewish. He has the merit of not mixing his metaphors, even if he is inclined to push them to extremes.

On a Jewish and Judaeo-Christian foundation Paul built up his own particular theological and christological edifice, in which Jewish occult lore had a prominent place. He had had mystical experiences; and it was on mystical lines that he developed the doctrine of the believer being in Christ and Christ in the believer. Related to this was the doctrine of the organic relationship between believers, and between Christ and the Church. These were demanded in the interests of Christian morality and solidarity, as was the doctrine of faith in safeguarding the status of Gentile converts.

In presenting the letters they have been divided into two groups, those written in the course of Paul's missionary activities and those written while a prisoner at Rome. As far as possible they have been placed in chronological sequence, with the approximate dates and places where written. We learn far more from this correspondence than appears in the *Acts* of the continuous conflict between Paul and the envoys of the central Christian authority at Jerusalem. In their concern for a loyal and united Christian Israel, true to the traditions of the fathers, the latter could not fail to be opposed to the creation of what amounted to a new religion, and they did their utmost to ruin and discredit Paul. They visited the communities he founded, and to a large extent succeeded in impressing the converts with their point of view. Paul reacted violently and bitterly, and seemingly with good reason, but it is important to appreciate that we have almost entirely his version of the controversy.

Aspects of this struggle are represented in nearly all the letters, particularly in the one addressed to the communities of Galatia. But in each centre there were also special problems. At Thessalonica there were some who expected the immediate return of Christ, and as a consequence had abandoned their occupations. The Corinthian believers presented Paul with numerous questions on various subjects. He had also to deal with the besetting Greek vices of factiousness and immorality. Evidently four letters were written to the Corinthian community, eventually compressed into two; and it is easier to follow the arguments if the original structure and order are tentatively restored.

The letter to the believers at Rome is of a different character. Paul had not visited this community and had had no hand in founding it. He therefore uses the notification of his plan to come to Rome on his way to Spain as a means of acquainting the community with his teaching as it affected both Jews and Gentiles. In what is virtually a treatise he amplifies the arguments used in the letter to the Galatians. The document forms a fitting conclusion to the First Series as a carefully reasoned statement of Paul's beliefs and convictions, boldly introduced by the challenging assertion that he is the envoy of a greater than Caesar charged with procuring the submission of all nations to the authority of his Lord.

———◆———

TO THE COMMUNITY AT THESSALONICA (1)

(Probably written from Corinth about A.D. 51)

Paul, Silvanus and Timotheus, to the community of Thessalonians in God the Father and the Lord Jesus Christ. May peace and prosperity be yours.

We invariably thank God for all of you, making mention of you in our prayers, continually remembering in the presence of God our Father the intensity of your faith, the ardour of your love, and the constancy of your hope in the Lord Jesus Christ.

I[1] know, brothers dear to God, how truly chosen you are, because my News came to you not merely with speech, but with power, with inspiration, and with strong conviction; even as *you* know the kind of man I was with you for your sakes. You became imitators of me, and of the Master, welcoming the Message in circumstances of great difficulty with fervent joy,[2] so that you became an example to all the believers in Macedonia and Achaia. For from you the Lord's Message resounded not only throughout Macedonia and Achaia, but indeed far and wide your faith in God has penetrated, so that there is no need for me to speak of it. The people of those parts themselves tell of the effect of my visit to you, how you turned from idols[3] to serve the Living and True God, and to await his Son from heaven, whom he raised from the dead, Jesus our rescuer from the coming Wrath.

You yourselves know, brothers, that my visit to you was by no means ineffective. Though I had previously suffered and been ill-treated, as you are aware, at Philippi,[4] I made bold in God with a great effort to give you God's News.[5] My appeal to you was without imposture or impure motives, neither did I use guile. I spoke as one approved by God as worthy to be entrusted with the News, not as one who seeks to please men, but God who tries my heart.[6] For I was never in speech a flatterer,

---

[1] Paul continues to use the first person plural as he writes in the joint names of his colleagues and himself. But here and in his other letters the singular has been used where Paul's views and experiences are concerned.

[2] Lit. 'joy of holy Spirit'.

[3] I.e. dead and false gods. Cp. 'the dead' (dead idols), *Aboth*, iii. 4.

[4] See above p. 223.   [5] See above p. 224-225.   [6] Cp. Prov. xvii. 3.

as you know, nor one with covetous designs, God is my witness, nor one who seeks human commendation, neither from you nor anyone else, though entitled to be of consequence as an envoy of Christ. Rather was I very tender with you, as if I were a foster-mother nursing her own children. Thus yearning over you, I was delighted to impart to you not only God's News but my very life, so dear had you become to me.

Only call to mind, brothers, my toil and drudgery. Night and day I laboured so as not to be a burden to you in any way while proclaiming God's News. You are witnesses, and God also, how correctly, honourably and blamelessly, I acted towards you believers, just as you know how I exhorted, encouraged and charged every single one of you, as a father his own children, to behave worthy of God who has invited you to share his sovereignty and state.

I do indeed thank God constantly for this, that on acceptance of God's Message as you heard it from me, you welcomed it not as a human message, but for what it truly is—God's Message, which is certainly operative in you believers. For, brothers, you became counterparts of the communities of God in Judea which are in Christ Jesus; for you yourselves have suffered similarly from your own countrymen as they from the Jews, who put to death the Lord Jesus and the Prophets, and hounded me out,[7] who incur God's displeasure, setting themselves against everyone, hindering me from speaking to the Gentiles that they might be saved and so filling up in every way the measure of their sins.[8] Thus 'Wrath to the full has fallen on them.'[9]

But though separated from you for a while, brothers, in presence not in mind, I have been exceedingly anxious and greatly longing to see your faces. Consequently I, Paul, wanted personally to visit you time and again, but Satan put difficulties in my way. For what, if not you, is my hope or joy or proud crown in presence of our Lord Jesus at his coming? It is you who are my glory and my joy!

So when I could bear it no longer, I was content to be left at Athens alone,[10] while I sent Timotheus, our brother and God's agent for the News of Christ, to sustain and encourage you in your faith, that none of you should wilt under these trials. You know yourselves that we are put here for this purpose; and further when I was with you I forewarned you, as you know, 'we are bound to have trouble', exactly as it turned out. So, as I say, being unable to bear it any longer, I sent to learn the state of your faith, in case the Tempter had tempted you, and my toil had been in vain.

But now, when Timotheus returned to me from visiting you, and gave me the good news of your loyalty and love, and that you always have a pleasant recollection of me and long to see

[7] See above p. 209.   [8] Mt. xxiii. 32, above p. 126.
[9] *Test. XII. Patr. (Test. Levi*, vi. 11)   [10] See above p. 225.

me, as I see you, this consoled me so far as you are concerned for all my anguish and distress. Now indeed I live again, since you stand fast in the Master. How can I sufficiently thank God on your account for all the happiness I enjoy because of you in the presence of our God! Night and day I supplicate beyond all bounds that I may be permitted to see your faces and make good any deficiencies in your faith. May God himself, our Father, and our Lord Jesus make it practicable for me to come to you!

The Lord make you increase and abound in love for one another and for all others, as my love goes out to you, so as to lift up your hearts blameless[11] in holiness in the presence of God our Father at the coming of our Lord Jesus with all his saints.

Further, brothers, I entreat and appeal to you in the Lord Jesus, that as you have received from me the manner in which you should conduct yourselves and be pleasing to God—as indeed you do conduct yourselves—so should you do better still. You know I gave you certain instructions on behalf of the Lord Jesus. Doing the will of God implies your consecration, that you keep clear of immorality, that each of you knows how to possess his own mate in purity and with respect; not swayed by lust like the Gentiles who do not know God,[12] that there be no meddling with or coveting what belongs to your brother;[13] for the Lord will avenge anything of that sort as I warned and solemnly told you. God has not called us to impurity but to consecration. Accordingly, whoever disregards this breaks faith not with men but with God, who has given us his Spirit which is holy.

As regards brotherly affection there is no need for me to write to you, for you yourselves are taught by God to love one another; and you do indeed practise it towards all the brothers throughout Macedonia. But I appeal to you, brothers, to do better still, and to make a real effort to be quiet and attend to your own business. Labour with your hands, as I have instructed you, that you may comport yourselves with dignity towards those outside,[14] and require no one's assistance.[15]

Now I do not want you to be ignorant, brothers, about those who are laid to rest, that you do not grieve like those who are without hope. For if we believe that Jesus died and rose again, so do we also that God by means of Jesus will carry off[16] as well as him those who are laid to rest. I tell you this by the word of the Lord, that we who are alive and survive till the coming of the Master will not forestall those who are laid to rest. The Master will himself descend from heaven with a cry

[11] As the offering was elevated in the Sanctuary.
[12] Cp. Ps. lxxix. 6.
[13] The 10th Commandment, Exod. xx. 17.
[14] See above p. 57, n. 23.
[15] Some Thessalonian believers, expecting the speedy return of Christ, were neglecting their employment. See the next letter to them.
[16] As booty from the thraldom of death.

254 THE LETTERS OF PAUL

of command, with arch-angelic voice and divine trumpet-blast, and the dead in Christ will rise first. Next we who are alive and survive will at once be caught up with them by clouds to meet the Master in the air; and so shall we be ever with the Master. Cheer one another, therefore, with this information.

As regards dates and times, brothers, there is no need for me to write to you, for you yourselves know perfectly well that the Day of the Lord will come like a thief in the night.[17] Just when they are saying, 'A peaceful night, and all's well', then suddenly destruction will be upon them like pangs on a pregnant woman, and they will have no chance of escape.[18] But you, brothers, are not in darkness, that the Day should catch you like a thief; for all of you are beings of the light[19] and beings of the day. We do not belong to the night or to darkness.

Well then, let us not slumber like others, but be wakeful and sober. For those who slumber slumber at night, and those who are drunkards are drunk at night. But let us who belong to the day be sober, clad in the corselet of faith and love, and helmeted with the hope of deliverance. For God has not destined us to Wrath, but to be preserved for Deliverance by our Lord Jesus Christ, who died for us, that at once—whether awake or sleeping—we should be alive with him. So encourage one another and fortify each other, as indeed you are doing.

But I do beg you, brothers, to acknowledge those who work so hard among you and act as your leaders in the Master, and advise you. Hold them in extra-special affection for their work. Be at peace among yourselves.

I appeal to you, brothers, give fair warning to the disorderly, encourage the fainthearted, stand by the weak, be patient with all. See to it that none renders to any injury for injury, but always do the right thing by each other and everyone else. Always be cheerful, pray constantly, give thanks for everything; for this is God's will in Christ for you. Do not still the Spirit, or scorn prophecies. Test everything: retain the good.[20] Refrain from anything that looks at all wrong.

Now may the God of peace himself sanctify you completely, and may you in your entirety, spirit, soul and body, be kept blameless till the coming of the Lord Jesus Christ. He who calls you is faithful, who indeed will accomplish this. Brothers, pray for us also.

Convey our regards to all the brothers with a chaste kiss. I adjure you by the Lord to have this letter read to all the brothers. The loving-kindness of our Lord Jesus Christ be with you.

---

[17] Cp. Mt. xxiv. 43; II. Pet. iii. 10.

[18] See Joel ii. 1-11.

[19] Lit. 'children of light'. Among the Jewish eclectic groups of the saints (Chasidim) the faithful Israelites called themselves the 'Children of Light', as opposed to the enemies of God the 'Children of Darkness'. Cp. the Dead Sea scrolls (*Manual of Discipline*).

[20] Probably based on a saying of Jesus frequently cited in the Patristic literature: 'Become skilled money-changers, rejecting some things, but retaining what is good.'

TO THE COMMUNITY AT THESSALONICA (2)

(Probably written from Corinth about A.D. 52)

Paul, Silvanus and Timotheus, to the community of Thessalonians in God our Father and the Lord Jesus Christ. May peace and prosperity be yours from God the Father and the Lord Jesus Christ.

We are bound invariably to thank God for you, brothers, as is only right, because your faith is so wonderfully increasing, and the love of each and all of you for one another is ever deepening; so that we ourselves boast of you in the communities of God, of your constancy and loyalty in all the persecutions and trials with which you have had to contend.

This is a proof of God's strict justice, in having treated you as worthy of the Kingdom of God, for which indeed you suffer. For that being so, it becomes just on God's part to repay affliction to those who afflict you, and to give you who are afflicted relief with us when the Lord Jesus is revealed from heaven with his mighty angels in flaming fire, inflicting retribution on those who do not acknowledge God and do not respond to the News of our Lord Jesus.[21] They shall pay the penalty of perpetual exclusion from the presence of the Master and the splendour of his majesty when he comes at that time to be praised by his saints and admired by all who have believed because our testimony to you was believed. To this end we invariably pray for you, that our God may make you worthy of your vocation, and enable you to accomplish every praiseworthy object and devoted deed which may serve to glorify the name of our Lord Jesus among you, and you in him, by the loving-kindness of our God and the Lord Jesus Christ.

Now I beg you, brothers, as regards the coming of our Lord Jesus Christ and our being gathered to him, not to take speedy leave of your senses or become agitated, either by a spirit intimation, or by a speech, or by any letter purporting to be from me, under the impression that the Day of the Lord has begun. Let no one deceive you in any way whatever; for it will not begin before the Defection has first taken place and the Lawless Man[22] has been revealed, the Doomed One who opposes and elevates himself above everything regarded as a god or as an object of worship, so that he himself sits in God's Temple

---

[21] Cp. DD, ii. 4, 'And power and might and great fury with flames of fire—all the angels of destruction—for them who turned aside out of the way and abhorred the statute.' See also Isa. lxvi. 15; Mic. v. 15; Ps. lxxix. 6.
[22] Belial, the Devil incarnate in apocalyptic thought. In rabbinical circles the name was interpreted as *Beli-'ol* (without yoke), without restraint of law.

claiming to be God.[23] Do you not recall that this is what I told you while I was still with you?

So now you know what is the retarding factor, that the Lawless One may be revealed at his proper time. Indeed, the process[24] of lawlessness is already at work, only there is one who is retarding it until his removal. And then the Lawless One will be revealed, whom the Lord Jesus will consume with the breath of his mouth and annihilate with the radiance of his presence,[25] that one whose coming is attended, in the way Satan works, by every kind of mendacious trickery practised on those who are perishing,[26] because they have not welcomed the love of truth so as to be spared. For that reason God will send them a spirit of delusion so as to believe the lie, that all may be condemned who have not credited truth, but have taken pleasure in falsehood.

But I am bound invariably to thank God for you, brothers dear to the Master, because God has chosen you from the very beginning for deliverance, for the acquisition of the glory of our Lord Jesus Christ, by that consecration of spirit and attachment to truth to which he called you by my News. So then, brothers, stand fast, and keep a firm hold on the traditions[27] you have been taught whether by my speech or correspondence.

May our Master himself, Jesus Christ, and God our Father, who has loved us and graciously granted us solid consolation and good hope, encourage and confirm your minds by every fair word and deed!

Finally, brothers, pray for me, that the word of the Lord may speed and be honoured as in your case, and that I may be delivered from inhumane and wicked men;[28] for faith is not found in everyone. But the Lord is faithful, and will establish you and shield you from harm. I have confidence in you in the Master, that you are following and will continue to follow my injunctions. The Lord direct your minds to the love of God and the constancy of Christ.

But in the name of the Lord Jesus Christ, brothers, I bid you shun every brother who behaves as a shirker, and not in accordance with the tradition you have received from me. You are well aware that you ought to copy me; for I was no shirker among you, neither did I accept free meals from anyone.[29] Rather with toil and hardship did I labour night and day so as not to be a burden to you in any way. Not that I have not the right; but that I personally should set you an example, so that you should copy me. That is why when I was with you I gave you this order,

---

[23] Cp. Isa. xiv. 13-14; Dan. xi. 36; Mt. xxiv. 15. The Emperor Gaius (A.D. 40) tried to set up his statue as God in the Temple at Jerusalem, but failed.
[24] Lit. 'mystery'.   [25] Cp. Isa. xi. 4; Mt. xxiv. 27.
[26] Cp. Rev. xiii, below p. 455.
[27] The doctrine handed on from teacher to disciple. See I. Cor. xi. 2, below p. 276, Rom. vi. 17.
[28] A Jewish morning supplication asks God for deliverance from arrogant and wicked men (AJP, p. 7).
[29] Lit. 'Neither did I eat anyone's bread for nothing.'

'He who will not work, neither shall he eat.' For I hear there are some among you behaving as shirkers, not busy but busybodies. I order and exhort in the Lord Jesus Christ such as these, that going quietly about their work they eat their own bread.

As for you, brothers, never hesitate to do the right thing; but if anyone pays no attention to what I say in this letter, mark that man, and have nothing to do with him, that he may be ashamed. Yet do not treat him as an enemy, but warn him as a brother.

Now may the Lord of peace himself give you peace always in all circumstances![30] The Lord be with you all.

The greeting I subjoin in my own, Paul's, hand. It is the mark of authenticity on every letter.[31] This is how I write. *The loving-kindness of the Lord Jesus Christ be with you all.*[32]

———◆———

TO THE COMMUNITIES OF GALATIA

(Probably written from Antioch in the early Summer of A.D. 53[33])

Paul the Envoy—not from any body of men or appointed by any man, but by Jesus Christ and God the Father who raised him from the dead—and all the brothers who are with me, to the communities of Galatia. May peace and prosperity be yours from God our Father and the Lord Jesus Christ, who gave himself for our sins to reclaim us from the present evil world in accordance with the will of our God and Father, to whom, be praise for evermore.[34] Amen.

I am amazed that you have so quickly turned your backs on the one who called you in Christ's mercy for some other version of the News. It is not really another, but there are certain people who are confusing you and want to alter the terms of the News of Christ. But even should I, or an angel from heaven, proclaim to you anything different to what I did

[30] See the Aaronic Benediction, Num. vi. 26.
[31] As is evident from these words, and an earlier reference in the letter, at least one forged letter in the name of Paul was in existence at this time, and had perhaps reached the Thessalonians. The practice was common and not considered so immoral in those days. The Nazarene 'Zealots for the Law' were no doubt responsible. These did all they could to turn Paul's converts against him, with considerable success, and did not scruple to pervert his teaching. See Rom. iii. 8, below pp. 299-300.
[32] The words italicized were added by Paul in his own handwriting in the original document. Most of Paul's letters were dictated.
[33] Some consider the letter may have been written as late as A.D. 57, perhaps from Corinth. In favour of this view is the likeness to the letter to the Romans.
[34] Paul constantly follows the practice of the pious Jew in adding a doxology when speaking of the ways of God.

proclaim to you, cursed be he! Having said that, I am going to repeat it. If anyone proclaims to you anything different to what you received, cursed be he!

Is it men I have to satisfy, or is it God? Or is it men I am trying to please? If I were still pleasing men I should be no servant of Christ. I must make it clear to you, brothers, that the News as proclaimed by me is no human contrivance, for I neither obtained it from anyone, nor was I taught it: it came through Jesus Christ's own revelation.

You have heard, of course, of my behaviour when I practised Judaism, how I ruthlessly hounded down God's Community and ravaged it, and how I advanced in Judaism far beyond many students of my own age; for none was more keenly enthusiastic than I to master the traditions of my ancestors. But when it pleased God, who separated me from my mother's womb and called me by his mercy, to reveal his Son to me that I should proclaim him to the Gentiles, I did not take immediate steps to consult any earthly authority, neither did I go up to Jerusalem to interview those who were envoys before me. Instead, I went away to Arabia, and returned again to Damascus. Not until three years had elapsed did I go up to Jerusalem to report to Cephas,[35] and I remained with him fifteen days. But I met none of the other envoys except James the Master's brother.[36] These are the facts I am giving you. Before God, I am telling no lie!

After that I went to the regions of Syria and Cilicia, and remained unknown by sight to the Christian communities of Judea. They only heard that 'he who formerly persecuted us now proclaims the Faith he once attacked', and they praised God for me.

After that, some fourteen years later, I again went up to Jerusalem with Barnabas, and also took Titus with me. I went there by a revelation and reported to them the terms of the News I preach to the Gentiles. This was privately to those of repute, in case I should strive or had been striving to no purpose. But there was no forcing of Titus, who accompanied me, to be circumcised, Greek though he was, despite the infiltrated false brothers who had crept in to spy out the liberty we enjoy in Christ Jesus in order to enslave us. Not for an instant did we strike our colours, so that the true character of the News might be preserved to you.

As for those of repute—whatever they were makes no difference to me: God takes no one at face value—they imposed on me nothing additional. Quite the contrary. When they saw that I had been entrusted with the News for the Uncircumcised, as Peter for the Circumcised—for he who stimulated Peter to envoyship of the Circumcised stimulated me also in

[35] The Hebrew form of the nickname Peter.
[36] Paul's account of his movements should be compared with the much later account in the Acts, above pp. 209-210.

going to the Gentiles—and when they realized the privilege that had been granted me, then James, Cephas and John, the reputed 'Pillars of the Faith,' extended to myself and Barnabas the right hand of fellowship. We were to go to the Gentiles, they to the Circumcised.[37] Oh yes, they did add one more thing, we were to remember the poor,[38] which personally I was only too ready to do.

So when Cephas came to Antioch I opposed him publicly, because he deserved censure. Before certain persons came from James he had eaten with Gentiles. But after their arrival he drew back and separated himself out of fear of those of the Circumcision. The other Jews played up to him, so that even Barnabas was carried away by their hypocrisy.

So when I saw that they were not acting in conformity with the true character of the News I said to Cephas in front of them all, 'If you a born Jew live like a Gentile, why do you force the Gentiles to keep Jewish ways? We who are of Jewish race and not Gentile sinners,[39] knowing that no one is exonerated by following regulations but by faith in Jesus Christ, even we have trusted in Jesus Christ so as to be exonerated by faith in Christ and not by following regulations; for by following regulations "not a single human being will be exonerated".[40] But if while seeking to be exonerated in Christ we ourselves are found to be sinners, does that make Christ sin's agent? God forbid! So if I rebuild what I have demolished it is I who become the transgressor of my own accord. For in law I have died in the legal sense, so as to live in the divine sense. I have shared Christ's crucifixion. I am alive, it is true, but strictly speaking it is not I who live, but Christ who lives in me. My present physical existence is by virtue of the life of God's Son, who loved me and gave himself for me. I am not going to be the one to refuse God's mercy. For if rectitude could be assured by law then Christ died in vain.'

You senseless Galatians, who has cast a spell over you, you before whose gaze Jesus Christ was publicly displayed[41] as crucified? I only wish to know this from you, did you receive the Spirit by following regulations or by the response of faith? Are you so senseless, that having made a start spiritually you are now going to end up physically? Have you experienced so much to no purpose—if it is to no purpose? Does he who mediates the Spirit to you, and effects miracles among you, do it by following regulations or by the response of faith, just as Abraham 'believed God, and it was accounted to him as rectitude'?[42]

[37] Cp. the account in Acts, above pp. 219-220.
[38] The poor saints of Jerusalem.
[39] Living in violation of the Divine Law. See above p. 54, n. 12.
[40] Cp. Ps. cxliii. 2.
[41] The word used signifies public placarding, but Paul probably had in mind the lifting up of the serpent in the wilderness. See Num. xxi. 9, and cp. Jn. iii. 14. He is speaking of his own preaching.
[42] Gen. xv. 6.

Observe, then, that it is those with faith who are the children of Abraham. And the Scriptures, foreseeing that God would exonerate the Gentiles by faith, proclaimed in advance the News to Abraham, 'in you shall all the nations be blessed.'[43] So it is those with faith who are blessed along with believing Abraham. All those who follow regulations are under a curse, for it is stated, 'Cursed is everyone who does not adhere to and observe all the precepts set down in the Code of Law'.[44]

Now it is evident that no one is exonerated before God by law, because 'the just shall live *by faith*'.[45] But the Law is not 'by faith': it stipulates that 'he who keeps the commandments shall live by them.'[46] Christ has released us from the Law's curse by becoming a curse on our behalf, for it is stated, 'Cursed is everyone hanged on a tree',[47] so that Abraham's blessing might come to the Gentiles by Jesus Christ, that we all should receive the promise of the Spirit by faith.

Brothers, I speak in human terms, even in human practice a covenant once ratified cannot be set aside or amended. The undertakings were clearly given to Abraham 'and to his seed'.[48] It does not say 'and to seeds', implying a number, but distinctly one, 'and to your seed', that is to say to Christ. So I say this, that the Law which came into force four hundred and thirty years later[49] cannot abrogate the covenant previously ratified by God, so as to nullify the promise; and God wanted to show his appreciation to Abraham by making a promise. Why then was the Law given? It was introduced to deal with infringements until such time as the promised Seed should come, drawn up in due form by angels acting through a spokesman.[50] Since, however, a spokesman does not act for one, while God is one, does that mean that the Law is at variance with God's undertakings? God forbid! Certainly if a law could have been given capable of conferring life, then rectitude would have been by law. As it is, the Scripture[51] classes all together as sinners, that the promise by faith in Jesus Christ might be granted to those who believe.

Before faith came we were under law's strict tutelage, we were classmates until the future faith should be revealed. Consequently, the Law was our disciplinarian till Christ came, so that we should be exonerated by faith. Now that faith has come we are no longer under a disciplinarian. You are all Sons of God by faith in Jesus Christ; for those who have been identified with Christ by immersion have assumed Christ's personality. It is impossible for there to be Jew or Greek, slave or

[43] Gen. xii. 3.
[44] Deut. xxvii. 26.
[45] Hab. ii. 4.
[46] Lev. xviii. 5.
[47] Deut. xxi. 23.
[48] Gen. xii. 3.
[49] The time refers to the sojourn of Israel in Egypt, Exod. xii. 40.
[50] I.e. the angels, by whom according to Jewish legend the Law was given, whose spokesman was the Angel of the Covenant.
[51] Ps. cxliii. 2.

freeman, male or female;[52] for in Jesus Christ you are all one and the same person. If you are in Christ you are 'the Seed of Abraham', heirs in accordance with the promise.

What I am saying is this, that so long as the heir is under age, though he is actually master of the estate his position hardly differs from that of a slave: he remains under supervisors and managers until the time fixed by his father. So it is with us. We too were under age, in subjection to the elemental forces of the universe. Then, when the set time had arrived, God sent out his Son, born of a woman, born under law, that those under law might be redeemed, that we might receive adoption as sons. And because you are now sons, God has sent his Son's spirit into our hearts, crying, 'Abba!' (Father!). Thus no longer is it a slave crying, but a son, and if a son, then by God's providence an heir also.

There was a time when not knowing God you were enslaved to those who in reality are no gods. But now acknowledging God, or rather being acknowledged by God, how comes it that you have turned back to the feeble and abject elemental forces? Do you intend to be enslaved to them all over again? You have begun to observe special days and months, seasons and years. I begin to fear for you that I may have been wearing myself out for you to no purpose.

Do become as I am, that I in turn may be as you are, I do entreat you. I assure you that you have not wronged me. You well know how through physical infirmity I proclaimed the News to you originally. But the temptation afforded you by my physical condition did not induce you to mock or express disgust. Instead, you welcomed me as if I were God's messenger,[53] as if I were Christ in person. What has become of the delight you exhibited? For I can testify that if need be you would have plucked out your eyes and given them to me. Have I become your enemy by being frank with you? They are paying court to you[54] for no good purpose: they really intend to ostracize you so that you should court them. It is good to be courted for a good purpose on all occasions, and not just when I am present with you, my children, for whom I travail once more until Christ is formed in you. I only wish I could be with you at this moment, and change my tone, for I am quite distracted about you.

Tell me, you that want to be under law, do you never listen to the reading of the Law. For it is stated that Abraham had two sons, one by the slave-girl and one by the free-woman. But while the child of the slave-girl was of physical origin, the child of the free-woman was born by promise. These are

52 The Jew daily thanks God that he has not made him a heathen, a slave, or a woman, in the order given here (AJP, pp. 5-6).

53 See Acts xiv. 12, above p. 218, where we learn how Paul was taken for Hermes (Mercury), messenger of the gods. In early Christian apologetics Jesus was likened to Mercury.

54 I.e. the advocates of Gentile obedience to the Law of Moses.

allegorical matters; for these women represent two covenants. The one is of Mount Sinai bearing children for servitude. This is Hagar—for in Arabia *hajar* means Mount Sinai[55]—and corresponds to the present Jerusalem which is in servitude with her children. But the Jerusalem Above[56] is free, which is our mother Sarah,[57] for it is stated,

> Rejoice, you barren one who do not bear!
> Cry out with joy, you who do not travail!
> For more are the children of the desolate
> Than of the woman who has a husband.[58]

Now we, brothers, like Isaac are children of promise. But just as then the child of physical origin persecuted the child of spiritual origin, so it is now. Yet what does the Scripture say? 'Cast out the slave-girl and her son, for the son of the slave-girl shall not share the inheritance with the son of the free-woman.[59] Consequently, brothers, we are not the children of the slave-girl, but of the free-woman, with the complete freedom Christ has given us. Stand firm, then, and refuse to be harnessed again to a yoke of bondage.

I, Paul, tell you plainly that if you become circumcised Christ is of no service to you. And I declare to every circumcised person that he is obligated to observe the whole Law. You have become severed from Christ, those of you who would be exonerated by law: you have fallen from grace. For it is spiritually, by faith, that we hold the expectation of rectitude; for in Christ Jesus it is neither circumcision nor uncircumcision that is efficacious, but faith stimulated by love.

You were running so well. Who brought you to a halt by making you lose confidence in the truth? That idea you have got never came from the one who called you. It takes little leaven to leaven the mass. I personally am convinced of you in the Master that you will not change your minds. He who is confusing you must bear the blame whoever he may be. And what of me, brothers? If I am still preaching circumcision, why am I still being persecuted? So much for the 'abolition of the obstacle of the cross'![60] It would be a good thing if those who unsettle you over circumcision would cut themselves off as well!

Now you have been called to freedom, brothers. That does not mean freedom merely as an excuse for physical indulgence:

---

[55] The Sinai Peninsula called by the Arabs Et-Tijahah.

[56] The heavenly Jerusalem believed to have been created by God in the beginning to be revealed in the Messianic Era. See Rev. xxi. 2.

[57] In the text the name is omitted, and perhaps also the author's explanation of the name, interpreted as 'noble'. It is possible that the passage has been tampered with in the interests of Gentile Christianity, for the quotation from Isaiah was later used to prove that more Gentiles than Jews had accepted Christ.

[58] Isa. liv. 1.

[59] Gen. xxi. 9-10.

[60] Paul seems here to be borrowing a phrase from the propaganda of the Zealots for the Law. The idea of a crucified Messiah was repugnant to Jews (see I. Cor. i. 23, below p. 268), and the death of Jesus had to be explained as the means whereby he entered into his glory. To the first Christians the crucifixion had no redemptive value.

it means that you are to serve one another by love. For the whole Law is summed up in this one precept, 'You are to love your neighbour or yourself.' [61] But if you bite and devour each other, take care that you do not exterminate one another. I say, therefore, conduct yourselves spiritually, and do not allow your physical passions to have their way. For the physical nature has passions contrary to the spiritual nature, and the spiritual nature contrary to the physical, because these are in opposition to one another. So you are not free to do as you please. Yet if you are spiritually guided you are not under law.

Now the deeds of the physical nature are obvious: they are adultery, impurity, sensuality, idolatry, sorcery, enmity, quarrelling, envy, passions, intrigues, dissensions, factions, malice, heavy drinking, revelling, and everything of the same description about which I have warned you, just as I am warning you now, that those who act in this way will not inherit the Kingdom of God. But the spiritual product is love, joy, peace, forbearance, kindliness, goodness, loyalty, gentleness, self-control. Against these no law is in operation. Those who are in Christ Jesus have crucified the physical nature with its passions and desires. If we are to live spiritually, let us also accept spiritual discipline. Let us not become self-assertive, defying one another, malicious to one another.

Brothers, if anyone has been detected in some fault, you who are spiritually-minded should correct him in a mild manner, having an eye on yourself in case you should be tempted. Bear one another's burdens, and thus carry out Christ's law. [62] But if anyone fancies himself to be somebody, when he is nothing of the kind, he suffers from self-delusion. Each must carefully examine his own work, and then he can have something to be proud of in his own right instead of in another's; for each must shoulder his own load. But let him who has the Message imparted to him share credit with his instructor.

Harbour no illusions. God is not to be hoodwinked. Whatever a man sows he will also reap. He who sows for his physical nature will reap decay as the physical consequences, while he who sows for the spiritual nature will reap Eternal Life as the spiritual consequences. Let us never grow weary of doing what is right; for by never relaxing we shall reap in due course. So as opportunity is afforded us let us labour for the welfare of all, particularly of our kinsmen in faith.

Look how I have written to you in large characters with my own hand! [63] Those who want to make a favourable impression in the physical sense press you to be circumcised, but only to evade persecution for Christ's cross. It is not as if these circumcised people were themselves observant. They only want you to be circumcised so that they can boast of your physical condi-

[61] Lev. xix. 18 (cp. Mt. xxii. 39-40; Rom. xiii. 9-10).
[62] Cp. Isa. liii. 4; Mt. viii. 27.   [63] I.e. as a mark of special distinction.

tion. For myself, God forbid that I should boast of anything but the cross of our Lord Jesus Christ, by which the world has been crucified to me, and I to the world! It is neither circumcision nor uncircumcision that counts for anything, but a new creation. To all who toe this line, peace and mercy be upon them, and upon the Israel of God.[64]

From now on let no one deal me any more blows, for I carry the scars of Jesus on my body.[65]

The loving-kindness of the Lord Jesus Christ be with your spirit, brothers. Amen.

———◆———

TO THE COMMUNITY AT CORINTH (1) [66]

(Written from Ephesus probably in A.D. 55)

EXCERPT ONE

. . . Am I not a freeman?[67] Am I not an envoy? Have I not seen Jesus our Master? Are you not the product of my labour for the Master? If I am not regarded by others as an envoy, surely I am by you, for you are the confirmation of my envoyship for the Master.

Here, then, is my reply to those who cross-examine me. Have I not the right to eat and drink? Have I not the right to take around with me a believing wife[68] like the other envoys, and the Master's brothers,[69] and Cephas? Is it only I and Barnabas who have no right to give up our occupations? Who ever goes on military service at his own expense? Who plants a vineyard and does not partake of its fruit? Who herds a flock and does not eat the curds obtained from the flock? Am I speaking in human fashion, or does not the Law say the same thing? Surely it is stated in the Law of Moses, 'You are not to muzzle the ox that treads out the corn'.[70] Is God concerned here with oxen, or speaking entirely for our benefit? For our benefit, surely, so that the ploughman should have something to expect

[64] Cp. Jewish prayer, 'May he bestow peace on us, and upon all Israel' (AJP, p. 54, 76, etc.). The 'Israel of God' or 'divine Israel' as distinguished from the physical Israel.

[65] Probably with reference to the flogging which Jesus underwent (Mk. xv. 15). Paul had already been flogged at Philippi and perhaps elsewhere (II. Cor. xi. 24-25, below p. 286).

[66] The existing two letters to the Corinthians are a combination of the original four. The first letter is referred to in I. Cor. v. 9, the second is largely represented by I. Cor., the third is mentioned in II. Cor. vii. 8, and the fourth corresponds to the greater part of II. Cor. The original first letter dealt in part with the subject of association with immoral persons. It is probable, as presented here, that I. Cor. ix. 1-x. 22 and II. Cor. vi. 14-vii. 1 belong to it.

[67] As compared with a slave, who had no rights.

[68] Lt. 'a sister-wife.'

[69] This suggests some missionary activities by the brothers of Jesus.

[70] Deut. xxv. 4.

from his ploughing, and the thresher from his part of the work. If we have sown spiritual seed in you, is it too much to expect if we reap material things from you? If you grant others that right, should you not much more to me, even if I have taken no advantage of that right, but have fended for myself entirely lest I should afford the slightest hindrance to the News of Christ. Are you ignorant that those who perform priestly duties partake of the Temple dues, and that those who serve the altar share in what is offered at the altar?[71] In the same way the Master has laid down that those who proclaim the News should live off the News.[72]

Greek foot race

Yet I have availed myself of none of these rights, and I have not mentioned them here with a view to getting anything for myself. I would sooner die first! Let no one take that as an empty boast. Granted that I do proclaim the News, there is nothing in that for me to boast of, for I am constrained to do it. Woe to me if I do not proclaim the News! Yet if I do it in a voluntary capacity I receive a reward. But if I am engaged to do it, it is my professional employment. What is the nature of my reward? It is that when I proclaim the News I can give it out free of charge by not exercising my rights.

But though I am in every sense a freeman, I have made myself everyone's slave so as to win over far more. So I have been a Jew to Jews to win over Jews. I have been subject to law to

[71] Cp. Lev. ii. 3; vi. 18.
[72] Cp. Lk. x. 7.

those under law—not being under law myself—to win over those under law. I have been alien to law to those without law— though not alien to God's law and legally bound to Christ—to win over those without law.[73] I have been subject to limitations to those with limitations,[74] to win over those with limitations. To everyone I have been as they are, that at all events I should save some. And whatever I do it is for the News, that I may assure my share in it.

Are you ignorant that though all the runners race on the course only one receives the prize? So run as if you meant to win. And every contestant exercises complete self-mastery; but they do it for a perishable garland, we for an imperishable. That is how I run, in no uncertain fashion, and that is how I fight, with no threshing the air. I pummel my body and make it my slave, in case having preached to others I should fail to pass the test myself.

I would not have you ignorant, brothers, that our ancestors were all under cover of the cloud and all passed through the sea, and all were immersed with the Mosaic immersion in the cloud and in the sea.[75] And they all partook of the same spiritual food[76] and drank the same spiritual drink; for they drank from that accompanying rock,[77] the rock that was Christ. But God was not pleased with the majority of them, and they were laid low in the wilderness.

Now these things have become illustrations to us not to covet what is bad, as they did; not to be idolaters as some of them were, as it is stated, 'the people sat down to eat and drink and rose up to play';[78] not to indulge in immorality, as some of them did, and twenty-three thousand fell in one day; not to tempt the Lord, as some of them did, and perished by snake bites; not to murmur, as some of them did, and perished by the destroyer. Now these things happened to those people to furnish illustrations, and they were recorded as a warning to us with whom the Consummation of the Ages has been reached. So let him who stands have a care lest he fall. No superhuman temptation has come your way. God is faithful: he will never allow you to be tempted beyond your strength, but along with the temptation he will provide a loop-hole also, to enable you to extricate yourself from it.

Consequently, dear friends, make good your escape from idolatry. I am talking to men of sense. Consider carefully what I say. Is not the cup of blessing we bless fellowship with Christ's blood? Is not the bread we break fellowship with Christ's

---

[73] See below p. 302, n. 209.
[74] Conscientious objection in matters of diet, etc.
[75] Exod. xiv. 19-21, 31.
[76] Exod. xvi. 15, the manna.
[77] Num. xvii. 6; xx. 8. In Jewish legend the rock was a crag like a beehive, which rolled along and accompanied the Israelites. When they camped it provided water as the people sang, 'Spring up, O well'. (Num. xxi. 17.)
[78] Exod. xxxii. 6.

body?[79] For we many are one loaf of bread, one body, since we all have a share of the one loaf of bread. Look at the physical Israel. Are not those who partake of the sacrifices in fellowship with the altar of sacrifice? Am I suggesting by this that an offering to an idol is anything, or that an idol is anything? Of course not. But what the Gentiles sacrifice they sacrifice to demons, and not to God, and I want you to have no fellowship with demons. You cannot drink the Lord's cup and the cup of demons. Neither can you share the Lord's table and the table of demons.[80] Are we to arouse the Lord's jealousy? Are we stronger than he?

Excerpt Two[81]

. . . Do not be ill-matched[82] with unbelievers. For what has rectitude in common with lawlessness? Or what fellowship has light with darkness? What harmony has Christ with Beliar? Or what share has the faithful with the faithless? And what agreement has the temple of God with idols? For we are the temple of the Living God, as God has said,

> *'I will dwell with them and walk with them,*
> *And I will be their God, and they my people.'*[83]
> *'Therefore come out from among them,*
> *And be separate,' says the Lord.*
> *'Have no contact with the unclean.*[84]
> *And I will admit you within,*
> *And I will be a Father to you,*
> *And you shall be my sons and daughters,'*[85]
> *Says the Lord of hosts.*

Having therefore these promises,[86] dear friends, let us cleanse ourselves from all physical and spiritual defilement, discharging our sacred duties[87] in the fear of the Lord . . .

[79] Referring to the ceremonial blessing of bread and wine (Heb. *Kiddush*) before the communal meal eaten by Christians on Sunday in commemoration of the Last Supper. See further below p. 277.
[80] In the Graeco-Roman world the sacrificial meal was regarded as the table of the god (e.g. 'the table of the Lord Serapis'). The Jews regarded their communal meal as the table of the Lord. See below p. 275, n. 119, and cp. *Aboth*, iii, 4.
[81] This excerpt may have followed the previous one almost directly.
[82] Lit. 'yoked with another kind', relating to the Law of Diverse Kinds (Deut. xxii. 9-11). A clean beast was not to be yoked with an unclean (see *Kilaim*, viii. 2).
[83] Lev. xxvi. 11-12.
[84] Isa. lii. 11.
[85] Cp. Jer. xxxi. 1, 9; Isa. xliii. 6.
[86] As just quoted. But see also Ezek. xxxvii. 21, 23, 28 (xi. 17, 20 in LXX), where in *v*. 17 of the Greek *eisdechomai* ('admit within') is used.
[87] As priests of God's temple.

TO THE COMMUNITY AT CORINTH (2)[88]

(Written from Ephesus probably in the early Autumn of A.D. 55)

Paul, by the will of God a chosen envoy of Jesus Christ, with Brother Sosthenes,[89] to the community of God at Corinth, consecrated in Jesus Christ as members of the holy assembly[90] in common with all who in every place invoke the name of our Lord Jesus Christ, their Master and ours. May peace and prosperity be yours from God our Father and the Lord Jesus Christ.

I invariably thank God for you, for the way he has favoured you in Christ Jesus, because he has so enriched you in him in every respect, both in speech and knowledge. Just as the testimony of Christ was so firmly established among you, so have you never lacked for any spiritual gifts while waiting for the revelation of our Lord Jesus Christ. He will keep you steadfast to the end, that you may be without reproach on the Day of our Lord Jesus Christ. God is faithful, who has chosen you for fellowship with his Son Jesus Christ our Master.

Now in the name of our Lord Jesus Christ I urge you, brothers, all to hold together and not to have divisions among yourselves, but to accommodate yourselves to the selfsame outlook and viewpoint. For it has been conveyed to me about you, brothers, by Chloe's people, that quarrelling is going on among you. I mean this, that you are variously saying, 'I side with Paul', or, 'I go with Apollos', 'I take Cephas's view', or, 'I take Christ's'. Has Christ been split up? Was Paul crucified on your behalf? Or were you immersed in the name of Paul? I am thankful I immersed none of you but Crispus[91] and Gaius, so that no one can say you were immersed in my name. Oh yes, I also immersed the household of Stephanas. Otherwise I do not recall that I immersed anyone else. For Christ did not send me out to immerse but to proclaim the News, and not with clever words either, in case Christ's cross should lose all its potency. The message of the cross may be foolish to those who are perishing, but to those who are being saved—to us—it is the power of God; for it is stated,

> *'I will destroy the wisdom of the sages,*
> *And nullify the intellect of the intelligent.'*[92]

What becomes of the sage, the scribe, the scholar of this world? Has not God made nonsense of the world's wisdom?[93]

---

[88] Commonly known as I. Corinthians. [89] Probably Paul's amanuensis.
[90] Answering to Heb. *mikra kodesh* (holy convocation) as in Exod. xii. 16.
[91] Former president of the synagogue at Corinth (Acts xviii. 8), above p. 226.
[92] Isa. xxix. 14. [93] CP. Isa. xxxiii. 18; xliv. 25.

For since in God's wisdom the world failed to know God by wisdom, it pleased God to save those who believe by the folly of preaching. For while the Jews demand a sign, and the Greeks require wisdom, we preach a crucified Christ, an obstacle to Jews and nonsense to Gentiles; but to those who are chosen—Jews and Greeks alike—a Christ who is the power of God and the wisdom of God. For God's 'folly' is wiser than men, and God's 'weakness' is stronger than men.

Look at the choice in your own case, brothers. There are not many sages among you in the world's sense, not many persons of consequence, not many highborn. Instead, God has selected what is foolish in the world to shame the wise, and what is weak to shame the mighty, and what is of base origin and treated with contempt God has chosen, and even what is non-existent[94] to bring to an end the existing order, that not a single human being should boast in God's presence. But you are his offspring in Christ Jesus, who was begotten to be wisdom to us from God, yes, and vindication, consecration and ransom; so that as it is stated, 'Let him who boasts do it in the Lord.'[95]

So when I came to you, brothers, I did not come disclosing to you the Divine Secret with imposing speech or wisdom; for I was determined to be conscious of nothing while among you but of Jesus Christ, and of him as crucified. And so it was in weakness, and in fear, and in great trepidation, that I arrived among you; and my speech and proclamation was with no persuasive words of wisdom, but with spiritual and phenomenal demonstration, so that your faith should rest not on human wisdom but on divine power. There is a wisdom we employ with the initiated; but it is a wisdom that has nothing to do with this world, or with the transient forces governing this world.[96] It is the Hidden Wisdom of God contained in a Mystery,[97] which God formulated of old to be our glory before the ages began, unknown to any of the forces governing this world; for had they known it they would never have crucified the Lord of glory. But as it is stated,

> What eye has never seen, nor ear heard,
> What never entered the mind of man,
> God has prepared for those who love him.[98]

Yet God has revealed it to us by the Spirit; for the Spirit delves into everything, even into the profundities of God. For who among men knows a man's ideas except the human spirit which is in him? So too none can know God's ideas except the Divine Spirit. Now what we have received is not the spirit of the created world, but the Spirit that emanates from God, so

[94] Possibly referring to the position of the slave, regarded literally in the Graeco-Roman world as a non-entity.
[95] Jer. ix. 24.
[96] The spirit-powers ruling the planet.
[97] Paul is here using the language of the Mystery cults.
[98] Isa. lxiv. 4.

that we may know what God graciously grants us to know.[99] Those are the things we speak of, not in the language that human wisdom provides, but in the fashion of spiritual instruction, bringing spiritually-equipped people into touch with spiritual realities. The materalist cannot entertain the ideas of the Divine Spirit: to him they are nonsense, and he cannot grasp them, because they have to be discerned spiritually. But the spiritually-equipped person discerns all these things, though they are to be discerned by no one unaided, for 'who has ever known the mind of the Lord, that he should teach him?[100] But we have Christ's mind.

It was impossible, however, brothers, for me to speak to you as spiritually-equipped people, only as physically-equipped, as infants in Christ. I had to feed you with milk rather than solid food, for you were not equal to it. Neither are you equal to it yet, for you are still at the physical stage. As long as there is rivalry and wrangling among you are you not physical and behaving in human fashion? Whenever someone comes out with, 'I take Paul's side', and another, 'I am with Apollos', are you not human? What then is Apollos, and what is Paul? Simply the agents, each as the Lord endowed him, by whom you believed. I did the planting, and Apollos did the watering, but God caused the growth. Consequently, neither the planter nor the waterer counts, only God the Grower. Both the planter and the waterer have the same standing, yet each will receive his individual reward according to his individual labour; for we are God's co-workers, and you are God's culture, God's structure. By virtue of God's favour bestowed on me, I, like a skilled master-builder, have laid the foundation, while another will build on it. Only let each take care in what way he builds on it. There can never be any other foundation laid than what has been laid, the foundation that is Jesus Christ. But upon it it is open to anyone to erect an edifice of gold, silver, precious stones, wood, straw, or rush. The material[101] in each case will be evident, for the Day will reveal it. Since fire will be the means of disclosure, the flame itself will prove what kind of material it is. If the material which anyone has used for building survives, he will receive a reward. If anyone's material is burnt up, he will pay the penalty, though he will be saved himself, but barely, as if he had come through the flame.

Do you not realize that you are God's temple, and that the Divine Spirit resides in you? If anyone dishonours God's temple God will dishonour him; for God's temple is holy, as you are meant to be.

Let no one delude himself. If any of you considers he is what passes for a wise man in this age, let him become a fool, so that he may become really wise; for this world's wisdom is folly to

---

[99] Deut. xxix. 29; *Amidah*, Bened. iv. 'Thou favourest man with knowledge,' (AJP, p. 46)
[100] Isa. xl. 13.   [101] Or, 'work'.

God, for it is stated, 'He catches the wise at their knavery',[102] and again, 'The Lord knows how trivial are the arguments of the wise'.[103] So let no one boast of individuals. Everything is yours as it is, whether Paul, Apollos, Cephas, the whole created world, life and death, the present and future, all is yours, and you are Christ's, and Christ is God's. Consequently, we should be regarded merely as Christ's assistants, stewards of the Divine Mysteries, which implies the requirement in stewards that they should be found trustworthy. So it is of small concern to me whether I am examined by your or any human standard. I do not even examine myself. I am not aware of anything to my detriment, but that does not exonerate me. It is the Master who will examine me. So do not judge prematurely, before the Master has come, who will bring dark secrets to light and reveal the heart's design; and then the praise that is appropriate will be accorded by God to each.

Now these things, brothers, I have applied figuratively to myself and Apollos for your benefit, that you may learn the truth by us 'Not beyond what is ordained',[104] so that you may not get puffed up over one as compared with another. For who has singled you out? Or what do you possess that you have not received?[105] And if you have received it, why do you boast as if you had not received it? Already you are glutted! Already you have grown rich! Already you have occupied the throne! And I only wish you had taken the throne, so that we too could reign with you. As it seems to me, God has kept us envoys for the end of the show, like those doomed to death;[106] for we have become a spectacle for the universe, for angels and men. We for Christ's sake are fools, while you in Christ are sensible people! We are weak, but you are strong! You stand in high esteem, while we are in disgrace! To this very moment we hunger and thirst, we are ragged and knocked about, vagrant and toil-worn, labouring with our hands. When insulted we are polite, when persecuted we submit to it, when cursed we are conciliatory. Right up to now we are treated as the scum of the universe, the offscouring of everything.[107]

I am not writing this to shame you, but as dear children of mine I am reminding you. Should you have ten thousand guardians in Christ, you do not have a number of fathers. It is I, I in Christ, who have begotten you by the News. Copy me, therefore, I entreat you. That is why I have dispatched Timotheus to you, who is not only a dear child of mine but loyal to the Master, to recall to you the course I follow in Christ, which

---

[102] Job v. 13.   [103] Ps. xciv. 11.
[104] The source of this dictum is not known, but cp. the saying of Paul's contemporary Johanan ben Zaccai, 'If you have learnt much Divine Doctrine claim no merit for yourself, for to that end you were created' (*Aboth*, ii. 8).
[105] Cp. I. Chron xxix. 14.
[106] Like condemned criminals in the arena.
[107] The metaphor is taken from the Athenian custom in the event of some dire calamity of throwing some of the human 'scum' of the city into the sea, to 'clean off' the guilt of the people.

I recommend everywhere to all the communities. There are some who are full of bluster under the impression that I shall not be visiting you. But if the Lord wills I shall be visiting you quite soon, and when I do I shall take cognizance not of the speech but of the spiritual power of the blusterers; for the Kingdom of God consists not in speech but in spiritual power. Which do you prefer, that I visit you with a stick or in a mild and affectionate spirit?

I am reliably informed that there is immorality among you, immorality such as has no parallel among the Gentiles, that one should have his father's wife. And you are full of elation, instead of grieving, to the end that the person responsible should be removed from among you. I, however, absent as I am in body but present in spirit, have already—as if I were present—condemned the perpetrator of such a crime in the name of the Lord Jesus. Before the assembled company of yourselves and my spirit, invested with the authority of the Lord Jesus, the sentence is that the person concerned be consigned to Satan for his physical destruction[108] that his spirit may be saved when the Day of the Lord comes.

There is no justification for your boasting. Are you not aware that 'a little leaven leavens the whole lump'? Get rid of the old leaven that you may be a new lump, once more in the unleavened state, for our passover—Christ—has been sacrificed.[109] Consequently, let us observe the festival, not with the old leaven, nor with the leaven of vice and immorality, but with the unleavened bread of purity and sincerity.

In my letter[110] I wrote to you not to keep company with immoral characters,[111] not specifically the immoral of contemporary society, any more than with usurers, extortioners and idolaters, for in that case you would have to exclude yourselves completely from society. But I am writing to you now not to keep company at all with anyone bearing the name of brother if he is immoral, or a usurer, or idolater, or foul-mouthed, or a drunkard, or extortioner. You are not even to take meals with such people. Is it for you to judge those outside[112] when you do not judge those inside? Leave God to judge those outside, while you 'put away the wicked from among you'.[113]

Has any of you with a grievance against his fellow the temerity to bring his case before the evil-doers instead of before the saints? Or are you ignorant that the saints are to judge the world? So if the world is to be judged by you, are you unqualified to deal with minor issues? Are you ignorant that we are to judge angels, let alone mundane matters? So if you have any

---

[108] The form of excommunication may have been akin to that of the Essenes. The expelled person was evidently expected to die.
[109] The passover sacrifice immediately preceded the Feast of Unleavened Bread. All the old leaven was destroyed before the festival.
[110] Two probable excerpts from this letter are given above pp. 264-267.
[111] See p. 54, n. 12, and *Sanhed*, iii. 3, where immoral persons with whom strict Jews did not consort are listed.
[112] See p. 57, n. 23.　　　　　　[113] Deut xxii. 24.

mundane issues let those be appointed to try them who are the most looked down on members of the community. I say this deliberately to shame you. Can it be possible that there is not a wise man among you competent to decide between one brother and another? But brother must go to law with brother, and before unbelievers too! It is already an admission of complete failure on your part that you have any causes between yourselves. Why not rather let yourselves be injured? Why not rather let yourselves be defrauded? Instead, you injure and defraud, and your own brothers too! Are you ignorant that evildoers shall not inherit the Kingdom of God? Do not delude yourselves. Neither the immoral, nor idolaters, nor adulterers, nor homosexuals, nor thieves, nor usurers, nor drunkards, nor the foul-mouthed, nor extortioners, shall inherit the Kingdom of God. That is what some of you were; but you have been cleansed, you have been consecrated, you have been exonerated by the name of our Lord Jesus Christ, and by the Spirit of our God.

'I am free to do everything.'[114] Yes, but everything is not advantageous. I am free to do everything, provided I do not fall into its power. 'Food is for appetite, and appetite for food', but God will do away with both the one and the other. For the body is not for prostitution, but for the Master, and the Master for the body. And the God who raised up the Master will also by his power raise us up. Are you ignorant that your bodies are the organs of Christ? Am I then to make the organs of Christ the organs of a prostitute? God forbid! Or are you ignorant that he who unites himself with a prostitute forms a single body, for 'the two', it is said, 'shall become one flesh'?[115] But he who unites himself with the Master forms a single spirit. Shun prostitution. Any other kind of sin a man may commit is independent of the body, but the immoral man sins against his own body. Or are you ignorant that your body is the temple of the holy Spirit which is in you, which you have received from God, and that you are not your own, having been acquired at a high price? Then praise God with your body.

Now to turn to the matters on which you have written me. It is preferable for a man not to have intercourse with a woman. But to avoid prostitution each should take himself a wife, and each woman should have her own husband. The husband should fulfil his obligations to his wife, and similarly the wife to her husband. The wife has not the control of her own body, but the husband. Similarly the husband has not the control of his own body, but the wife. Do not deprive one another, unless by agreement for a time to devote yourselves to prayer.[116] But then renew your unhealthy behaviour. I say this by way of accommodation, your association, so that Satan should not tempt you through

---

[114] This quotation and the one that follows may possibly have been contained in the letter from the Corinthians to which Paul is replying. See also below p. 276.
[115] Gen. ii. 24.   [116] Cp. Test. Naphtali, viii. 8.

not of instruction. I would prefer everyone to be as I am. But each has his own gift from God, one in this way, another in that. Though I do say to the unmarried and to widows that it is preferable for them to remain like me. Yet if they cannot exercise self-control they should marry; for it is decidedly better to marry than to burn.

For those who are married, however, I stipulate—not indeed I but the Master—that the wife is not to separate from her husband, and if she is separated she must remain unwed or be reconciled to her husband; and the husband is not to divorce his wife.[117] Beyond that, I say—not the Master—that if a brother has an unbelieving wife, and she is agreeable to living with him, he is not to divorce her. So with the wife who has an unbelieving husband, if he is agreeable to living with her, she is not to divorce her husband. For the unbelieving husband is consecrated by his wife, and the unbelieving wife is consecrated by the brother in faith. Otherwise your children would be impure instead of holy as they are now. But if the unbelieving partner insists on separation, let them separate. In such cases neither a brother nor a sister is under duress; for God has decreed that you should be at peace. And you, wife, how can you tell whether you will not save your husband? Or you, husband, how can you tell whether you will not save your wife?

Otherwise, 'to each as the Lord has assigned, for each as God has decreed.[118] So let him conduct himself, and so have I prescribed for all the communities. Let anyone who was circumcised when he was called not undo the operation. If he was called in uncircumcision let him not be circumcised. Circumcision is of no consequence, neither is uncircumcision: it is the keeping of God's commandments. Let each remain in the category in which he was called. Were you called as a slave, do not let it fret you; though if you have opportunity to procure your freedom use it to the full. For the slave called by the Master is the Master's freedman. Similarly the freeman who is called is Christ's slave. You have been acquired at a high price. Do not become slaves of men. Each as he was called, brothers, so let him continue before God.

Now as regards celibates I have no instructions from the Master, but I offer my opinion as one who has mercifully been permitted by the Lord to be continent. I consider, therefore, in view of the present stress that a man is best off if he is celibate. If you are united to a wife, do not seek to be free. If you are free of a wife, do not seek one; though if you should marry you have done nothing wrong. And if a girl should marry she has done nothing wrong either. But those who take this step face the cares of married life, which I would spare you.

Only I would urge this, brothers, time grows short. So from now on let those who have wives be as though they had none,

[117] Mk. x. 9, above p. 69.
[118] Source of quotation unknown, possibly a dictum of Paul's in his teaching.

and those who mourn as though they did not mourn, and those who rejoice as though they did not rejoice, and those who acquire as though they did not possess, and those who are on friendly terms with society as though they were unsociable; for the existing order is passing away. I would have you carefree. The unmarried man is concerned with the Master's affairs, how he may please the Master; but the married man is concerned with social affairs, how he may please his wife, and he is torn two ways. So too the unmarried woman and girl is concerned with the Master's affairs, that she may be devoted physically and mentally; but the married woman is concerned with social affairs, how she may please her husband. I am saying this in your own interest, not to hold you on a rein, but rather that not being pulled this way and that you may be more considerate and attentive to the Master. However, if anyone feels he is being inconsiderate to his maiden, should she be passing her bloom, and therefore he owes it to her, let it be as he wishes: he does nothing wrong. Let them be married. But he who maintains a firm resolve, not having necessity, and is in full control of his own will, and has determined in his own mind to keep his maiden inviolate, will do well. So he who marries his maiden does well, but he who does not marry will do better still.

A wife is bound for her husband's entire lifetime; but should the husband go to his rest she is free to marry whom she will, so long as he is a Christian. But in my opinion she is happier to stay as she is, and there I think I have the Spirit of God.

Now as regards offerings to idols, we are aware that all have knowledge. But knowledge puffs up while affection builds up. If anyone thinks he knows something, he still does not know it as well as he should: but if anyone is devoted to God, he is given insight by him. For example, as regards food offered to idols, we are aware that an idol has no real existence, and that there is no God other than the One. For even if there are so-called gods, whether of heaven or earth—since there are many 'gods' and many 'lords,' for us there is still only One God, the Father, from whom all things derive, and to whom we belong, and one Lord Jesus Christ, through whom all things come, and by whom we are. But this knowledge is not general. There are some who are so accustomed to the idea of idols that they eat such food as being actually offered to an idol, and their conscience being weak is defiled. But food will not bring us near to God; for neither by not consuming are we retarded, nor by consuming are we advanced. But take care that your 'right' does not prove a hindrance to those whose conscience is weak. For if anyone see you who have knowledge sitting at table in an idol temple[119] will not he whose conscience is weak conclude from this that there is some benefit to be gained by eating what is offered to idols? So the weak one will be ruined by the very thing you

[119] It was a pagan custom to send invitations to dine at the table of the god. See above p. 267, n. 80.

know, that brother of yours for whom Christ died. Consequently, by sinning against your brothers and wounding their weak conscience you are sinning against Christ. For that reason, if food makes my brother stumble, then rather than be the cause of that I will never eat meat again.[120]

I am free to do everything, but everything is not advantageous. I am free to do everything, but not everything is beneficial. Let no one study his own interests, but those of his fellow. Eat whatever is sold in the meat-market without making inquiries, for 'the earth is the Lord's with all it contains'. And if any unbeliever gives you an invitation, and you feel like accepting, eat whatever is placed before you without making inquiries. But if someone says to you, 'This is sacrificial food', then do not eat it, both for the sake of your informant and for conscience's sake. I say conscience, not yours but the other man's. But why should my freedom be governed by another man's conscience? If I partake with pleasure, why should I be abused over what I am thankful for? The answer is, that whether you eat or drink, or whatever you do, do everything for the glory of God. Be free from offence both to Jews and Gentiles, and to God's Community, just as I accommodate myself to everyone in every way, not studying my own convenience but that of the multitude, that they may be saved. Copy me, as I copy Christ.

I do thank you for reminding yourselves of me in every way, and for maintaining the traditions as I transmitted them to you. But I want you to know that the head of every man is Christ, while the head of woman is man, and the head of Christ is God. Every man who prays or prophesies with covered head dishonours his head, while every woman who prays or prophesies with unconcealed head dishonours her head; for it is exactly as if she were shaven. If the woman is not covered, let her also be shorn. If it is a shame for a woman to be shaven or shorn, let her be covered.[121] But it is not proper for a man to have his head concealed, being the image and glory of God;[122] but the woman is the glory of man. For man is not derived from woman, but woman from man;[123] and man was not created for the sake of woman, but woman for the sake of man.[124] For this reason the woman ought to wear some headdress[125] because of the angels. Beyond this, as relates to the Master, woman is not distinguished from man, nor man from woman. For just as the

---

[120] The argument is interrupted here by I. Cor. ix. 1-x. 22, which seems rather to belong to the previous letter mentioned in I. Cor. v. 9 (p. 272, n. 110). It is therefore printed above (pp. 264-267) in conjunction with II. Cor. vi. 14-vii. 1.
[121] Paul is speaking of married women. To go out with bare head was to act like a prostitute, and a Jewess could be divorced for so doing.
[122] Gen. i. 26.
[123] Gen. ii. 23.
[124] Gen. ii. 18.
[125] Lit. 'control over the head'. Exposure to the gaze of angels during worship, when the gates of heaven stood open, was no different to exposure to the gaze of men in the streets.

woman derives from man, so does the man owe his being to woman; and equally they derive from God.

Judge for yourselves whether it is seemly for a woman to be uncovered when praying to God. Does not nature itself teach you that when a man has fine tresses it is a disgrace to him? But when a woman has fine tresses it is her glory, for her tresses are given her as a natural drapery. If someone is inclined to be contentious on this issue, I can entertain no such practice,[126] nor the communities of God.

But here is news I do not appreciate, that when you assemble it is not for the better but for the worse. I learn first of all that when you hold your meetings there are divisions among you, and to a certain extent I believe it. Obviously there must be some variations among you, that those who are particularly worthy among you may be distinguished. But is not your coming together for the common purpose of eating the supper that is specifically the Master's? In partaking of this it is for each of you to have had his own supper beforehand. Yet one is famished and another is consumed with thirst. Have you no homes in which to eat and drink? Or do you mean to treat God's Community with contempt, and humiliate those who have no homes? What am I to say to you? Shall I commend you? This is something I cannot commend.

I indeed received from the Master what I have transmitted to you, that the Lord Jesus on the night he was betrayed took bread, and when he had given thanks broke it and said, 'This signifies my body broken on your behalf. Do this in commemoration of me.'[127] In the same way he took the cup after the meal, saying, 'This cup signifies the new covenant in my blood. Do this, as often as you drink it, in commemoration of me.' So as often as you eat this bread and drink this cup you are making mention of the Master's death until he returns. Consequently, whoever eats the bread or drinks the cup unworthily will be held responsible for the Master's body and blood. So let a man examine himself. and after that eat the bread and drink from the cup; for he who eats and drinks is eating and drinking a judgment on himself, not discerning the body. That is why many of you are infirm and ailing, and a number have gone to their rest. If we have passed judgment on ourselves we shall not be judged; but if we are judged by the Master we are punished, so as not to be condemned with the world. Consequently, my brothers, when you assemble to eat this meal for one another. But if anyone is famished let him eat at home, so that you do not come together for condemnation. As to other matters, I will settle these when I come.

Now about spiritual manifestations, brothers, I would not have you ignorant. You know the kind Gentiles you were as

<hr />

[126] I.e. as men covering their heads during worship, which is the Jewish practice to-day.
[127] See Lk. xxii. 19, above p. 185.

regards dumb idols, misguided just as you were led. So I must inform you that no one speaking by the Divine Spirit says, 'Cursed be Jesus!' And no one is able to say, 'Lord Jesus!' except by the holy Spirit. But there are different kinds of gifts, though the same Spirit, and different kinds of function, though the same Master, and different kinds of motivation, though the same God, who motivates everything universally. And to each has been given that particular spiritual manifestation which was suitable. For one has been given through the Spirit the faculty of wisdom, another according to the same Spirit the faculty of insight, and yet another the faculty of faith by the same Spirit. To another, still by the one Spirit, has been given gifts of healing, to another the effecting of miracles, to another prophecy, to another the discerning of the nature of spirits, to yet another variety of tongues, to another interpretation of tongues. For all these manifestations one and the same Spirit is responsible, allocating specifically to each at will.

For just as the body is a unity while possessing many organs, and all the organs of the body, though many, form a single body, so is Christ a unity. For by one Spirit we have all been immersed into one body, whether Jews or Gentiles, slaves or freemen, and we have all been given a draught of the one Spirit. For the body is no single organ, but many. If the foot should say, 'I am not part of the body because I am not the hand', is it therefore any less a part of the body? Or if the ear should say, 'I am not part of the body because I am not the eye', is it therefore any less a part of the body? If the entire body was eye where would be hearing? If the entire body was hearing where would be smelling? But we find that God has placed the organs in the body, every single one of them, exactly as he wanted. If it were entirely one organ, where would be the body? As it is, there are many organs but one body. The eye cannot say to the hand, 'I do not require you', nor can the head say to the feet, 'I do not require you'. Much more are those organs of the body found to be requisite which are more delicate, and those which seem of less consequence are those to which we devote far more attention. It is our unattractive features that come in for beautifying treatment, for which our attractive features have no need. But God interrelates the body to give added dignity to what is inferior, so that there may be no discrimination in the body, but that all the organs shall have the same concern for one another. So if one organ suffers, all the organs suffer with it, and if one organ is esteemed, all the organs rejoice with it.

Now you are Christ's body, and its respective organs, and God has placed these in the Community as follows: first envoys, second prophets, third teachers, next mediums, next those with gifts of healing, those with intuition, those who give guidance, and those with varied tongues. Are all envoys? Are all prophets? Are all teachers? Are all mediums? Have all gifts of healing? Do all speak in tongues? Are all interpreters? Make the higher gifts your aim. Yet let me point out to you a still better course to pursue.

Though I speak the tongues of men and angels, and have not love, I have become a clanging gong or clashing cymbal. Even if I possess the power of prophecy and know all mysteries and secret lore, and have such faith that I can remove mountains,[128] if I have not love I am of no account. Even if I share out my possessions[129] and give my body to be burnt, if I have not love it avails me nothing.

Love is long-suffering and kind. Love is never jealous, self-assertive, blustering or inconsiderate. It never seeks its own ends, is never irritable, keeps no score of wrongs, never rejoices at injustice, but delights in truth. Love is ever protective, ever trustful, ever hopeful, ever constant. Love never fails, but whether it is prophesyings, they will come to an end, or whether it is tongues, they will cease, whether it is knowledge, it will come to an end. For we only know imperfectly, and prophesy imperfectly. But when perfection is reached what is imperfect will come to an end. When I was a child, I talked like a child, I reasoned like a child, I argued like a child; but when I became a man I put an end to childish ways. So far I see indistinctly as in a mirror,[130] but then it will be face to face. So far I know imperfectly, but then I shall know as fully as I am known. At present faith, hope, and love, all three, continue, but the most enduring of them is love.

So pursue love, and make spiritual manifestations your aim, particularly the capacity to prophesy.[131] For he who speaks in a tongue addresses God, not his fellows, since no one can follow him. He is speaking mysterious things in spirit language.[132] But he who prophesies addresses his fellows for their benefit, encouragement and cheer. He who speaks in a tongue benefits himself, while he who prophesies benefits the community. I wish you could all speak in tongues, but preferably that you could prophesy; for he who prophesies is greater than one who speaks in tongues, unless he can interpret so that the community is benefited.

Supposing, brothers, that I were to come to you speaking in tongues, how should I benefit you if I did not also speak by revelation, by knowledge, by prophecy, or by teaching? It would be like inanimate objects that emit a sound, such as flute or harp. If no clear distinction of notes is rendered, how is it to be recognized what is being played on them? And if the trumpet sounds an uncertain call, who will prepare for battle? So with your tongues, if you do not utter plain speech how is it to be

---

[128] See Mt. xvii. 20.
[129] See Mk. x. 21.
[130] Mirrors of burnished bronze, etc., as then used.
[131] To prophesy was to give an inspired address. Prediction was only one element in prophecy.
[132] Speaking in tongues meant giving vent to sounds articulated as in speech, not necessarily belonging to any language used in human intercourse.

understood what you are saying? You will be talking to the air. Still more, as there happen to be such a variety of sounds in the world, and nothing is soundless, should I not know the implication of a sound I shall be a barbarian to the speaker, and he will be a barbarian to me. So with you, since you are ambitious for spiritual manifestations, aim at those which benefit the community, that you may excel. Therefore let him who speaks in a tongue pray for the ability to interpret. For if I pray in a tongue, my spirit is engaged in prayer, but my intellect is not functioning. Is it not desirable, therefore, that I pray not only with the spirit, but also with the intellect? Otherwise, if you only bless God in spirit, how is one who is unlearned to make the 'Amen' response at the end of your thanksgiving, since he does not know what you are saying? You are giving thanks fittingly, but the other is not inspired by it. I thank God I speak in tongues more than all of you, but in the community I would rather speak five words with my intellect to instruct others than ten thousand words in a tongue.

Brothers, do not be mentally childish, though in evil be as innocent as you please. But in mentality be adult. It is stated in the Law,

'By those of alien tongues and lips will I address this people, Yet for all that they will not heed me,' says the Lord.[133]

So tongues are a sign not to believers but to unbelievers, while prophecy is not for unbelievers but for believers. If therefore you hold a meeting of the whole community, and all speak in tongues, and unlearned people or unbelievers come in, will they not say you are mad? But if all prophesy, and an unbeliever or unlearned person enters, he will be convinced by all he hears, he will be searched by all he hears, and the secrets of his heart will be laid bare. And so, falling upon his face, he will worship God, declaring, 'Truly God is with you!'

Is it not desirable then, brothers, that when you come together each should have a psalm, an instruction, a revelation, a tongue, or an interpretation, so that everything contributes to edification? When someone speaks in a tongue, or perhaps two do so, or three at most, and then in turn, there should be one to interpret. If there should be no interpreter let the speaker in a tongue keep silence in the community and speak inwardly to God. And let two or three prophets speak, and the others draw conclusions. But if a revelation comes to anyone seated there let the previous speaker keep silence; for you can all continue prophesying after the one with the revelation has finished, since the spirits of the prophets remain under their control,[134] that all may learn and all be encouraged. God is a God of order, not of chaos.

---

[133] Isa. xxviii. 11.
[134] A revelation took precedence of every other form of spiritual message as it was a direct communication by the Spirit, with the one who gave it out acting merely as a medium not in control of what he said.

As is the practice in all the communities of the saints let the married women keep silence in the communities; for they are not entitled to speak, being in a subordinate position, as also says the Law.[135] If there is anything they wish to learn let them consult their husbands at home, for it is indecorous for married women to speak at meetings.

Did the Message of God go out from you, or did it in fact come to you? If anyone regards himself as a prophet or medium let him acknowledge that what I am writing to you is a commandment of the Master. If anyone is ignorant, however, let him be ignorant. Consequently, my brothers, be ambitious to prophesy and do not prevent speaking in tongues. But let everything be done decently and in an orderly manner.

Now I would draw your attention, brothers, to the News I proclaimed to you (which you accepted, on which you have taken your stand, by means of which you are being saved) in the very form in which I proclaimed it to you, if you have retained it, unless you believed in a heedless manner. For I delivered to you as fundamental what I had myself received, 'That Christ died for our sins in accordance with the Scriptures; that he was buried and raised up the third day in accordance with the Scriptures; that he was seen by Cephas, then by the twelve, after that on one occasion by more than five hundred brothers (some of whom are gone to their rest); after that he was seen by James, then by all the envoys.'[136] Last of all, as if by an untimely birth, he was seen even by me; for I am the most insignificant of the envoys, who does not deserve to be called an envoy, because I persecuted God's Community. But by God's mercy I am what I am, and his favour to me was not wasted, for I toiled harder than all of them, though not indeed I but God's favour that was with me. But whether it was myself or the others, this is what we proclaimed, and this is what you believed.

If then Christ was proclaimed as having been raised from the dead, how do some of you say that there is no resurrection from the dead? For if there is no resurrection of the dead, Christ cannot have been raised. And if Christ was not raised our proclamation was in vain, and our faith in vain, and we are exposed as false witnesses of God, since we have testified of God that he raised up Christ. This he cannot have done if the dead are not to be raised. For if the dead are not to be raised, neither can Christ have been raised. And if Christ has not been raised your faith is idle: you are still in your sins. Then too, all who have gone to their rest in Christ have perished. If we are merely to have hope in Christ in this life we are to be pitied above all men.

But in fact Christ *has* been raised from the dead as the first-fruits of those who have gone to their rest. For since by man

[135] Gen. iii. 16.
[136] This section has been placed within inverted commas as in the nature of a credo. It need not have been a written one.

came death,[137] so by man also came resurrection from the dead. For as in Adam all die, so also in Christ will all be brought to life, though each in his proper order, first Christ, followed at his coming by those who belong to Christ, then the remainder[138] when he has handed over the Kingdom to his God and Father after abolishing all other government, authority and power. For he himself must rule until 'he has put all enemies under his feet'.[139] The final enemy to be abolished is death,[140] for *everything* is brought into subjection beneath his feet. But when it is said, 'everything has been subjected',[141] it is obvious that this excludes the One who has made everything subject to him. When then everything is subjected to him, even the Son will be subject to the One who has subjected everything to him, that God may reign supreme.

Otherwise, what are they doing who are immersed on behalf of the dead? If the dead are not raised why be immersed on their behalf? And why am I risking my life all the time? 'I am ready to die any day', you say. Yes, that is your boast, brothers, which I make good in Christ Jesus our Master. If, in human terms, I have 'fought with wild beasts at Ephesus', how am I the gainer? If the dead are not raised, 'Let us eat and drink, for to-morrow we die'.[142] Oh no, do not delude yourselves! 'Bad company ruins good character.'[143] Sober up completely, and do not go to the bad; for some of you seem to ignore God's existence. I say this to shame you.

But someone may say, 'How are the dead raised, and what kind of body do they have?' You dunce! Surely what you sow does not spring to life before it dies! And what you sow you do not sow in the bodily form that will emerge, but as bare grain, perhaps of wheat, or possibly of other cereals. It is God who furnishes it with what body he wishes, each seed with its particular body. All flesh is not identical. There is the human, and besides that the flesh of animals, the flesh of birds, and the flesh of fish. There are also celestial and terrestrial bodies. But the glory of the celestial is one thing, and that of the terrestrial is another. Apart from the glory of the sun, there is the glory of the moon, and of the stars, and star even differs from star in glory. So is it with the resurrection of the dead. What is sown as perishable is raised imperishable. What is sown in humiliation is raised in honour. What is sown in weakness is raised in vitality. What is sown as a physical body is raised as a spiritual body. If there is such a thing as a physical body, there is also such a thing as a spiritual body. Just as it is stated, 'The first man (Adam) became a living soul',[144] so the last Adam became a

---

[137] Gen. iii.
[138] Processional order, the general, his staff, and then the main body of troops bringing up the rear. See Rev. xx. 4-6.
[139] Ps. cx. 1.
[140] See Rev xx. 14.
[141] See Ps viii. 6.
[142] Isa. xxii. 13.
[143] From Menander, Athenian dramatist, 342-291 B.C.
[144] Gen. ii. 7.

vitalizing spirit. It was not the spiritual that came first but the physical, and after that the spiritual. The first man was 'dust from the earth':[145] the second man was from heaven.[146] As is the nature of dust, so are the creatures of dust; and as is the heavenly nature, so are the heavenly beings. Just as we have worn the likeness of the dust nature, so shall we wear the likeness of the heavenly nature.

I tell you this, brothers, that flesh and blood cannot inherit the Kingdom of God, neither can the perishable inherit the imperishable. See, I will let you into a secret, we shall not all be laid to rest, but all of us will experience a change, in an instant, in the flicker of an eyelid, on the final trumpet note. For the trumpet will sound, and the dead will be raised up imperishable, and we shall experience a change. For this perishable nature must be invested with imperishability, and this mortal nature must be invested with immortality. And when this mortal nature has been invested with immortality, then the saying that is written will come true, 'Death has been swallowed up in victory'.[147]

> *Where, O death, is your victory?*
> *Where, O death, is your sting?*[148]

The sting of death is sin, and the strength of sin is the Law. But thanks be to God, who has given us victory through our Lord Jesus Christ!

Consequently, dear brothers, be firm and immovable, always fully engaged in the Master's work, knowing that your toil for the Master is not in vain.

Now as regards the fund for the saints, follow the same arrangement as I have made with the communities of Galatia. The day after the sabbath let each of you put by savings as he has prospered, so that collections do not have to be made when I come. Then when I come I will send whoever you designate by letter to convey your bounty to Jerusalem. If it is desirable that I should go too, they can travel with me.

I propose to visit you when I pass through Macedonia—for I intend to go through Macedonia—and perhaps I may settle down with you, or at least spend the winter, so that you can forward me on my further journey. I do not want to see you merely in passing; for it is my hope, if the Lord permits, to stay some time with you. I shall remain at Ephesus at any rate until Pentecost, for a wide and much frequented gateway has been opened to me, and there is considerable opposition. Should Timotheus come, be sure to put him at his ease, for he is as

---

145 *Ibid.*
146 According to the Jewish mystics God first created the Heavenly Man, the Archetype, who filled the universe and served as the pattern on which it was made. The earthly Adam was created in the likeness of this Heavenly Man, who in Paul's view incarnated in Jesus as the second Adam from heaven. See further his letters to the Asian communities, and those of Philippi and Colossae, below pp. 319-335.
147 Isa. xxv. 8.
148 Hos. xiii. 4.

much engaged in the Master's work as I am. So let no one be disrespectful to him. And forward him on his way in peace that he may come to me, for I am expecting him with the brothers.

Regarding Brother Apollos, I urged him strongly to visit you with the brothers, but he was very much against coming just now. However, he will come when convenient.

Be alert, stand firm in the faith, be manly and sturdy! I beg you, brothers, conduct all your affairs in a loving spirit. You know how the house of Stephanas was the firstfruits in Achaia, and how much it has devoted itself to ministering to the saints. It is for you to submit yourselves to people like these, and to all who collaborate and work so hard. I rejoice at the arrival of Stephanas, Fortunatus and Achaicus, which compensates for the lack of your presence; for they relieve my mind and yours. You should esteem such people.

The communities of Asia send you their regards. Aquila and Prisca[149] send you their regards in the Master together with the community at their house. All the brothers send you their regards. Convey our regards to one and all with a chaste kiss.

My personal regards in my own hand,
PAUL.

If someone[150] does not love the Master, let him be accursed.[151] *Maranatha!*[152]

The loving-kindness of the Lord Jesus be with you. My love to you all in Christ Jesus.[153]

◆

TO THE COMMUNITY AT CORINTH (3)[154]

(Probably written from Ephesus in the spring of A.D. 56)

COMMENCEMENT LACKING

Now I, Paul, personally entreat you by the mildness and moderation of Christ, I who am 'humble when in your presence, but overbearing towards you when absent'.[155] I pray that I do

149 See above p. 226.
150 Possibly a particular person is meant, who is never named, to whom Paul several times refers as being antagonistic to him. Alternatively read 'anyone'.
151 'Accursed' (*anathema*). Possibly we should read, 'let him be ardent again' (*anatherma*), cp. Mt. xxiv. 12.
152 Aram. 'Our Master, come!' Cp. Rev. xxii. 20.
153 The whole postscript was no doubt in Paul's own hand.
154 Corresponding to II. Cor. x-xiii. We have only the last part of this letter, but perhaps only a few introductory paragraphs are missing.
155 Here and in other places Paul appears to be quoting remarks adverse to himself which had been reported to him.

not have to be overbearing when I am present with the kind of persuasion I contemplate employing against those who reckon me as one who 'moves on the material plane'. In a material body I do move, but I do not fight with material weapons; for the weapons of my warfare are of no material character, but divine armaments for reducing strongholds, demolishing arguments, and every high and mighty position taken up in opposition to God's assured knowledge, bringing every design into subjection to the authority of Christ, and being ever ready to punish any insubordination once your submission is complete.

Face the facts squarely. If a certain individual is convinced he is acting for Christ, let him consider this as well, that as he acts for Christ so do I. For even if I should seem to boast unduly of my authority, which the Master has given me to build you up, not to pull you down, I would not be ashamed, so long as it does not appear as if I am bent on intimidating you with my letters. For 'his letters', says that individual, 'are weighty and powerful, but his physical appearance is insignificant and his speech is contemptible'. Let that individual mark this, that what I am in word by letter when absent that am I also in deed when present. I would not dream of classing or comparing myself with those who indulge in self-commendation; for these measuring themselves by themselves and comparing themselves with themselves cease to be relative. I will not boast so disproportionately, but in terms of the extent of the line the God of measurement has measured out for me, reaching as far as to you. Clearly I am not overreaching myself where my line did not extend to you, for right the way to you I was first with the News of Christ.[156] I do not boast 'beyond measure' where others have laboured, but I trust, when your faith has expanded, to have my own line considerably prolonged by you, so as to allow me to proclaim the News to the regions beyond you, instead of boasting along another's line where the ground was already covered. 'Let him who boasts boast in the Lord.'[157] For it is not the man who commends himself who is approved, but he whom the Lord commends.

O that you would put up with a little of my 'folly', or at least put up with me! For I am jealous for you with a divine jealousy; for I have bespoken you as a chaste virgin for one husband that I may give you to Christ. But I am afraid in case, as the Serpent beguiled Eve with his wiles, your minds should be corrupted from the simplicity and virtuousness to which Christ is entitled. For if someone who comes along can proclaim another Jesus whom I did not proclaim, or you can receive a different Spirit than you did receive, or a different News than you accepted, you can well put up with me. For I reckon myself in no way

---

[156] The passage is difficult to translate as the author is playing on the idea of measurement in more than one sense.
[157] Jer. ix. 24.

inferior to such super-envoys. Even if I am uncultured in speech, I am not in knowledge, and managed to make everything perfectly clear to you.

Did I make a mistake in abasing myself that you might be exalted, by proclaiming the News to you free of charge? I stripped other communities, taking payment to apply to your service. And when I was staying with you and went short I was a dead weight to no one, for my shortage was fully made up by the brothers who came from Macedonia. In every way I kept myself—and shall go on keeping myself—from being any burden to you. As Christ's truth is in me, I am not going to be denied this boast in the regions of Achaia! Why? Because I have no regard for you? God knows I have! But I make and am going on making this boast, that I may remove the pretext of those who want a pretext in that what they can boast of if they will be found to be my equals. Such people are false envoys, deceitful agents, masquerading as envoys of Christ. And no wonder, when Satan himself masquerades as an angel of light! So it is hardly surprising if his ministers masquerade as ministers of religion, whose fate will correspond to their actions.

I say again, let no one take me for a fool. But if they must, then accept me as a fool, so that I may do a little boasting. What I am saying then, I am not saying sensibly, but as in folly, on this basis of boasting. Since many boast in human fashion, I too will boast; for sensible as you are you gladly put up with fools. You even put up with it when somebody reduces you to cringing impotence, when somebody devours, grabs, makes a mat of you, and grinds your faces under his heel. I am speaking insultingly because I am so sick of it all. In whatever way anyone may make sweeping claims—I am keeping up this fool talk—so can I. Are they Hebrews? So am I. Are they Israelites? So am I. Are they the seed of Abraham? So am I. Are they agents of Christ? Mad as it sounds, I am even more so. My labours have been harder, my terms of imprisonment longer, my floggings beyond all bounds, my risks of death more frequent. Five times I received from the Jews forty strokes less one,[158] three times I have been beaten with Roman rods, once I was stoned,[159] three times shipwrecked, a night and day consigned to the deep. Often have I taken the road, in peril of rivers, in peril of brigands, in peril from my own nation, in peril from Gentiles, in peril in town, in peril in the country, in peril at sea, in peril from false brothers, in toil and hardship, often sleepless, in hunger and thirst, often fasting, in cold and in nakedness. On top of all this there has been my daily concern, the care of all the communities. Who is ailing, and I do not share his ailment? Who is offended, and I do not share his indignation?

If I must boast, I will boast of my disabilities. He who is

[158] Deut. xxv. 2-3. See JE. art. *Stripes*.
[159] Acts xiv. 19, above p. 219.

blessed for ever, the God and Father of our Lord Jesus, knows I am not lying. At Damascus the ethnarch of King Haretath picketed the city of the Damascenes to hem me in; but through a loophole I was let down the wall in a basket, and so escaped his clutches.

If I must continue to boast, undesirable as that is, I will come to visions and revelations of the Master. I know a man in Christ, who fourteen years ago—whether in the physical or astral state, I do not know, God knows—was caught up as far as the third heaven.[160] I know that this man—whether in the physical state or otherwise, I do not know, God knows—was caught up into 'the Garden'[161] and heard ineffable words which no human is permitted to utter. Of someone like this I will boast, but about myself I will not boast, only of my disabilities.

Even should I want to boast I should be no fool, for I state the truth. But I will refrain, in case anyone should think more of me than what he sees and hears. But with the transcendence of the revelations, in case I should be too elated, there was given me a spike in the flesh,[162] an emissary of Satan, to prod me. On this score three times I entreated the Master to make it leave me. But he told me, 'My favour is enough for you, for power is brought to full strength in weakness'. Most gladly, therefore, will I rather boast of disabilities, that the power of Christ may take up its quarters in me. So I am content with disabilities, assaults, physical punishments, persecutions and close confinements, for Christ's sake; for when I am weak then I am strong.

There, I have played the fool. You have driven me to it. For I ought to have had your championship; for in no way am I inferior to those super-envoys, even if I am of no consequence. Indeed, the marks of an envoy were produced among you persistently in signs, wonders and miracles. For in what were you outdone by the rest of the communities, except that I personally was no dead weight to you? Forgive me this injustice.

Observe, this is my third time of readiness to come to you. But I will be no dead weight to you; for I do not seek what is yours but *you*. For it is not the children who should provide for their parents but the parents for their children. Most gladly will I spend and be spent to safeguard you. If I love you so dearly, should I not be loved as much? But there it is, I did not burden you. But 'being naturally unscrupulous I took from you by a trick', eh? Was it by anyone I have sent to you that I defrauded you? I begged Titus to visit you, and with him I sent our brother. Was it Titus who defrauded you? Have we not acted in the same spirit, followed in the same steps? Do not think from this that I am defending myself. I am speaking before God in Christ. Everything I say, dear friends, is entirely for your benefit; for

---

160 These experiences may have taken place about A.D. 41 while Paul was in Tarsus, before Barnabas brought him to Antioch (Acts ix. 30: xi. 25).

161 'Paradise', the same as the third heaven, answering to the third degree of blessedness in Jewish occultism. See Talmud, *Chagigah*, 12a-b.

162 The complaint appears to have been rheumatic, perhaps sciatica.

I fear much in case when I come I shall not find you in the frame of mind I desire, nor you find me in the frame of mind you desire. I fear in case there should be strife, rivalry, high-feeling, faction, recrimination, vilification, protestation and uproar, in case at my coming my God should humiliate me in front of you, and that I should break down over many who have fallen into sin, and have not repented of the impurity, immorality and licentiousness of which they have been guilty.

This is my third time of coming to you. 'By the mouth of two or three witnesses every word shall be confirmed.'[163] I have said previously, and being absent now I give warning as if present a second time,[164] to those who have fallen into sin and to all the others, that should I come once more I will not spare, since it is proof you require that Christ speaks by me. He at least is not weak, but powerful among you. For though he was crucified from weakness, he lives now by the power of God. And though I am weak in him, I too live with him by the power of God. Test yourselves, examine yourselves, whether *you* are in the faith. Or do you yourselves not know that Jesus Christ is in you, whether by any chance you are frauds? But I trust you will realize that I am no fraud.

Now I pray God you may do no wrong in any way, not that I may be shown to be genuine, but that you may do the right thing even did I appear a fraud. For I have no power against the truth, only on behalf of truth. I am happy whenever I am weak and you are strong. This too I pray for, your restoration, That is why being absent I write as I do, that when present I should not have to employ severity, in accordance with the authority the Master has given me to build up, not to pull down.

Finally, brothers, rejoice, put yourselves to rights, take courage, be of the same mind, be at peace, and the God of love and peace be with you. Convey my regards to one and all with a chaste kiss. All the saints send you their regards.

The loving-kindness of our Lord Jesus Christ, the love of God, and the fellowship of the holy Spirit, be with you all.

---

[163] Deut. xix. 15.
[164] It is clear from the next letter that Paul had paid a short 'distressing visit' to Corinth, and that the present letter was in lieu of a second visit. He therefore thinks of his readiness to come again as a third visit.

TO THE COMMUNITY AT CORINTH (4)

(Probably written from Philippi in the summer of A.D. 56)

Paul, by the will of God an envoy of Christ Jesus, with Brother Timotheus, to the community of God at Corinth and to all the saints resident throughout Achaia. May peace and prosperity be yours from God our Father and the Lord Jesus Christ.

Blessed be the God and Father of our Lord Jesus Christ, Father of mercies and God of all comfort, who comforts us in all our afflictions, that we may be enabled to comfort those who are in any affliction with the same comfort we have received. Blessed be he, that just as a full share of Christ's sufferings has come to me, so equally have I had my full share of comfort through Christ. And whether I am afflicted for your comfort and well-being, or comforted for your comfort, which is a stimulus to the endurance of the same sufferings I suffer, my hope for you is constant, knowing that as we are fellows in suffering so are we in comfort also.

I would not have you ignorant, brothers, of the trying experience I have been through in Asia, how I was subjected to a weight so crushing in the extreme as to pass endurance, so that I had the gravest doubt whether I would survive. Rather for myself did I take it to be sentence of death, so that I should place no reliance on myself but on God who raises the dead. It was he who shielded me from imminent death, and shields me now, and whom I trust, with your co-operation in prayer on my behalf, to continue to shield me, so that thanksgiving to God on my account may be made by many persons for the kindness of so many towards me.

My pride, the testimony of my conscience, is this, that I have conducted myself in the world, not by means of any materialist philosophy but by divine mercy, in all innocence and utter sincerity, especially in my relations with you. I am therefore writing to you nothing but what you already well know or recognize, and I trust will ever recognize, as indeed to some extent you have acknowledged, that I shall be your pride when the Day of our Lord Jesus comes, just as you will be mine.

It was from this confidence that I purposed visiting you previously, that you might have a second pleasure, both by my passing via yourselves on the way to Macedonia and visiting you again on my return from Macedonia, when you would forward me on my way to Judea. Was I merely proposing this casually? Or when I make proposals do I do it in the ordinary casual way, so that my 'yes, yes', can equally mean 'no, no'? As God is true, my word to you is never 'yes-and-no'! For the Son of God, Jesus Christ, he who was proclaimed to you by us—by myself, Silvanus and Timotheus—did not come as a 'yes-and-no'. In him there came 'Yes', for every promise of God is fulfilled in him who is the 'Yes'. That is why, through him, we make the affirmation 'Amen'[165] to God in praising him. It is God who has secured both us and you for Christ, who has had us duly signed and sealed, and has given us the advance payment of the Spirit in our hearts. I call God as witness for my life, that it is to spare you I have not come again to Corinth! Not that I claim any jurisdiction over your faith: I am but a contributor to your happiness. In faith you have your own standing. But I made up my mind not to pay you another distressing visit, for if I distress you, who is going to cheer me except those I distress? So I wrote then and there[166] in case by coming I should be grieved by those who should give me joy, being convinced of all of you that it is my happiness that is the concern of you all. I wrote to you in great trouble and anguish of mind, shedding many tears, not to grieve you, but because of the very deep affection you know I have for you.

If a certain individual has caused distress, he has not caused me distress, at least not to an extent that I have to burden all of you with it. Let his censure by the majority suffice for that person, just as on the other hand it is for you to cheer and comfort him in case he should be completely overcome by the depth of his grief. Consequently, I entreat you to assure him of your affection. This was part of my object in writing, to ascertain your worth, whether you answer to all requirements. Whoever you forgive, so do I. Really, if anyone has to be forgiven, I am the one who has to be forgiven by you before Christ, in case Satan should catch me out; for I am not ignorant of his wiles.

Well, when I came to Troas in the interest of the News of Christ, and found a door opened to me by the Lord, I had no liberty of spirit because I did not find Brother Titus there. So taking leave of them I went off to Macedonia. Thanks be to God, who always leads men in triumph in Christ, and makes the perfume of the knowledge of him rise up through me in every place! For I am Christ's fragrance to God both among those who are being saved and among those who are perishing.[167] To the latter it is the odour of death leading to Death, while to the former it is the odour of life leading to Life. Who is adequate for such things? For I am not like the majority who water down God's message: I speak purely and plainly as from God, as standing in God's presence in Christ.

---

[165] 'So be it,' i.e. in the expression 'through our Lord Jesus Christ. Amen.'
[166] Namely the previous letter.
[167] As God's captive in Christ, Paul sees himself as a victim led along in the triumphal procession, and at the same time as the incense burnt in the victor's honour at various points on the route.

Have I begun to commend myself again? Or ought I like
some to have procured letters of commendation to you or from
you? Surely you are my letter, recorded on my heart, scrutinized
and perused by all men. It is plain for all to see that you are
Christ's letter composed on my behalf, recorded not in ink but
in the Spirit of the Living God, not on tablets of stone but on
tablets of the human heart.

Such is the confidence I have towards God through Christ. It
is not that I am adequate in myself to deal with anything as of
myself. My competence comes from God, who has qualified
me to act as an administrator of a New Covenant, not in letter
but in spirit; for the letter kills, but the Spirit vitalizes.[168]

Yet if the administration of death[169] in letters engraved on
stones was glorious, so that the children of Israel could not look
at Moses's face because of the transient shining of his face,[170]
how much more shall the administration of the Spirit be glorious? For if the administration of condemnation was glorious,
much more glorious still shall be the administration of vindication. Even what did shine could hardly be said to shine in
comparison with that surpassing glory. For if what was transient had a glory, much more glorious shall be that which is to
endure.

So having an expectation like this I speak plainly, and not like
Moses, who had to veil his face so that the children of Israel
could not look at the conclusion of what was transient. Their
perceptions were blinded; and down to this very day the same
veil over the implication of the Old Covenant remains unre-
moved, since it is in Christ that it is dispensed with. But till
to-day, whenever Moses is read, the veil lies upon their mind.
Yet whenever that mind 'shall be turned to the Lord' the veil
will be taken off.[171] 'The Lord' means the Spirit, and where the
Spirit of the Lord is there is freedom. So all of us, having our
face unveiled to the glory of the Lord, reflecting as in a mirror
the same image, are being transformed from glory to glory, as
from the Lord who is Spirit.[172]

Having this administration, therefore, as mercy has been
shown me, I am no shirker, but have renounced base subter-
fuges. I do not use cunning devices, nor water down God's
Message, but by plain truth make contact with every human
conscience in the sight of God. If my News is veiled at all, it
is veiled to those who are perishing, where the god of this world
has blinded the perception of the infidels, so that they should
not see clearly the luminosity of the News of the glory of Christ,
who is the image of God. For I do not proclaim myself but

---

[168] Cp. Jer. xxxi. 31-33.
[169] The giving of the Law at Sinai, in Paul's view. See above p. 283.
[170] Cp. Exod. xxxiv. 28-30.
[171] Exod. xxxiv. 34 (LXX).
[172] The process of transformation continues, as we reflect more and more of the
Spirit, until our final glorification at the resurrection, when we shall bear the
full likeness of the heavenly, the pristine image of God, like Adam when first
created. (Gen. i. 26).

Christ Jesus as Master, and myself as your servant for Jesus's sake, because it is the God who said, 'Let light shine out of darkness', who has illumined my mind with the luminosity of the knowledge of God's glory on the face of Christ.

I have this treasure in an earthen vessel,[173] however, that the superabundance of the power may be of God, and not emanate from myself. I am harassed on every side, but not hemmed in; in great straits, but not devoid of resources; hard-pressed, but not abandoned; struck down, but not destroyed,[174] always carrying around in my body the death-state of Jesus, that the life of Jesus may also be evident in my body. For ever I who live am delivered up to death for Jesus's sake, that the life of Jesus may also be evident in my mortal form. So then death is at work in me, but life in you.

Yet having the selfsame spirit of faith as is stated, 'I have believed, therefore have I spoken',[175] I too believe, and therefore speak, knowing that he who raised up Jesus will also raise me up with Jesus, and set me beside you. For all that has transpired is for your sake, that the mercy having been increased by the greater number sharing in it[176] the thanksgiving also may be multiplied to the glory of God.

So I am no shirker; but if my exterior self is disabled my inner self is daily renewed. The momentary lightness of my affliction achieves for me correspondingly a lasting weight of glory. I pay no regard to the things that are seen, but to those that are unseen; for the things that are seen are temporary, while those that are unseen are permanent. For I know that when my earthly makeshift dwelling is demolished I possess a building from God, a dwelling that is not manufactured, permanent in heaven. This is what I sigh for, longing to be under cover of my dwelling from heaven; for so sheltered I shall not be left out in the cold. Yes, that is what I, living in this hutment, sigh for, not wanting to be deprived of cover but to be under cover, so that what is mortal may be swallowed up by Life. God, who has acquired me for this very end, has given me the advance payment of the Spirit. So having every confidence, and knowing that while I am at home in the body I am absent from the Master—for I walk by faith and not by sight—I am both confident and content rather to be absent from the body and at home with the Master. That is why I strive so eagerly, whether present or absent, to satisfy him; for we must all stand revealed before Christ's tribunal, that each may be requited for his bodily actions, whatever he has done, either useful or worthless.

Sensible of the fear of the Lord, therefore, I persuade men,

[173] Cp. Jud. vii. 16; Jer. xxxii. 14. Paul speaks of his physical body.
[174] Paul is here using military terms.
[175] Ps. xcvi. 10.
[176] Paul refers to those who had been praying for his recovery from the serious illness mentioned at the beginning of the letter.

while my character stands fully revealed to God, and I trust also to your consciousness. I am not commending myself to you again, but furnishing you with grounds for boasting about me, that you may have something to set against those who boast on the basis of outward appearance instead of the heart. Whether I have been 'raving', it has been for God, or in my senses, it has been for you; for Christ's love deeply affects me. I have reached this conclusion, that as one died for all, all then were dead, and he died for all that those who live should live no longer for themselves but for him who died for them and rose again. From now on, therefore, we know no one in the physical sense. Even if we have known Christ in the physical sense, we do so now no longer.

Consequently, if anyone is in Christ, he is a new creation. The old relationships have gone, replaced by the new. It is all God's doing, who through Christ has reconciled us to himself, and has given us the administration of this reconciliation, the position being that in Christ God was reconciling the world to himself, not charging men's failings against them, and entrusting us with the Message of reconciliation. Accordingly, we plead on Christ's behalf, as though God were entreating by us, we beg you on Christ's behalf, 'Be reconciled to God'. He made him who knew no sin to be as sin for us, that we might be guiltless with God by him.

As a fellow-worker, I also beg you not to receive the mercy of God to no purpose, for he says,

> *'I have heard you at a time of receptiveness,*
> *And aided you on a day of deliverance.'*[177]

Assuredly now is the 'time of receptiveness', now is the day of deliverance'.

It is for me to create no difficulty of any kind, that no blame may attach to the administration. Rather in every way have I to commend myself as God's representative by much patience, afflictions, suffering and anxiety; by lashes, imprisonment and mob violence; by toil, vigil and fasting; by impartiality, insight and perseverance; by kindness, spiritual fervour and unfeigned love; by honest speech and divine power; by the right and left hand weapons of equity; by honour and dishonour, ill-fame and good-fame; as a deceiver yet true; as an unknown yet well known; as a dying man yet very much alive; as disciplined yet not brought to death; as grieved yet ever rejoicing; as poor yet enriching many; as possessing nothing yet owning everything.

Well, Corinthians, I have spoken frankly to you. I have bared my bosom. You have put no constraint on me, but you have put constraint on your own feelings. 'Now it's your turn to pay *me* back', as one says to children. Now you too bare your bosoms.[178]

Make room for me. I have wronged no one. I have harmed no

---

[177] Isa. xlix. 8.
[178] Omitting vi. 14-vii. 1, which is part of an earlier letter, see above p. 267.

one. I have defrauded no one. I am not saying this censoriously; for as I have said before, 'you are in my heart to die with and to live with',[179] I am filled with comfort. I am brim full of happiness despite all my trouble. For when I arrived in Macedonia I had no physical relief, but troubles on every side, 'conflict without and terror within'. But God, who comforts the depressed, comforted me by the arrival of Titus, and not only by his arrival but by the cheering report of you he brought, informing me of your longing for me, of your contrition, of your anxiety on my account, so that I was made happier still. Although I grieved you in the letter,[180] I have no regrets. Even if I had regrets, seeing that the letter in question had to cause you even an hour's distress, I am glad now, not that you were distressed, but because you were distressed into penitence, distressed indeed as God likes to see, so that you were in no way harmed by me. For pain of the divine kind produces penitence leading to restoration, not to be regretted; but pain of the world's kind produces death. Take this very case of grieving of the divine kind, how much concern it effected in you, instead of defensiveness, indignation, fear, complaint, passion and vindictiveness! In every way you have shown yourselves honourable in this affair. Therefore, though I wrote you as I did, it was not for the sake of the offender, not even for the sake of the victim, but that your concern for me might be plain to you in the sight of God.

That is why I have been cheered. And over and above my personal consolation I was made happier than ever by Titus's happiness, because all of you had set his mind at rest. So there has been no cause to retract anything I have boasted of to him about you. Rather, as I have spoken with complete truthfulness to you, so has the boast I made to Titus been equally truthful. And his heart overflows towards you at the remembrance of the submissiveness of you all as you received him with fear and trepidation. I am happy to have complete confidence in you.

Now I would inform you, brothers, of the divine favour granted to the communities of Macedonia, how during a most testing trial the excess of their joy set against the extremity of their destitution enhanced the lavishness of their generosity, so that to the best of their capacity, I declare, and beyond their capacity, of their own accord and with many entreaties, they begged me for the favour and fellowship of joining in the service for the saints.[181] It was not as I expected of them, but as they expected, that they gave first to the Master then to me by the will of God, so that I encouraged Titus that as he had begun so should he complete with you also the same expression of gratitude, that just as you excel in every way, in faith, in speech, in knowledge, and zeal of every kind, and also in the affection you

[179] Quoted probably from a part of the third letter, now missing.
[180] The last letter, above pp. 284-288.
[181] The collection of funds for the poor Saints of Jerusalem.

have for me, so should you excel in this expression of gratitude also.

I am not saying this as an order, but because of the zeal of others and in proof of the genuineness of your affection. For you know the graciousness of our Lord Jesus Christ, how being rich he impoverished himself for your sake, that you might be enriched by that poverty. But on this matter I do offer an opinion, for it is desirable that you should not only have initiated, but should maintain what you started a year ago. So now go on to complete what you have initiated, that as is the keenness to keep it up so will be the effectiveness of what is done. For if the keenness is there, whatever one may do is acceptable: it is not as if one does nothing. For it is not a question of others having relief while you are in difficulties, but that in fairness at the present time your superfluity should compensate for their shortage, so that in turn their superfluity may make up for your shortage, which will be only right and proper, as it is stated, 'He that had much had not too much, and he that had little did not go short'.[182]

Thank God for putting the same concern on your behalf into the mind of Titus, so that he welcomed the proposal, and being so very admirable he visited you initially of his own accord. I have now sent with him the brother approved in the service of the News throughout the communities,[183] and not only so but elected by the communities as my travelling companion in this expression of gratitude administered and pressed forward by me for the honour of the Master. In this way provision has been made that no one should find fault with me over this bounty which is administered by me; for I would be well-respected not only in the Lord's sight but also in the sight of men.[184] So I have sent with them my brother, whom I have proved to be admirable on so many occasions, and now more admirable than ever in the implicit confidence he places in you. So whether it is Titus, my associate and your fellow-worker, or my other brothers, envoys of the communities, they are a credit to Christ. Therefore furnish clear evidence in the sight of the communities in demonstration of your affection and of my boast about you to them.

It is really quite superfluous for me to be writing to you about this service to the saints, for I am aware of your keenness which is what I boasted about you to the Macedonians. 'Achaia,' I said, 'was all ready a year ago,' and your enthusiasm has stimulated many. Yet I have dispatched the brothers in case my boast about you should have been an empty one in this respect, so that, as I have been saying you are ready, should it happen that Macedonians accompany me and find you are not ready, I, not to say you, would be ashamed in face of this reality. I have

182 Exod. xvi. 18.
183 This unnamed brother has been thought by some to be Luke or Silas, but might also be either Tychicus or Trophimus. See above pp. 230-231.
184 Cp. Prov. iii. 4 (LXX); Rom. xii. 17.

considered it advisable, therefore, to propose to the brothers
that they should visit you in advance and set in motion that
previously announced goodwill-offering of yours, that the same
being promptly forthcoming it will be like a goodwill-offering
and not like an imposition.

There is this to add. 'He that sows sparingly will reap sparingly, while he that sows liberally will reap liberally.'[185] Let each
follow his heart's dictate, not acting grudgingly or from necessity, for 'the Lord loves a cheerful giver'.[186] God is able to lavish
every blessing upon you, so that always having sufficiency in
every way you may be more than adequate for every good deed,
just as it is stated,

> He has distributed his means;
> He has given to the poor:
> His beneficence endures for ever.[187]

He who supplies 'seed to the sower, and bread for food'[188] will
supply and multiply your produce, and increase the fruits of
your beneficence. So then, being enriched in every way for
every act of generosity, whatever is done evokes by my agency
thanksgiving to God. For the administration of this service
not only makes up the shortage of the saints, but is further augmented by the volume of thanksgiving to God; for in appreciation of this ministration the saints praise God for the strictness
of your conformity with the Good News of Christ and the
generosity of your fellowship with them and with all others.
And their future wishes for you are expressed in prayer on
your behalf because of God's overwhelming kindness to you.[189]
Thanks be to God for his incomparable gift!

CONCLUSION LACKING[190]

185 Cp. Prov. xi. 24 (LXX).
186 Prov. xxii. 8 (LXX).
187 Ps. cxii. 9 (LXX).
188 Isa. lv. 10 (LXX).
189 In extending to Gentiles participation in the Messianic Kingdom.
190 The rest of II. Cor. is reproduced as the third letter to the Corinthian community, above pp. 284-288. Probably little more than the concluding greetings
is missing from the fourth letter.

TO THE BELIEVERS' AT ROME[191]

(Probably written from Corinth early in A.D. 57)

Paul, servant of Jesus Christ, a chosen envoy, assigned to the proclamation of God's News, which he had previously announced by his Prophets in the Sacred Writings, concerning his Son, Jesus Christ our Master, born in the physical sense of the line of David, but potently demonstrated to be God's Son in the sanctified spiritual sense by resurrection from the dead.[192] By him I have obtained favour and envoyship to procure loyal submission to his authority on the part of all nations, among whom you likewise are summoned by Jesus Christ. To all God's dear ones in Rome, members of the holy assembly, may peace and prosperity be yours from God our Father and from the Lord Jesus Christ.

In the first place I thank my God through Jesus Christ for all of you that your faith is patent to the whole world. God is my witness, whom I serve devotedly in the cause of the News of his Son, that I never fail to make regular reference to you in my prayers, requesting that somehow at long last, God willing, I may succeed in reaching you. For I do so long to see you, that I may impart to you some spiritual gift for your confirmation, that is to say that I may find common encouragement with you through your and my mutual faith.

I do not want you to be in ignorance, brothers, that I have often proposed to visit you, though I have been prevented hitherto, in order that I may obtain some fruit of my labours among you as I have among other nations. I am indebted for such fruit both to Greeks and Barbarians, to the cultured and the uncultured; so I am naturally eager to have the opportunity of proclaiming the News among you in Rome also. For I am not ashamed of the News: it is God's means of deliverance for all who believe, whether Jews or Greeks. For by it God's justice is revealed by faith for faith, as it is stated, 'By faith the just shall live.'[193]

But God's wrath is revealed from heaven against all impiety and iniquity of men who wilfully suppress the truth, since they are well aware of the facts about God, for God has made these plain to them. For ever since the creation of the world those

---

[191] In this letter, in the nature of a treatise, Paul does not address himself to the community (*ecclesia*) at Rome, but to the believers there in general, Jews and non-Jews, giving a reasoned statement of his faith and position. He writes, indeed, as in some uncertainty as to whether they are Christians in his doctrinal sense.

[192] See Lk. xx. 36, above p. 182.

[193] Hab. ii. 4. 'Shall live', now and in the Messianic Era.

unseen qualities of his, his immaterial nature, power and divinity, could be clearly perceived, apprehended through his works. So that there is no excuse for them, when being acquainted with God they have neither praised nor thanked him as God, but indulged in idle speculations and obscured their senseless minds. Professing to be wise they have behaved with utter folly, and have converted the glory of the imperishable God into the portrayal of the likeness of perishable men, birds, four-footed beasts and reptiles. Therefore God has given them over to their hearts' desire for depravity, to the abuse of their bodies among themselves, they who have exchanged God's truth for a lie, and worshipped and served the thing created instead of the Creator, blessed be he for ever. Amen.

Consequently God has given them over to their infamous passion; for their females have changed the normal function into the abnormal. The males, too, abandoning the normal function with females, inflamed with lust for one another, males for males, have engaged in indecency, duly receiving the reward appropriate to their irregularity among themselves. And just as they have not admitted God to a place in their consciousness, so has God given them over to a corrupt mind, to behave in unseemly fashion, perpetrating every kind of iniquity, obscenity, cupidity and depravity.[194] They are brim full of malice, murder, quarrelsomeness, knavery and malignity, slanderers, libellers, anti-theistic, insolent, arrogant, brazen, contrivers of evil, defiant to parents, of low mentality, perfidious, lacking in affection, pitiless, the sort who well-knowing God's ordinance that those who are guilty of such behaviour deserve death, not only act in this way themselves, but applaud others who do so.

So there is no excuse for you, sir, whoever you may be, who sit in judgment; for in the very thing you judge others you condemn yourself, since you who judge act in the same way.

Now we know that God's sentence is a just one on those who have acted in this fashion. Do you reckon, therefore, you who judge those who have acted like this and yet do the same yourself, that you can escape God's sentence? Or do you affect to scorn the wealth of his consideration, forbearance and long-suffering, ignoring that God's consideration is designed to lead you to repentance, preferring on account of your hard and impenitent heart to store up wrath for yourself in the Day of Wrath and disclosure of God's just doom? He it is who will 'render to every man according to his deeds',[195] for those who by persistence in worthy actions seek glory, honour and immortality, it will be Eternal Life, while for those who are of a contentious nature and will not comply with the truth—but readily comply with falsehood—it will be wrath and anger. There

[194] Cp. Tacit. *Annals*, XV. xliv. 'The City of Rome, the common sewer into which everything infamous and abominable flows like a torrent from all quarters of the world.'
[195] Ps. lxii. 12.

will be affliction and anguish for every human being who engages in evil, first for Jew then for Greek; but glory, honour and peace for all who do good, first for Jew then for Greek; for there is no partiality on God's part.

As many as have sinned without law shall perish without law, and as many as have sinned under law will be sentenced by law, on the day God judges the hidden things in men's lives by Christ Jesus, according to my presentation of the News. For it is not the hearers of law who are right with God, but the keepers of law who are exonerated. When, therefore, such Gentiles as have no law act instinctively as the Law requires, these having no law are their own law. They thus display the operation of that law which is written in their hearts, their conscience endorsing such action, though in the meantime their reasoning faculties may be engaged in a mutual conflict of accusation and defence.[196]

Now you on the other hand are one who bears the name of Jew. You rely on law and boast in God.[197] You are acquainted with his will, and can make clear distinctions,[198] being instructed out of the Law. You are convinced that you are a guide to the blind, a light to those in darkness, a tutor of the backward, a teacher of infants, because in the Law you have the whole corpus of knowledge and truth.

Well then, you who teach others, do you never teach yourself? You who proclaim 'not to steal', do you steal? You who say 'not to commit adultery', do you commit adultery? You who detest idols, do you rob temples? You who boast in the Law, do you dishonour God by transgressing the Law? Surely, as it is stated, 'God's name is profaned by you among the heathen'.[199]

Circumcision is a definite advantage if you observe the Law; but if you are a lawbreaker your circumcision is converted into uncircumcision. So if the uncircumcised person observes the moral principles of the Law, is not his uncircumcision to be reckoned as circumcision? And has not that uncircumcision which is by nature the right, having carried out the Law, to judge you who in spite of both code and circumcision are a lawbreaker? For he is no Jew who is only one in appearance, nor is circumcision simply what appears physically. The real Jew is he who is one internally, and the real circumcision is that of the heart, spiritual not literal, whose praise comes not from men but from God.

What merit is there then in being a Jew? Or what advantage does circumcision confer? Much in every respect, primarily because the Jews were entrusted with the Oracles of God. What does it matter if some were untrustworthy? Does their untrust-

---

[196] Without God's Law as guide the Gentile cannot always be clear in mind as to what is right and wrong. See below p. 302, n. 209.
[197] In the daily affirmation, 'Hear, O Israel, the Lord is our God'.
[198] Between good and evil and between what is permitted and what is forbidden.
[199] Mal. i. 11-12.

worthiness invalidate God's fidelity? God forbid! If only God
be true, it matters not if every man be false, as it is stated,

> That you should have your words vindicated,
> And prevail when you are arraigned.[200]

But if our iniquity confirms God's rectitude, what are we to
say, that God is unjust to vent his wrath? (I am speaking
humanly.) God forbid! For in that case how can God judge the
world? But if God's truth has more redounded to his praise by
my untruth, why am I still adjudged a sinner? And why not, as
I am slanderously reported, and as some, whose condemnation
is richly merited, allege that I say, 'Let us do evil that good
may come of it'?

What then? Do we Jews come off any better? Not at all. For
we have already charged Jews and Greeks alike with sinful
behaviour, as it is stated,

> None is upright, not a single one.
> None gives heed: none seeks after God.
> All are defective, and worthless beside.
> None serves a useful purpose, not one.
> Their throat is a yawning grave:
> They employ their tongues for deceit.
> The venom of asps is between their lips,
> Filling their mouth with bane and bitterness.
> Their feet are swift to shed blood:
> Rack and ruin strew their path;
> And the way of peace they have not known.
> There is no fear of God before their eyes.[201]

Now we know that whatever the Law states it declares to
those who are governed by the Law, so that every mouth may
be gagged and all the world become accountable to God, since
by following regulations 'not a single human being will be
exonerated';[202] for through law comes acquaintance with sin.

But now, independent of law, the righteousness of God has
been made patent, attested both by the Law and the Prophets,
that righteousness of God which is by faith in Jesus Christ,
available to *all* who believe. (There is no distinction; for *all*
have sinned and failed to reach God's standard.) These, by
God's mercy, are freely exonerated through the discharge of
liability by Christ Jesus, by their reliance on his blood, whom
God has appointed as an expiatory sacrifice in demonstration
of his righteousness. In God's forbearance he overlooked the
sins of past generations in view of the demonstration of his
rectitude at the present time, so as to be both just himself, and
the exonerator of whoever places his faith in Jesus.

Where then does boasting come in? It is excluded. By what
law? Of regulations? No, by a law of faith; for we have

---

[200] Ps. li. 4.
[201] Associating Ps. xiv. 1-3; v. 9; cxl. 3; x. 7; Isa. lix. 7-8; Ps. xxxvi. 1.
[202] Ps. cxlii. 2.

reckoned that a man is exonerated by faith independent of legal regulations. For is he God of the Jews only, and not of the Gentiles? Surely of the Gentiles also, if God is truly One. He exonerates the circumcised by their faith, and the uncircumcised by means of their acquired faith. Are we using faith to invalidate law? God forbid! Rather are we confirming law.[203]

What then are we to say of Abraham, our ancestor in the physical sense? If Abraham was exonerated by regulations he may well boast, though not to God. For what does the Scripture say, 'Abraham relied on God, and it was credited to him as rectitude'.[204] To one who carries out stipulations his reward is not reckoned as a favour, but as a due. But to one who does not carry out stipulations, but relies on him who exonerates the ungodly, his faith is reckoned as rectitude, just as David speaks of the happiness of the man to whom rectitude is accounted independent of regulations:

> Happy are they whose illegalities are forgiven,
> And whose sins are covered over.
> Happy is the man against whom the Lord counts not sin.[205]

Is that happiness reserved for the circumcised, or is it not also for the uncircumcised? Surely we have said, his faith was credited to Abraham as rectitude. In what circumstances then was it credited, when he was in a state of circumcision or of uncircumcision? Not in a state of circumcision, surely, but in that of uncircumcision; for he received the mark of circumcision as a ratification of the rectitude arising from the faith he had while uncircumcised, so that he might be the father of all coming from uncircumcision who believe, that it might be credited to them also as rectitude. At the same time he became the father of circumcision to those who—not on account of circumcision alone—follow in the steps of the faith of our father Abraham which he had when uncircumcised.

For it was not by law that the promise was made to Abraham, or to his seed, that he should be 'heir of the world', but by rectitude deriving from faith. For if those based on law are heirs, faith is an empty thing and the promise is idle. The Law results in wrath, but where no law exists there can be no transgression either. Necessarily it is based on faith, so as to be a matter of favour, that the promise might be secured to *all* the seed, not only to that which is based on the Law, but also to that which is based on the faith of Abraham, who is our common ancestor, as it is stated, 'I have made you father of many nations'.[206] Anticipating this, he relied on God the 'Giver of life to the dead',[207] and the Namer of things as existing which as yet

---

[203] By propounding a law of faith.
[204] Gen. xv. 6.
[205] Ps. xxxii. 1-2.
[206] Gen. xvii. 5.
[207] *Amidah*, Bened. 2. (AJP, p. 45).

are non-existent. Against hope he relied on hope that he would be 'father of many nations', as expressed in the words 'so shall your seed be'.[208] His faith never weakened with consciousness of the impotence of his own body—he was nearly a hundred years old at the time—and of Sarah's incapacity for mother-hood. He did not challenge the promise of God incredulously, but fortified by faith he gave God credit, and was fully assured that what he had promised was practicable, and that he would carry it out. That is why it was 'credited to him as rectitude'.

Now it was not written in respect of Abraham alone that 'it was credited to him', but also in respect of us to whom it would subsequently be credited, of those who trust in him who raised up Jesus our Master from the dead, who was delivered up for our trespasses and raised up for our exoneration.

So being exonerated on a basis of faith we enjoy peace with God through our Lord Jesus Christ, by whom we have secured admission to that state of favour in which we now stand, and boast in the prospect of God's esteem. And not only this, we even boast in afflictions, knowing that affliction fosters patience, patience fosters experiment, experiment fosters expectation, and expectation never disappoints, because God's love has pervaded our minds by the holy Spirit which has been given us. Moreover, Christ, when we were still helpless, died in due course for the ungodly. Now hardly for a devout man would anyone die, though possibly for a good man someone might dare to die. But God proves his own love for us, because Christ died for us while we were still sinners. Much more, therefore, being now exonerated by his blood, shall we be delivered from wrath through him. If then, as enemies, we were reconciled to God by the death of his Son, much more, having become reconciled, shall we be delivered by his life. And not only this, we boast in God through our Lord Jesus Christ, by whose instrumentality we have obtained reconcilia-tion.

Consequently, as by one man's agency sin entered the world, and by means of sin death, so death became the common lot of mankind, for all have sinned. For up to the time there was law sin was in the world, though sin was not charged as such while no law existed.[209] Nevertheless, death reigned from Adam down to Moses, even over those who technically had not sinned in a manner corresponding to the transgression of Adam, who prefigured him who was to come. But the effect of the act of grace was very different to that of the transgression; for if by the transgression of one man the many died, far more has the mercy of God and the free gift in mercy represented

---

[208] Gen. xv. 6.
[209] Here as elsewhere Paul does not regard law as having existed until the revelation of the Divine Law to Moses. That is why he speaks of the non-Jewish nations as being without law. Josephus, the first century Jewish historian, takes much the same position in his treatises *Against Apion*, where he argues that Gentile philosophers and lawgivers borrowed from the Jews.

by the one man Jesus Christ transcended this for the many. Other, indeed, was the effect of the gift to what happened by one having sinned. The judgment for one transgression brought condemnation, while the act of grace for many transgressions brought acquittal. Where, by the transgression of one, death reigned on account of the one, far more will those who have obtained the advantage of mercy and the free gift of rectitude reign in life on account of the one, Jesus Christ.

So then as a single transgression led to condemnation for all mankind, so equally a single worthy action led to acquittal spelling life for all mankind. Just as by one man's disobedience the many were constituted sinners, so also by one man's obedience the many are constituted righteous. Law came in additionally to magnify the transgression; but where sin abounded mercy abounded still more, that as sin reigned by death so should mercy reign through rectitude in Eternal Life by Jesus Christ our Master.

What are we to say then? Are we to continue in sin that mercy may be magnified? God forbid! We who have died so far as sin is concerned, how can we still live in it? Can you be ignorant that those who have become associated with Christ by immersion, have become associated by it with his death? Through this association with him by immersion we are thus united with him in burial, so that as Christ was raised from the dead by means of the Father's glory, we too should conduct ourselves in newness of life. For if we have become identified with the manner of his death, surely we should be with his resurrection also, knowing this, that our former self has been associated in crucifixion to dispose completely of the sinful body, that we should no longer be enslaved to sin; for the dead has met all the claims of sin upon him. If we have died with Christ we believe that we shall also be associated in life with him, realizing that Christ having risen from the dead cannot be put to death again: death has no further power over him. As he died, he died permanently so far as sin was concerned, but as alive again, he lives to God. And so you no less can count yourselves dead so far as sin is concerned, but alive to God in Christ Jesus.

Therefore do not let sin rule your mortal body by obeying its lusts, nor offer your organs as instruments of iniquity where sin is concerned. Rather offer yourselves to God as alive from the dead, and your organs as instruments of rectitude to God. Sin shall not have dominion over you, for you are not under law but under mercy.

What then? Shall we sin because we are not under law but under mercy? God forbid! Do you not know that to whom you offer yourselves in obedience as slaves, to him you obey you are slaves, whether slaves of sin for death or of obedience for righteousness? But God be thanked that though you were slaves of sin you have since obeyed from the heart that model of teaching[210] which has been transmitted to you. Thus freed from sin, you have become enslaved to righteousness. (I am employing human terms because of the limitations of your physical nature.) For just as you offered your organs as slaves to uncleanness and lawlessness, for lawlessness, so have you now offered your organs as slaves to righteousness, for consecration. When you were slaves of sin you were freeman as regards righteousness. What fruit had you then from those things of which you are now ashamed? For the end of those things is death. But now having been freed from sin and having become enslaved to God you have your fruit in consecration, the end of which is Eternal Life. For death is the pittance sin pays, while God's bounty by Christ Jesus our Master is Eternal Life.

Can you be ignorant, brothers, for I am speaking to those familiar with law, that the Law is in control for as long as a man lives? For the wife subject to a husband is bound by law for the duration of her husband's life. But if the husband dies she ceases to be subject to marital control. It follows that if she becomes another man's during her husband's lifetime she will be pronounced an adulteress; but if her husband is dead she is free as far as the Law is concerned, so that she will be no adulteress if she then becomes another man's. Consequently, my brothers, you too have been freed in law by death through the body of Christ, so as to be able to become another man's, his who was raised from the dead, that we should be fruitful to God.[211] For when we stood in the physical relationship the sinful sensations induced by the Law actuated our organs to produce fruit for death. But now we are severed from the Law, that by which we were controlled being dead, so as to serve in a new way of the spirit and not in the old way of the letter.

What are we to say then? That the Law is sin? God forbid! But I should not have been acquainted with sin except through law; for I should not have known desire if the Law had not said, 'You are not to covet'. It was sin seizing the opportunity through the commandment that provoked in me every kind of desire; for apart from law sin was inert. I was alive once apart from law; but when the commandment came sin sprang to life, and I died.[212] So I found the commandment which was intended for life tended to death; for sin seizing the opportunity through the commandment completely beguiled me, and through it slew me. Consequently the Law is indeed holy, and the commandment is holy, just and good.

Did then what is good become death to me? God forbid! But sin, that sin might be apparent through the good, brought

[210] Perhaps a manual of instruction for believers on the lines of the *Didache* (*Teaching of The XII Apostles*). See also Rom. xvi. 17, below p. 316, n. 274.
[211] Paul thinks of the physical Christ as one man, and the Christ after resurrection as another. The believer is now, as it were, the wife of the new spiritual husband to bear him spiritual offspring.
[212] A Jewish child was not held responsible for his actions until after the age of 12 when he became *Barmitzvah* (Son of the Commandment).

about my death, that sin through the commandment might be exceedingly sinful. For we know that the Law is spiritual, but I on the other hand am physical, the cat's-paw of sin. I do not perceive what I am about; for I find myself doing not what I wish to do, but doing instead what I detest. So if I am doing what I do not wish to do, I grant that the Law is right. But there it is, it is not I that am doing whatever it is, but the indwelling sin in me. For I know that good does not reside in me, that is in my physical nature.[213] The intention is there, but the capacity to carry out what is right is not; for I do not do the good I intend, but the evil I do not intent. So if I do what I do not intend, it is no longer I who am doing it, but sin that dwells in me. I discover therefore the law, that whenever it is my intention to do right the wrong asserts itself in me. In my inner self I delight in the Law of God,[214] but I perceive another law in my organs, warring against the law of my mind and making me prisoner to the law of sin which exists in my organs. So there it is, I myself intellectually am bound to God's Law, but physically to sin's law. Miserable man that I am! Who will rescue me from this body of death?[215] Thanks be to God through Jesus Christ our Master!

So then there is now no condemnation whatever for those who are in Christ Jesus, for the law of the Spirit of Life in Christ Jesus has freed me from the law of sin and death. For the Law's powerlessness, due to its weakness because of the physical factor, was remedied by God sending his own Son in the likeness of sinful physical nature; and as regards sin he passed sentence on sin in Christ's physical being, so that the Law's claims should be satisfied so far as we are concerned, we who do not lead the physical but the spiritual life. For those who are physical are concerned with material matters, while those who are spiritual are concerned with spiritual matters. The materialistic mentality spells death; the spiritual mentality spells life and peace. That is because the materialistic mentality is hostile to God; for it is not subordinated to God's control, nor can it be. Those who have the physical outlook cannot please God.

Now you do not have the physical but the spiritual outlook, assuming that God's Spirit resides in you. Naturally, if anyone does not possess the spirit of Christ he does not belong to him. But if Christ is present in you it means that the body is dead as a vehicle of sin, but the spirit is alive as a vehicle of righteousness. And if the Spirit that raised up Jesus from the dead resides in you, then he that raised Christ Jesus from the dead will also give life to your mortal bodies by very reason of his Spirit indwelling in you.

[213] Cp. Ps. xxxviii. 3.   [214] Cp. Ps. cxix. 47, etc.
[215] Or 'dead body'. Perhaps with reference to the crime of the Etruscan king Mezentius, who bound living persons to dead bodies 'hand to hand and face to face' until they died a lingering ghastly death (Virgil, *Aeneid*, Bk. VIII, 481-488).

So then, brothers, we are under no obligation to our physical nature to live on the material plane; for if you live on the material plane you will surely die. Whereas if by the spiritual you put to death the practices of the body you will live; for it is those who are led by the Spirit of God who are sons of God. You have not received a servile spirit, to put you again in fear. It is a filial spirit you have received, whereby we cry 'Abba!' (Father!). The Spirit joins its witness to our spirit that we are God's children, and if children then heirs, first heirs of God, and then joint-heirs with Christ. In that case we suffer together so as to be ennobled together also. I personally count the sufferings of the present time as quite unworthy to be compared with the future glory that is to be revealed in us. The eager longing of the Creation itself waits expectantly for the revelation of the Sons of God. For the Creation is subject to dissolution, not of its own choice, but through him who subjected it, yet in expectation that the Creation itself would be freed from servitude to decay to share the glorious freedom of the children of God. We know indeed that the whole Creation groans and strains until now, and not it alone, but those who already enjoy the spiritual first-fruits—we ourselves—even they moan to themselves, waiting expectantly for the adoption, the redemption of their bodies. For we are kept alive on hope. But hope that is in sight is not hope; for when one *sees* where is there need for hope? But if we hope for what we do not see, then we persist in our expectant waiting.

Likewise the Spirit comes to the assistance of our limitations; for we do not know how to express ourselves adequately in prayer. But the Spirit itself makes intercession with speechless moans, and God who searches hearts knows what is the sense of the Spirit's utterances, that in God's way it is interceding for the saints. We know further, that for those who love God, for those called in accordance with his purpose, God makes everything turn out for the best. For, for those he had in view, he also planned in advance that they should come to resemble his Son, that thus he might be the eldest of many brothers. And those he purposed in advance he duly called, and those he called he duly exonerated, and those he exonerated he will duly ennoble.

What then are we to say to all this? If God is for us, who is there against us? He who did not withhold his very own Son, but delivered him up for us all,[216] will he not also with him gladly give us everything else? Who dare accuse God's Elect? When God exonerates, who is there that can condemn? When Christ has died, still more, has risen from the dead, is at God's right hand, and also intercedes for us, who is to separate us from Christ's love? Can affliction, or confinement, or perse-

---

[216] Cp. the offering up of Isaac by Abraham (Gen. xxii. 12), to which great spiritual significance was attached.

cution, or famine, or destitution, or danger, or sword? As it is stated,

> For your sake we are killed the whole day long;
> We are reckoned as sheep for the slaughter.[217]

Yet in all these circumstances we are easy victors through him who has loved us. I am convinced that neither death nor life, neither angels nor ruling spirits, neither present nor future, neither powers above nor powers below, nor any other created being, will be able to sever us from the love of God which is in Christ Jesus our Master.

I am telling the truth in Christ, I am not lying, my conscience bearing me witness in the holy Spirit, when I say that I am in great grief and continual mental distress. For I could entreat that I personally was outcast from Christ for my brothers' sake,[218] my kinsmen in the physical sense, who are Israelites, to whom belongs the Adoption,[219] and the Glory, and the Covenants, and the Lawgiving, and the Service,[220] and the Promises, whose are the Patriarchs, and above all from whom in the physical sense came Christ, blessed be God for ever. Amen.

There is no question of God's word having failed; for it is not all who spring from Israel who are Israel, neither because they are the seed of Abraham are all of them his children. For 'in Isaacs shall your seed be called'.[221] That is to say, not the children in the ordinary physical sense are the children of God, but the children of promise are reckoned as the seed. For this is how the promise went: 'About this time I will come, and Sarah will have a son'.[222] And not only so, but when Rebecca had also conceived by one, namely our father Isaac, it was told her, 'the elder shall serve the younger'.[223] This was before the children were born, when they had done nothing either good or bad, in order that the purpose of God as regards choice should stand not on a basis of conduct but of calling, just as it is stated, 'Jacob I have loved, but Esau I have hated'.[224]

What are we to say then? That there is injustice on God's part? God forbid! For he says to Moses, 'I will show mercy to whom I would be merciful, and have compassion on whom I would compassionate'.[225] It follows that it is a matter not of what one wants, or what one tries to do, but of God's mercy; for the Scripture says to Pharaoh, 'For this very reason I have

[217] Ps. xliv. 22.
[218] Cp. the prayer of Moses, Exod. xxxii. 32.
[219] I.e. as God's children.
[220] I.e. of the Sanctuary. The passage is liturgical, cp. AJP, p. 149. 'For the Law for the Service, for the Prophets . . .'
[221] Gen. xxi. 12.
[222] Gen. xviii. 10.
[223] Gen. xxv. 23.
[224] Mal. i. 2-3.
[225] Exod. xxxiii. 19.

raised you up, that through you I may display my power, and my name become known throughout the world'.[226] It follows that he is merciful to whom he wishes, and whom he wishes he makes obdurate.

You will then say to me, 'Why does he still blame anyone? For who is a match for his will?' If it comes to that, who are you, sir, to answer God back? Is it for the model to say to the modeller, 'Why did you make me like this?' Has not the potter in clay a perfect right to make out of the same lump one article as a thing of worth, another as a thing of no worth? Supposing that God, wishing to display his genius and demonstrate his ability, produced with immense pains crude articles prepared for destruction, in order to display the richness of his imagination on delicate articles which he had designed beforehand for distinction[227]—namely ourselves, whom he has called, not from the Jews alone but also from the Gentiles? He does indeed say in Hosea:

'I will call them my people, who were not my people,
And her beloved, who was not beloved,'
In the very place where it was said to them, 'You are
    not my people',
There shall they be called, 'Sons of the Living God'.[228]

Isaiah also cries concerning Israel, 'Though the number of the children of Israel is as the sand of the sea, only a remnant will be saved. For the Lord will make a full and summary settlement on earth'.[229] And as Isaiah said previously, 'If the Lord of hosts had not left us some seed, we should have become as Sodom, we should have been like Gomorrah'.[230]

What are we to say then? That the Gentiles who did not pursue righteousness have overtaken it, the righteousness that arises from faith, while Israel pursuing a law of righteousness has failed to attain it? That is so. Why? Because it was not by faith, but as by regulations. They stumbled at the stumblingstone, as it is stated,

'Lo, I place in Zion a stumbling-stone, a boulder to trip over;
But he who believes in him will not come to grief'.[231]

It is indeed my fondest desire, brothers, and the burden of my petition to God, that they should be saved. I can testify that they have a deep passion for God, though without discernment, for failing to perceive God's righteousness, while busy with trying to establish their own, they did not subordinate themselves

[226] Exod. ix. 16.
[227] The Greek conveys the full force of the metaphor because 'crude articles' equally means 'vessels of wrath' and 'delicate articles' means also 'vessels of mercy'.
[228] Hos. ii. 23.
[229] Isa. x. 22 with xxviii. 22.
[230] Isa. i. 9.
[231] Isa. viii. 14 with xxviii. 16 (LXX). 'In him', or 'In it', is an addition to the quotation, possibly taken from a collection of proofs from the OT that Jesus was the Messiah.

to God's righteousness. To all who believe, Christ is the end of law as regards righteousness; for Moses writes concerning the righteousness that is by law, that 'the man who acts up to it shall live by it'.[232] But the righteousness that is by faith speaks thus: 'Do not say to yourself, Who will ascend to heaven?' (that is, to bring Christ down) or, 'Who will descend into the abyss?' (that is, to bring Christ up from the dead). What it declares is, 'The word is very near you, in your mouth and in your mind'[233] (that is, the word of faith which we proclaim). For if you will affirm 'the word in your mouth' that Jesus is Master, and believe 'in your mind' that God raised him from the dead, you will be saved; for belief is by the mind for righteousness, and affirmation is by the mouth for salvation. The Scripture does indeed say, 'Everyone who believes in him will never come to grief'.[234] There is no distinction between Jew and Greek: the same universal Lord is sufficient for all who invoke him, for 'all who invoke the name of the Lord will be saved'.[235] How then are they to invoke him in whom they have not believed? And how are they to believe what they have not heard? And how are they to hear without a preacher? And how are they to preach unless they are sent? As it is stated, 'How fair are the feet of those who bring good news!'[236] But not all have responded to the news, for Isaiah says, 'Lord, who has credited our report?'[237] So then faith comes by hearing, and hearing through the proclamation of Christ.

But I say, have they not heard? Decidedly they have.

> Their voice has resounded throughout the earth,
> Their utterance to the utmost confines of the world.[238]

And I say, has Israel not known? First Moses says,

> 'I will make you jealous over what is no nation;
> Over a senseless nation I will anger you.'[239]

While Isaiah takes the liberty of saying,

> 'I have been found by those who did not seek me:
> I have become evident to those who never asked for me.'[240]

And of Israel he says, 'All day long I have stretched out my hands to a refractory and contradictory people'.[241]

I ask, therefore, has God rejected his people? God forbid! I too am an Israelite, of the seed of Abraham, the tribe of Benjamin. God has not rejected his people whom he knew of old. Or are you unaware of what the Scripture says in the person of

[232] Lev xviii. 5.
[233] Deut. xxx. 12-14.
[234] Isa. xxviii. 16.
[235] Joel ii. 32.
[236] Isa. lii. 7.
[237] Isa. liii. 1.
[238] Ps. xix. 4.
[239] Deut. xxxii. 21.
[240] Isa. lxv. 1.
[241] Isa. lxv. 2.

Elijah, where he speaks to God about Israel, saying, 'Lord, they have killed your prophets, thrown down your altars, and I alone am left, and they seek my life'? But what does his Interlocutor say to him? 'I have reserved for myself seven thousand men, who have not bent the knee to Baal'.[242] Just so at this present time by a merciful choice there is a remnant. If it is by mercy it is no longer by deeds, otherwise mercy would no longer be mercy.

What then? Israel has not found what it is seeking, but the chosen part has found it, while the rest were immobilized, exactly as it is stated, 'God has given them a spirit of stupor, eyes that do not see, and ears that do not hear, to this very day'.[243] And David says,

> Let their table become a snare and a trap,
> A hindrance and an obstacle to them,
> Let their eyes be dimmed that they see not,
> And their back be for ever bent.[244]

I ask, therefore, have they tripped in order that they should fall? God forbid! Rather that by their blunder salvation has come to the Gentiles, to stir them to emulation. But if their blunder is the world's enrichment, and their discomfiture the Gentiles' enrichment, how much more their complete achievement? (I am speaking now to you Gentiles.) In so far, then, as I am an envoy to the Gentiles I make much of my office, if in that way I can provoke my own kin to emulation, and save some of them. For if their loss has been the world's profit, what will their acquisition be but life from the dead? If the first-dough is holy, so is the whole lump,[245] and if the stem is holy, so are the branches.

Now if some of the branches have been pruned away, and you from a wild olive have now been grafted among them, sharing with them the sap-stream of the olive stem, do not lord it over the branches. For if you do lord it, remember that it is not you who carry the stem, but the stem you. You will say then, 'The branches have been pruned away that I might be grafted in'. Putting it fairly, they have been pruned away as lacking in trust,[246] while you by trust stand firm. So do not be arrogant, but fear. For if God did not spare the natural branches, neither will he spare you. Mark, then, the kindness and severity of God, severity towards those branches which drooped, kindness to you, provided you continue to merit his kindness. Otherwise, you too will be cut out, while they, unless they continue to remain without trust, will be grafted in again; for God can graft them in again. For if you were cut from an olive tree wild by nature, and grafted contrary to nature in a

[242] I. Ki. xix. 10, 18.
[243] Isa. xxix. 10 with Deut. xxix.4.
[244] Ps. lxix. 22-23.
[245] Cp. Num. xv. 18-21; Lev. xix. 23-24.
[246] 'Trust' may equally be read as 'faith'. The metaphor is difficult to reproduce.

cultivated olive, how much more shall these which are the natural branches be grafted into their own olive tree?

I would not have you ignorant of this secret, brothers, in case you should 'give yourselves airs',[247] that partial immobility has come to Israel until the full complement of Gentiles has come in; and so all Israel will be saved,[248] as it is stated,

> *The redeemer will come out of Zion:*
> *He will banish ungodliness from Jacob,*
> *For this is my covenant with them,*
> *When I take away their sins.*[249]

As regards the News they are out of favour for your sakes, but as regards the Choice they are dear to God for the Patriarchs' sakes;[250] for God never goes back on his acts of grace and his calling. Even as you once refused God obedience, but now have had mercy shown you in respect of their disobedience, so they also have now refused obedience in respect of the mercy shown to you, that they may obtain mercy. For God has classed all together as disobedient that he may show mercy to all.

Oh, the infinite wealth of God's wisdom and knowledge! How inscrutable are his judgments and mysterious his ways! Who has ever known the mind of the Lord, or who has been his counsellor? Or who has first given to him, that he must be repaid?[251] For from him, and through him, and in turn, are all things. To him be glory for ever. Amen.

I exhort you[252] therefore, brothers, by God's tender mercies, to offer your bodies as a holy living sacrifice well-pleasing to God, which is your plain religious duty. Do not accommodate yourselves to the age we live in, but transform yourselves by a mental renovation, so that you are competent to determine what is the good, well-pleasing, and perfect will of God.

By virtue of the favour bestowed on me, I ask every individual among you not to have a higher opinion of himself than he should, but to think of himself modestly, as God has allotted to each his share of credit. For just as we have many organs in one body, and all the organs do not perform the same function, so we are many persons in one body in Christ, and that body as a unity has its respective organs. Possessing then a variety of gifts according to the favour granted us let mutual regard be unfeigned. If the gift is for prophecy, let it be exercised with corresponding faithfulness. If it is for administration, let it be exercised in administration; if for teaching, let it be in teaching; if for exhortation, let it be in exhortation. He who has something to share, let him do it generously. He who super-

---

[247] Cp. Prov. iii. 7.
[248] 'All Israel have a share in the World to Come' (*Sanhed*. x. 1).
[249] Isa. lix. 20-21 with xxvii. 9.
[250] Cp. *Amidah*, Bened. I, 'Who bestowest loving-kindness, and possessest all things; who rememberest the pious deeds of the Patriarchs, and in love will bring a redeemer to their children's children' (AJP, p. 44).
[251] Cp. Ps. cxlv. 3: Isa. xl. 13-14; Job xxxv. 7; xli. 11.
[252] The paragraphs that follow are similar to those contained in the *Didache*, and may derive from an early 'Manual of Instruction'. See above p. 304, n. 210.

vises, let him do it diligently. He who does a kindness, let him do it cheerfully.

Let love be unfeigned. Repudiate what is evil. Cleave to what is good. In brotherly love be affectionate to one another. In honour give precedence to one another. In diligence do not be backward. In spiritual matters be ardent. Be willing slaves to the Master, joyful in hope, patient in affliction, persevering in prayer, sharing in provision for the necessities of the saints, ready with hospitality. Bless those who are so ready;[253] bless and do not curse. Rejoice with those who rejoice. Weep with those who weep. Be like-minded with one another. Do not be high and mighty, but consort with the humble. Do not give yourself airs.[254] Never return evil for evil. Be well-respected in the sight of all men.[255] If possible, where it rests with you, be at peace with everyone. Do not avenge yourselves, dear friends, but give anger a wide berth, for it is stated, 'Vengeance is mine, I will requite, says the Lord.'[256] Rather, 'If your enemy is hungry, feed him, if he is thirsty refresh him; for by so doing you will fill him with remorse.'[257] Do not be overcome by evil, but overcome evil with good.

Let every individual be subject to the responsible authorities; for there is no authority except from God, and those who are constituted hold their appointment from God.[258] Whoever, therefore, opposes the authority sets himself against the divine order, and those who resist it will duly receive punishment. Magistrates are not a terror to well-doers, but to evil-doers. If you would be free from fear of authority be of good behaviour, and you will earn its commendation; for the authority is God's administrator for your welfare. But if you do wrong, then be afraid, for he does not bear the sword without reason. In his capacity as God's administrator it is his official duty to inflict punishment on the evil-doer.

Of necessity you must be subject to the laws, not merely from considerations of punishment, but also of conscience, which applies equally to your payment of taxes. Those who levy them are God's officials regularly employed for this very purpose. Render to everyone their dues, tribute to whoever is entitled to it, tax to whoever is entitled to it, respect to whoever is entitled to it, honour to whoever is entitled to it. Owe nothing to anyone except regard for one another; for he who shows another love has met all the requirements of law. 'You are not to commit adultery, you are not to murder, you are not to steal, you are not to covet',[259] and whatever other commandment there

[253] The alternative rendering 'those who persecute' appears unsuitable in the context. The same word 'ready' has just been used in association with hospitality.
[254] Prov. iii. 7 (LXX).
[255] Prov. iii. 4 (LXX).
[256] Deut. xxxii. 35.
[257] Prov. xxv. 21-22.
[258] Of the Essenes it is said by Josephus, *Wars*, II. viii. 7, 'They swear to keep faith with all men, especially with the powers that be, since no ruler attains his office save by the will of God'. See also *Aboth*, iii. 2.
[259] Exod. xxii. 13-17.

may be, is summed up in this, 'You are to love your neighbour as yourself.[260] He who loves his neighbour will never do him an injury; so love is the sum total of law. This further, because I know the time, it is high time for you to awaken from sleep; for our deliverance is now much nearer than when we believed. The night is far advanced, the day is at hand. Let us therefore lay aside what belongs to the darkness, and put on the habits of the light. Let us conduct ourselves with daytime decorum, not in revels and carousals, not in sexual intimacy and licentiousness, not in wrangling and rivalry. Rather, invest yourselves with the Lord Jesus Christ, and make no provision for the fulfilment of physical desires.

Associate with the man who is weak in faith, but not for controversial arguments. For one believes he may eat anything, while another of weaker calibre keeps to a vegetarian diet. The man who eats must not be contemptuous of the one who does not. Neither must the man who does not eat condemn the one who does; for God has taken him into his service. Who are you to criticize another's retainer? To his own Master he stands or falls. And stand he will, for the Lord will see to it that he stands.

One man distinguishes one day above another, while someone else treats all days alike. Each must fully satisfy his own mind. He who observes a day observes it to the Lord, and he who eats every kind of food eats it to the Lord, because he thanks God for it. He who does not eat, his not eating is also to the Lord, for he too gives God thanks. None of us lives to himself, and none of us dies to himself. If we live, we live to the Lord, and if we die, we die to the Lord. Whether we live, or whether we die, we are the Lord's. That is why Christ died and came alive again, that he might have jurisdiction over both dead and living. Why then do you condemn your brother, or why do you treat your brother with contempt? We must all stand at God's tribunal, for it is stated,

'As I live', says the Lord, 'every knee shall bend to me,
And every tongue shall make full confession to God.'[261]

So then each of us must render an account of himself to God. Therefore let us no longer pass judgment on one another. Rather should you determine this, not to place any obstacle or impediment in your brother's way. I know and am convinced in the Lord Jesus that nothing is impure in itself,[262] but if someone considers anything to be impure, for him it is so. And if your brother is distressed by the food you eat, you are not behaving considerately. Do not by your food destroy one for whose sake Christ died. Do not let what is for your well-being be made a means of injury. For the Kingdom of God is not food and drink, but righteousness, peace, and joy in the holy Spirit. Who-

[260] Lev. xix. 18, cp. Mt. xxii. 40.
[261] Isa. xlv. 23.
[262] Cp. Mt. xv. 11.

ever in such matters serves Christ is both well-pleasing to God and agreeable to men.

So then let us follow the ways of peace[263] and the things that promote our mutual welfare. For a mere matter of food do not disrupt God's work. Everything is indeed clean; but it is a wrong thing for a man to be a means of offence by what he eats. The right course is neither to eat meat nor to drink wine, nor whatever else it may be that upsets your brother. As to the conviction you hold, hold it privately in the sight of God. Happy is the man who does not condemn himself by what he sanctions. But he who does discriminate stands condemned if he should eat, because it is not from conviction. For whatever is not done from conviction is sin.

It is the duty of those of us who are strong to bear the foibles of the weak, and not to gratify ourselves. It is for each of us to put his neighbour at ease so as to promote the general welfare. For even Christ did not please himself, as it is stated, 'The reproaches which they cast on you fell on me'.[264] Whatever indeed was set down was written entirely for our guidance, that through the sustaining power and encouragement of the Scriptures we should have hope. May God who sustains and cheers grant you to be likeminded with one another in accord with Jesus Christ, that in complete unanimity with one voice you may praise God, the Father of our Lord Jesus Christ!

Therefore associate with one another for the glory of God, just as Christ associated himself with you. For I say that Christ became a representative of circumcision, as God's honour required, so as to make good his promise to the Patriarchs, and that the Gentiles should praise God for his mercy, as it is stated,

> Therefore I will confess you among the Gentiles,
> And sing praises to your name.[265]

And again it says, 'Rejoice, O Gentiles, with his people',[266] and further,

> Extol the Lord, all you Gentiles,
> And praise him, all you peoples.[267]

And again it says, 'Rejoice, O Gentiles, with his people'.[266] and who arises to rule the Gentiles. In him shall the Gentiles hope.[268]

The God of hope so fill you with joy and peace in believing, that you overflow with hope by virtue of the holy Spirit!

Naturally, I personally am completely convinced of you, my brothers, that you are the very soul of kindness, fully provided with all essential knowledge, and most competent to admonish one another. But I have written to you more outspokenly than was warranted, simply to serve as a reminder to you, because of

263 Cp. Ps. xxiv. 14.
264 Ps. lxix. 9.
265 Ps. xviii. 49.
266 Deut. xxxii. 43.
267 Ps. cxvii. 1.
268 Isa. xi. 1, 10

the favour God has granted me that I should be the ministrant of Christ Jesus for the Gentiles, carrying out the rite of God's News, that the offering up of the Gentiles might be acceptable when consecrated by the holy Spirit. I hold therefore a privileged position in Christ Jesus in matters relating to God. I am not so audacious as to speak of anything which Christ has not effected by my agency, by virtue of signs and wonders, by virtue of the holy Spirit, to procure the obedience of the Gentiles in word and deed. So that from Jerusalem as far round as Illyricum [269] I have fully publicized the News of Christ. And thus have I most strenuously proclaimed the News, not where Christ's name was familiar, that I should not build on another's foundation, but rather as it is stated,

> They shall see, to whom he was not reported,
> And those who have not heard shall consider. [270]

That is why I have so frequently been prevented from visiting you. But now having nothing more that I may do in these regions, and having had a great longing these many years to visit you, whenever I travel to Spain I trust to have a sight of you in passing through, and to be forwarded by you on my way there after first making the most of my stay with you.

Just now, however, I am setting out for Jerusalem to render the saints a service; for Macedonia and Achaia have been pleased to make a contribution of funds for the poor among the saints at Jerusalem. [271] It has pleased them quite properly, since they are their debtors. For if the Gentiles have shared in their spiritual things, they in turn are obligated to minister to them in material things. When, therefore, I have performed this service, and deposited this benefit with them, I shall proceed via yourselves to Spain; and I know that when I come to you it will be with the full blessing of Christ.

Now I entreat you, brothers, by our Lord Jesus Christ, and by the bonds of spiritual affection, to aid me with your prayers to God on my behalf, that I may be protected from those in Judea who are disobedient, and that my mission to Jerusalem may be well received by the saints; so that coming on to you joyfully, God willing, I may take my rest in your company. The God of peace be with you all. Amen.

[272] My fellow-worker Timotheus sends you his regards, and so do my fellow-countrymen Lucius, Jason and Sosipater. (I, Tertius, who took down the letter, send you my regards in the Master.) My host Gaius sends you his regards, and so does the whole community. Erastus the city-treasurer sends you his regards, as does Brother Quartus.

[269] District east of the Adriatic roughly corresponding to modern Albania.
[270] Isa. lii. 15.
[271] See above pp. 228, 162, 294-296.
[272] Some regard Rom. xvi. 1-20, which is placed here in the Greek, as a short personal note sent with Sister Phoebe as the bearer of the letter, serving both to introduce her and to convey Paul's personal greetings to a number of individuals. This passage is therefore transferred to the end of the letter.

Now to him who can establish you in accordance with my presentation of the News and the proclamation of Jesus Christ, in accordance with the revelation of the mystery for long ages kept secret, but now disclosed through the Prophetic Scriptures by order of the Eternal God, and made known to all nations to procure their loyal submission, to the only wise God be praise through Jesus Christ for ever and ever. Amen.

COVERING NOTE

This is to commend to you Sister Phoebe, who is an administrator of the Cenchrea[273] community. Welcome her in the Master as befits saints, and assist her in whatever way she may require; for she has been of great assistance to many, including myself.

Give my regards to Prisca and Aquila, my fellow-workers in Christ Jesus, who have risked their necks on my behalf, and to whom not only I am grateful, but all the communities among the Gentiles. Then give my regards to my dear friend Epaenetus, Asia's first-fruits for Christ, also to Mary who has worked so hard for you. My regards to my fellow-countrymen and fellow-captives Andronicus and Junias, famed among the envoys, who also were in Christ before me. My regards in the Master to my dear friend Amplias, also Urban our fellow-worker in Christ, and my dear friend Stachys. My regards to Apelles approved in Christ, also to the family of Aristobulus. Give my regards to my fellow-countryman Herodion, also those of the family of Narcissus who are in the Master, and those hard workers in the Master Tryphena and Tryphosa. My regards to dear Persis, who has worked so hard in the Master, also Rufus, chosen in the Master, and his mother, and therefore mine. My regards to Asyncritus, Phlegon, Hermes, Patrobas, Hermas, and the brothers associated with them. My regards to Philologus and Julia, Nereus and his sister, Olympas too, and all the saints associated with them.

Convey my regards to one another with a chaste kiss. All the Christian communities send their regards.

Now I exhort you, brothers, to note those who create doubts and difficulties in opposition to the teaching you have learnt,[274] and keep away from them. Such as they do not serve the Lord Christ, but their own appetites, and by fair words and fine phrases seduce the minds of the guileless. But your obedience has become common knowledge. So I am quite happy about you, and only want you to be wise where good is concerned, uncontaminated where evil is concerned.[275] The God of peace will swiftly crush Satan under your heel.[276]

The loving-kindness of our Lord Jesus be with you all.

---

273 Seaport on east side of the Gulf of Corinth, see Acts xviii. 18, above p. 227.
274 Cp. *Didache*, iv.
275 Cp. Mt. x. 16.
276 The Old Serpent, Gen. iii. 15.

THE LETTERS OF PAUL OF TARSUS

SECOND SERIES

LETTERS FROM ROME

Preface to *Paul's Letters (Second Series)*

We are without the assistance of the *Acts* for knowledge of the closing years of Paul's life, and have to depend entirely on what can be gleaned from the second series of letters. From these it is clear that, although confined under guard in a rented apartment until his case was heard, Paul had full freedom of communication and the ministrations of his friends to solace him. He had every expectation of being set at liberty, and at one point was making plans for visits on his release. But he had enemies inside the Christian community as well as outside, who worked against him, and the first hearing was indecisive. The conditions of his imprisonment may have been made more rigorous, and finally he appears to have recognized that his death was inevitable even if for a time postponed. Some hold that he was freed and travelled to Macedonia and Asia, and was later rearrested and brought to Rome, and they would place his end in A.D. 66 or 67. The weight of evidence seems to the writer against this view, and it is accepted that Paul was confined in Rome until his death not later than the Spring of A.D. 64. The order and dating of the letters of this period have been governed by this hypothesis.

Scholars have drawn attention to the differences of style and vocabulary in some of the letters compared with the earlier ones, and in those to *Titus* and *I. Timotheus* to evidences of advanced Church government, thus throwing doubts on the Pauline authorship. Some would say that genuine Pauline material has been worked up by other hands. The arguments for some posthumous editing are very strong, but not conclusive.

What is notable about the letters to Philippi and the Asian communities is their mystical passages, where Paul employs occult doctrine to describe the nature of Christ and his relationship with the Church. The short letter to Philemon about his runaway slave Onesimus is delightful and appealing, and in those to Titus and Timotheus there is much to interest and inform about the organization of the Christian communities. But chiefly with this whole series one has to read with the thought of the imprisoned author constantly in mind. Through what he writes we can see how he encourages himself with prayer, with vision, and with spiritual song. We can see how he strives with counsel and clarification to leave a legacy that will assure the continuation of his life's work and convictions until the Messianic Era dawns. Studied from this viewpoint there is indeed much to touch the emotions and impress the reader with the nobility of soul of a great sufferer and a very courageous man.

TO THE COMMUNITY AT PHILIPPI

(Probably written from Rome about A.D. 61)

Paul and Timotheus, servants of Christ Jesus, to all the saints in Christ Jesus resident in Philippi, with their supervisors and administrators. May peace and prosperity be yours from God our Father and the Lord Jesus Christ.

I invariably thank my God for every recollection of you whenever I pray for you. I offer my petition with joy for the fellowship you have had with the News from the very beginning until now, being fully assured that he who promoted such well-doing in your case will maintain it to the Day of Jesus Christ. It is indeed right that I should so think of you all, because I have you so much at heart, all of you having shared in the privilege I have of being in fetters and of defending and championing the News. God is my witness how I long for you all with all the yearning of Christ Jesus! And so it is my prayer, that your love may bring you ever deeper insight and perception in distinguishing points of difference,[1] that you may be unalloyed and untarnished till the Day of Christ, laden with the fruit of rectitude that comes through Jesus Christ, to the glory and praise of God.

Now I want to tell you, brothers, that my circumstances have rather tended to the advancement of the News; for my fetters have publicized Christ to the whole praetorium[2] and everywhere else, and the majority of the brothers, having been fired with confidence in the Master by my fetters, have become much more venturesome, giving out God's Message fearlessly. Some of course do it out of envy and rivalry, but others proclaim Christ from goodwill. These do it out of regard, knowing that I am thus circumstanced for the defence of the News, while the former, who are not well-intentioned, announce Christ in a factious spirit, trying deliberately to make trouble for me in my fettered state. What does it matter? The main thing is, that whether in pretence or sincerity, Christ is proclaimed. For this I rejoice. But there is greater joy in store; for I know that this will be the salvation of me thanks to your prayers and the supply of the spirit of Jesus Christ, with the earnest hope and expectation I have that I shall in no way be put to shame, but that freely and fully, now as always, Christ will be magnified in my person, whether by life or death.

[1] Cp. Rom. ii. 18, p. 299, n. 198.
[2] Probably here the precincts of the court-house where Paul's case would be dealt with.

J.F.H.

Soldiers of the Praetorian Guard

It is useful[3] for me to live, and an advantage to die. But if I am to live physically it means an effort on my part, and I hardly know which to choose. I am in a quandary between the two, having the longing to depart and be with Christ, for that would be so much better, yet on the other hand to remain in the flesh is more essential for you. Finally convinced of this, I know I am to remain and be at the side of all of you for your advancement and joyfulness in faith, that your exultation in Christ Jesus may abound by me through my reappearance among you. Only let your ordering of affairs be worthy of Christ's News, that whether I come and see you or remain absent I shall hear word of you that you are continuing to be of one spirit, single-mindedly contending for the faith of the News, and not the least alarmed by the tactics of your adversaries. This is a sure sign of defeat for them, but deliverance for you, and this by God himself; for you have the privilege on Christ's account not only of believing in him but of suffering for his sake. Yours is the same kind of contest in which you have seen me engaged, and now learn that I am still engaging.

So if there is any encouragement in Christ you can give me, any consolation of affection, any fellowship of spirit, any deep concern and compassion, do fill me with the joy of it. So that in

[3] Reading *chrestos* for *Christos*.

thus thinking alike, having the same affection, being kindred souls with a common viewpoint, there will be no trace of rivalry, no trace of self-importance, but that humility of mind which regards others as superior to one's self, each studying not his own interests but those of his fellows. Let your disposition, indeed, be that of Christ Jesus, who though he had godlike form did not regard it as a prize to be equal to God,[4] but divested himself, taking the form of a servant. Appearing in human likeness, and disclosed in physical appearance as a man, he abased himself, and became subject to death, death by the cross. That is why God has so exalted him, that at the name of Jesus every knee, heavenly, earthly and infernal, should bend, and every tongue acclaim Jesus Christ as Master,[5] to the glory of God the Father.

Therefore, dear friends, as invariably you have been obedient, not only when I have been present, but much more creditably now in my absence, earn your salvation with fear and trembling; for it is God who is prompting you both to want and to carry out what is well-pleasing. Do everything without murmuring or argument, that you may be irreproachable and faultless, blameless children of God in the midst of a 'perverse and crooked generation',[6] in which shine out like luminaries in a dark universe, radiating a message of Life,[7] my proud proof on the Day of Christ that I have neither striven nor toiled in vain. But even should I be poured out as the libation and act of worship that your faith is called upon to make, I shall rejoice and congratulate you all, and similarly you will rejoice and congratulate me.[8]

Now I hope in the Lord Jesus to send Timotheus to you soon, that I myself may be heartened by knowing how you fare. I have no one better qualified, one who is genuinely concerned with how you fare; for most study their own interests, not those of Christ Jesus. But you know the worth of Timotheus, how he has served with me in the News like a son with his father. Him, then, I hope to send as soon as ever I have a clear impression of my prospects, though I am convinced in the Master that I shall be in a position before long to come personally. But I have considered it essential to send Brother Epaphroditus, my co-worker and campaigner and your envoy and minister to my needs, because he misses you so, and frets because you had heard that he was ailing. Indeed he was ailing, almost at death's

---

[4] Perhaps with reference to the sin of Satan. Cp. Isa. xiv. 12-14 where the king of Babylon is charged with this sin under the figure of Lucifer. Moses is said to have had a divine form, and as an infant to have grasped at the crown on Pharaoh's head. See Jos. *Antiq.* II. ix. 7.

[5] The Spirit-Christ, the heavenly Archetype, became incarnate in the human body of Jesus. The two natures were merged after the resurrection, thus as Jesus-Christ exalting the name of Jesus as being thereafter the name of the Spirit-Christ. Cp. Rom. i. 4. p. 297.

[6] Deut. xxxii. 5.

[7] Cp. Dan. xii. 3.

[8] Referring to the practice of mutual congratulation by the worshippers at the close of the festal service.

door, but God took pity on him, and not only on him but on me too, that I should not have one distress upon another. So I have sent him more expeditiously, that in seeing him again you may have joy, and I less sorrow. Give him, therefore, a joyful welcome in the Master, and hold such as he in high regard, for in doing the Master's work he came so near death, jeopardizing his life to make good your lack of opportunity to serve me.

Finally, brothers, rejoice in the Master.[9]

Here are the particular things I must mention to you, where indeed I do not falter while you are firm.

Beware of the dogs! Beware of the cowardly workers! Beware of the Incision![10] Is is we who are the Circumcision, we who are in service to God's Spirit and exult in Jesus Christ, and place no reliance on the physical, though I could well do so. If anyone else thinks he may rely on the physical, I even more so, circumcised as I was on the eighth day, of the race of Israel, the tribe of Benjamin, a Hebrew sprung from Hebrews, in observances a Pharisee, as regards zeal a persecutor of the Community, as regards legal rectitude irreproachable. But the very things that were an asset to me, these I regarded as a dead loss on Christ's account. Indeed, I definitely regard everything as a dead loss because of the excellence of the knowledge of Christ Jesus my Master, for whom all is well lost, and I regard it as so much rubbish, that I may gain Christ, and be found in him, not with my own rectitude which derives from Law, but with that which is through faith in Christ, the rectitude which derives from God on a basis of faith. My concern is to know him, and the power of his resurrection, to have kinship with his sufferings, entering as closely as possible into the manner of his death, if by any means I may attain the resurrection from the dead. There is no question of my having already obtained it, or of having already been perfected. But I pursue, if I may but overtake, even as I was overtaken by Christ Jesus. Brothers, I do not reckon myself to have overtaken as yet. But there is this at least, forgetting what lies behind, and reaching out to what is ahead, I drive hard at the mark for the prize of God's high calling in Christ Jesus.[11] But if you feel differently about it God will surely make this plain to you. The main thing is, to whatever extent we have forged ahead, to keep on the same course.

Copy me, brothers, and pay close attention to those who behave as I have set the example. For there are many, as I have often told you, and now tell you even with tears, who behave as enemies of Christ's cross, whose end is destruction, whose god

---

[9] The tone of the letter changes abruptly at this point. What follows represents either an afterthought as a result of some piece of news or is part of a second letter.

[10] The 'Zealots for the Law' had been *incising* themselves into the Pauline communities, in the interest of *circumcising* the Gentiles. At the entrance to Roman houses the legend Cave Canem (Beware of the Dog) was often to be read.

[11] See illustration p. 265.

is their appetite, and whose glory is in their shame, whose minds are on earthly matters. But our form of government originates in heaven, from which source we expect a Deliverer, the Lord Jesus Christ, who will transform the body of our humble state so that it corresponds to his glorious body by the power which also enables him to bring everything under his control.

Therefore, dear and desired brothers, my joy and crown, stand fast in the Master, my dear ones. I beg Euodia and Syntyche to be likeminded in the Master. Yes, I also ask you, true Synsyge,[12] to bring these sisters in faith together, who aided me in the News with Clement and the other co-workers of mine, whose names are in the Book of Life.

Rejoice in the Master always. I repeat, rejoice! Let your moderation be known to everyone. The Master is at hand. Have no anxiety, but always make your requests known to God by prayer and supplication with thanksgiving; and God's peace, which towers above[13] all reasoning, will stand guard over your minds and thoughts in Christ Jesus.

Finally, brothers, whatever is honest, whatever is reputable, whatever is just, whatever is pure, whatever is likeable, whatever is elevated, if there is something virtuous or laudable, concentrate on such things. Practise all you have learnt and received and heard and seen in me, and the God of peace be with you.

I have rejoiced in the Master greatly that now at last your thought for me could be given fresh expression, for indeed you had always thought that way but lacked opportunity. It is not out of considerations of want that I am saying this, for I have learnt to manage however I am situated. I have had experience of being reduced in circumstances and of having ample. I have been through the whole curriculum, to be replete and to be hungry, to have ample and to go short. I can cope with everything by him who strengthens me. You have none the less done a kindness in associating yourselves with my difficulties. Let me tell you Philippians that in the early days of the News, when I left Macedonia, there was not a single community which associated itself with me in this matter of giving and getting other than yourselves, so that even at Thessalonica you sent once and again a contribution for my needs. It is not that I am looking for gifts. What I am looking for is the yield that swells your credit account. I have indeed enough and to spare. I am fully supplied, having received from Epaphroditus what your means allowed, a sweet-smelling perfume, an acceptable sacrifice, well-pleasing to God. My God in turn will supply every need of yours in Christ Jesus by his wealth in glory. To God our Father be praise for ever and ever. Amen.

[12] Playing on the meaning of the name, 'Yoke-fellow'.
[13] Like a dominating and protective fortress.

Give my regards to every saint in Christ Jesus. The brothers who are with me send you their regards. All the saints send you their regards, particularly those of Caesar's household.

May the loving-kindness of the Lord Jesus Christ be with your spirit.

———————◆———————

TO THE COMMUNITIES OF ASIA

(The Ephesian Copy)

(Probably written from Rome about A.D. 61 or 62)

Paul, by the will of God an envoy of Christ Jesus, to the saints resident in [*Ephesus*][14] and to the faithful in Christ Jesus. May peace and prosperity be yours from God our Father and the Lord Jesus Christ.

Blessed be the God and Father of our Lord Jesus Christ, who has blessed us with every spiritual blessing in the heavenly spheres in Christ, just as in him God made choice of us in love[15] before the universe was founded, that we should be holy and blameless in his presence. For he designated us in advance for adoption as his own through Jesus Christ, as it pleased his will, to the great renown of the loving-kindness with which he has favoured us in the Beloved. In Christ we have redemption by his blood, absolution from transgressions, by virtue of the wealth of loving-kindness which God has lavished upon us, in having made known to us in all wisdom and understanding,[16] as it pleased him, the secret of his intention, which he purposed in Christ, for that ultimate Government when he shall have brought everything under Christ's jurisdiction, both in heaven and on earth. Yes, under him, in whom we too have our allotted place, assigned us in advance, according to the plan of God who makes everything work out in accordance with his design and intention; so that we should be to his great renown who (as Jews) set our hope in advance on Christ. In him also you (Gentiles) after hearing the Message of Truth, the

[14] While in some MSS. Ephesus is given as the destination, in others it is omitted. The letter is clearly of a general character intended for communities in Asia not founded by Paul, and of which he had information, probably through Epaphras, see the letter to Colossae. These may particularly have been Laodicea and Hierapolis. The members were of Gentile origin. The letter could not therefore have been written especially to the Ephesian Christians, but a copy was evidently preserved at Ephesus.

[15] See *Ahabah* prayer, 'Blessed art thou, O Lord, who has chosen thy people Israel in love' (AJP, p. 46).

[16] *Amidah*, Bened. IV, 'Thou favourest man with knowledge' (AJP pp. 39-40).

News of your salvation, and after believing in him, were sealed with the holy Spirit of promise, which is the advance payment on our inheritance, the promise to redeem what was purchased, to God's great renown.

Consequently, I too, having heard of the faith you have in the Lord Jesus,[17] which is common to all the saints, never cease

Coin of Tarsus

Coin of Ephesus

Coin of Philippi

giving thanks on your account, making mention of you in my prayers, that the God of our Lord Jesus Christ, the Father of glory, may give you a spirit of wisdom and revelation to acquire knowledge of him. I pray that with your mental vision illumined you may know the nature of the hope of God's calling, what is the glorious wealth of his inheritance in the

[17] See the preceding page, n. 14.

saints, and the surpassing extent of his power available to us who have believed. This was indicated by the operation of the mighty force God employed in the case of Christ in raising him from the dead and seating him at his right hand in the heavenly spheres high above every angelic Rule and Authority, Power and Dominion, and every entity that has existence not only in this world but in that which is to come. He has indeed 'put everything under his feet'[18] and over and above has given him headship of the Community, which is his body, the full dimension of him who fills the entire universe.[19]

You Gentiles too were once dead in the trespasses and sins in which you lived in conformity with the Aeon[20] of this world, the Archon[20] of the government of the lower atmosphere, the spirit of him who now animates the Children of Disobedience. We likewise, all we Jews, were once tarred with the same brush in the indulgence of our physical passions, fulfilling our physical desires and inclinations, and by nature Children of Wrath like the rest. But God being full of compassion because of the great love he had for us even when we were dead in trespasses, has brought us all back to life with Christ—it is by mercy you have been preserved—and has raised us up together, and seated us together in the heavenly spheres in Christ Jesus. For it is in mercy that you have been preserved through faith, not in any way by your own efforts, not by your own deeds—it is God's gift so that no one should boast. We are entirely his handiwork, created in Christ Jesus for those good deeds with which God pre-arranged that we should be occupied.

So bear in mind that you were once Gentiles in the physical sense, who are termed the Uncircumcision by those termed in respect of an operation in the flesh the Circumcision, because at that time you were without benefit of Christ, aliens to the body politic of Israel, and strangers to the covenants of promise. But now in Christ Jesus you who were once far off have been brought near by the blood of Christ. For he is our peacemaker, who has united both Jew and Gentile, having demolished the dividing partition-wall, and having in his person neutralized the cause of enmity, the Law of commandments set down in ordinances, so that the two should be welded in him into one new man, so making peace. Thus he has reconciled both to God by one body through the cross, having killed in his own person the enmity, and by his coming has brought news of 'peace to you the far off, and peace to the near',[21] be-

---

[18] Ps. viii. 6.

[19] It was believed that the Primordial Man, the Heavenly Man, stretched from earth to heaven. Christ and the Church are here the head and body of this Heavenly Man. See further p. 328, n. 28.

[20] Spirit powers subordinate to Beliar, the evil force controlling the existing world order.

[21] Isa. lix. 19. In the spiritual sense the Gentiles, barred in the Temple from the Court of Israel, have been given access by the blood of Christ.

cause through him by one Spirit we both have access to the Father.

So now you are strangers and foreigners no longer, but fellow-citizens of the saints, parts of God's house, having been built upon the foundation of the envoys and prophets with Christ Jesus himself as the coping-stone, where each block having been closely fitted together[22] grows course on course into a sacred fane in the Master, into which you too have been built as a spiritual abode of God.

To this end I, Paul, am the prisoner of Christ Jesus for you Gentiles. You must surely have heard of the administration of God's mercy granted me for your benefit, how by revelation he acquainted me with the secret, as I have briefly stated it above.[23] From this you may gather how well-versed I am in the Messianic mystery, which in other generations was never made known to mankind as now revealed under inspiration to God's holy envoys and prophets, the secret that by the News the Gentiles were to be joint-heirs, jointly incorporated, and joint-participants in the promise in Christ Jesus. Of this News I was made minister, by the gift of God's mercy granted me in accordance with the operation of his power. To me the least of all saints was this privilege given, that I should proclaim to the Gentiles the inexhaustible wealth of Christ, and publish the details of the secret kept hidden from the Aeons[24] by God who created all things; so that the wisdom of God in all its multitudinous aspects should now be made known through the Community to the Rulers and Authorities in the heavenly spheres, in accordance with the Plan of the Ages which God formed in Christ Jesus our Master. In him, by faith in him, we enter God's presence boldly and confidently. So I beg you not to take hardly my trials on your behalf, which are an honour to you.

To this end I bend my knees to the Father, from whom every order of being both in heaven and on earth derives its existence, that in accordance with the wealth of his glory he may grant you by his Spirit to be powerfully strengthened in the inner self, that the Christ may make his abode in your minds by faith, that being deep-rooted and well-founded in love you may be able to grasp with all the saints what is the Breadth, the Length, the Depth and the Height, that you may know, what indeed surpasses knowledge, the love of Christ, that you may be filled with the immensity of God.

Now to him who is supremely powerful to do infinitely more than we can ask or think, in accordance with the power that operates in us, to him be glory in the Community and in Christ Jesus to all generations for ever and ever. Amen.

---

[22] In the Temple at Jerusalem no mortar was used. The stones were closely fitted together.

[23] Above p. 324.

[24] According to Paul it had not been disclosed that Gentiles, by faith, were to form an integral part of the Messianic Community, the People of God.

I entreat you therefore, I the Master's prisoner, to behave in a manner worthy of the calling with which you have been called, with all humility and gentleness, with long-suffering, being patient with one another in love, striving to keep unity of spirit by the binding force of peace. There is one Body and one Spirit, just as you were called with one expectation of your calling, one Master, one Faith, one Immersion, one God and Father of all, and through all, and in all. And to each one of us there has been granted some favour corresponding to the extent of Christ's bounty, as it is stated,

> Having ascended on high he made captivity captive,
> and bestowed gifts on men.[25]

That he ascended implies that he also descended into the lower regions of the earth.[26] He who descended is the same as he who ascended to the uppermost part of the heavens,[27] that he might fill the universe. To some he gave gifts as envoys, some as prophets, some as preachers, some as pastors and teachers, for the training of the saints, for the work of administration, and the development of the Body of Christ, until we all reach unity of faith and knowledge of the Son of God, the Perfect Man, the measure of the stature of the full-grown Christ.[28] No longer should we be infants, tossed on the waves and swept this way and that by every wind of doctrine by the facile knavery of men practised in the contrivance of deceit, but speaking the truth in love we should grow up collectively to him, Christ, who is the Head, from whom the whole Body closely joined together and knit by every connecting joint, corresponding to the respective action of each separate part, the growth of the Body is promoted for its harmonious development.

This then I say and solemnly declare in the Master, that you are no longer to behave as the Gentiles behave in the levity of their minds. They, having their intellect dimmed, being aliens to the divine life through their ignorance and the obtuseness of their minds, being lost to decent feelings, have given themselves over to licentiousness, to indulge in every kind of impurity with avidity. But you have not so learnt what Christ means—that is if you have attended to him, and been instructed by him, as the truth is in Jesus—namely, that you should abandon what accords with the former mode of life of the old degenerate personality with its treacherous lusts, that you should have the temper of your minds renovated, and put on the new personality fashioned after God in rectitude and the sanctity of truth.

So abandoning falsehood 'let each speak the truth to his fellow.'[29] 'Be angry, yet sin not.'[30] Let the sun not set on your

---

[25] Ps. lxviii. 18.
[26] In the early Christian *Odes of Solomon* the descent of Christ to the underworld is described as the Head going down to the Feet. (*Ode* xxiii. 14.)
[27] The Seventh Heaven.
[28] Here the Body is to grow up to the Head, to the stature of the universe-filling Christ. See JE, Art. *Adam Kadmon.*
[29] Zech. viii. 6.   [30] Ps. xxxvii. 8.

anger, nor give the Devil his opportunity. Let him that stole steal no more. Instead let him toil, putting his hands to worthy employment that he may have something to give to any in need. Let no foul language pass your lips, only what is good for some constructive purpose, that it may give pleasure to the listeners. And do not grieve God's holy Spirit by which you have been sealed for the Day of Redemption. Put aside all bitterness and passion, anger, vituperation and abuse, and every kind of malice. Instead be kindly disposed to one another, large-hearted, merciful to each other as God in Christ has been merciful to you. Follow God's example, then, as dear children, and behave with affection, just as Christ loved you and offered himself for you as 'an offering and sacrifice of pleasing odour to God'. But let there be no mention among you of vice and any kind of impurity or lechery, as befits saints, nor obscenity, levity, or facetiousness, which are unbecoming. Preferably let there be thanksgiving. You surely know this, that no immoral person, nor impure, nor rapacious, which means an idol-worshipper, shall have any inheritance in the Kingdom of Christ and of God.

Let no one beguile you with empty words, for because of this the wrath of God falls upon the Children of Disobedience. Do not be of their company therefore; for though once you belonged to darkness, now in the Master you belong to light. Behave like Children of the Light[31]—the Light that has its fruit in every kind of goodness, in uprightness and honesty—approving what is acceptable to the Master. And have no fellowship with the unfruitful works of darkness, but rather refute them, though it is shameful to speak of the things such people do in secret. For whatever is refuted has light thrown upon it, since all visibility is due to light. This is why it is stated,

> 'Rouse yourself, sleeper,
> And arise from the dead,
> And Christ will shine on you![32]

Pay strict attention, therefore, to the way you behave, as wise people, not unwise, using the time profitably, for these are evil days. So do not be stupid, but comprehending, as to what are the Master's wishes. And do not get drunk with wine, in which is sottishness, but be filled spiritually, chanting psalms and hymns and spiritual odes, singing and making melody in your hearts to the Lord, above all invariably giving thanks to God the Father in the name of our Lord Jesus Christ.

Be submissive to one another in the fear of Christ, the wives to their husbands as to the Master; for man is the head of woman as Christ is the Head of the Community, being as he is preserver of the Body. But as the Community is subject to

---

[31] A term used by the Jewish pietists to denote the Elect.
[32] The early Christians like the Essenes used to sing hymns at dawn in praise of the 'Sun of righteousness', and these lines may be taken from one such hymn. See also Jn. i. 1-17, p. 389, n. 1.

Christ, so should wives be to their husbands in every way. Husbands, love your wives, even as Christ loved the Community and gave himself for her sake, that he might consecrate her, having been cleansed by the ritual bath of water,[33] so to speak, that he might take the Community to himself as a bride to be proud of, not having a spot[34] or wrinkle, or anything of the kind, as well as being chaste and unblemished. So ought husbands to cherish their wives as their own bodies. He who cherishes his wife cherishes himself; for no one ever hated his own flesh, but cares for and tends it, as indeed Christ does the Community, since we are members of his body. 'For this cause a man shall leave father and mother, and unite with his wife, and the two shall be one flesh.'[35] This is a great mystery: I am speaking here of the relationship of Christ and the Community. Just so every one of you too should thus love his wife as himself; and the wife should respect her husband.

Children, obey your parents, for it is rightly said, 'Honour your father and your mother',[36] which is the first commandment with a promise attached to it, namely, 'that it may be well with you, and that you may live long on the earth'. And you fathers, do not provoke your children, but bring them up in the discipline and admonition of the Lord.[37]

Slaves, obey those who in the physical sense are your masters with fear and trembling in singleness of mind as you obey Christ, not with service meant to catch the eye, like those who want to ingratiate themselves, but as slaves of Christ carrying out God's behests. Give service with real goodwill, as having the Lord in mind rather than men, knowing that each one, whether slave or freeman, has whatever good he may do treasured up by the Lord. And you masters, act in the same way towards your slaves, refraining from threats, knowing that both their and your Master is in heaven, and that with him there is no partiality.

Finally, make yourselves strong in the Lord and in the power of his might. Array yourselves in the full armour of God, so that you may stand up to the cunning of the Adversary. For we are not contending with mortals but with angelic Rulers and Authorities, with the Overlords of this dark state, the spiritual forces of evil in the heavenly spheres. Therefore take to yourselves the full armour of God that you may be able to withstand in the evil day, and having overcome completely to go on standing. Stand, therefore, with your loins girded with truth,[38] clad in the corselet of rectitude,[39] with your feet shod with the sureness of the News of peace.[40] To complete your equipment, hold before you the shield of faith with which you will be able to

---

[33] Baptism, under the figure of the ritual bath of purification taken by Jewish women, here prior to the marriage ceremony, *kiddushin* (consecration).
[34] Cp. Cant. iv. 7.
[35] Gen. ii. 24.
[36] Exod. xx. 12.
[37] Cp. Gen. xviii. 19.
[38] Cp. Isa. xi. 5.
[39] Cp. Isa. lix. 17.
[40] Cp. Isa. lii 7.

extinguish the flaming darts of the Evil One, and take the helmet of preservation, and the sword of the Spirit—which means God's Word. Pray at all times in the Spirit with every kind of petition and supplication for all the saints, being intent on this with all diligence and entreaty, and on my behalf, that fluent speech may be given me boldly to make known the mystery, on account of which I am an ambassador in chains, that even so placed I may speak as boldly as it behoves me to speak.

But so that you too may know the state of my affairs, how I fare, Tychicus,[41] that dear brother and loyal minister in the Master, will fully inform you. I have dispatched him to you for this express purpose, that you may know my concerns and that he may cheer your hearts.

Peace be with the brothers, and affection with faith, from God the Father and the Lord Jesus Christ. May prosperity be the portion of all who love our Lord Jesus Christ unfeignedly.

TO THE COMMUNITY AT COLOSSAE

(Place and time of writing as for the previous letter)

Paul, by the will of God an envoy of Christ Jesus, with Brother Timotheus, to the saints and faithful brothers in Christ at Colossae. May peace and prosperity be yours from God our Father.

I thank God, the Father of our Lord Jesus Christ, and invariably pray for you, having heard of your faith in Christ Jesus and the affection you have for all the saints on account of the Hope that lies before you in heaven. This Hope you first heard expressed in the True Message of the News, which reached you, as it has reached everywhere else in the world, producing fruit and increasing, again as it has done among you, from the very day you heard it and became truly conscious of God's mercy as you learnt it from our dear fellow-servant Epaphras. He is a faithful minister of Christ on your behalf, who also has informed me of your spiritual affection.

Accordingly, I too, from the day I heard, have never ceased to pray for you, and to request that you may be filled with the knowledge of God's will in all wisdom and spiritual comprehension, so as to behave in a manner worthy of the Master to his entire satisfaction by every good deed you do, producing fruit and increasing in the knowledge of God, endued by his glorious power with every capacity for much patience and long-suffering with joy.

I give thanks to the Father, who has qualified you to share

[41] The bearer of the letter, as also of the one to Colossae. He was one of Paul's lieutenants and emissaries.

the lot of the saints in Light, who has rescued us from the domination of Darkness and transferred us to the Kingdom of his dear Son, by whom we obtain redemption, absolution from our sins. He is the image of the Unseen God, the firstborn of all creation, that everything in heaven and earth might be founded on him, seen and unseen alike, whether angelic Thrones or Lordships or Rulers or Authorities. Everything was created through him and for him. He is the antecedent of everything, and on him everything was framed.[42] So also is he Head of the Body, the Community, that is to say, the fount and origin of it, the first-born from the dead, that in every connexion he might take precedence. For it pleased God that by him the whole should be governed, and through him—his making peace by the blood of his cross—to bring everything once more into harmony with himself,[43] whether on earth or in heaven. You yourselves were formerly alienated and hostile in attitude when engaged in evil deeds; but now Christ has reconciled you to God in his physical body by death, so as to present you before God chaste, blameless and irreproachable, assuming that you remain firm and unmoved in the Faith, and do not deviate from the Hope of the News which you have heard, which has been proclaimed to every creature under heaven, and of which I, Paul, was made a minister.

So I rejoice in my sufferings for your sake, and make good in my flesh the deficiencies of the Messianic Woes[44] for the sake of Christ's body, namely the Community, of which I was made a minister, in accordance with God's mandate granted me for you, to give effect to God's Message, the secret kept hidden from all ages and generations, but now published to his saints. To them God would make known what wealth of glory this secret holds for the Gentiles, namely Christ in you, the expectation of glory. He it is whom we proclaim, advising everyone and teaching everyone with all wisdom, that we may present everyone perfect in Christ. That is what I toil for, striving with his energy who so powerfully motivates me. Indeed, I wish you to know what a severe trial I am undergoing on your account, and on account of those at Laodicea, and of as many others as have never seen me personally, that their minds may be encouraged, being confirmed in their love and in the solid wealth of absolute certainty in knowledge of God's secret, yes of Christ himself, in whom are hidden all the treasures of wisdom and knowledge. I say this in case anyone should mislead you with specious arguments. For even if I am absent physically I am nevertheless with you in spirit, observing with pleasure your good order and the solidarity of your faith in Christ.

As, therefore, you have accepted Christ Jesus as Master, behave in his way, base yourselves and build yourselves on him,

[42] That is, on the model of the Heavenly Man, the Archetype of the Universe.
[43] I.e. with God.
[44] The 'Pangs of Messiah' which were to precede the birth of the Messianic Era.

and maintain yourselves in the Faith as you have been taught it, excelling in it with thanksgiving. Take care that no one gets hold of you with philosophy and worthless craft belonging to human tradition, to the elemental forces of the world instead of to Christ; for it is in him that the immensity of the divine wisdom corporately dwells, and it is in him—Head of all Rulers and Authorities—that you are made complete. It is in him too that you have been pared by a circumcision not man-made, by the stripping away of the physical body, by Christ's kind of circumcision, being buried with him by immersion. In him equally you have been raised up by faith in the might of God, who raised him from the dead. And you who were dead in transgressions and in your physical uncircumcision God has brought to life with him, having forgiven us all our transgressions. He not only cancelled the writ against us with its stipulations, which was adverse to us, but also took it right away, nailing it to the cross. After having despoiled the angelic Rulers and Authorities, he paraded them in public, having led them in triumph by the cross.[45]

Let no one judge you, therefore, in matters of food and drink, or in such a matter as a festival, new moon, or sabbath, which represent only a shadow of things to come, and of which Christ is the substance. Let no one arbitrarily influence you to fast and engage in the worship of angels,[46] inducing you to share his visions, being vainly puffed up by his physical mind and not holding to the Head, from whom the whole Body, connected and integrated by the joints and ligaments, grows in God's way.

If you have died with Christ to the elemental forces of the world, why as though still living in the world are you controlled by stipulations—'Do not handle! Do not taste! Do not touch!' which implies that everything contaminates[47] by its use—in accordance with human commandments and doctrines? Such prescriptions, indeed, seem to have some sense in them in subordination of the will, fasting and asceticism, but they are not really efficacious against physical indulgence.

If, therefore, you have been raised up with Christ, seek the things that are on high where Christ is, seated at God's right hand. Set your minds on the things that are above, not on what is on earth; for you have died, and your life has been secreted with Christ in God. When Christ, who enshrines our life, is revealed, then you too will be revealed with him in glory.

So treat your organs on earth as dead for fornication, impurity, lust, unlawful desire, and rapacity, which means idol-worship, things that bring the wrath of God. In such things you too once indulged when you led that kind of life. But now

[45] By dying a felon's death Christ not only lifted the curse of the legal statutes which made everyone guilty, but completely turned the tables, and by the cross triumphed over the angelic powers who had drawn up the Law. Cp. Gal. iii. 13, 19, p. 260, n. 50.
[46] The heavenly hierarchy very prominent in Jewish esoteric lore.
[47] Or 'sends to perdition'.

you must discard all alike, anger, rage, malice, abuse, foul-language. Do not lie to one another, having divested yourselves of the former man and his deeds, and having put on the new man, renovated in knowledge, in conformity with the likeness[48] of God who created him, where there can be no question of Greek and Jew, circumcision and uncircumcision, Barbarian, Scythian, slave or freeman, but of Christ wholly and completely. Put on, therefore, as God's Elect, saints and beloved ones, feelings of compassion, benevolence, humility, gentleness, long-suffering, bearing with one another and forgiving one another should any have a complaint against another. As the Lord has forgiven you, do you also forgive. And over and above these qualities put on love, which represents the band[49] that gives the finishing touch. And let Christ's peace direct your minds, the peace to which you were called as one Body. And be thankful. Let the Message of Christ dwell in you richly in all its wisdom, teaching and admonishing one another graciously by psalms, hymns and spiritual odes, singing to God in your hearts. And whatever you do by word or deed, do it all in the name of the Lord Jesus, giving thanks to God the Father by him.

Wives, be submissive to your husbands as is befitting in the Master. Husbands, love your wives and do not treat them harshly. Children, obey your parents in everything, for this is well-pleasing in the Master. Fathers, do not fret your children, in case they should be discouraged. Slaves, in everything obey those who are in the physical sense your masters, not with service that catches the eye like those who wish to ingratiate themselves, but in singleness of mind, fearing the Lord. Whatever you do, do it with real goodwill, as having the Lord in mind rather than men, knowing that you will receive from the Lord the recompense that is due. Serve the Lord Christ; for he who does wrong will be paid back for his wrong-doing, and there is no partiality shown. Masters, treat your slaves equitably and fairly, knowing that you too have a Master in heaven.

Apply yourselves constantly to prayer, being incited to it by thankfulness. At the same time pray for me, that God may give me opportunity for speech, to declare the secret of Christ on account of which I am fettered, that I should disclose it as it behoves me to speak. Behave with circumspection towards those who are 'outside', using the time profitably. Invariably let your speech be gracious, flavoured with salt, that you may know how to answer all and sundry.

As to my affairs, Tychicus, that dear brother and loyal minister and fellow-servant in the Master, will fully inform you. I have dispatched him to you for this express purpose, that you may know how I fare and that he may cheer your hearts, and with him faithful and dear brother Onesimus,[50] who is one of yourselves. They will tell you of all that goes on here.

[48] I.e. Christ, as the image of God.   [49] Either head-band or girdle.
[50] See the letter to Philemon.

My fellow-prisoner Aristarchus sends you his regards, as does Barnabas's relative Mark—about whom you have been advised: welcome him should he visit you—and so does Jesus known as Justus. They belong to the Circumcision, and they alone have been my co-workers for the Kingdom of God: they have been a great comfort to me. Epaphras, one of yourselves, a servant of Christ Jesus, sends you his regards. Invariably he contends for you at prayer times that you may stand, sound and fully assured, by the whole will of God. I can testify that he has put up a great fight for you, and for those of Laodicea and Hierapolis. Dear Doctor Luke sends you his regards, and so does Demas.

Give my regards to the brothers at Laodicea, also to Nympha and the community in her house. When this letter has been read by you arrange also for it to be read in the Laodicean community, and get their letter from Laodicea,[51] that you too may read it. And tell Archippus, 'See to it that you carry out the ministry you have received in the Master!'

My regards in my own hand,

PAUL.

Remember my fetters![52] Wishing you every happiness.

TO PHILEMON

(Written from Rome about A.D. 62)

Paul, prisoner of Christ Jesus, with Brother Timotheus, to our dear friend and co-worker Philemon, to our sister Apphia, to our fellow-campaigner Archippus,[53] and to the community in your house. May peace and prosperity be yours from God our Father and the Lord Jesus Christ.

Invariably I thank God, making mention of you in my prayers, learning of the affection and loyalty you have for the Lord Jesus and for all the saints, whereby the fellowship of your faith may prove effective in securing knowledge of every good thing that is ours in Christ. I have indeed been given much happiness and encouragement by your affection, brother, because through you the hearts of the saints have been refreshed.

Consequently, while regarding myself in Christ as quite at liberty to insist on the point, yet out of affection I prefer to appeal to you, being such as I am, that old man Paul, and also at present a prisoner of Christ Jesus. It is for a son of mine I appeal to you, one whom I have begotten in my bonds, Onesimus, who was previously worthless to you, but now is of very real worth both to you and me. I have sent him back to you,

[51] Either the letter to Asia known as Ephesians, or another which has not been preserved.
[52] I.e. in prayer.
[53] Mentioned at the close of the letter to Colossae.

which means I have parted with my own heart. I would much rather have kept him with me, so that he might have served me in your stead in the bonds of the News; but I did not wish to do anything without your consent, in case your kindness might seem obligatory instead of voluntary. Perhaps the reason he was parted from you for a while may be that you might have him wholly ever after, no longer as just a slave, but over and above a slave as a dear brother, particularly to me, but how much more so to you with a physical tie as well as in the Master?

So if you regard me as a kinsman, receive him as you would myself. If he has wronged you or owes you anything put that down to my account. I, Paul, put this in my own handwriting, 'I will make full restitution'. Need I say to you that you really owe me your own self? Well, brother, let me have some profit[54] out of you in the Master! Refresh *my* heart in Christ.

I am writing to you in full confidence of your compliance, knowing that you will do even more than I ask. At the same time prepare to have me also as your guest, for I anticipate that through your prayers I shall be granted to you.

My fellow-prisoner Epaphras[55] sends you his regards in Christ Jesus. So do my fellow-workers[56] Mark, Aristarchus, Demas and Luke.

The loving-kindness of our Lord Jesus Christ be with your spirit.

TO TITUS

(Probably written from Rome in A.D. 62)

Paul, servant of God, an envoy of Jesus Christ for purposes of faith of God's Elect, and for the knowledge of the Truth as it concerns devoutness in prospect of Eternal Life, which the never false God promised in the remote past and in due course revealed by his Message with the proclamation of which I have been entrusted by order of God our Saviour, to Titus my true son in our common Faith. May peace and prosperity be yours from God the Father and Christ Jesus our deliverer.

I left you in Crete with good reason, to tie up what loose ends were left and to ordain elders for each town as I directed you, assuming there is someone of blameless character, husband of one wife, having believing children, someone not open to the charge of profligacy or disorderliness. [For the supervisor should be irreproachable, as God's appointed steward, not domineering, not irritable, not a tippler, not a brawler, not mercenary, but open-handed, one who cares for goodness, is

[54] Playing on the name Onesimus, meaning 'serviceable', Onesimus had apparently run away from service with his master Philemon.
[55] See above p. 335.
[56] All these individuals are referred to in the letter to Colossae.

discreet, just, consecrated, disciplined, a close adherent of the trustworthy Message in terms of the Teaching, so that he may be able to exhort by sound instruction and confute opponents.][57] For there are many disorderly vapourizers and bamboozlers, particularly those from the Circumcision, people who must be muzzled, the kind who subvert whole households, teaching things they have no business to do from mercenary motives. One of themselves, an exponent of their own,[58] has said.

The Cretans, ever cheats, brute beasts and idle windbags.[59]

That is a true description. For that very reason rebuke them sharply, that they may be sound in the Faith, paying no heed to Jewish myths and enactments of men who have turned away from the truth. To the pure everything is pure, but to the polluted and unbelieving nothing is pure, because both their minds and consciences are warped. They profess to know God, but by their actions they disown him, being disgusting and mutinous, hopeless for any useful service.

It is for you to state what is consistent with sound teaching, to tell the older men to be sober, dignified, discreet, sound in faith, in love, in constancy. Tell the older women similarly to maintain a condition suited to a reverent nature, not to be spiteful, not addicted to drink, givers of good advice, so that they may influence the young women to be devoted to husband and children, to be sensible, chaste, domesticated, decent, submissive to their husbands, that God's Message may not come into disrepute. In the same way exhort the young men to be temperate. In every connexion you yourself should set an example of good behaviour, by purity of teaching, plain sense, and sound principles that cannot be impugned, so that he who is against us may respect our position, finding nothing detrimental to say about us.[60]

Slaves should be in subjection to their masters, giving entire satisfaction, not answering back, not pilfering, but giving proof of complete trustworthiness, that in every way they may be a credit to the teaching of God our Saviour. For God's mercy saving all men has displayed itself, instructing us that, abandoning impiety and worldly passions, we should live temperately, justly and devoutly in the present time, waiting for the blessed Hope and visible manifestation of the glory of the Great God and of our Deliverer Jesus Christ, who gave himself for us to free us from all our iniquities and to purify for himself a special people[61] eager for honest employment.

Declare these things, exhort and reprove, with every possible authority. Let no one treat you casually. Remind them to be

[57] This passage appears to be an interpolation or added note, and breaks the continuity of thought.
[58] Epimenides, Cretan poet and philosopher, in his poem on *Oracles*, quoted by Callimachus, *Hymn to Zeus*, 8.
[59] 'Windbags' (lit. paunches).
[60] Cp. Acts xxviii. 22. It is clear that already the Christians were in bad odour.
[61] Cp. Ezek. xxxvii. 23; Deut. xiv. 2.

subject to rulers and authorities, to be law-abiding, ready for every useful service, in no way abusive, to be free from pugnacity, equable, always exhibiting a mild demeanour towards everyone. I myself was once lacking in sense, ungovernable, erratic, a slave to various passions and pleasures, spending my time in resentment and jealousy, gloomy, hating others. But when the goodness and benevolence of God our Saviour became clear, not because of any righteous actions I had performed, but in accordance with his mercy, he saved me by the washing of rebirth and the renovating power of the holy Spirit which he lavished on me richly through Jesus Christ our Deliverer; so that being exonerated by that act of grace I became an heir in accordance with the expectation of Eternal Life.

This is a true saying, and I want you to be very positive about it, that 'Those who have believed in God should be concerned to offer themselves for honest employment'. This is a proper and helpful thing for men to do. But avoid foolish issues and genealogies, wrangles and legal quibbles; for they are unhelpful and senseless. Have no more to do with the dissentient man after giving him a first and second warning, seeing that anyone like this has turned away and erred deliberately, and stands self-condemned.

When I dispatch Artemas to you, or Tychicus,[62] do your utmost to come to me at Nicopolis, for I have decided to pass the winter there.[63] Afford the lawyer Zenas and Apollos every facility for their journey, so that they are short of nothing. Our people must really learn to offer themselves for honest employment to meet essential needs, so that they are not unproductive.

All here send you their regards. My regards to those who truly esteem me.

Wishing you all every happiness.

TO TIMOTHEUS (1)

(Probably written from Rome in A.D. 63)

Paul, envoy of Christ Jesus by appointment of God our Saviour and of Christ Jesus our Hope, to Timotheus my true son in faith. May prosperity, mercy and peace be yours from God the Father and Christ Jesus our Master.

As I begged you when you were leaving for Macedonia,[64] do stay on at Ephesus to impress on some there not to teach different doctrine, nor to concern themselves with myths and in-

---

[62] Bearer of the letters to Asia and Colossae. It is suggested that the Nicopolis where Paul proposed to spend the winter, assuming he was released, was the one in Epirus on the western coast of Greece.

[63] At the time of writing Paul evidently believed he would be at liberty to travel again. He had previously expressed his confidence in this more definitely in the letter to Philemon. On the whole it appears unlikely that he ever left Rome, though some read the text here and in I. Tim. in the sense that he did.

[64] Timotheus appears to have gone from Rome to Ephesus, and at Paul's request remained there.

terminable genealogies, matters which raise issues rather than
promote the divine government which rests on faith. The
essence of the precept still is love,[65] love out of a pure heart, a
clear conscience, and unfeigned faith. From these some, having
missed the mark, have gone off at a tangent into senseless talk,
wanting to be teachers of the Law, but neither understanding
what they are talking about, nor what they are really driving at.
We all know how valuable the Law is if it is consulted legiti-
mately. But we recognize none the less that the Law is not put
there for the upright, but for the lawless and refractory, the
impious and the sinners, the ungodly and profane, patricides
and matricides, those guilty of manslaughter, vicious persons,
homosexuals, man-traffickers, liars, perjurers, and whatever
else it may be that is opposed to sound teaching in conformity
with the News of the glory of the Blessed God with which I
have been entrusted.

I feel deeply grateful to the one who has empowered me, to
Christ Jesus our Master, that he considered me sufficiently
trustworthy to take into service, I who previously had been a
slanderer, a persecutor, and a man of violence. But I obtained
mercy because I acted unwittingly in unbelief; but our Master's
loving-kindness, together with the faith and love that is in
Christ Jesus, was more than adequate.

This is a true saying and deserving of unqualified acceptance,
that 'Christ Jesus came into the world to save sinners'. Of these
I am the foremost. But I obtained mercy for the very reason
that by me Christ Jesus might exhibit his full forbearance as a
general indication to those who would come to believe in him
for Eternal Life. To the imperishable invisible King of the
Universe, the Only God, be honour and glory for ever and
ever. Amen.

This signal[66] I transmit to you, son Timotheus, in conformity
with the prognostications about you, that in their sense you
may set out to wage a gallant campaign, in possession of faith
and a clear conscience, a campaign which some having declined have come to grief over the Faith. Among these are
Hymenaeus and Alexander, whom I have consigned to Satan
that they may be disciplined not to speak profanely.

In the first place, therefore, I require that petitions, prayers,
intercessions and thanksgivings be offered for everyone, for
kings and all holding positions of authority,[67] so that we may
pass a quiet and tranquil life in all godliness and gravity. This
is proper and well-pleasing in the sight of God our Saviour, who
desires everyone to be saved and come to acknowledge the
Truth. There is One God, and one intermediary between God
and Man, the man Christ Jesus, who gave himself as a ransom
for all, as will be proved in due course. To announce this I was

[65] Deut. vi. 5.
[66] The saying just quoted. Here and in the words that follow Paul uses the metaphor
of a military expedition by sea.
[67] See above p. 312, n. 258.

made a herald and envoy—I am telling the truth, I am not lying—a faithful and true teacher of the Gentiles.

I therefore desire the men everywhere to offer prayer, raising holy hands free from passion and controversy. Similarly, their wives should dress themselves unobtrusively, with modesty and moderation, not adorning themselves with lace and gold or pearl embroidery or expensive material, but with what is becoming for women professing to be religious, with kind actions. Let a wife learn passively with complete submissiveness. I do not permit a wife to teach, nor to exercise a husband's prerogative, but to be passive. For Adam was formed first, and then Eve. And it was not Adam who was beguiled, but the woman being completely beguiled fell into transgression. Yet she shall be saved by childbearing,[68] provided the couple remain faithful, affectionate and devoted, and also practice moderation.

This is a true saying, 'If anyone aspires to be a supervisor he desires honourable employment'. The supervisor ought therefore to be irreproachable, husband of one wife, sober, temperate, mannerly, hospitable, a good teacher, not truculent, nor pugnacious, but equable, pacific, free from avarice, managing his own household wisely, keeping his children in order with all gravity. For if anyone does not know how to manage his own household, how is he to take charge of God's community? He should not be a recent convert, in case by becoming conceited he meets with the Devil's fate. He ought also to be well spoken of by those 'outside', in case he falls into disrepute and the Devil's snare.

Administrators likewise should be grave, not gossipers, not addicted to liberal potations, not money-grubbers, holding the mystery of the Faith with a clear conscience. They should also first be on probation: then let them act as administrators when proved satisfactory. Their wives too should be grave, never malicious, sober, entirely reliable. Let administrators remain married to one wife, managing their children and their own households well. For those who act well as administrators acquire an influential status and great liberty of speech for the Faith that is in Christ Jesus.

I am writing you in this way, hoping to visit you shortly, but in case I am delayed, that you may know how life ought to be lived in the house of God, which is the Community of the Living God, the prop and stay of the Truth. Admittedly it is a great thing this mystery of devoutness, which in Christ[69]

> *Was made visible physically,*
> *Vindicated spiritually,*
> *Seen by angels,*
> *Proclaimed to the Gentiles,*
> *Believed in in the world,*
> *Taken up again in glory.*[70]

[68] Gen. iii. 16.   [69] 'Which in Christ' the text simply says 'who'.
[70] Possibly from a Christian hymn.

Now the Spirit categorically declares, 'In the latter times some will desert the Faith, paying attention to misleading spirits and pronouncements of demons, speaking falsely with intent to deceive',[71] having their own conscience seared, forbidding marriage, and requiring abstention from foods which God has created to be partaken of with thanksgiving by those who believe and fully understand the truth. For every provision of God is good, and by no means to be refused if it is accepted with thanksgiving; for it is consecrated by the recitation of the grace of God.

If you put these things to the brothers you will be a worthy minister of Christ Jesus, primed in the principles of the Faith and in the right teaching which you have consistently followed. But deprecate irreverent matters and old wives' tales. Train yourself for devoutness. 'Physical training is of limited usefulness, but devoutness is of unlimited usefulness, providing assurance both for the present life and for that which is to come.' This is a true saying and deserving of unqualified acceptance. That is why we toil and strive, because we have fixed our hope on the Living God, who is the Saviour of all men, particularly of believers. Impress and teach these things.

Let no one despise your youth; but set an example to believers by speech, by behaviour, by love, by faith, by purity. Devote yourself, until I come, to exposition, exhortation and instruction. Do not neglect the gift you have, which was bestowed on you by a prophetic intimation which accompanied your ordination by the elders. Exercise and develop these facilities, that your progress may be marked by all. Keep a firm hold on yourself and on the doctrine. Be true to them; for by doing so you will save both yourself and those who listen to you.

Do not reprimand an elder, but appeal to him as if he were your father, and to the younger men as brothers, to the older women as your mother, and to the younger women chastely as sisters. Care for widows who are lone widows. But where a widow has children or grandchildren let those first learn to discharge their filial duty and to make suitable return to the authors of their being, for this is well-pleasing in God's sight. But the lone and solitary widow has her hope in God, and gives herself to prayers and petitions night and day. The fast-living woman, however, is dead in life. Impress these things on them, that they may be irreproachable. So if any man does not provide for his own relations, and especially his own family, he has disavowed the Faith and is worse than an unbeliever.

Do not let a widow be put on the register[72] at a lower age than sixty, a woman who has been the wife of one husband, with testimonials to her kind actions, such as that she has brought up children, given hospitality to strangers, washed the feet of saints, relieved those in distress, or has been responsible for

71 Cp. Dan. viii. 23-26; Mt. xxiv. 10-12.
72 To receive communal support.

some other good deed. But decline to register the younger widows; for when they become capricious towards Christ they want to marry, earning condemnation for disregarding the first claim on their allegiance. At the same time they learn to be idle, going the round of houses; and not only to be idle, but also gossipers and meddlers, talking about what is none of their business. I therefore prefer the younger women to marry, to have children, keep house, and give no kind of pretext to the ill-disposed to indulge in abuse; for already some have gone off the road after Satan. Should any believers have widows to look after, let them give the assistance and not burden the community, so that lone widows may be provided for.

Let the elders who govern well be treated as deserving of twice as much consideration, particularly those who are occupied with speaking and instruction. The Scripture truly says, 'You are not to muzzle the ox that treads out the corn',[73] and 'the workman deserves his wages'.[74]

Do not admit an accusation against an elder unless it is supported by two or three witnesses. But publicly reprove those who do sin, that it may deter the others. I charge you before God and Christ Jesus and the elect angels[75] to maintain these principles without prejudice, doing nothing with bias.

Do not ordain anyone hastily, nor become involved in the sins of others. Keep yourself unpolluted.

Do not be a water drinker any longer, but take a little wine for the sake of your stomach and your chronic ailments. Some men's sins are patent, standing out for condemnation, but with others they are kept in the background. In the same way also their good deeds are patent; but even when they are not they cannot be concealed.

Let as many as are under the yoke as slaves regard their owners as deserving of every consideration, that the Name of God and the doctrine may not be brought into disrepute. But let not those who have owners who are believers be presumptuous towards them because they are brothers. Rather should they be meticulous in serving because those who are deriving the benefit of the useful service are believers and friends. Teach and advocate these things.

If anyone teaches anything different, and does not propound sound principles, those of our Lord Jesus Christ, and instruction that is consistent with godliness, he is befogged, knowing nothing clearly, crazy about issues and fights over words, which give rise to antagonism, rivalry, slanders, evil suspicions, and violent altercations of men whose minds are warped and bereft of truth, imagining good business to be the same thing as godliness. But godliness plus contentment is the best possible business; for we have brought nothing into the world, neither is there

[73] Deut. xxv. 4.
[74] Lk. x. 7; cp. Deut. xxiv. 15.
[75] Cp. Jos. *Wars*, II. xvi. 4, 'I call your Sanctuary and the sacred angels of God to witness'.

anything we can take out of it. Having food and shelter let us be content with these. Those who want to be rich expose themselves to temptations and pitfalls, and to many foolish and harmful cravings, which drag men down to ruin and perdition. The root of all the evils is avarice, and some having clutched at it have strayed from the Faith and racked themselves with many torments.

Do you, Man of God, fly from these things. But pursue rectitude, devoutness, faith, love, constancy and gentleness. Fight the gallant contest of the Faith to the finish. Put up a real struggle for Eternal Life, to which you were called. Having made the noble confession before many witnesses, I charge you before God the Source of all life,[76] and before Christ who made the noble confession before Pontius Pilate, to keep the injunction given you unsullied, unimpeachable, until the visible appearance of our Lord Jesus Christ, which the blessed and sole Sovereign will display in due course, the King of kings and Lord of lords, who alone is deathless, dwelling in unapproachable light, whom no man has seen, nor can see. To him be honour and everlasting might. Amen.

Impress on those who are rich in this present world not to be arrogant, nor to build their hopes on such an uncertain thing as riches, but on God who provides everything in profusion for our enjoyment. Impress on them to be beneficent, rich in kind actions, to be generous and public-spirited, storing up for themselves a useful fund for the future, so as to secure the Life worth having.

Guard what is committed to your care, Timotheus, avoiding the irreverent jargon and contradictions of the falsely termed 'Knowledge',[77] which some professing have fallen into error regarding the Faith.

Wishing you every happiness.

TO TIMOTHEUS (2)

(Probably written from Rome in A.D. 63)

Paul, by the will of God an envoy of Christ Jesus in conformity with the promise of Life that is in Christ Jesus, to his dear son Timotheus. May prosperity, mercy and peace be yours from God the Father and Christ Jesus our Master.

I am grateful to God, whom I serve with a pure conscience as did my forebears, as I am unremitting in mentioning you to him in my petitions, longing night and day to see you, very mindful of your tears, that I may be filled with joy. I

[76] Cp. I. Sam. ii. 6 (LXX).
[77] Gr. *Gnosis*.

cherish the recollection of your guileless faith, which first resided in your grandma Lois and your mother Eunice, and I am
sure does still in you. It is on this ground that I would urge you
to fan the flame of the divine gift imparted to you when I
ordained you; for God has not given us a spirit of timidity, but
of resolution, devotion and correction. So do not be ashamed
of the testimony of our Master, nor of me his prisoner, but
bear your share of hardship for the News as God enables you.
He has saved us and called us with a holy calling, not in
accordance with our actions, but in accordance with his own
purpose and mercy bestowed on us in Christ Jesus before the
Ages began, and now tangibly expressed through the visible
appearance of Christ Jesus our Deliverer, who has put Death
out of action and brought Life and imperishability into operation by the News of which I am appointed herald, envoy and
teacher. It is on this ground that I suffer as I do; but I am not
ashamed of it, for I know in whom I have put my trust, and am
confident that he is able to keep secure what I have entrusted
to him until that Day comes.

Hold firmly the outline of sound principles you have heard
from me by the faith and love that is in Christ Jesus. Keep safe
that noble deposit by the holy Spirit which resides in us. You
are well aware that all the Asiatic believers have turned from
me, among them Phygelus and Hermogenes. The Lord have
compassion on the household of Onesiphorus,[78] because he
often heartened me and was never ashamed of my chain; but
on arrival at Rome he made diligent inquiry for me and found
out where I was. The Lord grant him to find mercy[79] when the
Day comes. And the many ways in which he looked after me
in Ephesus you know better than anyone.

Be resolute therefore, my son, in the loving-kindness that is
in Christ Jesus, and what you have heard as from me through
many witnesses commit to reliable persons, who will be competent in turn to teach others. Bear your share of hardship
like a good soldier of Christ Jesus. No one going off to war
saddles himself with the responsibilities of life, since he aims
to satisfy his enlisting officer. Also if anyone contends in the
Games, he will not be crowned unless he adheres to the rules.
The farmer who has put in the labour ought to have first claim
on the produce. Note what I say. The Lord will grant you complete understanding. Always remember, Jesus Christ of the
lineage of David was raised from the dead in my presentation
of the News. For this I suffer hardship to the extent of imprisonment, like a malefactor. But God's Message is not
fettered. Because of that I submit to everything for the sake
of the Elect, that they too may obtain the salvation that is in
Christ Jesus, with eternal glory. It is a true saying,

[78] The passage appears to convey that Onesiphorus had died while in Rome.
[79] Lit. 'The Lord grant him to find mercy from the Lord', a Hebraism, cp. Gen.
xix. 24.

'If we have died with him, we shall also live with him;
If we are constant, we shall also reign with him;
If we disown him, so will he disown us;
If we are disloyal, he will still be faithful.'

For he cannot deny himself. Remind them of this, begging them most solemnly before God not to battle over words, which gains nothing, and only disconcerts the listeners. Be at pains to prove yourself competent to God, a workman who has no need to be ashamed, having kept to the straight line with the Message of Truth. But evade irreverent jargon. Those who employ it only further the progress of impiety, and their speech mortifies like a gangrene. Among them are Hymenaeus and Philetus, who have fallen into error regarding the Truth, saying that the resurrection has already taken place, and have overturned the faith of some. At least God's solid foundation stays firm bearing this stamp on it, 'The Lord knows those who are truly his',[80] and, 'Let all who pronounce the name of the Lord stand aside from iniquity'.[81] But in a large establishment there are not only vessels of gold and silver, but also of wood and earthenware, the ones for best and the others for common use. Should anyone make himself pure from the latter, he will become a vessel for best use, purified, fit for the Owner's employment, in complete readiness for every useful service.

Fly from youthful passions, but pursue rectitude, faith, love and peace, with those who invoke the name of the Lord with a pure mind. Deprecate foolish and idle issues, knowing that they breed strife. The Master's servant ought not to wrangle, but to be pacific towards all, instructive, forbearing, quietly correcting antagonists, so that perhaps God may give them a change of mind to realize the truth and be brought to their senses out of the Devil's snare, being recovered by him for that purpose.

You must know this, however, that in the Last Days hard times are in store; for men will be selfish, money-grubbing, brazen, arrogant, slanderous, defiant to parents, ungrateful, irreligious, lacking in affection, implacable, spiteful, uncontrolled, savage, disliking good, treacherous, headstrong, conceited, preferring pleasure to piety, maintaining a semblance of devoutness but denying its efficacy. Turn away from all such people; for from them come those who gain an entrance into households and captivate immature females, piled high with peccadilloes, swayed by whims and fancies, always learning, but never really able to grasp the Truth. In the same kind of way as Jannes and Jambres[82] opposed Moses, so do these men, warped in mind, unsound in the Faith, oppose the Truth. But

---

[80] Num. xvi. 5 (LXX).
[81] Cp. Num xvi. 26-7 (LXX).
[82] The legendary court magicians of Pharaoh.

they will make no further headway, for their folly will be patent to all, as indeed was that of those magicians.

But you have closely followed my teaching, method, presentation, faith, forbearance, devotion and constancy, the persecutions and sufferings I met with at Antioch, Iconium and Lystra,[83] the various kinds of persecution I underwent, from all of which the Lord rescued me. And indeed all who desire to live dutifully in Christ Jesus must expect persecution. But wicked men and imposters will flourish as time goes on, deceiving and being deceived. You, however, adhere to the things you have learnt and been convinced of, seeing from whom you learnt them, and that from infancy you have known the holy Scriptures, which have power to make you wise for salvation by faith that is in Christ Jesus. Each document is divinely inspired, and consequently advantageous for instruction, reproof, reclamation and moral discipline, so that the Man of God may be expert, fully equipped for every useful undertaking.

I charge you before God, and before Christ Jesus, who will judge the living and dead, and in view of his visible appearance and reign, proclaim the Message, apply yourself to this in season and out of season. Reprove, censure, exhort, with all forbearance and diligence. For the time will come when they will not tolerate sound teaching, but following their own desires will load themselves with teachers who tickle the ear, and will turn a deaf ear to the Truth, turning to myths instead. You, however, keep perfectly cool, endure hardships, do your duty as a standard-bearer of the News, fulfil the conditions of your service. For I am now on the eve of peace, and the time for my discharge is approaching. I have fought a gallant contest; I have completed the course; I have kept the Faith. There remains in store for me the crown to which I am entitled, which the Master, that honourable judge, will award me on that Day; and not me alone, but all who have delightedly welcomed his personal presence.

Do your utmost to come to me quickly, for Demas, loving the present world, has deserted me and gone off to Thessalonica, Crescens has gone to Gaul, Titus to Dalmatia. Only Luke remains with me. Pick up Mark and bring him with you, for he is valuable to me in administrative work, and I have dispatched Tychicus to Ephesus. When you come bring the book-wrap[84] I left with Carpus at Troas, also the books, particularly the parchments. Alexander the blacksmith has shown himself very ill-disposed towards me. The Lord will requite him in accordance with his actions.[85] Watch out for him yourself, for he is strongly opposed to our views. At the first hearing of my defence no one supported me: everyone deserted me.

[83] See Acts xiii-xiv. pp. 216-219.
[84] Or heavy jacket.
[85] Cp. Ps. xxviii. 4; II. Sam. iii. 39.

May it not be counted against them! But my Master supported and strengthened me, so that through me the proclamation might ring out, and all the Gentiles might hear it; and I was 'saved from the jaws of the lion'.[86] The Lord will continue to rescue me from every evil agency and preserve me for his heavenly Kingdom. To him be glory for ever and ever. Amen.

Give my regards to Prisca and Aquila, and to the household of Onesiphorus. Erastus is still at Corinth, while Trophimus I left ill at Miletus. Do your utmost to come to me before winter sets in.

Eubulus sends you his regards, so do Pudens, Linus, Claudia, and all the brothers.

The Lord Jesus be with your spirit. Wishing you every happiness.

[86] Cp. Ps. xxii 21, a Jewish stock phrase for the power of tyrannical rulers. See Jos. *Antiq.* XVIII. vi. 10; *Meg.* fol. 15b. Paul seems to have been remanded, but no longer now expected his freedom.

HOMILY ON
THE HIGH PRIESTHOOD OF CHRIST

To Jewish Believers

(HEBREWS)

Preface to the *Homily to the Hebrews*

THERE HAS BEEN much speculation as to the authorship and destination of this document. Eastern tradition ascribed the work to Paul; but it has long been recognized from the language, style and character of the book that it cannot have been written by him, though the author's viewpoint is in many respects Pauline. Among suggested writers a likely name is that of Apollos, Paul's esteemed fellow-worker. The description given of him in the *Acts* as an Alexandrian Jew, a learned man, well-versed in the Scriptures, is fully in keeping with what the document itself conveys. The author was evidently a man of erudition, who expounds ably in the fashion of the time. He is at home in the Greek language, which he uses with considerable literary skill, and with delight in shades of meaning and plays on words. For his Old Testament quotations he employs the Alexandrian text of the Septuagint Version, and he appears to be acquainted with the works of Philo, the Alexandrian Jewish philosopher of the first century A.D.

The Homily is directed to a particular community of Jewish Christians, who knew personally both the author and Timotheus, Paul's devoted assistant. This is important, as it indicates—assuming that these touches have not been introduced to make it appear that Paul was the author—that these believers were located in some city of Greece or Asia Minor where there was a considerable Jewish population. If we are to think of such a city where both Apollos and Timotheus worked the obvious choice is Ephesus. The document furnishes three other notable pieces of information, that the believers in question had suffered some persecution in the early days of their faith, that Timotheus had been imprisoned but was now released, and that the author was in all probability writing from Italy. The last we hear of Timotheus (*II. Tim.*) is that Paul had sent for him to come to Rome, where he may well have been imprisoned during the Neronian persecution. This, with the evidence of the book that the Temple in Jerusalem was still functioning, suggests a date for its composition about A.D. 65-67. Naturally, however, in the present state of our knowledge there can be no certainty as to authorship or date, and it is quite conceivable that the document is considerably later than it appears to be.

TO JEWISH BELIEVERS

(Hebrews)

At varying intervals and in varied fashions God spoke of old
to our fathers by the Prophets; but at the close of these times
he has spoken to us by a Son, whom he appointed heir to everything.[1] By him also he instituted the Aeons.[2] He, being the reflection of God's glory and the exact expression of his nature,[3]
bringing everything into being by the exercise[4] of God's power,
when he had effected an expiation for sins, sat down at the right
hand of the Majesty in the heavenly heights. In this respect he
is superior to the angels, in so far as he has obtained a more
exalted status than theirs. For to which of the angels did God
ever say, 'You are my son, to-day I have begotten you',[5] or
again, 'I will be a father to him, and he shall be a son to me'.[6]
Or again, when he introduced the Firstborn to his world estate,
he says, 'And let all God's angels pay him homage.'[7]

Now as regards the angels, God says,

> *Who employs spirits as his messengers,*
> *And fiery flames as his agents.*[8]

But as regards the Son.

> *'Your throne, O mighty one, is of eternal duration:*
> *A sceptre of justice is the sceptre of your dominion.*
> *You have loved rectitude and hated injustice;*
> *Therefore, O mighty one, your God has anointed you*
> *With coronation oil in the presence of your peers.'*[9]

Also God says,

> *'You in the beginning, lord, founded the earth,*
> *And the heavens are your handiwork.*
> *They will perish, but you will endure.*
> *They will all grow old like a garment,*
> *And like a robe you will fold them away.*
> *But you will be ever the same,*
> *And your years will never cease.'*[10]

[1] Cp. Gen. i. 28.
[2] Or 'Ages'.
[3] Gen. i. 26.
[4] Lit. 'expression' or 'utterance'.
[5] Ps. ii. 7 (LXX).
[6] II. Sam. vii. 14 (LXX).
[7] Deut. xxxii. 43 (LXX).
[8] Ps. civ. 4.
[9] Ps. xiv. 6-7.
[10] Ps. cii. 25-7.

And to which of the angels did God ever say,

> *'Be seated at my right hand,*
> *Till I make your enemies your footstool'?*[11]

Are they not all ministering spirits sent out for the service of those who are to obtain salvation?

That is why we ought to pay much closer attention to the things we have heard, so that we never let them slip. For if the Message spoken by angels[12] held good, and every failure or neglect brought just retribution, how are we to escape punishment if we should prove negligent of so great a salvation, which, originating with the Master's own declaration, was confirmed to us by those who heard him, and corroborated by God by signs and wonders, and by a variety of phenomena and distributions of holy Spirit at his discretion?

Now it was not to angels that God made subject that future world of which we are speaking; for in one place a certain writer has expressed it thus:

> *What is man, that you are mindful of him?*
> *Or the son of man, that you take account of him?*
> *You made him only slightly inferior to angels:*
> *You crowned him with dignity and honour.*
> *You set him over the work of your hands,*
> *And made everything subject to him.*[13]

By this 'making everything subject to him' he left nothing outside his control. As it is, we do not see as yet that everything has been made subject to him. But as regards being made 'only slightly inferior to angels', we do see Jesus by experiencing death having been 'crowned with dignity and honour', that thus in God's mercy he should taste death for all mankind. For it seemed fitting to God, for whom and by whom everything exists, in raising many sons to dignity, to perfect by sufferings the one responsible for their salvation. He indeed who sanctifies and those who are sanctified have all one parentage, for which reason he is not ashamed to call them brothers, saying,

> *'I will declare your Name to my brothers.*
> *I will praise you before the Community.'*[14]

And again, 'I will put my trust in him'.[15] And again, 'Here am I with the children God has given me'.[16]

Since, therefore, the children have human nature, so did he share it equally with them; so that by death he might put out of commission him who wields the power of death, namely the Devil, and release all those inhibited throughout their lives by

[11] Ps. cx. 1.
[12] The Law at Sinai given according to legend through the medium of angels. See Gal. iii. 19, above p. 260.
[13] Ps. viii. 4-6.   [15] Isa. xii. 2.
[14] Ps. xxii. 22.   [16] Isa. viii. 18.

fear of death. For where was the point of lending a helping hand to angels? It was the offspring of Abraham that needed a helping hand. Consequently it was essential for him to become in every respect like his brothers, that he might be a compassionate and trustworthy High Priest in matters relating to God, to propitiate for the people's sins; for having experienced temptation himself he is able to aid those who are tempted.

Wherefore, holy brothers, comrades of the heavenly calling, take note of Jesus the Representative and High Priest of our confession, how faithful he was to him who appointed him, as was Moses 'in all his house'.[17] But Jesus was thought worthy of greater dignity than Moses, in so far as he who has constructed the house derives more honour from it; for every house must be constructed by someone, though it is God who has constructed all things.

Now Moses indeed was faithful in all God's house as a privileged retainer, in proof of the things that were to be declared; but Christ was faithful as a son over his own house, the house which we represent, if we hold tenaciously to our confidence and pride in our Hope. So, as the holy Spirit says.

> 'To-day, should you hear his voice,
> Harden not your hearts as in the provocation,
> At the time of testing in the wilderness,
> Where your fathers tested me experimentally,
> And saw my activities for forty years.
> Therefore, I was grieved with that generation,
> And said, they are ever astray at heart,
> Never have they really known my ways.
> As I swore then in my anger,
> Never shall they enter my rest.'[18]

Take care then, brothers, lest there should be in any one of you an evil disloyal heart to make you revolt from the Living God. Rather exhort each other daily, while it can still be called 'to-day', in case any of you should be hardened by sin's subversive power. For we have become Christ's comrades, provided that we adhere steadfastly to the end to the fundamental basis of that association, in that it is said.

> To-day, should you hear his voice,
> Harden not your hearts as in the provocation.

For some having heard did provoke, though not all those who came out of Egypt under Moses. With whom then was it God was grieved for forty years? Was it not with those who had sinned, whose bodies fell in the wilderness?[19] And to whom did he swear they should not enter his rest, if not to those who were disobedient? So we see that they were prevented from entering by disaffection. Let us be deeply concerned, therefore, lest while

17 Num. xii. 7.
18 Ps. xcv. 7-11.
19 Ps. cvi. 26.

a promise of entering God's rest is left open any of you may seem to have missed it. For we too, just like them, have been recipients of Good News; but in their case the Message heard was of no avail because it did not come to grips with faith in the hearers. It is we who have believed who will enter God's rest, as he said, 'As I swore then in my anger, never shall *they* enter *my* rest', even though it is from labours that had been completed from the creation of the world. For in one place he speaks of the seventh day as follows: 'And God rested the seventh day from all his labours',[20] and again in this passage, 'Never shall they enter my rest'. Since, therefore, it is left open for some to enter it, and those who were first given the Good News did not enter because of disobedience, God again fixes a day, namely 'to-day', saying after a considerable interval by David as quoted,

> *To-day, should you hear his voice,*
> *Harden not your hearts as in the provocation.*

Had Joshua given the people rest, God would not here be speaking about another day later on. So a sabbath-keeping is left open for God's people. He who enters God's rest has himself rested from his own labours as God did from his. Let us therefore do our utmost to enter that rest, in case anyone should fall by the very same factor of disobedience. For God's Message is keen and eager, sharper than any double-edged dagger, piercing to the very juncture between soul and spirit, joints and marrow, and able to detect the feelings and intents of the heart. There is no created thing unnoticed by him, for everything is naked and exposed to the sight of him with whom we have to deal.

Having, therefore, a great High Priest who has passed through the heavens, Jesus the Son of God, let us hold fast to our confession. For we do not have a High Priest who cannot sympathize with our failings, having—though without sin[21]— been tempted similarly in every respect. Let us therefore confidently approach the Mercy Seat,[22] that we may obtain mercy and find favour so as to receive adequate aid. For every High Priest, being selected from men, appointed on behalf of men for divine duties to present offerings and sacrifices for sins, is capable of friendly sympathy with the ignorant and erring, since he himself is prone to failings, and for that very reason is obliged to bring offerings for sins[23] for himself, as well as for the people. And no one assumes the dignity on his own: he is called to office by God, as Aaron was. Thus even Christ did not raise himself to the dignity of High Priest: it was he who said to him, 'You are my son, to-day I have begotten you'.[24] As God also said elsewhere, 'You are a priest for ever after the

[20] Gen. ii. 2.
[21] The Logos (Word) has 'no participation in sin', Philo, *De Profug.* 20. He is also called by Philo 'High Priest'.
[22] Exod. xxv. 17.   [23] See Lev. iv. 3; xvi. 5-6.   [24] Ps. ii. 7.

order of Melchizedek'.[25] Christ, in the days of his physical existence, having offered petitions, and indeed supplications, with loud sobbing and tears to him who could save him from death,[26] was heard because of his piety. Though he was a son, he learnt obedience by what he suffered. And being perfected, he became for all who obey him the means of their eternal salvation, having been appointed by God High Priest after the order of Melchizedek.[27]

We are minded to say a great deal on this subject that is hard to explain since you have become dull of hearing. For when by this time you should be teachers, you again need someone to teach you the most elementary principles of the divine oracles. Yes, you have become in need of milk, not of solid food. For everyone who is at the milk-feeding stage is lacking in moral judgment; he is a babe. Solid food is for grown-ups, for those who from long practice have had their faculties trained to distinguish good from evil.

So leaving the subject of first Christian principles let us bring ourselves to maturity, not re-laying a foundation of repentance of our dead deeds, of faith in God, of instruction about immersions, ordination, resurrection from the dead and eternal judgment. This is what we must do, God permitting. For it is impossible for those who have once been enlightened, who have experienced the heavenly gift, and become sharers of the holy Spirit, and have truly experienced divine utterance[28]—the powers indeed of the world to come—and then have fallen away, to make a fresh start with repentance; for they have re-crucified the Son of God for their part, and held him up to scorn. For ground that absorbs the rain which falls frequently upon it, and bears vegetation suited to the use of those by whom indeed it is cultivated, will enjoy God's blessing. But if it produces thorns and thistles it is worthless and the next thing to a curse, and will end up in burning.

We are convinced, however, that the better fate carrying salvation with it will be yours, dear friends, even if we do speak in this way. God is not unjust. There has been no forgetfulness of your work on his part, nor of the love you have shown for his Name in ministering to the saints, and maintaining this ministry. And it is our desire that the same zeal should be exhibited by each of you, so as to make absolutely sure of the Hope to the very end, so that you do not become sluggish, but imitators of those who by faith and perseverance are entitled to the promises. For when God made a promise to Abraham he swore by himself, since he could swear by no one greater,[29] saying 'Assuredly, I will bless you and increase you'.[30] And so having

[25] Ps. cx. 4.   [26] I.e. in the Garden of Gethsemane.
[27] According to Philo, 'the Logos is shadowed forth by Melchizedek'.
[28] Speaking with tongues, or prophetic speech.
[29] Cp. Philo, *De Legg. Alleg.* iii. 72, 'Having well confirmed his promise even by an oath . . . for you see that God swears not by another—for nothing is superior to himself—but by himself, who is the best of all.'
[30] Gen. xxii. 16-17.

persevered, Abraham gained the promise. For men swear by
what is greater, and for them the oath in ratification marks
the conclusion of every controversy.[31] In this instance God,
being desirous of showing the heirs of the promise more definitely the unalterability of his purpose, negotiated by oath; so
that by two unalterable facts[32] impossible for God to falsify we
who have fled for refuge[33] might have strong incentive to grasp
the Hope extended to us. To this we cling as a safe and secure
anchor for the soul passing in behind the curtain,[34] where Jesus,
appointed permanent High Priest after the order of Melchizedek, has entered in advance on our behalf.

Now this Melchizedek, king of Salem, priest of the Most
High God, was he who met Abraham on his return from the
slaughter of the kings and blessed him, to whom Abraham
allocated a tenth of everything.[35] He is in the first place by
translation of his name 'king of righteousness', and in the second place king of Salem, which means 'king of peace', without
father, without mother, without ancestry, having neither beginning of days nor end of life.[36] Being therefore a representation of the Son of God, he remains priest in perpetuity.

Observe, then, what an important person he was to whom
Abraham—the Patriarch—gave a tenth of the spoils. Those
truly of the sons of Levi who possess the priesthood are entitled
in accordance with the Law to tithe the people, namely their
brothers, although sprung from the loins of Abraham. But this
man, not descended from them, has tithed Abraham and blessed
the holder of the promises. And beyond all argument it is the
inferior who is blessed by the superior. Again, in the one instance it is men subject to death who receive tithes, while in the
other[37] it is on record that he still lives on. As one might put it,
through Abraham even Levi who receives tithes has been tithed,
for he was still in his father's loins[38] when Melchizedek met
Abraham.

If, therefore, perfection had been by means of the Levitical
priesthood, for by that priesthood the people were given their
legislation, why was it still required that a different priest should
arise after the order of Melchizedek instead of carrying right
on after the order of Aaron? For the priesthood being altered,
of necessity an alteration of law is involved. For he to whom
these matters relate belonged to a different tribe, no member
of which was devoted to the service of the altar. For it is evident that our Master sprang from Judah, concerning which
tribe Moses said nothing about priesthood. And what is of
greater consequence, it is quite clear that a different priest is to

[31] Cp. Gen. xxi. 15.
[32] The promise and the oath.
[33] See I. Ki. i. 50.
[34] Cp. Lev. xvi. 15.
[35] See Gen. xiv. 18-20.
[36] Scripture makes no mention of Melchizedek's parentage, ancestry, birth or death.
[37] I.e. in the case of Melchizedek.
[38] Levi being Abraham's great-grandson not yet born.

arise after the order of Melchizedek, who is made priest not in terms of an evanescent commandment but by virtue of an indestructible life. For the testimony runs, 'You are a priest *for ever* after the order of Melchizedek'.

There has then been a definite setting aside of the previous commandment on account of its limitations and unsatisfactory character. For the Law perfected nothing, though it paved the way for a better prospect by which we draw near to God. And in so far as the change was not made without an oath-taking—for those other priests were installed without an oath-taking, but he with an oath-taking by him who swore to him, 'The Lord has sworn, and will not revoke his word: you are a priest for ever'—to that extent Jesus had surety of a better covenant. Now those others who are made priests are numerous, being prevented by death from continuing in office. But he, because he continues for ever, retains the priesthood in unbroken tenure. Consequently he is able to save absolutely those who approach God through him, since he is always alive to intercede on their behalf.

This was the kind of High Priest we required, one who is consecrated, guileless, undefiled, distinct from sinners, higher than the heavens, one who does not have daily necessity like other High Priests first to offer sacrifices for his own sins and then for the sins of the people; for this he did once and for all when he offered up himself. The Law indeed appoints men with failings as High Priests; but the terms of the oath-taking subsequent to the Law appoints a Son who has been permanently perfected.

To summarize what has been said, we have a High Priest of this sort, who has taken his seat at the right hand of the throne of the Majesty in the heavens, a ministrant of the sacred rites and of the True Tabernacle, which the Lord and not man set up.

Now every High Priest is appointed to present offerings and sacrifices, so it was necessary that this one too should have something to offer. If indeed he were on earth, he would not be a priest at all, there being already those who present the offerings in accordance with the Law. These serve as a token and shadow of the heavenly reality, as Moses was directed when about to carry out the construction of the Tabernacle. 'See', God said, 'that you make everything after the pattern shown you on the mountain.'[39] But now Jesus has obtained a more important ministration in so far as he is the negotiator of a better covenant, instituted by God on the basis of better promises. For if that first covenant had been entirely satisfactory, no occasion would have seen sought for a second. But expressing dissatisfaction God says,

[39] Exod. xxv. 40.

'Lo, the time will come,' says the Lord,
'When I will contract a new covenant
With the house of Israel and the house of Judah,
Not like the covenant I made with their fathers
On the day I took them by the hand
To lead them out of the land of Egypt.
For they did not adhere to my covenant,
So I left them to themselves,' says the Lord.
'But this is the covenant with the house of Israel
I will make after those days,' says the Lord.
'I will put my laws into their minds,
And on their hearts I will inscribe them.
Yes, I will be their God,
And they shall be my people.
And they shall teach no more each his fellow,
And each his brother, saying "Know the Lord";
For they all shall know me
From the least to the greatest of them.
For I will be merciful to their iniquities,
And their sins I will remember no more.' [40]

By saying 'a *new* covenant', he has rendered the previous one antiquated; and what is antiquated and decrepit is on the verge of extinction.

Yet, indeed, even the previous covenant had its regulations for worship connected with an earthly Sanctuary. For there was an outer Tabernacle erected in which was both the lampstand and the table with its display of loaves.[41] This was called the Holy Place. And beyond the inner curtain was a Tabernacle called the Most Holy Place, which had the golden censer and the ark of the covenant entirely overlaid with gold, in which was the jar containing manna, and Aaron's rod that budded, and the tablets of the covenant. Above the ark, overshadowing the propitiatory were the glorious cherubim, about which one cannot now speak definitely. But while these comprised the furnishings, it is only the outer Tabernacle that the priests enter regularly in the performance of their duties. Into the inner Tabernacle only the High Priest enters once a year, not without blood, which he offers up for his own and the people's sins of ignorance. By this the holy Spirit has indicated that the way into the Most Holy is not yet opened up so long as the outer Tabernacle, which served as an illustration down to the present era, still retains its function. In accordance with this both offering and sacrifices are presented incapable, so far as the conscience is concerned, of perfecting the worshippers simply by meat-offerings and drink-offerings and various lustrations, material regulations imposed until the Era of Revision.

But Christ having come as High Priest of the good things in

---

[40] Jer. xxxi. 31-34.   [41] The loaves of the Presence.

store, he has entered once and for all into the sacred precincts Above, through the better and more perfect Tabernacle that is not artificial, that is to say not of this created world,[42] not with blood of goats and calves, but with his own blood, procuring permanent redemption. For if the blood of goats and bulls, and the ashes of a heifer sprinkled on those who have incurred defilement, restores the ritual purity of the flesh, how much more shall the blood of Christ, who by his eternal spirit offered himself unblemished to God, purify our consciences from dead deeds to serve the Living God?

Consequently he is the negotiator of a new covenant; so that from a death having occurred in discharge of liability for violations of the previous covenant those who have been called may obtain the promise of the eternal inheritance. For where there is a covenant there must be provision of a death on the contractor's part. A covenant is ratified over corpses, otherwise it has no validity while the contractor lives. For this reason neither was the previous covenant inaugurated without blood; for when all the commandments of the Law had been recited by Moses to all the people, he took the blood of calves and goats, with water, scarlet wool and hyssop, and sprinkled both the book itself and all the people saying, 'This is the blood of the covenant which God has enjoined on you'.[43] And both the Tabernacle and all the utensils of the ritual he similarly sprinkled with blood. Indeed, according to the Law, practically everything is purified by blood, and without effusion of blood there is no absolution.

Of necessity, therefore, the representations of the heavenly realities were purified by such means, but the heavenly realities themselves with better sacrifices than these. For Christ has entered into no artificial Sanctuary, a copy of the true, but into heaven itself, there to appear in God's presence on our behalf. Neither has he entered that he may offer himself frequently, as the High Priest annually enters the sacred precincts with other blood;[44] for then he would have needed to suffer many times since the foundation of the world. As it is, he has appeared only once at the Consummation of the Ages to put away sin by his own sacrifice. And in so far as it is determined that men shall die but once, and after that follows judgment, so Christ also, being offered once to take away the sins of many,[45] will show himself a second time without sin to those who await him for their salvation.[46]

For the Law being a shadow of the good things in store, not the very image of the actualities, the High Priests can never with those sacrifices which they offer annually perfect for all time those who approach God. If they could, would not the

[42] It was believed that the earthly Sanctuary and also the city of Jerusalem were copies of the heavenly originals.
[43] Exod. xxiv. 8.   [44] Lev. xvi. 17.   [45] Cp. Isa. liii. 12.
[46] The people eagerly awaited the safe return of the High Priest from the Holy of Holies on the Day of Atonement as a sign of their salvation and the forgiveness of their sins.

sacrifices have ceased to be offered, because the worshippers, no longer having any consciousness of sins, would have been purified once and for all? But in these sacrifices there is an annual reminder of sins; for it is impossible for the blood of bulls and goats to take away sins. Consequently when Christ enters the world he says,

> 'Sacrifice and offering you have not desired:
> A body you have prepared for me.
> Holocausts and sin-offerings you have not welcomed.
> Then said I, Lo, I have come—
> In the roll of the book it is written of me—
> To carry out your will, O Lord.'[47]

Besides saying, 'Sacrifices and offerings, holocausts and sin-offerings, you have neither desired nor welcomed'—these being offered in accordance with the Law—he goes on to say, 'Lo, I have come to carry out your will'. He abolishes the former to establish the latter. By this 'will' we are consecrated through the offering of the body of Jesus Christ once and for all.

Moreover, every priest daily *stands* while officiating, and frequently offers the same sacrifices, which can never do away with sins. But this priest, having offered a single sacrifice for sins for all time, *sat down* 'at the right hand of God',[48] waiting thereafter for 'his enemies to be made his footstool'. For by one offering he has perfected for all time those who are consecrated. The holy Spirit is also our witness, for after having said, 'This is the covenant I will make with them after those days', the Lord says, 'I will put my laws in their hearts, and on their minds I will write them, and their sins and iniquities I will remember no more'. Where, then, there is absolution from these an offering for sins is no longer required.

Having therefore, brothers, confidence by the blood of Jesus to use the entrance into the sacred precincts which he has inaugurated for us, a way through the curtain fresh and vital, namely the way of his flesh, and having a supreme priest over the House of God, let us approach God with sincere minds and absolute faith, with hearts sprinkled from a bad conscience and our bodies washed with pure water. Let us adhere inflexibly to the confession of our Hope; for he who has promised is faithful. And let us vie with one another in intensifying our love and worthy actions, not neglecting assembling together, as is the custom with some, but encouraging one another, all the more as you see the Day approaching. For if we deliberately persist in sinning after receiving knowledge of the truth, no longer is there left a sacrifice for those sins, nothing but a dread foreboding of judgment and of an eager flame ready to devour the adversaries.[49] Anyone who has spurned the Law of Moses is put

---

[47] Ps. xl. 6-8.
[48] Ps. cx. 1. The author may be thinking of the fact that in the inner Temple only the king was permitted to be seated. *Sot.* fol. 41a.
[49] Cp. Zeph. i. 15-18.

to death without mercy on the testimony of two or three witnesses. Of how much more terrible a penalty do you think him deserving who has treated the Son of God with contempt, and has held the blood of the covenant by which he was sanctified as something vile, and has mocked the Spirit of mercy? We do indeed know him who has said, 'Vengeance is mine, I will requite',[50] and also, 'The Lord will judge his people'.[51] It is a terrible thing to fall into the hands of the Living God.

Recall those early days in which when you were illumined you endured a great bout of sufferings, partly as being yourselves the butts of insult and attacks, and partly as having fellowship with those who had been so treated. For you had sympathy with the prisoners, and you accepted with equanimity the seizure of your property, knowing yourselves to have a better and permanent possession. Do not cast away your confidence, then, which will have a substantial reward; for you will need all your constancy, so that when you have carried out the will of God you may obtain the promise.

> For only a very little longer.
> And the Coming One will come, and not delay.
> But my upright one shall live by faith.
> Yet should he draw back,
> My soul shall have no pleasure in him.[52]

But we are not of those who draw back to our destruction, but those with faith to gain our souls.

Now faith is the solid ground of our expectations, the proof of unseen actualities. By this faith the Elders had testimony borne to them. By it we apprehend that the Aeons were instituted by the divine utterance, so that what is seen did not proceed from any visible causes.

In faith Abel offered to God a greater sacrifice than Cain, by which testimony was borne to him as righteous, God himself testifying about his offerings; and by that faith, though dead, he still speaks.

In faith Enoch was translated without experiencing death, and was not to be found because God had translated him. But before he was translated it is on record that he pleased God. Now without faith it is not possible to please God, for he who approaches God must have faith in his existence, and that he rewards those who seek him out.

In faith Noah, deliberating about what was as yet unseen, and being prudent, constructed an ark to save his family, by which he passed judgment on the world, and became heir of that rectitude which rests on faith.

In faith Abraham obeyed, when called to set out for a region which he was destined to receive as an inheritance, and started out with no conception of where he was going. In faith he took

---

[50] Deut. xxxii. 35.   [51] Deut. xxxii. 36.
[52] Hab. ii. 3-4 (LXX), adapted and the order of the lines changed. In the source line 3 follows line 5.

up residence in the promised land, as in a foreign country, living in tents, as did Isaac and Jacob the co-heirs of the same promise. He waited for the city with foundations whose architect and builder is God. In faith also, when past the prime of life, he received capacity to beget children, because he held him to be faithful who had promised. And so there were begotten of one man, as good as dead, 'as the very stars of heaven for multitude, and countless as the sands on the seashore.'[53]

All these died in faith without having obtained the promises, but viewing them from afar, and hailing them, and confessing that they were 'strangers and sojourners on earth'.[54] People who speak like this make it clear that they are in quest of a homeland; for if indeed their minds were on that land from which they emigrated opportunity was theirs to return. As it is, they are reaching out for a better, namely a heavenly one. Therefore God is not ashamed to be called their God, for he has a city in readiness for them.

In faith Abraham when he was tested yielded up Isaac; and he who had received the promises offered up the only son of whom he had been told, 'By Isaac shall offspring be given you'.[55] He reckoned that God could even raise the dead, from whence indeed figuratively speaking he received Isaac back.

In faith Isaac also blessed Jacob and Esau in respect of what was to come.

In faith Jacob when dying blessed each of the sons of Joseph, and bowed upon the head of his staff.

In faith Joseph approaching his end made mention of the exodus of the children of Israel, and gave injunctions about his bones.

In faith Moses when born was hidden for three months by his parents, because they saw he was a fine child and were not afraid of the king's edict.

In faith Moses when grown up refused to be called the son of Pharaoh's daughter, preferring to endure adversity with God's people than to enjoy the temporary pleasures of sin. He deemed the reproach of Christ greater wealth than the treasures of Egypt; for he kept his eyes on the recompense. In faith he abandoned Egypt, fearless of the king's anger; for he was resolute in having the Invisible King in view. In faith he kept the Passover and the daubing of blood,[56] that the destroyer of the first-born should not touch the Israelites. In faith they crossed the Red Sea as on dry land; but when the Egyptians attempted it they were engulfed.

In faith the walls of Jericho fell after being circled for seven days.

In faith Rahab did not perish with the disobedient, because she received the spies peaceably.

And why should I continue? Time would fail me to tell of

[53] Gen. xxii. 17..   [54] Gen. xxiii. 4.   [55] Gen. xxi. 12.
[56] On the lintels and doorposts, Exod. xii. 22.

Gideon, Barak, Samson, Jephthah, of David too and Samuel, and the Prophets, who by faith conquered kingdoms, executed justice, won promises, stopped the mouths of lions, deprived fire of its power, escaped the devouring sword, from being weak were made strong, became mighty in battle and hurled back the ranks of the foe. Women by resurrection had their dead restored. Others had their limbs broken with clubs, refusing to accept release, to gain a better rising. Others were subjected to horse-play and flogging, and yet others to chains and imprisonment. They were stoned, burnt alive, tortured, sawn in two, and put to death by the sword. They went about in sheepskins and goatskins, in dire want, oppressed and ill-treated, men of whom the world was unworthy. They roamed over deserts and mountains, and lay in caves and holes in the ground. Yet all these, standing on record for their faith, did not secure the promise, God having had our best interest in view, that they should not be perfected without us.

This being the case, with such a dense throng of witnesses ranged about us, we too must throw aside every hampering conceit and closely-clinging sin. Let us run with grim determination our appointed course, keeping Jesus the starter and finisher of faith's race fixedly in mind, who for the sake of the bliss in store for him bore the cross, having scorned the shame, and has now taken his seat on the right hand of the throne of God. For think if you can of any who have had to endure such concerted opposition of sinners against themselves,[57] in case you get distressed and your hearts fail you. You have not resisted till you bled struggling against sin,[58] and you have completely forgotten the exhortation which appeals to you in filial terms,

> 'Son, make not light of the Lord's discipline,
> Nor be indifferent when reproved by him.
> For the Lord disciplines him whom he loves,
> And corrects every son he acknowledges.'[59]

Submit to discipline, since God treats you as sons; for where is the son whom his father does not discipline? But if you are without discipline of which all have their share, then you are bastards and not sons. Since, then, we have had those who were fathers of our physical being as disciplinarians, and we had a wholesome respect for them, shall we not much rather submit ourselves to the Father of our spirits, and live? For they indeed disciplined us for a brief time at their discretion, but he for our lasting good, that we may take after him in holiness. No discipline seems pleasant at the time: it is painful. But afterwards it repays those who are trained by it with the tranquil fruit of rectitude.

So tense the listless hands and the limp knees, and make firm straight tracks with your feet,[60] that the lagging step may not

[57] Cp. Acts iv. 25-27.   [58] Cp. Lk. xxii. 44.   [59] Prov. iii. 11-12.
[60] Cp. Job. iv. 3-4; Prov. iv. 25-26.

turn off the road, but rather recover ground. Follow peace with everyone, and that consecration without which no one will see the Lord, keeping a sharp look-out in case anyone is falling back from God's mercy, lest any bitter root springing up should cause inflammation and many be poisoned by it,[61] in case anyone should be immoral or unprincipled like Esau, who sold his birthright for a single meal. You know how when he wanted later to inherit the blessing he was rejected; for he discovered there was no opportunity left for his change of mind, though he tried tearfully to find it.

But you have not approached one who must grope,[62] nor to what is ablaze with fire, nor to murk, nor gloom, nor storm, nor trumpet-blast, nor to a Voice speaking,[63] which those who heard refused to have another word addressed to them;[64] for they could not bear what had been commanded, 'If even a beast touches the mountain it shall be stoned'.[65] Indeed, so awful was the spectacle that Moses said, 'I am terrified and trembling'.[66]

Instead you have approached Mount Zion, and the city of the Living God (heavenly Jerusalem), myriads of angels, the solemn assembly and gathering of the firstborn who are registered in heaven, God the judge of all, spirits of the just who have been perfected, Jesus the negotiator of a fresh covenant, and the spattered blood that speaks to better purpose than Abel's. Beware of disregarding the Speaker; for if they did not escape who refused to listen to him who conferred with them on earth, how much more we who turn our backs on him who confers with us from heaven? His voice then shook the earth, but now God has promised saying, 'Once more I will shake not the earth alone, but heaven also'.[67] And this 'once more' indicates a replacement of what is shaken, as with things that are made, that what is unshaken may endure. Therefore, because we are obtaining an unshaken Kingdom, let us feel the gratitude that will cause us to serve God acceptably with reverence and awe; for our God is an all-consuming fire.[68]

Let brotherly affection continue. Never neglect hospitality, for by giving it some have unwittingly entertained angels.[69] Remember those who are in bonds, as if you were bound with them, and those who are ill-treated, as having bodies yourselves.

Marriage is entirely honourable, and the undefiled marriage-bed; but God will judge the immoral and adulterous.

Let your nature be free from avarice. Be content with what you have, for God has said, 'I will never fail you nor desert

[61] Cp. Deut. xxix. 18.
[62] Like Isaac, who was blind, Gen. xxvii. 21 (LXX).
[63] Cp. Deut. iv. 11-12.
[64] Cp. Exod. xx. 19.
[65] Exod. xix. 12-13.
[66] Perhaps taken from an apocryphal work.
[67] Hag. ii. 6.
[68] Deut. iv. 24.
[69] Cp. Gen. xix. 1-2.

you'.[70] So that we may confidently say, 'The Lord is my helper, I will not fear. What can man do to me?'[71]

Remember your leaders, those who have declared God's Message to you. Copy their faith, closely observing the outcome of their manner of life.

Jesus Christ is the same nowadays and always, so do not be misled by varied and novel doctrines. It is well for the mind to be confirmed by loving-kindness, not by food, from which those who have argued about it have never gained any benefit. We have an altar off which those who serve the Tabernacle have no right to eat; for in the case of those beasts whose blood is brought into the sacred precincts by the High Priest for sin their carcases are to be burnt outside the camp.[72] Therefore Jesus too, that he might sanctify the people by his own blood, suffered outside the gate. So let us go out to him 'outside the camp', bearing his reproach;[73] for here we have no permanent city, we are seeking the one that is to come. Through him, therefore, let us continually offer to God 'the sacrifice of thanksgiving',[74] namely, 'the fruit of our lips',[75] confessing his Name.[76] But never neglect social service and fellowship, for with such sacrifices God is well-pleased.

Obey your leaders and give way to them, for they keep watch over your souls as those who must render an account, that they may do so with joy and not with sighing, for that would be detrimental to you.

Pray for us, for we trust that we have a good conscience, being anxious to live worthily in every way. But I particularly appeal to you for prayer that I may be restored to you sooner.

Now may the God of peace, who brought back from the dead that great shepherd of the sheep, our Lord Jesus, with the blood of a lasting covenant, equip you with every virtue to do his will, performing by you through Jesus Christ what is well-pleasing in his sight, to whom be glory for ever. Amen.

POSTSCRIPT

I beg you, brothers, bear with this message of exhortation, for indeed only to a slight extent have I given you orders. Let me add the news that Brother Timotheus has been released. If he comes soon I will see you with him.

Give my regards to all your leaders and all the saints. The Italians send you their regards.

Wishing you all every happiness.

[70] Josh. i. 5.
[71] Ps. cxviii. 6.
[72] Exod. xxix. 14.
[73] Like the scapegoat, Lev. xvi. 10.
[74] Lev. vii. 12.
[75] Hos. xiv. 2.
[76] I. Ki. viii. 33.

FOUR OPEN LETTERS

PETER
To Believers from the Gentiles in Asia
(I. Peter)

JAMES
To the Twelve Tribes in the Dispersion

JUDAS (JUDE)
To Believers from the Gentiles

'PETER'
To Believers from the Gentiles
(II. Peter)

Preface to the *Four Open Letters*

It was customary for the central Jewish Religious Authority in Palestine to address open or encyclical letters to the Jewish communities in other lands, advising on matters both religious and secular. The letters in this group, attributed to Peter, James and Jude, are Christian specimens of the same class of correspondence. The Jewish-Christian Authority, consisting of the Envoys and Elders at Jerusalem, regarded itself and was for a considerable time regarded as standing in the same relationship to the Christian communities elsewhere as the Sanhedrin at Jerusalem to the Jews of the Dispersion. The first head of the Nazarene Council was James the Just, the brother of Jesus, with Peter acting as a kind of vice-president. After the martyrdom of James about A.D. 62, and at the beginning of the Jewish war with Rome, the Nazarenes left Jerusalem for the region of Pella, east of the Jordan. There Simeon son of Cleophas, or Klopas, a name easily confused with that of Peter (Simeon Kephas), a cousin of Jesus, was elected president, and the Christian Sanhedrin included other surviving relatives of Jesus down to the beginning of the second century. Among them are mentioned James and Sokker, grandchildren of Jude, a younger brother of Jesus.

Appreciation of the existence of this Jewish-Christian Authority is essential not only for an understanding of these letters, but also for much else in the literary heritage of Christianity. Only now, as a result of research and discovery, is it beginning to be realized how substantial was the Jewish-Christian contribution.

The letter of Peter (*I. Peter*) has been placed first as there is a fair possibility that it was written by the Apostle from Rome about A.D. 65. It approximates more closely than the others to the type of letter written by Paul, and it has been held that the author was familiar at least with Paul's letter to the Roman believers (*Romans*) and his letter to Asian communities (*Ephesians*) written from Rome. The writer calls upon believers from the Gentiles to be of good behaviour under conditions of severe trial, and to give no offence to the authorities. The letter was composed in Greek though no doubt dictated in Aramaic to Silvanus (Silas). The curious commendation of the amanuensis may mean that Peter, ignorant of Greek, being unable to check what was written, was expressing his confidence that what he had said had in fact been set down.

There is a great deal less confidence in the authenticity of the letter of James, due to the good Greek in which it is written and to the lack of early references to the letter. It may be, however, that an early work, one of the earliest in the New Testament, was later discovered and made the groundwork of the present document. As evidence in favour of the letter's general antiquity much is made of the Judaic tone and the absence of a developed Christology. The document is related in spirit to the Jewish 'Wisdom' books in the Apocrypha. The author demands practical proof of faith in the performance of worthy and charitable actions, not merely an assertion of possessing it. Some would see in this an attack on Paul or on Pauline teaching. A difficulty in the way of accepting the work as genuine would be removed if it is allowed to have emanated from Jewish-Christian circles in the name of James, not necessarily the brother of Jesus, but perhaps that James the grandson of Jude to whom reference has been already made. He with his brother Sokker (perhaps Judas Sokker) are clearly stated by ancient tradition to have guided the Church in the closing years of the first century. They gained their living as farmers, and there are numerous allusions to land and farm in the letter.

Rural similes also occur in the short letter of Judas (Jude), who describes himself simply as 'brother of James'. Here again the writer could have been one of the brothers of Jesus, but the suggestion made above has stronger probability, that he was a grandson of that Jude of the same name. The letter attacks antinomian licentiousness in the Gentile-Christian communities and the author draws freely on Jewish apocryphal books to make his points. These works were highly venerated by the Jewish pietistic sects.

The fourth letter, claiming to be a second letter by Peter, is certainly pseudepigraphic. Both the external and even more the internal evidence is against the book's genuineness as the work of the Apostle. The writer has assumed Peter's identity in order to reinforce the message of Jude, which to some extent he has attempted to copy. His manner of referring to Christ, his acceptance of Paul's letters as Scripture, his allusions to the envoys, and his response to those who through the passage of time had become sceptical about the Second Advent, all reveal his late date. It has been held that the author was acquainted with the *Antiquities* of Josephus, and as the letter was also subsequent to that of Jude, its composition prior to the beginning of the second century is improbable.

OPEN LETTER TO THE GENTILE
CONVERTS IN ASIA

PETER

Peter, envoy of Jesus Christ, to the elect strangers[1] of the
Pontic, Galatian, Cappadocian, Asian and Bithynian areas
of the Dispersion, elected in accordance with the presci-
ence of God the Father, by spiritual consecration, to give
obedience[2] and to be sprinkled with the blood of Jesus
Christ. May abundant peace and prosperity be yours.

Blessed be the God and Father of our Lord Jesus, who in his
great loving-kindness has given us a new birth into a bright
and joyous hope by the resurrection of Jesus Christ from the
dead, into an imperishable, pure and fadeless inheritance that
has been kept safely in heaven for you, who by the power of
God are being safeguarded by faith for a salvation ready to
be revealed at the Last Time. In this you rejoice, even though
for a brief space now, as needs must be, you are saddened by
various trials; that the testing of your faith, so much more
precious than gold that perishes, yet is tested by fire, may result
in praise, esteem and honour at the revelation of Jesus Christ.

Him you love, never having set eyes on him, but believing in
him, still without seeing him, you yet rejoice with unutterable
and exalted joy, anticipating the final outcome of your faith,
the salvation of your souls. Prophets who have prophesied of the
mercy that would be yours have studied and investigated the
theme of this salvation, seeking to know the exact, or at least
the approximate date, which the spirit of Christ in them was
indicating when it testified in advance to the sufferings that
would befall Christ and the glory to follow. To them it was
revealed that it was not for themselves, but for you, they were
giving out those things which have now been reported to you
by those who have conveyed the News to you with holy Spirit
sent from heaven, things that angels long to pry into.

Brace your minds, therefore, remain calm and collected, expectant of the favour to be granted you at the revelation of
Jesus Christ. As obedient children, do not model yourselves on
your former lusts in your ignorance, but as the One who has
called you is holy, so be holy in all your behaviour, since it is
stated, 'You shall be holy, for I am holy'.[3] And as you address

---

[1] 'Elect strangers' may be a Christian equivalent of the Hebrew *Ger-zedek* ('a
righteous stranger'), technically a Gentile convert to Judaism. There can be little
doubt that believers of Gentile origin are intended here.
[2] I.e. to the proclamation of the One God and his Message.
[3] Lev. xi. 44.

yourselves to a Father who judges quite impartially in accordance with each individual's work, spend the remainder of the time of your sojourning reverentially, knowing that it was with no perishable materials, silver or gold, you were ransomed from your erroneous way of life handed down by your ancestors, but with the precious blood of Christ, as of a lamb without spot or blemish.[4] He was indeed foreordained before the foundation of the world, but only revealed at the end of the Ages for you who by him trust in God, who raised him from the dead and bestowed honour upon him, so that your faith and hope should be in God.

With your souls purified for sincere brotherly affection by obedience to the truth, love one another devotedly from the heart as those born anew not from a perishable life-germ but an imperishable, through the Message of the Living and Everlasting God. For,

> *All flesh is as grass,*
> *And all its glory as the flower of grass.*
> *The grass withers,*
> *And the flower drops;*
> *But the word of the Lord endures for ever.*[5]

It is that word which has been conveyed to you in the Good News.

Laying aside, therefore, everything base and deceitful, insincerities, jealousies and malicious gossiping, be eager like newborn babes for the pure and wholesome milk, once you have experienced how excellent the Master is, that you may grow to salvation by it. Coming to him, that precious stone,[6] rejected indeed by men, but chosen and prized where God is concerned, be built yourselves as precious stones into a spiritual dwelling, as a holy priesthood to offer up spiritual sacrifices through Jesus Christ acceptable to God, since it is contained in the Scripture,

See, I lay in Zion a chosen stone, a prized corner stone.
Whoever trusts in him will never come to grief.[7]

The honour, then, is for you who believe, but for the unbelieving, 'the stone which the builders rejected is made the coping-stone'[8] and 'a stumbling stone and boulder to trip over'.[9] They stumbled at the Message being disobedient, as indeed was ordained. But you are 'a chosen race, a royal priesthood, a holy nation,[10] a people for God's ownership',[11] that you may recite the merits of him[12] who has called you from darkness into his

---

[4] Cp. Lev. xxii. 18-20.
[5] Isa. xl. 6-8.
[6] Lit. 'living-stone'.
[7] Isa. xxviii. 16.
[8] Ps. cxviii. 22.
[9] Isa. viii. 14.
[10] Exod. xix. 6.
[11] Exod. xix. 5.
[12] Isa. xliii. 21 (LXX).

marvellous light, who once were 'no people', but now are God's people, who once 'had not obtained mercy', but now have received mercy.[13]

Dear friends, I appeal to you as strangers and sojourners to refrain from those physical lusts which are at war with the soul. Conduct yourselves honourably among the Gentiles, so that remarking your good behaviour in the very connexion in which they speak against you as evil-doers, they may praise God on the Day of Visitation.[14]

Give your obedience for the Master's sake to every human institution, whether it is to the emperor as paramount, or to governors as sent by him for the punishment of evil-doers and the commendation of well-doers; for so is the will of God, that you should silence the ignorant assertions of foolish men by well-doing. Give your obedience as freemen, or rather as slaves of God, not using your freedom as an excuse for depravity. Honour all, love the brotherhood, revere God, honour the emperor.

Domestic servants, be respectfully submissive to your masters, not only to those who are kind and considerate, but also to those who are wilful. For it is acceptable to God if for conscience's sake a man bears pain, suffering unjustly. But what virtue is it if you take it quietly when you are struck for your faults? But if you take it quietly when you suffer for well-doing, that is acceptable to God. To this indeed you were called, for Christ himself suffered on your behalf, leaving you a copy, that you should follow in his traces.[15] He committed no sin, nor did he employ deceit, when abused he did not return abuse, when suffering he uttered no threats, but left matters to him who judges justly. He himself in his own body carried our sins to the gibbet, that being 'taken from the earth' as regards sins we should live in rectitude; by 'whose bruise you have been healed'. For you were 'as sheep that have strayed', but now you have returned to the shepherd and guardian of your souls.

You wives, likewise, be submissive to your husbands, so that if any refuse acceptance of the Message they may be won over by the conduct of their wives with never a word said, having remarked the respectful virtuousness of your conduct. Of such women let not the adornment be the external one of braided hair, golden necklaces, or embroidered dresses, but the hidden one of the human heart in the imperishable beauty of a reposeful and gentle spirit, which is of great worth in the sight of God. It was thus the saintly women of old adorned themselves, who fixed their hope on God, being submissive to their husbands, as Sarah obeyed Abraham, calling him 'master'.[16] It is her daughters you are while you go quietly about your good work and

---

[13] Hos. ii. 23.   [14] See Isa. x. 3.
[15] Metaph. like a child tracing over the letters of a copybook. The copy is found in the account of the Suffering Servant in Isa. liii. on which the remainder of the paragraph is based in terms of Christ's experience.
[16] Gen. xviii. 12.

do not get nervously flustered.[17] You husbands likewise cohabit with your wives understandingly, giving satisfaction to the woman's requirements as the weaker vessel, as also being joint-heirs to the privilege of Life, that your prayers may not be obstructed.

The main thing is that all of you should be united, in sympathy with one another, affectionately disposed, kind-hearted, humble-minded, not returning evil for evil, or insult for insult, but on the contrary blessing, because for this you were called, that you should inherit a blessing.

> For he who desires a pleasant life
> And to see peaceful days,
> Let him keep his tongue from evil
> And his lips from speaking guile;
> Let him avoid evil and do good;
> Let him seek peace and pursue it.
> For the Lord's eyes are on the upright,
> And his ears are attentive to their prayer.
> But the Lord's face is against the evil-doers.[18]

And who is there who will harm you if you are zealous for what is good? But if you should suffer for righteousness's sake, you are indeed fortunate! But 'do not be afraid of the dread of them, neither be dismayed, and sanctify the Lord'[19] (namely Christ)[20] in your hearts, being ever ready to answer those who question you about the Hope that is yours, though mildly and respectfully with a good conscience, so that those who impugn your good conduct as Christians may be ashamed of what they say against you. It is indeed better, if that is God's will, to suffer for well-doing than for evil-doing; because Christ himself died for sins once and for all, the just for the unjust, to bring us to God, being put to death in the flesh but revived in the spirit, in which also Enoch[21] went and preached to the spirits in prison who formerly were disobedient while God's forbearance in Noah's time awaited the completion of the ark, in which a few, namely eight persons, were preserved by water. A counterpart of that water, the rite of immersion, not the removal of physical dirt but the request to God for a clear conscience, now preserves you also by the resurrection of Jesus Christ, who is at God's right hand, having passed into heaven, angels, authorities and powers having been made subject to him.

Christ, then, having suffered physically, arm yourselves with the like idea (for the physical sufferer has ceased to sin) so as to spend the remainder of your physical existence no longer

---

[17] Prov. iii. 25, though in a different connexion.
[18] Ps. xxxiv. 12-16.
[19] Isa. viii. 12-13.
[20] 'Namely Christ' may be an editorial addition. The quotation reads, 'the Lord himself' (LXX), 'the Lord of hosts himself' (Heb.)
[21] It has been credibly suggested that the name 'Enoch' has been accidentally omitted by an early copyist because of the immediately preceding ENOKAI ('in which also'). See *Enoch*, xiii.-xv. for his transactions with the errant angels.

controlled by human passions but by the will of God. It is enough to have devoted the time that has gone by to Gentile pursuits, when you indulged in various forms of licentiousness, sexual lusts, drinking bouts, revels, carousals and disorderly idolatries. They find it extraordinary that you do not join with them in the same excess of debauchery, and slander you. But they must render an account to him who stands ready to judge the living and the dead. That is why the News was proclaimed to the dead also, that they may be judged as men are judged physically, but live as God lives spiritually.

The climax approaches. Be temperate and sober, therefore, so as to attend to your prayers. Above all assiduously cultivate love among yourselves, for love atones for a multitude of sins.[22] Be ungrudging in your hospitality to one another. As each has been dowered, administer your particular gifts among yourselves as good stewards of God's varied favours. When one preaches, let it be as though it were with all the power at God's command, that in every connexion, through Jesus Christ, God may be glorified, to whom belongs the glory and domination for ever. Amen.

Do not be astounded, dear friends, at the fiery experience that has come to test you, as though something strange had happened to you. Rather rejoice that to some extent you share Christ's sufferings, so that at the revelation of his glory you may also rejoice exceedingly. If you are calumniated for Christ's sake, how fortunate you are, for the Spirit of glory and of God rests upon you! But let none of you suffer as a murderer, or as a thief, or as an evil-doer, or an interfering busybody, but if it is as a Christian, let him not be ashamed, let him praise God on that account, because it is the proper course for the Judgment to begin with the household of God. And if it begins with us, how will it end for those who have disobeyed God's News? 'If the righteous will scarcely be saved, where will the ungodly and the sinner come in?'[23] Wherefore let those who suffer for well-doing, in accordance with the will of God, commit their souls to a faithful Creator.

I beg the elders among you, therefore, I who am a fellow-elder and witness of Christ's sufferings, a sharer too in the glory that is about to be revealed, shepherd God's flock that is among you, not compulsorily but voluntarily, not self-interestedly but disinterestedly, not as domineering over your charges but as being examples to your flock. Then when the Head Shepherd appears you will obtain the evergreen wreath of honour.

Similarly, you younger men, subordinate yourselves to the elders. Always wear humility's apron[24] with one another, for 'God sets himself against the arrogant, but bestows favour on the humble'.[25]

[22] Prov. x. 12.
[23] Prov. xi. 31 (LXX).
[24] Humility is likened to the menial's apron.
[25] Prov. iii. 34.

Humble yourselves, therefore, under the mighty hand of God, that you may be exalted in due course, casting all your care upon him because he cares for you. Be sober, be alert! Your adversary the Devil is on the prowl like a roaring lion seeking prey. Resist him, steadfast in faith, knowing that the very same experiences are being faced by your fraternity elsewhere in the world. But the God of all mercy, who has called you to his eternal glory in Christ, after you have suffered a while will himself set, establish and strengthen you. To him be dominion for ever. Amen.

I have written to you thus very briefly by Silvanus,[26] a reliable brother as I hold, urging and affirming that this is the true grace of God. Stand in that.

Your elect sister-community in Babylon[27] sends you regards, as also does my son Mark. Convey my regards to one another with an affectionate kiss.

Peace be with all of you who are in Christ.

OPEN LETTER TO THE TWELVE TRIBES

JAMES

James, servant of God and the Lord Jesus Christ, sends greetings to the Twelve Tribes in the Dispersion.

Count it a most favourable occurrence, brothers, when you meet with various trying experiences, recognizing that the testing of your faith gives rise to constancy. But let constancy fulfil its complete function, so that you may be whole and hale, deficient in nothing. If any of you lacks wisdom, let him ask God, who gives to all bountifully and unstintingly, and it will be granted him. Only let him ask in faith with no misgiving, for the doubter is like a wave of the sea, driven by the wind and tossed hither and thither. Let not such a man, an indecisive character, vacillating in all his ways, expect to receive anything from the Lord.

Let the lowly brother rejoice when his circumstances are improved, but the well-to-do brother when his are reduced, for like the flower of grass he will pass away.[28] Once the sun has risen with its scorching rays it withers the grass, its flower drops, and its pleasant aspect is destroyed. Just so will the rich man shrivel in his tracks.

[26] The same as Silas, companion of Paul. The reliability is assumed to be in the capacity of interpreter and amanuensis, since Peter probably knew very little Greek.

[27] A Jewish apocalyptic designation of Rome. See Rev. xvii. 5; xviii. 2.

[28] Cp. Ps. xc. 3-7; Isa. xl. 6-8.

Happy is the man who holds out under temptation, for having been tested he will receive the award of Life, which God has promised to those who love him. Let no one say when he is tempted, 'I am being tempted by God'; for God is incapable of being tempted by evil and himself tempts no one. But each is tempted when beckoned and enticed by his own desires. Then when desire is embraced it begets sin, and sin once accomplished brings forth death. Do not delude yourselves, dear brothers. From Above comes every noble legacy and perfect gift, descending from the Supreme Luminary, which knows neither rising nor setting nor waxing and waning.[29] Of set purpose he begot us by the Message of Truth, so as to be in the nature of first-fruits of its creative activities.

You are aware of this, dear brothers. But let everyone be quick to hear, reluctant to speak, slow to be angry; for a man's anger does not serve the ends of divine justice. So clearing away every foul weed and rank growth in our moral nature, let us gently receive the implanted word that is able to save our lives.

Act on the Message, and do not merely listen to it, deluding yourselves. Whoever hears the Message and does not act on it is like a man who observes his natural appearance in a mirror. He takes stock of himself, but when he goes away he immediately forgets what he is like. But he who has looked into the untarnished law of liberty,[30] and stayed to gaze, being no forgetful listener but an active doer, will be blessed in what he does. If anyone deems himself devout,[31] not curbing his tongue but gulling his own mind, his devoutness is worthless, Pure and unalloyed devoutness in God's view is to care for the orphan and widow in their affliction and to keep oneself unsullied by the world.

Brothers, hold the faith of our Lord Jesus Christ with no partialities in your esteem. If a man with a gold ring splendidly dressed enters your synagogue, and there also comes in a poor man meanly dressed, but you show regard for the one wearing fine clothes and say, 'Please sit here where you'll be comfortable', while you say to the poor man, 'You can stand, or sit on the floor by my feet', are you not making distinctions among yourselves and letting evil considerations weigh with you?

Hearken, my dear brothers, has not God chosen the poor by the world's standard as rich in faith and heirs of the Kingdom he has promised to those who love him? But you have insulted the poor. Do not the rich oppress you and drag you into court? Do they not profane that fair name by which you are called? If you will but carry out that prince of laws in the

---

[29] Cp. Gen. i. 16, referring respectively to sun and moon, interpreting the astronomical terms employed.
[30] Here as elsewhere the writer alludes to the 'Law of the Gospel' in the Sermon on the Mount, interpreting the Law of Release, Deut. xv. 1-15.
[31] Scrupulous in religious observances like the Pharisees.

Scripture, 'You are to love your neighbour as yourself',[32] you will do well. But if you exhibit partiality you commit a sin, and are convicted by the Law as transgressors; for whoever may keep the whole Law, yet fail in one particular, becomes guilty in respect of all the rest. For he who said, 'Do not commit adultery', also said, 'Do not murder'. So if you do not commit adultery, yet commit murder,[33] you have become a transgressor of the Law. So speak, and so act, as those who will be judged by the law of liberty; for there will be judgment without mercy for him who has shown no mercy, while mercy will override judgment.

Of what avail is it, brothers, for someone to say he has faith, when he has no deeds to show for it? Can faith save him? If a brother and sister[34] are destitute, lacking even daily food, and one of you says to them, 'Go in peace. Mind you keep warm and take enough nourishment', but you give them no physical necessities for the purpose, what avails it? So with faith. Unless deeds spring from it it is dead in isolation.

One may put it this way. You have faith, you say, while I have deeds. Show me your faith independent of deeds, and I will show you my faith by my deeds. You believe there is one God, you say. It is well that you do believe it. But so do the demons, and they shudder. Can you not realize, you dunce, that faith without deeds is unproductive? Was not our father Abraham vindicated by his deeds when he offered his son Isaac upon the altar? Can you not see how faith assisted his deeds, and by his deeds his faith was perfected? And so the Scripture was fulfilled which states, 'Abraham believed God, and it was credited to him as rectitude',[35] and he was called 'the friend of God'.[36] You see, then, that a man is vindicated by the deeds, and not simply by faith. Was not Rahab the harlot likewise vindicated by her deeds, when she entertained the messengers and got them out another way? For as the body without the spirit is dead, so is faith without deeds.

Do not be all-inclusive teachers, brothers, knowing that we shall receive greater condemnation; for by attempting many things we fail in all. If a man makes no mistakes in a subject, he is an expert,[37] capable also of curbing the whole body. Look how we put bits in the mouths of horses to make them obey us, and so we steer their whole bodies. Look too at the ships. Large as they are and driven along by stiff breezes they are steered by a tiny rudder wherever the whim of the helmsman directs. Just so the tongue is an insignificant organ, but it boasts great things. Look how small a spark sets so mighty a forest ablaze! The very rule of misrule the tongue establishes among our organs: it is the soiler of the whole body and the inflamer of

---

[32] Lev. xix. 18.
[33] Exod. xx. 13-14. Murder here is metaphorical, cp. Mt. v. 21-22.
[34] Lit. 'brother or sister', but a married couple seems implied.
[35] Gen. xv. 6.   [36] Isa. xli. 8.   [37] Lit. 'a perfect man'.

the process of generation,[38] being inflamed itself by Gehenna.[39] Every species of beast and bird, reptile and marine creature, has been tamed by the human species. But the tongue no one can tame: it is an ungovernable evil, saturated with deadly poison. With it we bless the Lord our Father, and equally with it we curse men made in the image of God. This should not be, my brothers. Does a fountain gush fresh and brackish water from the same vent? Can a fig tree, my brothers, yield olives, or a vine figs? No more can salt water yield fresh.

Who among you claims wisdom and sagacity? Let him display his accomplishments by worthy conduct, with the moderation of wisdom. But if you have bitter jealousy and rivalry in your minds, do not boast and lie where truth is concerned. That wisdom never came from Above: it is earthly, materialistic and diabolical. For where bitter jealousy and rivalry exist, there will be found anarchy and every ugly business. But the wisdom from Above is first of all impartial, then peaceable, reasonable, persuasive, laden with mercy and beneficial fruits, free from favouritism and insincerity. For those who make peace the fruit of righteousness will be sown in peace.

What is the cause of your bellicose and pugnacious propensities? Is it not the animal instincts that war in your organs? You desire, but fail to acquire. You covet and envy, but you cannot secure. You battle and fight, but you do not possess by refusing to ask. You ask and then do not obtain, because you ask ill so that you can pander to your animal instincts. You adulterous creatures! Are you not aware that the world's intimacy means God's hostility? Whoever, therefore, wants to be a friend of the world renders himself an enemy of God. Or do you imagine that the Scripture states to no purpose, 'With *jealousy* does he desire the spirit which he has caused to dwell in us'?[40] Yet he bestows even greater loving-kindness, which is why it says, 'God sets himself against the arrogant, but bestows loving-kindness on the humble.'[41] Submit yourselves to God therefore, but oppose the Devil and he will fly from you.

> *Draw near to God*
> *and he will draw near to you.*
> *Cleanse your hands, you sinners,*
> *and purify your hearts, you double-minded.*
> *Afflict your souls,*
> *yes, mourn and weep.*
> *Let your laughter be turned to grief,*
> *and your joy to sorrow.*
> *Abase yourselves before the Lord,*
> *and he will raise you up.*[42]

---

[38] Perhaps implying unchastity, or the writer may hold Essene views on celibacy. James the Just was an ascetic.   [39] Hell fire.

[40] Not in the OT, probably from an apocryphal work regarded by the author as inspired. The source has not been traced.   [41] Prov. iii. 34.

[42] This poetic passage is not necessarily a quotation, though it may have been taken from a source unknown, perhaps liturgical. It reads like an exhortation before the Fast Day of Atonement.

Do not rail at one another, brothers. He who rails at his brother and condemns his brother rails at the Law and condemns the Law. But if you condemn the Law, you are no observer of the Law, but a judge of it. There is but one Lawgiver and Judge, who has power to preserve and destroy. Who are you, then, to judge your neighbour?

Come then, you who declare, 'To-day or to-morrow we will journey to this or that city, stay there a year, trade and make a profit', you who have no say in to-morrow's events. For what is your life? You are but a mist that is visible for a while and then vanishes. Instead of this you ought to say, 'If the Lord wills, we shall be alive and do so-and-so'. As it is you take pride in your idle boastings, and all such pride is wicked.

Come then, you rich, shed copious tears for the miseries that are coming upon you. Your riches have rotted and your clothes have become motheaten. Your gold and your silver are rusted over, and their rust will be evidence against you, and will eat into your flesh as a fire you have stored up for yourselves for the Last Day. See how the pay of the labourers who have reaped your meadows cries out, pay which you have held back, and the plaints of the harvesters have reached the ears of the Lord of hosts. You have grazed and gambolled upon the land, you have fattened yourselves up for a Day of Slaughter. You have condemned, you have murdered the upright. He does not resist you.[43]

Have patience then, brothers, till the coming of the Lord.[44] See how the farmer waits for the precious fruit of the earth, being patient until it can receive the early and late rain. So have patience yourselves, fortify your minds, for the coming of the Lord is at hand. Do not complain against one another, brothers, lest you are judged. Lo, the Judge stands at the door! Take the Prophets, brothers, who have spoken in the name of the Lord, as an example of suffering and fortitude. See how we eulogize those who have endured. You have heard of the constancy of Job, and you know its happy ending, how the Lord is full of compassion and tender mercy.[45] And above all, brothers, do not swear, either by heaven or earth, or with any other oath. Let your 'Yes' mean yes, and your 'No' mean no, lest you incur condemnation.[46]

Is any of you depressed? Let him pray. Is anyone cheerful? Let him sing psalms. Is any of you ailing? Let him summon the elders of the community, and let them pray for him after anointing him with oil in the name of the Lord. And the request in faith shall save the sick, and the Lord will raise him up. If he has committed sins they will be forgiven him. Confess your sins to one another, therefore, and pray for one another, that

---

[43] On this passage cp. Wisd. ii. 6-20. Cp. also Isa. liii. 7; Acts vii. 52.
[44] 'Coming of the Lord', perhaps Christ, but see Ps. xcvi. 13; Isa. xl. 10-11; Zech. xiv. 1-5.
[45] See Job. xlii. 10; cp. Num. xiv. 18.
[46] See above p. 94, n. 33.

you may be cured. The heartfelt petition of an upright man has great force. Elijah was a human being exactly like ourselves, and he prayed earnestly that it might not rain, and no rain fell on the land for three years and six months. Then he prayed again, and the heavens gave rain and the earth yielded its fruit.

Brothers, if any of you should stray from the Truth, and someone corrects him, be·sure that he who turns a transgressor from the error of his ways will save his own soul and atone for a multitude of sins.[47]

OPEN LETTER TO GENTILE COMMUNITIES

JUDAS

Judas, servant of Jesus Christ and brother of James, to the members of the communities dear to God the Father and kept by Jesus Christ.

While making every endeavour, dear friends, to write you on the theme of our common salvation, I have found myself obliged to write urging you to contend for the faith once and for all delivered to the saints. For certain people have managed to creep in, ungodly persons set down of old for judgment, converting the mercy of our God into licentiousness and disowning the Sole Sovereign and our Lord Jesus Christ.

I would remind you, therefore, though you once knew all this, how the Lord having saved the people from the land of Egypt afterwards destroyed those who did not believe. The angels too, who did not keep to their own province, but forsook their native habitat,[48] he has kept in close confinement[49] in subterranean gloom for the Judgment of the Great Day, even as Sodom and Gomorrah and the towns in their proximity, having after the same manner as these taken to obscene ways and indulgence in unnatural vice are presented as an example, suffering the penalty of perpetual burning.

Notwithstanding this, these dreamers similarly defile the flesh, defy disciplines, and speak slightingly of dignities. Yet even the Archangel Michael, when, at odds with the Devil, he argued about the body of Moses, did not care to make an abusive attack on him, but said, 'The Lord rebuke you!'[50] But these

---

[47] Cp. Ps. xxxii. 1-2.
[48] Gen. vi. 2; *Enoch*, xii. 4, 'the watchers of the heaven who have abandoned the high heaven . . . and have defiled themselves with women'.
[49] Or 'enduring fetters' (*Enoch*, xiv. 5).
[50] *Assumpt. Moses*, cp. Zech. iii. 2.

people speak slightingly of such things as they know nothing about, while in such things as they are familiar with instinctively, like brute beasts, in these they corrupt themselves. Woe to them! They have travelled the road of Cain, and plunged greedily for gain into the vice of Balaam, and perished in the mutiny of Korah.[51] These are the hidden snags sharing the entertainment of your love-feasts, feeding themselves fearlessly, empty clouds carried away by winds, trees that are autumn-blasted, and of barren, dead twice over, torn up by the roots, raging breakers of the sea foaming with their own shame, wandering stars for whom is reserved the blackness of darkness for ever.[52]

Concerning these men Enoch, the seventh from Adam, prophesied saying, 'Lo, the Lord comes with myriads of his holy ones to execute judgment upon all, and to convict all the ungodly of all their ungodly deeds for which they have been responsible, and of all the harsh things ungodly sinners have said against him'.[53] These men are complainers, bewailers of their lot, followers of their impulses, with mouths that speak fulsomely,[54] flattering people for some expected benefit.

You however, dear friends, recall the words spoken in advance by the envoys of our Lord Jesus Christ, when they told you, 'In the Last Time deceivers will come, followers of their ungodly impulses'.[55] These are the separatists, unspiritual materialists. You however, dear friends, develop yourselves in your most sacred faith, praying by the holy Spirit, retaining God's regard, awaiting the mercy of our Lord Jesus Christ for Eternal Life. Take pity on some, of course, and save them with eager resolution, snatching them from the blaze.[56] Take pity on others too, but save them with repugnance, loathing even the tunic soiled by the flesh.[57]

Now to him who is able to keep you steady, and enable you to stand proudly blameless in the presence of his glory, to the only God our Saviour, be glory, majesty, might and dominion, through Jesus Christ our Master, from all eternity, now, and to all eternity. Amen.

[51] The sequence 'travelled—plunged greedily—perished' bears some resemblance to the fate of the Gadarene swine, Mt. viii. 22, though this may not be intentional in making these allusions to the OT.
[52] Cp. *Enoch*, xviii. 14, 16.
[53] *Enoch*, i. 9.
[54] Cp. *Assumpt. Moses*, vi. 6-9.
[55] Mt. xxiv. 24; Acts xx. 29-31; I. Tim. iv. 1; II. Tim. iii. 1.
[56] Amos iv. 11; Zech. iii. 2.
[57] Zech. iii. 3.

OPEN LETTER TO GENTILE CONVERTS
IN ASIA
'PETER' (2)

Simeon Peter, servant and envoy of Jesus Christ, to those[58] who by the beneficence of our God and of our Saviour Jesus Christ have obtained a faith equal in privilege to ours. May abundant peace and prosperity be yours in the knowledge of God and of Jesus our Master.

Since God's divine power has granted us everything useful for life and piety through knowledge of him who has called us to his own nobility and virtue, by which those precious and marvellous promises have been given us, that having escaped by them the corruption the world is heir to by passion you may become sharers of the divine nature; for that very reason, having additionally brought to bear the utmost diligence, join virtue to your faith, knowledge to virtue, self-control to knowledge, constancy to self-control, piety to constancy, brotherly affection to piety, and love to brotherly affection. For where these qualities exist and abound they assure that you are neither uncultivated nor unfruitful where the knowledge of our Lord Jesus Christ is concerned. But in that man's case where these are not present, he is blind, being short-sighted, obtaining absolutely nothing[59] from his cleansing from his sins in the not so distant past.

Preferably therefore, brothers, use every endeavour to make your calling and choice certain, for by practising these qualities you will never come to grief. And thus an ample entrance will be afforded you into the Lasting Kingdom of our Lord and Saviour Jesus Christ.

I therefore intend always to remind you of these things, though you know them and are firmly established in the revealed truth. But I think it right, as long as I remain in this mortal frame, to keep you wide awake by reminder, knowing that the laying aside of my frame will come very soon now, as our Lord Jesus Christ has shown me. I will further endeavour to enable you after my departure to keep these things constantly in mind. For we have followed no cleverly contrived fables when we acquainted you with the power and presence of our Lord Jesus Christ, but were eye-witnesses of his majesty;

---

[58] Gentile converts who did not observe the Law of Moses.
[59] Lit. 'a blur' or 'blank' in accordance with the metaphor.

for he received from God the Father honour and glory when from the Supernal Glory language such as this was addressed to him, 'You are my dear Son, with whom I am well-satisfied'.[60] These were the very words we ourselves heard addressed to him from heaven when we were with him on the holy mount. And we possess the even more definitely Prophetic Message to which you will do well to pay attention, a Message that is like a lamp shining in a dismal place until daylight streams in and the morning star rises in your hearts. But this you must realize first of all, that no prophecy of Scripture is to be interpreted individually, for prophecy never came at human bidding: men spoke from God under compulsion of the holy Spirit.

Nevertheless there were false prophets among the people, just as there will be false teachers among you, who will introduce subversive principles, disowning even the Sovereign Lord who bought them, and bringing on themselves swift destruction. Many will follow them in their immoral courses, with the result that the True Way will be maligned. Yes, in their rapacity these false teachers will cheat you with their fabricated messages. But not for long will their judgment dawdle, or their destruction drowse. God did not spare angels who had sinned, but hurling them down to Tartarus consigned them to caverns of darkness, there to await judgment. He did not spare the ancient world, but saved Noah, eighth preacher of righteousness,[61] bringing a Deluge upon the world of impious men. The cities of Sodom and Gomorrah also he sentenced to be burnt to ashes, making them a warning of what is in store for the impious, but rescued virtuous Lot utterly prostrated by the licentious behaviour of the immoral people; for that virtuous man by what he saw and heard while living among them tortured his pure soul day after day with their lawless behaviour. If the Lord did these things he surely knows how to rescue the pious from temptation, and to keep the wicked under restraint for the Day of Judgment, particularly those who in their vile lust go in for unnatural vice and despise discipline. Daring, presumptuous, they are not the least overawed by dignities, speaking slightingly of them. Whereas angels who are greater in might and power than such dignities make no abusive attack on them before the Lord. These men, however, like natural brute beasts made for capture and destruction, speaking slightingly as they do of such things as they know nothing about, will surely perish in their corruption, suffering injury as the reward of inflicting injury.

These are the people who deem wantonness in the daytime a special pleasure: blots and disgraces, luxuriating in their seductive wiles, even when feasting with you, with eyes full of adultery that never rest a moment from sin, enticing unstable souls, and with a mind fully trained in gaining their ends. Off-

---

[60] Cp. Mt. xvii. 5.
[61] Eighth in succession to Seth. Cp. Jos. *Antiq.* I. iii. 1; Gen. v.

spring of execration! They have gone astray, abandoning the straight road, following in the steps of Balaam son of Beor,[62] who loved the fees of iniquity, but was reproved for his transgression: a dumb beast of burden speaking with a human voice checked the prophet's aberration. They are springs without water, tempest-driven spray, for whom the blackness of darkness is reserved. With their high-flown nonsensical talk they entice with their base physical passions those who have only just escaped from those who live in error. They promise them liberty, while they themselves are the slaves of corruption; for a man is enslaved by whatever he gives way to. For if, escaping from the world's pollutions by knowledge of the Lord and Saviour Jesus Christ, they are vanquished by being again enmeshed by them,[63] their last state is worse than the first.[64] Far better for them never to have known the way of righteousness, than knowing it to have gone back on the sacred injunction delivered to them. They only confirm what the true proverb says, 'The dog has returned to his vomit,[65] and the washed sow to her wallowing in the mire'.

The letter I am writing you now, dear friends, is my second, and my intention with these letters is to stimulate your clear thinking by reminder, that the words spoken beforehand by the holy Prophets and the injunction of the Lord and Saviour by your envoys may be brought back to you. In the first place you must realize this, that in the Last Days there will surely come scoffers, following their own desires and saying, 'What has become of the promise of his advent, for since the fathers fell asleep everything goes on exactly as it has done since the beginning of Creation?' They choose to ignore the fact that the sky and earth, formed by the word of God out of water and by water,[66] had been a long time in existence, yet the world of those days perished, inundated with water by these agencies.[67] By the very same word the present sky and earth have been stocked with fire, kept for the Day of Judgment and the destruction of ungodly mortals. There is this too that must not escape your notice, dear friends, that a single day with the Lord is as a thousand years, and a thousand years as a single day.[68] The Lord is not dilatory in fulfilling his promise as some reckon dilatoriness: he is forbearing to you, not wanting any to perish, but all to come to repentance.

Nevertheless the day of the Lord will come like a thief, when the sky will vanish with a roar, the elements will be disintegrated with intense heat, and of the earth and its occu-

---

[62] The alternative reading 'Bosor' may be original if intended as a word-play to represent 'basar' (Heb. flesh).
[63] Perhaps a metaphor taken from the retiarii, gladiators armed with net and trident.
[64] Cp. Mt. xii. 45.
[65] Cp. Prov. xxvi. 11.
[66] See Gen. i. 6-10.
[67] See Gen. vii. 11.
[68] Ps. xc. 4.

pants there will be left no trace. Since in this manner all these are to be disintegrated, what pure-living and devout persons ought you to be while eagerly expecting the Day of the Lord, in which the sky will go up in flames and the elements melt away with intense heat? Yet in accordance with God's promise we expect a new sky and a new earth[69] wherein righteousness dwells.

Consequently, dear friends, because we expect these things let us be anxious to be found by him in peace,[70] spotless and unblemished, and regard the forbearance of our Master as our salvation. Our dear brother Paul, according to the wisdom given him, has also written you to the same effect,[71] as indeed is true of all his letters where he speaks of these matters, letters in which there are certain things by no means easy to understand, which the unskilled and unstable twist to their own ruination as they do the rest of the Scriptures.[72] Being forewarned then, dear friends, be on your guard, so that you are not deprived of that firm support[73] by being led away by the error of unprincipled persons. Grow, then, in the favour and knowledge of our Lord and Saviour Jesus Christ, to whom be praise both now and for time eternal.[74]

[69] Cp. Isa. lxv. 17.
[70] Referring to Christ, his coming in peace and not in anger to punish.
[71] In his letter to the Asian Communities (Ephesians), cp. Eph. iii. 2-4; iv. 30; v. 6-8.
[72] By the author's time Paul's letters had evidently been collected and were accepted as Scripture.
[73] I.e. of the Scriptures.
[74] Lit. 'to the Day of Eternity'. A doxology with reference to Christ is another evidence of late date, as also is the expression several times used, 'Our Lord and Saviour Jesus Christ'.

THE WRITINGS OF JOHN

THE DISCOURSES OF THE LOGOS
(Gospel according to John)

ON THE THEME OF 'LIFE'
(I. John)

TO THE ELECT LADY AND HER CHILDREN
(II. John)

TO GAIUS
(III. John)

THE REVELATION OF JESUS CHRIST

THE DISCOURSES OF THE LOGOS

Preface to *John*

What are known as the Johannine writings consist of a Gospel, a tract, two letters, and a book of visions. They are the most puzzling documents in the whole New Testament collection. The first is anonymous, but is stated to contain the reminiscences of someone described as 'the disciple of whom Jesus was fond'. The tract (*I. John*) is also anonymous, but appears to be by the same writer as the two letters (*II. John* and *III. John*), the author of which calls himself 'the Elder' or 'Presbyter'. It is only the book of visions (*Revelation*) that is actually stated to have been recorded by a person of the name of John. On linguistic grounds alone it is almost certain that this John was not identical with the Elder or with the author of the Gospel in its present form; yet the *Revelation* is not wholly unrelated to the other documents.

The intimations of tradition are not sufficiently certain for any clear-cut pronouncement to be made. It is quite possible that both the Beloved Disciple and the Elder were called John, yet were two distinct persons, neither of them being—as was later supposed by some—the Apostle John the son of Zebedee, one of the Twelve. A letter has been preserved by Eusebius sent at the end of the second century by Polycrates, bishop of Ephesus, to Victor, bishop of Rome, in which he mentions that John the Beloved Disciple, who had once served as a High Priest, was buried at Ephesus. This man, probably the same as the 'John, the disciple of the Lord' referred to by Papias of Hierapolis, seems to have lived to an advanced age and to have died in the reign of Trajan. John the Elder, however, appears to have been a Greek, and a very uncompromising character. But the records are very confused, and the Beloved Disciple may also have been known as an Elder, the transmitter of certain traditions characteristic of the author of the *Revelation*. Whether there was any living relationship between the two cannot be determined; but that there was a literary relationship, either actual or subsequently arranged by a section of the Asian Church, there seems no good reason to doubt. To all intents and purposes the Greek Presbyter stepped into the shoes of the Jewish Priest.

The documents themselves are much more revealing of the personalities concerned, and fully confirm what the traditions only tentatively suggest. On the one hand, in the Gospel as it stands and in the Letters, we have a writer of good Greek, though very repetitious, a man with a non-Jewish background, strong views, and a very distinctive Christology. On the other hand, in the *Revelation*, we have a writer of barbarous Greek, whose native tongue seems to be Aramaic, a man who knows Palestine and Jerusalem well, is intimately acquainted with Jewish ritual and literature, and has been trained in Jewish mysticism. But there is this curious phenomenon. The Gospel contains, in the narrative portions, a great deal that is characteristic of the author of the *Revelation,* while the *Revelation,* in the Letters to the Seven Churches and some other passages, contains material which is typical of the writer of the Letters and the larger part of the present Gospel. The conclusion to which this points is that somehow in the Gospel and the *Revelation* the works of the Greek Presbyter and the Jewish Priest have been combined. In the Gospel the Greek Presbyter predominates, while in the *Revelation* it is the other way round.

Leaving the Letters and *Revelation* for further consideration in their respective Prefaces, let us briefly examine the peculiarities of the Fourth Gospel. A prolonged study has convinced the present editor and translator that we have here to do with separate literary contributions by two authors which amount to two distinct works. The underlying document, or source, much adapted and with many omissions, represents the reminiscences of the Beloved Disciple. He betrays his priestly office not only by exact references to Jewish ritual and Temple worship, but when he speaks of the priests not going into the praetorium to avoid defilement, and when he will not himself enter the tomb in which Jesus had been laid until he knows there is no corpse there. He is an acquaintance, possibly a relation, of the High Priest. Miracles of Jesus located by the Synoptic writers in Galilee are by him transferred to Jerusalem. He knows the topography well, and introduces and explains Aramaic words. It may have been his original intention to set out events in the life of Jesus in the form of a series of signs which establish that he was the Messiah, each introduced by the formula, 'After this', or 'after these events', a design which is still preserved down to AV. vii. 1, and is then abandoned until xix. 38. At various points expressions clearly reveal his knowledge of incidents contained in other Gospels, which are omitted in the text as we have it, but which may well have been in the underlying document. Early patristic quotations, and even fragments of an unknown Gospel (Egerton Papyrus I), reveal a form of certain sayings in the Fourth Gospel much closer in style and character to what we find in the Synoptics. It is said by various ancient authorities, including what are called the Anti-Marcionite Prologues, that the old Jewish Priest dictated his work. But in its original form that book, if it was ever published, is now lost.

The second work, which has so largely been imposed on and

superseded the other, is a Dialogue in the Greek Platonic tradition. It is in two parts, the first a Discourse of Jesus to the
Jews and the second a Discourse to the Apostles. The first part
has been chopped up, and most unskillfully inserted into
the Gospel incidents at different points and times, often
months apart and quite inappropriately, and out of the
Dialogue's natural order. The second part, also to some extent
in disarray, occupies Jn. xiii-xvii, section xi of the present
translation. Scholars have long recognized, even when regarding the Gospel as a unity, that there have been a number
of displacements, and that to restore continuity certain transpositions have to be made. These can only be tentative, and
those which the present editor has proposed do not in all cases
coincide with the proposals of others. The changes can be
followed by the student by means of the footnotes. One theory
which has been put forward to account for the state of the text
is that the Gospel had survived on separate strips of papyrus,
and that these were subsequently glued together to make a roll
with the unnumbered strips placed in the wrong order. This
does not seem a likely solution, and does not account for many
of the features of the book. Some careless amalgamations of
material there certainly have been, but it is of two distinct
types of work by different authors. It may well be that in the
heading of *I. John,* a tract which it has been held was meant
to introduce the Gospel, we have the actual title of the composite document, namely, 'On the Theme (or Message) of
LIFE' *(Peri tou Logou tes Zoes),* or in the briefer form of
the Latin Vulgate, *De Verbo Vitae.*

In the Dialogue document Jesus is the Divine Son of the
Father, whose earthly birth is not mentioned. He has come
direct from God and entered the world, and returns to God.
His human qualities almost entirely disappear. He addresses
the Jews as though not himself a Jew, and in disparaging
terms. The Law of Moses is 'your Law'. It is no wonder that
it has been suggested on the basis of some possible traditional
references that the Christian heretic Marcion of Pontus, who
opposed the God revealed by Jesus to the Creator God
(Demiurge) of the Old Testament, had some hand in the draft-
ing. The peculiarity of the Dialogue document, in keeping
with its nature, is that both the Jews and the Apostles appear
in it virtually as lay figures, enabling Jesus to make his points
by their interjection of unreal comments and questions. The
discourses of Jesus himself are full of repetitions. He speaks
indeed exactly as the author of *I. John* writes.

Even in the reminiscences of the old Jewish Priest there are
traces of the Elder's hand. These appear in certain comments
distinctive of this writer and also in the incidents themselves.
It is a feature of the Fourth Gospel, quite apart from the
Dialogue document, that much is related in conversational
terms, the meeting with Nicodemus and with the Samaritan

woman, the story of the man blind from birth. In these incidents the original account has been partially adapted in conformity with the Elder's views. One story, in a different style and quite out of place in its present position, cannot be the Elder's work. It is the story of the woman taken in adultery. Many MSS. omit it, or bring it in elsewhere. Papias of Hierapolis is said by Eusebius to have quoted a story like it which was in the *Gospel of the Hebrews*. It may nevertheless have been reported by the Beloved Disciple.

Who exactly the Beloved Disciple and Jewish Priest was is still an open question. Some scholars have suggested that he was Lazarus, whom Jesus raised from the dead. But it is by no means improbable that the man who is said to have taken the mother of Jesus into his home was the greatly trusted young owner of the house in which the Last Supper was held, the house which afterwards became the headquarters of the disciples. However this may be, the author of the present Gospel clearly distinguishes himself in two footnotes (Jn. xix. 35 and xxi. 24) from the Beloved Disciple of whose reminiscences he has availed himself. These footnotes are in the characteristic style of the Elder who is the author of the Letters of John, as may be seen especially by comparing Jn. xxi. 24 with I. Jno. 12. The last chapter of the Gospel also confirms the tradition that the Beloved Disciple lived to a very great age.

Finally, the Prologue to the Fourth Gospel is of some service both in locating and dating the book. This Prologue takes the form of an antiphonal chant, which could well be the very same that is mentioned by Pliny the Younger in his letter about the Christians (c. A.D. 112) sent when he was Governor of Bithynia to the Emperor Trajan. It will be remembered that the Beloved Disciple is said to have died in Trajan's reign and to have been buried at Ephesus. These links with Asia Minor are reinforced by the prominence given to the Apostle Philip in the Gospel. He is stated to have been buried at Hierapolis. Andrew and Thomas also, who are specially mentioned in the Gospel, are quoted among apostolic sources of information used by Papias of Hierapolis. The traditions would therefore appear to be authentic which make Asia Minor the region of publication of the Fourth Gospel; and since Trajan became emperor in A.D. 98 the book in its present form may approximately be dated about the end of the first decade of the second century.

THE GOOD NEWS OF JESUS CHRIST

John's Version

PROLOGUE[1]

In the beginning was the Word.[2]
And the Word was with God.
So the Word was divine.
He was in the beginning with God.
By him everything had being.
And without him nothing had being.[3]
What had being by him was Life.
And Life was the Light of men.
And the Light shines in the Darkness.
And the Darkness could not suppress it.

There was a man sent from God called John. He came as a witness, to testify about the Light, that all might believe through him. He was not himself the Light, but came that he should testify about the Light.

This was the true Light.
It illumines all who enter the world.
He was in the world, [and the world had being by him.]
But the world did not recognize him.
He came to his own domains.
And his own did not receive him.

On those who did receive him, those who believed in him,[4] he conferred the privilege of becoming children of God, who owed their being not to race, nor physical intention, nor to human design, but to God.

The Word took bodily form and dwelt with us.
And we beheld his glory.
Glory as of the Father's Only-begotten.
Full of loving-kindness and truth.

---

[1] The Prologue consists of a hymn interspersed with brief remarks. The hymn is antiphonal, the alternate lines being chanted as a response. Our book was published in Asia Minor early in the second century, and this hymn could well be the one mentioned by Pliny the Younger, when as Governor of Bithynia (c. A.D. 112) he wrote about the Christians to the Emperor Trajan, that 'they met on a certain fixed day before it was light and sang an antiphonal chant to Christ, as to a god'. See also *Acts of John*, 94-6.
[2] The *Logos*, the expressed concept, here personified.
[3] Cp. Prov. viii. 22-31.
[4] Cp. Jn. xii. 36, below p. 414.

John testified of him and proclaimed—these were his very words—'He who comes after me ranks before me; for he is my superior.'

For of his bounty we have all received.
Yes, mercy added to mercy.
For the Law was given by Moses.
Loving-kindness and truth came by Jesus Christ.

No one has ever seen God.[5] God's Only-begotten, who is in the Father's bosom, he has portrayed him.

I

Here is John's testimony when the Jews of Jerusalem sent priests and Levites to him to ask him, 'Who are you?' He admitted without the slightest hesitation, he clearly admitted, 'I am not the Messiah.'

Then they asked him, 'What then? Are you Elijah?'

'I am not,' he said.

'Are you the Prophet?'[6]

'No,' he replied.

Then they said to him. 'Who are you, that we may give an answer to those who sent us? What do you say of yourself?'

He said, 'I am a voice crying in the wilderness, "Level the Lord's road,"[7] as announced by the Prophet Isaiah.'

'They asked him further, 'Why then are you immersing if you are not the Messiah, nor Elijah, nor the Prophet?'

'I am immersing in water,' John replied. 'But there stands among you one whom you do not know, my successor, whose sandal-strap I am not worthy to unlace.'[b]

On the following day John saw Jesus approaching him and said, 'See, the Lamb of God who takes away the sin of the world! It is he of whom I said, "After me will come a man who ranks before me; for he is my superior." I did not know him, only that he would be revealed to Israel. That is why I came immersing in water.'

John testified further, 'I saw the Spirit flutter down like a dove from heaven and settle on him. I did not know him. I only knew that he who sent me to immerse in water told me, "The one on whom you see the Spirit descend and settle is he who will immerse in holy Spirit." I did see it, and have testified that he is the Son of God.'

The next day John was again standing with two of his disciples, and seeing Jesus go by, he said, 'There goes the Lamb of God!'

[a] Those who were sent belonged to the Pharisees.
[b] These things took place at Bethany-beyond-Jordan[8] where John was immersing.

[5] Cp. I. Jno. iv. 12.   [6] The expected Prophet like Moses.   [7] Isa. xl. 3.
[8] Probably meaning 'Place of a boat'. An alternative reading is Bethabara (Place of the crossing). The site of this particular ferry is uncertain; but it is likely to have been towards the southern end of the Jordan Valley.

His two disciples heard his exclamation and followed Jesus. Jesus turned and observing them following him said to them, 'What is it you want?'

'To know where you are staying, rabbi,'[a] they told him.

'Come and see,' he said.[b]

So they went along and saw where he was staying and remained with him the rest of the day. One of the two who was beside John and heard what he said was Andrew brother of Simon Peter. First thing in the morning he found his brother Simon and said to him, 'We have found the Messiah[c]!'

He brought him to Jesus, and when Jesus saw him he said to him, 'You are Simon son of John, are you not? You shall be called Kepha.[d]'

On the following day Jesus wished to leave for Galilee, and found Philip. 'Follow me!' Jesus said to him.[e]

Philip in turn found Nathaniel, and said to him, 'We have found him of whom Moses wrote in the Law, and the Prophets also, Jesus son of Joseph from Nazareth!'

'Whatever good can come out of Nazareth?' replied Nathaniel.

Philip said to him, 'Come and see.'

Jesus saw Nathaniel coming towards him, and said to him, 'Here is a true Israelite in whom there is no guile.'

'Have we met before?' Nathaniel inquired.

Jesus replied, 'I saw you before Philip called you, when you were under the fig tree'.[9]

'Rabbi,' said Nathaniel, 'you *are* the Son of God, you *are* the King of Israel!'[10]

Jesus said to him, 'Do you believe this because I told you I saw you beneath the fig tree? You shall see much more than that. I tell you for a positive fact,[11] you shall see the sky wide open and the angels of God ascending and descending on the Son of Man.'[12]

The next day but one there was a wedding at Cana of Galilee and the mother of Jesus was there. Jesus had also been invited to the wedding with his disciples. When they ran short of wine the mother of Jesus said to him, 'They have no wine.'

'What do you want with me, madam?' Jesus said to her. 'My time has not yet come.'

'Do whatever he tells you,' his mother said to the servants.

Now there were six stone water-jars standing there in ac-

---

[a] Translated, this means 'teacher'.

[b] It was about 4 o'clock.

[c] Translated, this means 'Anointed' (*Christos*).

[d] Meaning 'Rock' (*Petros*).

[e] Philip was from Bethsaida, the same town as Andrew and Peter.

[9] Cp. Zech. iii. 8-10, 'I will bring forth my servant the Branch . . . In that day, says the Lord of hosts, you shall call every man his neighbour under the vine and under the fig tree.'

[10] Cp. I. Chron. xxviii. 6; Ps. ii. 6-7.

[11] 'Positive fact' representing the double 'Amen'.

[12] Cp. Jacob's dream, Gen. xxviii. 12.

cordance with Jewish requirements for purification, each holding from eighteen to twenty-seven gallons.

'Fill the jars with water,' Jesus instructed the servants.

So they filled them to the brim.

Then he said to them, 'Now ladle it out, and serve it to the chairman of the banquet.'

So they served it.

When the chairman of the banquet tasted the water that had become wine, and had no knowledge of its source, though the servants who had drawn the water knew, the chairman called across to the bridegroom, 'Most people put out the best wine first, and the inferior when everyone is drunk. You have saved up the best wine till now.'

Jesus performed this, the very first of his signs, in Cana of Galilee, and revealed his quality: and his disciples believed in him.

II

After this Jesus went down to Capernaum, he, and his mother, and his brothers, and his disciples, but they did not stay there very long.

The Jewish Passover was approaching, and Jesus went up to Jerusalem. In the Temple he found the dealers in oxen, sheep and doves, and the money-changers sitting. And when he had made a lash of twisted rushes he drove them all from the sacred enclosure, sheep and oxen as well, and sent the money-changers' coins flying, and overturned their tables, while he told the dove-sellers, 'Take these out of here. Do not make a mart of my Father's house.' [a] [13]

The Jews wanted an explanation, and said to him, 'What sign have you to show us for acting like this?'

Jesus replied, 'Demolish this temple, and in three days I will raise it up.'

'This Temple has been under construction for forty-six years,' [14] said the Jews, 'and are you going to raise it up in three days?' [b]

While he was in Jerusalem for the Passover, for the festival, many believed in him when they saw the signs he performed. [c]

[a] His disciples remembered how it is stated, 'Zeal for your house shall consume me' (Ps. lxix. 9).

[b] But he spoke of the temple of his body. When, therefore, he had risen from the dead his disciples remembered that he had said this, and they believed the Scripture (Hos. vi. 1-2) and the saying Jesus had spoken.

[c] But Jesus did not trust himself to them since he knew all men, and had no need for anyone to speak on a man's behalf because he himself was well aware of that person's character.

[13] The Cleansing of the Temple is placed in Passion Week in the other Gospels and may be misplaced here.

[14] Herod the Great had begun the rebuilding of the Temple in 20 B.C. This would date this incident about A.D. 26.

There was one man who belonged to the Pharisees called Nicodemus, a member of the Jewish government. This man came to Jesus at night, and said to him, 'Rabbi, we know that you are a teacher come from God,[15] for no one can perform such signs as you do unless God is with him.'

Jesus replied, 'I tell you for a positive fact, unless one is born from Above[16] one cannot see the Kingdom of God.'

Nicodemus said to him, 'How can a man be born when he is old? Surely he cannot enter his mother's womb a second time and be born?'

Jesus answered, 'I tell you for a positive fact, unless one is born of water and spirit one cannot enter the Kingdom of God. What is born physically is physical, and what is born spiritually is spiritual. Do not be surprised at my telling you that you have to be born from Above. The wind[17] blows where it will. You hear the sound of it, but you do not know where it comes from or where it is going. So is everyone who is born of the Spirit.'

'How can this be?' Nicodemus inquired.

'You are a teacher in Israel,[18] and do not know this?' said Jesus. 'I tell you for a positive fact, we discourse of what we know, and testify to what we have seen; but you do not accept our testimony. If I tell you mundane things, and you are incredulous, how will you credit it if I tell you heavenly things? And no one has ascended to heaven but he who has descended from heaven, the Son of Man. And just as Moses elevated the serpent in the wilderness,[19] so must the Son of Man be elevated, that all who believe in him may have Eternal Life.' [a][20]

III

After these events Jesus went with his disciples into Judea, and spent some time there immersing people. John also was

[a] For God loved the world so dearly as to give his Only-begotten Son, so that all who believe in him should not perish but have Eternal Life. God did not send his Son into the world to condemn the world, but that the world might be saved through him. Whoever believes in him will not be condemned, but whoever does not believe in him has been condemned already, because he has not believed in God's Only-begotten Son. The condemnation consists in this, that Light has entered the world, but men held darkness dearer than light, for their deeds were evil. For everyone who does wrong hates the light, and does not come to the light, that his deeds may not be reproved. But whoever does right comes to the light, that it may be evident that his deeds are godly.[21]

[15] Cp. Mk. xii. 14 and parallels.
[16] This may equally be understood as 'born again'.
[17] The same Gr. word means both wind and spirit.
[18] A Jewish colloquialism. [19] See Num. xxi. 8-9.
[20] While much that was in his documentary source has been adapted by the author to bring the text into line with his ideas, some passages stand out as his distinctive contributions. Attention has been drawn to these wherever possible, or, as in the case of the present comment, they have been placed in the footnotes. See preface to the book.
[21] Lit. 'done in God'.

immersing at Aenon,[22] close to Salim, because there was an ample water supply; and the people came and were immersed, for John had not yet been thrown into prison.

When an argument started between the disciples of John and the Jews about purification, they came to John and said to him, 'Rabbi, he who was with you beyond Jordan, of whom you have testified, is immersing, and everyone is flocking to him.'

John replied, 'No one can receive anything unless Heaven has given it him. You can testify yourselves that I said, "I am not the Messiah, but am sent ahead of him." It is the bride-groom who has the bride. But the groomsman, who stands and listens to him, rejoices greatly at the bridegroom's voice. That joy of mine is now realized. He must grow greater and I grow less.'[a]

When then the Master learnt that the Pharisees had heard, 'Jesus is making and immersing more disciples than John,'[b] he left Judea and returned to Galilee.

Now he was obliged to pass through Samaria. In so doing he came to a Samaritan town called Shechem,[23] close to the plot of ground which Jacob gave his son Joseph.[24] Jacob's well was there. Jesus, exhausted from the journey, had just sat down on the well's rim,[c] when a Samaritan woman came to draw water.

Jesus said to her, 'Please give me a drink.'[d]

The Samaritan woman answered, 'How can you, a Jew, ask a drink from me, a Samaritan woman?'[e]

'If you only knew God's gift,' Jesus replied, 'and who it is who is saying to you, "Give me a drink," you would have asked him, and he would have given you living water.'[25]

'Sir,' she said, 'you have nothing to draw with, and the well is deep. How will you obtain this living water? Are you greater than our father Jacob, who gave us this well, and drank from it himself, and his sons too, and his cattle?'

Jesus answered, 'Whoever drinks this water will grow thirsty again, but he who drinks the water I will give him will never

[a] He who comes from Above is superior to all. He who is earthly remains earthly, and speaks in an earthly way. He who comes from heaven is superior to all. As he has seen and heard so he testifies, but no one accepts his testimony. Whoever does accept his testimony has confirmed that God is true; for he whom God has sent speaks the words of God, because God does not give him the Spirit stintingly. The Father loves the Son, and has placed everything in his hands. He who believes in the Son will have Eternal Life, while he who disobeys the Son will never see Life: God's wrath will abide on him.

[b] Though Jesus himself did not immerse, it was his disciples.

[c] It was about midday.

[d] His disciples had gone off to the town to buy food.

[e] Jews do not associate with Samaritans.

[22] Ain-nun, situated south-east of the modern Nablus.
[23] Following the correct reading of the Old Syriac. The Gr. reads Sychar.
[24] See Gen. xxxiii. 19, xlviii. 22.
[25] 'Living water' also means 'flowing water', cp. Jer. ii. 13, etc.

thirst any more; for the water I will give him will become a spring of water welling up inside him in Eternal Life.'

'Sir,' said the woman, 'give me this water, so that I shall never thirst, nor have to come here to draw.'

'Go and call your husband,' he said to her, 'and come back here.'

'I have no husband,' the woman replied.

Jesus said to her, 'You rightly say, "I have no husband," for you have had five husbands, and the man you have now is not your husband. There you have spoken the truth.'

'I see you are a prophet, sir,' said the woman. 'Our fathers worshipped on this mountain.[26] But your people say that at Jerusalem is the place where we ought to worship.'

'Believe me, madam,' Jesus told her, 'the time is coming when they will worship the Father neither on this mountain nor in Jerusalem. Your people worship one whom they do not know, our people worship One they do know.[a] Yes, the time is coming, indeed it is here already, when all true worshippers will worship the Father spiritually and sincerely,[b] for these are the kind of worshippers the Father seeks.'

The woman said to him, 'I know that Messiah will come.[c] When he is here he will tell us all about it.'

Jesus answered, 'I who speak to you am he.'

At this juncture his disciples returned, and were dumbfounded to find him talking to a woman.[d]

Abandoning her water-pot the woman then sped away to the town, and said to the men, 'You must come and see someone who told me everything I had done. Can he possibly be the Messiah?'

So they left the town and went out to him.

In the meantime his disciples had been begging Jesus, 'Rabbi, do eat.'

'I have food to eat that you do not know of,' he told them.

'Can someone have brought him food?' the disciples asked one another.

Jesus said to them, 'Food to me means to do the will of him who sent me and to complete his work. Do you not say, "Another four months and harvest will be here?" Look, I tell you! Raise your eyes, and see for yourselves how white is the land for harvesting![27] The reaper can already see his reward in view, and gather his crop for Eternal Life, so that the sower may re-

[a] For salvation comes from the Jews.
[b] God is Spirit, and those who worship him must do so spiritually and sincerely.
[c] The one called Christ.
[d] At any rate no one said, 'What are you inquiring about?' or 'Why are you talking to her?'[28]

[26] Mt. Gerizim, where stood the rival Samaritan temple.
[27] Referring to the approaching Samaritans.
[28] It was not considered proper for a rabbi to converse with a woman.

joice equally with the reaper. Herein the saying is verified, "It is one thing to sow, and another to reap." I have sent you to reap where you have done no work. Others have done the work, and you have had the benefit of it.'

Many of the Samaritans of that town believed in him through the woman's statement, 'He told me everything I had done.' So when the Samaritans reached him they begged him to stay with them. And he did spend two days there; and many more believed in him through his discourses, and they told the woman, 'Our belief is no longer due to what you said. We have heard him ourselves, and know that he really is the world's Saviour.'

When the two days had passed Jesus left there for Galilee, though he himself testified that a prophet is of no repute in his own homeland. Consequently when he reached Galilee the Galileans welcomed him only because they had seen everything he had done at Jerusalem during the festival.[a]

So he came once more to Cana of Galilee, where he had turned the water into wine.

Now there was an imperial officer whose son was ill at Capernaum. When he heard that Jesus had returned to Galilee from Judea, he went to him and begged him to come down and cure his son; for he lay at death's door. Jesus, however, said to him, 'Nothing will make you believe unless you see signs and wonders.'

'Do come down, sir,' urged the officer, 'before my child dies.'

'Go home,' Jesus replied. 'Your son will live.'

The man believed what Jesus told him and went away. He was well on the way down when his servants met him with the news that his son was alive. He asked them at what time he had shown improvement.

'Yesterday at one o'clock the fever left him,' they replied.

The father knew then that it was the very time Jesus had told him, 'Your son will live,' and he believed together with his whole household.

This then is the second sign Jesus performed, after he came from Judea to Galilee.

IV[30]

After these events Jesus crossed the Sea of Galilee.[b] A large crowd followed him because they saw the signs he performed on the sick.

Jesus climbed the mountain and sat down there with his disciples. The Jewish festival of Passover was approaching.[31]

[a] For they too had been at the festival.[29]
[b] The Sea of Tiberias.

[29] I.e. the Passover.
[30] Transposing Jn. vi. to follow Jn. iv. as required by the sequence of events. See below p. 399, n. 43.
[31] This is the second Passover to be mentioned. The author may intentionally have omitted certain intervening events which took place in Galilee.

When Jesus raised his eyes and observed a large crowd approaching him, he said to Philip, 'Where are we to buy bread for these people to eat?' [a]

Philip replied, 'Two hundred dinars' worth[32] of bread will hardly give each of them a piece.'

One of his disciples, Andrew, Simon Peter's brother, said to him, 'There is a lad here with five barley loaves and two small fish. But what good are they to so many?'

Jesus said, 'Get the men seated.' [b]

So the men sat down to the number of about five thousand.

Then Jesus broke the loaves, and when he had given thanks he distributed portions to those who were seated, and also as much as they wanted of the small fish. When they were satisfied, he said to his disciples, 'Gather up the fragments that are left over so that nothing is lost.'

So they gathered them up, and filled twelve baskets with the fragments of the five barley loaves left over from what they had eaten.

Then the people on seeing the sign he had performed said, 'This is surely the Prophet who was to come into the world!'

As soon as Jesus realized that they were about to come and carry him off to make him king, he withdrew again to the mountain alone.

When evening came his disciples went down to the sea, and going on board ship crossed over the sea to Capernaum. By this time it was dark, and still Jesus had not joined them, while the sea had become rough with a strong wind blowing. When, however, they had rowed some twenty-five or thirty furlongs, they saw Jesus walking on the sea and approaching the ship, and they were terrified.

But he said to them, 'It is I. Don't be alarmed!'

Then they readily took him on board, and at once the ship reached the short for which they had been making.

The next day the crowd standing on the far side of the sea realized that only one boat had been there, and that Jesus had not gone on board with his disciples, but that they had left on their own. Boats from Tiberias, however, put in close to the spot where they had eaten the bread after the Master had given thanks. So when the crowd was aware that neither Jesus nor his disciples were there any longer they took these boats and made for Capernaum in quest of Jesus. Having found him on the other side of the sea, they said to him, 'Rabbi, how did you get here?'

Jesus replied, 'I tell you for a positive fact, you do not seek me because you have seen signs, but because you ate the bread and were satisfied. Do not labour for the food that perishes, but

[a] He said this to test him, for he knew perfectly well what he intended to do.
[b] There was plenty of grass on the spot.
[32] About £8.

for the food that endures in Eternal Life, which the Son of Man will give you; for this the Father, God, has confirmed.'

'What must we do to carry out the works of God?'[33] they asked him.

'The work of God simply means this,' Jesus replied, 'that you believe in him whom God has sent.'

'What sign do you perform,' they said, 'that we may see it and believe in you? What miracle do you work? Our fathers ate the manna in the wilderness, as it is stated, "He gave them bread from heaven to eat." '[34]

Jesus said to them, 'I tell you for a positive fact, Moses did not give you the bread from heaven, but my Father will give you the real bread from heaven. God's bread is that which comes down from heaven and gives life to the world.'

'Sir,' they urged, 'never fail to give us that bread.'

'I am the bread of life,' Jesus told them. 'Whoever comes to me will never hunger, and whoever believes in me will never thirst any more. But as I have said to you, though you have seen you still do not believe.[35] Everyone whom the Father gives me will come to me, and none who comes to me will I ever reject; for I have come down from heaven not to carry out my own will, but the will of him who has sent me. The will of him who has sent me is this, that I must lose no part of whatever he has given me, but must raise it up on the Last Day. For the will of my Father is that whoever sees the Son and believes in him shall have Eternal Life, and I must raise him up on the Last Day.'

The Jews murmured about him, because he said, 'I am the bread that has come down from heaven', and said, 'Isn't he Jesus the son of Joseph, whose father and mother we know? How then can he say, "I have come down from heaven"?'

Jesus said to them, 'Do not murmur to one another. No one can come to me unless the Father who has sent me draws him, and I must raise him up on the Last Day. It is stated in the Prophets, "And they will all be taught by God."[36] Whoever has listened to the Father and learnt will come to me.[a]

'I tell you for a positive fact, whoever believes in me will have Eternal Life. I am the bread of life. Your fathers ate the manna in the wilderness and died. The bread that comes down from heaven is otherwise, that anyone may eat of it and not die. I am the living bread that has come down from heaven. If anyone eats of this bread he will live for ever. And the bread I will give for the life of the world is my flesh.'

[a] Not that anyone has seen the Father, except him who is from God: he has seen the Father.

[33] This reference to the works of God comes in abruptly, and is followed by dialogue material on the subject of 'the bread from heaven'. We have here, therefore, part of the Dialogue document inserted at this point because of the reference in the source to the feeding of the Five Thousand.

[34] Ps. lxxviii. 24 (LXX).

[35] Jesus had not exactly said this before, unless in a missing passage of the Dialogue. But cp. iv. 48, above p. 396.

[36] Isa. liv. 13.

The Jews then disputed with one another saying, 'How can he give us his flesh to eat?'

So Jesus said to them, 'I tell you for a positive fact, if you do not eat the flesh of the Son of Man and drink his blood you will not have life in yourselves. Whoever masticates[37] my flesh and drinks my blood will have Eternal Life, and I must raise him up on the last Day; for my flesh is true food and my blood is true drink. Whoever masticates my flesh and drinks my blood continues in me,[38] and I in him. Just as the Living Father has sent me, and I live through the Father, so he who masticates me will likewise live through me. This is the bread that has come down from heaven, not the kind the fathers ate, and died. He who masticates this bread will live for ever.'[a]

Many of his disciples when they heard this said, 'This is intolerable![39] How can one listen to such talk?'

Conscious that his disciples were murmuring about it, Jesus said to them, 'So this offends you, does it? Supposing you were to see the Son of Man ascend to where he was before? The Spirit is the life-giving agency: the physical counts for nothing. The words I have addressed to you are spirit, and they are life. But there are some of you who do not believe.[b] That is why I said to you that no one can come to me unless it is granted him by my Father.'

As a result many of his disciples parted company, and no longer associated with him.

Jesus then said to the twelve, 'Don't you also want to go?'

Simon Peter answered, 'Sir, to whom shall we go? You have the Message[40] of Eternal Life, and we have believed and are convinced that you are the Holy One of God.'

'Have I not chosen you, the twelve?' Jesus said to them. 'Yet even of you one is a traitor.'[41] [c]

V [43]

After these events there was a Jewish festival[44] and Jesus went up to Jerusalem.

Now at Jerusalem there is a bathing pool by the Sheep Gate,[45]

[a] Jesus said all this in the synagogue, while teaching in Capernaum.
[b] For Jesus knew from the very first who they were who did not believe, and who it was would betray him.
[c] He was speaking of Judas son of Simon Iscariot.[42] For it was he, one of the twelve, who was to betray him.

[37] Lit. 'munches' as of bread, or 'chews' as of meat.　　[38]Cp. I. Jno. ii. 24.
[39] 'Intolerable', lit. 'a stiff, or harsh, saying'. The author may be attacking here those who opposed his Christology (cp. I. Jno. ii. 19; II. Jno. 10; III. Jno. 8-10).
[40] Lit. 'Words'.　　[41] Gr. *diabolos*, one who accuses falsely.
[42] Perhaps the same as Simon the Zealot (Iananean), listed as one of the twelve envoys. Iscariot might mean 'One of the *Sicarii*' (cp. Jos. *Wars*, II. xiii. 3).
[43] Jn. v. is placed here after vi. which gives a better sequence of events. Jn. vii. follows awkwardly after vi, since in the latter Jesus is already in Galilee, while vii. 1 suggests that he has just left Judea for Galilee for a reason given in fact in Jn. v. 16.
[44] Either the Passover mentioned at the beginning of the previous section, or perhaps the festival of Pentecost following it.
[45] Or 'Market'.

which in Hebrew goes by the name of Bethzatha.[46] It has five porticoes. In these there were always lying a host of invalids, blind people, lame, and people with withered limbs, waiting for the water to bubble.[a] There was one man there who had been an invalid for thirty-eight years. When Jesus saw him lying there, and learnt that he had already been lying there a long time, he said to him, 'Do you wish to be cured?'

'Sir,' the invalid replied, 'I have no one to put me into the pool when the water is agitated, and while I am getting there someone else steps down before me.'

Jesus said to him, 'Rise, pick up your mattress, and walk!'

At once the man was cured, and took up his mattress and walked. That day was the Sabbath. So the Jews said to the man who had been cured, 'It is the sabbath, and illegal for you to carry your mattress.'

But he answered, 'He who cured me told me, "Pick up your mattress and walk".'[47]

They asked him, 'Who was it told you to pick it up and walk?'

The man who was cured did not know who it was.[b] Later, however, Jesus encountered him in the Temple, and said to him, 'See, you are cured now. Sin no more, or worse may befall you.'

The man went away and told the Jews it was Jesus who had cured him. It was for this reason that the Jews persecuted Jesus, because he did such things on the sabbath.[48]

'My Father is still at work,' Jesus replied, 'so I am working too.'

For this, then, the Jews in addition sought to kill him, because not only did he violate the sabbath, but also claimed God as his Father, putting himself on a level with God.

Therefore he answered and said to them, 'I tell you for a positive fact, the Son can do nothing on his own account, only what he sees the Father do. What he does the Son copies; for the Father loves the Son, and shows him whatever he does. And he will show him how to do greater miracles than this, that you may marvel. For just as the Father raises the dead and revives them, so will the Son revive whom he will. Neither does the Father judge anyone: he has entrusted all judgment to the Son, that all may honour the Son as they honour the Father. Who-

---

[a] For an angel of the Lord descended into the pool from time to time, and agitated the water. Whoever then got in first was cured of whatever complaint he was suffering from.

[b] For Jesus had moved off because of the crowd in the place.

[46] The reading Bethesda is incorrect. Bethzatha is Aram. probably meaning 'Place of Alkaline Salt'.

[47] Mk. ii. 9, above p. 54. The incident here appears to combine elements of the cure of the paralytic and of the man with the withered hand, which *Mark* locates in the synagogue at Capernaum. Cp. Jn. vi. 59, above p. 399, n. *a*.

[48] From about here until near the end of the section the continuity is broken by the introduction of another block of material that is distinctive of our author as compared with his source. It appears to have been inserted here because of the reference to curing on the sabbath.

ever does not honour the Son does not honour the Father who has sent him.

'I tell you for a positive fact, whoever hears my message and believes in him who has sent me will have Eternal Life, and will not come to judgment, but has passed from death to life.

'I tell you for a positive fact, the time is coming, indeed it is already here, when the dead will hear the voice of the Son of God, and those who hear it will live. For just as the Father has life in himself, so has he granted the Son to have life in himself, and has given him authority to execute judgment, because he is the Son of Man. Do not wonder at this, for the time is coming when those who are entombed will hear his voice and come forth, those who have done good to the Resurrection of Life, and those who have done evil to the Resurrection of Judgment.[49] I can do nothing on my own. As I hear I judge; and my judgment is just, because I am not serving my own interests but the interests of him who has sent me.

'If I were to testify on my own behalf my testimony would not be valid. There is someone else who testifies of me, and I know that the testimony he gives of me is valid. You sent to John, and he testified truly. It is not that I require human testimony: I am only saying this that you may be saved. He was a burning and shining light, and you were delighted for a time to bask in his light. But I have more important testimony than John's. The miracles which the Father has granted me to perform, the miracles I do, these testify of me that the Father has sent me. And he who sent me, the Father himself, has testified of me. You have never heard his voice, or seen his form, and his Message has no lodgment in you, because you do not believe in him whom he has sent. You pore over the Scriptures, because you think they will give you Eternal Life; and it is they which testify of me. Yet you do not want to come to me that you may have life.

'I do not require human praise, but I do know you, that you have not the love of God in you. I have come in my Father's name, and you do not receive me. If another should come in his own name you will receive him. How can you believe, you who receive praise from one another, but do not seek the praise that comes from the Only God? Do not think I will complain of you to the Father. Moses, the one on whom you have pinned your hopes, is the one who will complain of you. Had you believed Moses you would have believed me, for he wrote of me. But if you do not believe his writings, why should you believe my words?

[50] 'Did not Moses give you the Law? Yet none of you keeps the Law. Why do you seek to kill me?'

The crowd responded, 'You are demon-possessed! Who seeks to kill you?'

[49] Cp. Dan. xii. 2; Rev. xx.
[50] Transposing Jn. vii. 19-24 to follow Jn. v. 47.

Jesus said to them, 'I have performed one miracle and you are all amazed. Surely Moses gave you circumcision,[a] and you circumcise a man on the sabbath! If a man can receive circumcision on the sabbath that the Law of Moses may not be broken, why are you enraged with me because I have made a man whole on the sabbath? Do not judge by appearance. Judge justly.'

VI

After these events Jesus toured Galilee.[b] Now the Jewish festival of Tabernacles[51] was approaching. So his brothers said to him, 'Cross into Judea, that your disciples there too may see the miracles you perform. For no one does anything in secret if he seeks to be in the public eye. If you perform these miracles show yourself to the world.'[c]

Jesus replied, 'My time has not arrived yet, but any time is your time. The world cannot hate you, but it does hate me, because I testify of it that its deeds are evil. You go up for the festival. I am not going up yet for this festival, because my time has not yet come.'

Having said this he stayed on in Galilee. But after his brothers had gone up for the festival he too went up, not openly but secretly.

The Jews looked for him at the festival and inquired, 'Where is he?' And there was a great deal of murmuring about him among the crowds, some saying, 'He is a good man', while others said, 'No, he is leading the people astray.'[d]

The festival was already half over when Jesus went up to the Temple and taught there. The Jews were amazed and said, 'How has he acquired book-learning without having studied?'

Jesus replied, 'My teaching is not my own, but his who has sent me. Whoever wishes to do his will will know whether the teaching is God's or whether I am stating my own views. Whoever gives his own views seeks his personal glory, but he who seeks the glory of him who has sent him is sincere, and there is no falseness in him.'

[52] Then some of the Jerusalemites said, 'Isn't he the man they seek to kill? Yet here he is speaking freely, and they say nothing to him. Unless, of course, the rulers have recognized that he is the Messiah. Yet we know where this man comes from, while when the Messiah comes no one will know where he comes from.'

Jesus therefore proclaimed in the Temple as he taught, 'You

[a] Not that it derives from Moses; it derives from the Patriarchs.
[b] He would not tour Judea because the Jews sought to kill him.
[c] For neither did his brothers believe in him.
[d] No one, of course, spoke openly about him for fear of the Jews.

[51] The autumn harvest festival, when the people lived in booths (tabernacles) for seven days. See Lev. xxiii. 34, etc.
[52] Jn. vii. 25 here follows vii. 18. See n. 50, p. 401.

know me, and you know where I come from. And I have not come of my own accord. He who has sent me is indeed trust-worthy, whom you do not know. I know him, because I am from him, and he sent me.'

At this they sought to seize him, yet no one laid hands on him because his time had not yet come.[53]

Jesus now addressed them again saying, 'I am the light of the world. Whoever follows me will not walk in the dark, but have the light of life.'

The Pharisees said to him, 'You are testifying on your own behalf. Your testimony is not valid.'

Jesus replied, 'Though I testify on my own behalf my testimony is valid, for I know where I came from and where I am going. But you do not know where I came from nor where I am going. You judge by human standards, while I judge no one. But if I were to judge, my judgment would be valid because I am not alone. There is myself and him who has sent me. And in your Law it is stated that the testimony of two persons is valid. There is myself who am testifying on my own behalf, and there is the Father who has sent me who testifies on my behalf.'

'Where is your father?' they said to him.

Jesus replied, 'You neither know me nor my Father. Had you known me you would have known my Father also.'

He said these things in the treasury, as he taught in the Temple. And no one seized him because his time had not yet come.[54] Many of the people believed in him, and said, 'When the Messiah comes will he perform more signs than this man does?'

The Pharisees heard what the people were murmuring about him, so the head priests and Pharisees sent officers to arrest him.[55]

On the last day, the principal day of the festival,[56] Jesus stood and proclaimed, 'If anyone thirsts let him come to me and drink. "He who believes in me," as the Scripture says, "from his interior streams of living water shall flow." ' [57a]

Some of the people when they heard these words said, 'This is certainly the Prophet.' Others asid, 'He is the Messiah.' But the first replied, 'The Messiah will not come from Galilee.

[a] He said this with reference to the Spirit which those who believed in him were to receive. For as yet there was no Spirit, because Jesus was not yet glorified.

[53] From here until the end of Jn. xii. the text is in considerable disorder owing to the unskilful insertion of portions of the Dialogue document. The sequence of events as this may have appeared in the author's source has been seriously dislocated, while the Discourse of Jesus to the Jews (already begun above pp. 400-401) has had its continuity destroyed. The corrections of order which have been attempted are to be regarded as purely conjectural. At this point Jn. viii. 12-20 has been inserted between Jn. vii. 30 and 31.

[54] Here follows Jn. vii. 31-2.

[55] Omitting here Jn. vii. 33-6, transferred to follow xii. 32, below p. 413.

[56] Called 'The Great Hosanna'.

[57] Slightly varying Isa. xxviii. 16-17.

Doesn't the Scripture say that the Messiah will come from the line of David, and from David's village of Bethlehem?'

So there was a conflict of opinion among the people on his account. Some were for seizing him, but no one laid hands on him.

The officers then returned to the head priests and Pharisees, who asked them, 'Why have you not brought him?'

The officers answered, 'No man ever spoke like this.'

'Have you too been led astray?' said the Pharisees. 'Have any of the rulers or of the Pharisees believed in him? But these people who do not know the Law are accursed.'[58]

Nicodemus,[a] who was one of them, said to them, 'Does our Law condemn a man without first hearing what he has to say and knowing what he is doing?'

'Do you too come from Galilee?' they answered. 'Look for yourself, and you will find that the Prophet will not come from Galilee.'[59]

VII

[60][Then everyone went to his own house, but Jesus went to the Mount of Olives. At daybreak he was once more in the Temple, and all the people came to him, and he seated himself and taught them.

Then the scribes and Pharisees brought a woman caught committing adultery, and placed her before him saying, 'Teacher, this woman was caught in the very act of adultery. Now Moses in the Law commanded that such should be stoned.[61] But what do you say?'

They said this to tempt him, so that they could have grounds for charging him.[62] Jesus, however, bent down and drew on the ground with his finger. When they repeated their question he straightened up and said to them, 'Let whichever of you is sinless be the first to throw a stone at her.' And again he bent down and scrawled on the ground.

When they heard this, one by one they slunk away, beginning with the older men; and he was left alone with the woman in front of him.

Then Jesus raised himself and said to her, 'Madam, where are they? Has no one condemned you?'

'No one, sir,' she said.

Jesus told her, 'Neither do I condemn you. Go, and do not sin again in future.']

[a] The one who came to Jesus in the first instance.

[58] The uninstructed were scorned by the sages as boors (amme-haaretz).

[59] Alternatively, 'that no prophet will come from Galilee'.

[60] The passage within square brackets (Jn. vii. 53-viii. 11) is written in a different style to the rest of the book and is omitted in some MSS. In others it is placed elsewhere, including in one group after Lk. xxi. 37. The story seems to belong to the events of Passion Week, and may have been in our author's documentary source, a form of Gospel much closer to the Synoptics.

[61] Cp. Lev. xx. 10; Deut. xxii. 22.   [62] Cp. Mt. xix. 3; Lk. xx. 19-20.

[63]Then said Jesus to the Jews who believed in him, 'If you adhere to my message you will indeed be my disciples, and will come to know the truth, and the truth will liberate you.'

'We are Abraham's offspring,' they replied, 'and were never in slavery to anyone. Why do you say, "You will be freemen"?'

Jesus answered, 'I tell you for a positive fact, whoever commits sin is a slave. But the slave is not a permanent member of the household, while the son is.[64] So if the Son makes you free, you really will be freemen. I know you are Abraham's offspring, yet you seek to kill me because my message finds no place in you. I speak from personal experience of the Father, while you do only what you have heard from *your* father.'

'Abraham is our father,' they said to him.

'If you were children of Abraham,' Jesus told them, 'you would do Abraham's deeds. Yet here you seek to kill me, a man who has told you the truth which I have heard from God. Abraham did not do that. You do the deeds of your father.'

'We were not born illegitimately,' they protested. 'We have One Father, God.'[65]

Jesus told them, 'If God were your Father you would love me; for I emanated and came from God. I did not come of my own accord: he sent me. How is it you do not recognize my voice? It is because you cannot heed my message. You have the Devil for a father, and would carry out your father's behests. He was a manslayer from the very first, and could never abide the truth; for truth is alien to him. When he utters a lie he speaks his own language; for he is a liar and the father of lies. But because I speak the truth you do not believe me? Whoever belongs to God heeds the words of God. The very fact that you do not heed me proves that you do not belong to God.'

The Jews replied, 'Are we not justified in saying you are a Samaritan[66] and demon-possessed?'

Jesus answered, 'I am not demon-possessed. I honour my Father, and you dishonour me. I do not seek my own glory. There is One who seeks and decides that.

'I tell you for a positive fact, whoever holds fast to my message will never experience death.'

The Jews said, 'Now we are certain you are demon-possessed. Abraham died, and so did the Prophets, yet you say, "Whoever holds fast to my message will never experience

[63] When the interpolated incident is removed it is clear that Jesus had not left the Temple. He was presumably still teaching on the last day of the festival of Tabernacles. From Jn. vii. 31, 39 (above pp. 403-404) it is shown that many believed in him at this time, which was the reason why the head priests and Pharisees intervened. It seems best therefore to resume the Discourse at viii. 31 immediately after a reference to the belief of many Jews. The passage of the Discourse viii. 12-20 has already been restored to its probable position after vii. 30 (above p. 402-403). The passages viii. 21-30 and vii. 33-36 seem to belong to another part of the Discourse found in Jn. xii. (below pp. 413-414).
[64] Cp. Heb. iii. 5-6. This Homily may have been addressed to the community at Ephesus and therefore have been known by our Ephesian author. It represents an earlier stage in the development of the Logos doctrine.
[65] Cp. Mal. ii. 10.
[66] Implying 'idolatrous-heretic', a term of abuse.

death." Are you superior to our father Abraham who died, and to the Prophets who died? Who do you claim to be?'

Jesus answered, 'If I glorify myself, my glory amounts to nothing. It is my Father who glorifies me, whom you say is your God. Yet you are not acquainted with him, while I know him. Were I to say I do not know him, I should be like you, a liar. But I do know him, and hold fast to his message. Your father Abraham rejoiced that he would see my day:[67] he has seen it and is glad.'

The Jews said to him, 'You are not yet fifty, and Abraham has seen you!'[68]

Jesus told them, 'I tell you for a positive fact, I existed before Abraham was born.'

Then they picked up stones to throw at him. But Jesus hid himself, and left the Temple.

VIII

As Jesus went on his way he saw a man blind from birth, and his disciples asked him, 'Rabbi, who sinned, he or his parents, that he was born blind?'

Jesus replied, 'Neither he nor his parents sinned. He was born blind that he might afford an illustration of God's work. While daylight lasts we must do the work of him who has sent me. The night will come when no one can work. While I am in the world I illumine the world.'

Having said this, he spat on the ground and made clay with the saliva, and dabbed the clay on the man's eyes[69] and said to him, 'Go and wash in the Pool of Siloam.[a] '[70]

So he went away and washed, and returned with his sight.

His neighbours, and those who had known him previously when he was a beggar, said, 'Isn't he the man who used to sit and beg?'

Others said, 'Yes, that's the man.'

Others said, 'No, it isn't. But he's like him.'

'It is me,' the man said.

'How then were your eyes opened?' they asked him.

'The man called Jesus made clay and anointed my eyes,' he replied, 'and told me, "Go to Siloam and wash." So when I had gone there and washed I found I could see.'

'Where is he?' they inquired.

'I don't know,' he said.

They brought the former blind man to the Pharisees.[b] The Pharisees in turn asked him how he had obtained his sight. He

---

[a] To be translated 'Sent' (Heb. *Shiloah*, Ed.).
[b] It was the sabbath the day Jesus made clay and opened his eyes.

[67] Cp. Heb. vi. 12-vii. 10.
[68] Alternatively, 'And you have seen Abraham?'
[69] Cp. Mt. xx. 34.
[70] Located at the south-east corner of the city.

told them, 'He put clay on my eyes, and I washed, and now I can see.'

'This man is not from God,' said some of the Pharisees, 'for he does not observe the sabbath.'

But others said, 'How can a man who is a sinner[71] perform such signs?'

So there was a conflict of opinion between them.

Then they addressed the blind man again, 'What do you say of him for having opened your eyes?'

'He is a prophet,' he said.

But the Jews refused to credit that he had been blind and gained his sight until they had called the man's parents and asked them, 'Is this your son, whom you say was born blind? How then does he now see?'

'We know this is our son,' his parents replied, 'and that he was born blind. But we do not know how he can now see, and we have not the least idea who has opened his eyes. Ask him. He is grown up and can speak for himself.'[a]

Then they recalled the man who had been blind and said to him, 'Give God the praise. We know this man is a sinner.'

He replied, 'Whether he is a sinner I do not know. But one thing I do know, that I was blind and now I can see.'

They said to him, 'What did he do to you? How did he open your eyes?'

'I have already told you that,' he answered, 'and you took no notice. Why do you want to hear it again? Surely you are not wanting to become his disciples?'

Then they hurled abuse at him and said, 'You are his disciple. We are Moses's disciples. We know that God spoke to Moses; but him—we don't know where he is from.'

The man replied, 'That's what is so surprising, that you don't know where he is from; yet he has opened my eyes. We know that God does not listen to sinners, but he does listen to whoever is God-fearing and carries out his will. It is quite unheard of that anyone should open the eyes of one blind from birth. If he were not from God, he could never do it.'

'You dare to teach us, you misbegotten bastard!' they cried, and ejected him forthwith.

Jesus heard that they had ejected him, and when he had found him said to him, 'Do you believe in the Son of Man?'

He answered, 'Who is he, sir, for me to believe in him?'

---

[a] They spoke thus because they were afraid of the Jews. For the Jews had already agreed that if anyone confessed Christ he should be excommunicated.[72] That is why his parents said, 'He is grown up. Ask him yourselves'.

[71] See p. 54, n. 12.

[72] Nothing is known of any attempt in Palestine to exclude Jews from the Synagogue for accepting Jesus as Messiah before about A.D. 80. Even then the method was indirect, by including in the prayers a general curse on heretics, which obviously they would not be able to recite. There was no formal ban until much later. The word *aposynagogos* occurs only in this Gospel ((ix. 22; xii. 42; xvi. 2).

Jesus told him, 'You have not only seen him, but he is talking to you now.'

'I do believe, sir,' he said, and prostrated himself before him.

Then Jesus said, 'I came into this world as a judgment, that those who do not see should see, and those who do see should become blind.'

Some of the Pharisees who were there with him heard this, and said to him, 'Surely we are not blind?'

Jesus told them, 'If you were blind, you would be free from sin; but since you say, "We see," your sin remains.'

[73] Jesus addressed this saying to them; but they failed to grasp his meaning.

So Jesus spoke again. 'I tell you for a positive fact, I am the door to the sheep. All those who came before me are thieves and robbers; but the sheep have not listened to them. I am the door. Whoever enters by me will be safe, and will come in and go out, and find pasture. The thief only comes to steal and kill and destroy. I have come that they may have life and ever more life.

'I tell you for a positive fact, whoever does not use the door to the sheep-pen, but gets in another way, is a thief and a robber, while he who uses the door is a shepherd of the sheep. The doorkeeper lets him in, and the sheep not only listen to his voice, but he calls his own sheep by name, and leads them out. When his own sheep are all outside, he walks before them, and the sheep follow him because they know his voice. They will not follow anyone else, but run from him, because they do not recognize the voice of strangers.

'I am the good shepherd. The good shepherd will give his life for the sheep. But the hireling, not being the shepherd, with sheep that are not his own, when he sees the wolf coming abandons the sheep and runs away, leaving the wolf to ravage and scatter them, because the hireling has no concern for the sheep.

'I am the good shepherd, and know my own sheep, and they know me, just as the Father knows me and I know the Father, and I give my life for the sheep. There are other sheep I have, which do not belong to this pen. I must bring them in also, and they will listen to my voice, and there shall be one flock with one shepherd. That is why the Father loves me, because I give my life, that I may take it back. No one takes it from me: I give it of my own accord. I have the right to give it, and the right to take it back. This instruction I have received from my Father.'

There was a further conflict of opinion among the Jews over these words. Many of them said, 'He is demon-possessed and mad. Why do you pay any attention to him?'

[73] Placing Jn. x. 6-10 before 1-5.

Others said, 'These are not the ravings of a demoniac. Can a demon open the eyes of the blind?'

The Feast of Dedication[74] now took place at Jerusalem. It was winter, and Jesus was strolling in the Temple, in Solomon's portico. The Jews surrounded him, and said to him, 'How long are you going to keep us on tenterhooks? If you are the Messiah, tell us plainly.'

Jesus replied, 'I have told you, and you do not believe. The miracles I perform in my Father's name testify of me. But you do not believe because you do not belong to my sheep. My sheep listen to my voice, and I know them, and they follow me. And I will give them Eternal Life, and they will never perish, and no one shall wrest them from my hand. My Father who has given me everything is stronger, and no one can wrest anything from my Father's hand. I and the Father are one.'

Once again the Jews picked up stones to stone him.

Jesus said, 'I have shown you from the Father many notable miracles. For which of them are you going to stone me?'

The Jews answered, 'We are not going to stone you for a notable miracle, but for blasphemy, because you who are a man make yourself God.'

'Is it not stated in your Law,' Jesus replied, ' "I said, you are gods"?[75] If he called them gods to whom God's Message came, and there is no evading the Scripture, how can you say to him whom the Father consecrated and sent into the world, "You blaspheme," because I said, "I am God's Son"? If I do not perform my Father's miracles, do not believe me. But if I do, even if you do not believe me, believe the miracles, that you may realize and recognize that the Father is in me and I am in the Father.'

Then once more they attempted to seize him, but he escaped their clutches.

He went away again to the farther side of the Jordan, to the place where John had been immersing originally, and stayed there. Many came to him and declared, 'John performed no sign, but everything John said of this man was true.' And many there believed in him.

IX

Now a certain man was ill, Lazarus of Bethany, the village of Mary and her sister Martha.[a] So the sisters sent to Jesus to say, 'Master, your dear friend is ill.'

When Jesus heard this he said, 'This illness is not fatal, but

[a] It was the Mary who anointed the Master with perfume, and wiped his feet with her hair,[76] whose brother Lazarus was ill.

[74] Commemorating the rededication of the Temple of Judas Maccabaeus (165 B.C.). The festival falls in December.
[75] Ps. lxxxii. 6.
[76] See below p. 412.

for the glory of God, that the Son of God may be glorified by it.'[a]

After hearing that Lazarus was ill he remained where he was for a further two days. Only when these had expired did he say to his disciples, 'Let us return to Judea.'

'Rabbi,' his disciples protested, 'the Jews only recently attempted to stone you, and yet you are going back there?'

Jesus answered, 'Are there not twelve hours in the day? Provided one walks in the daytime one will not stumble, because one sees the light of this world. But if one walks at night, one will stumble, because one has not the benefit of the light.'

After saying this he paused, and then declared, 'Our friend Lazarus has fallen asleep, but I am going to awaken him.'

The disciples said to him, 'Master, if he has fallen asleep he will be all right.'[b]

Then Jesus told them plainly, 'Lazarus is dead. And for your sakes I am glad we were not there, that you may believe. Nevertheless let us go to him.'

Thomas, called Twin, said to his fellow-disciples, 'Let us go too that we may die with him.'

When Jesus arrived he found that Lazarus had already been four days in the tomb. Many of the Jews had come to condole with Martha and Mary for the loss of their brother.[c] As soon, therefore, as Martha heard that Jesus was coming she went out to meet him, while Mary remained seated indoors.[77]

'If only you had been here, Master,' Martha greeted Jesus, 'my brother would not have died. But even now, I know that whatever you ask God he will grant you.'

'Your brother will rise again,' Jesus told her.

'I know he will rise again in the resurrection on the Last Day,' Martha replied.

'I am Resurrection and Life,' Jesus told her. 'Whoever believes in me will live even if he has died, and everyone who lives[79] and believes in me will never die at all. Do you believe this?'

'Yes, Master,' she said. 'I fully believe you are the Messiah, the Son of God, who was to come into the world.'

When she had said this she went off and quietly called her sister Mary and said, 'The Teacher is here and asking for you.'

As soon as she heard that, she rose quickly and went to him.[d] Then the Jews who were in the house with her to console

[a] Jesus had a high regard for Martha and her sister and for Lazarus.
[b] Jesus was referring to his death, but they imagined he was speaking of normal sleep.
[c] Bethany was close to Jerusalem, only about two miles away.[78]
[d] Jesus had not yet entered the village, but was still at the spot where Martha had met him.

[77] In accordance with custom the chief mourners remained indoors seated on the floor or a low stool during the days of mourning.
[78] Gr. 'about fifteen stadia.'
[79] Until the Last Day.

her, seeing her get up quickly and go out, followed her, thinking she was going to the tomb to weep there. Mary, however, directly she came to the place where Jesus was, fell at his feet when she saw him, and said to him, 'If only you had been here, Master, my brother would not have died.'

When Jesus saw her weeping, and the Jews who accompanied her weeping, he groaned inwardly and was much upset.

'Where have you put him?' he asked.

'Come and see, sir,' they said.

Jesus wept.

'See how fond of him he was,' said the Jews, though some said, 'Could not he, who opened the eyes of the blind, have done something so that he would not have died?'

Still groaning, Jesus came to the tomb.[a] 'Remove the boulder!' he ordered.

The deceased's sister Martha protested to him, 'Master, by this time he will be putrefying. It is the fourth day.'

Jesus said to her, 'Did I not tell you that if you would believe you would behold God's glory?'

Then they removed the boulder.

Jesus raised his eyes heavenwards and said, 'I thank thee, Father, for having heard me. I know that thou dost always hear me, but I have said this because of the people standing by, that they may believe thou hast sent me.'

Having spoken thus, he called out loudly, 'Lazarus, come forth!'

The dead man emerged with his feet and hands strapped with bandages, and his face bound round with a cloth.

Jesus said to them, 'Unbind him, and let him go free.'

Many of the Jews who were visiting Mary and saw what he had done believed in him. But some of them went to the Pharisees and told them what Jesus had done. So the head priests and Pharisees convened a sanhedrin and said, 'What are we going to do, for this man performs many signs? If we leave him alone everyone will believe in him, and the Romans will come and take away both our place[80] and our nation.'

One of their number, Caiaphas, who was the reigning high priest,[81] said to them, 'It does not seem to have occurred to you that it is in your interest that one man should die for the people rather than the whole nation perish.'[b]

So that day they decided to kill him.

Jesus, therefore, no longer moved about openly among the

---

[a] It was a cave with a boulder placed across it.
[b] He did not say this of his own accord, but as the reigning high priest he prophesied that Jesus would die for the nation, and not for the nation only, but also that the widely scattered children of God should be gathered in one body.

[80] 'Place', probably meaning the Temple. See Jos. *Antiq.* XX. vi. 1.
[81] Lit. 'being high priest that year'. *Eniautos* can mean a term of years. The office was not an annual appointment.

Jews, but retired to the country close to the wilderness, to a town called Ephraim, and there stayed with his disciples.

X

Now the Jewish Passover was approaching, and many went up from the country to Jerusalem prior to the Passover to undergo purification. They looked out for Jesus, and remarked to one another as they stood in the Temple, 'What do you think, that he will not attend the festival?'[a]

Six days before the Passover, however, Jesus came to Bethany.[b] So they gave a dinner for him there. Martha waited at table, while Lazarus was one of those who dined with them. Mary then took a pound of genuine most expensive spikenard, and anointed the feet of Jesus, and then wiped his feet with her hair. The whole house was filled with the perfume of the ointment.

Then Judas Iscariot[c] said, 'Why wasn't this ointment sold for three hundred dinars[82] and the money given to the poor?'[d]

Jesus said, 'Leave her alone, that she may keep it for the day of my burial. You have the poor with you always, but you will not always have me.'

A considerable number of Jews got to know he was there, and came not simply on account of Jesus, but also to see Lazarus whom he had raised from the dead.[e]

The next day the vast crowd attending the festival, having learnt that Jesus was coming to Jerusalem, took palm-branches and went out to meet him shouting, 'Hosanna! Blessed is he who comes in the name of the Lord.[83] Blessed be the king of Israel.'

Finding a young ass, Jesus rode on it, as it is stated,

> *Never fear, daughter of Zion!*
> *See, your king is coming,*
> *Riding on an ass's colt!*[a][84]

[a] For the head priests and Pharisees had given orders that anyone who knew where he was should disclose it, so that they could arrest him.

[b] Where Lazarus lived, whom Jesus had raised from the dead.

[c] One of his disciples, who was about to betray him.

[d] He said this not because he was concerned about the poor, but because he was a thief and had the alms-bag, and pilfered what was put in it.

[e] The head priests had decided to kill Lazarus as well, because due to him many of the Jews went away and believed in Jesus.

[a] His disciples did not realize the significance of these things at first; but when Jesus was glorified then they recalled how this had been stated of him. Moreover, the people who had been with him when he called Lazarus from the tomb gave their testimony. This indeed was why the crowd met him, because they heard that he had performed this sign.

[82] About £12.   [83] Ps cxviii. 25-6.   [84] Zech. ix. 9.

The Pharisees thereupon said to one another, 'See for your-selves how helpless you are! Look, the whole world has gone after him!'

In fact among those going up to worship at the festival were some Greeks. These came to Philip of Bethsaida in Galilee with the request, 'Sir, we should like to meet Jesus.'

Philip went and told Andrew, and then Andrew and Philip told Jesus.

Jesus answered, 'The time has come for the Son of Man to be glorified!

'I tell you for a positive fact, unless the grain of wheat falls into the ground and dies it will remain solitary; but if it dies it will yield much fruit. Whoever loves his life will forfeit it, but whoever hates his life in this world will preserve it for Life Eternal. If anyone would serve me, let him follow me, and where I am there will my servant be also.[85] If anyone will serve me the Father will honour him.

'Just now my soul is deeply troubled. What am I to say? "Father, save me from this hour"? No, that is why I have come to this hour, Father, glorify thy name.'[86]

Then there came a voice from heaven, 'I have glorified it, and will further glorify it.'

The people who stood there and heard it said that it had thundered.[87] Others said, 'An angel spoke to him.'

Jesus answered, 'This voice did not come for my sake, but for yours. Now is the judgment of this world! Now shall the ruler of this world be cast out![88] While I, when I am lifted from the earth, will draw all men to me.'[a]

[89]Then Jesus said, 'For a brief space I shall be with you, and then I go to him who has sent me. You will seek me, but you will not find me, and where I shall be you cannot come.'

'Where is he going to that we shall not find him?' the Jews asked themselves. 'Surely he is not going to the Dispersion among the Greeks to teach the Greeks? What does he mean when he says, "You will seek me, but will not find me, and where I shall be you cannot come"?'

[90]Jesus repeated, 'I am going away, and you will seek me, and

[a] He said this to indicate the kind of death he was going to die.

---

[85] Cp. Lk. ix. 23-4.
[86] Reminiscent of the account of Jesus in the Garden of Gethsemane (cp. Mk. xiv. 33-36, above p. 39). The companions of Jesus then were Peter, James and John, as on the occasion of the transfiguration, when also there came a voice from heaven (cp. Mk. ix. 7, above p. 67).
[87] The same word in Greek is used for voice and sound.
[88] The inimical angel-power (Beliar), cp. Rev. xii. 9, below p. 454.
[89] Inserting here Jn. vii. 33-36 as required by xiii. 33. Perhaps on the basis of these words the apocryphal *Acts of Pilate* makes the Jews scour the country for Jesus after his resurrection. The material from this point until near the close of section x probably comes from the Dialogue document.
[90] Inserting here Jn. viii. 21-30, but transposing 26 and 29 and placing xii. 34 between them as required by the sense. As the text of xii. 32-38 stands in the Greek the people refer to Jesus having spoken of the lifting up of the Son of Man, when he had not said 'Son of Man', only 'I', when I am lifted from the earth.'

you will die in your sins. Where I am going you cannot come.'

The Jews then said, 'Is he going to kill himself, that he says, "Where I am going you cannot come"?'

'You are from below,' he replied, 'while I am from Above. You are of this world, while I am not of this world. I told you you will die in your sins; for unless you believe that I am he you will die in your sins.'

'Who are you?' they asked him.

Jesus replied, 'When you have lifted up the Son of Man, then you will realize that I am he. Of my own accord I can do nothing, but as the Father has taught me so I speak. And he who has sent me is with me. He has not left me on my own, for I always do what pleases him.'

The people responded, 'We have heard out of the Law that the Messiah will remain for ever. Why then do you say, the Son of Man must be lifted up? Who is this Son of Man?'

Jesus answered, 'First comes what I have yet to say to you. I have a great deal to say and to judge of you. He who has sent me is indeed true, and I tell the world only what I have heard from him.'[a]

When he said this many believed in him.

[91] Jesus then cried, 'Whoever believes in me, does not believe in me, but in him who has sent me. And he who sees me, sees him who has sent me. I have come as a light to the world, that everyone who believes in me should not remain in darkness. And if anyone hears my words and does not keep them, I will not judge him; for I did not come to judge the world, but to save the world. Whoever disregards me, and does not accept my words, has that which judges him. The Message I proclaim, that is what will judge him on the Last Day. For I do not speak of my own accord: it is the Father himself, who has sent me, who has given me his instruction what I am to say, and what I am to declare. And I know that his instruction means Eternal Life. What I say, then, is exactly what the Father has told me to say.'

[92] Then Jesus told them, 'The light will not be with you much longer. Walk while you have the light, lest darkness overtake you. He that walks in darkness does not know where he is going. While you have the light, believe in the light, that you may become sons of light.'

When Jesus had said this, he went away and was hidden from them. But though he had performed so many signs in their presence they did not believe in him, that the saying of the Prophet Isaiah might come true.

[a] They did not realize that he was speaking to them of the Father.

[91] Resuming at Jn. xii. 44-50.
[92] Continuing with xii. 35-43.

Lord, who has believed our report,
And to whom is the arm of the Lord revealed?[a][93]

XI

Now before the Passover festival, Jesus, knowing the time had come for him to pass over from this world to the Father, having cared for his own who were in the world, he cared for them to the last. At supper time, the Devil having already instigated Simon's son Judas Iscariot to betray him, Jesus, knowing that the Father had given everything into his keeping, and that he came from God and was going to God, rose from table, and after disrobing took a towel and tied it round him. Then he poured water into the basin, and proceeded to wash the disciples' feet, and to dry them with the towel that was about him.

He came to Simon Peter. 'Master,' he protested, 'are *you* going to wash my feet?'

'What I am doing,' Jesus replied, 'you do not understand now, but you will presently.'

'Never shall you wash my feet,' cried Peter.

'If I do not wash you,' Jesus answered, 'you are none of mine.'

'In that case,' Simon Peter said to him, 'do not wash just my feet, Master, but my hands and head as well.'

'He who has newly bathed,' said Jesus, 'only needs his feet washed to be completely clean. And you disciples are clean, though not all of you.'[b]

When he had washed their feet and resumed his garments Jesus sat down and said to them, 'Do you realize what I have done for you? You call me Teacher and Master, and you speak correctly, for so I am. If I then, the Teacher and Master, have washed your feet, you ought to wash each other's feet. I have set you an example, that you should do as I have done for you.

'I tell you for a positive fact, the servant is not superior to his

[a] The reason they were unable to believe was because Isaiah said further,

> *He has blinded their eyes,*
> *And hardened their minds,*
> *Lest they should see with their eyes,*
> *And understand with their minds,*
> *And return; and I must heal them.*[94]

Isaiah said this because he saw his glory, and spoke of him. As a matter of fact, however, even among the rulers many believed in him. But they did not openly admit it on account of the Pharisees, in case they should be excommunicated; for they had a higher regard for human praise than for God's praise.

[b] He knew who would betray him. That is why he said, 'Not all of you are clean'.

[93] Isa. liii. 1.
[94] Isa. vi. 9-10.

master,[95] nor the messenger to him who has sent him. If you know this, happy are you if you act upon it. I am not saying this to all of you—I know those I have chosen—but that the Scripture should be fulfilled, "He who has enjoyed my hospitality has lifted his heel against me."[96] I am telling you this before it happens, so that when it comes to pass you may believe that I am he.

'I tell for a positive fact, he who receives whoever I send receives me,[97] and he who receives me receives him who has sent me.'

When he had said this, Jesus was deeply moved and testified, 'I tell you for a positive fact, one of you will betray me.'

The disciples looked at each other uncertain to whom he was referring.

One of his disciples of whom Jesus was fond was reclining on his bosom.[98] So Simon Peter leaned over to him and said, 'Ask him who he means.'

Leaning back against the breast of Jesus he said to him, 'Who is it, Master?'

Jesus replied, 'It is the one for whom I dip the morsel and offer it to him.'

Then dipping the morsel he tendered it to Judas Iscariot son of Simon; and with the morsel Satan entered him.

Jesus then said to him, 'What you have to do, do quickly,'[a]

On receiving the morsel Judas went out at once. It was night.

When he had gone, Jesus said, 'Now the Son of Man is glorified, and God is glorified in him. God will both glorify him in himself, and glorify him immediately.

'My dear children, I shall be with you only a while longer. You will look for me, but as I told the Jews, so I say to you now, "Where I am going you cannot come." I give you a fresh instruction, to love one another. As I have loved you, so must you love one another. By this, your love for one another, everyone will recognize that you are my disciples.'

'Where are you going, Master?' Simon Peter inquired.

Jesus replied, 'Where I am going you cannot follow me now, but you will follow me later.'

'Why can't I follow you now, Master?' said Peter. 'I will give my life for you.'

'So you will give your life for me?' Jesus replied. 'I tell you for a positive fact, the cock will not have crowed before you deny me three times over.

[a] No one seated there knew why he said this to him. Some, however, imagined, since Judas had the alms-bag, that Jesus was telling him, 'Buy what we need for the festival', or that he should give something to the poor.

[95] Cp. Mt. x. 24.
[96] Ps. xli. 9.
[97] Cp. Mt. x. 40.
[98] The diners lay on their left sides on couches round the table with their feet outwards and their shoulders propped against their neighbour.

[99]Do not let your minds be troubled. Have faith in God, and have faith in me too. There are many apartments in my Father's house. Had it not been so I would certainly have told you, for I go to prepare accommodation for you. And if I go and prepare accommodation for you, I will come back and take you to myself, that where I am you may be also. And to where I am going you know the way.'

Thomas said to him, 'Master, we don't know where you are going, so how can we know the way?'

Jesus said to him, 'I myself am Way and Truth and Life. No one reaches the Father except by me. If you knew me, you would also perceive my Father. From now on you do know him, and have seen him.'

Philip said to him, 'Show us the Father, Master, and we shall be content.'

Jesus replied, 'Have I been with you all so long, yet you have not recognized me, Philip? He who has seen me has seen the Father. Why then do you say, "Show us the Father"? Do you not believe that I am the Father, and that the Father is in me? The words I speak to you I do not speak of my own accord: the Father who dwells in me performs his own miracles. Believe me, that I am in the Father, and the Father is in me. But if not, believe because of the miracles themselves.

'I tell you for a positive fact, he who believes in me will perform the same miracles as myself, and even greater miracles will he perform, because I am going to the Father. I will do indeed whatever you ask in my name, that the Father may be glorified in the Son. If you ask anything in my name I will do it.

'If you care for me, carry out my instructions; and I will beg the Father to give you another Adviser to be with you permanently, namely the Spirit of Truth, whom the world cannot receive, because it neither perceives him nor knows him. But you will know him, because he will dwell with you and be with you.[100] I will not leave you forsaken; I will come to you. Very soon the world will see me no longer, but you will see me, because I am alive; and you will live. When that time comes you will realize that I am in my Father, and you are in me, and I am in you. He who possesses my instructions and keeps them, he is the man who cares for me. He who cares for me will be loved by my Father. I too will love him, and manifest myself to him.'

Judas, not Iscariot, said to him, 'Why are you going to manifest yourself to us and not to the world?'

Jesus answered, 'If anyone cares for me he will heed my message, and my Father will love him; and we will come to him and make our abode with him. He who does not care for me

[99] Throughout the Discourse that follows there appear to be several cases of displacement. But since no narrative material intervenes no rectification has been attempted except in one case (see p. 418 and notes).
[100] Or 'in you.'

will not heed my word; yet the message you are hearing is not mine but the Father's who has sent me.

[101]'I am the true vine, and my Father is the cultivator. Every branch of mine that does not bear fruit he removes, and every one that bears fruit he prunes that it may bear finer fruit. You are already sound fruit through the Message I have proclaimed to you. Continue in me and I will continue in you. Just as the branch cannot bear fruit of its own accord unless it continues in the vine, so cannot you unless you continue in me.

'I am the vine, while you are the branches. He who continues in me, and I in him, will bear much fruit, because apart from me you are powerless. If anyone does not continue in me, he is cast off—as the branch is—and withers, and men gather such branches and throw them on the fire to be burnt. If you continue in me, and my words remain in you, you shall ask what you will and it shall be done for you. By this is my Father glorified, by your bearing much fruit and being disciples of mine. As my Father has loved me, so have I loved you. Retain my affection. If you obey my instructions you will retain my affection, just as I have obeyed the Father's instructions and retain his affection.

'I have spoken to you thus that I may have joy in you, and that your joy may be complete. It is my instruction that you love one another as I have loved you. No one has a love greater than that man's who will lay down his life for his friends. You are my friends if you carry out what I have enjoined on you. I call you servants no longer; for the servant does not know what his master is about. I have addressed you as friends, because I have acquainted you with everything I have heard from my Father. It is not you who have chosen me: it is I who have chosen you and placed you so that you may proceed to bear fruit, and that your fruit may endure, so that whatever you ask the Father in my name he will grant you.

'This is what I have enjoined on you, that you love one another. If the world hates you, you know that it hated me before it hated you. If you belonged to the world the world would be fond of its own. But because you do not belong to the world, since I have chosen you out of the world, therefore the world will hate you. Remember what I have said to you, "The servant is not superior to his master."[102] If they have persecuted me, they will also persecute you. If they have not heeded my message, neither will they heed yours. They will do all this to you on my account, because they do not know him who has sent me. If I had not come and spoken to them no sin would have been theirs; but now they have no excuse for their sin. He who hates me hates the Father also. If I had not performed such miracles before them as no one else ever did no sin would have been theirs; but now they have both seen and hated me

[101] Omitting here Jn. xiv. 25-31, and transferring these verses to their proper place following xvi. 33, below p. 420.
[102] See Jn. xiii. 16, above p. 415.

and my Father also, since the saying had to be fulfilled that is stated in their Law, "They hate me without cause." [103] When the Adviser comes, whom I will send you from the Father, the Spirit of Truth that emanates from the Father, he will testify of me, and you too shall testify, because you have been with me from the first.

'I have spoken to you thus that you may not be thrown off your balance. They will excommunicate you. The time will even come when anyone who kills you will think he is performing a sacred duty. They will do this because they have neither acknowledged the Father nor me. I have told you this, however, so that when the time comes you will recall that I said it to you. I did not speak of this to you before, because I was with you. But now I am going to him who sent me, [and none of you asks me, "Where are you going?"] [104] and because I have spoken to you thus your hearts are filled with grief. I am telling you the truth, however, that it is to your advantage that I depart. For unless I go the Adviser will never come to you. But if I go, I will send him to you. And when he comes he will convict the world in respect of sin, justice and judgment; sin, because they do not believe in me, justice, because I am going to the Father and you will see me no more, and judgment, because the ruler of this world will be judged.

'I have a great deal more to tell you, but you cannot receive it now. When he comes, however, the Spirit of Truth, he will initiate you into the full truth. He will not speak of his own accord, but say exactly what he hears, and convey to you what comes. [105] He will glorify me, because he will receive what is mine and convey it to you. Whatever the Father possesses is mine. That is why I say, he will receive what is mine and convey it to you.

'Soon you will no longer see me, but soon after you will behold [106] me.'

Some of his disciples asked the others, 'What does he mean when he tells us, "Soon you will no longer see me, but soon after you will behold me," [and, "I am going to the Father"?].' [107]

The others replied, 'We have no idea. What does he mean when he says, "Soon"?'

Jesus knew that they wanted to ask him, and said to them, 'You are questioning one another, are you not, about what I said, "Soon you will no longer see me, but soon after you will behold me"? I tell you for a positive fact, you will weep and wail, while the world will rejoice. You will mourn, but your mourning will be turned into joy. A woman is dismayed when she is about to give birth, because her time has come. But once

[103] Ps. xxxv. 19; lxix. 4.
[104] Either a gloss, or indicating a displacement, since Peter had in fact asked this question (xiii. 36, above p. 416).
[105] I.e. mediumistically. Alternatively, 'what is coming', the future.
[106] *Opsesthe*, suggesting an appearance of an abnormal nature.
[107] Probably a gloss. While these words had been used just before (Jn. xvi. 10, this page line 2), they had also been used some time back at xiv. 12, above, p. 418.

the babe is born she no longer remembers her pangs in her joy that a man-child is born into the world. So you too will grieve sorely now. But I will appear to you, and your hearts will rejoice, and no one will be able to take your joy from you. When that day comes you will not need to ask me anything. I tell you for a positive fact whatever you ask the Father he will grant you for my sake. So far you have asked nothing in my name. Ask, and you shall receive, that your joy may be complete.

'I have spoken to you enigmatically thus far. The time will come when I shall no longer speak to you enigmatically, but will inform you about the Father plainly. When that time comes you will ask in my name, and I will not say to you, "I will ask the Father on your behalf." The Father himself will love you, because you have loved me and believed that I came from the Father. I came from the Father and entered the world. Now I am leaving the world again and going to the Father.'

His disciples said to him, 'There, now you are speaking plainly and not enigmatically. Now we know that you know everything and need no one to question you. This makes us believe that you come from God.'

Jesus replied, 'So you do believe now? The time will indeed come, in fact it has come, when you will disperse each to his own home[108] and leave me completely alone. But I shall not be completely alone; for the Father will be with me. I have told you this so that you may be at peace where I am concerned. In the world you will have affliction, but take courage, I have overcome the world.

[109]'I have spoken to you thus while I am with you. But the Adviser, the holy Spirit, whom the Father will send in my name, will give you full instructions,[110] and remind you of everything I have told you. I leave you peace. I give you my own peace. I do not give it as the world gives it. Do not be distressed or dismayed. You have heard me say, "I am going away, but I will come to you." If you cared for me you would surely be glad that I am going to the Father, for the Father is superior to myself. I have told you now before it happens, so that when it happens you may believe.

'I shall not speak to you much more. The ruler of the world is coming, and in me he will get nothing, except that the world will know that I love the Father, and as the Father has given me commandment so I act. Rise, let us be going!'[111]

When Jesus had spoken thus, he lifted his eyes to heaven and said, 'Father, the time has come. Glorify thy Son, that thy Son may glorify thee, just as thou gavest him authority over all flesh, so that to all whom thou hast given him he should grant Eternal Life. Eternal Life consists in knowing thee, the only

---

[108] Cp. Mt. xxvi. 31, 56.   [109] Inserting here Jn. xiv. 25-31, see p. 418, n. 101.
[110] Lit. 'will teach you everything'.
[111] Cp. Mk. xiv. 42; Mt. xxvi. 46. From Jn. xii. 27-28 it is evident that the author was familiar with the story of the Agony in the Garden, but in the interests of the Discourse he has omitted it.

True God, and him whom thou hast sent, Jesus Christ. I have
glorified thee on earth by completing the work thou gavest me
to do. So now glorify me in thy dwelling place, Father, with the
glory I had with thee before the world existed.

'I have revealed thy name to the men thou gavest me out of
the world. Thine they were, and thou gavest them to me; and
they have heeded thy Message. They know now that everything
thou hast given me comes from thee; for the words thou gavest
me I have given them, and they have accepted and clearly understood that I have come from thee, and have believed that
thou hast sent me. I ask on their behalf—I do not ask on behalf
of the world, but for those thou hast given me—for they are
thine, and all that is mine is thine, and what is thine is mine,
and I am glorified in them. I shall no longer be in the world,
but they will be in the world, while I come to thee.

'Holy Father, keep in thy name those whom thou hast given
me, that they may be one as we are. While I have been with
them I have kept in thy name those whom thou hast given me,
and guarded them, and not one of them is lost except the
doomed one,[112] that the Scripture should come true.[113]

'But now I am coming to thee. So I am saying this in the
world, that they may experience the full measure of my happiness. I have given them thy Message, and the world has hated
them, because they are not of the world any more than I am of
the world. I do not ask that thou shouldst take them out of the
world, but that thou wouldst keep them from harm.[114] They are
not of the world any more than I am of the world. Consecrate
them by the Truth. Thy Message is Truth. Just as thou didst
send me into the world, so have I sent them into the world;
and on their behalf I have consecrated myself, that they too
may be consecrated by Truth.

'Neither do I ask on behalf of these alone, but also on behalf
of those who will believe in me through their report, that they
all may be one as thou, Father, art in me and I in thee, that they
also may be one in us, that the world may believe thou hast
sent me. So the glory thou hast given me I have given them,
that they may be one as we are one: I in them and thou in me,
that they may be perfected as one, that the world may know
that thou hast sent me, and that thou hast loved them as thou
hast loved me.

'Father, I desire that what thou hast given me, even these,
may be with me where I shall be, that they may see my glory
which thou hast given me; for thou didst love me before the
foundation of the world.

'Righteous Father, though the world has not known thee, I
have known thee, and these have known that thou hast sent
me. And I have made known thy name to them, and will make

[112] Lit. 'Son of Perdition'.
[113] Cp. Ps. cix. 7-8.
[114] Cp. Mt. vi. 13.

it known so that the love with which thou hast loved me may be in them, as I am in them.'

XII

When Jesus had spoken thus, he passed over the brook Kidron with his disciples, where there was an orchard into which he and his disciples entered.[a]

Judas, therefore, having obtained the cohort and officers from the head priests and Pharisees, went there with lanterns and torches and weapons.

Then Jesus, who knew everything that was to befall him, came out and said to them, 'Who are you looking for?'

'Jesus the Nazarene,' they replied.

'I am he,' he told them.

Judas himself, who betrayed him, was standing there with them. As Jesus said, 'I am he,' he[115] stepped back and fell prostrate.

Then Jesus asked him again, 'Who are you looking for?'

When they said, 'Jesus the Nazarene,' Jesus replied, 'I have told you I am he. So if it is only myself you want let these others go away.'[b]

At this juncture Simon Peter, who carried a sword, drew it and struck the high priest's servant,[c] severing his right ear.

'Return your sword to its sheath,' Jesus told Peter. 'Shall I not drink the cup the Father has given me?'[116]

The cohort with its tribune and the Jewish officers then laid hold of Jesus, bound him, and conducted him to Annas[117] in the first instance.[d] Simon Peter and another disciple followed Jesus. Now that disciple was a relative[118] of the high priest, and accompanied Jesus into the yard of the high priest's palace, but Peter was standing before the door outside. The other disciple, therefore, the relative of the high priest, went out and spoke to the woman doorkeeper and secured Peter's admission.

The woman then said to Peter, 'Aren't you one of the man's disciples?'

'No, I'm not,' he said.

The servants and officers had lit a charcoal brazier, because

---

[a] Judas, who betrayed him, was familiar with the spot, because Jesus often resorted there with his disciples.

[b] That the saying he uttered, 'I have lost none of those thou hast given me', should come true.[119]

[c] The servant's name was Malchus.

[d] He was father-in-law of Caiaphas, who was the reigning high priest. It was Caiaphas who had counselled the Jews, 'It is advisable that one man should die for the people.'

[115] The text reads 'they', which may of course be intentional, but 'he' seems more appropriate, since otherwise the reference to Judas is superfluous.
[116] Another indication of the author's knowledge of the Agony in the Garden.
[117] Annas son of Seth, appointed high priest by Quirinius in A.D. 7.
[118] Reading *gnotos* instead of *gnostos* 'acquaintance'. See preface.
[119] See Jn. xvii. 12, above p. 421.

it was cold, and stood warming themselves. So Peter stood with them, and warmed himself too.

Meanwhile, the high priest had been questioning Jesus about his disciples and about his teaching.

Jesus answered, 'I have spoken quite openly to the world. I have invariably taught in the synagogue and in the Temple,[120] where all the Jews congregate, and have said nothing secretly. Why do you ask me? Ask those who have listened what I said to them. They know what I said.'

When he said this, one of the officers who was standing by struck Jesus and said, 'Is that the way to answer the high priest?'

Jesus replied, 'If I have spoken wrongly, say exactly what is wrong; but if rightly, why do you strike me?'

Then Annas sent him bound to the high priest Caiaphas. Simon Peter was still standing warming himself.

Then they said to him, 'Aren't you one of his disciples?'

He denied it and said, 'No, I'm not.'

One of the high priest's servants[a] said, 'Didn't I see you in the orchard with him?'

Once more Peter denied, and immediately a cock crowed.

From Caiaphas they conducted Jesus to the praetorium. It was early morning, so they did not enter the praetorium in case they should be defiled, and so prevented from eating the passover. Pilate therefore went out to them and said, 'What charge do you bring against this man?'

'Had he not been a criminal,' they replied, 'we should not have handed him over to you.'

'In that case,' said Pilate, 'take him yourselves and sentence him in accordance with your law.'

The Jews answered, 'We have no power to execute anyone.'[b][121]

Pilate then went into the praetorium and summoned Jesus, and said to him, 'Are you the king of the Jews?'

Jesus replied, 'Are you asking this of your own accord, or did others suggest it to you about me?'

'Am I a Jew?' said Pilate. 'Your own people and the head priests have handed you over to me. What have you done?'

Jesus replied, 'My kingdom is not of this world.[122] Had my kingdom been of this world my supporters would have struggled to prevent my being handed over to the Jews. My kingdom, however, is not from that source.'

'You are a king then?' Pilate said to him.

[a] He was a kinsman of the one whose ear Peter had severed.
[b] That the saying of Jesus should come true by which he had indicated the kind of death he would die.[123]

[120] Cp. Mt. xxvi. 55.
[121] According to Jewish tradition the Sanhedrin was deprived by the Romans of power to try capital cases about A.D. 30, forty years before the destruction of the Temple.
[122] The Messiah's kingdom was that of the World to Come, the Kingdom of God in the Messianic Era.
[123] See Jn. xii. 32-33, above p. 413.

Jesus replied, 'As you say, I am a king. The reason I was born and came into the world was to testify to the truth. All who own the truth listen to my voice.'

'What does truth mean?' Pilate said to him.

When he had said this he went out again to the Jews and told them, 'I can find nothing whatever against him. But you have a practice that at the Passover I should release one person for you. Do you then wish me to release the king of the Jews for you?'

They shouted back, 'Not this man, Bar-Abbas!'[a]

Pilate then had Jesus flogged, and the soldiers plaited a victor's wreath out of thorns and set it on his head, and draped round him a crimson cloak, and saluted him with, 'Hail, king of the Jews!', and struck him.

Once more Pilate went out, and said to them, 'I am going to bring him out to you, that you may know that I find nothing whatever against him.'

Then Jesus came out, wearing the thorn wreath and the crimson cloak, and Pilate announced, 'Here he is!'

When they saw him, the head priests and their supporters shouted, 'Crucify him, crucify him!'

Pilate said to them, 'Crucify him yourselves, for I find nothing against him.'

The Jews replied, 'We have a law, and in accordance with that law he ought to die, because he claimed to be God's son.'

When Pilate heard this he was even more alarmed, and went back into the praetorium and said to Jesus, 'Where do you come from?'

But Jesus gave him no reply.

Pilate then said to him, 'Have you nothing to say to me? Do you not know that I have power to release you and power to crucify you?'

Jesus replied, 'You could have no power over me at all unless it was given you from Above. Consequently he who handed me over to you is more to blame than you are.'

Because of this Pilate endeavoured to release him. But the Jews shouted, 'If you release him, you are no friend of Caesar's. Whoever claims to be king is in opposition to Caesar.'[124]

When Pilate heard these expressions he brought Jesus out and seated him[125] on the tribunal in the place called the Tiled Court, but in Hebrew *Gabbatha*,[b][126] and said to the Jews, 'Here is your king!'

'Off with him, off with him! Crucify him!' they shouted.

Pilate said to them, 'Am I to crucify your king?'

---

[a] Bar-Abbas was a brigand.
[b] It was the preparation day of the Passover, about six o'clock in the morning.[127]

[124] See p. 80, n. 94.
[125] Or 'took his seat'.   [126] Aram. *Gabbetha* (the Platform).
[127] Lit. 'the sixth hour' (Roman reckoning) corresponding to the first hour (Jewish reckoning).

The head priests responded, 'We have no king but Caesar.' Then Pilate handed him over to them to be crucified.

So they took Jesus, and carrying his own cross he went out to what was called Skull Place, that is to say in Hebrew *Golgotha,* where they crucified him, and along with him two others on either side, with Jesus in the middle. Pilate also wrote a notice and posted it up on the cross, to this effect, 'Jesus the Nazarene, King of the Jews'.

Many Jews read the notice, because the place where Jesus was crucified was close to the city, and it was written in Hebrew, Latin and Greek. So the Jewish head priests said to Pilate, 'Do not put "King of the Jews", but "He said, I am King of the Jews".' Pilate replied, 'What I have written I have written.'

Now when the soldiers crucified Jesus they took his clothes and divided them into four lots, one lot for each soldier, leaving the tunic over. Now the tunic was seamless throughout, woven in one piece. So they said to one another, 'Don't let us tear it, but draw lots for it and see who gets it.' [a]

Standing by the cross of Jesus were his mother, and his mother's sister, Mary the wife of[128] Clopas, and Mary of Magdala. Then Jesus, noticing his mother and the disciple of whom he was fond standing there, said to his mother, 'Madam, this is your son.' Then he said to the disciple, 'This is your mother.' From that time the disciple took her into his own home.

After this, Jesus conscious that all was now over said, 'I am thirsty.' [b] There was a jar full of vinegar placed there. So they saturated a sponge with vinegar, fixed it on a spike,[129] and put it to his mouth. When he had received the vinegar he said, 'It is all over', and bowing his head yielded up his spirit.

Then the Jews,[c] that the bodies should not remain on the cross on the sabbath,[d] requested Pilate that their legs might be broken and the corpses removed.

So the soldiers went and broke the legs of the first, and of the other man crucified with him. But when they came to Jesus, as they saw he was already dead they did not break his legs; but one of the soldiers with his lance pierced his side, and there came out blood and water.[e]

[a] That the Scripture should come true, 'They divided my garments among them, and for my clothing they cast lots' (Ps. xxii. 18). This is exactly what the soldiers did.
[b] That the Scripture should be accomplished (Ps. lxix. 21).
[c] As it was the preparation day.
[d] For that sabbath was a high day.
[e] He who saw it has stated this, and his statement is completely trustworthy, and he knows he is telling the truth, that you too may believe. For this happened that the Scripture should come true, 'Not a bone of his shall be fractured' (Ps. xxxiv. 20, LXX), and still another Scripture says, 'They shall look at him whom they have pierced' (Zech. xii. 10).

[128] Or 'daughter of'.   [129] Reading *hysso* for *hyssopo* (hyssop), the scribal error probably being due to the fact that in Greek the word following commences with 'p'.

XIII

[130]After these events, Joseph of Arimathea[a] asked Pilate's leave to remove the body of Jesus, and Pilate committed it to him. So he went and removed the body. Nicodemus[b] also went, carrying a compound of myrrh and aloes weighing about seventy-five pounds.[131] Then they took the body of Jesus, and wrapped it in swatches of linen with the spices.[c]

Now in the locality where Jesus was crucified there was an orchard, and in the orchard a new tomb in which no one had ever been laid before. There then they laid Jesus.[d]

On the day after the sabbath Mary of Magdala came very early to the tomb while it was still dark, and saw that the boulder was removed from the tomb. So she ran to Simon Peter and the other disciple of whom Jesus was fond and told them, 'They have removed the Master from the tomb, and we[132] don't know where they have laid him.'

So Peter and the other disciple set out and came to the tomb. They both ran there together; but the other disciple outdistanced Peter and reached the tomb first, and stooping down saw the linen wrappings lying there. He did not go in however. Then following him came Simon Peter, and entered the tomb. There he saw both the wrappings and also the cloth that had covered Jesus's head, not lying with the wrappings, but apart, folded up by itself. Then the other disciple, who had reached the tomb first, also went in, and saw for himself and believed.[e] Then the disciples returned home.

Meanwhile Mary stood outside the tomb close by weeping. As she wept she peered into the tomb and saw two angels sitting there, one at the head and one at the feet where the body of Jesus had lain.

'Madam, why are you crying?' they said to her.

'Because they have taken away my Master,' she replied, 'and I don't know where they have laid him.'

When she had said this she turned round and saw Jesus standing there, though she did not realize it was Jesus.

Jesus said to her, 'Madam, why are you crying? Who are you looking for?'

[a] He was a disciple of Jesus, but kept the fact secret for fear of the Jews.
[b] The one who first of all came to Jesus by night.
[c] As is the Jewish burial custom.
[d] On account of the Jewish preparation day, because it was close by.
[e] For so far they had not understood the Scripture that he must rise from the dead.

[130] 'After these events.' The division of the text introduced by these words is regularly employed up to Jn. vii. 1 (above section vi), and is then dropped until resumed here.
[131] Gr. 'one hundred litras'. A litra was equal to 12 oz.
[132] The plural suggests the author's awareness that the other women had also been at the tomb (cp. Mk. xvi. 1-8, above p. 82).

Thinking he was the gardener, she said to him, 'Sir, if you have moved him, tell me where you have put him and I will take him away.'

Jesus said to her, 'Mary!'

She turned and said to him in Hebrew, *'Rabboni!'* [a]

'Do not detain me,'[133] Jesus said to her, 'for I have not yet ascended to the Father. Go to my brothers, and tell them, "I am ascending to my Father and your Father, to my God and your God."'

Mary of Magdala went and informed the disciples, 'I have seen the Master,' and gave them his message.

The evening of that day, the day after the sabbath, when the doors had been bolted where the disciples were for fear of the Jews,[134] Jesus came and stood before them, and said to them, 'Peace be with you.' So saying he showed his hands and side.

The disciples were delighted to see the Master.

Again he said to them, 'Peace be with you. As the Father has sent me, so am I sending you.'

With this he expelled a deep breath, and said to them, 'Receive the holy Spirit! Those whose sins you forgive will be forgiven, and those whom you condemn will be condemned.'

Thomas, however, one of the twelve, who was called Twin, was not with them when Jesus came. So the other disciples told him, 'We have seen the Master.'

But he replied, 'Unless I see the scar of the nails in his hands, and insert my finger in the nail scars, and insert my hand into his side, I shall not believe it.'

Eight days later the disciples were again indoors, and this time Thomas was with them. When the doors were bolted Jesus came and stood before them, and said, 'Peace be with you.'

Then he said to Thomas, 'Bring your finger here where my hands are, and bring your hand and insert it into my side, and do not be incredulous but believing.'

Thomas answered, 'My Lord and my God!'[135]

Jesus said to him, 'You have believed because you have seen me. Happy are they who have believed without seeing!'

Many other signs did Jesus perform in the presence of his disciples, which have not been recorded in this book. But these have been recorded that you may believe that Jesus is the Messiah, the Son of God, and by believing have Life on his account.

[a] That is to say, 'Teacher!'

[133] Or, 'Do not cling to me'.
[134] According to the uncanonical *Gospel of Peter* the disciples were in hiding because they were being sought for by the Jews in the belief that they were intending to set fire to the Temple.
[135] The author may have put this expression into the mouth of Thomas in response to the fact that the Emperor Domitian had insisted on having himself addressed as 'Our Lord and God'. Suet. *Domit.* xiii.

EPILOGUE

After these events Jesus revealed himself again to the disciples at the Sea of Tiberias. He appeared in this way. Simon Peter, Thomas called Twin, Nathaniel from Cana of Galilee, the sons of Zebedee, and two other disciples of his, were together. Simon Peter said to them, 'I am going fishing.'[136]

'Very well,' they told him, 'we will come with you.'

So they went on board the boat; but that night they caught nothing. When morning came there was Jesus standing on the shore.[a]

Jesus then hailed them, 'Have you anything to eat there, lads?'

'No,' they replied.

'Cast your net on the right side of the ship,' he told them, 'and you will find fish.'

So they cast the net, and now they could hardly haul it in for the quantity of fish.

At this, the disciple of whom Jesus was fond said to Peter, 'It is the Master!'

As soon as Simon Peter heard it was the Master, he tied his smock round him[b] and leapt into the sea. But the other disciples came to shore in the dinghy[c] dragging the net full of fish.

As they landed they saw a charcoal fire burning and a small fish with bread being baked.

'Bring some of the small fish you have just caught,' Jesus said to them.

So Peter went aboard and drew the net to land full of large fish, a hundred and fifty-three of them; yet in spite of there being so many the net was not broken.

'Come and breakfast,' said Jesus.

None of the disciples had the temerity to ask him, 'Who are you?' knowing it was the Master.

Jesus came and took the bread and distributed it to them, and the fish as well.[d]

When they had breakfasted, Jesus said to Simon Peter, 'Simon son of John, do you love me more than these others?'

'Of course, Master,' he replied. 'You know I am devoted to you.'

'Tend my lambs,' he told him.

[a] The disciples did not actually know it was the Master.
[b] He was naked.
[c] They were not far from the shore, only about a hundred yards.
[d] This was now the third occasion on which Jesus had appeared to the disciples after rising from the dead.

[136] The *Gospel of Peter* also makes some of the disciples go to the sea with Peter, but the extant fragment breaks off at this point.

Again he asked him for the second time, 'Simon son of John, do you love me?'

'Of course, Master,' he replied. 'You know I am devoted to you.'

'Shepherd my sheep,' he told him.

For the third time he asked him, 'Simon son of John, are you devoted to me?'

Peter was vexed that he asked him a third time, 'Are you devoted to me?' and said to him, 'You know everything, Master. You must know I am devoted to you.'

'Tend my sheep,' Jesus said to him. 'I tell you for a positive fact, when you were young, you fastened your girdle and went wherever you wished. But when you are old, you will stretch out your hands, and someone else will fasten you and convey you where you will not wish.' [a]

Having said this, he added, 'Follow me.'

Turning round, Peter noticed that the disciple of whom Jesus was fond had been following.[b] Seeing him, Peter said to Jesus, 'What about him, Master?'

Jesus replied, 'Supposing I wish him to remain until I come, what concern is that of yours? You follow me.'[c]

[a] He said this in indication of the kind of death by which he would glorify God.[137]

[b] The one who reclined on his breast at the supper, and said, 'Master, who is it who will betray you?'

[c] Thus the saying got about among the brothers that that disciple would not die, though Jesus never told him he would not die, he only said, 'Supposing I wish him to remain until I come, what concern is that of yours?' He is the disciple who testified to these matters and recorded them, and we know that his testimony is trustworthy. There is also much else that Jesus did, which if every item were to be recorded I[138] very much doubt if the world itself could find room for the books that would have to be written.

[137] According to tradition Peter was crucified by the Romans head downwards.
[138] The author, or editor, seems here clearly to distinguish himself from the Beloved Disciple whose records he has been using. Cp. III. Jno. 12, below p. 437.

Preface to the *Letters of John the Elder*

THREE LETTERS by John, the Elder not the Apostle, are extant. About the authenticity of the first there has never been any serious question. Neither can there be any real doubt regarding the genuineness of the other two, though naturally, being so short and containing no teaching that was not already in the first, they would tend to be disregarded.

Strictly the first letter is not a letter at all, but a tract or homily. In the present version it is suggested that the opening sentence is really the title and sub-title. The word *peri*, 'concerning', or 'on the subject of', is constantly used in Greek descriptive titles; and certainly *The Theme of 'Life'* is the subject of this document. Life as appearing in Christ and Life as possessed in him. The same thought is frequently expressed in the Elder's version of the Fourth Gospel. Some have held that the letter or tract was published with the Gospel as a kind of commendation of it. See the preface to the Gospel.

The second and third letters are real letters, the former written to an unnamed community of believers, 'the Elect Lady and her Children', and the latter to Gaius, possibly an influential member of the same community. The letters reveal the clash of personalities as well as the conflict of beliefs that was taking place in the Asiatic communities in the first quarter of the second century, where certain heretical teachers were beginning to appear and propagate their doctrines. In defence of his Christology, very different to that of the earlier disciples, the Elder speaks his mind bluntly, and fully in keeping with the stories handed down about his uncompromising nature. That same voice speaks with the lips of Jesus in the Discourses in the Fourth Gospel and in the *Letters to the Seven Communities* inserted in the *Revelation*. It is consistent and unmistakable. Yet with friends it can be surprisingly sweet and tender.

Especially in the tract, or first letter, there are so many allusions to the Gospel that it would disturb the reading to list them. As we have seen, the author has so united his own work with that of the Beloved Disciple that here he can range himself beside him and speak of 'we' who have seen and touched Jesus. We cannot tell whether it was through modesty or due to the Elder, that the name of the Beloved Disciple is never mentioned in the Gospel.

LETTER OF JOHN (I)
ON THE THEME OF 'LIFE'[1]

He who was from of old, whom we have heard, whom we have seen with our own eyes, whom we have inspected, and whom our hands have touched.

Not only was Life made visible, but we have seen it, and solemnly affirm this, and proclaim to you that Eternal Life which was with the Father and was made visible to us.

Him whom we have seen and heard we proclaim to you also, that you too may have fellowship with us. And the fellowship, our fellowship, is with the Father and with his Son Jesus Christ; and we are writing this to you that your[2] joy may be complete.

It is the very same Message we have heard from him which we are conveying to you, that 'God is Light, and there is no trace of darkness in him'. If we say, 'We have fellowship with him', and walk in the dark, we lie, and are not keeping to the truth. But if we walk in the light we have fellowship with one another, and the blood of his Son Jesus cleanses us from all iniquity. If we say, 'We have not sinned', we make him a liar, and his word is not in us.

I am writing this to you, dear children, that you may not sin; but should anyone sin we have an intercessor with the Father, Jesus Christ the Just. He is a propitiator where our sins are concerned, and not only ours but those of the whole world. We are conscious that we know him in this way if we obey his instructions. He who says, 'I know him', but does not obey his instructions is a liar, and truth is not in him. Whoever obeys him, in him truly the love of God is accomplished. In this way, we are conscious that we are in him. He who says he continues in him ought himself to behave as he behaved.

Dear friends, it is no new instruction I am sending you, but an old one which you had from the very first. The old instruction is the Message you have heard. Yet I *am* sending you a new instruction, something that holds good both for him and for you, that the darkness is passing away, and the True Light already shines. He who claims to be in the light and hates his brother is still in the darkness. He who loves his brother continues in the light, and in it there is no pitfall. But he who hates his brother is in darkness, and walks in the dark, and does not know where he is going, because the darkness has blinded his eyes.

I am writing to you, dear children, because your sins are forgiven for his sake. I am writing to you, fathers, because you

---

[1] These words are here regarded as the title of the tract, 'Life' being personified and manifested in Jesus Christ. Alternatively read, 'On the Word of Life'. See prefaces to John and to these letters. [2] Alternative reading 'our'.

have known him who is from of old. I am writing to you, youths, because you have overcome the Evil One.

I have written to you, children, because you have known the Father. I have written to you, fathers, because you have known him who is from of old. I have written to you, youths, because you are strong and the word of God remains in you, and you have overcome the Evil One. Do not love the world, nor what is in the world. If anyone loves the world, there is no love of the Father in him. For everything that is in the world, desire of the flesh, desire of the eyes, and the hollow sham of life in general, belongs not to the Father, but to the world. And the world with its desire is passing away, while he who does the will of God will endure for ever.

Children, it is the Last Hour. And as you have heard, 'Antichrist will come', well, there are plenty of antichrists in existence now, by which fact we know it is the Last Hour. They went out from us, but they did not belong to us. Had they belonged to us they would surely have remained with us. They went out, indeed, to make it clear that they all do not belong to us. You, however, are consecrated by the Holy One. You do know, all of you. I have not written to you because you do not know the truth, but because you do know it, and because no lie has any connexion with the truth.

Who but he is a liar, who denies that Jesus is the Christ? He is the Antichrist, he who denies the Father and the Son. Whoever denies the Son cannot have the Father either. He who confesses the Son has the Father also. As for you, let what you have heard from the beginning continue in you. Should what you have heard from the beginning continue in you, then you will continue both in the Son and in the Father. And this is the promise he has made us, the promise of Eternal Life.

I have written this to you regarding those who would deceive you. As for you, the consecration you have received from him will continue in you, and there will be no need for anyone to teach you, since his consecration will teach you about everything; and this will be truth and no lie. So as it has taught you, continue in him.

And now, dear children, continue in him, so that whenever he shall appear we may meet him confidently on his arrival, and not shrink from him in shame. If you are aware that he is just, you must also know that everyone who does justice is born of him. Look what love it is the Father has bestowed on us, that we should be called Children of God. And that is what we are. That is why the world does not recognize us, because it did not know him. Yes, dear friends, we are Children of God now, though it is not yet evident what we shall be. We only know that when he appears we shall be like him, for we shall behold him as he is. And everyone who has this expectation purifies himself, as he is pure.

Whoever commits sin commits lawlessness. Sin, indeed, is

lawlessness. And you know that he appeared to take away sin, and in him there is no sin. Whoever continues in him does not sin, while whoever sins has neither seen him nor known him.

Do not deceive yourselves, dear children. He who executes justice is just, as he is just. He who commits sin belongs to the Devil; for the Devil has continued to sin from the beginning. To this end the Son of God appeared, that he might undo the Devil's works.

Whoever is born of God does not commit sin,[3] because his seed remains in him; and he cannot sin, for he is begotten of God. This is what differentiates the Children of God from the Children of the Devil. Whoever does not do justice does not belong to God, nor does he who does not love his neighbour. For the very declaration you have heard from the beginning is that we should love one another, and not be like Cain, who belonged to the Evil One, and slew his brother. And why did he slay him? Because his own deeds were evil, while those of his brother were good.

Do not be in the least surprised, brothers, if the world hates you. We know indeed that we have passed from Death to Life, because we love the brothers. He who does not love his brother continues in Death. Whoever hates his brother is a manslayer, and you know that no manslayer has any continuance of Eternal Life in him. We have known what love is from the fact that the Son of God[4] laid down his life for us. We too ought to lay down our lives for our brothers. But he who has worldly means, and observes his brother in need, and withholds his compassion from him, how does the love of God continue in him? Let us not love, dear children, merely in speech and word, but in deed and reality. In this way we shall know that we belong to the Truth, and shall relieve our minds in his presence should our minds accuse us; for God is greater than our minds and knows everything. Should our minds not accuse us, dear friends, we shall have confidence towards God, and whatever we ask for we shall obtain from him, because we obey his commandments and do what is pleasing in his sight. And it is his commandment that we should believe in his Son Jesus Christ, and that we should love one another as Christ enjoined on us. Whoever obeys his instructions continues in him, and he in him who obeys. And the way we recognize that he continues in us is by his spirit which he has given us.

Do not credit every spirit, dear friends. Examine the spirits to find out whether they are from God, because many false prophets are abroad in the world. You will recognize the spirit from God in this way: every spirit which confesses that

---

[3] By sin the author here seems primarily to mean sexual relations. Much is made by early writers of John's celibacy, and cp. Rev. xiv. 4.
[4] The text simply reads 'he'.

Jesus Christ has come in the flesh is from God, while every spirit which does not admit the reality of Jesus is not from God.[5] And this is the spirit of Antichrist, which you have heard will come.

Now you, dear children, belong to God, and have overcome the antichrists;[6] for he who is in you is greater than he who is in the world. They belong to the world. That is why they speak in a worldly way and the world listens to them. We belong to God. He who knows God will listen to us, while he who does not belong to God will not listen to us. This is how we shall discern the spirit of truth and the spirit of error.[7]

Love one another, dear friends, because love is from God, and everyone who does love is born of God and knows God. He who does not love does not know God; for God is Love. God's love has been made evident to us in this way, that God sent his Only-begotten Son into the world that we might have Life through him. This is where love comes in, not in our having loved God, but in his having loved us, and having sent his Son as propitiator where our sins were concerned.

If God so loved us, dear friends, we too ought to love one another. No one has ever yet seen God; but if we love one another God continues in us, and his love is perfected in us. This is how we know that we are continuing in him and he in us, because he has given us some of his own Spirit, and we have seen and testified that the Father has sent the Son as saviour of the world. Whoever confesses that Jesus is the Son of God, God continues in him and he in God. We ourselves have known and have believed the love which God has for us.

God is Love, and he who continues in love continues in God, and God continues in him. It is in this way that love is perfected in our case, so that we should have confidence on the Day of Judgment; because as he is so are we in the world. There is no such thing as fear in love. Rather does utter love expel fear. For fear causes timorousness: he who is afraid is not perfect in his love. We love, because God loved us in the first place. If anyone says, 'I love God', yet hates his brother, he is a liar. For he who does not love his brother whom he has seen, cannot love God whom he has not seen. Indeed, we have this very commandment from him,[8] that he who loves God must love his brother also.

Whoever believes that Jesus is the Christ is begotten of God, and whoever loves him who begot loves him who is begotten of him. It is when we do love God and keep his commandments that we realize that we love the Children of God. Love of God consists in our obeying his commandments. And his commandments are not burdensome, for whatever is begot-

[5] The author here opposes the Docetists, those who said that Jesus Christ had had no real physical existence. He only appeared to be a man and to suffer.
[6] Or false prophets. The text simply reads 'them' (cp. ii. 18).
[7] Or, 'detect the true spirit and the false spirit'.
[8] See Deut. vi. 5; Lev. xix. 18; Mt. xxii. 37-9.

ten of God overcomes the world. The victory that overcomes the world lies in our faith. Who is it overcomes the world but he who believes that Jesus is the Son of God? He it is, Jesus Christ, who has gone through water and blood,[9] not only water, but water and blood. Now it is the Spirit that affirms this, because the Spirit is Truth. For there are three that give their testimony, the Spirit, the water, and the blood, and the three are in complete accord. If we accept the evidence of men, the testimony of God is greater, because it is indeed the testimony of God that he has given regarding his Son. He who believes in the Son of God has the evidence in himself. He who does not believe God has made him a liar, because he has not credited the testimony which God has given regarding his Son. The evidence consists in this, that God has given us Eternal Life, and that this Life is in his Son. He who possesses the Son possesses Life. He who does not possess the Son of God does not possess Life.

I have written this to you—those who believe in the name of the Son of God—that you may be aware that you do possess Eternal Life. The confidence we have, then, where God is concerned is this, that if we ask anything which is in accordance with his will he will listen to us. And if we know that he listens to our requests, we know equally that we shall obtain whatever it may be we have asked him for.

If anyone sees his brother committing a sin that is not deadly, he shall ask, and God will grant him life. This applies to those who commit sins which are not deadly. There is such a thing as deadly sin.[10] I am not suggesting that he should pray in respect of that. Every iniquity is of course sin, but there is such a thing as sin that is not deadly.

We know that whoever is born of God does not sin, since he who was begotten of God keeps him, and the Evil One does not get hold of him. We know that we belong to God, while the whole world is devoted to the Evil One. We know too that the Son of God has come, and has given us insight so that we should know the True One.[11] And in his Son Jesus Christ we are in the True One. He is the True God and Eternal Life. Guard yourselves from idols, dear children.

[9] The baptism of water and the baptism of blood (Mk. x. 38; Lk. xii. 50), the crucifixion. The Fourth Gospel stresses the water and blood that came out when the side of Jesus was pierced (Jn. xix. 34).

[10] What the author would think of as deadly sins are listed in Rev. xxi. 8.

[11] See Jn. xvii. 3. It is in such passages that there is a suspicion of Marcionism. There is a curious statement found in fourth century prefaces to the Fourth Gospel that the Old Priest John cast out Marcion because of his contrary opinions. Marcion had brought him writings from the brothers at Pontus. But the Old Priest, though credited with being a centenarian, must have been dead a good many years before Marcion became active. The tradition is none the less important in view of Marcionite tendencies in the Johannine documents.

LETTER OF JOHN (II)
TO THE ELECT LADY AND HER CHILDREN

The Elder, to the Elect Lady and her children, whom I truly love for the Truth's sake, and not only I but all indeed who have known the Truth, which continues in us and will be with us for ever. There will be loving-kindness, mercy and peace with us from God the Father, and from Jesus Christ the Son of the Father, in truth and in love.

I was extremely happy to find children of yours following the truth, as we were commanded by the Father. So now I put it to you, Lady, not as sending you a new injunction, but one we have had from the beginning, that we should love one another. And the love consists in this, in our living in accordance with his commandments. In order that you may follow it, this is what the injunction to love one another[12] means, as you have heard from the beginning. For many deceivers are abroad in the world, those who do not admit Jesus Christ as having come in the flesh.[13] Here is 'the Deceiver' and 'the Antichrist'! Be on your guard, so that we do not lose what we have laboured for, but receive a full reward. Whoever goes beyond, and does not remain within Christ's teaching, will not possess God. It is he who remains within the teaching who will possess both the Father and the Son. If anyone comes to you and does not bring this teaching, do not receive him into your homes, do not even bid him welcome; for he who bids him welcome shares in his evil deeds.

Having so much to say to you, I do not want to do it with paper and ink. I am hoping instead to come and see you, and speak to you personally, that your[14] joy may be complete.

The children of your Elect Sister send you their regards.

LETTER OF JOHN (III)
TO GAIUS

The Elder, to dear Gaius,[15] for whom I have a genuine affection.

First and foremost, dear friend, I trust you are well and prosperous, as prosperous as your soul is. You may be sure I was

[12] 'To love one another'. These words are implied though not in the text.
[13] See p. 434, n. 5.   [14] Or 'our'.
[15] Evidently a person of some means and influence, probably belonging to the community addressed in the previous letter.

extremely happy when brothers came and testified to your sincerity, as you follow the True Faith. There is no greater satisfaction for me than to hear that my children are following the True Faith.

You are doing a creditable thing, dear friend, whatever you may do for the brothers and to some extent for strangers. They have given evidence of your affection before the community, and you will do well to forward them on their way in a manner worthy of God; for they have set out for his Name's sake taking nothing from the Gentiles. We ought therefore to sponsor such as they, that we may be co-workers with the Truth.

I have written something to the community.[16] But Diotrephes, who fancies himself as their leader, finds no room for us. Consequently, if I do come, I shall raise the matter of his behaviour, fooling me with worthless words. And not content with that, he will not entertain the brothers either, and those who wish to do so he prevents, and expels them from the community.

Do not copy the bad example, dear friend, but the good. The well-doer belongs to God. The evil-doer has not seen God. Everyone speaks highly of Demetrius,[17] and so does Truth itself. And we too pay our tribute, and you know that our testimony is trustworthy.[18]

I have a great deal to say to you, but I will not do it with ink and pen. I hope however to see you shortly, and then we will have a personal talk.

Peace be with you. The friends send you their regards. Give the friends individual greetings from us.

[16] Possibly referring to the previous letter.
[17] Perhaps the bearer of these letters.
[18] Cp. Jn. xxi. 24, above p. 429, note c.

Preface to the *Revelation*

The *Revelation* belongs to a class of Jewish visionary writings which had developed in the period of the Hasmonean dynasty (160-60 B.C.), and flourished for some centuries after, especially among the eclectic bodies in Judaism, whose members were largely responsible for their composition. This literature drew much of its imagery and apparatus from Babylonian and Persian religious concepts and pictorial presentations. The Jewish mystics borrowed and extended the range of symbols, adapting their significance to their own monotheistic faith. They also employed them to provide a dramatic commentary on past and present events, and a prophetic forecast of the future. Through dreams and visions and homilies put into the mouths of ancient patriarchs and seers, the ways of God were justified to generations of his people experiencing suffering and calamity. The seer is often taken to heaven and from that celestial region he sees the march of events on earth from the divine viewpoint. There is judgment on Israel for its sins, but after the judgment there will be deliverance for the faithful, the destruction of the wicked and the oppressor, and finally the Messianic Era. It is important to appreciate that the authors of these books never deal with the remote future: they are concerned with contemporary conditions and what lies almost immediately ahead. Where they furnish a review of the past it·is to build up their case, and to satisfy the historic requirements of the period in which the individual lived whose name the actual writer has borrowed, Enoch, Abraham, Moses, etc.

The apocalyptic books represent a particular art form in which the initiated among the saints were instructed. They were trained in the eschatological interpretation of the Scriptures (their hidden references to the Last Times), and in the science of symbol and cipher, by which the full meaning of the images, numbers, and colours used, could be understood. Lacking much of that equipment we cannot now determine the significance of all the allusions; but by studying many examples of the literature which are extant we can sufficiently master the method to obtain a considerable part of the sense.

The *Revelation* (or *Apocalypse*) *of Jesus* is such an excellent specimen of the literature that it can only have been written by an expert, one moreover who was acquainted with the Temple and its ministries, and conversant ·vith the eschatological interpretation of the *Song of Moses* (Deut. xxxii). The writer thinks in Hebrew, and the sounds of certain Hebrew words enter into the visions. He writes however in clumsy Greek. If the name of John, given in the book as the seer and recorder, belongs to the original work and is not a pseudonym, he may be identified with the Beloved Disciple, a former Jewish priest, who according to tradition settled at Ephesus after having been exiled to the island of Patmos off the coast of Asia Minor.

John is said to have seen the visions towards the end of the reign of Domitian (A.D. 95-6), when the Christians were suffering great persecution, particularly in Asia Minor, refusing to acknowledge the Emperor's deity. The tradition may well be correct, since it comes from sources sufficiently near in time and locality, and it receives strong support from the contents of the book itself. If the author was indeed the Beloved Disciple we learn much from the work about himself and his background. He first appears in the Fourth Gospel as a disciple of the prophetic preacher John the Baptist, so that his association with the Jewish pietist and mystical groups is likely enough. The Fourth Gospel also suggests that he was a priest, as was stated of him by Polycrates, bishop of Ephesus a century later. Certainly it is improbable that anyone not a priest could have known so much about the Temple of Jerusalem as does the author of the *Revelation*.

The work now is not quite in its original form. Both the beginning and the end have been altered and are in some confusion. There are also some interpolations in the body of the document. As it stands the visions are set within the framework of a letter addressed to seven Christian communities in Asia, each of which is given a separate message. These messages and some other passages and phrases have quite a different character, tone, and doctrinal viewpoint, reminding us forcibly of the Fourth Gospel Dialogue document. The additions and changes may therefore be due to the Elder, who seems to have taken over John the Priest's literary material. In the present version square brackets are used to distinguish many of these elements. The whole question of authorship, however, is too difficult and complex for any final judgment, and there is room for the view that a non-Christian apocalypse has been utilized.

As to the structure, the series of visions is in two parts, the first dealing with the Judgment on Israel, and the second with the Judgment on the Nations (especially Rome); and there is an intentional parallelism between them. In Book I the earthly scene is Palestine; in Book II it is the Roman Empire. Yet the story is continuous, commencing with the events preceding the Jewish War with Rome and culminating in the destruction of the Empire, the coming of the Messianic Era, and the Last Judgment. It is possible to identify many of the allusions from contemporary records and other apocalyptic writings, but certainty in every case there cannot be. To assist the reader the notes to this work and references to other books have been somewhat enlarged, and cross headings have been inserted. It is hoped that these will make the *Revelation* less mysterious. It would be missing the whole purpose of the book, however, if it was imagined to be simply history and prophecy presented through images and symbols. Its greatness lies in the fact that it exhibits human affairs as seen by the Eternal Presence on the Throne. Through inspired literary creation it asks and answers the question, 'Shall not the Judge of all the earth do right?'

THE REVELATION OF JESUS CHRIST

PROLOGUE

The Revelation of Jesus Christ, which God gave him to show to his servants what must shortly transpire. So he made it known by communicating it through his angel to his servant John, who in turn gave out God's Message and the testimony of Jesus Christ so far as he saw.

Happy is he who reads and those who hear the terms of the prophecy, and who heed the matters recorded in it; for the time is at hand!

'I am the Alpha and the Omega,' says the Lord God, who Is and Was and Shall be,[19] the Almighty.[20]

[John, to the seven communities in Asia. May peace and prosperity be yours from him who Is and Was and Shall be, and from the seven spirits which are before his throne, and from Jesus Christ the trustworthy witness, the first-born from the dead, and the ruler of earthly kings.

To him who loved us and has freed us from our sins by his blood and has given us kingship as priests to God his Father,[21] to him be glory and dominion for ever. Amen.

He will indeed come with clouds, and every eye will behold him,[22] including those who pierced him,[23] and all the tribes of the earth will mourn because of him. Even so. Amen.]

Vision of the Angel-Messiah

I John, your brother and associate in the persecution, and also in kingship and constancy in Jesus, was on the island called Patmos for the sake of God's Message and the testimony of Jesus. I became ecstatic on the Lord's day, and heard behind me a loud voice like a trumpet horn[24] saying, 'Set down in a book what you see[25] [and dispatch it to the seven communities, to Ephesus, Smyrna, Pergamum, Thyatira, Sardis, Philadelphia and Laodicea]'.

I turned to face the voice that addressed me; and when I had turned round I saw seven golden lampstands, and in front of the lampstands a human figure clad in an ankle-length robe,

---

[19] Cp. *Targ. Pal.* at Deut. xxxii. 39.
[20] Transferring i. 8 to its proper position after verse 3.
[21] Cp. Exod. xix. 6; I. Pet. ii. 5.   [22] Cp. Dan. vii. 13; Mt. xxvi. 64.
[23] Zech. xii. 10.   [24] The *shofar* (ram's horn trumpet), cp. Ezek. iii. 12.
[25] Cp. Tobit. xii. 20.

clasped at the breast with a golden girdle. His head and hair were white as wool, white as snow, and his eyes like a fiery flame. His feet were like burnished bronze, as if heated white-hot in a furnace, and his voice was like the booming of many waters. In his right hand he held seven stars, and from his mouth projected a sharp two-edged sword. His whole aspect was like the sun in full blaze.[26]

When I saw him I fell at his feet as though dead. But he laid his right hand upon me and said, 'Do not be afraid. I am the First and the Last,[27] and the Living One. I was dead, but now I am alive for evermore, and hold the keys of Death and Hades. Write, therefore, what you see, what is happening now, and what will transpire afterwards. [As to the implication[28] of the seven stars which you see in my right hand and of the seven golden lampstands, the seven stars are representatives of the seven communities, and the seven lampstands are the seven communities themselves.]

Messages to the Seven Communities

'To the representative of the community at Ephesus write as follows:

'Thus says he who holds the seven stars in his right hand, he who walks among the seven golden lampstands, "I know your works, your labour and your constancy, and that you cannot stand the wicked, but have tested those who call themselves envoys, when they are not, and have found them to be liars. You have shown constancy, and have borne much for my name, and have not grown weary. I have against you, however, that you have forsaken your former love. Recall, then, the state from which you have fallen, and repent, and be as you used to be. Otherwise, if you do not repent, I will come and remove your lampstand from its position. It is at least creditable that you detest the deeds of the Nicolaitans[29] as I do."

'Let the discerning take note of what the Spirit says to the communities, *"I will grant the victor the right to eat from the Tree of Life[30] which is in the Garden of God."*

'To the representative of the community at Smyrna write as follows:

'Thus says the First and the Last, who was dead and revived, "I know your affliction and poverty, yet you are rich, and I know the impudence[31] of those who claim to be Jews,[32] when

---

[26] Cp. the description of the Ancient of Days, Dan. vii. 9, and that of the High Priest Simon son of Onias in Ecclus. 1. 5-11. According to the Jewish Christians, 'Messiah was created, like one of the archangels, yet greater . . . a manlike figure, invisible to men in general.' See also *Enoch*, xiviii. 3-7.

[27] The First Man (*Adam Kadmon*), the Archetypal Man, who was incarnate in Jesus. the Second Adam or Last Man. See I. Cor. xv. 45. [28] Gr. *mysterion*.

[29] Believed to be a semi-Gnostic sect, followers of a certain Nicolaus.

[30] *Test. Levi*, xviii. 11.

[31] Lit. 'blasphemy.' [32] This may allude to the false envoys (ii. 2), or to non-Jewish Christians seeking to avoid persecution by claiming to be Jews, since Judaism was a faith authorized by the Romans and Christianity was not.

they are not, but are a synagogue of Satan. Do not be afraid of
what you are to suffer. The Devil is going to throw some of you
into prison, that you may be tested, and you will experience
persecution for ten days. Be loyal, even unto death, and I will
give you the award[33] of Life."

'Let the discerning take note of what the Spirit says to the
communities. *"The Victor shall not be harmed by the Second
Death."*[34]

'To the representative of the community at Pergamum write
as follows:

'Thus says he who has the sharp two-edged sword, "I know
where you live, where Satan's seat is,[35] and that you hold fast
to my name, and did not deny my Faith even at the time when
Antipas my loyal witness was slain among you, there where
Satan dwells. Yet I have a few things against you, that you
have there adherents of the teaching of Balaam, who instructed
Balak to lay a trap for the children of Israel, to make them
eat food dedicated to idols, and to indulge in sexual vice. So
do you likewise have adherents of the teaching of the Nicolaitans. Repent, then, or else I will come swiftly and fight them
with the sword of my mouth."

'Let the discerning take note of what the Spirit says to the
communities, *"I will give the victor the hidden manna.*[36] *I will
also give him a white pebble with a mystic name*[37] *graven on it
known only to him who receives it."*

'To the representative of the community at Thyatira write as
follows:

'Thus says the Son of God, who has eyes like a fiery flame
and feet like burnished bronze, "I know your works, and your
love, your faith, service and constancy, and that your latest
works exceed the former. Yet I have against you that you let
that Jezebel woman, who calls herself a prophetess, not only
teach, but beguile my servants into indulgence in immorality
and eating food dedicated to idols. I have given her time to
repent, but she has no intention of repenting of her immorality.
I will indeed send her to bed, and send those who have committed adultery with her great affliction, unless they repent of
their deeds; and I will slay her children by Death. And all the
communities shall know that I am he who investigates minds
and motives,[38] and I will requite each of you in accordance
with your deeds. To you, then, I say, and to the rest at Thyatira
who have not accepted this teaching, and have not known what
they call 'the profundities of Satan', I will lay upon you no
additional burden to what you already carry. Hold fast to that
till I come."

---

[33] Lit. 'the garland' (victor's wreath).
[34] After the resurrection to Judgment. See Deut. xxxiii. 6 (*Targ. Pal.*).
[35] Centre of Emperor-worship.   [36] Cp. *Apoc. Baruch*, xxix. 8.
[37] Cp. Rev. iii. 12; xix. 12; Isa. lxii. 2; lxv. 15.
[38] Lit. 'examines kidneys and heart' (Jer. xi. 20).

' *"I will give the victor, and him who takes care of my inter-tests to the end, authority over the nations, and he shall herd them with an iron-shod staff, as earthenware jars they shall be crushed,*[39] *as I have received authority from my Father; and I will give him the Morning Star."* Let the discerning take note of what the Spirit says to the communities.

'To the representative of the community at Sardis write as follows:

'Thus says he who has the seven spirits of God and the seven stars, "I know your works, that you have a name for being alive, but are really dead. Rouse yourself, and rally what remains, that is on the verge of extinction, for I have not found your affairs satisfactory in the sight of my God. Recall, therefore, what you have seen and heard, heed it and repent. If you fail to rouse yourself I will come like a thief, and you will not know at what hour I shall come upon you.[40] Yet you have a few persons at Sardis who have not soiled their garments, and they shall walk with me in white, because they are worthy."

' *"The victor shall be clad in white garments, and I will not erase his name from the Book of Life, but own his name in the presence of my Father and in the presence of his angels."*[41] Let the discerning take note of what the Spirit says to the communities.

'To the representative of the community at Philadelphia write as follows:

'Thus says the holy one and true, who has the key of David, who opens and none shall close, and closes and none shall open, "I know your works, that you have a little strength and have kept my Message, and have not denied my name. I have indeed set before you an open door, which none shall be able to close. Lo, I will make them members of Satan's synagogue who claim to be Jews, when they are not, but lie. Yes, I will make them come and grovel at your feet, and know that I have loved you. Because you have kept my Message with constancy, I too will keep you from the hour of trial that is about to come upon the whole world, to try the inhabitants of the earth. I shall come very soon. Hold on to what you have, that no one may take your award."

' *"I will make the victor a pillar in the Temple of my God, and he shall never go outside it again. And I will engrave on him the name of my God, and the name of the City of my God, New Jerusalem, which will descend from heaven from my God, and my own new name."* Let the discerning take note of what the Spirit says to the communities.

'To the representative of the community at Laodicea write as follows:

[39] Cp. Ps. ii. 8-9.   [40] Cp. Lk. xii. 39.   [41] Cp. Lk. xii. 8.

'Thus says the Amen,[42] the trustworthy and reliable witness, the beginning of God's creation, "I know your works, that you are neither frigid nor fervent. It would be better if you were either frigid or fervent. So because you are tepid instead of frigid or fervent, I am going to spit you out of my mouth, because you say, 'I am rich and prosperous, and in need of nothing', and do not realize that you are wretched and pitiable, poor, blind and naked. I recommend you to buy from me gold refined in the furnace, that you may be truly rich; and white robes, that you may be clothed, that the shame of your nakedness is no longer exposed; and eye salve to anoint your eyes, that you may see. Those whom I care for I reprove and discipline. Strive, therefore, to make amends. Lo, I stand at the door and knock. Whoever hears my voice and opens the door, I will come in to him and dine with him, and he with me."

'"*I will give the victor the right to sit beside me on my throne, just as I was victorious and have sat beside my Father on his throne.*" Let the discerning take note of what the Spirit says to the communities.']

BOOK I

Vision of the Court of God

After this I saw, and, lo, a door stood open in heaven, and the first voice I had heard speaking to me, that was like a trumpet horn, said, 'Ascend here,[43] and I will show you what will happen hereafter.'

At once I was in ecstasy, and there in heaven was placed a throne, and upon the throne a Presence was seated. And he who sat there presented to the gaze the brilliance of jasper and the fiery glow of the sardius, while an iridescence of emerald hue encircled the throne. Surrounding the throne were twenty-four other thrones, and upon these were seated twenty-four Elders clothed in white raiment with golden garlands upon their heads; and from the throne proceeded lightning flashes, voices, and peals of thunder.[44]

Seven flaming torches flared before the throne (which are the seven spirits of God), and also before the throne lay a glassy sea like crystal. At the base of the throne on all sides of it were four Living-Creatures[45] studded with eyes in front and at the back. The first Living-Creature resembled a lion, the second a calf, the third had a human face, and the fourth resembled a flying eagle. These four Living-Creatures, each one

---

[42] See II. Cor. i. 20, above p. 290.   [43] In Heb. '*Ale-hena,*' onomatopoeic.
[44] The scene is the court of the heavenly Temple, where the heavenly King is seated in state. Attending him are the Elders corresponding to the twenty-four courses of priests, Levites and laymen, of the earthly Temple. On the glory of the Lord see Ezek. i. 28.
[45] Cp. Ezek. i.

of them possessing six wings studded with eyes all over and underneath, never pause day or night from saying,

'Holy, holy holy, is the Lord God Almighty,[46]
Who Was, and Is, and Shall be.'

And whensoever the Living-Creatures render praise, honour and thanksgiving to him who sits on the throne, to him who lives for ever and ever, the twenty-four Elders prostrate themselves before the throne, and worship him who lives for ever and ever,[47] and lay their garlands before the throne, saying,

'Worthy art thou, O Lord our God,
To receive praise, honour, and might;
For thou hast created all things,
And by thy will they existed and were created.'

A Lamb receives the Sealed Book of Prophecy

Now I saw in the right hand of him who sat on the throne a small scroll with writing on both sides secured with seven seals.[48] I also saw a stalwart angel proclaiming in a loud voice, 'Who is worthy to open the scroll and break its seven seals?'

But no one in heaven, nor on earth, nor beneath the earth, was able to open the scroll or to look at it. I wept a great deal because no one worthy was found either to open the scroll or to look at it. But one of the Elders said to me, 'Do not weep. See, the Lion of the tribe of Judah, the Stock of David, has prevailed to open the scroll and its seven seals.

Then I saw standing in front of the throne and the four Living-Creatures, and in front of the Elders, a Lamb, as though it had been butchered. It had seven horns and seven eyes (which are the seven spirits of God dispatched to every part of the world). And it came and took the scroll from the right hand of him who sat on the throne. When it had taken the scroll, the four Living-Creatures and the twenty-four Elders prostrated themselves before the Lamb, each holding a lyre and golden bowls full of incense (which represent the prayers of the saints). And they sang a new song, saying,

'Worthy art thou to take the scroll,
And to open up its seals;
For being slain, thou didst buy
With thy blood for God
Those of all tribes and tongues,
Of peoples and of nations,
And for our God hast made them
Kings and priests to reign on earth.'

Then I saw, and heard the voice of many angels round the throne, and the Living-Creatures, and the Elders, numbering

[46] Cp. Isa. vi. 2. On the angelic doxologies see AJP, p. 39.
[47] In the Temple priests and people prostrated themselves when the ineffable Name of God was pronounced by the high priest.   [48] Cp. Ezek. ii. 10.

myriads of myriads and thousands of thousands, crying aloud,

> *'Worthy is the butchered Lamb,*
> *To receive power and wealth,*
> *And wisdom and strength,*
> *And honour and glory and praise.'*

And every created thing in heaven, and on earth, and beneath the earth, I heard saying,

> *'To him that sitteth on the throne,*
> *[And to the Lamb]*
> *Be praise and honour and glory,*
> *And dominion for ever and ever.'*

And the four Living-Creatures said, 'Amen'. And the Elders prostrated themselves and worshipped.

The Lamb breaks the Seals

Then I saw that the Lamb had opened one of the seven seals. And I heard one of the four Living-Creatures say like a clap of thunder, 'Come!'

I looked, and there was a white horse, and its rider carried a bow, and a victor's wreath was given him, and away he rode conquering and to conquer.

And when he had opened the second seal I heard the second Living-Creature say, 'Come!'

And there came out another horse, fiery red this time. Its rider was permitted to take peace from the earth, so that men should slaughter one another; and to him was given a great scimitar.

And when he had opened the third seal I heard the third Living-Creature say, 'Come!'

I looked and there was a black horse, and its rider had a pair of scales in his hand. And I heard among the four Living-Creatures what sounded like a voice saying, 'A quart of wheat for a denar, and three quarts of barley for a denar; but do not harm the oil and the wine.'[49]

And when he had opened the fourth seal I heard the voice of the fourth Living-Creature say, 'Come!'

I looked, and there was a livid horse. The name of its rider was Death, and Hades attended him.

To these four was given power over a quarter of the earth, to slay with the sword, with famine, and with pestilence, and by the wild beasts of the earth.[50]

And when he had opened the fifth seal I saw below the altar the souls of those butchered for the word of God and the testi-

---

[49] Famine prices are to rule, but wine and oil used for the Temple services are to be exempted. Cp. Jos. *Wars*, V. xiii. 6.
[50] Ezek. xiv. 21. Prayer was regularly recited by the Jews asking God to 'keep from us the enemy, Pestilence, Sword, Famine, and the pangs of Death'. These are the four horses and their riders. The white horse represents Plague and its rider carries a bow to shoot plague-arrows. The red horse represents War. The black horse represents Famine and its rider carries a pair of scales. The livid horse and its rider represent Death.

mony which they bore. They were crying aloud, 'How long will it be, holy and true Sovereign Lord, before thou dost judge and avenge our blood on those who dwell on earth?'[51]

Then there was given to each of them a white robe,[52] and they were told to remain quiet for a while longer until the number of their fellow-servants and brothers should be completed, who were about to be slain as they had been.

When he opened the sixth seal I saw that a great earthquake resulted; and the sun grew black as goat's hair cloth, and the full moon turned blood red, while the stars of heaven fell to earth[53] like unripe figs shed from a fig tree when shaken by a tempest. The very heavens rebounded like a scroll rolling up,[54] and every mountain and island was dislodged from its place. The kings of the earth, the statesmen and generals, the rich and the powerful, and every slave and freeman, hid themselves in dens and mountain clefts,[55] and cried to the mountains and cliffs, 'Topple over us, and hide us from the presence of him who sits on the throne, and from the wrath of the Lamb; for the terrible day of their wrath has come, and who will be able to endure it?'

Preservation of Loyal Israel

After this I saw four angels standing at the four corners of the earth, restraining the four winds of the earth so that no wind should blow on land and sea, nor on any tree.

Then I saw another angel mount up from the sunrise holding the seal of the Living God. And he cried aloud to the four angels charged with harming the land and sea, 'Do not harm the land, nor the sea, nor the trees, before we have marked the servants of our God on their foreheads.'[56]

I heard the number of those who were marked: it was a hundred and forty-four thousand out of all the tribes of Israel.

From the tribe of Judah twelve thousand were marked;[57]
From the tribe of Reuben twelve thousand;
From the tribe of Gad twelve thousand;
From the tribe of Asher twelve thousand;
From the tribe of Naphtali twelve thousand;
From the tribe of Manasseh twelve thousand;
From the tribe of Simeon twelve thousand;
From the tribe of Levi twelve thousand;

[51] Cp. Deut. xxxii. 43. Jewish legend speaks of the blood of Zechariah son of Jehoiada, murdered in the Court of the Priests, crying out for vengeance until it was appeased by the slaughter of ninety-four thousand priests and Israelites by Nebuzaradan. Christian sources repeat the story with the father of John the Baptist as the victim, and Titus as the avenger by slaying the Jewish priests in A.D. 70.

[52] Jewish candidates for the priesthood if found without blemish were given white robes, and if rejected black robes.

[53] Cp. Joel. ii. 10; Mt. xxiv. 29.   [54] Cp. Isa. xxxiv. 4.   [55] Isa. ii. 19.

[56] Before the judgment begins the saints are marked with the cruciform Hebrew letter *tau* (Ezek. ix. 4) that they may escape injury as the Israelites did in Egypt when the angel of death passed through Egypt.

[57] Judah heads the list as the royal tribe. Dan. is omitted as the tribe given over to idolatry. (*Test. Dan.* v. 4).

From the tribe of Issacher twelve thousand;
From the tribe of Zebulon twelve thousand;
From the tribe of Joseph twelve thousand;
From the tribe of Benjamin twelve thousand.

The Redeemed of the Gentiles

After this I saw, and there was a vast concourse, impossible to count, from every nation, tribe, people, and tongue, standing before the throne [and before the Lamb], clad in white robes with palm branches in their hands. And they cried aloud saying, 'Hosanna [58] to our God, who sits upon the throne [and to the Lamb].'

Then all the angels where they stood about the throne, and the Elders, and the four Living-Creatures, prostrated themselves before the throne and worshipped God saying.

'Amen. Blessing, glory, wisdom, thanksgiving, honour, power and might, be to our God for ever and ever.' [59]

Then one of the Elders put the question to me, 'Who are these arrayed in white robes, and where do they come from?'

'You know that, sir,' I replied. Then he told me, 'These are they who have come out of the Great Persecution, and have washed their robes and made them white in the blood of the Lamb. That is why they are before the throne of God, and minister to him day and night in his Temple. And he who sits upon the throne will dwell among them. They shall neither hunger nor thirst any more, nor shall the sun scorch them, nor any heat; [60] for the Lamb who is before the throne will tend them, and guide them to well-springs of Waters of Life, and God will wipe away all tears from their eyes.'

Vision of the Seven Angels with War Horns

And when he had opened the seventh seal there was silence in heaven for about half an hour. [61]

Then I saw the seven angels who stood before God, [62] and they were given seven war horns. And another angel came and stood at the altar with a golden censer, and a large quantity of incense was given him so that he should offer the prayers of all the saints at the golden altar before the throne. And the smoke of the incense bearing the prayers of the saints ascended before God from the angel's hand. Then the angel took the censer and filled it with fire from the altar and cast it upon the earth, and there were thunders, and voices, and lightnings, and an earthquake.

[58] Lit. 'salvation'. The seer beholds the Elect of the Gentiles who have been gathered in (Mt. xxiv. 31). They appear before God as the Jews appeared before him in the earthly Temple at the Feast of Tabernacles (the feast of ingathering), bearing palm branches and singing their Hosannas.
[59] Such eulogistic responses were used in the Jewish liturgy.
[60] The redeemed here are possibly the Gentile Christians martyred in the Neronian persecution of A.D. 64. Many had been turned into flaming torches. See on the language Isa. xlix. 38 and Deut. xxxii. 24.
[61] In the Temple, when the incense was offered, the people retired from the court and prostrated themselves in silent prayer and adoration.
[62] These are the seven archangels (*Enoch*, xx).

Then the seven angels with the seven war horns prepared to sound an alarm.[63]

The first angel sounded, and a hail of fire mingled with blood rained upon the earth. A third of the land was burnt up, a third of the trees were burnt up, and a third of the vegetation was burnt up.[64]

The second angel sounded, and something like a great flaming mountain was hurled into the sea. A third of the sea turned to blood, a third of the animate creatures in the sea died, and a third of the shipping was disabled.[65]

The third angel sounded, and a great meteor blazing like a torch fell from heaven and landed on a third of the rivers and wells of water. The meteor was called Wormwood; and a third of the waters turned to wormwood, and many people died of the waters that were made bitter.[66]

The fourth angel sounded, and a third of the sun was eclipsed, and a third of the moon, and a third of the stars; so that a third of them was blotted out, and the day lost a third

[63] 'For these things they sound the alarm in every place, for blasting, mildew, locusts, caterpillars, evil beasts, and the sword' (*Taanith* vi). For the judgments on Israel, which follow, the seer has drawn upon the eschatological interpretation of the *Song of Moses* (Deut. xxxii). Verses 20 to 35 in the Aramaic paraphrase read as follows: 'And he said, I will take away from them the favour of my countenance: it will be seen what will be their end; for they are a perverse generation, children who have no faith. They have made me jealous by that which is not God; they have angered me by their vanities. I also will provoke them to jealousy by a people which has not been a people, by the foolish Babylonian people will I provoke them. For an east wind strong as fire shall go out before me, and blaze in the might of my anger, and burn to the lowest hell. It shall consume the land with its produce, and set the foundations of the mountains aflame. And when they dwell in Babel they will serve their idols. For I have spoken in my word to array calamities against them, the plague-arrows of my vengeance to destroy them. I will make them go into captivity in Media and Elam, in the captivity of Babel, the house of Agag, who are like demons gaping with famine, and the corpses devoured by birds, and to stricken evil spirits of the moon, to Lillin and to spirits big with evil. And the Greeks who bite with their teeth like wild beasts will I send against them, and will shake them by the hands of the Syrians venomous as basilisks, the serpents of the dust. A people who will come from beyond the land of Israel shall consume them with the stroke of the sword, and those who are left in the land of Israel will I throw into the terror of death . . . their young men shall perish, their maidens, their sucklings, with their men and their elders . . . For the works of this people are like the works of the people of Sodom, and their evil counsels like those of the people of Gomorrah; their wicked thoughts are as serpents' heads; bitter therefore to them is their punishment which makes desolate . . . So shall be the bitter cup of the curse, which they are to drink in the day of their punishment, and cruel as the head of asps . . . Vengeance lies before me, and I will recompense them at the time when their foot shall move to the captivity; for the day of their destruction is at hand, and the evil which is prepared for them makes haste' (*Targ. Pal.*). All the evils of the four Beasts of Daniel's vision (vii), Babylon, Medo-Persia, Greece and Syria, are combined for the seer in the sufferings of the Jews before and during the war with Rome (A.D. 67-70).

[64] All the blasts signify judgments on Israel. These are couched in visionary and prophetic language, but yet reflect conditions in Palestine during the Roman war. The first blast suggests the punitive expedition of Cestius Gallus which signalized the outbreak of hostilities. 'He overran the countryside, sacking everything in his path and burning the surrounding villages' (Jos. *Wars*, II. xviii. 9).

[65] Cp. the battle of Joppa, when the Jewish ships were wrecked and broken up on the rocks, and many of the sailors killed themselves, 'so that a wide area of sea was red with their blood' (*Wars*, III. ix. 3). Also the battle of the Sea of Galilee: 'One could see the whole lake red with blood and covered with corpses.' (*Wars*, III. x. 9).

[66] During the war there was poisoning of the wells and fountains. Josephus records that during a terrific heat-wave in the summer of A.D. 67 many died of thirst (*Wars*, III. vii. 32).

of its visibility and the night likewise.[67]

   Then I saw and heard a lone eagle flying in midheaven screaming 'Alas,[68] alas, alas, for the inhabitants of the earth, because of the remaining blasts of the horns of the three angels who are about to sound!'[69]

   Then the fifth angel sounded, and I saw that a meteor from heaven had fallen to earth. To it was given the key of the vent of the Abyss, and it opened the vent of the Abyss, and smoke ascended from the vent. Out of the smoke swarmed locusts on to the earth, and they were given the kind of power that scorpions of the earth possess. They were told they must not harm the grass, nor any vegetation, nor any tree, only those human beings who do not have the divine seal on their foreheads. They were not to kill them, only to torment them for five months. The kind of torment they were to inflict was to be like that of a scorpion when it stings a man. In those days men will seek death, but will not find it; they will long to die, but death will fly from them.

   The appearance of the locusts[70] was like horses accoutred for battle. On their heads were golden crests, and their features were like human features. They had manes like women's tresses, and their teeth were leonine. They had scaly fronts like steel breastplates, and the whirr of their wings was like cavalry charging into battle. They had tails like scorpions equipped with stings, and it was in their tails that their power lay to hurt men for five months. They had a king over them, the angel of the Abyss, whose name in Hebrew is Abaddon, but in Greek he is called Apollyon.

   One calamity is over, but there are still two calamities to follow.

   Then the sixth angel sounded, and issuing from the golden altar that was before God I heard a solitary voice saying to the sixth angel with the war horn, 'Free the four angels chained beside the great river Euphrates!'[71]

   So the four angels were freed, who had been reserved for this very hour and day and month and year, to slay the third of men. The host of horsemen numbered twice a myriad myriad.[72] I heard the number of them.

---

[67] Perhaps referring to the murder by the revolutionaries of many of the aristocracy and eminent citizens of Jerusalem (*Wars*, IV. iii. 4f).

[68] In Heb. '*Oyé*', onomatopoeic, *oee*.

[69] The previous judgments have preceded the advance of the Roman armies on Jerusalem. The eagle may symbolize the opening of the last stage, the coming of war to the capital, scene of the final judgments.

[70] The fifth blast releases upon the land a swarm of demonic locusts. This is the locust army of Joel ii, the 'incursion of the *shedim*' of *Apoc. Bar.* xxvii. 9, and the combined forces of all the inimical empires of *Targ. Pal.* on Deut. xxxii. (see above p. 449, n. 63). From the description of the locusts the seer appears to have the Roman army in mind where he is not drawing on the prophetic imagery. They wear crested helmets with horsehair tails (like women's tresses), and are clad in mail, cp. Jos. *Wars*, III. v. 5-6 on the equipment of the Roman cavalry and infantry. The army had 'quickfirers' for discharging arrows called 'scorpions' (*Wars*, V. i. 3).

[71] In a Syriac *Apocalypse of Ezra* the four angels are four kings. (See below n. 72.)

[72] For the symbolic number of 200,000,000 cp. Ps. lxviii. 17.

In the vision this is how I saw the horses and their riders.[73] They had breastplates of fiery hue, smoke-blue and sulphur-yellow. The heads of the horses were leonine, and from their mouths belched fire and smoke and sulphur. By these three plagues the third of men were slain, by the fire, the smoke, and the sulphur, which belched from their mouths. The power of the horses lay in their mouths and in their tails; for their tails were like serpents, possessing heads, and it is with these they inflict injury.[74] Yet the rest of men, who were not killed by these plagues, did not repent of the works of their hands, but continued to worship demons, and idols of gold and silver, bronze and stone and wood, which can neither see, nor hear, nor move. Nor did they repent of their murders, their sorceries, their immorality, and their robberies.[75]

Vision of the Angel with the Small Scroll

Then I saw another mighty angel descend from heaven, clad in cloud and with a rainbow on his head. His face was like the sun, and his legs like pillars of fire, and in his hand he held a small open scroll. He set his right foot on the sea and his left foot on the land, and cried aloud as though a lion were roaring.[76]

When he cried the seven thunders responded, and when they did so I was about to set down what they said. But there came a voice from heaven saying, 'Seal up what the seven thunders have said, and do not write it down.'

Then the angel I had seen take his stand upon the sea and land raised his right hand to heaven and swore by him who lives for ever and ever, who created heaven and all that is in it and earth and all that is in it, and the sea and all that is in it, that there will be no further interval, but that in the days when the seventh angel shall sound his horn God's mystery will be at an end, as he declared to his servants the Prophets.[77]

Then the voice from heaven which I had heard addressed me again and said, 'Go and take the small scroll that lies open in the hand of the angel standing on sea and land.'

So I went to the angel and said to him, 'Give me the small scroll.'

[73] An invading host from the East was part of current apocalyptic expectation, with the Parthians particularly in view. The demonic horsemen historically join the Romans in the attack on Israel, and in fact four eastern kings, Antiochus of Commagene, Agrippa II. Soemus of Emesa, and the Arab Malchus furnished cavalry and archers, (Jos. *Wars*, III. iv. 2), The Parthian king Vologses offered to supply the Romans with 40,000 mounted archers (Tacit. *Hist.* iv. 51; Suet. *Vespas.* 6).
[74] The Parthians twisted their horses' tails to points and the archers could shoot backwards. Symbolic animals with serpent-headed tails are featured in ancient mural paintings.
[75] Cp. Deut. xxxii. 37-38; Jos. *Wars*, IV. ix. 10.
[76] Cp. Dan. x. 5-6.
[77] Dan. x. 5-6; cp. Deut. xxxii. 39-43.

'Take it and digest it,' he replied. 'It will make your stomach bitter, though in your mouth it will be sweet as honey.'[78]

So I took the small scroll from the angel's hand and digested it; and it was sweet as honey in my mouth, but when I had eaten it my stomach was made bitter. And I was told, 'You must prophesy further concerning many peoples, nations, tongues, and kings.'

The Two Witnesses

There was now given me a cane like a measuring-rod[79] with the order, 'Rise, and measure the Temple of God, and the altar, and compute those who worship there; but exclude the court outside the Temple, and do not measure that, since it is given to the Gentiles, and they will tread the Holy City under foot for forty-two months.[80] But I will cause my two witnesses to prophesy for twelve hundred and sixty days clothed in sackcloth. (These are the two olive trees and the two lampstands which stand before the Lord of the earth.)[81] If anyone purposes to harm them fire will issue from their mouths and devour their enemies; so if anyone should seek to harm them that is how he will be killed. They have the power to shut heaven, so that no rain will fall during the period of their prophecy, and they have power over water, to turn it into blood, and to smite the earth with every kind of plague as often as they wish.

'When they have concluded their testimony, the Beast who rises from the Abyss will make war on them, and overcome them, and kill them, and leave their corpses lying on the square of the Great City[82] which in the spiritual sense is called Sodom[83] and Egypt, where also their Master was crucified. And some of the people, tribes, tongues and nations will observe their corpses during three and a half days, and will not permit their corpses to be interred. And those who dwell on earth will rejoice over them and make merry, and send gifts to one another, because these two prophets tormented those who dwell on earth.'

But after the three days the breath of life from God entered them, and they stood on their feet;[84] and great fear seized those who saw them. Then they heard a loud voice from heaven saying to them, 'Ascend here!' And they ascended to heaven in

[78] Ezek. ii. 9-iii. 3.   [79] Cp. Ezek. xl. 3; Cp. Jos. *Wars*, VI. v. 4.
[80] Dan. xii. 7.
[81] Though the judgments on Israel are now far advanced a final opportunity of repentance and relief is given if they will but heed the two faithful witnesses, perhaps the Law and the Prophets (Mt. xxii. 40; Lk. xvi. 31) symbolized by Moses and Elijah (Mt. xvii. 3), as shown by the powers given them. Cp. Zech. iv. on the two olive trees.
[82] The seer may have in his mind's eye the high priests Ananus and Jesus murdered in Jerusalem, whose bodies were cast out without burial (Jos. *Wars*, IV. v. 2).
[83] 'I believe that, had the Romans delayed to punish those reprobates, either the earth would have opened and swallowed up the city, or it . . . would have tasted anew the thunderbolts of Sodom' (*Wars*, V. xiii. 6).
[84] Cp. Ezek. xxxvii. 9; Hos. vi. 2.

a cloud while their enemies watched them. That very hour there was a great earthquake, and the tenth part of the city collapsed. Seven thousand people were killed in the earthquake, while the rest were frightened and offered praise to the God of heaven.

The second calamity is over. The third calamity will follow speedily.

Then the seventh angel sounded, and loud voices in heaven proclaimed, 'The dominion of the world has become the dominion of our Lord and his Anointed, and he shall reign for ever and ever.'

And the twenty-four Elders who were seated before God on their thrones prostrated themselves and worshipped God saying,

'We give thanks unto thee, Lord God Almighty, who Wast and Art, because thou hast taken to thee thy great power and hast reigned. The heathen raged;[85] but thy wrath has come, and the time for the dead to be judged, and for reward to be given to thy servants the Prophets, and to the Saints, and to those both high and low who revere thy Name, the time to destroy those who destroy the earth.'[86]

Then the Temple of God in heaven was opened, and the Ark of his Covenant was revealed in his Temple.[87] And there were lightning flashes, and voices, and peals of thunder, and an earthquake, and heavy hail.

BOOK II

Vision of the Woman and the Dragon[88]

Now there appeared in heaven a great sign, a Woman clothed with the sun, with the moon beneath her feet, and upon her head a wreath of twelve stars. She was with child, and cried out in her pangs straining to be delivered.

Another sign also appeared in heaven. This took the form of a great fiery Dragon with seven heads and ten horns, whose tail carried away a third of the stars of heaven and flung them to earth. The Dragon stood before the Woman who was about to give birth, so that when her child was born he could devour it.

She bore a son, a male child, who is to herd all nations with

---

[85] Cp. Ps. ii. 1; xlvi. 5-6.

[86] The judgments on Israel are now ended, and those upon the heathen are about to commence. From this moment, the sovereignty of God over the world is specifically exercised, where before only his sovereignty over his own people was apparent.

[87] To mark the new development the curtains of the heavenly Sanctuary are drawn aside disclosing the Ark of God's Covenant. God's people are in his care. In the synagogues still the Ark containing the sacred scrolls of Scripture is opened at the most solemn moments in the service.

[88] This version introduces the events recorded in Book II. The Woman and the Dragon in the astrological sense are constellations symbolizing the Creative Wisdom and Chaos, while terrestrially they are Loyal Israel (cp. Gen. xxxvii. 9), mother of the Messiah, and the tyrant adversary embodied in the Roman Empire.

an iron-shod staff;[89] but the child was snatched away to God and to his throne.[90] The Woman fled to the wilderness, where she has a place prepared for her by God, for her to be cared for there for twelve hundred and sixty days.[91]

Then war broke out in heaven. Michael[92] and his angels fought the Dragon, and the Dragon and his angels fought, but did not prevail, neither was a trace of them left any longer in heaven. The great Dragon was flung out, the primeval Serpent called Devil and Satan, deceiver of the whole world. Yes, he was flung to earth, and his angels along with him.

Then I heard a loud voice in heaven say, 'Now indeed the salvation, power, and dominion of our God, and the authority of his Anointed has become effective; for the accuser of our brothers, who accused them before God day and night, has been flung out. They overcame him by the blood of the Lamb, and the declaration of their testimony, and did not cling to life till death should claim them. Rejoice, therefore, O heavens, and all who dwell there! But alas for land and sea; for the Devil has come down to you in a great rage, knowing that his time is short.'

When the Dragon found himself flung to earth, he pursued the Woman who had given birth to the male child. But the Woman was given the two wings of the great eagle,[93] so that she might wing her way to the wilderness, to her place there, where she is to be cared for for a time, times, and a half, from the presence of the Serpent.

Then the Serpent spouted water after the Woman like a river, to carry her away with a flood. But the earth aided the Woman, and the earth gaped and swallowed the river which the Dragon spouted from his mouth.[94] So the Dragon was enraged against the Woman, and went off to make war with the remainder of her offspring, who observe the commandments of God and hold the testimony of Jesus; and he stood on the sand of the sea.

Vision of the Two Beasts

Now I saw a Beast with ten horns and seven heads rise out of the sea.[95] On his horns were ten crowns, and on his head blas-

---

[89] Ps. ii. 9.
[90] According to a Jewish legend the Messiah was spirited away at birth and these is a similar legend about the infant John the Baptist. Another version of the latter legend says that his mother fled with him to a mountain which opened to receive them into safety when Herod's soldiers were killing the babes in Bethlehem.
[91] Historically, Vespasian, after the fall of Jerusalem, tried to seize those who were of Davidic descent, but the family of Jesus had made good their escape to the wilderness beyond Jordan.
[92] Guardian angel of Israel, Dan. x. 4, 21.   [93] Cp. Exod. xix. 4; Deut. xxxii. 11.
[94] There may be an historical allusion here to the Jordan being in flood when the Nazarenes were escaping to the wilderness beyond. A dragon was supposed to lurk in the river sucking up the water when the river was low and spouting it out when it was in spate. Cp. Job. xl. 23; Odes of Sol. xxii. Josephus tells of Jewish refugees unable to escape the Romans because of the flooded Jordan (Wars, IV. vii. 5).   [95] Cp. Dan. vii.

phemous titles. The Beast I saw was like a leopard, with the feet of a bear, and the jaws of a lion. And the Dragon conferred on him his own power and throne, and great authority. One of his heads was as if wounded to death, but his death stroke had been healed.[96] The whole earth was in awe of the Beast, and worshipped the Dragon because he conferred authority on the Beast. They worshipped the Beast too, saying,

'Who is like the Beast?
Who can fight with him?'[97]

He was permitted to use boastful and blasphemous language, and allowed to do so for forty-two months. And he opened his mouth in profanity against God, maligning his Name and his dwelling-place, everything of a heavenly nature. He was also permitted to make war with the Saints and to overcome them, and was given authority over every race, and people, tongue and nation. And all who dwell on earth will worship him, everyone whose name has not been written from the foundation of the world in the Book of Life [of the butchered Lamb].

Let the discerning take note. *If anyone is destined for captivity, to captivity he will go. If anyone is destined to death by the sword, by the sword must he be slain.*[98] Here is where the constancy and loyalty of the Saints is required.

Then I saw another Beast rise out of the land.[99] He had two horns like a lamb, but he spoke like a dragon. He exercises all the authority of the first Beast in his presence; and he causes the earth and all who dwell in it to worship the first Beast whose death stroke was healed. He also performs great signs, making fire from heaven fall to earth in the sight of men, and so deceives those who dwell on earth by the signs he is permitted to perform in the presence of the Beast, telling those who dwell on earth to make an image of the Beast who had the dagger thrust[100] and yet lived. He was also permitted to animate the image of the Beast, so that the image of the Beast could speak, and he causes such as refuse to worship the image of the Beast to be slain. He further causes all, both high and low, rich and poor, free and slave, to receive a stamp on their right hand or forehead,[101] so that none should be able to buy or sell unless he has the stamp either of the name of the Beast or of the number of his name.

[96] The heads are Roman emperors. The one wounded to death may be either Nero or Domitian, who met violent ends. The stroke was healed because the Imperial regime continued.
[97] A blasphemous parody of Exod. xv. 11. Cp. Agrippa's speech: 'Almost every nation under the sun does homage to the Roman arms'. (Jos. *Wars*, II, xvi. 4.)
[98] Cp. Jer. xv. 2. Exile or death are the penalties for treason against the emperor.
[99] The two Beasts appear in Jewish legend as Leviathan (the Beast from the Sea) and Behemoth (the Beast from the Land). See *Enoch*, lx. 6-10; *Apoc. Bar.* xxix, 4. Here the former represents the Roman Empire and the latter the Imperial cult chiefly practised in Asia.
[100] The emperor's statue. Domitian insisted on worship and required to be addressed as 'Our Lord and God'. He was killed by a dagger thrust (Suet. *Dom.* xvii), as was Nero.
[101] Cp. Deut. vi. 8. All, of whatever occupation, must use the Imperial stamp which was affixed to deeds of sale, etc.

This is where wisdom is required. Let him who has the wit to do so compute the numerical value of the Beast; for it is calculated in man's way. His number is 616.[102]

The Elect on Zion

Then I saw, and there on Mount Zion stood the Lamb, and with him a hundred and forty-four thousand who had [his name and] the Name of the Father written on their foreheads.[103]

And I heard a sound from heaven like the booming of many waters and like the peal of heavy thunder. The sound I heard was also like that of harpers playing their harps. They were singing a new song before the throne, and before the four Living-Creatures, and the Elders; but none but the hundred and forty-four thousand redeemed from the earth could learn the song. [These are they who have not been defiled with women: they are celibate.] These are they who attend the Lamb wherever he goes: they are the redeemed out of mankind, the firstlings belonging to God[104] [and the Lamb], and in their mouths no falsehood was found: they are faultless.[105]

Final Warning to the Gentiles

Now I saw another angel flying in mid-heaven with a firm and final ultimatum to deliver to those who dwell on earth, to every nation, tribe, tongue and people, in these terms, 'Revere God, and offer praise to him, for the time of his judgment has come. Worship him, therefore, who made heaven and earth, the sea and the springs of water.'

Another, a second angel, followed crying, 'Great Babylon has fallen, has fallen,[106] she who made all nations drink the strong wine of her immorality.'

Yet another, a third angel, followed these, proclaiming loudly, 'Whoever worships the Beast and his image, and receives his stamp on forehead or hand, shall surely drink the strong wine of God which is mixed undiluted in the goblet of his wrath,[107] and shall be tortured by fire and sulphur in the

---

102 Some MSS. read 666, but the more difficult number is more probable. Greek and Hebrew letters have a numerical value, and those of the Beast added together give the required total. The stamp as used in the Empire was Greek, and bore either the name of the emperor with the year of his reign, or the latter followed by 'of Caesar'. The solution of the puzzle depends on the period at which the seer is writing, and from tradition and from the details given this appears to be the end of the reign of Domitian (assassinated in A.D. 96), when according to ancient tradition the Revelation was seen (Euseb. *Eccl. Hist.* Bk. III xvii-xviii). From known examples of the Imperial stamp that of A.D. 95-96 would probably read ΙΔ ΚΑΙΣΑΡΟΣ (14th year of Caesar's reign), which adds up to 616 (14+20+1+10+200+1+100+70+200). The addition of the letter 'N' (Nero?) = 50 would bring the total to 666. See further *Sibyl. Orac.* Bk. V. 39-40.
103 The Elect have now all passed over and stand on the heavenly Mount Zion.
104 Exod. xiii. 12.
105 It is possible that the whole scene is an interpolation, and not simply the bracketed words.
106 The fiat against Rome has gone forth. Cp. Isa. xxi. 9.
107 Cp. Jer. xxv. 12-17.

presence of the holy angels [and in the presence of the Lamb]. The smoke of their torment will ascend for ever and ever. Those who worship the Beast and his image, and whoever receives his stamp, will have no respite day and night.'

Here is where the constancy of the Saints is required, those who keep God's commandments and are loyal to Jesus.

Then I heard a voice from heaven saying, 'Write this down. Happy are the dead who die in the Master[108] from now on!'

'Even so,' the Spirit agrees, 'that they may rest from their toil, for their deeds accompany them.'

Vision of the Two Harvests[109]

Then I looked, and there was a white cloud, and seated on the cloud a manlike figure[110] with a golden garland on his head and a sharp sickle in his hand. And another angel emerged from the Temple calling loudly to him who was seated on the cloud, 'Use your sickle and reap, for the time to reap has come. Earth's harvest is fully ripe.'

So he who sat on the cloud brought down his sickle upon the earth and the earth was reaped.

Now another angel emerged from the Temple in heaven, and he too had a sharp sickle. Another angel with power over fire emerged from the altar and shouted to the one with the sharp sickle, 'Use your sharp sickle, and gather the clusters of earth's vineyard, for its grapes are quite ripe.'

So the angel brought down his sickle, and gathered earth's vintage, and cast it into the great winepress of the wrath of God. And the winepress was trodden outside the city, and blood gushed from the winepress to the height of the horses' bridles sixteen hundred furlongs away.[111]

The Saints from the Gentiles approve God's Judgment

Now I saw another great and amazing sign in heaven, seven angels with the seven last plagues; for by these plagues the wrath of God will be accomplished.

I also saw what looked like a glassy sea veined with fire, and those who had come off conquerors from the Beast, and his image, and the number of his name, were standing by the glassy sea holding harps of God. They sing the song of Moses,[112] the servant of God, [and the song of the Lamb] as follows:

---

[108] I.e. as Christians.
[109] The two harvests may be understood as those of Mercy and Judgment. The reapings are symbolical acts. The first is a corn harvest signifying the ingathering of the saints, while the second is a vintage harvest signifying the ingathering of sinners.
[110] 'A manlike figure.' See p. 441, n. 27.
[111] Cp. Isa. lxiii. 3 and *Enoch*, c. 1-3: 'Brothers will fall in death . . . until it streams with their blood like a river . . . And the horses will walk up to the breast in the blood of sinners, and the chariot will be submerged to its height'.
[112] 'The Song of Moses', i.e. Deut. xxxii with Exod. xv. 1-18. Those who have remained loyal throughout the persecution of Domitian stand on the brink of the Red Sea of fire and sing the triumph song.

'Great and marvellous are thy works,
Lord God Almighty.
Just and true are thy ways,
O everlasting King.[113]
Who shall not fear thee, O Lord,
And glorify thy name?
For thou alone art holy.
For all nations shall come
And worship before thee;[114]
For thy judgments are revealed.'

Vision of the Seven Angels with Golden Bowls

After this I saw that the shrine of the Tabernacle of Testimony in heaven had been opened, and the seven angels with the seven plagues emerged from the shrine robed in pure shining white linen clasped at the breast with golden girdles. Then one of the four Living-Creatures handed the seven angels seven golden bowls filled with the wrath of God, who lives for ever and ever.[115] And the Temple was filled with smoke from the glory of God and his might,[116] and none might enter the Temple until the seven plagues of the seven angels had been accomplished.

Then I heard a loud voice from the Temple telling the seven angels, 'Go, and empty the seven bowls of the wrath of God on to the earth!' [117]

So the first angel went and emptied his bowl on the land, and an evil and malignant ulcer broke out on the men who had the stamp of the Beast, and who worshipped his image.

The second angel emptied his bowl into the sea, and it turned like the blood of a corpse, and everything in the sea that had the breath of life died.

The third angel emptied his bowl on the rivers and springs of water, and they turned to blood.

Then I heard the angel of the waters say, 'Just art thou who Art and Wast, the Holy One, that thou hast judged thus; for they have shed the blood of saints and prophets, and thou hast given them blood to drink as they deserve.'

And I heard the altar say, 'Even so, Lord God Almighty. True and just are thy judgments.'

---

[113] Cp. on these lines *Targ. Onkel.* at Deut. xxxii. 4: 'Ascribe ye greatness unto our God, the Mighty One whose works are perfect, for all his ways are justice . . . just and true is he'.

[114] Cp. Exod. xv. 11 and Ps. lxxxvi. 8-10.

[115] Again there comes a solemn moment before the judgments on the nations commence. The symbol of bowls is used appropriately in accordance with Ps. lxxix. 6-7.

[116] Isa. vi. 4.

[117] The judgments intensify those previously inflicted on Israel, and are also reminiscent of the Plagues of Egypt (cp. 1. Pet. iv. 17). They are still future, but the seer may have had in mind the great eruption of Vesuvius (cp. *Sibyl. Orac.* Bk. IV. 130-136), the fire of Rome in the reign of Titus (A.D. 79-81), and the plague 'such as was scarcely ever known before' (Suet. *Titus*, viii).

The fourth angel emptied his bowl on the sun, and it was permitted to scorch men with fire. And men were scorched with a burning heat, and blasphemed the Name of God who had control over the plagues; yet they did not repent so as to offer him praise.

The fifth angel emptied his bowl on the seat of the Beast, and his realm was plunged into darkness. And they gnawed their tongues in agony, and blasphemed the God of heaven because of their agony, and because of their ulcers; yet they did not repent of their deeds.

The sixth angel emptied his bowl on the great river Euphrates, and its stream was dried up, that the way of the Kings of the East might be prepared.[118]

The Dragon gathers his Forces

Now I saw issue from the mouth of the Dragon, and the mouth of the Beast, and the mouth of the False Prophet three foul spirits like frogs. These are the spirits of wonder-working demons, on a mission to the kings of the entire world, to gather them together for the battle of the Great Day of God Almighty.[119] And they gathered them together to the place called in Hebrew ARMAGEDDON.[120]

'I will surely come like a thief. Happy is he who is on the alert and retains his garments,[121] lest he go about naked and they see his shame.'

Then the seventh angel emptied his bowl on the air. And a loud voice issued from the Temple, from the throne, saying, 'It is done!' Then came lightning flashes, voices, and peals of thunder, and a great earthquake such as there had never been since man was on the earth, so prolonged and so violent a quake. The Great City was split into three parts, and the cities of the Gentiles fell, and Great Babylon was remembered before God to be given the goblet of the strong wine of his wrath. Every island vanished, mountains disappeared from existence, and a fierce hail, the stones weighing about a talent,[122] rained on men from heaven. And men blasphemed God because of the plague of hail, for the plague of it was indeed terrible.

---

[118] The eastern forces are to come this time not as allies but as enemies of Rome. 'Then shall come to the west the strife of war stirred up, and the exiled man of Rome (Nero redivivus), lifting up a mighty sword, crossing the Euphrates with many tens of thousands' (*Sibyl. Orac.* Bk. IV. 137-9).

[119] Cp. I. Ki. xxii. 19-23 for the source of the thought of the foul spirits enticing the kings to battle.

[120] Probably an adaptation of the Hebrew 'Rama-Gad-Yavan' (Rama of Gad of the Greeks) perhaps a contemporary name of the ancient Ramoth-Gilead (I. Ki. xxii. 20). Gad-Yavan as a place name occurs in the Mishnah (*Zab.* i. 5). Cp. Arimathea for the Hebrew *Ramathaim*. In the O. T. story one of the kings concerned is Jehoshaphat (the Lord is Judge), with which the seer may have linked the prohecy of Joel iii. 9-17 calling all nations to the valley of Jehoshaphat, 'for there will I sit to judge all the heathen round about'.

[121] In the Temple the captain of the guard went the rounds at night, and if any of the watch was found dozing at his post he set fire to his garments with his torch (*Midd.* i. 2).

[122] This was the weight of the stones thrown by the Roman engines (Jos. *Wars,* III. vi. 9). The enemy now receives his own with interest.

Vision of the Woman on the Scarlet Beast

One of the angels with the seven bowls now came and spoke to me and said, 'Come, and I will show you the judgment of the Great Harlot who sits on many waters,[123] with whom the kings of the earth have committed immorality, and the inhabitants of the earth have been intoxicated with the wine of her immorality.'

He conveyed me in spirit to the desert; and there I saw a Woman seated on a Scarlet Beast studded with blasphemous titles, and which had seven heads and ten horns. The Woman was arrayed in purple and scarlet and decked out with gold, precious stones and pearls. In her right hand she held a golden goblet filled with abominations and the foulness of her immorality.[124] On her forehead there was written the significant title, 'Great Babylon, Mother of Harlots and Earth's Abominations'.

I saw the Woman intoxicated with the blood of the Saints, and the blood of the martyrs of Jesus, and I marvelled greatly at the sight of her.

The angel said to me, 'Why are you amazed? I will tell you the significance of the Woman, and of the Beast with seven heads and ten horns that carries her. The Beast you have seen was, and is not, and is about to rise out of the Abyss and go to destruction.[125] Those who dwell on earth will be amazed, whose names have not been written from the foundation of the world in the Book of Life, when they see that the Beast was, and is not, yet still is.[126]

This is where the intelligent mind is required. The seven heads are seven hills[127] on which the Woman is seated. And there are seven kings;[128] five have fallen, one is, and the other has not yet come; but when he does come he will only continue for a short time. The Beast which was, and is not, he is himself the eighth, and is of the seven, and will go to destruction. The ten horns you have seen are ten kings who have not yet received their kingdom, but will receive royal authority with the Beast for one hour. They will be united in their resolve to offer their royal power and authority to the Beast. They will fight

[123] See Jer. li. 12-13. Here the woman is Rome. 'Then shall the world be ruled beneath a woman's hand, and obey her in all things' (*Sibyl. Orac.* Bk. III. 75).

[124] The image of the woman seated on a beast and holding in her hand a goblet may well have been taken from a representation on a coin or mural decoration.

[125] The Beast is the Imperial power which supports Rome (almost literally true of the emperors' care of the city of Rome and its citizens) and in particular Nero, who 'was, is not, yet still is', since his return was expected. He is 'about to rise from the Abyss'.

[126] 'Was, and is not, yet still is.' While the words may have a special meaning they are also the deliberate perversion of 'Who Is, and Was, and Shall be', used of God.

[127] The seven hills of Rome.

[128] The interpretation again depends on the period of which the seer is writing. If this was the end of Domitian's reign the five kings may be the emperors Gaius (first to order his statue to be worshipped), Claudius, Nero, Vespasian, and Titus. The one 'who is' will be Domitian, and the one who follows and reigns only a short time will be Nerva (A.D. 96-98). The eighth who is of the seven will be the returned Nero.

with the Lamb; but the Lamb will overcome them, for he is supreme lord and king, and those who are on his side are called, chosen, and loyal.

'The waters you have seen,' he told me, 'where the Harlot is seated, are peoples and masses, nations and tongues. Both the ten horns you have seen, and the Beast, will hate the Harlot, and make her naked and solitary, and devour her flesh, and burn her with fire;[129] for God has put it into their minds to execute his will, and to be united in resolve to offer their royal power to the Beast until God's pronouncements are accomplished. And the woman you have seen is that Great City which exercises sovereignty over the kings of the earth.'

The Doom of Rome

After this I saw another angel with great authority descend from heaven, and the earth was illumined by his glory. With stentorian voice he cried, 'Great Babylon has fallen, has fallen, and become the habitation of demons, and the haunt of every foul spirit, and the haunt of every foul and hateful bird;[130] for all nations have drunk the strong wine of her immorality, the kings of the earth have committed immorality with her, and the merchants of the earth have grown rich through her insatiable desires.

Then I heard another voice from heaven say 'Leave her, my people, lest you participate in her sins, and partake of her plagues; for her sins have piled up to heaven, and God has remembered her iniquities.[131] Treat her as she has treated you, and doubly so, in accordance with her deeds.[132] In the very goblet she mixed for others mix double for her. To the extent that she has glorified herself and waxed wanton, by so much render to her anguish and sorrow. For she says to herself, "I sit a queen, and am no widow. Sorrow I shall never know." Therefore in a single day her plagues shall come, death and sorrow, and famine,[133] and by fire she shall be consumed; for mighty is the Lord God who judges her.[134]

'The kings of the earth, who have committed immorality and been wanton with her, shall mourn and lament over her when they see the smoke of her conflagration, keeping their distance from fear of her torment, and saying, "Alas, alas, for that great

[129] Nero-Antichrist and his ten allies, 'the Kings of the East', will attack and destroy Rome.
[130] Cp. Isa. xiii. 19-22; xxxiv. 14.   [131] Cp. Jer. l. 8; li. 9.
[132] Jer. l. 15; Ps. cxxxvii. 8.   [133] Isa. xlvii. 8-9.
[134] With the general picture may be compared *Sibyl. Orac.* Bk. IV. 158-179; 'And from heaven a great star shall fall on the dread ocean and burn up the deep sea, with Babylon itself and the land of Italy, the cause that many of the Hebrews perished, holy and faithful, and the people of truth . . . Woe to thee, thou city of the Latin land, all unclean, thou maenad circled with vipers, thou shalt sit a widow on thy hills . . . Knowest thou not the power and design of God? But thou saidst, "I am alone, and none shall despoil me." Yet now shall God who lives for ever destroy both thee and thine . . . Abide thou alone, thou lawless city, wrapt in burning fire. Inhabit thou in Hades the gloomy house of the lawless'. The judgment on Rome is parallel with that on Jerusalem, but greater. Cp. Lam. i. 1-2; iv. 22.

city Babylon, that mighty city! In a single hour your judgment has come!"

'The merchants of the earth shall mourn and lament over her;[135] for now there are none to buy their cargoes, cargoes of gold and silver, precious stones and pearls, fine linen and purple, silk and scarlet, loads of aromatic timber and articles of ivory, articles of rare woods, bronze, iron, and marble, cinnamon and spices of the orient, incense, myrrh and frankincense, wine and olive oil, wheat and fine flour, sheep and cattle, horses and chariots, and bodies and souls of men.

'The luscious fruits your soul craved for are gone from you. All your fads and fancies are gone from you, and never shall you indulge them more.

'The traders in these things, who have been enriched by her, shall anchor at a distance from her torment, mourning and lamenting, and saying, "Alas, alas, for that great city, which was arrayed in fine linen, purple and scarlet, and decked out with gold, precious stones and pearls! All that wealth is gone, gone in a single hour!"

'And every navigator and voyager, the sailors and seafarers, standing at a distance will cry as they watch the smoke of her conflagration, "Where is the like of this great city?" Throwing dust on their heads, they will mourn and lament, crying, "Alas, alas, for that great city, by whose ample means all with ships at sea were enriched! All is gone, gone in a single hour!"

'But rejoice over her, O heaven, and you Saints, Envoys, and Prophets; for God has executed your judgment on her.'

Then a strong angel lifted a stone like a huge millstone, and flung it into the sea, exclaiming, 'Thus with violence shall that great city Babylon be thrown down, and never rise again![136] Never again shall the music of harpists, musicians, flautists, and trumpeters, be heard in you![137] Never again shall craftsmen of any craft be found in you! Never again shall the sound of a mill be heard in you! Never again shall the light of a lamp shine in you! Never again shall be heard in you the voice of bridegroom and bride! Your merchants were the princes of the earth; for all nations were bewitched by your spells. But in her was found the blood of Prophets and Saints, and of all who were butchered on earth.'

The Paeans of Praise in Heaven

After this I heard the sound of a mighty throng in heaven saying,

> 'Hallelujah.[138]
> Salvation, glory, and power,
> Be unto our God;

[135] Cp. the prophecy against Tyre, Ezek. xxvii.
[136] Cp. Jer. li. 63-4, and see above n. 135.   [137] Cp. Ezek. xxvi. 13-14.
[138] See the opening of the festal Hallel Psalms (cxiii-cxviii), which were sung in the Temple by the choir.

For true and just are his judgments.
He hath judged the Great Harlot,
Who corrupted the earth with her vice;
And hath avenged at her hands
The blood of his servants.[139]

Once more they said, 'Hallelujah. Her smoke shall ascend for ever and ever.'

Then the twenty-four Elders and the four Living-Creatures prostrated themselves and worshipped God who sits on the throne, saying, 'Amen. Hallelujah', while a voice issuing from the throne said,

'O sing unto our God,
All ye his servants,
Ye who revere him
Both high and low.'[140]

Then I heard the sound as of a vast concourse, like the booming of many waters, and like peals of heavy thunder, saying,

'Hallelujah.
For the Lord our God Almighty reigneth.
Let us be glad and rejoice,[141]
And render praise to him;
For the Lamb's wedding-day is here,
And his spouse hath made herself ready.'

She was permitted to be robed in pure shining white lined.[142] (The fine linen represents the state of righteousness of the Saints.)

Then he said to me, 'Write this down. Happy are those who are invited to the wedding-banquet of the Lamb. These are God's very words,' he added.

At this I prostrated myself at his feet and worshipped him. But he said to me, 'Forbear! I am only the fellow-servant of you and your brothers who have the testimony of Jesus. Worship God.' (The testimony of Jesus means the spirit of prophecy.)

The Battle with the Beast

Now I saw heaven open, and there was a white horse whose rider is faithful and true, and who judges and fights with justice. His eyes were like a fiery flame, and on his head were

[139] Cp. *Targ. Pal.* at Deut. xxxii. 43: 'Rejoice ye nations, and ye people of the house of Israel; for he hath avenged the blood of his servants which was shed.' Once more the seer employs the *Song of Moses.*
[140] Cp. Ps. cxiii. 1; cxv. 11.
[141] Cp. Ps. cxviii. 24.
[142] The garment of ministering priests in the Temple in a state of ceremonial purity.

many crowns with a title engraved on them which no one but himself understands. He was clad in a robe spattered with blood,[143] and bore the name 'The Word of God'.

Behind him on white horses followed the heavenly hosts, clad in pure white linen, while from his mouth there projected a sharp two-edged sword with which to smite the nations. He shall herd them with an iron-shod staff;[144] and it is he who shall tread the winepress of the wrath of God Almighty.[145] On his robe and upon his thigh he bears the title, 'Supreme King and Lord'.

Then I saw an angel standing in the sun, and he shouted loudly to all the birds that fly in midheaven, 'Come, flock to the great feast of God, and devour the flesh of kings, and the flesh of captains, and the flesh of warriors, and the flesh of horses and their riders, and the flesh of all alike, free and slave, high and low.'[146]

Now I saw the Beast, and the kings of the earth, and their hosts, assembled to do battle with the rider on the horse and his hosts. And the Beast was captured, and with him the False Prophet who performed signs in his presence by which those who had received the stamp of the Beast and worshipped his image had been deceived. Both of them were flung alive into the Lake of Fire burning with sulphur![147] while the rest were slain by the sword of the rider on the horse, which projected from his mouth; and all the birds were glutted with their flesh.[148]

The Millennium and Fate of the Dragon

Then I saw an angel descend from heaven with the key of the Abyss and a heavy chain in his hand. And he seized the Dragon, the primeval Serpent, who is the Devil and Satan, and bound him for a thousand years, hurled him into the Abyss, and locked and sealed him up; so that he should deceive the nations no more till the thousand years were ended. Thereafter he has to be freed for a brief period.

I also saw thrones and those who were seated on them, to whom judgment was referred, together with the souls of those beheaded for the testimony of Jesus and for the sake of God's Message. These had not worshipped the Beast or his image,

[143] Cp. Isa. lxiii. 1-4.
[144] Ps. ii. 9.
[145] Isa. lxiii. 3.
[146] Cp. Ezek. xxxix. 17-20.
[147] Cp. *Apoc. Bar.* xl. 1-3; 'The last leader of that time will be left alive, when the multitude of his hosts will be put to the sword, and be bound, and they will take him up to Mount Zion, and my Messiah will convict him of all his impieties . . . Afterwards he will put him to death, and protect the rest of my people . . . And his (Messiah's) principate will stand for ever, until the world of corruption is at an end, and until the times aforesaid are fulfilled.'
[148] Cf. *Sibyl. Orac.* Bk. IV. 697-8: 'The very earth shall drink the blood of the slain, and the beasts shall be glutted with their flesh.'

and did not receive his stamp on their forehead or hand; and they lived and reigned with the Messiah for a thousand years. The rest of the dead, however, did not come to life until the thousand years were ended.

This constitutes the First Resurrection. Happy and blessed is he who shares in the First Resurrection. Over such as these the Second Death has no power. They will be priests of God and the Messiah, and will reign with him a thousand years.

When the thousand years have ended Satan will be freed from his prison, and will go out to deceive the nations that are in the four corners of the earth, Gog and Magog, and assemble them for battle, the number of whom is as the sand of the sea. Across the breadth of the earth they came up, and encircled the encampment of the Saints and the Beloved City.[149] But fire fell from heaven and devoured them, and their deceiver the Devil was flung into the Lake of Fire and sulphur where the Beast and False Prophet already were; and they will be tormented day and night for ever and ever.

The Last Judgment and Final Age

Then I saw a great white throne, and him who sat on it, from whose presence earth and heaven fled and were lost to view. And I saw the dead, high and low, standing before the throne; and the books were opened.[150] Another book was also opened, that of Life, and the dead were judged according to their deeds by what was recorded in the books. The sea presented the dead who were in it, and Death and Hades presented the dead who were in them, and they were judged each one according to their deeds. Then Death and Hades were flung into the Lake of Fire. This, the Lake of Fire, is the Second Death, and whoever was not found inscribed in the Book of Life was flung into the Lake of Fire.

Now I saw a new heaven and a new earth.[151] The previous heaven and earth had passed away, and the sea no longer existed. I also saw the City, the New Jerusalem, descending from heaven from God in all her glory, like a bride adorned for her husband.[152]

I also heard a loud voice from the throne say, 'Behold, God's dwelling-place is with men, and he will dwell among them.[153] And they shall be his people, and God himself will be with them and wipe all tears from their eyes, and there shall be no more death. Neither shall there be sorrow, nor mourning, nor grief any more. The old conditions have passed away.[154]

[149] Cp. on this passage Ezek. xxxviii-ix; Joel iii; Zech. xiv.
[150] Dan. vii. 10.
[151] Cp. Isa. lxv. 17; *Enoch*, xlv. 4-5, xci. 16; and *Targ. Jer.* at Deut. xxxii. 1.
[152] Cp. Isa. lxi. 10, and *Test. Dan*, v. 12-13: 'And the saints shall rest in Eden, and in the New Jerusalem will the righteous rejoice, and it shall be unto the glory of God for ever. And no longer shall Jerusalem endure desolation, nor Israel be led captive: for the Lord shall be in the midst of it.'
[153] Cp. Ezek. xlviii. 35.
[154] Isa. xliii. 18-19.

Then he who sat on the throne said, 'Lo, I make everything anew.' He said also, 'Write this down, for these words are trustworthy and true.'

[Then he said to me, 'It is done. I am the Alpha and Omega, the Beginning and the End. To the thirsty I will give freely of the spring of the Water of Life. The victor shall inherit all this, and I will be his God, and he shall be my son. But the cowardly, the disloyal, the vicious, the murderous, the immoral, sorcerers, idolaters, and all liars, shall have their portion (which is the Second Death) in the Lake that burns with fire and sulphur.']

Vision of the New Jerusalem[155]

Now there came one of the seven angels who had the seven bowls filled with the seven last plagues, and said to me, 'Come, and I will show you the Bride, the Lamb's wife.'

He conveyed me in spirit to the summit of a huge and lofty mountain[156] and showed me the Holy City Jerusalem which had descended from heaven from God, possessing the glory of God. The brightness of it was like some precious stone, like polished jasper. It had an immense and high wall with twelve gates, and at the gates were twelve angels, while engraved on them were names, those of the twelve tribes of the children of Israel.[157] On the east were three gates, on the north were three gates, on the south were three gates, and on the west were three gates. The wall of the City had twelve foundation-stones, and on these were the twelve names of the twelve envoys of the Lamb.

Now he who talked to me had a golden measuring-reed,[158] so that he could measure the City, with its gates and wall. The City lay foursquare, the length and breadth of it being the same. His measurement of the City with the reed came out at twelve thousand furlongs.[159] The length, the breadth, and the height of it were identical. Its wall measured a hundred and forty-four cubits, man's standard of measurement[160] (which means angel's standard). The wall was constructed of jasper, and the City itself of pure gold like clear glass. The foundations of the City's wall were adorned with all kinds of precious stones;[161] the first foundation-stone with jasper, the second with sapphire, the third with chalcedony, the fourth with emerald, the fifth with onyx, the sixth with sardius, the seventh with

155 It has been considered that this section has been moved down from its original position in the previous section, perhaps to allow for the Epilogue, which is itself in some disorder.
156 Isa. ii. 2; Ezek. xl. ii. Jewish legend suggested that the mountains Tabor, Carmel, and Zion, would be piled on one another, and Jerusalem set on top of them.
157 See Ezek. xlviii. 30ff.
158 Cp. Ezek. xl. 3.
159 The measurements are symbolical. Cp. the 144,000 (12 times 12,000) of ch. vii.
160 Perhaps referring to the ordinary cubit, about 18 inches, rather than the special cubit of Ezekiel, about 21 inches.
161 Isa. liv. 11-12.

chrysolite, the eighth with beryl, the ninth with topaz, the tenth with chrysoprase, the eleventh with jacinth, and the twelfth with amethyst. The twelve gates were twelve pearls, each gate a single pearl; and the streets of the city were of pure gold like transparent glass.

I saw no Temple in it; for the Lord God Almighty is its Temple [and the Lamb]. The City requires neither sun nor moon to shine on it; for the glory of God illumines it[162] [and its lamp is the Lamb]. The nations will walk by the light of it, and the kings of the earth will bring their splendour into it.[163] The gates of it shall never be shut from day to day[164] (for there will be no night there). They will admit the glory and pride of the nations into it, but there shall never enter it anything profane,[165] or anything that causes idolatry[166] or deceit, only those who are inscribed in the Book of Life [of the Lamb].[167]

Then he showed me the river of the Water of Life clear as crystal flowing from the throne of God[168] [and the Lamb] down the middle of the street of the City. And on either side of the river grew the Tree of Life bearing twelve kinds of fruit, yielding its fruit for each month respectively, while the leaves of the tree were for the healing of the nations. There will be no more anything accursed. The throne of God [and of the Lamb] will be in the City, and his servants will minister to him, and behold his face, and his name shall be on their foreheads. There will be night no more, neither will they have need of the light of lamp or light of the sun; for the Lord God will shine upon them, and they shall reign for ever and ever.

Epilogue

I, John, heard and saw all this, and when I had seen and heard I prostrated myself to worship at the feet of the angel who had shown me these things. But he said to me, 'Forbear! I am only the fellow-servant of you and your brothers the Prophets, and of those who heed the prophetic words of this book. Worship God.'

Then he[169] said to me, 'These words are trustworthy and true, and the Lord God of the spirits of the Prophets has sent his angel to show his servants what must shortly transpire. *I shall come very soon. Happy is he who heeds the prophetic words of this book.*'

[170] He further instructed me, 'Do not seal up the prophetic words of this book, for the time is at hand. Let the unjust re-

---

[162] Isa. lx. 19-20.   [163] Isa. lx. 3.
[164] Isa. lx. 11.   [165] Isa. lii. 1.
[166] Lit. 'abomination'.
[167] Only those ordained to enter shall go into the New Jerusalem (*Baba Bathra*, fol. 75b.).
[168] On this passage see Ezek. xlvii. 1-12.
[169] The speaker is once more the Angel-Messiah, the angel of Jesus, of the beginning of the book.
[170] Either the whole Epilogue, or at least from here, is probably an addition.

main unjust, the vile continue vile, and let the just still do justice, and the holy remain consecrated. *I shall come very soon. And my reward will be with me to requite each according to his deeds.*

'I am the Alpha and Omega, the First and the Last, the Beginning and the End. Happy are those who wash their robes, that they may have a claim upon the Tree of Life and enter by the gates into the City. Outside are the dogs, the sorcerers, the immoral, murderers, idolaters, and all who love and practise what is false.

'I, Jesus, have sent my angel to testify these things to you for the communities. I am the stock and scion of David, the bright morning star.'

Both the Spirit and the Bride say, 'Come!' Let the hearer too say, 'Come!' Let him who is thirsty come. Let whoever will take the Water of Life freely.

I testify to all who hear the prophetic words of this book, that if anyone shall add to them, God will add to him the plagues set down in this book.[171] And if anyone subtracts from the words of the book of this prophecy, God will subtract from him his share in the Tree of Life, and in the Holy City, the matters recorded in this book.

He who testifies to these things says, *'I shall come very soon.'* Amen. Come, Lord Jesus!

[The loving-kindness of the Lord Jesus Christ be with the Saints.][172]

171 Cp. Jos. *Against Apion*, i. 8: 'How firmly we have given credit to those books of our nation (i.e. the Old Testament) is evident by what we do; for during so many ages as we have already passed no one has been so bold as either to add anything to them or take anything from them.' Ancient Jewish tombstones found in Phrygia invoke the curses written in Deuteronomy (xxvii–xxix) on anyone tampering with the grave.
172 The work in its present form is framed in a letter, cp. i. 4.

INDEX OF PERSONS AND PLACES[1]

[1] All references in this Index relate solely to the text of the New Testament itself. Places are shown in italics. In certain cases a brief description of persons and places has been added.

INDEX OF REFERENCES[1]

THE OLD TESTAMENT AND APOCRYPHA

[1] All references in this Index relate to the General Introduction and Footnotes.

THE TARGUMS[1]

APOCALYPTIC AND PSEUDEPIGRAPHIC LITERATURE

ROMAN, GREEK AND JEWISH AUTHORS

---

[1] Aramaic Paraphrases of the Old Testament.

[2] Commonly known as the *Targum of Jonathan ben Uzziel*.

[3] The so-called 'Zadokites' were a Jewish sect, probably forming some part of the Essenes, which had entered into a 'New Covenant', and lived in distinct communities in Palestine. Some of their literature has recently been recovered from caves close to the Dead Sea in the foothills near Khirbet Qumran. The *Damascus Document*, however, was found much earlier in the lumber room of a synagogue in Old Cairo (Fostat). Its fragments were published by Dr. Schechter in 1910.

RABBINICAL LITERATURE (THE MISHNAH[1])

RABBINICAL LITERATURE (THE TALMUD[2])

EARLY CHRISTIAN LITERATURE

SPECIAL SOURCES

---

[1] The Jewish 'Oral Law' as compiled by Rabbi Judah the Patriarch at the close of the Second Century A.D. The order of the tractates has been followed.
[2] The Talmud consists of the Mishnah together with the Gemara (Rabbinical discussions on the Minhnah). TJ before the name of a tractate refers to the Palestinean rescension (*Talmud Jerushalmi*) compiled towards the close of the Fourth Century A.D. All other references are to the Babylonian rescension compiled about a century later.

The Mentor Philosophers

The entire range of Western speculative thinking from the Middle Ages to modern times is presented in this series of six volumes, which are unique in the low-priced field. Each book contains the basic writings of the leading philosophers of each age, with introductions and commentary by noted authorities.

"A very important and interesting series."
—Gilbert Highet

50 cents each

THE AGE OF BELIEF: The Medieval Philosophers
edited by Anne Fremantle (#MD126)

"A well-chosen sampler of the writings of the great philosophers of the fifth to 15th centuries."
—Saturday Review Syndicate

THE AGE OF ADVENTURE: The Renaissance Philosophers
edited by Giorgio de Santillana (#MD184)

"That most romantic, fertile and productive period of modern civilization—the Renaissance."
—The Pioneer (India)

THE AGE OF REASON: The 17th Century Philosophers
edited by Stuart Hampshire (#MD158)

"The New American Library has earned the gratitude of tens of thousands . . . by providing them with such intellectual fare at so cheap a price."
—Shankar's Weekly (India)

THE AGE OF ENLIGHTENMENT: The 18th Century Philosophers
edited by Isaiah Berlin (#MD172)

"Mr. Berlin . . . has one of the liveliest and most stimulating minds among contemporary philosophers."
—N. Y. Herald Tribune

THE AGE OF IDEOLOGY: The 19th Century Philosophers
edited by Henry D. Aiken (#MD185)

". . . a rounded and sympathetic presentation of the 19th century . . . most distinct intellectual contribution."
—The New York Times

THE AGE OF ANALYSIS: 20th Century Philosophers
edited by Morton White (#MD142)

"No other book remotely rivals this as the best available introduction to 20th century philosophy."
—N. Y. Herald Tribune

The MENTOR Religious Classics

The Papal Encyclicals *edited by Anne Fremantle.* The most important pronouncements of the Popes through the ages, in their historical context. (#MD177—50¢)

Of the Imitation of Christ *by Thomas à Kempis.* The great 15th century classic of devotional literature, translated by Abbot Justin McCann. (#MD193—50¢)

The Meaning of the Glorious Koran *An Explanatory Translation by Mohammed Marmaduke Pickthall.* The complete sacred book of Mohammedanism, translated with reverence and scholarship. (#MD94—50¢)

The Song of God: Bhagavad-Gita. The Hindu epic translated by Swami Prabhavananda and Christopher Isherwood. (#M103—35¢)

The Way of Life: Tao Tê Ching *by Lao Tzu.* A new translation by R. B. Blakney of a masterpiece of ancient Chinese wisdom. (#MD129—50¢)

The Sayings of Confucius *translated by James R. Ware.* The wise teachings of the ancient Chinese sage in a new translation. (#MD151—50¢)

The Teachings of the Compassionate Buddha *edited by E. A. Burtt.* The basic texts, early discourses, the Dhammapada, and later writings of Buddhism. (#MD131—50¢)

The Upanishads: Breath of the Eternal. The wisdom of the Hindu mystics, translated by Swami Prabhavananda and Frederick Manchester. (#MD194—50¢)

To Our Readers

We welcome your comments about any SIGNET, SIGNET KEY, or MENTOR Book. If your dealer does not have the books you want, you may order them by mail, enclosing the list price plus 5¢ a copy to cover mailing. Send for our free catalog. The New American Library of World Literature, Inc., 501 Madison Avenue, New York 22, New York.